IRELAND NORTH AND SOUTH
Perspectives from Social Science

D1587490

PROCEEDINGS OF THE BRITISH ACADEMY · 98

IRELAND NORTH AND SOUTH
Perspectives from Social Science

Edited by
ANTHONY F. HEATH, RICHARD BREEN
& CHRISTOPHER T. WHELAN

Published for THE BRITISH ACADEMY
by OXFORD UNIVERSITY PRESS

Oxford University Press, Great Clarendon Street, Oxford OX2 6DP

Oxford New York
Athens Auckland Bangkok Bogota Bombay
Buenos Aires Calcutta Cape Town Dar es Salaam
Delhi Florence Hong Kong Istanbul Karachi
Kuala Lumpur Madras Madrid Melbourne
Mexico City Nairobi Paris Singapore
Taipei Tokyo Toronto Warsaw

and associated companies in
Berlin Ibadan

Published in the United States by
Oxford University Press Inc., New York

British Library Cataloguing in Publication Data
Data available

ISBN 0–19–726195–7
ISSN 0068–1202

Typeset by J&L Composition Ltd, Filey, North Yorkshire
Printed in Great Britain
on acid-free paper by
Creative Print and Design Wales
Ebbw Vale

Contents

Notes on Contributors

Paul Bew is Professor of Irish Politics at The Queen's University, Belfast. He read Modern History at Cambridge (MA, Ph.D., 1968–74) and is author of five books on modern Irish history and co-author of seven others. Most recently author of *Ideology and the Irish Question* (1998).

John Bradley is a Research Professor at the ESRI in Dublin. He has published extensively on the economics of the island of Ireland, with particular focus on North-South interactions, as well as on the economic implications of Structural Funds and the Single Market in the EU periphery. He currently directs an ACE-Phare project on the transition of CEE economies to EU membership.

Richard Breen holds the Chair in Social Stratification and Inequality in the Department of Political and Social Sciences at the European University Institute, on extended leave of absence from The Queen's University, Belfast. His most recent books include *Censored, Sample Selected and Truncated Regression Models* (1996); *Social Class and Social Mobility in the Republic of Ireland* (with C. T. Whelan, 1996); and *Class Stratification: A Comparative Perspective* (with D. B. Rottman, 1995). He is a Member of the Royal Irish Academy.

John D. Brewer is Professor of Sociology at The Queen's University, Belfast. He was a Visiting Fellow at Yale University in 1989, and Visiting Scholar at St John's College, Oxford, 1992. He taught formerly at the University of East Anglia and the University of Natal. He has researched and published extensively on the sociology and politics of divided societies, including policing issues and crime, and has participated in four international study groups on aspects of South African policing and its future. His major publications cover South Africa, Northern Ireland, policing and various aspects of qualitative sociology. His books include *After Soweto* (1986); *The Police, Public Order and the State* (1988, second edition in 1996: co-author); *The Royal Irish Constabulary: An Oral History* (1990); *Inside the RUC: Routine Policing in a Divided Society* (1991); *Black and Blue: Policing in South Africa* (1994); and *Crime in Ireland 1945–95* (1997).

David Coleman is Reader in Demography at the University of Oxford. His research interests include the comparative demographic trends and convergences in the industrial world and their socio-economic consequences; immigration trends and policies and the demography of ethnic minorities. His books include *The State of Population Theory: Forward from Malthus* (ed. with R. S. Schofield, 1986); *The British Population: patterns, trends and processes* (with J. Salt, 1992); *Europe's Population in the 1990s* (ed., 1996) and *Ethnicity in the 1991 Census. Volume 1: Demographic characteristics of ethnic minority populations* (ed., with J. Salt, 1996). He has been the joint editor of the *European Journal of Population* since 1992.

Geoffrey Evans is a Fellow of Nuffield College, Oxford. He has written numerous articles on comparative political sociology and voting behaviour, is a co-author of *Understanding Political Change* (1991) and editor of *The End of Class Politics* (forthcoming). A member of the British Election Study team since 1987, in recent years he has conducted survey research into social and political divisions in Northern Ireland and directed ESRC and EU funded studies of social and political change in thirteen post-Communist societies.

Tony Fahey is a sociologist in the Economic and Social Research Institute, Dublin. His research interests include various aspects of the family and family policy, demography and religion. His most recent book (with John Fitzgerald) is *Welfare Implications of Demographic Trends* (1997).

Brian Girvin is Senior Lecturer in Politics, University of Glasgow. His publications include *Between Two Worlds* (1989); *The Right in the Twentieth Century* (1994); *The Green Pool and the Origins of the Common Agricultural Policy* (ed. with R. T. Griffiths, 1995) as well as numerous contributions on Irish history and politics, comparative politics and nationalism. He is completing *Nationalism and Political Culture in Ireland: The Clash Between Modernity and Tradition* and *The Universal Nature of Nationalism* (forthcoming).

Andrew Greeley is Professor of Sociology at the University of Arizona and the University of Chicago, as well as a sometime visiting Professor at the University of Cologne and Honorary Senior Fellow at the National University of Ireland. His academic books are *Religion as Poetry* (1995) and *Religious Change in America* (1989).

Graham Gudgin is the Director of the Northern Ireland Economic Research Centre, the office of which he has held since the Centre was established in 1985. Prior to this, he was a Senior Research Officer in the Department of Applied Economics, University of Cambridge and Economics Fellow of Selwyn College, Cambridge. His research specialism is regional economic issues with particular reference to the economy of

Northern Ireland. His most recent publications are on the growth of small firms and on unemployment in Northern Ireland.

Bernadette C. Hayes is Reader in Sociology at The Queen's University, Belfast, Northern Ireland. She has also held appointments at the University of Surrey and the Australian National University. She has published widely in the area of gender, social stratification, religion and politics. Her most recent publications include articles in the *British Journal of Sociology*; *Comparative Political Studies*; *European Sociological Review*; *Electoral Studies* and the *Journal of the Royal Statistical Society*.

Anthony Heath, FBA is Professor of Sociology at the University of Oxford and Official Fellow of Nuffield College, Oxford. His research interests include the sociology of education and social class, ethnicity and political behaviour. He has been the Director of the British Election Studies since 1983 and is the co-Director of the ESRC's Centre for Research into Elections and Social Trends. His books include *Origins and Destinations* (1980, co-author); *Social Mobility* (1981); *How Britain Votes* (1985, co-author); *Understanding Political Change* (1991, co-author); and *Social Research and Social Reform* (1992, co-editor).

Bill Lockhart is Director of EXTERN and of its Centre for Independent Research and Analysis of Crime (CIRAC). He has been a Visiting Fellow at the Institute of Criminology, University of Cambridge, Chairman of the Northern Ireland Branch of the British Society of Criminology and Member of the Editorial Board of the *Howard Journal of Criminal Justice*. He is author of, among others, *Crime Statistics and Surveys in Northern Ireland* (1992); *Remands in Custody in Northern Ireland; Report for the Standing Advisory Commission on Human Rights* (1993); *Car Theft in Belfast* (1993); and *Crime in Ireland 1945–95* (1997).

Ian McAllister is Director of the Research School of Social Sciences at the Australian National University. Previously he held appointments at the University of New South Wales, the University of Strathclyde, and the University of Manchester. His research interests are in the areas of comparative political behaviour, political parties, voters and electoral systems. He is the author of *Political Behaviour* (1992); *Dimensions of Australian Society* (1995, co-author); *The Australian Political System* (1995, co-author); and *Russia Votes* (1996, co-author).

John McCartney is a Ph.D. candidate at the School of Public Policy, Economics and Law at the University of Ulster and a member of the Structural Funds Evaluation Unit in the Department of Trade, Employment and Enterprise in the Republic of Ireland. His main research area is workplace innovations in the Republic of Ireland and he is author of a number of articles on this theme. Currently, he is writing a book on the topic, provisionally entitled *Reshaping Labour Market Institutions in Ireland.*

Eithne McLaughlin is Professor of Social Policy at The Queen's University, Belfast. Her research interests include unemployment, labour supply and social security policy, as well as family policy and community care, in both British and Irish welfare regimes. She is the author of *Flexibility in Work and Benefits* (1994); *Paying for Care – lessons from Europe* (co-author, 1993); *Work and Welfare Benefits* (1989); *Policy Aspects of Employment Equality in Northern Ireland* (ed., 1996); *Understanding Unemployment: new perspectives on active labour market policies* (1992); and *Women, Employment and Social Policy in Northern Ireland: a Problem Postponed?* (1991). She has also authored and co-authored articles on these topics in *Ageing and Society*; *Journal of Area Studies*; *Journal of Social Policy*; *The Political Quarterly*; *Policy and Politics*; *Health and Social Care*; *Journal of European Social Policy*; *International Social Security Review*; and *Women's Studies International Forum.*

Philip J. O'Connell received his BA and MA degrees from University College Cork, and his Ph.D. from Indiana University. He taught at the University of North Carolina, Chapel Hill, before returning to work at the ESRI in 1991. He has conducted a wide range of research on labour market and social policy issues, and undertaken numerous evaluation projects of EU Structural Funds programmes. From 1995 to 1997 he served as a consultant advisor to the European Commission on education, training and the labour market in Ireland. He is co-author, with Frances McGinnity, of *Work Schemes? Active Labour Market Policy in Ireland* (1997), and co-editor, with Jerry Sexton, of *Labour Market Studies: Ireland* (1996).

Pat O'Connor is Professor of Sociology and Social Policy at the University of Limerick. Gender has been a dominant pre-occupation of her work to date. Her publications have ranged over a wide area – including *Friendships between Women* (1992); *A Study of the Barriers to Women's Promotion in the Health Services* (1995); and *A Time of Change: Women in Contemporary Irish Society* (1998). Her current research revolves around the relationship between the family and the state; women's experiences within organisational structures and the issue of consensual control. She has recently completed a study of a Community Mother's Programme; a case study of a semi-state development agency while a preliminary international study of young people's attitudes to work and family is in progress.

Paula Rodgers is a social policy worker for Save the Children, formerly Research Fellow in the Department of Sociology and Social Policy at The Queen's University, Belfast. She has a doctorate from The Queen's University, Belfast for a thesis on voluntary aid agencies, part of which was published as *The Charity Box Speaks Back*, by the Sociological Association of Ireland in 1996. She has extensive experience of qualitative research and is co-author of *The Northern Ireland Civil Service: Policy and Practice in the Employment of People with Disabilities* (1994); *An Examination of Training Provision for People with Disabilities in Northern Ireland* (1994); *Policy and Provision for People with Disabilities in Higher and Further Education* (1994) and *Crime in Ireland 1945–95* (1997).

David B. Rottman is the Associate Director of Research at the National Center for State Courts in Williamsburg, Virginia. Between 1975 and 1992 he worked at the Economic and Social Research Institute in Dublin, Ireland. He is the co-author of *Understanding Contemporary Ireland* (1990); *Class Stratification: A Comparative Perspective* (1995); and *Dispensing Justice Locally* (1998).

Sally Shortall lectures in sociology at The Queen's University, Belfast. Her main research interests are rural development policy, women on farms, and change in farming, and she has published on these topics over the past ten years. Her book, *Power and Property—Women and Farming* will be published in 1999.

Richard Sinnott is Lecturer in Politics and Director of the Centre for European Economic and Public Affairs at University College, Dublin. He is the author of *Irish Voters Decide: Voting Behaviour in Elections and Referendums since 1918* (1995) and co-author (with Jean Blondel and Palle Svensson) of *People and Parliament in the European Union: Participation, Democracy and Legitimacy* (1998).

Paul Teague is currently a Visiting Fellow at Cornell University, and a Professor in the School of Public Policy, Economics and Law, University of Ulster. His main research interest is the industrial relations consequences of European integration. He is the author of a number of books on this topic including *The European Community: the Social Dimension* (1989); *Industrial Relations and European Integration* (with John Grahl, 1994). He has recently completed a new study, *The Crisis of Social Europe.*

Christopher T. Whelan is a research sociologist at the Economic and Social Research Institute, Dublin. He was joint editor with John H. Goldthorpe of *The Development of Industrial Society in Ireland*, Proceedings of the British Academy, 79 (1992); editor of *Values and Social Change in Ireland* (1994);

and co-author with Brian Nolan of *Resources Deprivation and Poverty* (1996). He has also contributed to a range of academic journals on topics such as unemployment, poverty, education, social mobility and psychological distress.

Preface

This volume is the outcome of a Symposium held at Nuffield College, Oxford, 6–9 December 1996, and sponsored by the British Academy with support from the Royal Irish Academy. The chapters were completed before the Good Friday agreement of 1998 and thus have not been able to take account of this very important development.

Our work has been greatly helped by the discussants at the Symposium, the referees who commented on the papers, and staff at the British Academy and at Nuffield College. We would particularly like to thank Iain Bryson, Roy Foster, John Goldthorpe, Chelly Halsey, Damian Hannan, Roger Hood, Naomi McCay, Jane Pearce, Bob Rowthorne, Emer Smyth, Brendan Whelan, Mandy Roberts and Rosemary Lambeth.

We also wish to thank the Warden and Fellows of Nuffield College for their support for the Symposium.

AFH, RB, CTW

Problems of, and Prospects for, Comparing the Two Irelands

DAVID B. ROTTMAN

Introduction

THE OBSTACLES TO COMPARING THE TWO IRELANDS ARE FORMIDABLE. Certainly few North to South comparisons have been undertaken in any of the social sciences. Obstacles to such comparisons assume two main forms. The first form of obstacle includes the standard bundle of theoretical and methodological problems that beset any comparative project. However, problems of theory and method are compounded when the countries to be compared are drawn from the ranks of small, 'open' political units and when, as in Ireland, there is no established tradition of undertaking comparative research on which to build. Assertions and assumptions abound in Irish social science about Ireland's place in the world, but comparative research efforts are few in number and often informal in application. The unequal political statuses of the North and South are also troubling. That a state is being compared to a statelet or a semi-state are ways of expressing the difference.

The second form of obstacle lies within the perspectives of the scholars making the comparison rather than the task per se: they fall within the social psychology of comparative analysis. Briefly stated, the intellectual and world views of scholars from neither the North nor the South encourage the development and application of a comparative perspective embracing both Irelands. Few direct comparisons of the North and South have been undertaken. Scholars in the South do not regard the North as a useful or appropriate point of comparison. And scholars in the North do not regard the South as a fruitful point of comparison. Social psychological obstacles to North/South comparisons are to some degree independent of the theoretical and methodological problems associated with

Proceedings of the British Academy, **98**, 1–33. © The British Academy 1999.

comparative analysis. They need to be understood, however, in the context of the structure of the social sciences in Northern Ireland and in the Republic.

This paper initially examines the problems of, and prospects for, comparing the two Irelands in the following way. The next section reviews the role of comparative thinking and research in Irish social science, establishing the context within which North to South comparisons are conducted. Then, the theoretical and methodological problems associated with undertaking a macro-level comparison between the Republic and the North are addressed. Those problems do not justify the indifference with which scholars North and South have treated the case on the other side of the border. This leads to consideration of the social psychological dimension to comparing the two Irelands. The ultimate objective of this paper is reached in its final section, which looks at the prospects for using comparisons between the Republic of Ireland and Northern Ireland to better understand contemporary Ireland, North and South.

The Comparative Tradition in Irish Social Science

A somewhat stylised account of the introduction and development of comparative work in Irish social science might go like this.[1] Comparative inquiry can often be traced to foreign scholars who located in Ireland in order to conduct field work or to find employment during the 1960s and 1970s. For many, a primary motivation was to obtain data that would add the Irish 'case' to an existing area of comparative inquiry. Scholars interested in aspects of 'modernisation' tended to gravitate to the South; those interested in ethnic conflict and the fate of 'settler societies' went northward. Broader outside interest in Northern Ireland as a comparative case was inhibited by its presumed uniqueness and the predominance of sectarian conflict in the province's life and social institutions. Social inquiries in Northern Ireland, whether qualitative or quantitative, focused on comparisons between Protestants and Catholics.

This legacy remained of some consequence as Irish social science itself became more self-confident and more reliant on systematic data during the 1970s. A large number of aspiring social scientists followed a path from Irish universities and research institutions to specific post-graduate programmes in North America and Britain and then back to employment

---

[1] My characterisation neglects nuance in pursuit of general tendencies and relates primarily to sociology, social psychology and political science, but also applies to the lack of North to South comparisons in economics. My particular focus is on sociology, my own field and the social science most concerned with establishing generalisations.

in Ireland. They returned with the theoretical perspectives and research methodologies then dominant in their place of study, along with their Ph.D.s. This cohort of new scholars created a strong potential for comparative thinking and research in Irish social science. That potential was realised in ways that varied by discipline and whether the returnee was based in the South or the North. There were also differences among the various university departments and, more generically, between academic and research institutions.

There are both intellectual and structural aspects to the differential use made of comparative thinking and research in Irish social science. In terms of intellectual aspects, a basic consideration is the status that is given to imported theories when seeking an understanding of contemporary Ireland. Here, I would identify two orientations. One orientation stresses a critical application of general theories to the Irish case. General theories guide the research and analysis, and place Ireland in context; the research findings are used to illuminate and refine the same general theories. In short, Ireland is used as a critical case to establish the adequacies of competing explanatory theories. This orientation is broadly characteristic of political science in Ireland, notably in the way that theoretical perspectives have been used to better understand and explain Irish nationalism, and the phenomenon of Irish nationalism then used to further develop those international perspectives.[2]

A second orientation makes a far less critical application of general theories. In this usage, theories are presumed to provide concrete representations of macrosocial units and can thus be used to 'read off' the details of and explanations for the Irish case, treating Ireland as a point in a continuum established from such frameworks as modernisation theory or Structural Marxism. Applicability is viewed as unproblematic. Ireland is not treated as a strategic case to test or improve a general theory.[3] Such an orientation is inimical to meaningful comparative analysis.

---

[2] Good examples of this orientation include the work by various Irish scholars on nationalism (for example, Coakely, 1980; 1990; Garvin, 1987) and on the social bases of party affiliation and voting behaviour (Laver, 1992 and Mair, 1992 contribute thorough reviews of the large Irish literature on the topic). Within sociology, a critical, reflexive use of prominent theories is evident in studies of the relationship of industrialism to social mobility (Breen and Whelan, 1994; 1995; 1996), the national distinctiveness of socio-religious values (Kelley and de Graaf, 1997); education (Raftery and Hout, 1993), and rural sociology (Hannan, 1979; Hannan and Cummins, 1992). Examples of critical applications of general theories to Ireland are scattered through work in other subfields, for example, criminology (Rottman, 1980; McCullagh, 1996) and the role of the state (Breen et al., 1990; O'Connell and Rottman, 1992).

[3] Applications to Ireland of Structural Marxism, the World System perspective, and dependency theory provide the most dramatic examples of this orientation, but the more subtle assumptions implicit in modernisation theory can also be damaging.

Problems of explanation concerning Northern Ireland are both more and less likely than those concerning the Republic to be framed comparatively. There is a body of work which seeks to explain political instability and ethnic conflict in the North comparatively (e.g., Wright, 1987; Guleke, 1988).[4] However, such studies are exceptions. Most social science exercises in explanations treat Northern Ireland in isolation (McGarry and O'Leary, 1995: 311–12). The tendency to treat Northern Ireland as *sui generis*, lacking in obvious points of comparison, carries over to work focused on institutions and processes, not on conflict.

In the Republic, comparative work in sociology and in some aspects of political science became concentrated in Irish research institutions. This situation in part reflects traditional patterns in which international scholars became affiliated with specific such institutions, which tended to be more hospitable to outsiders, more quantitatively oriented (and, in particular, more open to survey methods) and more active in international networks than were university departments.[5] Institutes also had the financial and organisational wherewithal to carry out large-scale survey research. As a result, the influence of comparative thinking and data ran narrowly through Irish sociology, being marginal to the manner in which some university departments defined their role.

The social sciences in the North and South developed differently in ways that had implications for the growth and shape of comparative thinking and research. Generally, the various social science fields matured earlier in the South, especially in terms of a social science of Irish society (O'Dowd, 1995). This reflects both the foundation provided by visiting anthropologists, sociologists and political scientists in the South, and the cohorts of young scholars returning to Ireland with degrees from the elite British and North American universities. Also, the application of social science theories and perspectives to Ireland was unproblematic to many social scientists in the North, but viewed as problematic in many of the subfields of sociology, political science and economics as pursued in the Republic.

These differences in part reflect the demographics of the social science communities in the two parts of Ireland. The inflow of non-Irish social scientists was far greater in Northern Ireland than in the Republic. Currently, about one-half of the academic staffs of Northern universities

---

[4] McGarry and O'Leary (1995: Chapter 8) offer the most comprehensive review and appraisal of the theories that have been applied comparatively and the cases that have been selected for comparison.

[5] This is far less applicable to academic Irish political science, which during the 1960s and 1970s became linked to a number of international centres of comparative politics (notably Strathclyde in Scotland and Leiden in the Netherlands).

are from outside of Ireland, primarily from Britain (McVeigh, 1995: 112).[6] The smaller inflow into the Republic was motivated in large measure by interest in Ireland and the strategic case that it represents. However, most non-Irish social scientists in the North seek positions in the North to pursue specialised fields of inquiry through participation in British professional associations and networks. The Sociological Association of Ireland, for example, never developed a broad represen- tation of Northern-based social scientists. Within Northern Ireland, university academic departments are fractured according to place of origin and politics, a demarcation that often divides those who have a primary interest in describing and explaining Irish phenomena from those with more general pursuits. In the less fractured academic depart- ments of the South (at least according to politics and place of origin), consideration of Northern Ireland raises sensitivities that do not encourage pursuit of comparative questions. In other words, 'The North' is thought of as a problem of politics and morality, not one of social science.[7]

By the 1990s, Ireland had shifted from being the passive subject of comparative research to active involvement in its development inter- nationally, particularly in political science and economics, but also within some subfields of sociology such as stratification.[8] Ireland is recognised as a strategic, even critical, test case for theories and Irish scholars con- tribute to the international development of their areas of expertise.[9] International data collection efforts have yielded a significant, if not overwhelming, body of comparable survey data on Northern Ireland and the Republic. Funding and sponsorship for North to South compar- isons, previously lacking, received a boost from the New Ireland Forum, particularly in the Republic.

---

[6] In 1985, 7 of the 23 sociologists in Southern universities and 15 of the 22 in Northern universities were from outside of Ireland (Lee, 1989: 626).

[7] In the view of a Southern-born social scientist on the faculty of a Northern university, 'To many intellectuals—conservative, liberal and socialist—Northern Ireland was simply a back- ward province of Britain . . . the Northern Ireland problem was posed as a series of choices: archaic religious passions versus secular humanism, terrorism versus the rule of law, benighted nationalism versus pluralism' (O'Dowd, 1990: 37–8).

[8] Yet the National Economic and Social Council commissioned a Norwegian (Lars Mjøset) to undertake the first methodologically sound international perspective on Irish socio-economic and institutional development.

[9] Pyle's (1990) study of sex discrimination in the Republic is an example. Studies derived from data collected through panel surveys at the Economic and Social Research Institute in Dublin also adopted a comparative stance on topics such as poverty (e.g., Nolan and Callan, 1993; Nolan and Whelan, 1996).

Social Stratification

The study of social stratification in Ireland began with anthropological work, predominately describing rural communities that could serve as deviant, and strategic, cases for structural functionalist theory (but with a notable urban exception—Humphreys' [1966] study of Dubliners). Sociological investigation of the dynamics of social class as a feature of an emerging industrial society was substantially advanced by the work of the English sociologist Bertram Hutchinson, who joined the staff of the Economic and Social Research Institute in the mid-1960s. His two surveys of social mobility in Dublin (in 1968 and 1972), which replicated research he had previously undertaken in Brazil, reflected Hutchinson's primary concern with the impact of modernisation on structured social inequality. Hutchinson's legacy (Hutchinson, 1969; 1973) included a tradition of stratification analysis linked to the prevailing international standards of theory and methods (Glass, 1954). It also embraced data sets that subsequently provided the basis for the first genuine class analysis in the Republic (Whelan and Whelan, 1984) and the first comparative mobility studies involving the Republic (Breen and Whelan, 1985, comparing a Dublin sample to data from England and Wales).

Stratification research in Northern Ireland originated in efforts to understand the relative strength of religion and class as bases for stratification, with particular reference to the weakness of working-class organisations (e.g., the studies reported in Cormack and Osborne, 1983; 1991).[10] The first major stratification inquiry, undertaken by a North American sociologist, was a part of a comparison of conflict relations in Northern Ireland and New Brunswick, Canada (Augner, 1975). A specially drawn sample from the 1971 Census was used to compare the occupational composition of Protestant and Catholic males.

Both Northern Ireland and the Republic were included in comparative discussions on social mobility carried out through international networks associated with the International Sociological Association's Research Section on Mobility. An all-Ireland social mobility study was undertaken by John Jackson, then at The Queen's University, Belfast through funding by the UK Social Science Research Council. Although Jackson's survey produced detailed data for large samples from the North and South, the comparative potential went unexploited for some time, although basic work on Northern Ireland mobility patterns resulted (Miller, 1986).

---

[10] In this line of inquiry, the work of social anthropologists is often crucial (Harris, 1972). In Northern Ireland, but not in the Republic, a tradition of urban anthropology developed often, but not exclusively, at comprehending the religious divide.

Subsequently, secondary analysis of Hutchinson's data (Breen and Whelan, 1985) and Jackson's data by an American sociologist (Hout and Jackson, 1986; Hout, 1989) explicitly took an all-island comparative purpose, and gave international prominence to consideration of Irish mobility patterns.

The widespread social mobility surveys of the 1970s transformed contemporary study of social class and class mobility (exemplified, notably, in the work of Erikson and Goldthorpe, 1992). In that context, Ireland, and particularly the Republic, offered a crucial test case for the relationship between industrialisation and social mobility, one in which 'history must carry at least as great a weight as theory' (Goldthorpe, 1992: 414).[11]

Social class, social mobility and their links to state strategies and polices, became the central concern of sociological work undertaken at the ESRI in the South, largely through secondary analysis of national surveys. There was also a strong emphasis on the link between social classes and the state in major analyses of society and societal conflict in Northern Ireland (e.g., Bew *et al.*, 1995). The empirical base of such studies, however, was limited to Irish surveys and official statistics, and the comparative dimension remained implicit.[12]

Values and Attitudes

The study of Irish values and attitudes also began as a search for Irish survey data that could speak to the generalisability of international findings on the structure and correlates of values and attitudes. The context was the work of Almond and Verba (1965) that pushed comparative political science beyond its preoccupation with institutions to embrace a new agenda of comparative civic (or political) culture. Scholars around the world quickly sought to add new national cases to the five considered by Almond and Verba.

Indeed, political culture became the topic of the first Irish attitudinal survey with a comparative context. Raven and Whelan (1976: 18) sought to 'study the way in which people perceive the institutions concerned with the

[11] 'Ireland offers an outstanding opportunity for testing empirically certain claims, central to the theory [the liberal theory of industrial society], that concern the effects of industrial development on processes of social stratification, and on the nature and extent of social inequality' (Goldthorpe, 1992: 419). Strategic advantages of the Irish case include the extent of documentation that is available, the role of liberal theory ideas and institutions (World Bank, OECD, IMF) in fostering Irish industrialisation, and, crucially, sequencing in which modernisation preceded industrialisation.

[12] Outsiders are perhaps more conscious of the potential for the Irish case to be illuminated by, and contribute to, the development of general theories concerning state-building (Weitzer, 1990; Lustick, 1993).

management of their society and their own role in relation to them'. The principle researcher, John Raven, was a British social psychologist on the staff of the ESRI concerned with understanding the development of different types of societies through comparative study. Raven had been conducting pilot studies to establish Irish-specific attitudinal measures and scales for a broad-based social survey, but needed to combine resources with Stein Larsen, a Professor at the Institute of Sociology at the University of Bergen, to get a survey into the field. The agreed upon topic was Irish civic culture, replicating Almond and Verba's perspective while also incorporating questions pertaining to specific Irish concerns.[13]

Public opinion poll data provided the underpinnings for many academic analyses of sectarian conflict in Northern Ireland, augmented by three substantial social surveys designed by academics (the classic study by Rose, 1971, and surveys by Moxon-Browne, 1983 and Smith, 1987). After the imposition of Direct Rule, some, but not all (e.g., the General Household Survey) of the official British government social surveys were gradually extended to cover random samples of the Northern population. An independent institute, Social and Community Planning Research, also used a sufficiently large sample from Northern Ireland to support separate analysis, leading to an annual *Social Attitudes in Northern Ireland* report.

The capabilities of survey research were used directly to understand attitudes relating to the Northern conflict. Coordinated surveys were conducted in Northern Ireland (Moxon-Brown, 1983) and in the South (Davis and Sinnott, 1979) under the auspices of the Committee for Social Science Research in Ireland, which itself began as a vehicle for administering a Ford Foundation grant designed to develop the social sciences in Ireland. Controversy surrounding the interpretation of the survey data from the Republic may have blunted the attractiveness of North to South comparisons (Davis *et al.*, 1980), but the feasibility of such research was amply demonstrated.

The prestige of social surveys in the South was enhanced by Ireland's inclusion in the ten-nation 1981 European Values Study Group survey, which sought to examine 'the moral and social values systems prevailing in Europe'. Results from the Irish survey provided the basis for extensive public discussion of major contemporary political and social issues, including those relating to Northern Ireland, which also participated in the survey (Fogarty *et al.*, 1984). In particular, the survey findings were interpreted to show that the values of the people of the two Irelands were closer

---

[13] The standing of attitudinal research in the South was enhanced by another replication (MacGréil, 1977; 1991), which examined 'prejudice and tolerance' among Dubliners using the constructs and survey items developed in the United States for the study of race relations.

to one another than to the rest of the British Isles or Continental Europe. Questions from the 1981 survey were repeated in a 1990 survey, again conducted in both the North and South. The results of the international survey have been widely analysed, and the two Irish cases treated as crucial to interpreting the direction and structure of national value systems (e.g., Kelley and De Graaf, 1997). Irish scholars have examined the link between social change and Irish values in the Republic to challenge the very concept of Irish conservatism and uniqueness that makes it so attractive a case for outsiders and to relevant general theories (Whelan, 1994).

Generic and Specific Problems of Theory and Method

Both Irelands also have been compared to a wide, even exotic range of countries.[14] But most such comparisons are informal, and many are ad hoc. Very few include both Northern Ireland and the Republic of Ireland. The more rigorous comparisons—of class voting and of social mobility, for example—stand for limiting consideration to other industrial capitalist societies and often include both the North and the South as cases. Here, Ireland is often treated strategically, using general theory to inform analysis of Irish structures and processes and using the results to refine theory itself.

To better understand the reasons for this limited and specialised use of the comparative method, I address five questions with specific reference to Ireland and Irish social science. How to compare? How to select the appropriate cases for a comparison? Which cases are truly independent of one another? How to overcome the limitations of small numbers of cases to work with (the small-N problem). And, finally, what kinds of theories should guide comparisons?[15]

---

[14] Ruane and Todd (1996: 4) note that 'Northern Ireland has been compared, *inter alia*, with Canada, South Tyrol, Algeria, the southern US, Bohemia, Prussian Poland, ex-Yugoslavia, the Armenian-Azerbaijan frontier, and implicitly with societies such as Fiji and Burundi'. This reflects the focus on ethno-religious conflict and political instability. While the Republic has been compared to Latin America (Kirby, 1992) and rapidly industrialising Southeast Asia, most comparisons are to the OECD member states in Europe, North America and the Antipodes.

[15] Goldthorpe (1997) highlights the 'black box' problem of processes and connections that lie between the causes and effects that we can observe. I chose, however, to stress problems of selecting cases, which I believe are pervasive in comparisons undertaken by Irish social scientists.

How to Compare?

Selecting a method for comparison is often presented as a choice between two broad approaches to knowing: the quantitative (variable-oriented) and the qualitative (or case-oriented).[16] The variable-oriented, quantitative approach operates through a probabilistic logic and is usually directed at achieving explanation and generalisation in the context of a general theory: it tests abstract hypotheses drawn from general theories (Bollen, 1993: 335). Erikson and Goldthorpe's (1992) analysis of the relationship between class origins and class destinations, measured at the individual level, as it varies among ten industrialised nations adheres to this basic logic, although they lack sufficient cases for a full operationalisation.[17]

The case-oriented, qualitative approach seeks to be holistic, is fundamentally deterministic in its approach to causation (if that is the objective), and stresses what is historical and unique. The aspiration is to treat nations as meaningful wholes. Weitzer's (1990) comparison of Zimbabwe to Northern Ireland as settler societies or Hechter's (1975) study of internal colonialism within the British Isles exemplify this approach. The qualitative approach can be adapted to consider a large (by the standards of macrosocial comparison) number of cases and be multivariate and to reflect a conjunctural form of causal reasoning (Ragin, 1987).[18] Proponents of qualitative studies notably Tilly (1984) and Ragin (1987) claim to occupy a privileged position in their ability to overcome the problems associated with comparative analysis. Their position seems doubtful, however; 'the logic of good quantitative and good qualitative research designs do not fundamentally differ'—they share the same logic of inference despite their different styles (King *et al.*, 1994: 4; see also Goldthorpe, 1997).[19]

Most comparisons are quantitative (based on Ragin's criteria): in recent

---

[16] Comparisons can also be used to illustrate, to establish the limits of existing theory, and to generate hypotheses, all uses that stop short of pursuing causal explanations (Satori, 1993; Skocpol and Somers, 1980) or as a method for achieving control (Smelser, 1976).

[17] Separate analyses in the volume examine social fluidity in Australia, Japan and the United States, countries that are often regarded as exceptions to the general pattern.

[18] Specifically, Ragin offers a 'qualitative comparative method' based on Boolean algebra that seeks to merge features of both the qualitative and quantitative approaches, but adheres to the basic logic of case-oriented comparisons.

[19] Qualitative studies incorporate causal reasoning through J. S. Mill's method of agreement (appropriate where the cases have the same value on the dependent variable) and his method of difference (appropriate where the cases differ on the dependent variable). The surface appeal of such explanatory reasoning is misleading (see the critiques by, among others, Goldthorpe, 1991; 1994; 1997; Lieberson, 1992) 'Application of Mill's methods to small-N situations does not allow for probabilistic theories, interaction effects, measurement errors, or even the presence of more than one cause' (Lieberson, 1992: 117).

Anglo-American sociology only 5 per cent of articles and 21 per cent of books are qualitative (Bollen *et al.*, 1993: 339). However, Ireland North and South have more frequently been considered through qualitative comparisons. Would-be comparativists treating Ireland, and perhaps especially Northern Ireland, as a holistic case face some difficulties. The difficulty in identifying the most appropriate basis for comparison is exacerbated by Ireland's distinctiveness as a part of Europe's North Atlantic periphery. Ireland also is exposed 'to two quite different force-fields—one "European" (which makes it similar in some respects to Scotland, Wales, Brittany or Galicia), the other "colonial" (giving it some of the characteristics of the settler societies of the New World)' (Ruane and Todd, 1996: 269).[20]

Are the Cases 'Independent'?

Ireland presents a particular application of what is known as Galton's Problem, which challenges the presumed independence of cases in comparative analyses.[21] The shared cultural patterns or policy choices of nation-states observed in comparative research may reflect processes of diffusion, from one to the other or from a third case to both, rather than the workings of general causal processes operative within societies. The influence of international institutions such as the World Bank or European Union makes the true independence of national cases questionable, as do the demands imposed by a global economy on the small open economies of many nations and regions.

Such concerns have a clear applicability to Ireland. The Republic and Northern Ireland share a significant administrative inheritance, both of institutions and of political traditions. Both were strongly influenced by changes in British public policy after 1922 and constrained by a shared marginal location within the global economic system. Certainly the same set of international institutions associated with economic development left their marks on the political and economic institutions of both North and South. Across a broad spectrum of comparisons related to public institutions and public policy choices and outcomes, the two Irelands might not

---

[20] Ruane and Todd (1996: 4–5) relate this ambiguity of 'context' to three problems of the comparative method that lead them to proceed cautiously with comparisons: the cultural base of 'meaning'; multideterminism through the interaction of several variables, and the duality of 'contexts' as simultaneously 'internal' and 'external'. However, a sophisticated methodological literature responds to such concerns (see, especially, King *et al.*, 1994).

[21] So named in recognition of Sir Francis Galton's critique of a paper examining the laws of marriage and descent delivered in 1889 to the Royal Anthropological Institute in London (Elder, 1976: 217). Even today, however, few macrocomparisons are attentive to the problem.

be truly independent cases. This concern has particular relevance to the Republic's inclusion in comparative studies seeking to explain the size, scope and nature of welfare states (O'Connor and Brym, 1988; O'Connell, 1994).

There is a body of thought, notably Irish adherents to dependency theory or the world-system perspective, that underestimates the value of treating the South, and for a different set of reasons, the North, as true explanatory units—as cases for comparative analysis. Existing applications of the world-system perspective to Ireland, however sophisticated, tend to be framed as absolutes. The approach taken is too deterministic, reading off a set of characteristics from Ireland's place in the world system. In terms of the North, although there are strong precedents for giving regions within nation-states an independent status, it seems preferable to treat the North in terms of its specific political status.

The most fundamental question is the continuing explanatory relevance of structures and processes within Ireland, relative to the dictates of the global economic and political order. Globalisation is a set of processes that are turning the world into 'a single place' (Robertson, 1992: 396). The term also denotes the current phase of capitalism. 'An integrated and co-ordinated global division of labour' replaced monopoly capitalism, in which 'the world economy could be understood as an aggregation of reasonably distinct national economies; production . . . organised within national boundaries' (Gereffi, 1994: 208). Neither national economies nor state policies may retain sufficient autonomy to be of prime interest in comparative analyses. Consequently, Irish stratification processes, for example, may be shaped more by the international than the national division of labour.

Treating the Republic and the North as explanatory units does require that their institutions and policy-making apparatuses have the capability to shape the national characteristics of interest. Participation in the global economy limits the choices available in formulating national or regional policy. Certainly the Republic's dependence on investments by multinational firms and the North's dependence on subsidies from the British Exchequer make their economies vulnerable to outside influences (Kennedy, 1989). But the strength of such influences is overstated in world-system-based explanations of Ireland's pattern of developments. Or, more precisely, the countervailing national factors are systematically undervalued.

Another important consequence of the application of world-system and similar perspectives to Ireland is that its slot in the world system is seen as translating automatically into a weak state (O'Hearn, 1995). A more compelling case can be made, however, that a form of a state-centred theory is essential for comprehending developments in Southern Ireland since Independence (Rottman *et al.*, 1982; Girvin, 1989; Breen *et al.*, 1990; and O'Connell and Rottman, 1992). Similarly, the work of Bew and his colleagues (1995) on the Northern state would seem to suggest that it retained considerable explanatory force through its various manifestations.[22]

In comparative research, 'boundaries around place and time periods define cases' (Ragin, 1987: 5). The island of Ireland is an awkward place to fix such boundaries of time and place. Political and economic boundaries have coincided rarely in the modern period. A clear split in the economies of the North and the South was evident in the middle of the nineteenth century (Bradley, 1996: 147). State-building North and South came later for the most part, but preceded partition. Changes in the British Administration between 1880 and 1920 forged two civil services, one in Dublin and the other in Belfast, that were easily grafted onto the two new states (McCogan, 1982; McBride, 1991).[23]

What can be done with Small-Ns?

Can meaningful comparisons be made between two cases (North and South) or among the small number of countries that are likely to be relevant to both North and South? This, the small-N problem, is pervasive: most comparative studies in the areas of stratification and of race and ethnic relations are based on five or fewer cases and a significant proportion embrace only two cases (Bollen *et al.*, 1993: 228). Some of the most influential comparative works of the post-Second World War period are based on small numbers of cases (Skocpol, 1979; Moore, 1966). The problems encountered with small-Ns, however, apply equally to these qualitative studies. Variables must exceed cases by a ratio that can be established empirically (King *et al.*, 1994: 213–17). Thus, ultimately, the small-N problem is one of too little data, not of the choice of method (Goldthorpe, 1997).

---

[22] There may be, however, unexploited possibilities in terms of how a perspective derived from dependency theory can breathe some new life into old subjects. McCullagh (1996: Chapter 5), for example, draws upon some ideas from dependency theory to explain crime patterns in the Republic. Explanation there, however, requires a version of dependency perspective so 'soft' as to be heretical.

[23] The independence of the North and South as 'cases' can also be viewed as under threat from the growth of supranational forms of government such as the European Union. However, the EU's member states retain a largely unrestricted role in key policy areas such as education, industrial relations, social welfare and taxation—which collectively filter world-system effects on national populations (Castles, 1988).

Comparisons embracing the North and South can either be one-on-one or include other cases that are relevant and appropriate to the purpose of the comparison. Either option raises the small-N problem: there are too many variables and too few cases.[24] Consideration of a small number of cases, the typical situation for comparisons involving Ireland, has other consequences. Reliance on a small number of cases highlights the specifics from the history and circumstances of the countries considered (Tilly, 1984: 76). Small-N comparisons bring out dissimilarities, in contrast to larger comparisons, which tend to reveal similarities. And findings of dissimilarity present more difficult problems of interpretation than do those indicating similarity. The explanation of differences between nations 'requires more explicit consideration of historical, cultural, and political-economic particularities than does the lawful explanation of cross-national similarities' (Kohn, 1987: 717).

In small-N situations, the tension between general causal arguments and the historically contingent is likely to be strong. Indeed, history is often central to comparative work on Ireland. How does one incorporate the distinctive history of the island and of the North and South in this century into comparisons? To some, comparisons must be framed to incorporate the specifics of history. This makes it difficult for theory to guide comparative projects. Others, notably Goldthorpe (1997) argue that 'history exposes the limits of theory', a view he has related to the potential for the Irish case to sharpen understanding of the relationship between industrialisation and the openness of class structures (Goldthorpe, 1992).

How to Select Comparable Cases?

The selection of cases is the main choice available to a qualitative comparativist (King *et al.*, 1994: Chapter 4; Sartori, 1994). It is also fundamental to the task of quantitative comparativists. For both types of comparisons, the objective is to select the cases that maximise leverage over the causal hypotheses under consideration and to eliminate confounding variables. The most common approach is to select cases that are as similar as possible (Bollen *et al.*, 1993: 331). The other common strategy, the selection of cases that are as different as possible, is rarely applied to Ireland.

Case selection is related to the fundamental question of whether Northern Ireland and the Republic of Ireland can validly be selected for inclusion in a comparison. Do the discrepant political statuses of the two

---

[24] Stated differently, a problem arises when 'we have more inferences than implications observed' (King *et al.*, 1994: 119), a problem as applicable to qualitative comparisons as it is to quantitative ones.

Irelands—the North as a region of the UK and the Republic as a nation-state, make a true macrocomparison possible?[25]

Macrocomparative social science uses the attributes of macrosocial units to offer explanations (Ragin, 1987: 5–7). The 'unit of explanation' (what accounts for the observed results), must be societal or otherwise macrosocial; the 'unit of observation' (the one used for data collection and data analysis) is the individual.[26] Typically, the macrosocial explanatory unit is the nation-state, although units within nations, including regions, can meet these criteria (Elder, 1976: 218–19).[27]

There are a number of approaches to resolving the problem of when the North and South can be compared, either to one another or in a broader comparison. The first two strategies seek to meet Ragin's (1987) assumption that the nation-state or other macrosocial entity serves as the explanatory unit. A third approach meets Kohn's (1987: 714) lower standard for cross-national research: studies that are explicitly comparative in that they 'utilize systematically data from two or more nations'. A fourth strategy treats the Irish case to test ('confirm or infirm') a theory or perspective (Kazancigil, 1994). The fifth strategy is a 'side by side' comparison in which findings from one case are used informally to illuminate findings from the other case.

Nation-State to State or Nation

Definitions of a nation-state abound, with several alternatives that are particularly relevant to the task in hand. Charles Tilly in his sweeping interpretations of European history, prefers the general label of national state: 'states governing multiple contiguous regions and their cities by

[25] Indeed, one Southern sociologist whose views I respect greatly described a North/South comparison to me as being tantamount to comparing North Dakota to Canada. But there are precedents for such a study. The study of the status attainment process, which dominated the field of stratification during the 1970s and beyond, was based on a survey of young men in the state of Wisconsin. A small industry emerged in which national samples from other countries were, in essence, being compared to natives of Wisconsin.

[26] Ragin (1987: 5) offers as an example the link between social class and political party preference: 'If a study seeks to explore the link between various configurations of industrial society and that link, it is comparative. However, if the objective is to use data from various countries to test a hypothesis stating that people follow their economic interest when voting, the social scientist would have avoided concretizing any macrosocial unit and thereby would have avoided engaging in comparative social science.'

[27] Przeworski and Teune (1970) offer a more restrictive definition of comparative social science because they exclude instances in which the dependent variable is an aggregation of individual level data (e.g., national literacy rates or unemployment rates). Dependent variables in their programme describe relationships that are measured at the level of the individual.

means of centralized, differentiated, and autonomous structures'. Such entities are rare, but even rarer are those that he terms nation-states:

> . . . a state whose people share a strong linguistic, religious, and symbolic identity. Although states such as Sweden and Ireland now approximate that ideal, very few European national states have ever qualified as nation-states.[28] (1993: 2–3)

The nature of the Irish state has generated much debate in the South. Unfortunately, much of the discussion has revolved around issues of 'autonomy' and 'capacity' without producing a clear outcome. Proponents of a strong, autonomous state may have been over eager to apply the then popular state-centred approach to Ireland. However, such an approach does seem to provide an explanation of such key features of the Republic as the growth and shape of its welfare state (O'Connell and Rottman, 1992).

It may be that centralisation, rather than 'autonomy' is the real consideration about the two Irelands when framing a comparative project. The UK and the Republic of Ireland are among the more centralised of the EU countries. Centralisation complicates a direct comparison because so many aspects of government in the North are established in London and not in Belfast. Such a conclusion, though, emphasises the 'state' component of the nation-state.

There nevertheless are strong precedents for including both North and South in a comparative project. Erikson and Goldthorpe (1992: 53), for example, treat Northern Ireland, Scotland, England and Wales, and the Republic of Ireland as independent *national* units in their study of comparative social mobility. The first three of those units are treated as 'the component parts of a larger, multinational state'. Sufficient variation in social fluidity is found among those component parts to make a strong claim for their separate consideration. While Northern Ireland is one of eleven official regions of the United Kingdom, its institutional distinctiveness suffices to justify its treatment as a case in some comparative projects.

Nation-State to Region-State

Regions of countries can stand alone as the units for macrosocial comparison if justified by the specific topic that is the reason for the comparison (Elder, 1976: 218–19). The concept of a 'region-state' offers one possible basis for framing North to South comparisons. A 'region-state' is a:

---

[28] Chase-Dunn (1989) and Giddens (1985) offer alternative definitions with different implications for the conduct of comparative analysis.

> ... natural economic zone that has important advantages for successfully competing in the global economy: 'The primary linkages of region states tend to be with the global economy and not with their host nations. . . . A region-state must be small enough for its citizens to share certain economic and consumer interests but of adequate size to justify the infrastructure . . . necessary to participate economically on a global scale'. (Ohmae, 1993: 80)

Region-states are thus focused on the global economy, while nation-states are focused on domestic politics. Ohmae (1993: 81) asserts that a region-state is defined by economies of scale in consumption, infrastructure and professional services (rather than in production) and, further, that where this obtains, religious, ethnic and racial divisions are unimportant.

A more sociological formulation of a region-state potentially offers a gateway to direct North/South comparisons. To Giddens (1984: 122), region:

> ... always carries the connotation of the structuration of social conduct across time-space. Thus there is a strong degree of regional differentiation, in terms of class relationships and a variety of other social criteria, between the North and the South in Britain. The 'North' is not just a geographically delimited area but one with long-established, distinctive traits.

Applications of the 'new regionalism' to the political sociology of Scotland bear this out by identifying three 'places' (in effect, regions) in which economic base, demography, culture and politics combine (Agnew, 1987: Chapter 7).[29] Discounting the significance of regional differences in the socio-economic institutions within nation-states may promote aggregation error.[30]

A solid sociological definition of a region-state would open up new possibilities for comparisons between small open economies (such as the South) and small open regions, such as the North. Bradley (1996: 4, 32–3, 55) strongly advocates such a stance, while also noting issues for which the different statuses of state apparatuses North and South make direct comparison inappropriate. Such comparisons need not focus on economic issues directly. Regional institutions and culture can provide a sufficient rationale for treating the North and the South as cases meriting the same explanatory status. Comparative studies of public trust and confidence in

---

[29] The extent to which regional differences within nations are of consequence to structured social inequality may be linked back to processes in the global economy. Region is more important in weak states (that is, economically uncompetitive nations), such as Britain, than in strong states, such as Sweden (Vogler, 1985: 168–72).

[30] A North/South comparison would seem a natural vehicle for addressing Joe Lee's claims concerning entrepreneurship in the South or the various contending claims as to which forces most strongly condition Irish economic performance, a question addressed by Mjøset (1992) for the South without particular reference to the North (see Bradley, 1996: 34).

government, for example, can treat the North and South as equivalent units of analysis (see the 21 nation study by Nye *et al.*, 1997).[31]

Context to Context

If we specify that the nation (usually nation-state) is the *context* of study rather than its object (which is its role in the Ragin approach), opportunities for comparative research expand greatly. The national context can be formally incorporated into the comparison, as it was in Kelley and De Graaf's (1997) study of religious beliefs that included both national (the context) and parental religiosity as explanatory factors in a 15 country study. However, any study qualifies for this general strategy if it primarily seeks to test the generality of findings and interpretations about how various social institutions operate or how social structures impinge on individuals (Kohn, 1987: 714).[32] Much, perhaps most, of the social science research undertaken in the North or in the South would seem to qualify for this specification of comparative work.

Deviant or Strategic Case Analysis

Selection to achieve diversity is associated with the selection of deviant or strategic cases for analysis. This has been frequently applied in Ireland, for example, in the context of the relationship between industrialisation and class mobility (Breen and Whelan, 1995; this volume).[33] In this scenario the hypotheses drawn from a general theory suggest that Ireland is either a deviant case (it modernised before it industrialised) or is an outlier to the general pattern observed through the analysis of cases (it is the least 'open' of the industrial nations). In a sense, such deviant case analyses explore the boundary between theory and history (Goldthorpe, 1997; Kazancigil, 1993).

---

[31] Kohn is agnostic about whether the nation-state has a special status in comparative research, noting that 'we learn something about the importance or lack of importance of the nation-state by discovering which processes transcend national boundaries and which processes are idiosyncratic to particular nations or to particular types of nations' (1987: 725).

[32] Kohn (1987: 725) usefully distinguishes comparative, cross-national and cross-cultural research, and notes how they differ from cross-societal and cross-systemic research.

[33] Arensberg and Kimball, and their mentor W. Lloyd Warner, were perhaps the first to seize upon the strategic potential of the Irish case. The sociology department of Harvard University had developed a central hypothesis through the application of the ethnographic methods and theories used to study primitive societies to a New England city ('Yankee City'). Then, 'in a setting far different but still in some ways closely comparable to the American scene . . . they would try to give it [their hypothesis] a greater precision' (1940/68: *xxx*).

Side-by-Side Comparisons

Here, the nation still serves as the context for the research, but the comparisons are informal and implicit. Comparisons are informal because the researcher does not employ a theory that indicates which characteristics of the macrosocial units are important or why they are important as explanations for the phenomena being studied. There is usually no explicit interest in generalising from the collection of nations under scrutiny. Rather, comparisons are made of industrial relations or crime trends in several countries in the hope that doing so clarifies patterns and sharpens interpretation of findings in each nation or in the primary nation of interest.

Most North/South comparisons take this form. The Republic and Northern Ireland are discussed in successive sections of a chapter or article (Rottman, 1989; Brewer, 1996) or in successive chapters of an edited volume (e.g., O'Hearn, 1995; O'Dowd, 1995). The two 'cases' engage at a distance and discursively rather than analytically.

Side-by-side comparisons are desirable and may be a necessary first step toward comparative analyses fitting the specifications of Kohn or Ragin. Too often, though, the informal and implicit nature of side-by-side comparison promotes interpretations that are based, in effect, on stereotypical views of particular nations and their peoples: their entrepreneurial abilities, their mind sets, or a vague reference to 'their histories'.

What Kinds of Theories are Helpful?

Often, the theories that have been applied to the North or the South, and are thus available for application to North/South comparisons, stifle comparisons. Dependency and world-system perspectives deny either Ireland independent status as explanatory units. Similarly, structural functionalism (for which the Republic was one of the last refuges) and modernisation theory are based on a presumed convergence of nations, due to the logic of industrial society. In all of these theoretical perspectives, what transpires within nations is of limited significance relative to what occurs on a larger stage.

There is a more specific problem. These theoretical frameworks all suffer from inattention to macro-to-micro linkages. All comparative analyses need to be attentive to the often neglected 'micro' foundations of macrosociology (Erikson and Goldthorpe, 1992: 1; Goldthorpe, 1992: 141–2).[34]

---

[34] The principle of methodological individualism is that 'all social phenomena are ultimately explicable in terms of the actions of individuals and of their intended and unintended consequences . . . What methodological individualism denies is not the reality of social phenomena but rather that there are supraindividual actors or ("subjects") . . . whose action can or must be understood independently of and prior to, that of individuals in the context of,

Explanations of differences between the North and South premised on the projects or interests of various social classes or of the state are unconvincing in my view. Macro-level explanations for North/South differences need to specify, for example, why *individuals* occupying similar class positions in the North and in the South behave differently as voters or trade union members (Breen and Rottman, 1995). Here, rational choice (or action) theory offers a basis for connecting macrosocial processes and the behaviour of individuals. It is not the only vehicle for making that connection, but it has been applied to topics of clear relevance to a comparison of North and South (Hechter, 1986; Meadwell, 1993).

The Nature and Role of Vision

The theoretical and methodological problems associated with comparative analysis, although formidable, cannot fully account for the paucity of social science work embracing both the North and South of Ireland. Instead, explanations for the reciprocal neglect of the island's other 'case' require reference to what I term the social psychology of comparisons.

A social psychological dimension is generic to comparative analyses, affecting which problems and which cases are regarded as appropriate for such treatment.[35] Lipset (1990; 1996), for example, notes the pattern in North America for United States social scientists to ignore the 'case' to their North, but for nothing to be written by their Canadian counterparts *without* a comparison to the United States. Why this is so is a question to be answered primarily within the sociology of knowledge, not within the logic of the comparative method. In a consideration of problems of comparing Northern Ireland and the Republic, however, social psychological issues are more acute.

The international literature provides little guidance for these problems of vision. Indeed, in some measure however, the problem is specific to 'these islands':

---

say, some theory of history or the functioning of social systems' (Erikson and Goldthorpe, 1992: 1, fn 1).

[35] Related issues include why some kinds of social science theory are popular in some regions and nations but not in others and why some social structures and processes are viewed as problematic in some places but not in others. Kohn (1987: 713, fn 1) summarises analyses of the varying fortunes of comparative studies in American (US) sociology, and the internationalisation of that discipline since the 1960s, including the rise in cross-national collaborations.

> . . . studies of contemporary Irish society, history and politics have tended to
> suffer from a habit of viewing Irish affairs as unique, in part, a consequence
> of 'the usual British Isles parochialism'. (Garvin, 1996: 1)

There are, however, features of the intellectual climate generally, and of
Irish social sciences, that differ between North and South, creating different visions of the island's other case. I treat these separately, beginning with
the Republic.

Southern Perspectives

The 'spirit of an age' (Lee, 1989: 619) during the formative years of Irish
social science inhibited comparative work. Declan Kiberd (1996: 574) sums
up the atmosphere of the 1960s and 1970s in this way:

> To many southerners, the north seemed a Neanderthal place, caught in a
> historical time-warp, inhabited by paranoiacs who couldn't trust one another,
> much less the outside world. The south liked to think of itself as superior,
> affluent, urbane and forward-looking; the north, according to such thinking,
> was trapped in a woeful, repetitive past.

Kiberd (1996: 573–5) places this lack of interest and sense of connection in
the context of the coincidence of 'the Troubles' with the Republic's long-
delayed emergence into a period of affluence and dynamism. It was also a
period in which Catholicism became primarily a private, rather than public
identity: 'In the new emerging Ireland, religion was to be a private affair.'
The result was a weak solidarity with the nationalist community in the
North: 'A plague on both your houses' was a common response. In Sean
O'Faolain's (1969: 165) words, the population of the South was 'weary of
the past'.[36]

Simply put, the North was not regarded as an appropriate point of
reference for Southern social science:[37]

---

[36] An alternative interpretation is that the Lemass era's preoccupation with material success
reflected a belief that Southern economic development was the most practical and promising
expression of nationalism. A modern, prosperous South might be less objectionable to
Northern unionists as part of a united Ireland (Brown, 1985: 279–80).

[37] When I joined the staff of the ESRI in September, 1975, the North was very much in the news.
It was not frequently discussed in the Institute, being, I think, regarded as a topic for conversa-
tion with family and friends, not with colleagues. However, Roy Geary, the formidable first
Director of the ESRI, and perhaps the most distinguished social analyst Ireland has produced,
worked in collaboration with Northern statisticians and economists. Also, the Professors of
Economics at The Queen's University and the New University of Ulster served on the ESRI's
Council. Northern social scientists published articles in the *Economic and Social Review.* So my
sense was and is that the ESRI was atypically engaged with its Northern counterparts.

The Irish contemporary historian finds himself in the unusual position of being simultaneously insider and outsider. He cannot pronounce on both Northern Ireland and the Republic from the same perspective, relying on the same silent assumptions. A truly comparative history of North and South has yet to be adequately conceived, much less completed. Southern Irish historians, like myself, are likely to be as ambivalent toward the North as are citizens of the Republic in general. If it was a striking achievement of an impressive generation of Irish historians to 'exorcise passion' from the study of the Irish past, it did so largely by evading the challenge of contemporary history. (Lee, 1990: *xiv*)

However, there was from the 1980s onwards a growing interest in using cross-national comparisons to enhance understanding of structure and processes in the Republic. Comparative references to other small Western European countries became commonplace in Irish social science. Girvin (1989), for example, used several groups of comparisons in his analysis of development in Ireland. One comparative reference for him is the experience of Greece, Portugal and Spain. He also made use of comparisons to Austria, Finland and Switzerland. Indeed, the title of his book, *Between Two Worlds,* reflects his claim for Irish distinctiveness, with the Republic falling between the situation of high growth and high living standards of countries such as Denmark, Finland and Austria and the situation of low growth and low living standards of such countries as Greece, Brazil and Argentina. Other writers were more taken by the parallels between the Republic and Latin America. An interest in those parallels dates back to Independence, and has been reinforced through the influence of Liberation Theology in more recent years (Kiberd, 1996: 272, 572; Kirby, 1992).[38]

Lee's (1989) *Ireland: Politics and Society* was published in the same year as Girvin's book and also made extensive and imaginative use of comparative material. The extensive publicity and discussion that Lee's book generated solidified the emerging status of comparative work, making it fashionable and almost obligatory. Kiberd (1996: 645–6), for example, argues that an 'insistence on the value of comparisons' was Joe Lee's greatest contribution to Irish scholarship, breaking through a tradition that insisted on Irish exceptionality. However, he notes that Lee's comparisons:

---

[38] As Smith (1995, 38) notes, 'Too often, the construction of nations has been equated with state-building. But state-building . . . is not to be confused with the forging of a national cultural and political identity among often culturally heterogeneous populations.' This claim, developed in light of the experience in contexts such as the Philippines and Ethiopia applies to Northern Ireland, and argues for a focus on institutions and culture that, even if in contention, are Northern Ireland, not UK phenomena.

. . . were all with smaller European countries, which did not undergo the long nightmare of colonial expropriation and misrule, much less wave after wave after wave of massive emigration. Had he widened his field of vision, he might have conceded that in many respects the Irish achievement has been remarkable.

Kiberd's concern is based largely on the case of Greece, the EU's other European post-colonial nation, which tends to be outside of Lee's comparative scope.

Still, the new popularity of interpretations founded upon comparisons in the South has not extended to broad consideration of the North as a case. There are some exceptions, notably in economics (Bradley, 1996),[39] the sociology of education (Breen, Heath and Whelan, this volume), and social mobility (Breen and Whelan, this volume).

Northern Perspectives

The general failure of Irish social scientists to seek analytical leverage through North/South comparisons does parallel the curious scholarly silence in the North about the sectarian Northern state (O'Leary, 1993). O'Leary offers a concise but devastating history of the Northern state that makes the silence from the academic community so deafening:

> Why at no time during those years [before 1969] did the academics of Queen's University of Belfast—the University of Ulster was scarcely off the ground by 1968—provide the guidance that other societies have come to expect from intellectuals? (O'Leary, 1993: 155)[40]

O'Leary's tenure as a professor at The Queen's University, Belfast suggests that he possessed relevant insider and self-knowledge. However, he raises the question at the end of his contribution and leaves it unanswered.[41]

During the 1970s, the social sciences in Northern Ireland became

---

[39] Some fundamental commonalities between North and South have been noted, such as a shared record as being among the 'striking economic failures of this century' (Lee, 1989: xiii).

[40] Hill and Marsh (1993) point to the role played by Basil Chubb in the South as what was absent in the North. However, after 1969, Northern-based social scientists became rapidly engaged in addressing political and social issues. It is fair to say that by the 1990s the degree of engagement with issues of the day in the North rivalled or exceeded that found among social scientists based in the South.

[41] This claim of mutual neglect can be extended to Irish economists: 'In the past each region saw its peripherality *not* in the context of the island of Ireland, encompassing—in an entirely benign way—the similar plight of the other region, but in a more exclusive way that placed little value on the market potential of the other region or of the island economy as a whole' (Bradley, 1996: 32). Bradley goes on to note that the North is understood as one of the eleven UK sub-regions, while the South is viewed as a small peripheral member state of the EU (1996: 33).

vigorous in productivity and in 'relevance' (Whyte, 1990). Of course, 'the Troubles' can explain much of the change, but other factors are important. Considerations include the presence of a new generation of Irish social scientists, many trained in the United States (or in the South), rather than the UK and previously noted all-Ireland social science research committees and funding.

But this new vigour did not generate a look southward for comparative inspiration. University departments remained fractured, with Britain the main frame of reference for many academics.[42] Many scholars mirrored the Southern view of the Republic's uniqueness. Here, however, the South's uniqueness is rooted in the dominance of the Catholic Church, economic failure, debilitating emigration, poor public service provision and dependence upon EU largesse (Ruane and Todd, 1996: 256–9). The South was easy to dismiss by Northern Protestants and Catholics alike as irrelevant to understanding their situations.

Prospects for Comparing the Two Irelands

Comparative research is demanding of time, effort and resources. The task of comparing Northern Ireland and the Republic of Ireland presents further obstacles. There is a weak tradition of systematic comparisons on which to build: the use of the comparative method has been a weakness, not a strength of Irish social science. Scholars in one part of the island operate through mind sets that render the structures and processes of the other part irrelevant to understanding and explaining. Moreover, the different political statuses of the North and South restrict the kinds of topics, questions and hypotheses that sensibly can be approached comparatively.

Cross-national comparisons also have a unique capacity to illuminate, to test alternative explanations, and to explain. North/South comparisons, either one-on-one or with a set of other purposefully selected cases, have much to offer. Useful comparisons can range from those in which countries (or regions) serve as explanatory units to less ambitious forms of context-to-context or side-by-side studies. It should be recognised, however, that the lower the ambition, the lower will be the contribution.

What needs to be done? Comparisons that treat the Irish case—North, South, or both—strategically to apply and test general theories have delivered dramatic increases in knowledge. The North has served this role in relation to settler societies and the South in relation to the origins and

---

[42] A Southern-born, United States-trained sociologist returning to an academic post in the North during the mid-1970s claims that 'I seemed to have become an outsider in what I had hitherto regarded as my own country' (O'Dowd, 1990: 34).

consequences of structured social inequality. Such comparisons are demanding intellectually but do not presuppose the availability of precisely comparable international data.

A shift from reliance on qualitative comparisons and toward quantitative ones is also needed to realise the contribution to theory and understanding that the comparative method can yield. Scholars in both North and South seem reluctant to exploit the body of data now available from international surveys through secondary analysis. Irish universities need to provide the training required for macrocomparisons and to instill the value of systematic comparative thinking. Some of the problems that I label social psychological are doubtless products of the forms of professional socialisation prevalent in Irish economics, history, social psychology and sociology over recent decades.

This leads directly to the issue of how to select the cases for comparison. A promising development is the concept of 'families of nations, defined in terms of shared geographical, linguistic, cultural and/or historical attributes and leading to distinctive patterns of public policy outcomes' (Castles, 1993a: *xiii*).[43] This offers the potential to develop and test explanations that simultaneously consider the effects of Irish national characteristics and those associated with one or more 'families' to which Ireland belongs. It also provides a basis for filling in the ranks of other countries to include when comparing North and South.

In terms of true macrolevel comparisons, Northern Ireland and the Republic of Ireland are suitable cases along with other cases for comparisons concerning crime and crime victimisation, social mobility, poverty, voting behaviour, labour market entry and educational participation. Certainly, the other part of the island is a more plausible comparative case than England or the Netherlands for many purposes. Moreover, Ireland can be viewed as a naturally occurring experiment in which one macrosocial case became two cases. Interconnections between the North, South and Britain also offer potential insight into, for example, the treatment of minorities in new states. For example, an understanding of public opinion and political party behaviour in the North and South is a product of a three-way interaction of Northern Ireland, the Republic of Ireland and the British government.

Comparative thinking depends on the application of theory. There are

---

[43] A good starting point might be the claim that the Republic of Ireland does not belong within the English-speaking family of nations: 'Our view is that to include Ireland would distract the analysis for its main objects, which is to establish what it is about the other five English-speaking nations which made them seek to refashion the relationship between state and economy to a degree unparalleled elsewhere in the world of capitalism (Castles, 1993b: 5).

'traditions' of theory and research that link North and South. One such link is the importance attributed to the state and to social class by Bew and his colleagues (e.g., Bew *et al.*, 1995) in the North and by ESRI sociologists (e.g, Rottman and O'Connell, 1982; Breen *et al.*, 1990; O'Connell and Rottman, 1992) in the South. Both theoretical perspectives seek to explain social change through an investigation of the evolving link between class and state. It is likely that both perspectives would be sharpened through an application to the island's other case. A specific application to the educational systems of the two jurisdictions is particularly apt, touching on an important topic in the literature on nations and nationalism (e.g., Gellner, 1983).

Theoretical perspectives from the literature on ethnicity and class stratification also resonate well with the macro-level issues raised by a comparison between the Republic of Ireland and Northern Ireland. One set of theories relate to the interrelationship of class and ethnicity, notably those offered by Parkin (1979) and Hechter (1975). Another approach is through the work of Charles Tilly (1996) on citizenship, identity and social history.

The ability of theory to frame North/South comparisons will depend, in part, on the degree to which attention is paid to the micro-foundations of macro-level theories. The comparative method is blunt and sterile if it operates entirely at the macro level of nations or regions. Indeed, true cross-national comparisons use the individual as the unit of data collection.

Finally, the social psychological barriers to North/South comparisons need to be recognised and addressed. Scholars in the South are clearly more comfortable framing comparisons to Australia, Japan or the Netherlands than to Northern Ireland. Comparative work in the North tends to be framed to locate other cases with sustained political instability and ethnic conflict. A region can serve as a unit of explanation or as the context for comparisons. There is an unrealised potential for the North to stand as a point of comparison with the Republic.

A paper reciting the difficulties of comparative research might seem destined toward a gloomy set of conclusions about the prospects for North/South comparisons. There is however scope for one-on-one comparisons between Northern Ireland and the Republic of Ireland, and for more broadly drawn comparative efforts embracing both Irelands and other cases. Given the number of studies comparing the Republic to Australia or to Switzerland and the North to Lebanon and South Africa, it is difficult to comprehend how reasons of theory or method can push the North and South beyond one another's comparative reach.

Acknowledgements. I am grateful for critical reviews of earlier drafts, suggestions, encouragement and editorial advice provided by John Bradley, Richard Breen, Roger Hanson, Ciaran McCullagh, Kieran McKeown, and Chris Whelan.

References

Agnew, J. A. (1987) *Place and Politics: The Geographical Mediation of State and Society*, Boston: Allen and Unwin.

Arensberg, C. M. and Kimball, S. T. (1968) *Family and Community in Ireland*, Second Edition, Cambridge Mass.: Harvard University Press (first edition, 1940).

Augner, E. A. (1975) 'Religion and Occupational Class in Northern Ireland', *Economic and Social Review*, 7(1): 1–18.

Bew, P. and Patterson, H. (1982) *Seán Lemass and the Making of Modern Ireland 1945–66*, Dublin: Gill and Macmillan.

Bew, P., Gibbon, P. and Patterson, H. (1995) *Northern Ireland 1921–1994: Political Forces and Social Classes*, London: Serif.

Bollen, K., Entwisle, B. and Alderson, A. (1993) 'Macrocomparative Research Methods', *Annual Review of Sociology*, 19: 321–51.

Bradley, J. (1996) *Exploring Long-Term Economic and Social Consequences of Peace and Reconciliation in the Island of Ireland*, Consultancy Studies No. 4, Forum for Peace and Reconciliation, Dublin: Stationery Office.

Breen, R., Hannan, D., Rottman, D. and Whelan, C. (1990) *Understanding Contemporary Ireland: State, Class, and Development in the Republic of Ireland*, London: Macmillan.

Breen, R. and Rottman, D. (1995) 'Class Analysis and Class Theory', *Sociology* 29(3): 453–73.

Breen, R. and Rottman, D. (1998) 'Is the National-State the Appropriate Geographical Unit for Class Analysis?', *Sociology* 32: 1–21.

Breen, R. and Whelan, C. T. (1985) 'Vertical Mobility and Class Inheritance in the British Isles', *British Journal of Sociology*, 36: 176–92.

Breen, R. and Whelan, C. T. (1994) 'Measuring Trends in Social Fluidity: The Core Model and a Measured Variable Approach Compared', *European Sociological Review*, 10: 259–72.

Breen, R. and Whelan, C. T. (1995) 'Gender and Class Mobility: Evidence from the Republic of Ireland', *Sociology*, 29: 1–22.

Breen, R. and Whelan, C. T. (1996) *Social Mobility and Social Class in Ireland*, Dublin: Gill and Macmillan.

Brewer, John (ed.) (1996) *The Police, Public Order and the State: Policing in Great Britain, Northern Ireland, the Irish Republic, the USA, Israel, South Africa, and China*, New York: St. Martins Press.

Brown, T. (1985) *Ireland: A Social and Cultural History*, London: Fontana.

Burawoy, M. (1985) *The Politics of Production in Factory Regimes Under Capitalism and Socialism*, London: Verso.

Carnoy, M. (1993) 'Multinationals in a Changing World Economy: Whither the Nation-State?' in M. Carnoy, M. Castells, S. Cohen and F. Henrique Cardoso (eds), *The New Global Economy in the Information Age: Reflections on Our Changing World*, University Park, Pa.: The Pennsylvania State University Press.

Carnoy, M., Castells, M., Cohen, S. S. and Henrique Cardoso F. (1993) 'Introduction' and 'Epilogue', in M. Carnoy, M. Castells, S. Cohen and F. Henrique Cardoso (eds), *The New Global Economy in the Information Age: Reflections on Our Changing World*, University Park, Pa.: The Pennsylvania State University Press.

Castles, F. (1988) *The State and Political Theory*, Princeton, NJ.: Princeton University Press.

Castles, F. (1993a) 'Introduction' in F. Castles (ed.), *Families of Nations: Patterns of Public Policy in Western Democracies*, Aldershot: Dartmouth Publishing.

Castles, F. (1993b) 'Changing Course in Economic Policy: the English-speaking Nations in the 1980s' in F. Castles (ed.), *Families of Nations: Patterns of Public Policy in Western Democracies*, Aldershot: Dartmouth Publishing.

Chase-Dunn, C. (1989) *Global Formation: Structures of the World-Economy*, Cambridge Mass.: Blackwell.

Coakley, J. (1980) 'Independence Movements and National Minorities: Some Parallels in the European Experience', *European Journal of Political Research*, 8: 215–48.

Coakley, J. (1990) 'National Minorities and the Government of Divided Societies: a Comparative Analysis of some European Evidence', *European Journal of Political Research*, 18: 437–56.

Cormack, R. J. and Osborne, R. D. (eds) (1983) *Religion, Education, and Aspects of Equal Opportunity in Northern Ireland*, Belfast: Appletree.

Cormack, R. J. and Osborne, R. D. (1991) 'Disadvantage and Discrimination in Northern Ireland' in R. J. Cormack and R. D. Osborne (eds), *Discrimination and Public Policy in Northern Ireland*, Oxford: Clarendon.

Davis, E. E. and Sinnott, R. (1979) *Attitudes in the Republic of Ireland Relevant to the Northern Ireland Problem*, Dublin: Economic and Social Research Institute.

Davis, E. E., Sinnott, R., Baker, T. J., Hannan, D. F., Rottman, D. B. and Walsh, B. M. (1980) *Some Issues in the Methodology of Attitude Research*, Dublin: Economic and Social Research Institute.

Deflem, M. and Pampel, F. C. (1996) 'The Myth of Postnational Identity: Popular Support for European Unification', *Social Forces*, 75(1): 119–43.

Elder, J. W. (1976) 'Comparative Cross-National Methodology', *Annual Review of Sociology*, 2: 209–29.

Erikson, R. and Goldthorpe, J. H. (1992) *The Constant Flux: A study of Class Mobility in Industrial Societies*, Oxford: Oxford University Press.

Firebaugh, G. and Beck, F. D. (1994) 'Does Economic Growth Benefit the Masses?', *American Sociological Review*, 59(5): 631–53.

Fogarty, M., Ryan, L. and Lee, J. (1984) *Irish Values and Attitudes: The Irish Report of the European Value Systems Study*, Dublin: Dominican Publications (for the Conference of Major Religious Superiors).

Garvin, T. (1987) *Nationalist Revolutionaries in Ireland*. Oxford: Clarendon Press.

Garvin, T. (1996) *1922: The Birth of Irish Democracy*, Dublin: Gill and Macmillan.

Gellner, E. (1983) *Nations and Nationalism*, Cambridge, Mass.: Blackwell.

Gereffi, G. (1994) 'The International Economy and Economic Development' in

N. Smelser and R. Swedberg (eds), *The Handbook of Economic Sociology*, Princeton, NJ: Princeton University Press.

Giddens, A. (1984) *The Constitution of Society: Outline of the Theory of Structuration*, Cambridge: Polity Press.

Giddens, A. (1985/1987) *The Nation-State and Violence*, Berkeley: University of California Press.

Girvin, B. (1989) *Between Two Worlds: Politics and Economy in Independent Ireland*, Dublin: Gill and Macmillan.

Glass, D. V. (ed.) (1954) *Social Mobility in Britain*, London: Routledge.

Goldthorpe, J. H. (1991) 'The Uses of History in Sociology: Reflections on Recent Tendencies', *British Journal of Sociology*, 42(2) (June).

Goldthorpe, J. H. (1992) 'Employment, Class, and Mobility: A Critique of Liberal and Marxist Theories of Long-term Change' in H. Haferkamp and N. Smelser (eds), *Social Change and Modernity*, Berkeley: University of California Press.

Goldthorpe, J. H. (1992) 'The Theory of Industrialism and the Irish Case' in J. Goldthorpe and C. Whelan (eds), *The Development of Industrial Society in Ireland*, Oxford: Oxford University Press.

Goldthorpe, J. H. (1994) 'The Uses of History in Sociology: A Reply' *British Journal of Sociology*, 45(1) (March).

Goldthorpe, J. H. (1997) 'Current Issues in Macrosociology', *Comparative Social Research*, 6.

Gordon, D. M. (1994) 'The Global Economy: New Edifice or Crumbling Foundations?' in D. Kotz, T. McDonough and M. Reich (eds), *Social Structures of Accumulation: The Political Economy of Growth and Crisis*, Cambridge University Press.

Guelke, A. (1988) *Northern Ireland: The Internationalist Perspective*, Dublin: Gill and Macmillan.

Hannan, D. F. (1979) *Displacement and Development: Class, Kinship, and Social Change in Irish Rural Communities*, Dublin: The Economic and Social Research Institute.

Hannan, D. F. and Commins, P. (1992) 'The Significance of Small-Scale Landholders in Ireland's Socio-Economic Transformation', in J. H. Goldthorpe and C. T. Whelan (eds), *The Development of Industrial Society in Ireland*, Oxford: Oxford University Press.

Harris, R. (1972/1986) *Prejudice and Tolerance in Ulster: a Study of Neighbours and Strangers in a Border Community*, Manchester: Manchester University Press.

Hechter, M. (1975) *Internal Colonialism: The Celtic Fringe in British National Development, 1536–1966*, London: Routledge and Kegan Paul.

Hechter, M. (1986) 'Rational Choice Theory and the Study of Ethnic Relations', in J. Rex and D. Mason (eds) *Theories of Race and Ethnic Relations*, New York: Cambridge University Press.

Hill, R. and Marsh, M. (eds) (1993) *Modern Irish Democracy: Essays in Honour of Basil Chubb*, Dublin: Irish Academic Press.

Hout, M. (1989) *Following in Father's Footsteps: Social Mobility in Ireland*, Cambridge Mass.: Harvard University Press.

Hout, M. and Jackson, J. (1986) 'Dimensions of Occupational Mobility in the Republic of Ireland', *European Sociological Review*, 2: 114–37.

Hughes, M. R. (1997) 'Sample Selection Bias in Analyses of the Political Democracy and Income Inequality Relationship', *Social Forces*, 75(3): 1101–17.

Humphreys, A. J. (1966) *New Dubliners: Urbanisation and the Irish Family*, London: Routledge and Kegan Paul.

Hutchinson, B. (1969) *Social Status and Inter-Generational Social Mobility in Dublin*, Dublin: Economic and Social Research Institute (GRS Paper No. 48).

Hutchinson, B. (1973) *Social Status in Dublin: Marriage, Mobility and First Employment*, Dublin: Economic and Social Research Institute (GRS Paper No. 67).

Kazancigil, A. (1994) 'The Deviant Case in Comparative Analysis, High Stateness in a Muslim Society: the Case of Turkey' in M. Dogan and A. Kazancigil (eds), *Comparing Nations: Concepts, Strategies, Substance*, Cambridge Mass.: Blackwell.

Kelley, J. and De Graaf, N. D. (1997) 'National Context, Parental Socialization and Religious Belief: Results from 15 Nations', *American Sociological Review*, 62(4) 639–59.

Kennedy, L. (1989) *The Modern Industrialisation of Ireland 1940–1988*, Dublin: The Economic and Soical History Society of Ireland.

Kiberd, D. (1996) *Inventing Ireland*, Cambridge Mass.: Harvard University Press.

King, G., Keohane, R. and Verba, S. (1994) *Designing Social Inquiry*, Princeton NJ: Princeton University Press.

Kirby, P. (1992) *Ireland and Latin America: Links and Lessons*, Dublin: Gill and Macmillan (for Traocaire).

Kohn, M. L. (1987) 'Cross National Research as an Analytic Strategy', *American Sociological Review*, 52 (December): 713–31.

Laver, M. (1992) 'Are Irish Parties Peculiar?' in J. H. Goldthrope and C. T. Whelan (eds), *The Development of Industrial Society in Ireland*, Oxford: Oxford University Press.

Lee, J. J. (1989) *Ireland 1912–1985: Politics and Society*, Cambridge: Cambridge University Press.

Lieberson, S. (1992) 'Small *N*'s and Big Conclusions: an Examination of the Reasoning in Comparative Studies Based on a Small Number of Cases' in C. Ragin and H. Becker (eds), *What is a Case? Exploring the Foundations of Social Inquiry*, Cambridge: Cambridge University Press.

Lijphart, A. (1971) 'Comparative Politics and the Comparative Method', *American Political Science Review* 65 (3): 682–98.

Lipset, S. M. (1990) *Continental Divide: The Values and Institutions of the United States and Canada*, New York: Routledge.

Lipset, S. M. (1994) 'Binary Comparisons: American Exceptionalism—Japanese Uniqueness' in M. Dogan and A. Kazancigil (eds), *Comparing Nations: Concepts, Strategies, and Substance*, Cambridge Mass.: Blackwell.

Lipset, S. M. (1996) *American Exceptionalism: A Double-Edged Sword*, New York: W. W. Norton.

Lustick, I. S. (1993) *Unsettled States, Disputed Lands: Britain and Ireland, France and Algeria, Israel and the West Bank-Gaza*, Ithaca: Cornell University Press.

McBride, L. W. (1991) *The Greening of Dublin Castle: The Transformation of*

Bureaucratic and Judicial Personnel in Ireland, 1892–1922, Washington DC: Catholic University of America Press.

McCogan, J. (1982) *British Policy and the Irish Administration*, London: George Allen & Unwin.

McCullagh, C. (1996) *Crime in Ireland: A Sociological Introduction*, Cork: Court University Press.

McGarry, J. and O'Leary, B. (1995) *Explaining Northern Ireland: Broken Images*, Oxford: Blackwell.

MacGréil, M. (1977) *Prejudice and Tolerance in Ireland*, Dublin: College of Industrial Relations.

MacGréil, M. (1991) *Religious Practice and Attitudes in Ireland*, Maynooth: Survey and Research Units, Department of Social Studies, St. Patrick's College.

McMichael, P. (1990) 'Incorporating Comparison within a World-Historical Perspective', *American Sociological Review*, 55(3) 385–97.

McVeigh, R. (1995) 'The Last Conquest of Ireland? British Academics in Irish Universities', *Race and Class*, 37(1): 109–21.

Mair, P. (1992) 'Explaining the Absence of Class Politics in Ireland' in J. H. Goldthorpe and C. T. Whelan (eds), *The Development of Industrial Society in Ireland*, Oxford: Oxford University Press.

Martz, J. D. (1994) 'Comparing Similar Countries: Problems of Conceptualization and Comparability in Latin America', in M. Dogan and A. Kazancigil (eds), *Comparing Nations: Concepts, Strategies, and Substance*, Cambridge Mass.: Blackwell.

Meadwell, H. (1993) 'Transitions to Independence and Ethnic Nationalist Mobilization', in W. J. Booth, P. James and H. Meadwell (eds), *Politics and Rationality*, Cambridge: Cambridge University Press.

Miller, R. (1986) 'Social Stratification and Mobility', in P. Clancy, S. Drudy, K. Lynch and L. O'Dowd (eds), *Ireland: A Sociological Profile*, Dublin: Institute of Public Administration.

Mjøset, L. (1992) *The Irish Economy in a Comparative Institutional Perspective*, Dublin: National Economic and Social Council, Report No. 93.

Moore, B. (1966) *Social Origins of Dictatorship and Democracy*, Boston: Beacon Press.

Moxon-Browne, E. (1983) *Nation, Class and Creed in Northern Ireland*, Aldershot: Gower.

Nolan, B. and Callan, T. (eds) (1993) *Poverty and Policy in Ireland*, Dublin: Gillard Macmillan.

Nolan, B. and Whelan, C. T. (1996) *Resources, Deprivation and Poverty*, Oxford: Clarendon Press.

Nye, J., Zelikow, P. and King, D. (1997) *Why People Don't Trust Government*, Cambridge Mass.: Harvard University Press.

O'Connell, P. J. (1994) 'National Variation in the Fortunes of Labor: a Pooled and Cross-Sectional Analysis of the Impact of Economic Crisis in the Advanced Capitalist Nations', in Janoski and A. M. Hicks (eds), *The Comparative Political Economy of the Welfare State*, Cambridge: Cambridge University Press.

O'Connell, P. J. and Rottman, D. (1992) 'The Irish Welfare State in Comparative

Perspective' in J. H. Goldthorpe and C. T. Whelan (eds), *The Development of Industrial Society in Ireland*, Oxford: Oxford University Press.

O'Connor, J. S. and Brym, R. J. (1988) 'Public Welfare Expenditures in OECD Countries', *British Journal of Sociology*, 39: 47–68.

O'Dowd, L. (1990) 'New Introduction' to Albert Memmi, *The Colonizer and the Colonized* (tr. H. Greenfield), London: Earthscan.

O'Dowd, L. (1995) 'Development or Dependency? State, Economy and Society in Northern Ireland' in P. Clancy, S. Drudy, K. Lynch and L. O'Dowd (eds), *Irish Society: Sociological Perspectives*, Dublin: IPA.

O'Faolain, S. (1979) *The Irish* (Revised Edition), Harmondsworth: Penguin.

O'Hearn, D. (1995) 'Global Restructuring and the Irish Political Economy', in P. Clancy, S. Drudy, K. Lynch and L. O'Dowd (eds), *Irish Society: Sociological Perspectives*, Dublin: IPA.

Ohmae, K. (1993) 'The Rise of the Region State', *Foreign Affairs*, 72(2) (Spring): 78–87.

O'Leary, C. (1993) 'Northern Ireland, 1921–72: Misshapen Constitutional Development and Scholarly Silence', in R. Hill and M. Marsh (eds), *Modern Irish Democracy: Essays in Honour of Basil Chubb*, Dublin: Irish Academic Press.

Orridge, A. W. (1981) 'Uneven Development and Nationalism', *Political Studies*, 19(1): 1–15.

Orridge, A. W. (1982) 'Uneven Development and Nationalism II', *Political Studies*, 19(2): 181–90.

Parkin, F. (1979) *Marxism and Class Theory: A Bourgeois Critique*, New York: Columbia University Press.

Pyle, J. L. (1990) *The State and Women in the Economy: Lessons from Sex Discrimination in the Republic of Ireland*, Albany: State University of New York Press.

Przeworski, A. and Teune, H. (1970) *The Logic of Comparative Social Inquiry*, New York: Wiley.

Raftery, A. and Hout, M. (1993) 'Maximally Maintained Inequality: Expansion, Reform and Opportunity in Irish Education, 1921–1975', *Sociology of Education*, 66: 41–62.

Ragin, C. C. (1987) *The Comparative Method: Moving Beyond Qualitative and Quantitative Strategies*, Berkeley: University of California Press.

Ragin, C. C. (1992) 'Introduction: Cases of "What is a Case?"' in C. Ragin, Charles and H. Becker (eds), *What is a Case? Exploring the Foundations of Social Inquiry*, Cambridge: Cambridge University Press.

Raven, J. and Whelan, C. T. (1976) 'Irish adults' Perceptions of their Civil Institutions and Their Own Role in Relation to Them', in J. Raven, C. Whelan, P. Pfretzschner and D. Borock (eds), *Political Culture in Ireland: the Views of Two Generations*, Dublin: Institute of Public Administration.

Robertson, R. (1992) 'Globality, Global Culture, and Images of World Order' in H. Haferkamp and N. Smelser (eds), *Social Change and Modernity*, Berkeley: University of California Press.

Rose, R. (1971) *Governing Without Consensus: An Irish Perspective*, London: Faber and Faber.

Rose, R. and Garvin, T. (1983) 'The Public Policy Effects of Independence: Ireland as a Test Case', *European Journal of Political Research*, 11: 377–97.

Rottman, D. B. (1980) *Crime in the Republic of Ireland*, Dublin: Economic and Social Research Institute.

Rottman, D. B., Hannan, D., Hardiman, N. and Wiley, M. (1982) *The Distribution of Income in the Republic of Ireland: A Study in Social Class and Family Cycle Inequalities*, Dublin: Economic and Social Research Institute.

Rottman, D. B. (1989) 'Crime in Geographical Perspective', in R. W. G. Carter and A. J. Parker (eds), *Ireland: A Contemporary Geographical Perspective*, London: Routledge.

Rottman, D. and O'Connell, P. (1982) 'The Changing Social Structure of Ireland', *Administration*, 30(3).

Ruane, J. and Todd, J. (1996) *The Dynamics of Conflict in Northern Ireland: Power, Conflict and Emancipation*, Cambridge: Cambridge University Press.

Sartori, G. (1994) 'Compare Why and How: Comparing, Miscomparing and the Comparative Method', in M. Dogan and A. Kazancigil (eds), *Comparing Nations: Concepts, Strategies, and Substance*, Cambridge Mass.: Blackwell.

Skocpol, T. and Somers, M. (1980) 'The Uses of Comparative History in Macrosocial Inquiry', *Comparative Studies in Society and History*, 22: 174–97.

Skocpol, T. (1979) *States and Social Revolutions*, Cambridge: Cambridge University Press.

Sklair, L. (1991) *Sociology of the Global System*, New York: Harvester Wheatsheaf.

Smelser, N. J. (1976) *Comparative Methods in the Social Sciences*, Englewood Cliffs NJ: Prentice-Hall.

Smith, D. (1987) *Equality and Inequality in Northern Ireland, Part III: Perceptions and Views*, London: Policy Studies Institute.

Smith, A. D. (1995) *Nations and Nationalism in a Global Era*, Cambridge: Polity Press.

Tilly, C. (1984) *Big Structures, Large Processes, Huge Comparisons*, New York: Russell Sage Foundation.

Tilly, C. (1992) *Coercion, Capital, and European States, AD 990–1992*, Cambridge Mass.: Blackwell.

Tilly, C. (1996) 'Citizenship, Identity and Social History' in C. Tilly (ed.), *Citizenship, Identity and Social History*, Cambridge: Press Syndicate of the University of Cambridge.

Vogler, C. (1985) *The Nation State: The Neglected Dimension of Class*, Aldershot, Hants: Gower.

Weitzer, R. (1990) *Transforming Settler States: Communal Conflict and Internal Security in Northern Ireland and Zimbabwe*, Berkeley: University of California Press.

Whelan, C. T. and Whelan, B. J. (1984) *Social Mobility in the Republic of Ireland: A Comparative Perspective*, Dublin: The Economic and Social Research Institute.

Whelan, C. (ed.) (1994) *Values and Social Change in Ireland*, Dublin: Gill and Macmillan.

Whyte, J. (1990) *Interpreting Northern Ireland*, Oxford: Clarendon.

Wright F. (1987) *Northern Ireland: A Comparative Analysis*, Dublin: Gill and Macmillan.

The History of Economic Development in Ireland, North and South

JOHN BRADLEY

Introduction

COMPARATIVE DISCUSSION OF THE TWO ECONOMIES of Ireland is a very recent phenomenon.[1] Limited communication over the years between Northern and Southern researchers, as they drifted apart in intellectual space, led to a lack of shared knowledge about the different parts of the island. Northern researchers tended to look exclusively to Britain (Harris, 1991) while Southern researchers tended to be more preoccupied with European and world arenas (Bradley *et al.*, 1995).

However, a much longer time horizon is needed in order to understand the historical socio-economic processes that operated on the island and which led to the very different economic development experiences of North and South. The violence that escalated in the late 1960s did not take place in a vacuum. Rather, the unfolding of events was conditioned by political and socio-economic factors inherited from the past. It is for others to paint this wider picture. We merely sketch some narrower economic aspects of the island's development before and after partition.

Although we will focus mainly on economic issues, we are aware of the dangers of a simplistic claim that economic factors predetermine political choices (McGarry and O'Leary, 1995). What we wish to investigate, however, is the extent to which past economic developments in Ireland were influenced by such forces as technology, geography, factor endowments, demography, external economic and social events, etc. The predominantly

[1] This paper draws on material from a report prepared for the Dublin-based Forum for Peace and Reconciliation (Bradley, 1996).

Proceedings of the British Academy, **98**, 35–68. © The British Academy 1999.

political-historical tradition of much research and writing on island developments has tended to down-play these economic aspects.[2]

We first present a schematic historical overview of the island economy for the period 1750–1960, i.e., from the time when the first aspects of a modern Irish economy emerged in the early stages of the British industrial revolution to just before the outbreak of Northern civil unrest in the late 1960s. The political consequences of this earlier period of demographic upheaval and regionally skewed economic development were enormous and facilitated the partition of the island economy in 1921.

We then narrow our focus to the 1960–96 period, during which both regions broke with past patterns of development that had their origins in the nineteenth century. Here we restrict our analysis to economic issues, having previously outlined the broader historical-economic setting of the preceding period. We go on to describe how industrial policy on the island was planned and executed in recent decades, at a time when economic cooperation between the two contiguous regions was difficult, if not impossible. We show that at times the emphasis of industrial and regional policy was very different within each of the two regions and argue that this may have led both to a sub-optimal outcome for the island as a whole and may also have been a contributing factor in the onset, duration and severity of the Northern civil unrest. We conclude with some observations on the recent dynamic growth performance of the South (the so-called 'Celtic tiger') as compared with the North.

The Origins of the Two Economies: 1750–1960

Key Historical Events

The Act of Union. Ireland was on the move in the latter half of the eighteenth century. Under a devolved parliament, however imperfect its structures, economic and social advances were being made at a time when the early effects of the industrial revolution in Britain were beginning to spill over into adjoining countries. From the start of the nineteenth century the Act of Union fundamentally changed the terms on which Ireland would relate to the global super-power on its doorstep. After the Union, policy making adjusted to control from London and there was no protection from the full rigours of competition with the hegemonic British economic giant.

---

[2] A recently published study of the period 1780–1939 gives central place to economic developments in Irish history (Ó Gráda, 1994). Economic aspects are also integrated into an historical narrative by Bardon (1992). However, the highly critical analysis of the 'failure' of Southern development in the twentieth century by Lee (1989) is itself open to criticism for its limited international comparisons and anachronistic economic perspective.

However, to claim that all economic progress stopped after the Union is grossly simplistic, and in recent years a number of historians have sought to correct the excesses of this ultra-nationalist view (Johnson and Kennedy, 1991; Ó Gráda, 1994). The classic statement of the Nationalist economic thesis was contained in the writings of George O'Brien (O'Brien, 1918; 1921), whose central claim was that the absence of political autonomy during the eighteenth and nineteenth centuries condemned Ireland to economic stagnation and decline.[3] Johnson and Kennedy (1991) summarise O'Brien's thesis as follows:

i. Considerable economic benefits had been conferred on Ireland during the brief period of legislative autonomy that occurred between 1782 and 1800;

ii. The Act of Union was followed by a long period of economic decline which adversely affected public finance, agriculture and industry, the causes of which can be directly attributed to the provisions of the Act and the absence of any autonomous local legislative power;

iii. The strong performance of the economy of the north-east region of the island, centred on Belfast, is explicable in terms of conditions of special advantage that only applied to Ulster;

iv. The system of land tenure was a long-standing source of Irish economic weakness, but once again Ulster was in a privileged position relative to the rest of the country.

The revising historians challenge the factual basis for at least three of the above four claims. The first is held to be inconsistent with the fact that while in many regions of Ireland economic indicators did improve during the last two decades of the eighteenth century, they improved even more in the aftermath of the Union and up to the onset of the Great Famine in the mid-1840s. Indeed, the Irish parliament had opposed protectionism and favoured free trade. Johnson and Kennedy concluded that:

> Expansion in agriculture and industry in the period 1750–1800 owed little to Irish parliamentary action. The dynamic of growth was supplied by the market, organisational and technological changes associated with the rise of urban, industrial capitalism in Britain. (1991: 16)

Neither is the second claim borne out by closer examination of the facts. The net contribution made by the Irish exchequer to Britain was considerably less of a burden when recycled Imperial expenditures undertaken in Ireland were included. The Act of Union ensured continued access

---

[3] A related theme originates from the Marxist interpretative tradition, suggesting that Ireland's economic link with British capitalism has on occasion and in some sectors been malign (Munck, 1993). Crotty (1986) further develops the interpretation of Ireland as an example of capitalist colonisation.

for Irish agricultural goods to the expanding British market, and a sector-by-sector examination of the performance of Irish industry shows up the weakness of the nationalist case in blaming the Union. Nor does the success of the north-east region appear to have been built on a land tenure system which encouraged the accumulation of capital. Were it not for the advent of the Great Famine, Johnson and Kennedy's conclusion is difficult to fault on strictly economic grounds in the context of the nineteenth-century environment:

> Economic conditions for the exercise of autonomy in the first half of the nineteenth century were far less favourable (than in the second half). Being a region of the UK economy was then, perhaps, the optimal arrangement for Ireland. (1991: 28)

The Great Famine. The calamity of the Great Famine, the causes of which had been building up for decades, tore asunder the fragile social and economic fabric of the island and in particular exposed the economic weakness of the densely populated Western regions. In his examination of the causes of Ireland's poor economic performance in the nineteenth and twentieth centuries, Mjøset places the post-Famine population decline at the centre of a vicious circle, interacting with and exacerbating what he calls a weak 'national system of innovation' (Mjøset, 1992).[4]

By devastating the population through death and emigration, the Famine prevented the emergence of a dynamic home market for local industry. By bearing most heavily on the more agricultural South, it further accentuated separation from the North and by setting in train a tradition of emigration ('exit'), it dampened internal pressures for economic reform and innovation ('voice').

The main legacy of the Famine was a gross distortion of the evolution of Ireland's population after the middle of the nineteenth century and the creation of the conditions for a very uneven spread of the second Industrial Revolution to Ireland during the second half of that century. Ó Gráda has commented that: 'No other 19th century European society endured such an ecological jolt' (Ó Gráda, 1994: 235), and concludes that:

> The Great Irish Famine is a grim reminder of how narrowly the benefits of the first Industrial Revolution had been spread by the 1840s. Nearly a half century of political and economic union had made little or no impression on the huge gap between Irish and British incomes, nor was it enough to shield Ireland from cataclysm. (Ibid.: 208)

---

[4] A national system of innovation is defined by Mjøset as encompassing the institutions and economic structures which affect the rate and direction of innovative activities in the economy (Mjøset, 1992: 43–50).

Partition.   There were strong elements of an economic rationale, seen from Belfast, for partition in the first two decades of this century, at a time when the economy of the north-east of Ireland, centred on that city, was at its zenith. A subsequent irony was that the strong and successful Northern industries—mainly linen, shipbuilding and associated heavy engineering—were the ones that suffered seriously in the aftermath of partition, except for a revival during the abnormal circumstances of the Second World War. However, partition was irrelevant to the long-term decline of these Northern sectors, since their pattern of decline was simply mirroring a wider British phenomenon.

The sundering of the engineering/industrial North from the agricultural/ food processing South destroyed any possibility, if there were such, of building intra-island synergies. The centrifugal bonds of identity, tradition and allegiance were simply too strong for the centripetal forces of economic rationality. After partition, official statistics show that North-South trade diminished, sources of supply adjusted, and economic planning on the island accommodated to partition, even if political rhetoric did not (Stationery Office, 1985).

The view has been often expressed that the partition of Ireland was an economic as well as a political disaster. It has been suggested that the loss of Belfast was a one-off event that exacerbated a post-colonial economic vicious circle, since the South was separated from the only surviving industrial centre on the island (Mjøset, 1992: 10). However, the dramatic post-First World War reversal in the fortunes of the North's two main industries (linen and shipbuilding) raises questions about how much they would have provided innovation and resources for the industrialisation needed in the mainly agricultural South. It is almost certain that the South's urgent need to construct its industrial sector from an almost zero base, at a time when the world was moving from *laissez faire* to protectionism, would have caused serious North-South policy disputes in any 32-county Ireland.[5]

Key Economic Issues

Socio-economic issues can sometimes be closely related to a single historical event: for example, the Famine dominates all other explanations of the unique pattern of Irish demographics. However, they are usually associated with a series of events, no one of which is dominant. We identify three such

---

[5] Insight into tensions in the world economy between maintaining policies of *laissez faire* or retreating behind protectionism in the early 1930s is provided by Keynes' Finlay lecture, delivered at University College Dublin in 1932 (Keynes, 1933).

socio-economic events: demographics, emigration and decline; economic geography and the North-South divide; and economic relations of the island with the rest of the world.

Demographics, emigration and decline. Two defining features of Irish demographics stand out clearly. The first, concerning population growth, is illustrated in Figure 1, where a comparison is made with a range of other smaller European nations (data are taken from Mjøset, 1992). Of the ten comparison countries, only Ireland showed a decline in population between 1840 and 1910. In 1840 Ireland contained more people than Benelux, while by 1910 Benelux had three times as many as Ireland.

The second feature concerns the extent of Irish migration, where Figure 2 makes a comparison with a subset of the three other nations (Denmark, Norway and Sweden) that displayed non-trivial migration behaviour at least sometime during the period 1851 to 1960. Only for a short period towards the end of the nineteenth century did emigration rates (i.e., emigration per thousand of the population) come anywhere near the high Irish rates.

However, there can be no simple explanation for Ireland's poor economic performance in terms of emigration, particularly in the twentieth century, since this is both a cause and an effect of slow growth originating from other failures in the economy. Explanations become circular, and the real challenge is to include emigration in a broader study of the Irish pattern of development.

Mjøset uses the notion of a vicious circle linking two key Irish characteristics: population decline via emigration, and a weak national

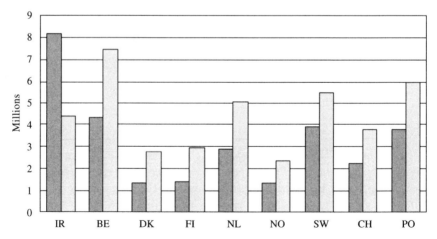

Figure 1. Irish population growth in an international context. ■■■ 1840, ☐ 1910. IR = Ireland, BE = Belgium, DK = Denmark, FI = Finland, NL = Netherlands, NO = Norway, SW = Sweden, CH = Switzerland, PO = Poland.

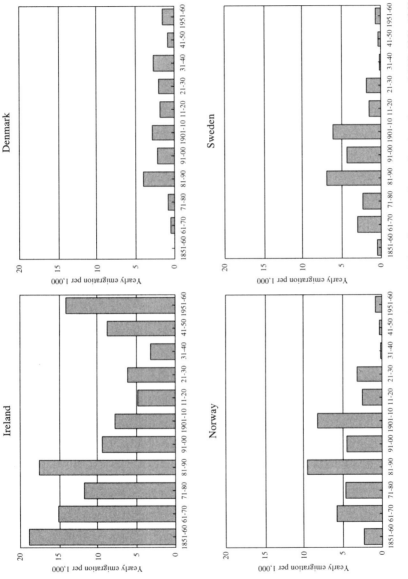

Figure 2. Irish emigration patterns in an international context. Migration rates (annual emigration per 1,000) 1851–1960 for Ireland, Denmark, Norway, and Sweden.

system of innovation (Mjøset, 1992: 50–67). These two mechanisms re-inforce each other negatively through the social structure: the pastoral bias of agrarian modernisation, paternalistic family structures, sluggish growth of the home market and a further marginalisation through weak indus-trialisation. Many of the elements in the weak national system of innova-tion arise in the context of the economic geography of nineteenth-century Ireland, to which we now turn.

Economic geography and the North-South divide. A striking feature of the geography of economic activity is that it often occurs in forms that are highly concentrated spatially because of the presence of increasing returns to scale and agglomeration economies that come from the more intense economic interactions that proximity encourages (Krugman, 1991). Continental Europe has a manufacturing triangle containing the Ruhr, Northern France and Belgium. Within Britain, the first stage of the Industrial Revolution concentrated in specific areas: Lancashire for cotton, the Clydeside and Liverpool for shipbuilding, Birmingham for engineering and manufacturing. Hence, it was not entirely surprising that when the Industrial Revolution came to Ireland in the latter half of the nineteenth century, it developed in a geographically concentrated form.

However, Ireland's industrialisation was never to emulate Britain's generalised economic and technological leap forward. Rather, it was to involve a few specific sectors (brewing, linen, shipbuilding), and selected locations (mainly Belfast and Dublin), and by-passed much of the rest of the country. What is of interest is that the concentration of the key sectors, linen and shipbuilding, came to be located almost exclusively in the north-east corner of the island. The fortunes of sectors such as cotton, linen, wool, shipbuilding and distilling during the first half of the nineteenth century have been documented (Ó Gráda, 1994: 273–313). Factors influen-cing the success or failure included access to energy resources (mostly imported coal), the role of entrepreneurship (where the importation of techniques, finance capital, capital goods and skilled workmen played a crucial role, North and South), the possible deterrent role played by crime and civil unrest, and the price of labour (where lower Irish wages were offset by lower productivity).

Recent advances in economic growth theory and economic geography provide compelling insights into how the area centred on Belfast developed rapidly as the only region in Ireland that fully participated in the latter phases of the Industrial Revolution (Krugman, 1991). The greater Belfast region took on all the attributes of an 'industrial district', i.e., a geo-graphically defined productive system characterised by a large number of firms that are involved at various stages and in various ways, in the production of closely interrelated products.[6] Most strikingly, a decline in population of almost 55 per cent occurred during the years 1841 and 1951 in the area that was eventually to become the Republic of Ireland, compared with a decline of only 17 per cent in the area that was to become Northern Ireland (Mjøset, 1992: 222). Population actually grew in the area around Belfast, to the extent that by the year 1911 the population of the Belfast area (386,947) had greatly outstripped that of Dublin (304,802).

Economic relations of the island with the rest of the world. The political incorporation of Ireland into the United Kingdom in 1801 generated forces that also led to a comprehensive economic and trade integration. The full extent of this integration after more than one hundred years of Union is illustrated in Figure 3 for the case of the South. This figure shows the UK-Irish trade position from just after partition to the year 1950. The proportion of Southern exports going to the UK showed only a very small reduction from 99 per cent in 1924 to 93 per cent by 1950.

The failure of the South to diversify away from an almost total export dependence on the UK had serious consequences for its economic performance when compared to a range of other small European countries.[7] The reluctance of the new Southern administration to deviate too much from British policy norms is well documented (Fanning, 1978). The inability of the new Northern administration to deviate in any significant way at all from UK-wide policy simply reflected the extremely limited scope for local autonomy that was provided for in the 1920 Government of Ireland Act under which its local parliament (Stormont) functioned.

Starting from a position of almost full economic integration within the UK, it is hard not to be sympathetic with Southern policy makers as they considered their limited options. The eventual break with *laissez faire* that came with the first change of administration in 1932 was not, in fact, such a dramatic step, since protection had been creeping into the international economy during the 1920s and the world financial system that had supported free trade was being rocked to its foundations.[8]

The difficulties faced by the South in breaking free from the economic embrace of the UK can be understood using the concept of 'webs of dependency' (Wijkman, 1990). It was hardly surprising that these islands

---

[6] Bardon (1982) provides an account of the political, social and economic aspects of the rise of linen and ship-building in mid- and late nineteenth century Belfast.

[7] Mjøset (1992) is a seminal study of Southern economic under-performance that draws carefully from a wide European literature on social and economic development. Lee (1989) is more discursive political-historical narrative.

[8] See Keynes (1933) for contemporary reflections on free trade and protection. Kenwood and Lougheed (1992) analyse the impact of the First World War on the workings of the international economy and its subsequent collapse during the 1930s.

John Bradley

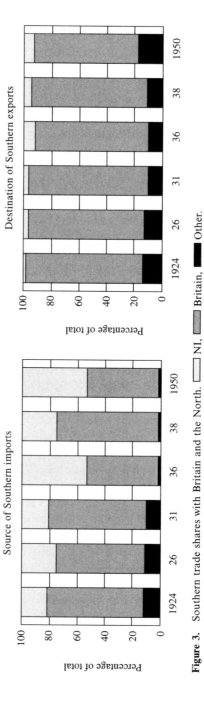

Figure 3. Southern trade shares with Britain and the North.

formed a particularly strong web of dependency, continuing from Southern independence well into the 1960s. While Southern policy makers may have been less assertive and innovative than was desirable, in the absence of a robust industrial sector there is probably very little that could have been achieved to accelerate an earlier economic decoupling of the South from Britain. The consequences for the South followed inexorably. In the words of Mjøset:

> Ireland became a free rider on Britain's decline, while Austria and Switzerland were free riders on Germany's economic miracle. Even Belfast specialised in lines of production which fitted into the general British orientation: textiles and shipbuilding. (Mjøset, 1992: 9)

The strong web of dependency between the South and the UK only began to weaken after the shift to foreign direct investment and export-led growth that followed the various 'Programmes for Economic Expansion' in the late 1950s and during the 1960s. Figure 4 shows the behaviour of the shares of Southern exports going to the UK, and Southern imports originating in the UK, for the period 1960 to 1992. The forces that brought about this changed pattern of behaviour are further explored below.

Legacy: the Two Economies in the 1960s

The South embarked on a path of political independence with an economy that was without significant industrialisation, but was dependent on mainly agricultural exports to the British market. The North achieved a degree of

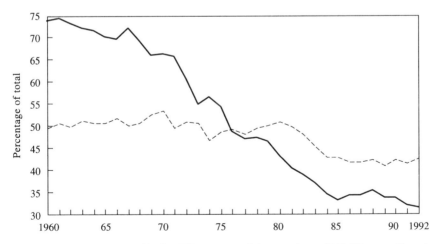

Figure 4. Southern trade with the UK: export and import shares 1960–92. ——— Export share, - - - - Import share.

regional autonomy within the UK at a stage when the perilous state of its strong industrial base was still hidden in the aftermath of the economic boom created by the First World War.

Between 1921 and the early 1960s there were many changes in the North and South, but few of major significance compared with the legacy of the pre-1922 period.[9] The South attempted to construct an industrial base behind a protective barrier of high tariffs. The North's staple industrial specialisations continued to decline, with a temporary period of growth during and immediately after the Second World War. Both regions entered the 1960s in a state where major policy changes were needed, even in a situation where the North had been moderately successful during the 1950s in attracting British investment in the area of textiles, artificial fibres and other petroleum-based products. What was not anticipated was that the outbreak of civil unrest would make this transformation much more prolonged and difficult than it would have been in a period of peaceful economic transition.

Some important insights can be learned from the economic history of the island over the last century and a half. First, the modern features of the island economy were clearly present from the middle of the nineteenth century. These included a weak island industrial base, other than in the north-east corner of the island; the interaction of population growth with weak economic performance that was to appear as a mixture of unemployment/under-employment and emigration; a vicious circle of interaction between emigration and a weak ability to create a national system of innovation; and an almost complete integration into and dependence on the British economy. Only after a period of national crisis was a sustained effort made in the South to address these problems with the publication of *The First Programme for Economic Expansion* in 1958 (Government of Ireland, 1958). Parallel efforts made in the North during the 1950s and 1960s produced a rate of Northern industrial-based growth that for a short while exceeded that of Britain (Farley, 1995). However, subsequent efforts may have been hampered by a lack of appropriate regional policy instruments and by the effects of the outbreak and persistence of the Troubles from the late 1960s.

The Two Economies During the Troubles: 1960–90

Although North and South share many economic characteristics and problems, the published literature contains few attempts to place analysis

[9] We return to developments in the period between 1930 and 1960 later in the context of regional policy. See also Kennedy, Giblin and McHugh, 1988.

within a common regional economic framework. Rather, the North is usually discussed in the context of the eleven sub-regions of the United Kingdom (Harris, 1991) and the South in the context of small peripheral member states of the EU (Bradley, Herce and Modesto, 1995).

In this section we examine four aspects of economic performance North and South during the period of the Northern 'Troubles'. The first issue concerns the central role played by manufacturing, where behaviour in both regions was strikingly different. The evolution of the public sector is then discussed, where again there are major differences in behaviour. We then examine labour market performance, where there are many similarities between North and South. Finally, we discuss public and private sector financial balances that are at the centre of regional economic governance.

The Manufacturing Sector

Over the period 1932 to 1960 there had been rapid growth of indigenous industry in the South, protected from international competition by high tariff barriers. By the late 1950s it was clear that protectionism had long outlived its usefulness and that few of the so-called infant industries had matured and become sufficiently competitive to generate much in the way of exports (O'Malley, 1989).

The changes forced on Irish policy-makers by economic collapse in the late 1950s were fundamental and far-reaching. The *Control of Manufactures Act*, which prohibited foreign ownership, was abolished and replaced by a policy that systematically cultivated FDI through a zero corporate profits tax on manufactured exports (replaced in 1980 by a flat rate of 10 per cent on all manufacturing), attractive investment grants and a complete dismantling of most tariff barriers within less than a decade.

Much of the performance of the Southern Irish economy during the following three decades can be explained in terms of the quite phenomenal growth of export-oriented FDI in manufacturing, from a zero base in the late 1950s to a situation in 1993 where almost 60 per cent of gross output and 45 per cent of employment in manufacturing is in foreign-owned export-oriented firms (Barry and Bradley, 1997).

Northern Ireland, of course, always functioned in a regime of free trade, with full access to the large British and Commonwealth markets. British policy as applied in the North included a regional employment premium scheme of wage subsidies, as well as other subsidy and grant-based policies. However, as we have seen, its main industrial sectors were in decline, and the region failed to attract sufficient FDI to offset the job losses.

Since both regional Irish home markets were so small, the domestic manufacturing sectors, North and South, simply could not efficiently supply all their different needs through import substitution. Rather, they needed to specialise in a narrow range of products, sell in highly competitive export markets, and import the goods not produced at home. As they moved to such specialisation, the two most striking aspects of manufacturing activity on the island over the last three decades are that total employment has remained almost unchanged (359,000 in 1960 compared with 343,000 in 1990), while a dramatic shift in favour of the South was taking place (Figure 5). Thus, the island industrial development in recent decades came to resemble a type of zero-sum game.

The evolution since the 1960s of aggregate Northern and Southern manufacturing employment is shown in Figure 6. While Northern manufacturing employment stagnated and declined, Southern employment rose steadily. The decline of Northern manufacturing (admittedly from a very high base) had serious consequences for the wider Northern economy. However, despite a strong growth in output, the performance of Southern manufacturing employment was not impressive until very recently.

What caused the Northern manufacturing decline? There is a certain amount of research on the economic effects of civil unrest, but no very convincing conclusions (see Harris, 1991). Even so, the inability of the North to attract inward investment to anything like the extent of the South can probably be blamed on the uncertainty and disruption of the Troubles as well as on world economic conditions. However, the fact that the

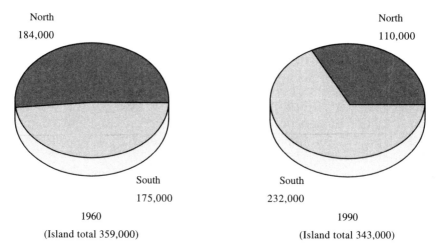

Figure 5. Changing size of Northern and Southern manufacturing employment.

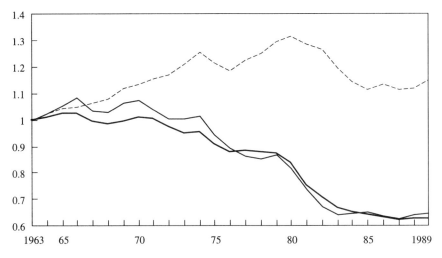

Figure 6.   The evolution of manufacturing employment: North, South and UK.
- - - - South, —— North, —— UK. Index: Base 1963=1.0

Troubles coincided with a serious crisis in Northern industrial policy
suggests that it is useless to attempt to pin the subsequent decline on the
Troubles alone (Munck, 1993: 60–4). The performance of the Southern
manufacturing sector, on the other hand, may look flattering in comparison with the North, but contains a disturbing difference between the
inability of the Southern indigenous sector to grow and compete internationally, and a more rapid growth of the less employment intensive
foreign-owned sector (NESC, 1992).

Concerning the possible role of policy flexibility, comparison of
Northern employment performance with aggregate UK performance
shows that Northern Ireland was merely tracking a wider UK manufacturing decline (Figure 6), without the parallel strong growth of
private services that occurred in the more prosperous core British
regions. The North, together with other relatively poorer peripheral
British regions, appears to have been unable to arrest this decline with
the limited range of policy instruments and the level of support available
(NIEC, 1992: 21), and comparisons with Scotland tend to reinforce this
finding (Ibid.: 38–43).

The Public Sector

Employment in the public sector (i.e., public administration, defence,
health and education) grew rapidly in both North and South from the

mid-1960s to the late 1980s. In Figure 7 we show public sector employment as a fraction of private sector employment (i.e., manufacturing, market services and agriculture). This is a measure of the 'burden' carried by a region's private sector to the extent that regional tax revenue supports public activities.[10]

What Figure 7 illustrates is that the Northern public sector, relative to the size of the private sector, is dramatically larger than its Southern counterpart. The relationship between the exposed manufacturing sector (which is forced to match world prices and is driven mainly by external demand) and the public sector is a particularly interesting one. In the South the need to finance public sector expansion by immediate or deferred taxation (i.e., debt creation) drives a 'wedge' between wage costs borne by employers in manufacturing and the value of take-home pay spent by employees. Hence, public sector expansion can crowd out employment in the exposed manufacturing sector through loss of competitiveness as unions drive up nominal wages to restore their members' real standard of living. This tended to happen in the South during the 1980s and was a cause of serious loss of manufacturing jobs (Barry and Bradley, 1991).

In the North, on the other hand, there is now no direct link between the size of the public sector and the need to finance it exclusively from Northern Ireland tax resources. Part of the explanation of the behaviour of the public/private employment ratio can be attributed to the need for the North to catch up with the higher British levels of public services. However, the increase in the size of the public sector can still crowd out the exposed manufacturing sector through the effect of the lower rate of regional unemployment in driving up wage rates.

Labour Market Problems

A shared feature of the two labour markets over the past three decades has been an enduring high rate of unemployment. In Figure 8 we show unemployment rates for North, South and Britain. Figures 9(a) and (b) show the annual change in the working-age population superimposed on net migration from each region.

The common pattern of behaviour of unemployment is striking. During the 1980s, both Irish regions suffered much higher rises in unemployment rates than occurred in Britain. However, the patterns of labour migration and population growth are quite dissimilar in the two Irish regions. In the

---

[10] A special factor driving up the numbers employed in the Northern public sector over the past 25 years has been the need to increase the size of the security forces.

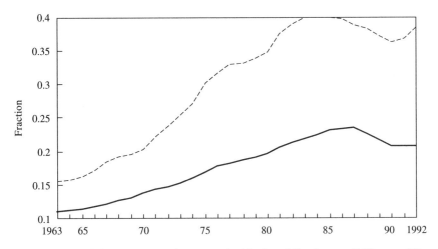

Figure 7.   Public/private sector employment ratio: North and South. ——— ROI, - - - - NI.

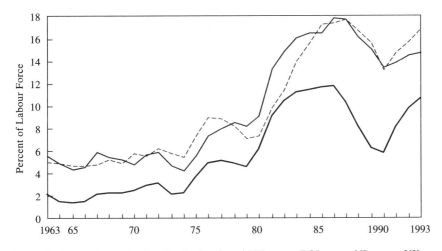

Figure 8.   Unemployment rates: North, South and UK. - - - - ROI, ——— NI, ——— UK.

case of the South, migration was net outward during the 1960s, became strongly net inward during the expansionary 1970s, and reverted to net outward for most of the 1980s. In the last few years net-outward migration has ceased, due to relative improvements in the Irish market and in Social Welfare entitlements. In the case of the North, migration was more modest

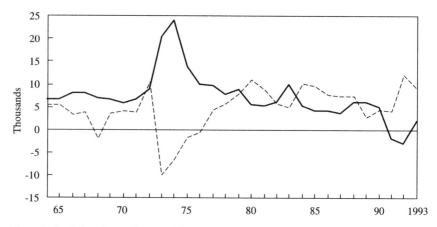

Figure 9(a).   Migration and net working-age population change: North. ——— Migration,
- - - - Population change.

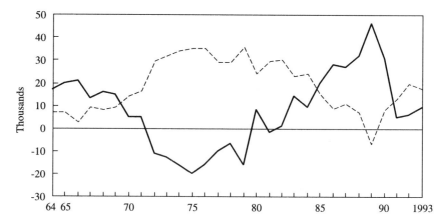

Figure 9(b).   Migration and net population change: South. ——— Migration,
- - - - Population change.

and steady, other than during the years 1971–72, a period of serious civil
unrest.[11]

A further characteristic of Northern and Southern labour markets is that
the fraction of those who are long-term unemployed (defined as greater than
one year) has become very high (Figures 10[a]) and [b]). Furthermore, in the
North this has been associated with pockets of long-term unemployment in

---

[11] Ó Gráda and Walsh (1995: 273–4) touch on another aspect of emigration from the North,
namely the traditionally higher rate of emigration by Catholics compared to that of other
religious groups, and the reversal of this pattern in the period 1971 to 1991.

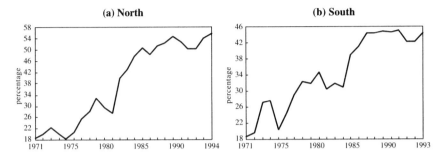

Figure 10.   Long-term unemployment rates, North and South.

areas that have suffered most from violence, shown in the grouping of regions on the right of the histogram (Figure 11[a]). The regional variation in unemployment rates was not so pronounced in the South (Figure 11[b]), at least not at the level of regional subdivision shown in the graph.

In summary, the deterioration of the Northern labour market from the late 1970s and throughout the 1980s was replicated in the South, where over-shooting of employment growth after the fiscal expansions of the late 1970s was unsustainable. In both regions a serious problem of structural or long-term unemployment emerged. Economic studies in the South indicate that unemployment rose initially as a result of world recession, higher taxes and population growth pressure (Barry and Bradley, 1991). Sociological studies show that a key characteristic of long-term unemployment is low skill levels, and that working class marginalisation arises from the rapid and uneven nature of class transformation in Ireland and changing patterns of emigration (Breen *et al.*, 1990). These factors clearly operated in the North as well, but were overlaid by 'community' and 'location' issues whose interpretation has been an area of great controversy in Northern socio-economic research (McGarry and O'Leary, 1995).

Paying the Bills: Regional Balance Sheets

After the introduction of direct rule in 1972, any attempt to maintain even an approximate link between tax revenues and public expenditures in the North was broken and public spending since then has been related to need, defined by British standards and unconstrained by local revenue-raising powers. If a regional balanced budget had continued to be required, as it had been to some extent during previous decades, Canning *et al.* (1987) suggest that some 50,000 fewer public sector jobs would have been sustainable, with less induced market sector employment as a consequence.

There is no disputing that the Northern economy is now a financial

(a) North

Regional distribution of unemployment
North (June 1987)

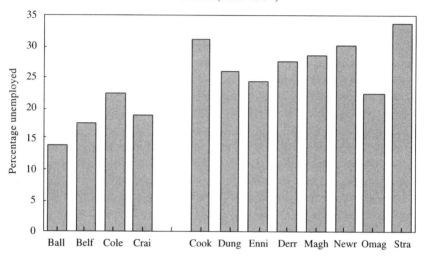

(b) South

Regional distribution of unemployment
South (1979 and 1993)

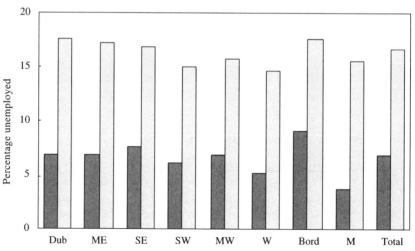

Figure 11. Regional unemployment rates, North and South. ▰ 1979, ☐ 1993.

burden on the British government and the region has lost its previous self-sustaining capacity.[12] Northern industry, the main source of wealth creation, stagnated and the public sector is now financed through large-scale subsidies from Britain.[13] Estimates of this burden vary, but the regional public sector deficit appears to have climbed to over 25 per cent of regional GDP by the early 1990s (Bradley, 1996: 50–5).[14]

Whereas the link between tax revenue and public expenditure in the North, considered as a separate region, has been broken, policy makers and tax payers in the South enjoy no such luxury. For as long as British tax payers accept the current system of financing the Northern deficit, the deficit is only a residual item of limited economic consequence within the UK (McGregor *et al.*, 1995). On the other hand, deficit-financing in the South represents a very real constraint on public policy initiatives. Prior to 1980, public expenditure in the South grew rapidly, driven mainly by an increase in public sector employment. The ratio of public to private sector employment has however been consistently lower than in the North (see Figure 7). Even as Southern tax rates were raised, the PSBR grew, reaching almost 16 per cent of GNP in 1981. The ratio of national debt to GNP peaked at about 130 per cent in the mid-1980s. Since an increasing portion of debt was denominated in foreign currencies, interest payments were an outflow from the economy and devaluations of the Irish pound within the EMS during the first half of the 1980s further increased the debt burden. Driven in large part by the PSBR, the current account of the balance of payments also moved into serious deficit.

During the early 1980s tax rates were raised sharply and public capital expenditure curtailed. However, further adjustment was inevitable since the South had run up against the budget constraint that the North has never had to face. The fiscal adjustment, when it came after 1987, was extraordinarily and unexpectedly severe. Public expenditure fell, even measured in nominal terms, between 1987 and 1988. A combination of buoyant world demand, falling interest rates, and a devaluation of the Irish pound (£IR) against sterling within the EMS, boosted Southern growth and

---

[12] The limited data available indicate that Scotland and Wales are also in receipt of net transfers from London, albeit smaller ones on a per capita basis than in the case of the North (Blake, 1995). Data for the UK regional current account balance of payments are not available.

[13] In a recent study of the Northern public sector, Smyth (1993) states that: 'Expansion of the public sector of Northern Ireland has been a surrogate for autonomous growth, a buttress against political instability and remains the dominant feature of the region's economy'.

[14] The Northern estimates are based on an approximate attribution of UK indirect taxes to Northern Ireland, and assume that receipts are confined to revenue generated from the North's own economic activity (Bradley, 1990).

enabled the debt/GNP ratio to be cut significantly. More recently, the disciplines of the EMS (particularly prior to the broadening of the currency bands in August 1993) and the explicit commitments in the Maastricht Treaty now constrain the Southern government from moving away, even temporarily, from fiscal rectitude.

Surprisingly, far from depressing Southern GNP, as might have been predicted by Keynesian analysis, the economy grew strongly in the years after the 1987 adjustment and the current account moved strongly into surplus. Giavazzi and Pagano (1991) claimed that causation underlay this correlation and argued that the South's experience during the years 1987 to 1990 was a case of 'expansionary fiscal contraction'.[15] However, this view is controversial.[16]

Industrial and Regional Development in Ireland

We turn now to a more detailed exploration of industrial activity. Our first theme concerns enterprise and industrial organisation, where there is widespread recognition of the centrality of the manufacturing sector and the fact that past Irish performance in this area left much to be desired. We have seen that the North suffered from a serious problem of deindustrialisation that was part of a wider British pattern of decline. Problems in the South concerned mainly the weakness of the indigenous sector and over-dependence on inward foreign direct investment.

Our second theme concerns geographical and sectoral organisation of the island economy, an issue that was relevant to the manner in which the island developed in the nineteenth century and to how it came to be politically partitioned in the early twentieth century. Successful emulation by Ireland of rapid growth regions elsewhere in the world is likely to need appropriate supporting domestic policies, and recent Northern and Southern industrial policy studies have indeed begun to draw similar lessons from the new literature of industrial organisation (Stationery Office, 1992; NIGC, 1995).

---

[15] In an expansionary fiscal contraction (EFC), public expenditure cuts will reduce the need for future high taxes. This will be foreseen by a rational, optimising private sector which will immediately increase consumption and investment, possibly more than offsetting the contractionary effects of the cuts.

[16] Bradley and Whelan (1997) incorporated forward-looking expectations into a Southern macro-model and found that the strong performance of private consumption could not be accounted for convincingly by expectational effects related to personal income and consumption. Their preferred explanation focuses on the unexpectedly strong growth in the world economy which occurred during the adjustment.

Enterprise and Industrial Development

Present-day industrial policy, both North and South, could be very crudely characterised as a process whereby national and regional agencies (the IDA in the South and the IDB in the North), using a wide range of incentives, bid for subcontracting roles from global multinational firms and then attempt to influence the allocation of these activities over their respective regions in order to satisfy conflicting mixtures of economic, social and political criteria. However, the very success of inward investment to the island has tended to conceal rapid changes that are taking place in the international marketplace, many of which have served to return the focus of attention to regions as natural units of production (Sabel, 1989). Discussions of industrial policy have begun to take account of how the environment within which firms operate has been changing rapidly, with important consequences for the growth of successful clusters of modern innovative firms (Porter, 1990; Best, 1990).

Public policy can be invoked to influence an otherwise poor regional competitiveness position. The most extreme forms of intervention consist of import quotas and/or tariffs, methods that were used in the South during the protectionist period from the 1930s to the early 1960s. The preferred approach in recent decades involves subsidies to labour and capital combined with lower rates of corporate taxation in the South. Indeed, a striking similarity between North and South is the vigour with which state intervention is directed to enhance otherwise mediocre levels of international cost competitiveness, mainly through low corporate taxation in the South and high (though recently declining) subsidy rates in the North. Analysis indicates that while the effective exchequer cost of the Northern and Southern incentive packages are quite similar (NIEC, 1995), the South's tax-based measures may be more efficient in economic terms (i.e., lower 'deadweight' costs) than the Northern subsidy-based measures.

The economies of North and South are individually small, with populations of about 1.6 and 3.6 million respectively. Northern Ireland is not only separated geographically from Britain, but also appears to be very weakly integrated into the supply side of the British economy, even if demand for Northern output is dominated by the British market. This lack of supply-side integration with Britain is due in part to the problems created by the past 25 years of the Troubles. Improvements in access transport and the stability that peace may bring will probably alleviate this situation over time, but is unlikely to ever place the North on a par with the rest of the British economy, at least from the supply-side perspective. Rather, it is likely to remain the case that the North will always be geographically as well as economically peripheral to Britain.

The situation in the South relative to the countries that provide the bulk of Southern foreign direct investment (i.e., the US, Britain and the rest of the EU) has strong analogues with the North. For example, the Southern economy is not central to the strategic planning of US-based firms, other than as a highly profitable location for production of products mainly designed, developed and tested elsewhere, and a location where a very high quality labour force is available. The branch plant nature of foreign firms located in the South tends not to encourage the building of strong performance on the Porter 'diamond'.[17] Dependence purely on external investment is unlikely to generate the type of cumulative self-sustaining growth that is a characteristic of successful international growth poles.

Spatial Issues: Infrastructure, Clusters and Regional Development

Pre-1960 Irish experience. The protectionist policy regime in the South also ensured that the natural growth of inter-firm cooperation within given local specialisations would never happen, and that firms would be unlikely to survive when tariff barriers were dismantled in the 1960s (Ó Gráda, 1994: 398). Inter-firm cooperation and industrial 'districts' failed to develop from the 1930s to the 1950s, largely as a result of an industrial policy that minimised the likelihood of geographic clustering in a not very successful effort to spread employment more evenly throughout the regions. It is not surprising that the resulting weak indigenous sector performed so poorly when faced with stiff international competition in the 1960s after tariff barriers were lowered.

We have already seen that the situation in the North was very different. Here, the size of crucial sectors such as shipbuilding (Belfast) and linen (Dungannon-Newry-Belfast) ensured the existence of considerable scale economies. The extraordinary success of the north-east region, centred on Belfast, meant that this was the only Irish region that fully participated in the latter stages of Britain's industrial revolution.

However, after partition, Northern Ireland's problem became one of stagnant or declining world demand for its main products, combined with a failure to restructure into newer product areas. The negative effects on Belfast's satellite towns were serious as the growth pole process went into reverse. By the 1950s much of Northern indigenous industry suffered from the problems of its Southern counterpart: dispersal, small size and inward orientation.

---

[17] The Porter competitiveness 'diamond' consists of factor conditions, demand conditions, supporting industries and firm structure/strategy (Porter, 1990).

Post-1960 Southern experience. While the north-east growth pole centred on Belfast had arisen during the nineteenth century in an era of *laissez faire*, the debate on concentration versus dispersal in the South was revived in the 1950s and 1960s in the context of public policy initiatives designed to tilt the balance predominantly in one direction or another. The Buchanan Report was a comprehensive statement of the key issues for the South, while the Matthew report was an earlier statement of issues in the North (Buchanan, 1969; Matthew, 1963). The subsequent public debate, North and South, is illuminating and decisions taken in the early 1970s still largely shape both economies.

The first suggestion of a switch to a more spatially selective industrial policy in the South appeared in the year 1958 in *Economic Development*, the background document from which the *First Programme for Economic Expansion* drew its inspiration. The debate on growth centres versus dispersal flourished during the early- to mid-1960s, culminating with the commissioning of the Buchanan Report in 1966. Buchanan proposed a new policy orientation that embodied the growth centre idea, namely that 75 per cent of new industrial employment over a twenty-year period should be concentrated into a limited number of urban areas. In particular, the development of two national growth centres at Cork (in the south) and Limerick (in the south-west) was intended to enable them to attain a sufficient size to compete effectively with Dublin (in the east).

These proposals generated a vigorous and sometimes acrimonious debate, with the government reluctant to implement them, opting essentially for a continuation of the previous policy of dispersal. The formal rejection of the policy of concentration was eventually embodied in the first five-year plan of the Industrial Development Authority (IDA), published in 1972, and formal growth centre policy was quietly dropped.

A major economic argument against the promotion of growth poles made by the IDA was that improvements in transport and communications had greatly increased the locational flexibility of industry and that this was reflected in the ability of the weaker regions, outside the proposed Buchanan growth centres, to attract and support foreign direct investment. IDA policy was formulated in terms of systematic regional dispersal, accompanied by a comprehensive programme of fully serviced industrial sites and advance factories, and greater locational variability in grants made available.

To the extent that IDA policy was indeed targeted at a redistribution of manufacturing employment more evenly throughout the country, it was quite successful. By the late 1970s the earlier bias in favour of Dublin had been largely removed and all the other regions had improved their position. The success in dispersing new manufacturing employment to the regions was accompanied by a more modest, but nevertheless significant, convergence in regional per capita incomes in the South.

Such an equitable regional outcome might suggest that concentration was not necessary to ensure both strong national and regional growth. However, a different, less benign interpretation can be made based on specific features of the Southern experience of foreign direct investment, which was the main source of post-1960 industrial growth. Re-reading Buchanan today with hindsight forces one to reconsider his rather unsettling questions in the context of subsequent developments.

The foreign-owned industries locating in the South were originally, and largely remained, branch plants, seldom becoming involved in the core stages of product design and development, these activities remaining abroad with the foreign parent company. Rather they were involved in relatively routine assembly and manufacturing processes, often at the standardised stage of the product cycle. However, most small nations start by importing their technology, and the most common way to do this is to encourage foreign direct investment and to train the labour force in the servicing of this investment, simultaneously working to try to increase the level of indigenous competence.

Did these branch plants, against a background of spatial dispersal, begin to interact with each other, gradually taking on increasingly complex tasks and moving towards the earlier stages of the product cycle (i.e., 'maturing' products or, eventually, 'new' products)? The Irish evidence here is difficult to interpret, with international commentators tending to be more optimistic than domestic analysts. For example, Castells and Hall (1994) in their analysis of 'technopoles' comment that:

> New countries and regions emerge as successful locales of the new wave of innovation and investment, sometimes emerging from deep agricultural torpor, sometimes in idyllic corners of the world that acquire sudden dynamism. Thus, Silicon Valley and Orange County in California; . . . Silicon Glen in Scotland; the electronics agglomeration in Ireland. . . .

One interpretation of the Southern experience could be that, far from being a late-comer, the South, after executing an extraordinary policy *volte face* in the 1960s, was among the early countries to benefit from the production, transportation and communication advances that first generated internationally mobile investment flows on a large scale in the late 1950s.[18] With an early start, a comprehensive range of incentives and a high level of human capital, the IDA succeeded in attracting an impressive share of this investment. Since these branch plants required little in the way

---

[18] O'Malley (1989) develops the 'late-comer' thesis as an explanation of the poor Southern manufacturing performance since Independence.

of interaction with the local economy, they could be dispersed among different regions.

While the policy of dispersal had little effect on multinational branch plants, which were relatively self-sufficient and sourced only a small fraction of their inputs in Ireland, any anticipated synergies between foreign firms and between foreign and indigenous firms, were probably very seriously impeded.[19] Given the complexities of the Irish industrialisation process, it is difficult to make an absolutely convincing case that the policy of dispersion of multinational branch plants definitely did impede the development of synergies between foreign and indigenous firms. However, there are many direct and indirect indications that what synergies did come about were at best weak. For example, although industrial output and exports grew rapidly in the key areas where foreign-owned multinational firms dominated (e.g., chemicals, pharmaceuticals, computers, instrument engineering), the employment response was attenuated both in these key sectors themselves and in the industrial and service sectors that would be expected to benefit from synergies (NESC, 1995). Furthermore, IDA work on targeting foreign-indigenous synergies (e.g., the National Linkage Programme) is designed to strengthen what are admitted to be weak linkages.

Geographic dispersion was obviously not the only issue at the root of the problem of weak foreign-indigenous synergies.[20] In addition, the gulf that existed between the new high technology foreign-owned firms and existing largely traditional indigenous industries was probably too large to bridge satisfactorily during the first decades of the export-led growth strategy. Although the inter-firm synergies may have been weak, there were direct benefits to the Southern economy in terms of conventional income multiplier effects. A further important benefit came through human capital and labour market externalities, as the expansion of the Southern education system after the mid-1960s interacted with the demand of the foreign sector for an increasingly skilled labour force. After three decades of large-scale inward investment, the position in the South is now transformed and these are the kind of factors underlying more recent strong growth performance.

---

[19] The main incentive for attracting inward investment, i.e., the low corporate tax regime, was itself an obstacle to linkage development within Ireland. The transfer pricing activity which it encourages is most easily operated where branch plants in Ireland maintain their major supply links with affiliate plants located abroad.

[20] In the eighteenth and nineteenth centuries industries needed to cluster close to sources of energy (coal, water, etc.) and at transport hubs near large centres of population. However, in the latter part of the twentieth century the concept of geographical distance has been diluted and redefined by dramatic improvements and cost reductions in communications technologies.

Post-1960 Northern experience. Policy on sub-regional development within the North was relatively weak and passive from the immediate post-war period until the mid-1960s, tending to accommodate to a focus on expanding the north-east sub-region around Belfast. As late as 1962 the Hall report on the economy of Northern Ireland devoted little attention to regional imbalances or to the active use of public policy to redress these imbalances, even in light of the serious unemployment in areas west of the Bann (Derry, Enniskillen, Strabane), and to the south of Belfast (Newry, Dungannon) (Hall, 1962).

However, the Belfast Regional Survey and Plan was the first of a series that began to focus on sub-regional imbalances (Matthew, 1963). Unlike the South, where physical planning tended to follow behind economic planning, economic plans for the North up to the mid-1970s accepted the essentials of the physical strategy as put forward in the Matthew Report. The growth centres as designated by Matthew had a clear concentration on the eastern sub-region.

The Wilson Report further promoted the concept of growth centres, and worked on the assumption that successful regional development would be accompanied by internal migration: people moving to jobs, rather than jobs moving to people (Wilson, 1965). A major change in regional policy was heralded by the Quigley Report in 1976. An acknowledgement of the segmentation of Northern labour markets and the relatively low rate of internal migration led to the conclusion that:

> It is simply a fact that no regional policy (whatever its success in promoting investment or raising GDP or reducing unemployment) will be judged satisfactory which fails to remove the unemployment black spots.[21] (Quigley, 1976: 17)

From the mid-1970s, it could be said that regional policies in both North and South eschewed any narrow focus on growth centres and became a pragmatic blend of concentration and dispersal that attempted to bring spatial equity to the island, with as little loss of economic efficiency as possible.

A final aspect of the Northern sub-regional policy debate concerns its implications for the spatial distribution of Government sponsored employment in relation to the religious composition of the population (Bradley *et al.*, 1986). Contrasting with the scattered nature of the Catholic majority areas, the non-Catholic community forms a reasonably solid contiguous group in the east-central region of Northern Ireland. Any economic policy

---

[21] The failure of Craigavon, a 'new' Northern town, to generate self-sustaining growth is an aspect of migrational difficulties within the North (Bardon, 1992: 717).

that facilitated further concentration on the east-central region, either passively or actively, could not avoid the relative neglect of the large areas with Catholic majorities. Figure 12 shows manufacturing 'location' ratios for the entire period 1949 to 1981, together with two sub-periods: the passive policy period 1949 to 1963, and the active policy period, 1964 to 1981.[22]

Although there is no overall difference for the entire period, there is a marked difference between the two sub-periods, with Catholic majority areas faring better during the later 'active' policy period than during the earlier 'passive' period. Had the situation been reversed, and had the relatively deprived areas with Catholic majorities benefited more in both employment and housing during the first period rather than the second, then perhaps some of the underlying causes of the outbreak of civil unrest in the late 1960s might have been alleviated.

Summary. Our brief examination of the previous and the present stance of industrial policy, both North and South, suggests that the normal processes of clustering and regional concentration eventually were impeded both by the branch-plant nature of the investment and by a public policy of geographical dispersal. The only example of an Irish self-sustaining 'industrial district', i.e., Belfast during the period from the mid-nineteenth century to the early decades of the twentieth, declined thereafter. More recent policy has deliberately promoted regional dispersal, almost certainly at some expense to strict economic efficiency criteria.

However, after more than three decades of exposure to foreign direct investment, the South has succeeded in attracting sufficient firms in the computer, instrument engineering, pharmaceutical and chemical sectors to constitute sectoral 'agglomerations' or 'clusters'.[23] The incentives used in the South to attract and hold these firms were tax breaks, grants and a well educated and trained work-force. With the exception of tax-based incentives, similar policies were used in the North to attract inward investment, albeit in a climate dominated by negative factors associated with the Troubles.

Conclusions

We have described how the island of Ireland has experienced a variety of radically different political regimes since the first phases of the British

---

[22] Location ratios measure how a region's share of total national employment in any sector compares with its share of national population.

[23] At present the Southern agglomerations and clusters are of a rather weak variety and are quite unlike the dynamic clusters in regions like Silicon Valley and Route 128 in the US. Nevertheless, Ireland has become an attractive location for certain high-technology activities simply because of the presence of other similar industries.

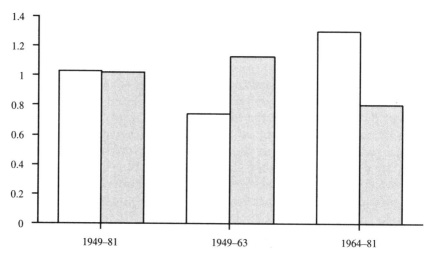

Figure 12. Northern location ratios: 1949–63 and 1964–81. ⬜ Catholic majority, ▨ non-Catholic majority.

Industrial revolution: colonisation with a limited form of self-government prior to 1800; full incorporation into the United Kingdom between 1800 and 1920; and then partition into two parts, with Northern Ireland remaining within the UK (but with a local parliament and limited policy autonomy) and the rest of the island achieving full independence. Economic development, policy-making institutions and performance in the island have reflected these different regimes and have been largely shaped by them.

We suggested that economic preconditions for the political partition of the island were in place at least three decades before the end of the last century and we surveyed the key economic issues of this crucial period in history: the abnormal demographics of the island; the economic geography of the North-South divide; and the almost total economic dependence of the island on the British economy.

Radical transformations have taken place during the past three decades in both economies of Ireland, introducing dramatic differences in the relative performance of North and South. Overlaying these differences is the civil unrest (or so-called 'Troubles') that casts a shadow over the recent economic development of Northern Ireland. A detailed discussion of the reasons for the stronger performance of the South relative to the North in the last decade would require a separate paper.[24] Basically five key factors

---

[24] For a full treatment of the recent Southern growth experience, see Bradley *et al.*, 1997. Using certain measures (e.g., GDP per capita), the South has even surpassed the UK, although the welfare implications of such comparisons are complex.

are involved in the South's dynamic performance: the changing demographic structure and the role of inward migration in preventing skill shortages; the steady build-up of human capital after the educational reforms in the 1960s; the major improvements in physical infrastructure, particularly since 1989 as a result of the EU Community Support Framework; the extreme openness of the economy, export orientation to fast growing markets and products, together with benefits stemming from the completion of the Single European Market (*1992*) and from massive FDI inflows;[25] and the stable domestic macroeconomic policy environment.

The role played by large-scale British financial support in sustaining the standard of living in the North has perhaps served to mask the true nature of the differences in performance between North and South. The situation in the North would appear to be rather less advantageous than in the South for each of the above five factors. Northern demographic trends remain out of line with the European norms to which the South has converged. The problems associated with the selectivity of the Northern education system are treated elsewhere in this volume. Economic openness is less beneficial to the North than is the case in the South, since the North's export orientation is mainly to the slower growing British markets and to more traditional products. The overhang of the large financial subvention and fears about its possible reduction has introduced uncertainty to Northern medium-term economic planning. In fact the only exception where the relative position of the North is better than the South is in the state of physical infrastructure, and this is changing rapidly.

Adverting to the uneasy relationship between economics and politics mentioned at the start of this essay, the *Economist* recently posed the following question: might success and self confidence (in the South) bring the island closer to an even greater prize—peace in the North? The conclusion drawn was unusually optimistic:

> As prosperity lightens the burdens of history, Britain and the Republic should develop a more relaxed relationship, based on shared economic interests and unforced mutual respect. With time, the border between North and South could come to seem unimportant, reconciling Northern nationalists to its existence and Northern unionists to closer links with the South. Miracles do happen, you know: look at the Irish economy. (*Economist*, 17 May 1997)

---

[25] An examination of the impact of *1992* on the Greek, Irish, Portuguese and Spanish economies is available in Barry *et al.*, 1997.

References

Bardon, J. (1982) *Belfast: An Illustrated History*, Belfast: The Blackstaff Press.

Bardon, J. (1992) *A History of Ulster*, Belfast: The Blackstaff Press.

Barry, F. and Bradley, J. (1991) 'On the Causes of Ireland's Unemployment', *Economic and Social Review*, 22(4): 253–86.

Barry, F. and Bradley, J. (1997) 'FDI and Trade: the Irish Host-Country Experience', *The Economic Journal*, 107: 1798–1811.

Barry, F., Bradley, J., Hannan, A., McCartan, J. and Sosvilla-Rivero, S. (1997) *Single Market Review 1996: Aggregate and Regional Aspects—the Cases of Greece, Ireland, Portugal and Spain*, London: Kogan Page.

Best, M. (1990) *The New Competition: Institutions of Industrial Restructuring*, Cambridge: The Polity Press.

Blake, N. (1995) 'The Regional Implications of Macroeconomic Policy', *Oxford Review of Economic Policy*, 11(2): 145–64.

Bradley, J., Hewitt, V. and Jefferson, C. (1986) *Industrial Location Policy and Equality of Opportunity in Assisted Employment in Northern Ireland 1949–1981*, Belfast: Fair Employment Agency.

Bradley, J. (1990) 'The Irish Economies: Some Comparisons and Contrasts', in R. Harris, C. Jefferson, and J. Spencer (eds), *The Northern Ireland Economy*, London: Longmans.

Bradley, John (1996) *An Island Economy: Exploring Long-Term Economic and Social Consequences of Peace and Reconciliation in the Island of Ireland*, Dublin: Stationery Office.

Bradley, John and Whelan, K. (1997) 'The Irish Expansionary Fiscal Contraction: A Tale from One Small European Economy', *Economic Modelling*, 14(2): 175–201.

Bradley, John, Herce, J-A. and Modesto, L. (1995) 'Modelling in the EU Periphery: the HERMIN project', *Economic Modelling*, 12(3): 219–333.

Bradley, John, Fitz Gerald, J., Honohan, P. and Kearney, I. (1997) 'Interpreting the Recent Irish Growth Experience', in D. Duffy, J. Fitz Gerald, I. Kearney and F. Shortall (eds), *Medium-Term Review: 1997–2003*, Dublin: The Economic and Social Research Institute.

Breen, R., Hannan, D., Rottman, D. and Whelan, C. (1990) *Understanding Contemporary Ireland*, Dublin: Gill and Macmillan.

Buchanan, C. (1969) *Regional Studies in Ireland*, Dublin: An Foras Forbartha.

Canning, D., Moore, B. and Rhodes, J. (1987) 'Economic Growth in Northern Ireland: Problems and Prospects', in P. Teague (ed.), *Beyond the Rhetoric*, London: Lawrence and Wishart.

Castells, M. and Hall, P. (1994) *Technopoles of the World: The Making of 21st Century Industrial Complexes*, London: Routledge.

Crotty, R. (1986) *Ireland in Crisis: A Study of Capitalist Colonial Underdevelopment*, Dingle: Brandon Book Publishers.

Fanning, R. (1978) *The Irish Department of Finance 1922–58*, Dublin: The Institute of Public Administration.

Farley, N. (1995) 'A Comparative Analysis of the Performance of the Manufacturing Sectors, North and South: 1960–1991', in J. Bradley (ed.), *The Two Economies of Ireland*, Dublin: Oak Tree Press.

Giavazzi, F. and Pagano, M. (1991) 'Can Severe Fiscal Contractions be Expansionary? Tales of Two Small European Countries', in *The NBER Macroeconomics Annual 1991*, Cambridge: The MIT Press.

Government of Ireland (1958) *Economic Development*, Dublin: Stationery Office.

Hall, R. (1962) *Report of the Joint Working Party on the Economy of Northern Ireland*, London: HMSO.

Harris, R. (1991) *Regional Economic Policy in Northern Ireland 1945–1988*, Aldershot: Avebury.

Johnson, D. S. and Kennedy, L. (1991) 'Nationalist Historiography and the Decline of the Irish Economy: George O'Brien Revisited', in S. Hutton and P. Stewart (eds), *Ireland's Histories: Aspects of State, Society and Ideology*, London: Routledge.

Kennedy, K., Giblin, T. and McHugh, D. (1988) *The Economic Development of Ireland in the Twentieth Century*, London: Routledge.

Kenwood, A. and Lougheed, A. (1992) *The Growth of the International Economy 1820–1990*, London: Routledge.

Keynes, J. M. (1933) 'National Self-Sufficiency', *Studies*, 22: 177–93.

Krugman, P. (1991) *Geography and Trade*, Cambridge: The MIT Press.

Lee, J. J. (1989) *Ireland 1912–1985: Politics and Society*, Cambridge: Cambridge University Press.

Matthew, R. (1963) *The Belfast Regional Survey and Plan*, London: HMSO.

McGarry, J. and O'Leary, B. (1995) *Explaining Northern Ireland: Broken Images*, Oxford: Blackwell.

McGregor, P., Swales, K. and Ying, Y. P. (1995) 'Regional Public-Sector and Current-Account Deficits: Do They Matter?', in J. Bradley (ed.), *The Two Economies of Ireland*, Dublin: Oak Tree Press.

Mjøset, L. (1992) *The Irish Economy in a Comparative Institutional Perspective*, Report No. 93, National Economic and Social Council, Dublin: The Stationery Office.

Munck, R. (1993) *The Irish Economy: Results and Prospects*, London: Pluto Press.

National Economic and Social Council (NESC) (1992) *The Association Between Economic Growth and Employment Growth in Ireland*, Report No. 94, Dublin: The Stationery Office.

National Economic and Social Council (NESC) (1995) *The Determinants of Competitive Advantage in Selected Irish Sectors*, Dublin: The Stationery Office.

Northern Ireland Economic Council (NIEC) (1992) *Inward Investment in Northern Ireland*, Belfast: Northern Ireland Economic Council.

Northern Ireland Economic Council (NIEC) (1995) *The Economic Implications of Peace and Political Stability for Northern Ireland*, Belfast: Northern Ireland Economic Council.

Northern Ireland Growth Challenge (NIGC) (1995) *Northern Ireland Growth Challenge: Interim Summary of Progress*, Belfast.

O'Brien, G. (1918) *The Economic History of Ireland in the Eighteenth Century*, London: Maunsel.

O'Brien, G. (1921) *The Economic History of Ireland from the Union to the Famine*, London: Longmans.

Ó Gráda, C. (1994) *Ireland: A New Economic History 1780–1939*, Oxford: Clarendon Press.

Ó Gráda, C., and Walsh, B. (1995) 'Fertility and Population in Ireland, North and South', *Population Studies*, 49: 129–37.

O'Malley, E. (1989) *Industry and Economic Development: The Challenge for the Latecomer*, Dublin: Gill and Macmillan.

Porter, M. (1990) *The Competitive Advantage of Nations*, London: Macmillan.

Quigley, G. (1976) *Economic and Industrial Strategy for Northern Ireland: Report by the Review Team*, Belfast: HMSO.

Sabel, C. (1989) 'Flexible Specialisation and the Re-emergence of Regional Economies', in P. Hirst and J. Zeitlin (eds), *Reversing Industrial Decline*, Oxford: Berg Publishers.

Smyth, M. (1993) 'The Public Sector in the Economy', in P. Teague (ed.), *The Economy of Northern Ireland*, London: Lawrence and Wishart.

Stationery Office (1985) *The Economic Consequences of the Division of Ireland Since 1920*, New Ireland Forum, Dublin: The Stationery Office.

Stationery Office (1992) *A Time for Change: Industrial Policy for the 1990s*, Dublin: The Stationery Office.

Wijkman, P. (1990) 'Patterns of Production and Trade', in W. Wallace (ed.), *The Dynamics of European Integration*, London: Pinter.

Wilson, T. (1965) 'The Report of the Economic Consultant', in *Economic Development in Northern Ireland*, Cmd. 479, Belfast: HMSO.

Demography and Migration in Ireland, North and South

D. A. COLEMAN

Introduction

THE RECENT DEMOGRAPHY OF IRELAND has been dominated by contrasts with the rest of the world and within itself. Ireland became highly exceptional among the populations of Europe by the mid-nineteenth century and has remained so almost up to the end of the twentieth. Ireland's remarkable example—North and South—has challenged any attempt to establish general rules for the demographic behaviour of modern industrial societies. One task of this chapter is to document this contrast with the rest of the industrial world, to attempt to explain it and to see how far, and why, Ireland's exceptionalism is now drawing to a close. Another is to analyse the internal contrasts between the demographic regimes in the island of Ireland, between and within North and South, and to evaluate possible explanations for them.

The Irish Question in Demography

Irish demographic exceptionalism is readily demonstrated. As late as 1970, for example, Irish fertility, whether measured by the total period fertility rate (TFR) or by the completed fertility of cohorts of women (see Coleman, 1996; Sardon, 1990) was by far the highest of any Western developed country. The TFR indicates the average family size per woman implied by the continuation of the fertility rates of the year in question. In 1970 the TFR in the Irish Republic was 3.87 and in Northern Ireland 3.25. In the same year, the mean TFR of 18 West European countries was 2.41 and of 14 Central and Eastern European countries was 2.30. The Irish

Proceedings of the British Academy, **98**, 69–115. © The British Academy 1999.

Republic TFR in 1970 was more than three standard deviations from the West European mean (Figure 1).

In that year, with the exception of Albania (5.16), Irish fertility had no equal or even close rival anywhere on the continent of Europe. Even in 1990, after 20 years of decline, the TFR in the Irish Republic (2.19) was still exceeded only by that of Iceland in Western Europe (2.3), by Albania (3.0) and Moldova (2.39) elsewhere in Europe, and—slightly—by that of Northern Ireland (2.26). By 1993 the TFR in the Irish Republic (1.93) and in Northern Ireland (2.0) had for the first time fallen below the level required to replace the population in the long run (conventionally taken to be 2.1) and by 1994 had fallen further to 1.87 and 1.92 respectively. The Irish demographic transition is now over, although for the time being it has left Irish fertility at the top end of the European range.

Western Europe has been notable, over several centuries, for its unusual pattern of delayed marriage and high level of lifelong spinsterhood (Hajnal, 1965; 1982). From the mid-nineteenth to the late twentieth century Ireland was, along with Sweden, one of the most extreme examples of this pattern, with marriage often delayed until women were approaching age 30

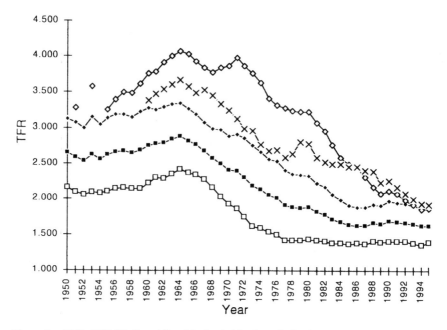

Figure 1. TFR 1950–95, Republic of Ireland, Northern Ireland and mean of 15 Western European countries +/− one standard deviation. (■) West European mean TFR, (□) mean − one standard deviation, (◆) mean + one standard deviation, (◇) RoI TFR, (×) NI TFR. *Sources*: Eurostat (1996), Council of Europe (1996), National Demographic Yearbooks.

and avoided altogether by at least a fifth of the population. Even today about 20 per cent of Irish women now in their fifties have remained childless, notwithstanding the average high fertility. Despite delayed marriage, illegitimate births continued to be rare in Ireland until recently; a remarkable testimony to social control, helping to make Ireland 'a unique entity in terms of her demography of sexuality' (Szreter, 1996: 16). Age at first marriage in Ireland is still late compared with most European countries (in 1992 mean age of marriage of spinsters was 27.0, the oldest in the 15 countries of the EU except for Denmark, Iceland and Sweden), although the picture is now clouded by the novel rise of cohabitation.

Generalisations about Ireland's demography are complicated by the overlapping in Ireland of a demographic regime described above, characteristic of the Irish Catholic population and another less marked variant of the Western pattern—with somewhat earlier marriage, lower celibacy and lower marital fertility—typical of the Protestants of the North and the South. In the North, the Protestants—or at least non-Catholics—now comprise about 58 per cent of the population (Compton, 1996), in the South about 5 per cent. Because of higher Catholic fertility, and in the South through emigration and assimilation, these proportions have fallen from 65 per cent and 10 per cent respectively in 1911. However, the Northern Irish Protestants do not share the same regime as their co-religionists in Scotland, England and Wales, but a distinctive Irish version of it, with higher fertility until recently and persistently higher mortality than in the rest of the UK.

The potentially very rapid population growth made possible by high fertility both in the South and the North has been, in most years, more than balanced by the highest proportional rate of emigration in the industrial world. A few developed countries already experience population decline because their death rates exceed their birth rates. The Irish Republic is still the only developed country which, in many recent years including 1995, has seen its population fall through net emigration despite a positive natural increase. As a consequence of high fertility, the Irish population is the most youthful in the industrial world with 24 per cent of the population under age 15 in 1996 and only 11 per cent aged 65 and over, and a mean age of 33.6 years (24 per cent and 13 per cent in Northern Ireland in 1993). By contrast the under 15s comprised 18 per cent of the population of the 15 EU countries in 1995. However, the Irish population is now ageing relatively fast as fertility has declined: in 1981 the under 15s comprised 30 per cent of the population and the mean age was 30.8 years (CSO, 1997). Among European countries with populations over 1 million, the Irish Republic was until 1996 alone in Europe in having no legal provision for divorce. Since a reform of the law in Belgium in 1990, the Irish Republic is also alone in Europe in not permitting abortion for any purpose other than the saving of the life of the mother, and that only on the strictest conditions. For more on all these matters, valuable summaries of the demographic scene in Ireland may be found in (e.g.) Kennedy, 1994; Compton, 1995; Ó Gráda and Walsh, 1995.

Data and Their Difficulties

Demographic data on Ireland, North and South, past and present, are relatively limited. As always in historical demography, much ink continues to be spilled over insoluble controversies about premodern population size and vital rates. Contemporary estimates of population size began with William Petty's in 1697, based on the surveys for the hearth tax. The first completed census was held in 1821 following an earlier abortive attempt in 1813, but the census in Ireland was not considered to be reliable until that of 1841, the first to be based on a household canvass. Pre-census estimates of Irish population remain controversial.

The parish registers of baptisms, burials and marriages, so useful to historical demographers elsewhere since Henry's technical innovations, scarcely exist in usable form in Ireland. Civil registration of births, marriages and deaths did not begin until 1864 (except for Protestant marriages from 1844) and the returns are incomplete. There are also serious difficulties, up to the end of the nineteenth century, in relating aggregate vital events (births, marriages and deaths) to the local populations at risk (Teitelbaum, 1984; Ó Gráda, 1991). In the twentieth century both census and vital registration have been much improved. Even so, there was no census in 1921 and since then two parallel series of data, for the Irish Republic and for Northern Ireland, have complicated study.

Official demographic data for the Irish Republic and for Northern Ireland are limited compared to those available for most other Western countries, although this author has always found the offices themselves to be invariably helpful. For example annual birth data for Northern Ireland are not related to a population at risk by age, so it is difficult to compute fertility rates. In the official publications from both parts of Ireland, time-series of means and demographic indices are sparse. For example, no published series of mean age at marriage for the Republic extends before 1960 and none is more recent than 1990 (the 1992 data given above were from Eurostat, 1996). However, data on births by birth order and age of mother relate to all births, not just to births within marriage as in Northern Ireland. Time-series of such indices as the expectation of life at birth for the Republic of Ireland are published annually by Eurostat (1996) and by the Council of Europe (1996) but not by the CSO. Unlike most censuses in Western Europe, that in Ireland North and South asks a (voluntary) question on religious affiliation, following a pattern begun in 1861.

Data from Northern Ireland are only sub-national data; these are not usually as comprehensive as those for a whole country. However, the problem really works the other way round: Northern Ireland suffers from its lack of integration into the UK. Like Scotland it has its own Registrar-General, but the resources of that office cannot match those available to the Office of Population Censuses and Surveys (now ONS) which publishes data for England and Wales, and the data are not as comprehensive as for England and Wales, or even for its regions. The limitations of demographic data for Northern Ireland restrict those for the whole UK. The total fertility rate cannot be determined for Northern Ireland before 1960, and therefore not for the UK either. Other data published for the 'United Kingdom' by the Council of Europe and by Eurostat (despite warnings by ONS) in fact refer only to England and Wales. Even today the Northern Ireland TFR is not published in the Annual Report but must be sought in the Annual Report of the Chief Medical Officer (DHSS, 1994). Mean age at first marriage was not published at all before 1962 and until the late 1970s was only given one year at a time in the text of the report .

Response to the census in Northern Ireland has been compromised in some years by non-cooperation and in 1981 by Republican violence. Data from the General Household Survey and the Labour Force Survey are now available. The first comprehensive fertility survey in Northern Ireland was not held until 1983 (Compton and Coward, 1989). However, a demographic review was published in 1995 (Compton, 1995) and a question on marital fertility was posed in the 1991 census (unlike that of 1981).

Data on migration are poor in most countries, particularly so in Ireland. Until 1922, migration to Britain and between Southern and Northern Ireland was 'internal' migration and was not directly counted except through sea passenger statistics. Census statistics on birthplace and on previous residence partly compensate for this lack. No controls have existed in peacetime on the border between North and South. Since 1922 the Irish Republic and the United Kingdom have formed a Common Travel Area whereby entry to one permits entry to the other without further check. Neither of the UK's sources of direct immigration data, the Home Office data on settlement and the International Passenger Survey of all incoming and departing passengers, applies to movements with the Irish Republic. Other UK sources, such as the National Health Service Central Register, the annual Labour Force Survey and Social Security statistics, in conjunction with Irish Republic sources and those from other countries, permited indirect estimates to be made (Geary and Ó Gráda, 1987) at various times in the past.

In the Irish Republic, no direct comprehensive data on immigration or emigration are published in the absence of controls on the movement of persons in and out (Garvey, 1985). Indirect or survey-based estimates are published by the Central Statistical Office from the annual Labour Force Survey, the continuous Country of Residence Inquiry of passengers at airports and seaports, and social security statistics, amended retro-spectively by the Census. The Irish Labour Force Survey includes a unique supplementary question on the intended country of destination of persons resident in the previous year who have since emigrated, and the CSO publishes annual data on the intended future residence of married couples. These sources enable gross and net international migration statistics to be published (Sexton, 1994). These Irish statistics, along with data from the British Labour Force Survey, National Health Service Register and National Insurance records, now permit annual estimates of gross and net movement between the UK and the Irish Republic to be made (see OPCS, 1996: MN table a) although they have not yet been published separately.

Northern Ireland is part of the UK's international and national migra-tion system. Although the UK receives and sends substantial numbers of international migrants each year, and has in recent years been a net recipient of immigration even before asylum claimants are considered, Northern Ireland is remote from these international movements except for those involving the Irish Republic. That apart, most of its migration is with the other parts of the UK. In the absence of any system of national registration, movement can only be measured indirectly, for example through the NHS Central Register, which records changes of registration with medical practi-tioners. Otherwise, migration is estimated in net terms from birthplace data and from migration questions in the census and the Labour Force Survey.

The History and Survival of the Irish Demographic Regime

When the curtain goes up on Irish demographic history in the eighteenth century it reveals unusually rapid population growth. The Malthusian model suggests that this exceptional growth was encouraged by the ease of setting up and supporting a family through potato cultivation (Connell, 1950) in an immobile egalitarian rural society dominated by partible inheritance. This view appears to have stood the test of time: recent research has if anything reinforced the classic model of pre-famine Irish population, characterised by high rates of natural increase driven by high marital fertility (Clarkson, 1981; Dickson et al., 1982; Kennedy and

Clarkson, 1993), although there is less agreement on whether pre-famine marriage was early by European standards. Irish population growth from 1753 to 1821 was already exceptional, being then the highest in Western Europe (Figure 2): on average 1.3 per cent per year between 1750 and 1845 according to Mokyr and Ó Gráda (1984: 476), or 1.4 per cent between 1791 and 1821; Daultry *et al.*, (1981: 625). Population more than doubled in the eighteenth century, having possibly doubled also during the seventeenth. But such growth was not sustainable. Ireland did not experience the agricultural or industrial revolutions so important to England's later economic success, and which enabled it to sustain a large population with a growing standard of living in the later eighteenth and early nineteenth centuries. Without such developments the catastrophe of the famine forced the population into a new regime in order to survive new circumstances.

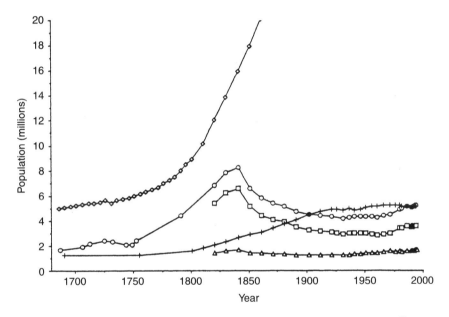

Figure 2. Population Trends, Great Britain and Ireland 1686–1994 (millions). (O) All Ireland population, (□) RoI population, (△) NI population, (◇) E&W population, (+) Scotland population. *Note*: No data for Wales could be found before 1801. Following the ratios in the 1801–21 censuses, 3% has been added to the England population before 1801. For Ireland before 1821, the average of the range of estimates of Dickson *et al.* (1982) was used. *Sources*: England before 1801: Wrigley and Schofield (1981) table A3.1, Scotland before 1801: Tyson (1995), Ireland before 1821: Dickson *et al.* (1982), Republic of Ireland from 1821: Central Statistics Office (various years), Northern Ireland from 1821: Registrar-General (Northern Ireland) various years, England and Wales 1801 onwards: Office for Population Censuses and Surveys (various years), Scotland 1801 onwards: Registrar-General Scotland (various years).

Little is known about marriage and fertility in Ireland before the 1840s. In the general prevalence of partible inheritance, farms could be and were subdivided; new land was also cultivated. But the favoured mechanism for accelerating population growth, the lowering of the age at marriage, has its critics. The 1841 census, for example, suggests that mean age of marriage just before the famine was an unexceptional 24–25 for women and 27–29 for men (Mokyr and Ó Gráda, 1984: 477). These estimates are supported by rare surviving enumerators' returns for Antrim, although these also suggest that mean age at marriage had increased a little since the beginning of the century (Morgan and Macafee, 1984). Marital fertility does appear to have become exceptionally high by European standards before 1840, possibly through changes in breastfeeding patterns connected with potato cultivation (Schellekens, 1993). Infant mortality around 1841 was higher than average in Europe (220–225 per 1,000 live births: Mokyr and Ó Gráda, 1984: 484). But adult mortality may have fallen, partly because the potato increased the subsistence base. Smallpox may have been checked by inoculation in the eighteenth century, especially on the East coast, but not to the same extent as in Britain.

The components of a distinctive Irish demographic regime became discernible by the mid-nineteenth century: exceptionally late marriage with low levels of illegitimacy or cohabitation; 'natural' high fertility within marriage; correspondingly low levels of overall fertility compared with other nineteenth-century populations. By this time, and possibly much earlier, most households were based upon the nuclear family. Before and after the famine, mortality is thought to have been moderate by the contemporary standards, possibly because of the low level of urbanisation and the avoidance of subsequent subsistence crises through emigration.

The whole system was overshadowed, and its peculiar nineteenth-century features made possible, by the institutionalisation of high rates of emigration. Emigration, especially from Ulster, had been substantial even before the famine, especially to North America: perhaps three quarters of the 250,000 to 400,000 emigrants from 1700–1776 were Protestants (Miller, 1985: Ch. 4). The conventional wisdom is that the elevated levels of emigration after the famine, and its continuation almost to the present day, became the cornerstone of an Irish demographic regime also characterised by continuing high marital fertility, delayed marriage, frequent celibacy and impartible inheritance. This enabled high rates of natural increase to continue for over a century without feeding back onto population size, to a greater degree than elsewhere in Europe (Table 1). After the famine, Irish population declined throughout the nineteenth century, until the 1950s; a trend unique in Europe for a country although

Table 1. Republic of Ireland, average annual population change (1871–1996).

Period beginning	Population change	Natural increase	Net migration	Rates per 1,000 population Population growth	Rates per 1,000 population Natural increase	Rates per 1,000 population Net migration
1871	−18,317	31,855	−50,172	−4.6	8.1	−12.7
1881	−40,133	19,600	−59,733	−10.9	5.3	−16.3
1891	−24,688	14,954	−39,642	−7.4	4.5	−11.9
1901	−8,214	17,940	−26,154	−2.6	5.6	−8.2
1911	−11,180	15,822	−27,002	−3.7	5.2	−8.8
1926	−357	16,318	−16,675	−0.1	5.5	−5.6
1936	−1,331	17,380	−18,711	−0.4	5.9	−6.3
1946	1,119	25,503	−24,384	0.4	8.6	−8.2
1951	−14,226	26,652	−40,877	−4.9	9.2	−14.1
1961	15,991	29,442	−13,451	5.5	10.2	−4.6
1971	46,516	36,127	10,389	14.5	11.3	3.2
1981	8,231	28,837	−20,606	2.4	8.3	−5.9
1991	19,063	18,426	637	5.3	5.2	0.1

Source: CSO.

not uncommon for provinces of a country. There was therefore no demographic incentive for a reduction in marital fertility.

The Irish Question in historical demography, however, never seems to be quite settled. The post-famine novelty of relatively late marriage has been questioned; some sceptics doubt whether the famine inaugurated a new demographic regime (Kennedy, pers. comm.). Furthermore, the famine was not unique to Ireland. It is difficult to see how the famine itself could account for permanently higher levels of emigration once conditions had returned to normal in the 1850s; a problem also for the somewhat parallel case of the Scottish Highlands (Flinn, 1977: 32–8, 421–38), unless there was a widespread perception that the old ways were no longer sustainable. Higher levels of emigration, however, are beyond doubt and the gradual predominance of impartible inheritance after the famine must have been important in sustaining it (Ó Gráda, 1993: Ch. 5). The death rate, although slightly lower in the nineteenth century than in more urbanised Britain, appears to have been relatively more unfavourable to females and for longer. As many emigrants were women, Ireland thereby acquired an unusual sex ratio (only recently lost) with more males than females. This depressed the marriage chances of men, giving some substance to its depiction earlier this century as 'a nation of elderly bachelors'.

Ireland's Migration Pattern

Neither Ireland's population trends nor its fertility can be understood without considering emigration. The basic fact about Ireland's demography, over the last 150 years, is that emigration of up to half of each birth cohort has overwhelmed the substantial natural increase in the population and caused numbers to decline. Emigration is the most distinctive feature of Ireland's demography, even more than its high birth rate, in per capita terms the greatest of all the European nineteenth-century diasporas. By the mid-twentieth century it was only in Ireland that emigration still had such a powerful effect upon the national population, continuing to limit total size and permitting the continuation of unusually high fertility. During the renewed exodus of the 1880s, provoked by agricultural depression and the Land Wars, emigration primarily to North America exceeded natural increase by two- or threefold. The 1950s saw emigration on almost the same scale, this time to the UK, attracted by postwar economic growth; a pattern slightly paralleled by that of Finland and Sweden.

Other countries, especially on the north-western fringes of Europe, also had high emigration rates: especially Norway and also Sweden, Finland and the UK, particularly Scotland (Baines, 1991). More emigrants left from Britain and from the German-speaking populations, but the rate was lower. While heavy emigration rates depressed population growth widely, Ireland is exceptional in that emigration put population growth into reverse. However, the Scottish Highlands and Islands—not dissimilar in agricultural terms—also suffered irreversible depopulation through emigration after the famine (Flinn, 1977); Scottish population growth as a whole was also slowed by emigration in the late nineteenth century and slightly reversed from 1921 to 1931 (Anderson and Morse, 1993) and again in the 1970s and 1980s (some of the latter migration being to the Irish Republic).

Since the 1880s, emigration has, in very broad terms, been declining except during the 1950s, and fell below a net annual loss of 20,000 people after the Second World War. Irish population ceased to decline in the 1950s. In 1972, the Irish Republic gained population through migration for the first time in peacetime (Figure 3). As that also coincided with a rise in natural increase the population grew relatively fast for a time (Figure 4). Both are reasonably attributed to the marked revival in the Irish economy in the middle to late 1970s.

The end of that episode of prosperity led to a marked elevation of unemployment and a resumption of emigration from the early 1980s, peaking at a net loss of 43,900 in 1989 (about 1 per cent of the population). Up to about 1990, about 60 per cent of postwar emigrants went to the UK and most were unskilled. In the 1990s, more have gone to the United States and to the EU. Most earlier migrants were unskilled; more recently they have been much better educated and more mobile. Since 1993, while unemployment continues at a high level, exceptional economic growth

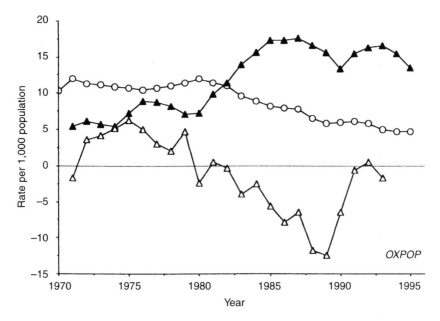

Figure 3. Irish Republic: Rates of natural increase, unemployment and net migration 1970–95. (O) RoI Rate of Natural Increase (per 1,000 population), (▲) RoI Unemployment (% of workforce), (△) RoI Crude Migration Rate (per 1,000 population). *Sources*: Central Statistics Office, OECD.

rates, associated with strong overseas investment in new manufactures and services and EU aid, have led once more to modest positive net immigration (6,200 in 1992, 5,600 in 1996). As in the 1970s, most of the immigrants were return migrants, although Ireland is now also attracting high-level foreign labour. However, migration is now volatile: 1994 and 1995 again saw a return to a small net outflow, of 5,500 and 1,700 persons respectively (Sexton, 1994; CSO, 1996; OECD, 1997: 116–19).

A notable feature of the demography of Ireland, compared with the rest of Europe, is the absence of any substantial foreign population, especially from outside Europe. Few international migrants have settled in Ireland (except returned expatriates of Irish origin) throughout the last century and beyond. In 1996 total foreign population in the Irish Republic was 95,500 (2.7 per cent) of whom 63 per cent were from the UK and only 15 per cent from outside the EU or the United States. Only 7 per cent of the population was born outside the Republic; 5.3 per cent in the rest of the British Isles and 1.7 per cent outside it. In 1991 only 1 per cent of the residents of Northern Ireland were born outside the British Isles (0.5 per cent each from the Commonwealth and from foreign countries); 91.4 per cent of its residents had been born in Northern Ireland, 4.1 per cent were

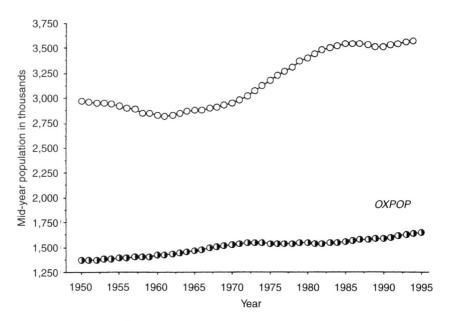

Figure 4. Estimates of mid-year population, Northern and Southern Ireland 1950–95.
(O) RoI mid-year population (1,000s), (◑) NI mid-year population (1,000s). *Sources*: Central
Statistics Office, Registrar-General, Northern Ireland.

from the rest of the UK, 2.2 per cent from the Republic of Ireland (CSO,
1997: table 21, DHSS/RGNI, 1992: table 7). Few of the UK's numerous
non-European ethnic minority populations have settled in Northern
Ireland; between 7,000 and 10,000, mostly Chinese (about 0.5 per cent of
the population: Belfast Multi-Cultural Resource Centre, pers. comm.).

The Irish Republic until recently lacked general immigration legislation
beyond the Aliens Act 1935, which covered rights of residence and employment. Gross and net flows with the (non-UK) EU are roughly balanced,
and not more than 7,000 per year each way since 1989. Few residence and
work permits are granted to non-EC nationals, mostly for special skills.
Some 3,600 work permits were granted in 1992, and demand is increasing.
In relation to population, numbers of work permits are about the same as
are granted by the United Kingdom, but the Irish figures include renewals
as well as new issues. The most numerous are to nationals of the United
States, Canada and Japan, India and Pakistan.

So far, there are no organised non-European 'ethnic minority' populations in the Republic. The rise of asylum claiming in the Republic, however,
may change that. Only a few tens of asylum claims per year were made in
the Republic up to the early 1990s (19 in 1986, 39 in 1992, 91 in 1993, 362
in 1994, 424 in 1995, not including some Bosnian 'programme' refugees:

data from Department of Justice, Equality and Law Reform). In the absence of specific asylum legislation, administrative procedures were drawn up in 1985 in consultation with UNHCR. The 1996 Refugee Act set out in transparent statutory form the status and rights of persons recognised as refugees and procedures for recognition, with generous provisions. Not surprisingly, according to press reports (Murdoch, 1997), asylum seekers have now discovered the Irish Republic. Asylum claims, mostly from Eastern Europe and notably by Romanian gypsies, increased to 1,179 in 1996 and to 2,312 by the end of July in 1997. Relative to population, the latter figure if annualised is comparable to that in the UK.

Ireland's Fertility Transition

Ireland's post-1841 fertility and marriage regime has been put into European perspective by the Princeton group's international demographic project (Coale and Watkins, 1986; Teitelbaum, 1984). In the absence of data suitable for the calculation of total fertility rates, indices of indirect standardisation were used (Coale et al., 1975). These 'Princeton' indices relate the fertility and marriage patterns of populations to the benchmark of the Hutterite (Anabaptist Protestant) religious enclaves of the rural United States (Hostetler and Huntington, 1996), which had in the 1950s the highest levels of fertility ever recorded. These indices enable the birth rates of populations with very different age-structures to be compared reliably with minimal data. They vary from 1.0 to 0, with 1.0 equalling Hutterite fertility. By dividing the index for all women (I_f) into that for married women (I_g) an index of marriage (I_m) showing the relative influence upon fertility levels of marriage patterns can be determined (1.0 = universal early marriage and therefore no limiting influence of marriage). Low levels of I_g suggest that some form of family limitation is being adopted within marriage. From the 1870s—and in a few cases much earlier—most European populations began to adopt family planning within marriage. Ireland in general did not, except for some Protestant communities and urban elites from about 1900 (David and Sanderson, 1990), although despite the indifference to demographic transition of the rural majority in Ireland there is some evidence of some 'spacing' of births even in parts of rural Ireland around that time (Ó Gráda, 1991).

Overall Irish fertility (I_f, Figure 5) was distinctive in Europe by the later nineteenth century because it was relatively low, not because it was high, thanks to delayed and avoided marriage. By remaining relatively constant in the century that followed, it came to appear distinctively high by the 1920s, exposed to view by the receding tide of fertility almost everywhere

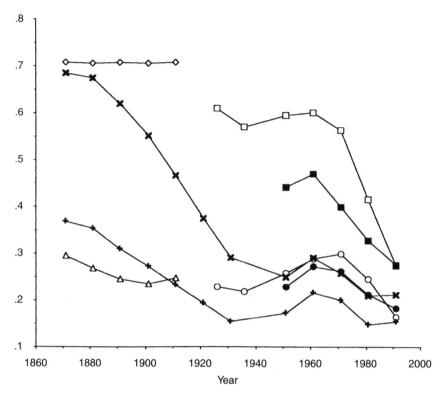

Figure 5. Princeton Indices I_f and I_g for Ireland and England and Wales 1871–1991. (○) I_f RoI, (□) I_g RoI, (△) I_f all Ireland, (◇) I_g all Ireland, (+) I_f England & Wales, (×) I_g England & Wales, (●) I_f NI, (■) I_g NI. *Note:* The pre-1961 values given here for Ireland are those of Teitelbaum, not the higher estimates of Ó Gráda. *Sources:* Teitelbaum, 1984; Coale and Watkins, 1986; CSO; OPCS; Registrar-General (Northern Ireland), various years.

else. I_g (marital fertility) from 1871 to 1911 shows only modest decline in Ireland (recent work contradicts the earlier picture of no decline at all and suggests a fall from a higher level of about 0.825 in 1881 to 0.735 in 1911; Ó Gráda, 1991). I_g fell almost everywhere else. Before the transition, for any given age at marriage, Irish fertility was little higher than that of Scotland or of England and Wales. Overall, it resembled the Scottish pattern of lower nuptiality and higher marital fertility rather than the English pattern (Anderson and Morse, 1993). But Ireland did not join in the substantial decline in marital fertility in Scotland and England after the 1870s which followed the adoption of family limitation in marriage. This reduced British I_g to 0.25 by 1961 when in Ireland it remained at 0.60 (after some decline which will be discussed later). Instead of family planning, the trend of I_m shows that in Ireland, but not in England or Scotland, there was a substantial further reduction in nuptiality, thus increasing age at marriage still further and reducing the proportions of those ever marrying. This is usually interpreted as a partial response through marriage to those pressures which in England and Scotland were resolved through family planning.

Urban women tended to marry earlier than rural women. The adoption of fertility control by some urban women around the turn of the century brought their fertility back in line with that of the traditionally later-marrying population (David and Sanderson, 1988). Different parts of Ireland were already diverging in fertility, which rose somewhat in rural Galway while it fell in Antrim, Down and Belfast. Throughout this period the proportion of births outside marriage remained very low. Illegitimacy fell throughout Europe in the nineteenth century; those at risk would have been the most avid customers of the new knowledge of contraception. No such decline is evident in Ireland, although illegitimate births may have suffered from under-registration.

Twentieth-Century Fertility Trends to 1995

Irish fertility declined slowly in the first three-quarters of the twentieth century; an increasingly anomalous example of persistent high fertility. The fertility levels of England and Ireland parted company around 1910. By then, the 1911 census shows that fertility differences between the Protestant and Catholic populations of Northern Ireland were already discernible: a difference in completed family size of 0.3 children from the marriages of the 1880s. Protestant fertility, however, remained higher than on the British mainland, (Ó Gráda, 1984). In fact overall, natural increase in Northern Ireland was higher than in the Republic until 1969 (Figure 6) although that was partly due to a higher death rate in the Republic. From 1960, the first year from which the TFR statistic is available, the fertility trends in North and South Ireland are remarkably similar (Figure 7), and still uniquely high in Europe. In the baby boom which began in the 1950s the TFR rose to a peak of 4.1 in 1964, a figure matched only by New Zealand among the Western countries. More than in most Western countries, the Irish baby boom was a result of earlier births. There was no increase in completed family size, which fell from a peak around the mid-1950s (births to mothers born in the mid-1930s). Both completed family size and TFR declined substantially from the late 1970s onwards. In that respect Irish period fertility trends have most in common with those of Roman Catholic, Southern European countries (e.g., Spain, Portugal).

The Irish baby boom followed the weakening of the unique Irish

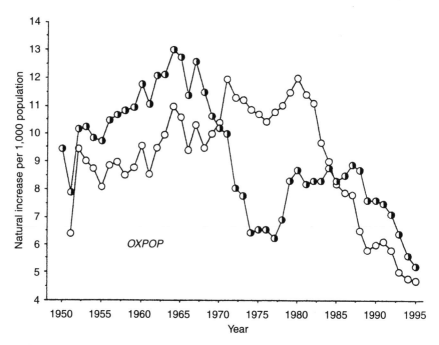

Figure 6. Natural increase per 1,000 population, Northern and Southern Ireland 1950–95.
(○) RoI Rate of Natural Increase, (◑) NI Rate of Natural Increase. *Sources*: CSO, Registrar-General (Northern Ireland) various years.

pattern of very late marriage (see Kennedy, 1989). Even in 1960, mean age at first marriage was still 31 for bachelors and 28 for spinsters, and by 1977 women were marrying at average age 24. Earlier marriage had started to become popular in other European countries a quarter of a century earlier, in the late 1930s (e.g., England and Wales). This late decline in mean age at marriage (which brings forward childbearing) temporarily inflated the TFR and to some extent concealed the substantial decline in marital fertility from the 1970s (Sexton and Dillon, 1984). The Irish baby boom was unusual in another way. Despite a higher TFR, the number of births did not rise in proportion because the maternal generations producing the babies were relatively small. Therefore Ireland lacks the very characteristic West European 'bulge' of an expanded baby-boom age structure around age 30; instead, the most numerous cohorts are now around age 15. The decline of large families after 1960 is reflected in the reduction of high order births (Figure 8). In the 1960s, almost one half of all births occurred in families where there were at least three children already—way above the European average. By the late 1970s this proportion had fallen to just over a quarter and in 1995 was 15 per cent. Correspondingly, first births

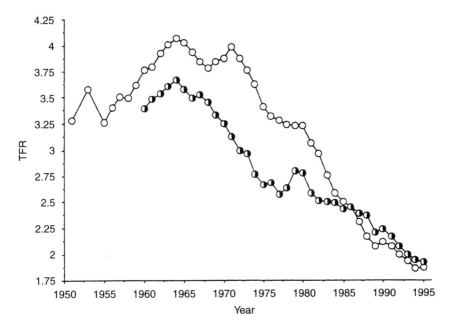

Figure 7. Total Fertility Rate, Northern Ireland and Irish Republic, 1950–95. (O) RoI TFR, (◑) NI TFR. *Sources*: CSO, Registrar-General (Northern Ireland) various years..

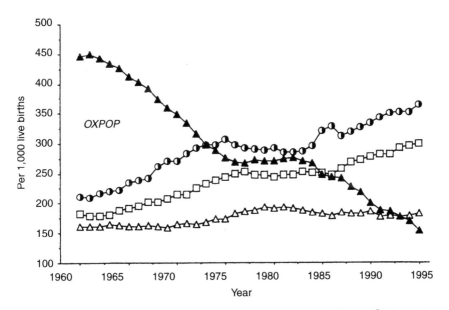

Figure 8. Irish Republic: births by birth order 1960–95, per 1,000 total births. (◑) Proportion 1st births, (□) Proportion 2nd births, (△) Proportion 3rd births, (▲) Proportion 4th births. *Source*: CSO (various years).

increased from about one in five in 1960, to over one in three in 1995—still substantially less than in other Western societies, however, where on average 40 per cent of births are first births.

Everything started to change between 1970 and 1980. TFR and natural increase, which up until then had seemed relatively immune to the example of decline elsewhere in Europe, moved sharply downwards and have continued downwards ever since. Mean age at first marriage, having reached a low of 24.0 years in 1979, several years after most of the rest of Europe, started to rise again, as it has in other European countries. The Irish TFR fell below the replacement level (2.1) in 1992 for the first time in history. By 1995 it was 1.85; still higher than in most European countries but no longer requiring graphs to be re-scaled to accommodate it. As elsewhere in Europe, in part these declines in fertility can be attributed technically to the delay of childbearing. Mean age at first birth, still over 27 years of age in the Irish Republic in 1960, fell to a low point of 25 between 1971 and 1982 and since then has risen to 27 by 1995. Even at its lowest this was late by European standards: elsewhere the mean age at first birth fell to as low as 22. However, Ireland has become less distinctive than it was in that respect. As until recently almost all births were legitimate, these trends were closely linked with movements in mean age at first marriage, which has since increased, along with the rest of Europe. But that trend is complicated by the new rise of cohabitation and illegitimacy, noted below.

The 'Second Demographic Transition' in Ireland

The 'first demographic transition' is the term given to the acquisition of low levels of mortality and fertility over the course of the last century or more; whereby expectation of life for both sexes rises to over 70 years and average family size falls to around two children. While a two-child family was achieved in most Western countries some time in the 1930s, Ireland has only reached this level of fertility in the last few years. In that respect it is 60 years behind the times.

In the meantime, before the first transition is quite over in Ireland, it has become commonplace to speak of a second demographic transition in the Western industrial world. This is not so much distinguished by trends in overall fertility and mortality, but rather by new patterns of sexual behaviour, contraception, abortion, cohabitation and illegitimacy. The proposition is that since the 1960s there has been a marked and discontinuous upward trend in all these phenomena. Behaviour once rare and stigmatised has become accepted or even normal. Their increase in most Western societies is hardly in doubt (see van de Kaa, 1987). However, they have reached very different levels in different countries. Critics of the concept (e.g., Cliquet, 1991) doubt the discontinuous nature of the change, detecting its signs at an earlier date. The new patterns of inter-personal behaviour and living arrangements are associated with declines in traditional behaviour such as religious affiliation. They are convention-ally associated with the spread of more individualistic, 'post materialistic' ideas made possible by the satisfaction of material needs through economic growth and welfare (Inglehart, 1977; De Graaf and Evans, 1996). Those who adopt the new patterns of behaviour—notably cohabitation—tend to have non-traditional attitudes towards parental and legal authority, sexual freedom and especially show little interest in religion (Lesthaeghe and Moors, 1996).

Ireland North and South have begun the second demographic transi-tion with some gusto, before they have even quite finished the first: a 'compressed' demographic transition (Kennedy, 1989). In both places, illegitimate births, once very rare (25 per 1,000 live births in 1960), have increased sharply since the 1970s, and the trend between North and South is scarcely to be distinguished (Figure 9). Although still only half the level of that in Scotland and England and Wales, rates in 1995 were well beyond

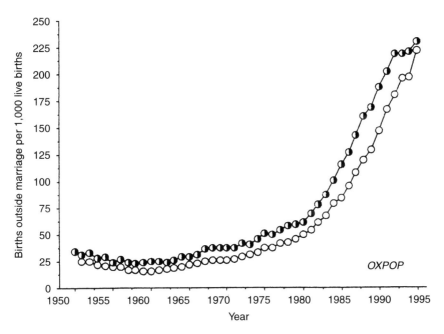

Figure 9. Northern and Southern Ireland: illegitimacy ratio 1950–95 (births outside marriage per 1,000 live births). (O) RoI Illegitimacy Ratio, (◑) NI Illegitimacy Ratio. *Sources*: CSO, Registrar-General (Northern Ireland).

any historical level and have comfortably exceeded levels in other European countries (Italy, Spain, Germany, Netherlands) even though starting from a lower position. This indicates a startling change in attitudes; the end of a tradition of sexual restraint before long-delayed marriage (Szreter, 1996). The social changes which are hastening the end of the first Irish demographic transition are, at the same time, ushering in the second, with more sexual freedom and a plurality of family forms.

Data on cohabitation are less easy to come by. The Irish LFS is silent on the topic and cohabitation only featured as a question in the Irish census in 1996. That revealed 3.9 per cent of 'family units' to be cohabiting, 40 per cent of them with children. Responding to the change in the times, the UK census has asked about remarriage as a separate category since 1981 and in 1991 introduced a separate category of 'living as married', i.e., cohabiting. While the question was asked on the Northern Ireland 1991 census forms, responses have not been routinely tabulated. However, special tabulations show that there were about 8,000 cohabiting unions in the province, about 2.4 per cent of all unions (Compton, 1995)—much less than in England and Wales (11 per cent in 1994), and it seems less than in the Republic in 1996. In only about one half of the partnerships were both partners single. Most lived in the east of the province; many fewer in the Catholic and rural west. Cohabiting partners were predominantly less educated than average, and likely to be unemployed and living in public housing—a more pronounced 'underclass' profile than shown by their counterparts in England and Wales. And while in England and Wales much of the recent increase in illegitimate births has occurred to such unions, this does not seem to be the case in Northern Ireland, where only 2,575 cohabiting women had children (there are about 5,000 illegitimate births per year in Northern Ireland), suggesting that much more of the illegitimacy in Northern Ireland is of the 'traditional' kind (Compton, 1995) where the girl is left holding the baby.

This is, however, a complex kind of sexual revolution. What is the point of a second demographic transition without abortion or divorce? Yet the first is officially absent in the Irish Republic and both are less developed in Northern Ireland than in the rest of the UK. In the Irish Republic the beginning of the impressive upward trends in illegitimacy coexisted with a reaffirmation, in the June 1986 referendum, of the 1937 constitutional ban on divorce, overwhelmingly supported by 63 per cent against 36 per cent. The same electorate voted in 1983 for the incorporation into the constitution of the prohibition of abortion. No other major European country forbade divorce. In the last ten years, however, there has been a radical turnaround. Following another referendum in November 1995, the Family Law (Divorce) 1996 Act became law in February 1997 to permit divorce on grounds of 4 years separation. The first (exceptional) case went through the Irish courts on 17 January 1997. Irish laws are now more in line with those of the rest of Europe. Separation, annulment and desertion, and divorce abroad, have substituted to some extent for the absence of domestic divorce arrangements in the Irish Republic, creating a large backlog of candidates for the new law. In 1986 there were 37,245 separated persons in Ireland (in proportional terms, a larger number than in England); by 1996 this had doubled to 87,800.

In Northern Ireland, divorces increased from 1,653 in 1983 to 2,200 in 1995. It is not possible to compute synthetic indices of divorce for Northern Ireland, but a simple comparison with marriages celebrated in the same year gives a rate of 165 divorces per thousand marriages in 1983 and 250 per thousand in 1995, or alternatively a rate per 1,000 married population of 2.5 to 3.4 respectively. These are about a quarter of the corresponding rates in England and Wales, with the implication that current rates of divorce in Northern Ireland would end about 10 per cent of marriages by their 25th wedding anniversary. The possible impact of the new liberalisation of divorce in the Irish Republic is given by divorce rates for Catholics in Northern Ireland, where the rate per 1,000 married population is 2.3 compared with 3.4 for the whole population (Compton, 1995: Table 8.12). These patterns of divorce naturally give Northern Ireland and Southern Ireland very different population distributions in relation to marital status, and also ensure that almost all weddings in the South, unlike those in the North, are first marriages (the decline in the death rate has ensured that weddings of widows and widowers are now relatively rare).

Abortion reform, however, is still in the future. The prohibition of abortion in cases other than the most severe medical emergency is only shared among major countries by Belgium (until 1990) and (since 1990) Poland. In Northern Ireland, the provisions of the 1967 Abortion Act do not apply, and the much more restrictive provisions of the Criminal Justice Act (Northern Ireland) 1945 still obtain (which permitted abortion but only on stricter medical grounds). Accordingly residents both of Northern Ireland and of the Irish Republic seek abortions in Britain, almost entirely in England and Wales (there were, for example only 12 abortions on non-residents of Scotland out of 11,143 performed in Scotland in 1995). Up to 1,800 residents of Northern Ireland annually have obtained abortions in England and Wales in recent years. Access to British abortion facilities has brought the Northern Ireland abortion ratio up from (at least) 59.2 per 1,000 live births in 1985 to (at least) 64.9 in 1995. These figures are based upon data on abortions performed in England and Wales only to non-residents. While the abortion ratio for women resident in the Irish Republic (based on the same source of data) was (at least) 62.5 per 1,000 live births in 1985, the ratio had increased to 93.4 in 1995; higher than some other European countries (Figure 10).

Contrasts in Demographic Regime Within Ireland

The Irish demographic regime can be compared by religion and national origin in three areas in the British Isles; in the Irish Republic and in Northern Ireland between Catholics and Protestants, and in Great Britain (where most Catholics in the British Isles now live) both between Catholics and Protestants and between the Irish born and British born (see Spencer, 1982). Here there is only space for comparisons within Northern Ireland.

Throughout most of the twentieth century Northern Ireland shows the sharpest demographic contrast between any two neighbouring communities in Europe outside Kossovo in Serbia. Since the 1920s two different demographic regimes have emerged, preserved by a religious and political divide. Overall, the TFR in Northern Ireland was 3.39 in 1961, 3.13 in 1971, subsequently falling fast to 2.64 in 1978. It first fell below replace-

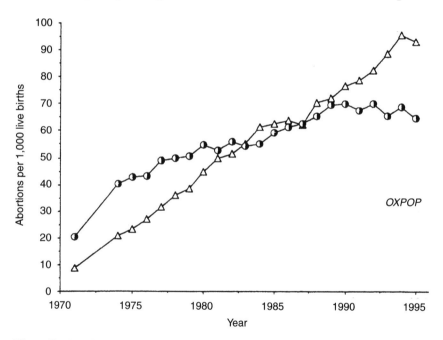

Figure 10. Northern and Southern Ireland, abortion ratio 1971–95. (△) RoI Abortion Ratio, (◑) NI Abortion Ratio. *Note*: Abortions carried out in England and Wales. *Sources*: OPCS Abortion Statistics Series AB table 25, table 6.11.

ment level (to 2.0) in 1993 and fell further to 1.92 in 1995. For most of the postwar period it was somewhat lower than that of the Republic, especially during the worst period of violence between 1969 and 1980; it has now been undershot by the rapid fertility decline in the Republic.

Comparisons between the numbers and growth rates of the Roman Catholic and non-Catholic populations in Northern Ireland have attracted particular interest because of their possible constitutional implications; specifically that if Roman Catholics became a majority then the electorate of the province might vote in a referendum to leave the United Kingdom. However, it is important to keep in mind that confessional adherence by no means translates simply into political preference; for example, the 1991 Northern Ireland Social Attitudes Survey indicated that 4 per cent of Protestants favoured a United Ireland while 35 per cent of Catholics favoured retention of the links with the UK (Jardine, forthcoming).

The census in Ireland has asked a voluntary question on religious affiliation since 1861, and this tradition is continued in both North and South. In 1971 it has been estimated that 10 per cent did not reply to it (mostly Roman Catholics; Compton, 1982) and 20 per cent in 1981, when a Republican campaign of non-cooperation was mounted against the census. However, partly due to a change of mind among nationalist politicians, response to the 1991 census was encouraged and non-response rates to the question on religion were lower (7.3 per cent). It may be that Protestants were more likely not to respond (Compton, 1996). For whatever reason, that census was the first to reveal that those claiming adherence to a Protestant denomination were no longer a majority (Macourt, 1995). For the first time also the response 'no religion' became a fully-fledged category (62,692 responses). Falling away from religion is thought to be more common among non-Catholics. Corrected data suggest that the Northern Ireland Catholic population has increased from 34 per cent of the total in 1951 to 42 per cent in 1991 (Jardine, forthcoming).

Data on the relative fertility and other demographic parameters of the Roman Catholic and non-Catholic populations are unsatisfactory, indirect and controversial (see, e.g., Spencer, 1982; Macourt, 1995; Compton, 1996). But for obvious reasons they are the subject of much interest. When the UK census asked a question on previous births, as it did from 1911 until 1971, then the fertility of the two communities could be compared. A retrospective fertility question was also asked at the 1991 census in Northern Ireland (not in the rest of the UK). Unfortunately the question was only asked in respect of married women. The results, which would therefore only be of limited interest, had not been published by July 1997. Data on religious affiliation are not collected on the registration of births. Estimates of annual births can be made nonetheless. Residential segregation is so strong (Boal, 1981; Boal and Douglas, 1982), exacerbated by the violence since 1969, that estimates of births to the major religious groups can be made from the local geography of their occurrence. Sources from the churches themselves (Spencer, 1977) using baptismal records are also used. There are few conversions and not more than 5 per cent of unions are thought to have been religiously mixed in 1991 (Compton, 1996)—many fewer than would be expected in any other European country between groups of such size.

The fertility differential between Roman Catholics and others, which first became obvious in statistics in the 1920s, widened considerably up to the 1950s. In 1961 Catholic TFR in Northern Ireland (derived from census data) was 4.6 compared to the Protestants' 3.0 (averaged over all women); in 1971 the difference was 4.1 to 2.8. However measured, Roman Catholic fertility in the 1970s was between 40–50 per cent higher than Protestant (Compton, 1981) and was probably higher than in the Republic of Ireland (Coward, 1980). When standardised for marriage the difference was widened; on average Roman Catholics marry later than Protestants. The 1983 Northern Ireland Fertility Survey (NIFS), the first of its kind in the Province (Compton and Coward, 1989), together with earlier data from the census, underlined the differences between Catholic and Protestant fertility regimes. Catholics were more likely to be married but married later. Their higher fertility arose from a lower level of childlessness (8 per cent compared with 12 per cent), shorter birth intervals (by 33 per cent) and later stopping: the average Catholic family took 9.5 years to complete compared with 7.5 years in Protestants.

Nonetheless the survey showed a gradual decline of completed family size in both communities (Figure 11) from the marriage cohorts of 1920 (5.29 and 3.56 births per woman respectively) to those of 1963 (4.09 and 2.80 respectively). In percentage terms the Roman Catholic 'advantage' had hardly changed (49 per cent and 46 per cent respectively) although in absolute terms it has shrunk from 1.7 births to 1.3 over the two periods. Statements on intended fertility suggested that the Catholic marriages of 1982/83 would yield 2.93 children compared with 2.49 to Protestants (Compton and Coward, 1989: Table 4.2). According to these authors, fertility might converge between the 1990s to early in the next century. So far, the simple data on births and deaths which are available suggest that this has not yet happened. Around 1990 the Catholic birth rate was estimated to be just under 20 per 1,000 with a death rate about 9 per 1,000; compared with 14–15 and 11.5 per 1,000 respectively for the non-Catholic population (Compton, 1996). The rate of natural increase (excess of births over deaths) and therefore effectively the rate of population growth except for migration remains about three times higher among the

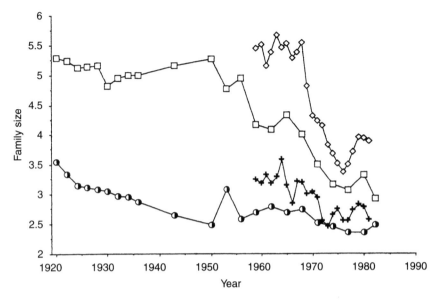

Figure 11. Northern Ireland fertility trends 1920–83. (□) Roman Catholic Completed Family Size by marriage cohort, (◑) Protestant Completed Family Size by marriage cohort, (◇) Roman Catholic Total Marital Fertility Rate, (+) Protestant Total Marital Fertility Rate. *Note:* To facilitate comparison, data for marriage cohorts are located 28 years after the year of marriage (i.e., at approximate mean age of childbearing). Data for fertility rates are located on the year to which they apply. CFS = Completed Family Size (a cohort measure of actual completed fertility). TMFR = Total Marital Fertility Rate (a period measure of the average completed family size of married women assuming the continuation of current rates). *Sources:* Data from Crompton and Coward (1989). CFS data beyond marriage cohorts of 1964 based on intentions.

Catholic compared with the non-Catholic population; about 1 per cent compared with about 0.3 per cent.

The effect of net emigration on the size of the religious communities is even harder to assess. Up to the 1961 census it was estimated that most emigrants (60 per cent) were Roman Catholics (Barritt and Carter, 1972), therefore partly compensating for the Roman Catholic fertility 'advantage'. Between 1971 and 1991 this proportion may have diminished to 50 per cent, therefore still reducing the Catholic population somewhat more than the non-Catholic. A range of projections indicate that while the numerical gap between the two communities is certain to narrow, a Catholic majority is by no means inevitable and in any case would be unlikely to emerge for the next 30 years or so. The situation may 'eventually settle down to a rough numerical equivalence' (Compton, 1996: 280).

Family Planning and Religion

There have been no formal restrictions on contraception in Northern Ireland in the twentieth century. Contraception in the Irish Republic was made illegal in the 1920s although the letters to Marie Stopes and other sources reveal considerable unmet demand at the turn of the century. It finally came out of the closet in the 1970s. A Supreme Court decision in 1973 (McGee) established the legality of contraceptive sale for 'bona fide' purposes (whatever they are), a provision formalised by legislation in 1979. By 1982 there were 48 clinics of various kinds employing 2,000 people (Nic Ghiolla Phadraig, 1984). In 1985 further legislation made non-medical contraceptives of all kinds available to anyone aged over 18 years without prescription. Contraceptive supply was still hedged with impediments quite recently: in February 1991 the Virgin Megastore in Dublin was fined £500 in the High Court for selling condoms and was told that it had 'got off lightly'.

The rather limited surveys on family planning suggest that practice in the Irish Republic is rapidly converging with the rest of the industrial world. By 1975, 66 per cent of a sample of 600 married couples had used some form of birth control, 37 per cent had used 'natural' (church approved) methods, 19 per cent had used the pill and 10 per cent other artificial methods. This seemed a very high level of use in view of the reported ideal family size of 5.6 children. Family planners, as usual, were from higher social classes, were better educated and younger. Few who avoided contraception mentioned specifically religious reasons, although 13 per cent thought the pill 'immoral' (Wilson-Davis, 1982). In a sample a few years later in a Dublin maternity hospital 81 per cent of the married mothers had used some form of contraception: 61 per cent the pill, 13 per cent other (mostly artificial) methods, only 7 per cent 'natural' methods. Twenty per cent of the married women's pregnancies had been unwanted, 89 per cent of those of the single women. Among the latter 64 per cent had used no method of contraception; a legacy of weak knowledge and supply of family planning (Greene et al., 1989). Twenty-eight per cent had considered abortion in the UK: in the early 1980s 37 per cent of pregnant single women in Ireland may have sought abortion in the UK (Dean, 1984).

In Northern Ireland around the same time most Roman Catholics in the NIFS—74.1 per cent—approved the principle of family planning, 8 per cent had no opinion and 17.9 per cent disapproved; 90.3 per cent of Protestants approved, with only 4 per cent having no opinion. But the evangelical Protestant Fundamentalists (less than 10 per cent of all Protestants in the sample) shared Catholic reservations; almost half the Catholics who disapproved did so on moral grounds. Twenty-six per cent of Roman Catholics had never used birth control, compared with 13 per cent of Protestants; 22 per cent had only ever used natural means but 52 per cent had used artificial means: 40 per cent the pill, 16 per cent condoms, 10 per cent IUD. Only 5 per cent had been sterilized (Table 2). Family planning has rapidly gained favour among Catholics in Northern Ireland, 66 per cent of those married before 1955 had never used family planning and only 15 per cent had used artificial methods. But among Catholics married after 1974, only 14 per cent had never used family planning and 69 per cent had already used artificial methods. Corresponding Protestant figures for the later cohort were 4 per cent and 92 per cent respectively. A rapid transition of Roman Catholic behaviour was nearly completed even by the 1980s and among the most educated women occupying high-status jobs, denominational difference in contraceptive practice had already disappeared. Furthermore, 14 per cent of Roman Catholics favoured a liberalisation of abortion legislation in Northern Ireland, as did 52 per cent of Protestants and 21 per cent of Protestant Fundamentalists.

Table 2. Northern Ireland 1983. Attitudes and practice towards contraception by religious denomination.

	Denomination							
	Protestants		Protestant Fundamentalists		Roman Catholics		All Denominations	
	%	N	%	N	%	N	%	N
Attitudes								
Approve FP	90.3	1,412	77.2	132	74.1	851	83.5	2,480
No opinion	3.8	60	8.8	15	8.0	92	4.6	167
Ever-use								
Never used FP	13	205	21	35	26	293	19	533
Natural only	7	100	6	10	22	251	13	361
Artificial only	63	975	41	86	33	376	50	1,437
Both	17	265	22	38	19	209	18	512
Selected methods, ever-use								
Safe + Billings	9	139	13	22	36	415	20	576
Condom	42	651	37	62	16	183	31	896
IUD	14	222	19	33	10	116	13	371
Pill	57	883	42	72	40	456	50	1,472
Sterilization	17	267	16	27	5	57	12	366

Source: Compton and Coward, 1989: Table 5.1, 5.8. (NIFS).
Note: Totals of ever-use may exceed 100.

The Mortality Transition

In the last quarter of the nineteenth century, expectation of life (e_0) in Ireland (for both sexes) was relatively high by European standards and exceeded that of England and Wales, as might be expected in a predominantly rural population. This advantage was lost in the twentieth century, but since the Second World War overall mortality has converged although Northern Irish mortality rates remain higher than those of England and Wales. In 1992, expectation of life for women was 79 years in the Irish Republic and in England and Wales, and 78.3 in Northern Ireland. For the last two decades both parts of Ireland have shared the same improved trend (Figure 12).

In detail, causes of death in both parts of Ireland are distinctive. Northern Ireland suffers the highest levels of Ischaemic Heart Disease (IHD) in the world, with the South not far behind. In these as in other respects, Ireland is a prominent exemplar of mortality characteristics common to other North European countries. Deaths from stroke and respiratory diseases are also very high. On the other hand, compared with the rest of the UK, death rates from cancer of the (female) breast and of the uterine cervix are lower in Northern Ireland, although both the UK and Ireland as a whole, and Northern Europe as a whole, suffers high breast cancer rates compared with the rest of Europe (Levi *et al.*, 1995). The former differences with the rest of the UK are plausibly accounted for by regional differences in diet (Fehily *et al.*, 1990) and possibly smoking;

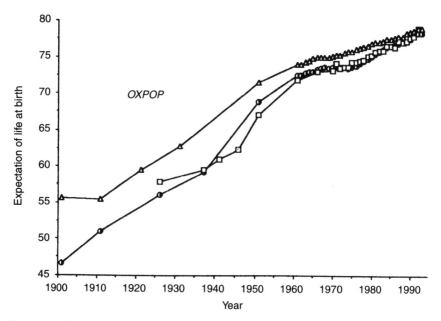

Figure 12. Expectation of life at birth, females, Northern and Southern Ireland, England and Wales 1901–94. (◑) e_0 Northern Ireland (females), (□) e_0 Republic of Ireland (females), (△) e_0 England and Wales (females). *Sources*: CSO, Registrar-General (Northern Ireland), OPCS.

the latter by (past) differences in childbearing and in sexual behaviour. Although perinatal mortality is relatively low in both parts of Ireland, neural tube defects (spina bifida and related conditions) are especially frequent in Ireland and among the Irish (Leck and Lancashire, 1995).

This author has not located explicit comparative studies of mortality in North and South published since 1981. However a crude comparison of the percentage causes of death in 1993 reveals a near-identity in North and South in the percentage of all deaths attributed to cancer of the lung and of the female breast, and of respiratory disease (pneumonia + bronchitis, emphysema only). Deaths from IHD and from stroke in the North are higher than in the South (which itself ranked fifth in the industrial world in 1985; Shelley *et al.*, 1991); deaths from motor vehicle traffic accidents, relatively high in North and South, are higher in the South as a proportion of all deaths (Central Statistics Office, 1994; Registrar-General Northern Ireland, 1995). Despite the high incidence of total abstinence (Fehily *et al.*, 1990), alcohol-related disease is still more prevalent among the Irish (especially males) both in Ireland and in the UK (Harrison *et al.*, 1993; Carney and Sheffield, 1995). Infant mortality (deaths under age 1 per 1,000 live births), formerly higher in the Irish Republic than in Northern Ireland or England and Wales has also converged since the war. Indeed, since the early 1980s the infant mortality rate in the Irish Republic has been the lowest of the three; it was 5.9 per 1,000 live births in 1994, compared with 6.1 in Northern Ireland and 6.3 in England and Wales.

Ireland has also had a distinctive pattern of mortality differentials according to sex. Earlier this century, Ireland was unusual in Europe in that women still lived no longer than men. Elsewhere such a pattern was only to be found in a few other predominantly rural societies such as Italy and Bulgaria. It is found today only in the less-developed world, especially northern parts of the Indian sub-continent (Ruzicka, 1984) although in the past excess female mortality was relatively common in the rural West. Between 1840 and 1910, in about 60 per cent of Western countries female mortality exceeded that of males around age 10, and in about 30 per cent around age 30 (Stolnitz, 1955a; 1955b). The life table for Ireland in 1891 showed a female deficiency of nearly one year of life, declining to 0.4 years by 1901 and becoming slightly positive by 1911. By 1891 the female excess in England and Wales was already 4 years (Figure 13). The first English life table of 1840 ($e_0m = 40.2$ years) showed female life expectation at birth to be already 2.0 years higher than that of males, an advantage which in London had been evident since the days of John Graunt. However, in Ireland at that time, females had the same expectation of life as males in Irish towns outside Dublin (30 years) and one year less than men in rural districts (29 years: Kennedy, 1973a: 45). Female excess mortality was a

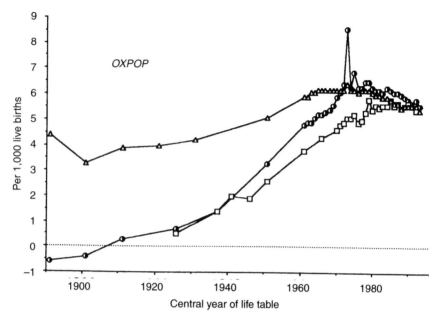

Figure 13. Excess expectation of life at birth of females over males, Northern and Southern Ireland, England and Wales 1891–91. (⬤) Northern Ireland e_0 difference, (□) Republic of Ireland e_0 difference, (△) England and Wales e_0 difference. *Sources*: CSO, Registrar-General (Northern Ireland), OPCS.

rural, not an urban problem, in Ireland as elsewhere. Even in 1961 the female excess expectation of life was just under 4 years in the Irish Republic—about 2 years less than in other developed countries. The 1981 life table shows a truly modern pattern. The female advantage in the Irish Republic in 1992 (5.4 years) was little less than the average for the industrial world (6.3 years).

In the less-developed world today, excess female mortality is attributed to the systematically disadvantaged position of females in such societies, not just to maternal mortality. Patterns of male dominance were also prevalent in European rural societies in the past, with similar consequences (Johansson, 1991). Such behaviour persisted in the Irish countryside longer than elsewhere (Kennedy and Clarkson, 1973: Chapter 3) and was statistically salient because the total population remained unmodernised and rural for so long. A further factor may be a rise in deaths from tuberculosis (TB), to which young females, and people of Irish origin, appear to be more vulnerable than males. Such an increase might be associated with the late mobility transition in Ireland, which brought large numbers of immunologically naive country people into contact with a wider population and its diseases (B. Benjamin, pers. comm.). Between 1974 and 1984 Irish TB mortality was still the highest in the EC (Barry, 1992).

Female excess deaths disappeared faster in the more urbanised Northern Irish population than in the Irish Republic. However, the rapid relative increase in female life expectancy since the late 1960s in Northern Ireland may owe less to relative improvement in female health than to excess male mortality from diseases such as IHD, in which Northern Ireland is world leader. The peaks of male mortality in 1973 and following years shown in the graphs are attributable to deaths from terrorist activity, which have a disproportionate statistical effect because of the relative youth of many of the victims. There was also an increase in road traffic accident deaths, mostly young males, in Northern Ireland, indirectly related to the security problems.

Accounting for Fertility Decline

These trends present us with a number of interesting problems, particularly in respect of the birth rate. Crucial questions, most of which are not successfully answered here, include:

1 Why did fertility in Ireland take so long to decline?

2 Now that it has fallen to more average European levels, how to account for the decline?

3 What will happen next—does Ireland face a southern European future of very low fertility, like Italy and Spain, or will geography triumph with higher rates typical of north-west European countries (some Catholic, such as Belgium)?

4 Will the low birth rate eventually kill off the emigration culture and high unemployment by making labour scarce at last?

5 How do we account for the differences and the similarities between South and the North?

Analysis at the county level was valuable in identifying demographic pioneers and their characteristics at the onset of the demographic transition (Teitelbaum, 1984) and has yielded futher valuable insights into recent decline (Sexton and Dillon, 1984; Ó Gráda and Walsh, 1995). This promising line of inquiry had to be neglected here for want of space, despite the striking polarisation of the distribution of the Irish Republic population, with 42 per cent still rural and 26 per cent living in the capital; both the highest proportions in Western Europe.

Otherwise, these issues are complicated by the lack of agreement about the answers to more general problems, of which the Irish demographic question is just a sub-plot: for example why European fertility began to decline in the first place (Coale and Watkins, 1986; Cleland and Wilson, 1987); how do we explain the subsequent level and variation of fertility and the rise of the second transition (van de Kaa, 1996). Explaining Ireland's exceptionalism is an additional problem perched on top of an already unsteady theoretical superstructure.

Changing Preferences for Families

The EU's Eurobarometer surveys of attitudes showed that ideal family size in Ireland fell from 3.62 in 1979 to 2.79 in 1989, compared with EU averages of 2.2 and 2.1 respectively, the highest in the 12 in both cases. What altered values or economic rationalities lie behind the declining ideal family size and the acceptability, or necessity, of family planning? In most European countries, the problems of explaining the once-off fertility trans-ition to small family sizes, the baby boom and subsequent low and often fluctuating birth rates are sequential and separate. In the Irish case they are somewhat telescoped. Studies of the demographic transition in Europe have not revealed any one single key which can specify the timing of the onset of decline. Nonetheless, high fertility normally wilts in the face of the increased costs of higher quality children in a modern economy; the effects of near-universal literacy and higher education standards (especially among women), an open society offering rewards to those skills and education; the parallel erosion of traditional and religious influences aided by greater geographical mobility and urbanisation, and the movement of married women into the workforce. Some research emphasises economic rationality, some the autonomous importance of the diffusion of indivi-dualistic ideas emphasising self-realisation in prosperous economies (Lesthaeghe, 1983; Simons, 1986; Cleland and Wilson, 1987).

Different models may be appropriate for different periods of time and be eclipsed when circumstances change. Especially since the late 1950s, Irish economy and society has been changing in ways which would be expected to lead to a fertility decline simply from the varied propositions of the demographic transition noted above. Better off, less agricultural, more urbanised literate societies have lower birth rates (Kennedy, 1989). Up to the 1950s Ireland was a rural society where 40 per cent worked on the land. Since then Irish employment has shifted to urban, manufacturing and service jobs: only 15 per cent worked in agriculture in 1987 and 10 per cent in 1995, compared with 24 per cent in manufacturing and 53 per cent in services. However, the rural population, 54 per cent in 1961, was still 42 per cent in 1996. Movement from rural smallholdings undermined one of the main props of long-delayed marriage or celibacy. The education reform of 1967 removed costs from secondary education—a late reform now clearly bearing fruit in economy and society. Elsewhere such economic changes have usually brought small family size, often at a much earlier stage as in the rural societies of prewar Italy, Greece and Bulgaria, but in Ireland the effects seem to have been delayed. Formal economic analyses of the Irish fertility decline are lacking, which might show whether the decline is in line with that experienced elsewhere or whether, as seems likely, Irish fertility levels have been for some time out of line with Irish economic and social development. Easterlin's ingenious cohort size model receives little support in the Irish case (Wright, 1989).

Women in the Workforce

In most European societies, the demographic transition has been more or less complete for half a century, establishing a two-child norm on which the short-term factors of employment and the economic cycle can re-establish their influence once clear of the overwhelming downward trend of transition. A simple Malthusian model, operating primarily through the effects on mens' wages in facilitating earlier marriage and more children, can account in part for the upturn of the baby boom but not for its decline. It has been displaced from favour by econometric 'new home economics' models. These present a new rationality of fertility taking into account the post-1950s movement of women into the workplace and its effects on household income and women's independence (de Cooman et al., 1987; Ermisch, 1996). These retain the 'Malthusian' ability to relate fertility to male earnings, but additionally incorporate the new opportunity costs of childbearing arising from married women's participation in the workforce. That element is expected to depress, not elevate fertility as household income increases. However, the system moves on. Those models, once reasonably well supported, look less convincing in Scandinavia (Kravdal, 1992). There, welfare arrangements have it seems made childbearing and work no longer alternative choices, enabling fertility to rise even in the face of high women's workforce participation. NHE models have also been challenged (Murphy, 1992) on more general grounds. Causation here can and does work both ways—declines in fertility facilitate women's work— and it is not always clear which is the stronger.

Does any of this make sense in the Irish case? Inspection of the trend of fertility shows that we should be particularly interested in the events around 1980, when the birth rate (TFR, I_g, rate of natural increase) started a sharp and so far unreversed decline. In 1971 only 7.5 per cent of married women in Ireland were in the workforce compared with over 40 per cent in most Western countries. That increased threefold to 23.1 per cent by 1988, then the lowest in the EC except for Spain (Courtney, 1990) and to 40.7 per cent by 1995, according to the Labour Force Survey. At young ages workforce participation of married women is only slightly below the EC average (51.4 per cent in 1988 compared with 58.2 per cent at ages 15–24). However, older married women are much less likely to be in work: 45.5 per cent at age 25–34 compared with the EC's 59.1 per cent, 29.7 per cent at age 35–44 against the EC's 58.5 per cent (Eurostat, 1991). The cross-sectional correlation of women's workforce participation rates with fertility is low (West Germany has only average rates, Italy below average). Time series correlations work better. Figure 14 is at least suggestive, but it also accommodates equally plausibly a relationship with the more classical economic

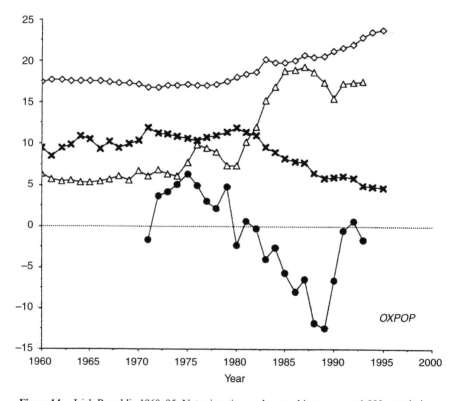

Figure 14. Irish Republic 1960–95: Net migration and natural increase per 1,000 population, male unemployment and female workforce participation %. (△) Male unemployment %, (●) Crude Migration Rate (net migrants per 1,000 population), (×) Rate of Natural Increase per 1,000 population, (◇) Female workforce participation rate %/2. *Note*: The female workforce participation rate in per cent has been divided by two in order to fit the data onto the same scale. *Sources*: CSO, OECD.

variable of rising unemployment. A simple model is presented in Figure 15, relating fertility to female workforce participation rates in four countries. Where workforce participation has been higher for longer (Sweden) and where welfare compensation is high, women's work no longer depresses fertility. In Ireland where neither is true the statistical effect is still strong. Figure 16 shows actual and fitted values for the TFR in the Irish republic from 1950 to 1995 in relation to male and female workforce participation. The fit is good but the utility of the model crucially depends upon the fit

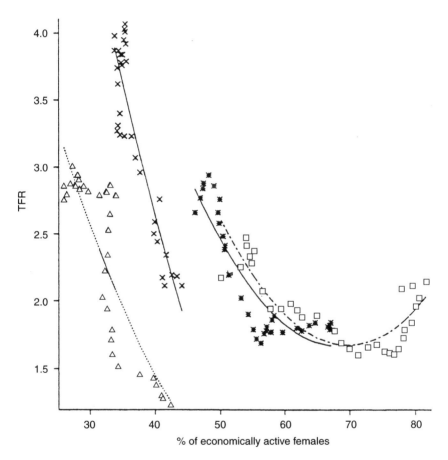

Figure 15. Observed and fitted values of total fertility rates, selected countries 1960–90. (Δ) Spain (actual data), (········) Spain (fitted), (×) Republic of Ireland (actual data), (———) Republic of Ireland (fitted), (∗) United Kingdom (actual data), (———) United Kingdom (fitted), (□) Sweden (actual data), (–·–·) Sweden (fitted). *Note*: Model: TFR = k + a.economic activity (female) + b.country + c.economic activity (females)^2 + d.country.economic activity (females). Fitted by GLIM. *Sources*: EUROSTAT (1997); OECD (1995); national demographic yearbooks.

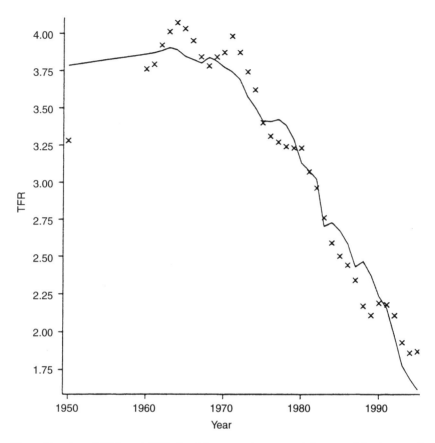

Figure 16. Actual TFR and TFR fitted by regression on workforce participation trends, Republic of Ireland 1950–95. (×) Actual TFR, (——) Fitted value. *Note*: Model TFR = k + a.economic activity (females) + b.economic activity (males). r² = 0.95. The fitted line is irregular because the data are graphed on the y axis according to calendar year. Were the dependent and independent variables to be graphed against each other in a bivariate plot then the regression line would, of course, be a straight line. *Sources*: CSO, OECD (1995).

before 1970, when TFR began to decline. Unfortunately, data on workforce participation are scarce before 1960. Space does not permit futher statistical exploration of possible causal factors. Both 'end of transition' and 'women's workforce participation' factors are likely to be working together to depress Irish fertility; the compensating effects of elaborate childcare provision are not (yet) present.

Ideological explanations of fertility change, noted earlier, have gained ground because of the inadequacy of socio-economic models (Cleland and Wilson, 1987; Lesthaeghe, 1983) and because they can account for some anomalies, although without adequate theoretical explanation of cause. Ireland returns conservative scores in European attitude surveys, as do other relatively high fertility countries such as England and France, where religiosity is much lower (Simons, 1986). In the European Values Survey 1981 round, Ireland scored by far the highest rating for 'familism' and 'religiosity', and by far the lowest on the measure of 'nonconformity' (Lesthaeghe and Meekers, 1986).

A Catholic Explanation?

The most potent ideology in Ireland is Roman Catholicism and the obvious explanation for the persistent high birth rate of the Irish fertility regime is the dominance of the Roman Catholic Church in Ireland, the pronatalism of its doctrines translated into demographic consequences by Irish religiosity. Irish religiosity is surely higher than anywhere else in Western Europe. According to the 1991 European Values Survey, 85 per cent of Roman Catholics in the Irish Republic claimed to attend services at least once a week (85 per cent in 1981), and 73 per cent in Northern Ireland (93 per cent in 1981). Irish Catholics must be the only population in Europe to go to church almost as often as they have sex. Protestants in the Republic and in Northern Ireland also attended more regularly than in England and Wales, but the sample size makes detailed figures unreliable. At a different level, the influence of the Roman Church, whose 'special position' is recognised in the Republic's constitution, has been evident in government policy on, for example, abortion and contraception.

There are, however, too many international exceptions (Quebec, and Italy and Spain, with the lowest birth-rates in the world) to allow a simple confessional hypothesis to pass unchallenged. Quebec, where fertility was particularly high until the 1960s, may then have seemed a close parallel. Catholics with a strong sense of identity were in a minority position in historical circumstances which had given the Church great prestige and influence. They were distinguished by a different culture, language and religion; until the 1960s the population was mostly rural. The collapse of the old high fertility regime, and of church influence, were particularly dramatic. By the 1980s Quebec's fertility rate (TFR = 1.4) was much lower than the rest of Canada (although it has since recovered somewhat). However, in Quebec the retreat from religion was more marked than in Ireland; it may therefore not be a good parallel. If populations effectively cease to be Catholic they cannot be expected to display 'Catholic' fertility any more.

More generally, 'Catholic fertility' simply does not work as a general proposition. Roman Catholic influence, independent of socio-economic status, can only be shown to be important where Roman Catholicism acquired particular authority through being a focus for the national sentiments of a disadvantaged minority in a larger population (Day, 1968). This formulation helps to account for the apparent Polish and Irish exceptions. In both, the Catholic Church was, into this century, the only institution surviving as a focus for national identity during the absorption of the society into a wider polity. In both, fertility remained high into the 1980s. However, neither has been a 'minority' for seventy years. Any survival of this effect for religious reasons in Ireland, independent since 1922 in a way that Poland was not from 1939–89, may seem surprising. But the political conflicts which aligned Roman Catholicism with nationalism and thus preserved its status have not yet disappeared in North or South, although they have been eroded in the South by prosperity and a more settled political regime, urbanisation, education and the media, perhaps especially by the 1967 reforms and by television. The ease of return migration from the UK in the postwar period may have helped to diffuse different attitudes, whereas earlier in the century the example of Protestant family planners in Ireland itself may have been shunned.

The preference of Irish Catholics, and especially of Northern Catholics for larger families—however now eroded—cannot be explained away by any socio-economic or any other standardisation. They seem to have been a genuine difference in preference (Ó Gráda and Walsh, 1995). The particularly high fertility of Catholics in Northern Ireland, higher than in the South (Coward, 1980), has, it seems, correctly been held up as a specific example of the 'minority status effect' (Siegel, 1970) on birth-rates (Kennedy, 1973b). Ireland has once again been exceptional in being a rare example of Catholicism—and all it was aligned with—actually having an effect on demography.

In Ireland today, Catholicism now seems to be 'customised' or 'compartmentalised'; its adherents accepting some parts, rejecting others, to meet their new preferences and the realities of their economic lives, as must be the case with all populations of practicing Catholics with low birth rates. Public opinion surveys in the 1980s showed that a majority of adults in Ireland (especially young people), even though most continued to be church-goers, no longer accepted the Catholic Church's teaching on contraception and instead approve its use, mirroring the responses in Northern Ireland. The same population in the Republic which reaffirmed by referenda the continuing ban on abortion in 1983, and on divorce in 1986 was also starting to embrace the 'second demographic transition'.

Can parallels be found in other Catholic countries? Catholic France and Belgium, with their secular constitutions, embraced controlled fertility long ago and offer few (religious) comparisons. Italy and Quebec maintained moderate and higher fertility respectively until the 1970s, then declined fast to lower levels. Most spectacularly, Spain and Portugal preserved relatively high fertility until about 1980, which then declined rapidly to become almost the lowest in the world at the time of writing. In these four cases, more than in Ireland, the Church suffered a sharp loss of prestige, with declining vocations, Mass attendance, the failure of campaigns against divorce and abortion, and a transformation of personal behaviour. The most abrupt of these transitions occurred in Spain and Portugal where the Church suffered from too close an association with autocratic regimes overturned in 1975. The rejection and obliteration from memory of the *ancien régime* and its ideological baggage is still one of the driving forces behind Spanish politics and its dedication to a new identity in the EU. No such cataclysm occurred in Ireland, where many are happy both to go to Mass and to visit the chemist. Nonetheless, there is some parallel in that the institutions of the Irish state, including its understanding of the Church's special position, were developed in the 1930s. In their romantic terminology and lack of class base the major political parties still seem to belong to a somewhat different world from those in most European polities.

The Emigration Factor

Other factors need to be invoked to explain the persistence of high fertility so long after independence and so long after all other European Catholic countries have adopted a low fertility regime. The Irish case is complicated by the survival of the strong emigration tradition begun in the 1840s. This has permitted high levels of natural increase to co-exist with declining population size for over a century. It has exported demographic feedbacks which otherwise might have depressed fertility. Without emigration, population growth and density would have become uncomfortable many decades ago, increasing land values, access to agricultural holdings, rents and prices. It would have been difficult to create jobs at the rate of population growth which otherwise would have occurred with high fertility. Studies on other high-fertility, high-emigration countries (e.g., Puerto Rico; Mosher, 1980) suggest that emigration and fertility decline can be regarded as alternative 'multiphasic' demographic responses to the problems posed by population growth (Davis, 1963). These 'multiphasic' options provide a useful escape clause for demographers as well as for the Irish. Long-term high emigration retards the modernisation of fertility. In a few countries, mostly relatively small, size and geographical location allow mass emigration to be a partial alternative to the limitation of

fertility. Ireland, some of the Caribbean islands and remote upland provinces of larger countries (e.g., Scottish Highlands; Flinn, 1977: Parts 5, 6)
are among them. Emigration may have other, selective effects on cohorts,
leaving behind the more conservative (Walsh, 1972). Negligible immigration has meant less exposure to alternative attitudes to fertility, religion
and authority.

Past emigration derived from fundamental imbalances in the Irish
economy, North as well as South, especially chronic unemployment, itself
powered by 'relentless' high rates of natural increase (Gudgin and O'Shea,
1993). Emigration had become 'traditional'; an accustomed means of resolving problems, facilitated by the links preserved with the large numbers of
previous Irish emigrants in the UK, the United States and elsewhere.
Twenty-five per cent of the university graduates as recently as 1987–1998
have emigrated (Shuttleworth, 1993). Despite recent declines in the birth
rate, the age-structure will ensure high rates of entry to the potential labour
force, and hence continuing pressures to emigrate during the 1990s
(Sexton, 1994; Kennedy, 1994: Chapter 6). But the situation shortly after
the turn of the century will change dramatically, and demographic and
economic change should finally end the traditional Irish emigration regime.

What Future?

The distinctive Irish fertility regime is nearly over, and will join those of
Quebec, Spain, Portugal and other Catholic countries as questions of
recent history rather than of the contemporary world. Will Irish fertility
become indistinguishable in pattern from that of the rest of Europe? Not
necessarily. Some distinctive patterns such as the particularly low fertility
of Germany and its neighbours have persisted for almost two decades.
While 'Catholic fertility' has disappeared in the industrial world, other
differences concerned with sexual behaviour have not. Although cohabitation and illegitimacy are growing in almost all industrial countries, they are
doing so at very different rates and from different starting points. The
southern Catholic countries have lower levels of cohabitation and illegitimacy than others. Ireland, with its high illegitimacy rates, is behaving more
like its north-west European neighbours (some of which, such as France
and Belgium are of course also predominantly Catholic) than its Southern
coreligionists. However, Ireland today does not enjoy the kind of welfare
support for families which is provided in France or Belgium, let alone that
available in Scandinavia.

Despite that, this author expects that fertility in Ireland will stabilise in
most parts of Irish society at a level more typical of north-west than of

southern Europe (that is with a TFR about 1.7–1.8) and with correspondingly high rates of illegitimacy. There is some speculative circumstantial
evidence for this supposition. The English-speaking world shares common
demographic behaviour to a surprising degree: especially in terms of the
pattern, trend and level of fertility, divorce, illegitimacy rates, and other
characteristics such as cause of death. In these respects Britain resembles
the United States, Canada, Australia and New Zealand more than its
European neighbours (Coleman, 1997). As these overseas societies are all
to a considerable degree still Anglo-Hibernian in origin, it may be that the
common factors, whatever they are, will make their demography a good
model for Ireland's future as well.

Acknowledgements. Many thanks are due to the staff of the Registrar-General and of
the Census Office, Belfast, and to the staff of the Central Statistical Office, Dublin,
for their efficient and patient responses to repeated requests for unpublished or
obscure data. Tarani Chandola did the GLIM modelling. Tony Fahey, Graham
Gudgin, Liam Kennedy and Richard Breen offered many helpful comments and
corrections. David Robertson provided valuable data on attitudes. All errors, of
course, remain my own. Some of the work for this paper, relating to the OXPOP
project on international demographic comparisons, was supported by a grant from
the ESRC (award no. L315253006) and by the World Society Foundation, Zurich.

References

Anderson, M. and Morse, D. J. (1993) 'High Fertility, High Emigration, Low
    Nuptiality: Adjustment Processes in Scotland's Demographic Experience
    1861–1914' part 1, *Population Studies*, XLVII(1): 5–26.
Baines, D. (1991) *Emigration from Europe 1815–1930*, London: Macmillan.
Barritt, D. P. and Carter, C. F. (1972) *The Northern Ireland Problem: a Study in
    Group Relations.* 2nd edn, London: Oxford Paperbacks.
Barry, J. (1992) 'Avoidable Mortality as an Index of Health Care Outcome—
    Results from the EC Atlas of Avoidable Death', *Irish Journal of Medical
    Science*, 161(8): 490–2.
Boal, F. W. (1981) 'Ethnic Residential Segregation, Ethnic Mixing and Racial
    Conflict: a Study in Belfast, Northern Ireland', in G. C. K. Peach, V. Robinson
    and S. Smith (eds), *Ethnic Segregation in Cities*, London: Croom Helm.
Boal, F. W. and Douglas, J. N. H. (eds) (1982) *Integration and Division: Geo-
    graphical Perspectives on the Northern Ireland problem*, London: Academic
    Press.
Carney, M. W. P. and Sheffield, B. F. (1995) 'Alcoholism Diagnosis and Celtic
    Names', *Irish Journal of Psychological Medicine*, 12(3): 95–100.
Central Statistics Office (1989) *Statistical Abstract*, 1989 (and earlier), Dublin:
    Central Statistics Office.
Central Statistics Office (1990) *Statistical Bulletin*, Sept. 1990 Volume LXV No. 3.

Central Statistics Office (1992) *Report on Vital Statistics 1989*, Dublin: Central Statistics Office.

Central Statistics Office (1994) *Vital Statistics. Fourth Quarter and Yearly Summary 1993*, Dublin: Central Statistics Office.

Central Statistics Office (1996) *Vital Statistics. Fourth Quarter and Yearly Summary 1995*, Dublin: Central Statistics Office.

Central Statistics Office (1997) *Census 1996: Principal Demographic Results*, Dublin: Central Statistics Office.

Clarkson, L. A. (1981) 'Irish Population Revisited, 1687–1921', in J. M. Goldstrom and L. A. Clarkson (eds), *Irish Population, Economy and Society: Essays in Honour of the late K.H. Connell*, Oxford: Clarendon Press.

Cleland, J. and Wilson, C. (1987) 'Demand Theories of the Fertility Transition: an Iconoclastic View', *Population Studies*, 41: 5–30.

Cliquet, R. L. (1991) *The Second Demographic Transition: Fact or Fiction?*, Strasburg: Council of Europe.

Coale, A. J. and Watkins, S. C. (eds) (1986) *The Decline of Fertility in Europe*, Princeton: Princeton University Press.

Coale, A. J., Hill, A. G. and Trussell, T. J. (1975) 'A New Method of Estimating Standard Fertility Measures from Incomplete Data', *Population Index*, 41: 182–210.

Coleman, D. A. (1983) 'The Demography of Ethnic Minorities', in *Biosocial Aspects of Ethnic Minorities, Journal of Biosocial Science Supplement*, No. 8, Cambridge: Galton Foundation.

Coleman, D. A. (1996) 'New Patterns and Trends in European Fertility: International and Sub-National Comparison', in D. A. Coleman (ed.), *Europe's Population in the 1990s*, Oxford: Oxford University Press.

Coleman, D. A. (1997) 'Britain's Place in Europe's Population', Paper presented to the ESRC Conference 'Population and Household Change', London, Policy Studies Institute April 1997.

Compton, P. (1981) *The Contemporary Population of Northern Ireland and Population Related Issues*, Belfast: Institute of Irish Studies, Queen's University.

Compton, P. A. (1982) 'Fertility, Nationality and Religion in Northern Ireland', in D. A. Coleman (ed.), *The Demography of Immigrants and Minority Groups in the United Kingdom*, London: Academic Press.

Compton, P. A. (1995) *Northern Ireland: Demographic Review*, Belfast: Northern Ireland Economic Council.

Compton, P. A. (1996) 'Indigenous and Older Minorities', in D. A. Coleman and J. Salt (eds), *Ethnicity in the 1991 Census Volume 1: Demographic characteristics of the ethnic minority populations*, London: HMSO.

Compton, P. A. and Coward, J. (1989) *Fertility and Family Planning in Northern Ireland*, Aldershot: Avebury.

Connell, K. H. (1950) *The Population of Ireland 1750–1845*, Oxford: Clarendon Press.

Connolly, S. J., Houston, R. A. and Morris, R. J. (1995) *Conflict, Identity and Economic Development in Ireland and Scotland 1600–1939*, Preston: Carnegie.

Cooman, E. de, Ermisch, J. and Joshi, H. (1987) 'The Next Birth and the Labour Market: a Dynamic Model of Births in England and Wales', *Population Studies*, 41: 237–68.

Council of Europe (1996) *Recent Demographic Developments in Europe 1996*, Strasburg, Council of Europe (and earlier).

Courtney, D. A. (1990) 'Women, Parenthood and Labour Force Activity in Ireland during the 1980s', Paper presented to the Council of Europe Seminar on Present Demographic Trends and Lifestyles, Strasburg 1990.

Coward, J. (1980) 'Recent Characteristics of Roman Catholic Fertility in Northern and Southern Ireland', *Population Studies*, 34: 31–44.

David, P. A., Mroz, T. A., Sanderson, W. C., Wachter, K. W. and Weir, D. R. (1988) 'Cohort Parity Analysis: Statistical Estimates of the Extent of Fertility Control', *Demography*, 25(2): 163–88.

David, P. A. and Sanderson, W. C. (1988) 'Measuring Marital Fertility Control with CPA', *Population Index*, 54(4): 691–713.

David, P. A. and Sanderson, W. C. (1990) 'Cohort Parity Analysis and Fertility Transition Dynamics: Reconstructing Historical Trends in Fertility control from a Single Census', *Population Studies*, 44(3): 421–45.

Davis, K. (1963) 'The Theory of Change and Response in Modern Demographic History', *Population Index*, 21(4).

Day, L. H. (1968) 'Nationality and Ethnic-Centrism: Some Relationships Suggested by an Analysis of Catholic-Protestant Differentials', *Population Studies*, 22: 25.

Dean, G. (1984) *Termination of Pregnancy, England 1983. Women from the Republic of Ireland*, Dublin: Medico-Social Research Unit.

De Graaf, N. D. and Evans, G. (1996) 'Why are the Young more Post-Materialist? A Cross-Natural Analysis of Individual and Contextual Influences on Post-Materialist Values', *Comparative Political Studies*, 28: 608–35.

Department of Health (1990) *1987 Annual Report on Vital Statistics*, Dublin: Central Statistics Office.

DHSS (1994) *The Health of the Public in Northern Ireland. Annual Report of the Chief Medical Officer 1994*, Belfast: Department of Health and Social Services.

DHSS/Registrar-General Northern Ireland (1992) *Northern Ireland Census 1991 Summary Report*, Belfast: HMSO.

Dickson, D., Ó Gráda, C. and Daultrey, S. (1982) 'Hearth Tax, Household Size and Irish Population Change 1672–1821', *Proceedings of the Royal Irish Academy 82C*, 6: 125–50.

Ermisch, J. (1996) 'The Economic Environment for Family Formation', in D. A. Coleman (ed.), *Europe's Population in the 1990s*, Oxford: Oxford University Press.

Eurostat (1991) *A Social Portrait of Europe*, Luxemburg: Office for Official Publications of the European Communities .

Eurostat (1996) *Demographic Statistics 1996*, Luxemburg: Office for Official Publications of the European Communities (and earlier issues).

Eurostat (1997) *Labour Force Survey Results 1995*, Luxemburg: Office for the Official Publications of the European Communities.

Eversley, D. E. C. (1989) *Religion and Employment in Northern Ireland*, London: Sage.

Fehily, A. M., Barker, M. E., *et al.* (1990) 'The Diets of Men in 4 Areas of the UK: the Caerphilly, Northern Ireland, Edinburgh and Speedwell Studies', *European Journal of Clinical Nutrition*, 44(11): 813–17.

Flinn, M. (1977) (ed.) *Scottish Population History from the 17th Century to the 1930s*, Cambridge: Cambridge University Press.

Garvey, D. (1985) 'The History of Migration Flows in the Republic of Ireland', *Population Trends*, 39: 22–30.

Geary, P. T. and Ó Gráda, C. (1987) *Post War Migration between Ireland and the UK: Models and Estimates*, Working Paper No. 49, Dublin: Centre for Economic Research, University College Dublin.

Greene, S. M., Joy, M.-T., Nugent J. K. and O'Mahoney, P. (1989) 'Contraceptive Practice of Irish Married and Single First-Time Mothers', *Journal of Biosocial Science*, 21(4): 379–86.

Gudgin, G. and O'Shea, G. (1993) *Unemployment Forever? The Northern Ireland Economy in Recession and Beyond*, Belfast.

Hajnal, J. (1965) 'European Marriage Patterns in Perspective', in D. V. Glass and D. E. C. Eversley (eds), *Population in History*, London: Arnold.

Hajnal, J. (1982) 'Two Kinds of Preindustrial Household Formation System', *Population and Development Review*, 8(3): 449–94.

Harrison, L., Carrhill, R. and Sutton, M. (1993) 'Consumption and Harm – Drinking Patterns of the Irish, the English and the Irish in England', *Alcohol and Alcoholism*, 28(6): 715–23.

Henripin, J. *et al.* (1978) *La fin de la revanche du berceau*, Quebec:

Hostetler, J. and Huntington, G. E. (1996) *The Hutterites of North America*, New York: Harcourt Brace College Publishers.

Inglehart, R. (1977) *The Silent Revolution: Changing Values and Political Styles among Western Publics*, Princeton: Princeton University Press.

Jardine, E. F. (forthcoming) 'Demographic Structure in Northern Ireland and its Implications for Constitutional Preference. A paper to the Statistical and Social Inquiry Society of Ireland', 5 May 1994, *Journal of the Social and Statistical Inquiry Society of Ireland*.

Johansson, S. R. (1991) 'Welfare, Mortality and Gender. Continuity and Change in Explanations for Male/Female Mortality Differences over Three Centuries', *Continuity and Change*, 6(2): 135–77.

Kennedy, F. (1989) *Family, Economy and Government in Ireland*, General Research Series Paper No. 143, Dublin: Economic and Social Research Institute.

Kennedy, L. and Clarkson, L. A. (1993) 'Birth, Death and Exile: Irish Population History 1700–1921', in B. J. Graham and L. J. Proudfoot (eds), *An Historical Geography of Ireland*, London: Academic Press.

Kennedy, L. (1994) *People and Population Change: a Comparative Study of Population Change in Northern Ireland and the Republic of Ireland*, Dublin and Belfast: Co-operation North.

Kennedy, R. E. (1973a) *The Irish: Emigration, Marriage and Fertility*, Berkeley: University of California Press.

Kennedy, R. E. (1973b) 'Minority Groups and Fertility: the Irish', *American Sociological Review*, 38: 85.

Kravdal, Ø. (1992) 'The Weak Impact of Female Labour Force Participation on Norwegian Third-Birth Rates', *European Journal of Population*, 8(3): 247–63.

Leck, I. and Lancashire, R. J. (1995) 'Birth Prevalence of Malformations in

Members of Different Ethnic Groups and the Offspring of Matings Between them', *Journal of Epidemiology and Community Health*, 49(2): 171–9.

Lee, J. (1981) 'On the Accuracy of the Pre-famine Irish Censuses', in J. M. Goldstrom and L. A. Clarkson (eds), *Irish Population, Economy and Society*, Oxford: Clarendon Press.

Lesthaeghe, R. (1983) 'A Century of Demographic and Cultural Change in Western Europe', *Population and Development Review*, 9: 411–36.

Lesthaeghe, R. and Meekers, D. (1986) 'Value Changes and the Dimension of Familism in the European Community', *European Journal of Population*, 2: 225–68.

Levi, F., Lavecchia, C., Lucchini, F. and Negri, E. (1995) 'Cancer Mortality in Europe 1990–92', *European Journal of Cancer Prevention*, 4(5): 389–417.

Macourt, M. P. A. (1995) 'Using Census Data on Religion as a Key Variable in Studies of Northern Ireland', *Environment and Planning A 27*, 4: 593–614.

Meghen, P. J. (1970) Ch. 2 'The Census of Population', Ch. 3 'Vital statistics', *Statistics in Ireland*, Dublin: Insititute of Public Administration.

Miller, K. A. (1985) *Emigrants and Exiles: Ireland and the irish Exodus to North America*, New York: Oxford University Press.

Mokyr, J. and Ó Gráda, C. (1984) 'New Developments in Irish Population History, 1700–1850', *Economic History Review*, 2nd ser XXXVII, 4: 475–88.

Morgan, V. and Macafee, W. (1984) 'Irish Population from the Pre-Famine Period: Evidence from County Antrim', *Economic History Review*, 37(2): 182–96.

Morris, C. and Compton, P. (1985) '1981 Census of Population in Northern Ireland', *Population Trends*, 40: 16–20.

Mosher, W. D. (1980) 'The Theory of Change and Response: an Application to Puerto Rico 1940–1970', *Population Studies*, 34: 45–58.

Murdoch, A. (1997) 'Why Irish Eyes aren't Smiling on the Great Romanian invasion', *The Independent*, 23 May: 8.

Murphy, M. (1992) 'Economic Models of Fertility in Post-War Britain—A Conceptual and Statistical Re-interpretation', *Population Studies*, 46: 235–58.

Nic Ghiolla Phadraig, M. (1984) 'Social and Cultural Factors in Family Planning', in *The Changing Family*, Dublin: University College.

OECD (1995) *OECD Historical Statistics 1960–1993*, Paris: OECD.

OECD (1997) *Trends in International Migration. SOPEMI Annual Report 1996*, Paris: OECD.

Ó Gráda, C. (1984) *Did the Catholics always have Larger Families? Religion, Wealth and Fertility in Rural Ulster before 1911*, Centre for Economic Policy Research Discussion paper No. 6, London: CEPR.

Ó Gráda, C. (1991) 'New Evidence on the Fertility Transition in Ireland 1880–1911', *Demography*, 28(4): 535–48.

Ó Gráda, C. (1993) *Ireland Before and After the Famine: Explorations in Economic History 1800–1925*, 2nd edn, Manchester: Manchester University Press.

Ó Gráda, C. and Walsh, B. (1995) 'Fertility and Population in Ireland, North and South', *Population Studies*, 49(2): 259–79.

OPCS (1995a) *Abortion Statistics 1993 Series AB No. 22*, London: HMSO.

OPCS (1995b) *Birth Statistics 1993 Series FM1 No. 22*, London: HMSO.

OPCS (1996) *International Migration Statistics Series MN*, London: HMSO.

Petty, W. (1687) 'Treatise of Ireland', in C. H. Hull (ed.), *The Economic Writings of Sir William Petty*, Cambridge: Cambridge University Press.

Registrar-General (1982) *Fifty-Ninth Annual Report of the Registrar-General 1980* (and earlier), Belfast: HMSO.

Registrar-General Northern Ireland (1995) *Annual Report 1993, No. 72* (and earlier), Belfast: HMSO.

Ruzicka, L. T. (1984) 'Mortality in India: Past Trends and Future Prospects', in T. Dyson and N. Crook (eds), *India's Demography: Essays on the Contemporary Population*, New Delhi: South Asian Publishers.

Ruzicka, L., Wunsch, G. and Kane, P. (eds) (1989) *Differential Mortality: Methodological Issues and Biosocial Factors*, Oxford: Clarendon Press.

Sardon, J.-P. (1990) *Cohort Fertility in Member States of the Council of Europe*, Population Studies No. 21, Strasburg: Council of Europe.

Schellekens, J. (1993) 'The Role of Marital Fertility in Irish Population History 1750–1840', *Economic History Review*, XLVI(2): 369–78.

Sexton, J. J. (1994) *A Review of Irish External Migration, Past and Present*, Dublin: Economic and Social Research Institute (ESRI).

Sexton, J. J. and Dillon, M. (1984). 'Recent Changes in Irish Fertility', *Quarterly Economic Commentary*, May 1984: 21–40.

Shelley, E., O'Reilly, O., Mulcahy, R., *et al.* (1991) 'Trends in Mortality from Cardio-Vascular Disease in Ireland', *Irish Journal of Medical Science*, 160: 5–9.

Shuttleworth, I. (1993) 'Irish Graduate Emigration: the Mobility of Qualified Manpower in the Context of Peripherality', in R. King (ed.), *Mass Migration in Europe: the Legacy and the Future*, London: Belhaven.

Siegel, B. J. (1970) 'Defensive Structuring and Environmental Stress', *American Journal of Sociology*, 76: 11.

Simons, J. (1986) 'Culture, Economy and Reproduction in Contemporary Europe', in D. A. Coleman and R. S. Schofield (eds), *The State of Population Theory: Forward from Malthus*, Oxford: Basil Blackwell.

Spencer, A. E. C. W. (1977) 'The Relative Fertility of the Two Religious-Ethnic Communities in Northern Ireland 1947–1977', *Transactions of the Sociological Society of Ireland 1977–8*.

Spencer, A. E. C. W. (1982) 'Catholics in Britain and Ireland: Regional Contrasts', in D. A. Coleman (ed.), *The Demography of Immigrants and Minority Groups in the United Kingdom*, London: Academic Press.

Stolnitz, G. J. (1955a) 'A Century of International Mortality Trends I', *Population Studies*, IX: 24–55.

Stolnitz, G. J. (1955b) 'A Century of International Mortality Trends II', *Population Studies*, X: 17–42.

Summers, R. and Heston, A. (1991) 'The Penn World Table (Mark 5): An Expanded Set of International Comparisons', *Quarterly Journal of Economics* (May 1991).

Szreter, S. (1996) *Falling Fertilities and Changing Sexualities in Europe Since c. 1850: A Comparative Survey of National Demographic Patterns.* Working Papers in Demography No. 62: 35. Canberra: Australian National University Research School of Social Sciences.

Teitelbaum, M. S. (1984) *The British Fertility Decline: Demographic Transition in the Crucible of the Industrial Revolution*, Princeton: Princeton University Press.

Tyson, R. E. (1995) 'Contrasting Regimes of Population Growth in Ireland and Scotland during the Eighteenth Century', in S. J. Connolly, R. A. Houston and R. J. Morris (eds), *Conflict, Identity and Economic Development: Ireland and Scotland, 1600–1939*, Preston: Carnegie.

Van de Kaa, D. J. (1987) 'Europe's Second Demographic Transition', *Population Bulletin*, 42(1).

Van de Kaa, D.J. (1996) 'The Second Demographic transition Revisited: theories and expectations', in G. C. N. Beets *et al.* (eds), *Population and Family Life in the Low Countries 1993 Late Fertility and Other Current Issues*, Amsterdam: Swets and Zeitlinger.

Walsh, B. M. (1972) 'Ireland's Demographic Transformation 1958–70', *Economic and Social Review*, 3: 251–75.

Wilson-Davis, K. (1982) 'Fertility and Family Planning in the Irish Republic', *Journal of Biosocial Science*, 14: 343–58.

Wright, R. E. (1989) 'The Easterlin Hypothesis and European Fertility Rates', *Population and Development Review*, 15(1): 107–22.

Family and State

TONY FAHEY & EITHNE MCLAUGHLIN

Introduction

ONE OF THE DIFFICULTIES IN DEALING with the question of similarities and differences between the family in Ireland north and south of the border is that we do not know enough about the family in the two regions separately. There have been no in-depth studies of the family in the Republic since Hannan's work on the rural family in the 1970s[1] and none on the urban family since Humphreys' research of the late 1940s (Humphreys, 1966). The record of research on this subject in the North is, if anything, even weaker.[2] The one area where data are readily available and some analysis has been carried out in both parts of the island—demographic aspects of family behaviour—is the subject of David Coleman's chapter in this volume and so outside our brief here.

In the absence of the information needed for a broad approach to North-South comparisons of family patterns, the present paper focuses on the narrower question of state-family relations in the two jurisdictions. This focus is of interest not only as a comparative case study of family policy but also as a perspective on the origins and nature of the two states.

---

[1] See Tovey (1992) for an insightful review both of Hannan's work and of the tradition of rural ethnographic research, dating back to Arensberg and Kimball (1940/1968), out of which it grew.

[2] As in the Republic, family studies in the North began within the rural/ethnographic framework in the shape of Rosemary Harris's research in a rural community in the North in the early 1950s (Harris, 1972/86; see also Leyton, 1970; 1975). However, only ten of almost 6,000 entries in the 1982 bibliography of Northern Irish social science material (Rolston et al., 1983) were indexed under 'family', and none of these studied the family in depth. A more recent bibliography on women in Northern Ireland (Montgomery and Davies, 1990) showed a similar picture.

Proceedings of the British Academy, **98**, 117–140. © The British Academy 1999.

Diverging projects for the family were built into the processes which led to the fracturing of the colonial state in Ireland in the late nineteenth and early twentieth centuries and to the emergence of new state formations on the island following partition. Catholic nationalism in the South, and the independent state which it created in 1921, was overwhelmingly rooted in a 'peasant' or small-farm society and in the anachronistic family system that entailed, while Northern unionism was heavily committed to capitalist industrialisation and (despite many reservations) to the industrialised family forms which went with it. These differences were far from absolute, given the strong agrarian connections of Unionism and the many accommodations with urban industrialisation reached by Catholic nationalism. But they were enough to affect the nature of the two states and to influence the way they approached family issues.

Because concerns related to the family were built into the dynamic which created the two states, we have to think of state-family interactions as a circular relationship rather than a one-way action of the state on family life. A comparative analysis must therefore go beyond a decontextualised focus on family policy and consider historical, macro-level factors affecting both the family and the state which provide the background to the more recent evolution of state-family interactions in the North and the South.

The present paper pursues these issues, first, by providing a broad overview of the historical development of state-family relations in the North and the South. This is dealt with in the following section, which examines the pre-partition era and the colonial legacy, and in the section following that, which outlines post-partition developments. To illustrate the way broad contextual factors filter down to the details of family policy, the paper then presents a case study of a particular field of family policy— child protection—where North/South differences in the role of the state have been especially acute, and which has been the focus of considerable recent policy attention in both states. The final section provides a summary and conclusion.

Family and State Prior to Partition

The pervasive influence of the colonial link with Britain on the development of Irish social policy prior to, and following, independence is often described in terms of the importation of British social policy into Ireland. However, the legacy of the colonial state on family policy goes beyond simple 'importation' and beyond social policy in the usual sense. The state in Ireland in the latter half of the nineteenth and early twentieth centuries evolved a two-stranded approach to issues affecting the family, one strand of which comes under the heading of social policy as normally defined, but the other strand of which was oriented to agrarian concerns and affected social and family structures through mechanisms not normally considered a part of social policy. We will now look at these two strands in turn.

The Industrial Strand

One of the two strands derived from the model of state intervention in the market system which had been developing in Britain since the pre-industrial period. Since its major proximate influences lay in the social and political circumstances of capitalist industrialisation in Britain, we will refer to it here as the 'industrial' strand of British social policy in Ireland. The more distant origins of this aspect of social policy lay with the pre-industrial Poor Law and was influenced by the Poor Law heritage until well into the twentieth century. The Poor Law was legislated much later in Ireland (1703) than in England (1601) and was never as extensive in Ireland, North or South, as in Britain. In contrast to England, the Irish poor had no legal or statutory right to be provided with relief, under either the 1703 Act or the Irish Poor Law Relief Act of 1838, (O'Connor, 1995: 66). In addition, implementation was weak and only three workhouses existed in the eighteenth and early nineteenth centuries.

One of the important legacies of the eighteenth-century Poor Law for family policy in Ireland was the abiding fear of the state as a possible agent of proselytism which it created. The reorganisation of the poor law along the lines of the British model in 1838 attempted to distance social welfare provision from such proselytism, but the issue continued to inform the development of child custody, guardianship and adoption law in the Republic in the present century (O'Halloran, 1994; see section 4 below).

Modern industrial social policy proper began after 1900, as social provision in Britain began to move away from a Poor Law basis towards modern social welfare principles. Three of the key developments—old age pensions in 1908, child protection, also in 1908 (The Children Act), and social insurance for employees in 1911—were applied in Ireland. A fourth development, health insurance, though installed in Britain, was fought off in Ireland by the medical profession in the period 1912–18 (Barrington, 1987). These measures, alongside the remaining elements of the Poor Law, laid the foundations for much of the welfare system in the post-partition period in Ireland, though, as we shall see in the next section, to quite different effect in the Free State than in the North.

The Agrarian Strand

The second strand of state intervention in social and family structures in Ireland arose as a response to land agitation and separatist politics in rural Ireland in the latter decades of the nineteenth century (and thus we refer to it here as the agrarian strand of British policy in Ireland). In an attempt to deal with these political pressures (to 'kill Home Rule with kindness'), the British state threw its liberal economic principles to the winds and instituted a massive programme of state intervention in Irish rural society. The components of this programme which were significant from a family point of view were fourfold.

First and most important was the reform of land tenure, which was brought about through a series of land acts initiated in the 1870s and largely completed by the 1920s. Under the aegis of the Land Commission established in 1881, this radical reform transferred ownership of some 15 million of the 17 million acres of land in Ireland from a small landlord class to a large class of family farmers. It thereby made small family farmers into the largest class in the Irish social structure.

The second component was the programme of regional economic development launched by the setting up of the Congested Districts Board in 1891, a unique experiment in state-led development at the time. This programme was directed at the poor rural areas in the west, the boundaries of which eventually comprised one-third of the area of the country. Its primary remit was to consolidate and enlarge the myriad of tiny and often fragmented small holdings in the west by buying up and redistributing land, but it also aimed to develop economic infrastructure and fishing, by investing in land drainage, farm buildings, stock breeds, roads, ports, fishing fleets and housing. By 1919 it had built or improved close to 10,000 houses, as a result of which the worst classes of rural hovels and cabins were largely eliminated from the Board's counties (Aalen, 1992: 143–4).

The third component of agrarian policy was the housing programme for landless agricultural labourers brought about through the Labourers' Acts, the first of which was passed in 1883 and the most important of which was passed in 1906. These acts were 'closely linked to, indeed almost corollaries of, the various Land Acts' and amounted to 'the first public housing programme in the British Isles and probably in Europe' (Aalen, 1992: 138, 140). By 1921, 48,000 houses (for rental tenure) had been constructed under the programme, as a result of which 'by the First World War Irish rural labourers were among the best housed of their class in Western Europe' (Ibid.: 146).

The final component of agrarian policy has been little noted in historical accounts but provided an important adjunct to the other components noted above. This was the broad educational drive conducted through the National School System, the Department of Agricultural and Technical Instruction and the Congested Districts Board to raise standards of domesticity in rural households, focusing on cleanliness, diet, clothing and, most of all, on the diligence and home-making skills of the housewife (Bourke, 1993: 236–61). While the impact of this drive is hard to assess, it is notable as a further dimension of state activity in a central area of rural family life.

These components together amounted to a programme of state intervention in social and economic life in rural Ireland which was without parallel in any other major region, urban or rural, in western Europe at the time. Some elements of that programme, especially rental housing provision for rural labourers, clearly presaged later urban social housing activities and so are easy to grasp in conventional social policy terms. The backbone of the overall programme however, lay in the land reform activities of the Land Commission and the Congested Districts Board. These amounted to a quite distinctive kind of intervention, in that they were directed at the sphere of production (that is, focusing mainly on access to land and other rural capital, including housing), where social policy characteristically intervenes in the sphere of exchange (that is, focusing on the distribution of income and basic consumption necessities). Their effect was to push the family toward the centre of the system of agricultural production and to displace the market towards the edge. Land and labour, the two key factors of production in the rural economy, were largely decommodified and reorganised on a family basis (i.e., they were 'familised'). The treatment of land as a capital asset to be accessed through the rental or purchase market was largely supplanted by a view of land as a family possession, to be transferred through intra-family bequest (Crotty, 1966; Hannan, 1979). Rural wage labour likewise declined and was replaced by family labour (Fitzpatrick, 1980), in keeping with the design of new farm holdings as *family* production units (thus, uneconomic holdings were understood as those which could not support a family unit). Only in regard to the sale of output (and to a lesser extent, the purchase of inputs) did the market continue to be an important focus of the small-farm economy. Even here, non-commercial, non-capitalist orientations were prominent, so that much of farm output was geared to own-use consumption on the farm and subsistence standards of living rather than to the maximisation of commercial opportunities (Crotty, 1966).

Thus, agrarian policy promoted a family-based *alternative* to the capitalist production system in the countryside, even though the capitalist market economy continued to provide the wider, though often remote, context in which family farming operated.[3] In consequence, the property-owning, family production unit, with a considerable degree of economic self-sufficiency, became the dominant family form of rural Ireland. That family form was characterised, to some degree at least, by the range of family practices which together have been labelled the 'stem family' (a focus on impartible inheritance and family continuity on the land, the 'match' and the dowry system of marriage, delayed marriage, patriarchal control over adult children, the frequent occurrence of the three-generational household, etc.).[4] It would be an exaggeration to say that the agrarian policies of the colonial state in Ireland were the ultimate cause of this development, or that this outcome was the conscious intention of state policy, but agrarian policy was undoubtedly the proximate means by which it was brought about and sustained within the wider capitalist environment.

The social and family dimensions of agrarian policy became more explicit as the land reform project was appropriated by Catholic nationalism in the final decades of British rule in Ireland. The political and literary elite of the new nationalist movement and the clerical leadership of the Catholic Church joined forces to generate a far-reaching ideological glorification of the small family farm and to elevate the pastoral idyll into a framework for emerging national identity. This outlook defined the countryside as the repository of true moral values and contrasted the authentic rural way of life with the social and moral danger of the city (exemplified in Patrick Pearse's pledge that there would be 'no Glasgows and Pittsburgs' in a free Ireland). Conservative, patriarchal and stable forms of family organisation were central both to this worldview and to the reality of the small-farm economy which underlay it. The groundwork was thus laid for the powerful rural focus of state ideology and state practice in the post-partition Free State, the consequences of which had a major effect on family policy as well as on the broad lines of national development in independent Ireland.

The Development of Family Policy Post-Partition

After partition, the divergences in family policy between North and South turned at a very general level on the differing emphasis given to the two

---

[3] There is an extensive literature on the precise nature of the relationship between the 'peasant' economy and the capitalist economy in modern economic conditions. See Tovey (1992) for a review of this literature in the Irish context.

[4] The precise definition of the stem family is a matter of debate, as is the question of the prevalence of its various features in rural Ireland (from a large literature, see, e.g., Hannan 1979; Gibbon and Curtin, 1983).

strands of the pre-partition legacy described in the previous section. In the Free State, the agrarian strand dominated and had implications for family life in the wider society at the level of values, rhetoric and 'moral' legislation, as well as on certain material issues. The industrial strand suffered from this dominance and limped along in a neglected condition for more than two decades, before reviving in the post-war period. In the North, the agrarian strand persisted in the form of a supportive stance towards agriculture and the family farm (or owner-farmer, the term favoured today by the main Unionist political party; UUP, 1997), but it lacked the ideological significance it acquired in the South. The industrial strand, which by the post-war period had evolved closer to the modern welfare state, took centre stage, reflecting British developments. However, the imperatives posed by a contested territory and political conflict meant that industrial social policy in Northern Ireland developed differently from that of Britain in a number of ways. Certain features of public administration in Northern Ireland, especially the large role played by unelected administrative bodies (or 'quangos', to use a more recent term), also left a distinctive imprint on social policy in the North.

The South—a Catholic Model of State Intervention

The state in independent Ireland from the 1920s to the 1960s has been described as minimalist in its approach to social issues and as particularly reluctant to intervene in what was constructed as the 'private sphere' of the family. This minimalism is normally explained as a consequence of the anti-statist stance of Catholic social teaching, as well as of the straitened revenue resources of the state (see, e.g., Breen *et al.*, 1990; Kiely and Richardson, 1995). There is some truth in this view, in that certain kinds of state intervention were resisted by Catholic social teaching and did not take place in Ireland in this period. But this is only part of the picture, since an alternative model of state intervention, much of it derived from the agrarian strand of British policy in Ireland, was quite congenial with Catholic social principles and was applied with some enthusiasm in the post-independence period, particularly under De Valera in the 1930s.

The twin pillars of this 'Catholic' model of state intervention were, first, an emphasis on widely distributed family ownership of key kinds of capital (especially land and housing), and second, the strict moral regulation of public and private life along Catholic lines. In connection with land as a form of capital, state policy focused on the completion of tenant purchase (which was largely achieved by the end of the 1920s), the continuation of land re-distribution towards small-holders,[5] a range of financial supports for farmers such as the easing of annuity obligations arising from tenant purchase (Rumpf and Hepburn, 1977: 124), and aspirational gestures such as the pledge by the state in the 1937 Constitution (Article 45.2.iv) to maximise the numbers of families living on the land. In the event, measures such as these proved insufficient to rescue agriculture from the inherent lack of commercial dynamism in the small farm system and its crippling dependence on the unprofitable British market. Even so, they reflected a quite interventionist effort on the part of the state to protect and support the small farm economy, for social as well as economic reasons, and thus to give some substance to the pastoral flavour of nationalist rhetoric.

On the housing front, though state intervention was slow to take off after Independence, it soon became exceptional both in its extent and in the degree to which it was directed at the goal of owner-occupation. One strand of this intervention was in the form of state aid to private house building for owner occupation, which was to remain a remarkably constant and prominent feature of Irish government policy from the 1920s to the 1980s, at which point it began to be scaled down (Aalen, 1992: 158; Kaim-Caudle, 1965; Power, 1993). The other strand, public housing, though long-standing in rural areas, took off in urban areas in the 1930s in the form of urban slum clearance programmes. Thenceforth, the scale of the public housing programme, combined with generous state aid to private house building, meant that state support for housing in Ireland was exceptionally high by European standards. For example, in the mid-1950s capital originating from government accounted for 75 per cent of total capital investment in housing in Ireland, the highest such share in Europe (the comparable figure for the UK was 56 per cent and for Sweden 36 per cent—Ó hUiginn, 1959–60: 63). The sale of public housing to tenants, which was initiated in the 1930s with a scheme of tenant purchase for rural cottages built under the Labourers' Acts, was an important element in the spread of home ownership. By the early 1990s, two-thirds of the housing built by local authorities (amounting to some 200,000 dwellings) had been transferred to tenant ownership and this accounted for a quarter of the total stock of owner-occupied housing (Fahey and Watson, 1995). Today, the Republic has the highest share of housing in owner-occupation (at 80 per cent) in western Europe.

---

[5] Between 1921 and 1953, the Land Commission (into which the Congested Districts Board was merged in 1923) bought up and re-distributed to small holders some 1.2 million acres of land (Rumpf and Hepburn 1977: 124; see also Nolan 1988).

Where the Catholic model defined state promotion of widespread property ownership as necessary to the foundations of healthy family and social life, it demanded strong state support for Catholic moral regulation as an essential part of the cultural superstructure. The new independent state responded appropriately, with a particular focus on sex, reproduction, gender and childhood discipline. Censorship (1929), the banning of artificial contraceptives (1935) and the drive to control occasions of youth immorality (such as The Public Dance Halls Act 1935) were the main measures in the sexual and reproductive arenas. The promotion of a domestic role for women was pursued in the 1930s through the 'marriage bar' against female employment in teaching and the public service, and, for working-class women, the introduction of 'protective' legislation against 'unsuitable' work practices such as nightwork and heavy manual labour (Pyle, 1990). The family articles in the 1937 Constitution, which emphasised patriarchal rights, the domestic role of women and a Catholic view of the impermissability of divorce, represented the culmination of this trend.

In regard to childhood, the protective impulse reflected in The 1908 Children Act stagnated (see below) and a disciplinary impulse took over. The School Attendance Act of 1926 brought into being an extensive and harsh policing of childhood, over and above that already in place in the schooling system itself. In the 1940s, when this kind of policing was at its peak, prosecutions for non-attendance at school rose to over 10,000 per year, while warning visits to children's homes by school attendance enforcers may have reached between 15 and 20 per cent of the relevant population (Fahey, 1992). Industrial schools, to which persistently truant children could be committed, were little more than prisons. In ordinary schools too, a harsh regime of corporal punishment was tacitly endorsed.

Catholic enthusiasm for state intervention in support of small-scale family capital and Catholic family morality entailed as a corollary a suspicion of state schemes of income distribution and other social services. In consequence, compared to the flurry of activity on the property and moral fronts, the distributive front represented by industrial social policy remained moribund in independent Ireland until the 1940s. Little movement toward social welfare principles of social provision took place, as a result of which the British Poor Law had a stronger contemporary role in Ireland than in Britain. The much-hated home assistance scheme lived on (though in ever-narrowing form) until the 1970s (Yeates, 1995; Ó Cinnéide, 1970). Old-age pension rates, notoriously, were cut back in the period 1924 to 1928, and no increase over 1924 rates took place until 1948 (Carney, 1985). There was little development of social insurance—by 1926, for example, only one in five of the Irish labour force was insured against unemployment, though social insurance coverage was extended to provide widows' and orphans' pensions in 1935 (Yeates, 1995).

By the 1940s and 1950s, the demonstration effects of social welfare developments in other countries (such as the National Health Service and the Beveridge plan in Britain) became increasingly difficult to resist in Ireland. In addition, the growing contrast between social stagnation in Ireland and social progress abroad led to a crisis of confidence in national performance as a whole and in the capacity of Catholic models of social action to deliver the required progress. Catholic influence remained strong in some areas of social policy, such as health and education, and hindered the expansion of the role of the state, but other developments, such as the expansion of social security provision under the 1952 Social Welfare Act, indicated the declining capacity of Catholic social principles to cope with modern social policy concerns. A new phase of social policy development began to emerge at that time, with the introduction of children's allowances in 1944, The Social Welfare Act of 1952 and The Health Act of 1953.

Since the 1970s, the Catholic model of social action has been virtually abandoned, even though certain elements of that tradition live on under a more secular umbrella. A protective attitude towards family farming and the rural way of life persists in public policy, and indeed has been given new life, in the shape of the Common Agricultural Policy since Ireland joined the EEC in 1973. Likewise, the predilection for home-ownership as a goal of public policy has persisted and been normalised by policy movements in the same direction throughout Europe (not least in Thatcher's Britain). However, national development thinking in the 1960s switched its attention to urbanisation and industrialisation as the engines of future national progress. With that, the rural was edged somewhat towards the margins of national life, and family farming made complex adjustments to its more commercialised and urbanised environment (Hannan and Katsiaouni, 1977; Hannan and Commins, 1992).

The Catholic moral heritage in the fields of sex and marriage became more and more contentious. The initial major challenge came from an increasingly liberal Supreme Court in the 1960s and 1970s, most notably in the McGee judgement in 1973 which struck down the legal ban on contraceptives as unconstitutional. The growing feminist movement and associated liberalising campaign were aided at crucial points by the commitments to gender equality arising from the Treaty of Rome. Implementation of the various Equality Directives from Europe by successive Irish governments has been slow and reluctant, as a result of which the process extended over the whole of the 1970s, 1980s and early 1990s (Mahon, 1995). A concern for women's status was also to the forefront in The Succession Act, 1965, the introduction of social welfare support for unmarried mothers in 1973 (Conroy Jackson, 1993; McLaughlin and Rodgers, 1997), the introduction of barring order procedures in the family courts (1976, 1981 and 1996) as a remedy for domestic violence, and the extensive powers to protect the interests of dependent spouses and children incorporated into the radical overhaul of legal separation procedures in 1989.

A conservative counter-attack against the liberal agenda came in the form of the campaign for the insertion of an anti-abortion clause into the constitution in the early 1980s. The concern of those who initiated the campaign was that existing anti-abortion legislation might one day be overturned either by the Supreme Court in Ireland or as a result of legislation enacted in Europe. The campaign led to a constitutional referendum in 1983, in which a two-to-one majority voted to accept a constitutional amendment guaranteeing the right to life of the unborn. However, judicial rulings in 1992 on what the amendment implied as far as foreign abortions were concerned caused the issue to erupt again and necessitated further referendums on questions related to foreign abortions in November of that year (see Girvin 1994 for a full account). At the time of writing, it is declared government policy to have a further referendum on detailed legislation on abortion in the foreseeable future.

Conservative forces scored another resounding victory in 1983 when a government-sponsored referendum to remove the ban on divorce from the constitution was defeated by a two-to-one majority. However, in a second run at the same question in November 1995, the government of the day carried through a pro-divorce constitutional amendment, though the margin of victory, at less than one per cent of the vote, could scarcely have been tighter. In the aftermath of that referendum, the government set up a Commission on the Family to investigate the relationship between public policy and family life. This Commission had not yet reported at the time of writing.

The North—the Impact of Conflict on Industrial Social Policy

Although social policy in the North is often described as following that of Britain, in the pre-war period (1920–39) social welfare support in Northern Ireland owed more to the pre-partition legacy of Ireland as a whole than to developments taking place in Britain. For example, the Poor Law continued in Northern Ireland until the end of the Second World War,[6] whereas in

---

[6] During the inter-war period the total number of people in receipt of Poor Law relief in Northern Ireland never fell below 9,741. In 1939 5,035 people were still being maintained in workhouses (Evason et al., 1976).

Britain, Boards of Guardians were abolished in 1929 and their functions transferred to local authorities. This was to change after the war when the British Treasury agreed to underwrite the bulk of the introduction of the Beveridge welfare state in the North. Nevertheless the post-war Northern welfare system remained distinctive, as Unionist politicians, civil servants and professionals sought to achieve the (populist) benefits of the British welfare state through means which '[were] more in keeping with Unionist principles than those adopted in the system across the water . . . These Unionist principles were seen as being the protection of freedom for the individual and minimal state intervention.' (Connolly, 1990: 99). In addition, many unionist politicians and thinkers were quick to argue that the introduction of the welfare state 'proved' that the Union must stay and pointed to the 'less advanced' welfare system in the South.

Modifications to the Beveridge welfare system took three forms: firstly, tighter restrictions on entitlement to cash benefits; secondly, a greater role for unelected administrative bodies; and thirdly, more restrictive distributive public services and normative family law. All of these were related to the wider politics of the divided Northern state. Describing the development of social policy in the North as following an industrial path is, then, insufficient, insofar as it was shaped by the contested nature of the northern state as well as by the modernism and industrialism of Britain. The more restrictive conditions attached to some of the principle cash benefits, for example, were intended to protect the boundaries of the Northern state and inhibit population movement from the South to the North. Thus, a residence qualification of five years out of the last ten was introduced to establish entitlement to unemployment benefit to 'safeguard against infiltration from Eire' (Ibid.: 92). Similarly, the Family Allowances Act in Northern Ireland applied a residence test to British subjects not born in the UK, to aliens and to those from the Republic, with a stipulation that the family must have been resident in the UK in two out of the last three years (Ibid.: 90–1). Family Allowances were one of the most contentious elements of the post-war welfare package, and debate around them embodied and expressed the (still present) Unionist fears of higher demographic growth among the nationalist compared with the unionist Northern populations. Thus, the initial enabling Bill sought to give fourth and subsequent children less than the British benefits, partly in order to prevent Catholics in the North obtaining more benefit from this family policy than Protestants, and partly from a belief that generous Family Allowances would encourage 'undesirable' (i.e., Catholic) breeding.

The second type of modification of British industrial social policy—the greater role of unelected administrative bodies—reflected Unionist ideology of the 'small state' (at least in social affairs). The 1948 Health Services Act and the 1946 Public Health and Local Government Act, among others, established a range of bodies with no parallels in Britain. These were centralised (having mostly removed functions and responsibilities from local authorities); they had members appointed by a Minister rather than elected by some appropriate constituency; they were relatively autonomous from the sponsoring Ministry; and were responsible for planning, policy, administration. Such bodies (or 'quangos' in contemporary language) were not 'corporatist' in the sense of incorporating a range of 'social partners', and were justified in political debate in terms of the inadequacies of the machinery of local government (Birrell and Murie, 1972; 1980). Ditch (1988) views the impetus for the establishment of these bodies at the expense of local authorities as the result of the power and influence of the Northern Ireland Civil Service. Whether that is so or not, the significance of these institutions was the way they provided opportunities for the representation, and influence, of key professional groups, such as doctors, planners, social workers, senior representatives of the voluntary sector and religious organisations, in the delivery and development of social policies.

The result, albeit for different reasons, was a similarity with the South, through the influence of professional and religious organisations on the shape and content of social policy, especially those areas which might be included within the remit of family policy. This was obvious in the way that both the Orange Order and the main Churches influenced education policy and laws on 'moral' issues such as homosexuality (Connolly, 1990: 117–18). However, it was also related to the third difference between Northern and British social policy—more restrictive distributive policies. Expenditure in 'family' areas (as well as housing) never reached equivalent levels to Britain, a problem which has continued, at least in respect of social services, since Direct Rule.

By the late 1960s, there were, then, parallel services and reciprocal benefits in the North and Britain but Northern Ireland had not simply transplanted British 'industrial' social policy. Rather, as Ditch (1988) argues, the Stormont government had devised its own principal of 'differential universality', reflecting the symbolic significance of social security benefits as status indicators of the link with Britain (and its putative welfare state) on the one hand, and as a token for attraction-avoidance via-à-vis the Republic of Ireland on the other. Meanwhile, public and welfare services—or distributive family policies—were more restrictive than in Britain and religious and professional organisations had greater influence on normative family policies.

Social Policy and 'Direct Rule'

Since 1972 and the introduction of 'Direct Rule', policy making within Northern Ireland has come much more within the overall thrust of British policies (Connolly, 1990: 127), but some of the distinctiveness of the earlier period remains. For example, the greater reliance on 'corporate' bodies instead of local authorities has continued. Indeed it has been expanded by the removal of remaining social welfare responsibilities from local councils and their transfer to existing or new administrative bodies (such as the Health and Social Services Boards and the Northern Ireland Housing Executive). The original reliance on administrative bodies in the North may have reflected Unionist ideology of the 'small state'. However, in some areas at least (such as child protection, which is surveyed in the next section of this paper), and particularly since 1972, the outcome has been the opposite.

'Direct Rule' has been associated with a rise in spending on social welfare, though there is reason to doubt that this rise has been sufficient to achieve 'parity of outcome' in terms of distributive family policies. Although spending per head had become higher in Northern Ireland than Britain by the late 1970s, once migration, different administrative arrangements and higher levels of social and economic need are taken into account, the apparently higher figure reduces dramatically, if not completely.[7] It is, of course, difficult to establish whether parity of outcome exists in relation to distributive family policies, whereas it is relatively easy to ascertain parity in relation to social security, where entitlements rest on individuals' rights prescribed by law. However, continued under-provision in relation to preschool provision (Hinds, 1991) and social care services (McLaughlin *et al.*, 1997) have been documented for the late 1980s.[8]

In the normative arena, differences between Britain and the North have also continued. Abortion, for instance, is available in substantially more restricted circumstances than in Britain, the age of consent for heterosexual sex remains one year higher than in Britain, and decriminalisation of

---

[7] In 1962/63, Northern Ireland's identifiable public expenditure was 8 per cent lower than England's, 7 per cent less than Wales' and 24 per cent less than Scotland's. By 1977/78, Northern Ireland's position had become much more favourable, when the comparable figure was 41 per cent above England and Wales and 13 per cent above Scotland. Connolly (1990) points out that the NIEC analysis of 1985/86 public expenditure showed that apparent over-expenditure reduced from 39.3 per cent to 5.4 per cent, once migration, different administrative arrangements and the cost of implementing new 'national' (i.e., UK) policies were taken into account.

[8] McLaughlin *et al.* (1997) found that at the end of the 1980s, individuals with the same degree of disability, needs for care, and marital circumstances, were less likely to receive either residential or intensive domiciliary care in the North than their counterparts in Britain.

homosexuality was achieved only under pressure from the European Court of Human Rights. The North remains characterised by a cultural conservatism in the normative family arena. This phenomenon is not analytically separate from that of political conflict given the religious fundamentalism associated with the politics of the divided Northern state.

Child Welfare/Protection

This section documents the substantial differences between the North and South of Ireland in the balance between private and public family law regarding children and associated differences in outcomes. At the heart of these differences has been a greater reliance on private family law (and thus on parental rights) in the South, leading to limited powers of state intervention, and a much greater reliance on public family law in the North and with that a more interventionist role for the state in child welfare. These differences are of interest here as they illustrate how the broad features of policy regimes documented in previous sections are reflected at the level of detailed policy. At the same time, the match between the general character of a regime and detailed policies is by no means straightforward. The balance between family rights versus state interventionism in the realm of child protection may not necessarily be replicated in other aspects of family policy and is not explicable by reference to general, essentially ideological, principles such as the boundary between the public and private spheres. The social construction of these spheres is nuanced and variable so that in the South, a strong ideology of family privacy in relation to child custody, guardianship and adoption coexisted with a strongly interventionist stance in relation to school attendance and 'moral' areas such as contraception and sexual behaviour (Fahey, 1995). Meanwhile in the North, the supposed 'small state' favoured by Unionism, and hence the greater role of administrative bodies in the North than in Britain, paradoxically increased rather than reduced intervention in the 'private sphere', at least in relation to child welfare and protection (as is shown below).

The Legal Framework of Parental Rights

The legal foundations of parental rights in the South rest on Articles 41 and 42 of the Constitution. Few powers for direct state intervention exist (see below). Married parents are prohibited from shedding absolutely or acquiring rights exclusive of the other parent in respect of the child of a marriage under Article 42. But married parents have considerable discretion, free from state intrusion, to make care arrangements which fall short of adoption (if these are agreed by both parents). The unmarried mother is permitted under private family law to personally place her child in the care of whomsoever she wishes,[9] with or without the intention of permanently transferring all rights to that person. Non-consensual arrangements can be reviewed[10] but in the case of married parents, this must be at the instigation of a parent or guardian of the child in question, not that of statutory authorities. As a result, in the South, the interface between matrimonial, care and adoption proceedings has been 'virtually watertight' (O'Halloran, 1994: 146). Professional assessment from the perspective of the welfare of the child has been a discretionary rather than standard statutory requirement in both matrimonial custody and adoption proceedings.

In the North, the introduction of The Guardianship of Infants Act shortly after partition (1925), established much greater powers of direct intervention by the State, deriving from the principle of 'the welfare of the child'. Subsequently, both before and after the introduction of Direct Rule, few legislative initiatives regarding guardianship, custody and child care developed in Britain were introduced in the North. However, the particular development of public administration in the North led to an unusual integration of medical, social work and administrative structures with the judicial institutions which supervise marriage breakdown, especially from the 1970s onwards. For example, The 1973 Matrimonial Causes Act established that statements providing information about the future care of children, arrangements for maintenance and so on, had to be approved by a judge before divorce could be granted, and s/he could order a welfare report to be prepared focusing on the needs of the child/ren. The judiciary could decide whether the welfare of a child would be best met through adoption, matrimonial or wardship proceedings and could transfer proceedings between them. The necessary public administration corollary of this legal framework—the growth of the health and social services (see below)—introduced mechanisms for monitoring the standard of childcare and 'led to the present position where socially approved standards must be met if parents are to retain their *prima facie* right to the custody of their children' (O'Halloran, 1994: 28). The exercise of private parental rights by

[9] The relative rights of unmarried mothers and fathers are unclear, though in both guardianship and adoption proceedings, the rights of non-custodial natural fathers in practice have been weak. Though the unmarried mother thus has a *prima facie* right to custody and to control the upbringing of her child, judicial opinion is divided as to whether this is of constitutional or merely statutory origin (O'Halloran, 1994: 16).

[10] Under Part II of The Guardianship of Infants Act 1964, in respect of unmarried parents, and The Judicial Separation and Family Law Reform Act 1989, in respect of married parents.

married and unmarried parents have been equally subject to the interventionist powers of Health and Social Services agencies or the judiciary when child welfare considerations are deemed to arise.

Intervention in the Interests of Child Protection

As statutory authorities in the South can assume parental duties, but not rights, most intervention has taken place at the request of parents who have a right to request help from the health boards. Until 1991, the only powers which permitted a coercive intervention by a health board (i.e., which involved the assumption of both parental rights and duties) had their origins in the pre-partition era—the emergency intervention and place of safety procedures of The Children Act 1908. These were replaced by The 1991 Child Care Act (Parts III and VI) but the new provisions also contained a very guarded approach to emergency intervention.[11] Paragraph 18 of The 1991 Child Care Act placed a generalised duty on health boards to identify children at risk of neglect and to provide related services but this brief is informed by 'the principle that it is generally in the best interests of a child to be brought up in his own family' (O'Halloran, 1994: 158). Thus, although the Act represents an important step away from the previous non-interventionist stance, permanent provision (including adoption, see below) remains based on 'complete failure' of parents both in the present and for the future of the child's life as a minor, a much stricter criterion than in the North or Britain. The result of the South's largely non-coercive approach to child welfare was that, as recently as 1985, 73 per cent of children in health board care were there with the voluntary consent of their parents, that is, 'by parental invitation and in support of an intended long-term continuation of care in the family of origin' (O'Halloran, 1994: 149).

Until 1952, there was no legislation permitting adoption, consensual or non-consensual (since married parents were not permitted to place their children for adoption under the Constitution, and unmarried parents could make whatever private arrangements they wished). O'Halloran (1994) argues that it was concerns about proseleytism which caused the absence of adoption legislation in the Republic (such legislation had occurred in England and Wales in 1926, Northern Ireland in 1929 and Scotland in 1930). Public pressure from two quarters led to the introduction of such

[11] A health board social worker must first apply to a District Court judge demonstrating 'reasonable cause'; following the issuing of a Care Order by the Court, the health board is permitted to care for the child without parental consent in the family of origin, or with fosterparents, in residential care, or through adoption. The length of the order is determined by the court, not the health board.

legislation—from those who had 'adopted' illegitimate babies and were in a state of legal insecurity, and from the Catholic Church. The latter developed concerns that without an adoption law there were opportunities for Protestant couples to acquire the illegitimate children of Catholics and then use the law to permanently resist any claim for their return (Whyte, 1980).

However, provision for adoption in the South remains limited because of tight circumscription of the power of statutory authorities to place children who are in long-term care in adoption against their parents' wishes. Parental rights cannot be terminated on the basis of culpability alone. There is no direct legal link between a statutory health board duty to secure immediate protection for a child known to be at risk and the adoption process which rests in the main on the discretionary decision of a relinquishing parent. It has been largely through voluntary admissions to care under the 1952 Act, rather than the involuntary provision under the 1908 Act, that children have passed from parental care into the adoption process. Movement of children from care to adoption has been low, so that (somewhat ironically) a distinguishing feature of Irish child-care policy has been the consistently high number of children remaining in residential care for long periods. In more recent times, through the 1988 and 1991 Child Care Acts, health boards have greater opportunities to facilitate prospective non-consensual adoption applications by making 'placements with a view to adoption'. However, the parental failure which resulted in a Care Order being made continues to be insufficient in itself to warrant a similar outcome in adoption proceedings.[12] These features of the Republic's family law are testament to the singular influence of the Constitution on the autonomy of the marital family unit and integrity of parental rights vis-à-vis the claims of third parties in relation to a child's welfare interests.

In the North, until the mid-1970s, the majority of children in care were also there on a voluntary basis (i.e., at their parents' request or with their parents' approval), but since then, the majority of children in care in Northern Ireland have been there involuntarily. This seems to have been the result of The Children and Young Persons Act (NI) 1968 (under which parents in the North only had the right to request access to care for their children from the statutory sector if such action was clearly in the best interests of the child, not the parent). The establishment of Health and Social Services Boards and the expansion of such public services after the

---

[12] O'Halloran (1994) notes that a probable result of the 1991 arrangements will be that the 'care population' in the Republic will accelerate as compound growth rates result from more annual coercive committals and there continue to be few discharges because of restrictions on non-consensual adoptions.

introduction of 'Direct Rule' have also promoted this outcome. Health and social services agencies can assume both parental rights and duties if a professional assesses a child as in need of care and protection and admits children to residential care facilities on a temporary basis. Long-term care and responsibility for a child (whether residential, foster or adoptive) without parental consent has been relatively easily obtained by health and social services boards through the use of wardship proceedings. Wardship proceedings mean that the veto of a 'culpable parent' to arrangements being made for their child could be overcome. The grounds for dispensing with parental consent provided for a wide definition of 'welfare' and used the statutory ground of 'reasonableness' (rather than 'compelling reasons' as in the South).

Whether in care on a voluntary or compulsory (through wardship proceedings) basis, a child in Northern Ireland could, on the initiative of a Health and Social Services Board, be made available for an adoption placement. O'Halloran's view (1994: 188) is that:

> The fact that freeing orders may be utilised by the Boards in respect of the children of non-culpable parents provides a vivid illustration of the extent to which interventionism is now given effect through the provisions of substantive law in Northern Ireland.

The high degree of coercive intervention in the North, mainly through the use of wardship proceedings, means that non-consensual adoptions have became the 'anchor tenant' of Health and Social Services' Boards childcare programmes (O'Halloran, 1994: 134). This has been exacerbated since 1987, when The Adoption (NI) Order restricted parental rights to give or withhold consent to adoption. O'Halloran notes that the extent of coercive interventionism has historically been stronger in the North than in Britain, as a result of close cooperation between the judiciary and the Health and Social Services Boards, firstly under wardship proceedings and more latterly under The Adoption Order. The extent of change likely to be introduced as a result of the implementation of The Children's Order 1996 is difficult to assess, though the explicit intention is to reduce the use of institutional care for children and to develop more modes of intervention which maintain children in their families of origin.

Overall, the greater interventionism characterising the North has meant that the proportion of children in care has been more than double that in the South, and, as noted above, has been largely involuntary. In parallel, the numbers of social workers employed in the South (in relation to the size of the population) has been about half that in North (O'Halloran, 1994: 193). However, the questions, which for many will seem to be the key questions, raised by these comparisons between North and South must remain unanswered. What have been the costs and benefits of interventionism in the North, and on whom have those costs and benefits fallen? Has that interventionism resulted in a higher level of welfare for children in the North than the South? Or has interventionism in the North served more to control (some) parents than to benefit children? And if so, which parents? Data on the social class and political-religious status of parents and children affected by the practice of interventionism in the North is not available, though it might be anticipated that the well-established link between poverty and state intervention, and the higher incidence of poverty among the Catholic than Protestant communities in the North, resulted in the former community disproportionately experiencing judicial and professional intervention. There are undoubted benefits to children arising from protection from physical, emotional and sexual abuse within their families of origin. However, these benefits are tempered by the costs for children attached to the often unsatisfactory nature of traditional policy responses—institutional and foster care, and adoption—and the failure to develop other, more satisfactory, broad-based and preventative policies directed at families of origin and the wider cultural, social, economic and political environment which both permits and gives rise to abuse, and particularly abusive forms of masculinity. Whether the more child-centred, interventionist orientation of policy in the North compared to the South can be viewed as less patriarchal, more protective of vulnerable individuals and in that sense more egalitarian, depends, then, on the balance of answers to these questions rather than on any simple comparison of levels of interventionism.

Conclusion

This chapter has argued that the historical contrast between the agrarian, anti-colonial foundations of the state in the South compared to the industrial, metropolitan orientation of the state in the North is central to an understanding of the evolution of state-family relations in the two regions. Catholic nationalism generated much of its political dynamism and social ideology in the context of the land reform movement of the late nineteenth and early twentieth centuries. That movement nurtured the small-farm family into a dominant position in the social structure of the countryside, principally by means of a heavily interventionist set of agrarian policies which it won from the colonial state from the 1880s onwards. Given both its numerical preponderance and its ideological dominance in nationalist thinking, that family form was established as a core of the social system in the state established after Independence. The Southern state, therefore, was partly founded on a particular family model, i.e., the family as a property-owning production unit, with a considerable degree of self-sufficiency and only limited contact with the capitalist market. That model also entailed a vision of what the state's role in family life should be, involving state support for a wide, family-based distribution of capital (especially land and housing) and a strictly Catholic and patriarchal regulation of moral life. Conversely, it entailed a minimalist view of the state's role in income distribution and in other social services identified with industrial models of social policy. All of these factors can be seen coming together in the South's distinctive private and public family law (for example, the distinction between married and unmarried parents, the long absence of adoption legislation, and the very limited powers of statutory authorities in child protection).

Although the state in the North also had a strong agrarian dimension, heavy industrialisation in the north-east, coupled with the North's subsumption into the UK state, meant a stronger emphasis on urban industrial family forms and associated policies. Family policy in the North, therefore, was drawn in the direction of British social policy, but developed distinctive elements—principally more restrictive distributive and normative policies, and a greater role for 'quangos' or 'corporate bodies' in the development and administration of social policies. The conservatism facilitated by the latter in the normative arena from the 1940s onwards, together with the religious fundamentalism generated by the politics of the divided Northern state, has been similar in some ways to the moral conservativism of Catholicism in the South. The complex balance of similarity and difference between Britain and the North can be seen in the field of child protection and family intervention. In that area, new forms of interventionist legislation in Britain often have not been introduced in the North, but new forms of public administration have developed in the North instead, leading to a higher rather than lower levels of intervention in the 'private sphere'.

Since the 1960s, the Catholic agrarian tinge to state-family relations in the Republic has faded a great deal, though a strong focus on the social fabric of the countryside is still evident, for example, in the Common Agricultural Policy. The general tenor of family policy has therefore tended to converge towards that in the North. In the 1990s, public debate in the South about the position of women in the family, abortion, child sexual abuse, divorce and adoption has intensified so that family issues are at the forefront of political debate and public controversy, a situation not paralleled in the North. Such convergence as has occurred between North and South in this period is by no means complete, since both the institutional and moral heritage of earlier periods still affects state actions on the family on the two sides of the border. The extent of the gap is particularly clear in the area of child protection and family law. As we have shown, even The 1991 Child Care Act in the South has not come close to the high degree of interventionism characterising the Northern state since the 1970s, with its tradition of legitimisation by the judiciary of the professional belief system represented by Health and Social Services Boards.

References

Aalen, F. H. A. (1992) 'Ireland' in C. Pooley (ed.), *The Comparative Study of Housing Strategies in Europe, 1880–1930*, Leicester: Leicester University Press.

Arensberg, C. and Kimball, S. T. (1940/1968) *Family and Community in Ireland*, Cambridge, Mass.: Harvard University Press.

Barrington, R. (1987) *Health, Medicine and Politics in Ireland 1900–1970*, Dublin: Institute of Public Administration.

Birrell, D. and Murie, A. (1972) 'Social Services in Northern Ireland', *Administration*, 20(2).

Birrell, D. and Murie, A. (1980) *Policy and Government in Northern Ireland*, Dublin: Gill and Macmillan.

Bourke, J. (1993) *Husbandry to Housewifery: Women, Economic Change and Housework in Ireland, 1890–1914*, Oxford: Clarendon Press.

Breen, R., Hannan, D., Rottman, D. and Whelan, C. (1990) *Understanding Contemporary Ireland*, Dublin: Gill and Macmillan.

Carney, C. (1985) 'Old Age Pensions', *Administration* 33: 4.

Connolly, M. (1990) *Politics and Policy-making in Northern Ireland*, Hemel Hempstead: Philip Allan.

Conroy Jackson, P. (1993) 'Managing Mothers: the Case of Ireland' in J. Lewis (ed.), *Women and Social Policies in Europe*, Aldershot: Edward Elgar.

Crotty, R. (1966) *Irish Agricultural Production: Its Volume and Structure*, Cork: Cork University Press.

Ditch, J. (1988) *Social Policy in Northern Ireland Between 1939–1950*, Aldershot: Avebury.

Evason, E., Darby, J. and Pearson, M. (1976) *Social Need and Social Provision in Northern Ireland*, NUU, Occasional Paper in Social Administration.

Fahey, T. (1992) 'State, Family and Compulsory Schooling in Ireland', *Economic and Social Review*, 23(4): 369–95.

Fahey, T. (1995) 'Privacy and the Family: Conceptual and Empirical Reflections', *Sociology*, 29(4): 687–702.

Fahey, T. and Watson, D. (1995) *An Analysis of Social Housing Need*, Dublin: Economic and Social Research Institute.

Fitzpatrick, D. (1980) 'The Disappearance of the Irish Agricultural Labourer, 1841–1912', *Irish Economic and Social History*, 7: 66–92.

Gibbon, P. and Curtin, C. (1983) 'Irish Farm Families: Facts and Fantasies', *Comparative Studies in History and Society*, 25.

Girvin, B. (1994) 'Ireland: Moral Politics and Abortion Referendums', *Parliamentary Affairs*, 47(2): 203–21.

Hannan, D. F. (1979) *Displacement and Development: Class, Kinship and Social Change in Irish Rural Communities*, Dublin: Economic and Social Research Institute.

Hannan, D. F. and Commins, P. (1992) 'The Significance of Small-Scale Landholders in Ireland's Socio-Economic Transformation', in J. H. Goldthorpe and C. T. Whelan (eds), *The Development of Indusrial Society in Ireland*, Oxford: Oxford University Press.

Hannan, D. F. and Katsiaouni, L. (1977) *Traditional Families? From Culturally Prescribed to Negotiated Roles in Farm Families*, Dublin: Economic and Social Research Institute.

Harris, R. (1972/1986) *Prejudice and Tolerance in Ulster: a Study of Neighbours and Strangers in a Border Community*, Manchester: Manchester University Press.

Hinds, B. (1991) 'Child Care' in C. Davies and E. McLaughlin (eds), *Women, Employment and Social Policy in Northern Ireland: a Problem Postponed?*, Belfast: Policy Research Institute.

Humphreys, A. (1966) *New Dubliners: Urbanisation and the Irish Family*, London: Routledge and Kegan Paul.

Kaim-Caudle, P. (1965) *Housing in Ireland: Some Economic Aspects*, Dublin: Economic and Social Research Institute.

Kiely, G. and Richardson, V. (1995) 'Family Policy in Ireland' in I. Colgan McCarthy (ed.), *Irish Family Studies: Selected Papers*, Dublin: Family Studies Centre, University College Dublin.

Leyton, E. (1970) 'Spheres of Inheritance in Aughnaboy', *American Anthropologist*, 72: 1378–88.

Leyton, E. (1975) *The One Blood: Kinship and Class in an Irish Village*, St. John's: Institute of Social and Economic Research, Memorial University of Newfoundland.

Mahon, E. (1995) 'From Democracy to Femocracy: the Women's Movement in the Republic of Ireland', in P. Clancy, S. Drudy, K. Lynch and L. O'Dowd (eds), *Irish Society: sociological perspectives*, Dublin: Institute of Public Administration.

McLaughlin, E. and Rodgers, P. (1997) 'Mothers not Workers: Single Mothers in the Republic of Ireland' in S. Duncan and R. Edwards (eds), *Single Mothers in Comparative Perspective*, London: Taylor & Francis.

McLaughlin, E., Parker, G., Porter, S., Bernard, S. and Boyle, G. (1997) *The Determinants of Residential and Nursing Home Care in Northern Ireland*, Belfast: DHSS.

Montgomery, P. and Davies, C. (1990) *Women's Lives in Northern Ireland Today: A Guide to Reading*, Centre for Research on Women, University of Ulster, Coleraine.

Nolan, W. (1988) 'New Fields and Farms: Migration Policies of State Land Agencies, 1891–1980', in W. J. Smyth and K. Whelan (eds), *Common Ground: Essays on the Historical Geography of Ireland*, Cork: Cork University Press.

Ó Cinnéide, S. (1970) *A Law for the Poor: A Study of Home Assistance in Ireland*, Dublin: Institute of Public Administration.

O'Connor, J. (1995) *The Workhouses of Ireland: the fate of Ireland's poor*, Dublin: Anvil Books.

O'Halloran, K. (1994) *Adoption in the Two Jurisdictions of Ireland*, Aldershot: Avebury.

Ó hUiginn, P. (1959–60) 'Some Social and Economic Aspects of Housing: an International Comparison', *Journal of the Statistical and Social Inquiry Society of Ireland*, 20(3): 36–70.

Power, A. (1993) *Hovels to High Rise: State Housing in Europe since 1850*, London, Routledge.

Pyle, J. (1990) 'Export-led Development and the Underemployment of Women: the Impact of Discriminatory Development Policy in the Republic of Ireland' in K. Ward (ed.), *Women Workers and Global Restructuring*, New York: Cornell University, ILR Press.

Rolston, B., Tomlinson, M., O'Dowd, L., Millar, B. and Smyth, J. (1983) *A Social Science Bibliography of Northern Ireland 1945–1983*, Belfast: QUB.

Rumpf, E. and Hepburn, A. C. (1977) *Nationalism and Socialism in Twentieth Century Ireland*, Liverpool: Liverpool University Press.

Tovey, H. (1992) 'Rural Sociology—Ireland', *Irish Journal of Sociology*, 2.

Ulster Unionist Party (UUP) (1997) *Election Manifesto*, Belfast: UUP.

Whyte, J. (1980) *Church and State in Modern Ireland 1923–1979*, Dublin: Gill and Macmillan.

Yeates, N., with Stolz, P. (1995) *Unequal Status, Unequal Treatment: the Gender Restructuring of Welfare—Ireland*, Working Paper of the Gender and European Welfare Regimes Project, Human Capital Mobility Programme of the EC, Dublin: WERRC, UCD.

The Religions of Ireland

ANDREW GREELEY

North of the border are the best Protestants in the world. South of the border there are the best Catholics in the world. There are very few Christians in the whole lot of them.

Frank O'Connor

Well I don't trust the Prots up here much, but I'll tell you one thing: I trust them more than I do them Catholic fockers down below.

Northern Irish Catholic with Republican sympathies.

There is no doubt that Northern Catholicism was a church of the ghetto.

Fionnuala O'Connor

Introduction

I TAKE IT THAT MY ASSIGNMENT in this chapter is to investigate the possible differences between, or possibly among, the religions of Ireland and ascertain whether there is any convergence taking place in these religions. I further assume that my responsibility, given my training and experience, is to undertake this task through the analysis of existing social survey data sets. I leave it to those who study the same phenomenon from the viewpoint of history or anecdotal comparisons or lived experience—exercises which I do not deprecate—to collect and analyse their own survey data if their impressions seem incompatible with those I find in my data. While I am not unfamiliar with the literature of Irish history, I do not propose to discuss that literature, which is beyond my professional competence, in this paper. I note that Akenson (1993) discusses differences between Irish Catholics and Irish Protestants, using data from countries to which both groups have migrated and refutes all of the

Proceedings of the British Academy, **98**, 141–160. © The British Academy 1999.

hypotheses about Irish Catholic inferiority that have been popular in Irish historiography.[1]

I also note that as I remarked in a recent article (Greeley, 1996) everyone takes surveys. Anyone who generalises about Ireland has listened to people, observed phenomena, analysed the words and observations, and generalises from them. The survey analyst differs from others who offer generalisations only in that he is explicit about his sample, questions, methods, and the limited nature of his generalisations.

I propose to work with three data sets, the 1991 International Social Survey Program (ISSP) study of religion, the 1993 International Social Survey Program study of environmental attitudes and the 1990 European Value Study (EVS). The data have been collected for these three surveys by reputable data collection agencies. In Ireland by the ESRI and in Northern Ireland by SCPR and British Gallup. All samples were probability samples and all interviews were face-to-face.

Because the studies in Ireland and Northern Ireland[2] were different projects, they represent valid samples of both regions but when one combines them they do not represent valid samples of the whole island. One can legitimately compare the two regions but one cannot estimate to the whole island, unless one weights for the relative size of the two populations. Moreover, sample sizes make it impossible to consider any but the three major religions of the island—Southern Catholics, Northern Catholics and Northern Protestants. In Ireland in the 1991 study, for example, there were 67 respondents who were not Catholic—30 Anglicans (Church of Ireland) and 30 with no religious affiliation.

---

[1] For reasons that escape me Akenson ignores analysis of large data sets pooled from surveys in the United States which explore the continuing differences between Irish Catholics and Irish Protestants, which in fact reverse the conclusions of many of those who write about religious differences in Ireland. Irish Protestants (equal in number to Irish Catholics) are more likely to be rural and southern and less likely to be economically, socially and educationally successful. Irish Catholics are now the most successful gentile group in the United States. They exceeded the national average of college attendance for those of college age in the first decade of the present century. It is remarkable indeed, is it not, the impact of sea air on the alleged deficiencies of the Irish Catholic character? Akenson is not the only scholar to ignore these findings. So do most US scholars. Economist Thomas Sowell dismisses the findings with the airy comment that no American Protestant would admit to being Irish!

[2] I use these terms without any political connotations. I do note however that the latter governmental unit includes only six of the nine counties of historic Ulster.

The case bases for the three surveys were as follows:

	Southern Catholics	Northern Catholics	Northern Protestants
ISSP 91	935	275	483
ISSP 93	892	225	411
EVS	2,084	160	295

No survey is perfect. Each of the three on which I base this analysis has flaws. The ISSP data are collected in a fifteen-minute module which in each of the participating countries is added to another study. The questions are hammered out at frequently acrimonious yearly meetings. I will not attempt to defend the collective decisions of my colleagues, many of whom are neither interested in nor sensitive to religion.

The EVS data set is based on a large mixtum-gatherum of survey items derived from the collective unconscious of the survey fraternity, especially as this fraternity has been shaped by the various Gallup organisations around the world. The study in both its 1981 and 1990 manifestations is utterly without theoretical orientation other than the assumption that religion is declining. (See Whelan, 1994 for an intelligent use of the EVS data and Ester, Halman, and deMoor, 1993, for a use of the same data which does not inform the reader that the measure of 'secularisation' changed in the second survey). Moreover, unlike the ISSP data which are available for all users as soon as they are archived at Zentralarchiv (ZA) in the University of Cologne, the investigators of the EVS in various countries are notably anal retentive with their data. One does one's best with the data that are at hand. Anyone who insists on better data is welcome to try to raise the money to fund a better project.

At the time of writing (1996/97) the EVS data is six years old, the ISSP data five and four years old. It is doubtful that the kind of attitudes with which my analysis is concerned have changed much in recent years. If one wants fresh data, then one may do one's own survey, though the lag behind data collection and report writing in international studies is usually between two and three years.[3]

Finally, I have no way of connecting the religious attitudes and behaviours which I will report with political unrest in Ireland. Civil unrest and violence is so rare in the countries studied in both the ISSP and the EVS that no thought has been given to concentrating on that subject.

[3] I am aware of the remarkable drop in the Irish birth rate in the five years from 1991 to 1996, but I do not see how that affects the present project. The rejection of Catholic birth control teaching is hardly new in Ireland.

Moreover, it does not require many people to launch a riot or a pogrom and not many more to support a secret army. The Irish are not, however, a people who are given to demonstrations in numbers higher than in most other countries. Seventeen per cent of Southern Catholics, 24 per cent of Northern Catholics, and 27 per cent of Northern Protestants have participated in demonstrations as compared to a 23 per cent average in the Values Study. Short of much more elaborate research one can only speculate about the relationship between the findings I will report and possibilities of peace in Ireland. The political surveys indicate that members of all three communities overwhelmingly supported the peace process. There are no data which would enable us to judge whether religion has any impact on the 'hard men' (and the 'hard women').

There are two issues to be faced in this analysis: what are the religions of Ireland and are the differences between or among the religions diminishing. It would seem at first consideration that there are patently two religions, Catholicism and Protestantism. Catholics in the North and South are led by a single hierarchy, ministered to by priests taught at the same seminaries, taught by the same kinds of religious orders of brothers and nuns and engage in the same kinds of religious devotions. But there is a possibility that after years of repression (either seventy-five or three hundred, depending on when one wants to start counting) Northern Irish Catholicism might have diverged somewhat from its Southern counterpart. In fact the data suggest strongly that the latter is the case: there are three religions in Ireland. In O'Connor's (1993) words 'Segregated, shut-in Belfast is a hundred miles and a world away from the fizz and frivol of Dublin pub talk . . . A minority faith behaves differently.'

In the absence of time series data[4] one must approach the issue of the diminution of differences by comparing the young and the university educated in the three populations to see if the differences among them are less than the differences among the total populations. In fact, there is little evidence of a decline in religious differences among the three religions of Ireland, as much as a good secularist might hope that such a decline (which they take to be inevitable) might contribute to the peace process.

Survey research often proves that what everyone knows to be true is not true at all. Survey research on Ireland sometimes goes further than that: it suggests that what everyone knows cannot possibly be true is in fact true. Thus for example Ward and Greeley (1990) have demonstrated in an analysis of the EVS data, that the Irish (Ireland in the sense used in this paper) are the most tolerant of the English-speaking peoples of diversity

---

[4] The ISSP was due to repeat its religion study in 1998.

among neighbours and the most likely to approve of homosexual marriage ceremonies. The tolerance of diversity can be explained when one takes into account religion. In England, Ireland and Northern Ireland, Catholics are more tolerant. Holding religion constant, there is no difference in tolerance among the three countries. One should approach the study of Irish religion with a readiness to be surprised.

Theoretical Orientation

For reasons I have explained elsewhere (Greeley, 1995) I do not consider the 'secularisation' model of religion to be useful. It is, in my judgment reductionist and weak in its explanatory power. It reduces religion to a dependent variable and pays little attention to its role as a predictor variable. Indeed the secularisation theory does not seem to be useful in understanding religious behaviour anywhere in Europe (Jagodzinski and Greeley, 1997). More to the point in the present instance, in the case of Ireland as Whelan and his colleagues have demonstrated, it does not provide all that many insights. My own approach focuses on the 'story' role of religion: a religion is a story (or a series of interconnected stories) which purport to explain the meaning and purpose of life. Religion is experience before it is reflection, poetry before doctrine, story before it is anything else and story after it is everything else. Religions will vary not only in their basic orientations but in how these orientations adapt to different sets of circumstances.

This approach led me to expect that there would be three religious stories in Ireland—an expectation which nothing in the 'secularisation' model could have anticipated. It seemed to me that the different social and political environments in which Northern and Southern Catholics found themselves would produce quite different stories, stories which would account at some level for the situation in which both groups found themselves and perhaps strengthen the existing differences. I did not expect that either age or education would lead to convergence of these two different religious stories, both Catholic, but Catholic in very different environments. Nor did I expect that there would be any convergence in the different Catholic and Protestant stories in Ireland.

ISSP 91: World View, Faith and Devotion

The first two variables in Table 1, which are drawn from the 1991 International Social Survey Program study of religion, are based on a series of questions about fundamental world views:

Table 1. Religions of Ireland (ISSP) (% Different from Southern Catholic[1]).

	All		Higher Education		Under 35	
	North Catholic	North Protestant	North Catholic	North Protestant	North Protestant	North Catholic
Pelagian	−8	−15	−8	−15	−8	−19
Calvinist	11	12	22	29	28	22
Faith	19	14	22	19	19	18
Devotion	4*	−31**	11	−29	7	35
Superstition	12	8	4	10	21	9
Sexual Morality	4*	−8**	−11	−14	−4	−15
Tough on Crime	−15*	21**	0	−13	−18	−19
Cheat	8	−12**	10	−10	7	−16
Feminism	0*	−10**	0	−8	3	−11
% Very Happy	−7	0*	3	5	9	−4
Hrs Work	−15	−13	−6	−4	7	7
Church-State	0*	−12**	9	11	7	18

Key   * Not significantly different from Southern Catholics

        ** Significantly different from both Northern and Southern Catholics

Note: 1. In proportion above mean on factor scale.

There is very little people can do to change the course of their lives.
The course of our life is decided by God.
Life is meaningful only because God exists.
Life is meaningful only if you provide meaning yourself.
We each make our own fate.

Four variables constitute the SUPERSTITION factor:

Good luck charms sometimes do bring good luck.
Some fortune tellers really can foresee the future.
Some faith healers really do have God-given healing powers.
A person's star sign at birth or horoscope, can affect the course of their future.

Two variables serve as a short hand measure for FEMINISM in ISSP 91:

A husband's job is to earn money; a wife's job is to look after home and family.
Family life suffers when a woman has a full time job.

Finally a series of items attempted to measure attitudes towards Church-State relationships:

Politicians who do not believe in God are unfit for public office.
It would be better if people with strong religious beliefs held public office.
Do you think that churches and religious leaders in this country have too much power?

The first three variables cluster on a factor I call CALVIN[5,6] because it seems to indicate a sense of predetermination or predestination. The fourth and fifth variable cluster on a factor which I name after PELAGIUS, a monk who did battle with Saint Augustine on the issue of whether humans could do good without God's help. Pelagius, who was Irish, held that they could. Southerners are significantly[7] more likely to be PELAGIANS, Northerners more likely to be CALVINISTS. There are no significant differences between the two Northern communities. Among those who have attended university and those under thirty-five, the differences persist. The old battle line between the Irish monk and the African bishop continues in the modern world, most notably, it would seem, along the boundary which separates the six counties from the twenty-six.

Factor scores were computed for a wide variety of variables in the three studies. Then the scores were dichotomised and the proportions above the means for the three religious groups were calculated. Thus Northern Catholics were eleven percentage points more above the mean on the CALVIN scale than were Southern Catholics, and Northern Protestants were twelve percentage points more above the mean than Southern Catholics. Both differences are statistically significant. Thus one concludes that on this scale Northerners, whether Catholic or Protestant, are more inclined to CALVINISM than are the Southerners, but that Catholics and Protestants in the North do not differ significantly with one another.[8]

Then the populations are divided into those who have had university education and those who have not. Far from diminishing the differences

---

[5] Calvin, like most of the Protestant leaders was in fact an Augustinian. Augustine in his later life took a profoundly pessimistic view of human nature. Humankind could do nothing by itself. It was utterly dependent on God's mercy. He sharply divided nature and grace, saying that God owed humans nothing. Pelagius saw a much smoother development of nature into grace and was far more optimistic about humankind. The Greeks defended Pelagius (and have never considered Augustine a saint). Thomas Aquinas leaned more in the Pelagian direction than in the Augustinian. It is fascinating that, insofar as our scales measure the two strains of the Western Catholic heritage, Ireland is divided between the Augustinian North and the Pelagian South. As we shall see, the old debate between the North African and the Irishman continues to be live in Ireland today, with the border between the six and the twenty-six counties also marking the border between the two theologies. In fact, the Irish score higher on the PELAGIAN scale than any other population in the ISSP.

[6] Factor names are in caps to remind the reader that they are nothing more than labels for a cluster of intercorrelations.

[7] The convention is followed in the tables of using an * to indicate the absence of statistical significance between either of the two Northern groups and Southern Catholics. Two ** indicates a *significant* difference between Northern Protestants and both Catholic groups.

[8] The factor scores were first computed for the entire sample and for the three communities. There were no basic differences in the various calculations. PELAGIUS and CALVIN did not correlate and hence could not be combined into one scale.

between North and South on CALVIN, a university education seems to exacerbate them because such an education leads to a more notable decline in CALVINISM among Southerners than among Northerners.

Tables 1, 3 and 4 in this chapter summarise the differences among the three religions of Ireland. The first two columns of each table present the differences in comparison of Northern Catholics and Northern Protestants with Southern Catholics.[9] The second two columns depict the differences among those who have attended universities. The third two columns represent the differences among those who are less than thirty-five years old.[10]

Thus CALVIN wins in the North (and presumably St Augustine) and the Irish monk wins in the South. Insofar as our measures tap fundamental world views, Northern Catholics are as pessimistic as their Protestant neighbours, perhaps because the culture of the six-county majority has been absorbed by the minority community.[11] The 'story' of the meaning of life which Northern Catholics tell is more like that of the Northern Protestants than that of the Southern Catholics.

On matters of religious FAITH (God, heaven, hell, life after death, bible) Northerners are also substantially more faithful than Southerners. Neither youthfulness nor higher education diminishes these differences. However, Catholics in both regions have higher levels of DEVOTION (prayer and church attendance) than their Protestant counterparts, differences which again are immune to youthfulness and higher education.[12] Protestants are significantly lower than both Catholic groups in their devotions.[13]

---

[9] The percentages are the B statistic in dummy variable multiple regression analysis in which Protestants and Northern Catholics are compared with Southern Catholics. Statistical significance is generated by the regression equation.

[10] Numbers representing the 'left hand' bars are omitted for the sake of making an already complicated chart less confusing than it might be. The issue is not differences among the older and the less educated, but among the younger and the more educated.

[11] Table 2 enables the reader to compare the three Irish communities in the context of percentage responses to individual questions in other countries; Britain and the United States. Thus the Southern Irish would seem to be the most Pelagian and the Northerners the most Calvinist not only in Ireland but in all three countries.

[12] This does not mean that younger Catholics are more faithful or devout than their elders, but only that the differences persist even among the young and educated, though in all three groups their levels of faithfulness persist even though the absolute levels may have declined. Younger Catholics are somewhat less likely to go to church regularly than older Catholics, but they remain more likely to attend than younger Protestants and at the same level of difference.

[13] Table 2 shows that in the five communities being considered Irish Catholics are more likely to attend Church regularly than Irish Protestants and than Americans and British. Nine out of ten in Ireland and the United States believe in God as opposed to seven out of ten in Britain, Far from being the result of faith, magic seems incompatible with it.

Thus, while Northern Catholics are similar to Northern Protestants in their world view, they are similar to Southern Catholics in both their faith and their devotion, perhaps this '*via media*' is what one would expect from a group which is pulled by two different cultures.

ISSP 91: Superstition and Morality

There were four questions in the 1991 ISSP project which measured attitudes towards superstition and magic—astrology, good luck charms, fortune tellers and faith healers. Greeley and Jagodinksi have both analysed these items and the factors which they form and report that rates of magic are lowest in countries where religious faith is strong (Ireland) and in countries where it is weakest (East Germany). In countries which are in between (Britain and West Germany) magic seems to have the strongest appeal.

The Northern Irish, both Catholic and Protestant, are significantly higher on the magic scale than the Southern Catholics and are not significantly different from one another. Among the university-educated Catholics, the difference between Northerners and Southerners disappears, though not among the young. The difference between Southerners and Northern Protestants is not affected either by youthfulness or education.[14]

The results of my analysis so far suggest that a key question in this project is on what variables Northern Catholics will be more like their Protestant neighbours and on what variables they will be more like their Southern co-religionists.

On the matter of sexual morality (premarital, extramarital, same sex sexuality) they are more like their Southern co-religionists; indeed, they are more orthodox than the Southerners and than their Northern neighbours. A group under pressure might well elect to emphasise those aspects of a religious culture that the leaders have most strongly proposed as essential. The Vatican is more likely to be concerned about abortion than about fortune tellers.[15]

The Irish Catholics however, have one of the highest rates of opposition

---

[14] Britons are, as previous research would lead us to expect, more likely (Table 2) to believe in fortune tellers than any of the three Irish communities.

[15] Table 2 shows that barely half of Southern Catholics support abortion in the case of a defective child as opposed to 43 per cent of Northern Catholics, almost seven-eighths of Northern Protestants. In Britain the rate is 92 per cent and in the US (in this survey) 83 per cent. In the US Catholic attitudes towards abortion are indistinguishable from the national average. Attitudes towards premarital sex in Ireland are a ten year cohort behind those in the United States—the rate of approval among Irish in their thirties, is the same as that of Americans in their forties.

to the death penalty of any country in the world and the Northern Irish are even more likely to oppose it than their Southern neighbours, perhaps because they see some of their young men as potential targets for the death penalty or perhaps because they have less confidence in the legitimacy of the criminal justice system (Table 2). Thus on a factor which combines support for the death penalty and for harsh sentences for criminals, Irish in the North are significantly more tolerant than Irish in the South and Protestants are significantly less tolerant than are Catholics in either community. Among university-educated Catholics, there is no significant difference between Catholics and Protestants. Ireland, incidentally has one of the lowest murder rates in Europe and Northern Ireland has the lowest rate of non-political crimes in the United Kingdom.

However, Irish Catholics in both regions are more likely to approve of cheating on taxes and government compensation forms and Northern Catholics are also significantly more likely to think it is all right to cheat the government than do Northern Protestants. Professor Liam Ryan explains this lack of scruple as a survival of the old feudal sense of community which distrusts the modern state. It is also possible that the consoling Catholic doctrine that tax laws are 'purely penal' (bind in conscience only to accept punishment if one is caught) plays a part in this relaxed attitude. Well trained in casuistry that they are (especially by their Jesuit teachers) the Irish can be depended on to know about 'purely penal' laws.

Table 2.   Ireland Compared to Other Countries (%).

	South Catholics	North Catholics	Protestants	Britain	USA
Own Fate	71	59	59	60	63
Predetermined	53	55	62	21	40
Fortune Tellers	26	30	32	41	—
Family Suffer (Disagree)	45	44	38	43	48
Tax Cheat (Not Wrong)	34	38	21	26	17
Abortion OK Defect	52	43	86	92	83
Pro Death Penalty	37	19	64	33	50
Attend Weekly	71	90	26	17	44
Church too much Power	36	32	33	28	23
% Very Happy	40	33	39	33	37
Job satisfaction	52	48	35	19	31
God	97	98	95	94	71
Obedient Children	35	58	51	32	39
Nuclear Threat	44	37	23	21	25

Two variables serve as a short-hand measure for FEMINISM in ISSP 91:

> A husband's job is to earn money; a wife's job is to look after home and family.
> Family life suffers when a woman has a full-time job.

On the FEMINISM scale Irish Catholics in both regions are more likely to take a feminist position than are Northern Protestants who are significantly lower in their support for FEMINISM than are Catholics. Indeed (Table 2) there is no difference between Irish Catholics and Britons or Americans on this issue.[16] Neither youthfulness nor education have an impact on these differences.

ISSP 91: Happiness, Work, Church and State

Although it was claimed recently in *Society* magazine that Scandinavians report the highest levels of psychological well-being as measured by the 'happiness' item; in fact the Irish of whatever religious persuasion have the highest score, though it is lower among Catholics in Northern Ireland than in the South. As Table 2 demonstrates, however, Northern Irish Catholics are slightly higher than Americans, and significantly higher on this measure than Britons.

Despite their happiness (or perhaps because of it) the Southern Irish work longer hours than members of the other two communities, almost forty-four hours a week as opposed to slightly under forty for the Northerners. If number of hours worked is a sign of the Protestant Ethic, then Irish Catholics are the last Protestants in Europe. These differences disappear among the young and the well educated, one of the rare times in the present analysis that we discover that youthfulness and education do lead to a convergence in behaviour.

Finally a series of items attempted to measure attitudes towards Church-State relationships:

> Politicians who do not believe in God are unfit for public office.
> It would be better if people with strong religious beliefs held public office.
> Do you think that churches and religious leaders in this country have too much power?

---

[16] Many years ago, British Gallup did a study of attitudes towards the role of women in the then nine Common Market countries. On the more than thirty variables, the Irish and the Danes were in either first or second place on every one. It does not follow, I hasten to add, that Irish feminists have no just grounds for complaint. It only follows that matters were worse in other countries.

Catholics are more likely than Protestants to think that Church leaders have too much power. Neither education nor youthfulness diminish this cross-border difference. Moreover (Table 2), on the third item Southern Catholics are more likely than Britons or Americans to think the Churches have too much power—arguably because they do.

A Fourth Irish Religion?

In the above analysis I combined all Christians who were not Catholic in the North into one category as a preliminary strategy. The question remains, however, whether there might be a fourth Irish religion, Northern Church of Ireland. Therefore, I compared Presbyterians (217) and Anglicans (167) on the variables in Table 1. On two of them was there a statistically significant difference: Presbyterians were fifteen percentage points higher on the DEVOTIONAL scale and, not surprisingly, eleven points higher on the CALVINIST scale. If one compares Northern Anglicans with Southern Catholics[17] one will find inevitably, given the previous analysis, that the two groups differ significantly on many of the measures available in the ISSP data. Catholics are more DEVOUT, less MORAL, more satisfied with the relationship between CHURCH and state, more PELAGIAN, more tolerant of CRIME and of those who CHEAT.

On the measures used in this project therefore there does not appear to be a fourth religion in Ireland.[18] Yet devotion and world view might be considered the most important of the religious measures in Table 1. On both measures Northern Anglicans are different from both Southern Catholics and Northern Protestants, less devout than either Catholics or Presbyterians, less Pelagian than Southern Catholics and less Calvinist than Presbyterians. If devotion and world view are defining character-istics of religion, then Ireland indeed has a fourth religion—Northern Anglican.

Finally I compared Northern Anglicans and Southern Anglicans and found only one significant difference: Southern Anglicans are significantly more likely to have high scores on the FEMINISM scale than are Northern Anglicans—58 per cent versus 33 per cent.

---

[17] One cannot add the thirty Southern Anglicans to the Northern Anglicans because, as explained earlier, they would not represent a valid sample of all the Anglicans in Ireland, save if a complicated weighting process were used. Such a process, given the small number of southern Anglicans, would be at best precarious.

[18] I excluded the 30 Anglicans in the South so as to hold 'country' constant in the analysis described in this paragraph.

ISSP 91: Summary

Protestants in the North differ systematically from Catholics in the South on all items except personal happiness. Clearly then, as these indicators measure religious differences, there are two different religions on the island, not completely different, but different enough. Southern Catholics are more PELAGIAN, less CALVINIST, more faithful, more devout, less superstitious, more sympathetic to criminals, more likely to cheat the government, more likely to be strict on sexual morality, more feminist, more likely to work longer and more opposed to the power of the Church. They do not however differ from Protestants in the proportion who are very happy. Only in hours of work do education and age seem to diminish the difference.

Northern Catholics are somewhere between the two. In world view, faith, superstition and hours of work, they are more like their Protestant neighbours. However, they are stricter morally and more 'faithful' than the Southern Catholics and even more sympathetic to criminals. They do not differ from Southerners in their devotion, their propensity to cheat the government, their feminism and their views on Church and State.

There does not appear to be a fourth religion in Ireland because Presbyterians and Anglicans in the North differ from one another only in their levels of religious devotion and in adherence to a Calvinist world view.

Tentatively we may conclude that this 'third' Irish religion is the result of tension between the culture in which they live as a hated minority and the religious culture they are taught in their churches and schools. Does this greater similarity with Northern Protestants suggest they might be more open to accommodation? Or is it more probable that the culture conflict might increase their hostility?

The data do not enable us to make a choice. If I were forced to speculate I would lean to the latter alternative.

EVS 1990

In the Value Study many scales were administered to respondents which might be interpreted as linked somewhat to religion. The most obvious is the FAITH scale which replicates the finding reported about the FAITH scale in the ISSP study: Northerners are more FAITHFUL than Southerners.

The EVS however, presented a different measure of moral absolutism:

> Here are two statements which people sometimes make when discussing good and evil. Which one comes closest to your point of view?

There are absolutely clear guidelines about what is good and evil. These always apply to everyone, whatever the circumstances.

There can never be absolutely clear guidelines about what is good and evil. What is good and evil depends entirely upon the circumstance at the time.

Southern Catholics are not different from Northern Catholics in their moral absolutism as measured by this item. However, Northern Protestants are more absolutist than Southern Catholics on this measure.

Northerners of both religions are more likely to want children who are obedient and hard working than are Southern Catholics. In fact as Table 2 shows Southern Catholics are similar in this respect to Americans and Britons while Northerners, both Catholic and Protestant, are very different. This seems to be a case of the minority group absorbing the values of the majority group through psychological processes of emulation mixed with dislike. Catholics in the South are under no pressure to do the same thing.

There are more protests (petitions, lawful and unlawful demonstrations, boycotts, occupation of buildings) in Northern Ireland than in the Republic, a finding which is hardly surprising. Moreover, when demonstrations are considered separately, they are also more likely to be found in the two Northern communities. As noted earlier, protests and demonstrations are more frequent in the North than the EVS average and less frequent in the South.

Table 3.   Religions of Ireland (EVS) (% Different from Southern Catholic).

	All		Higher Education		Under 35	
	North Catholic	North Protestant	North Catholic	North Protestant	North Protestant	North Catholic
Faith	17	7	14	7	22	7
Moral Absolutism	4*	6	0	6	0	5
Docile Children	21	24	27	26	23	27
Protests	9	5	7	8	3	9
Demonstrate	11	9	7	12	9	16
Tolerance	−5	−7	−6	−7	−5	−9
Civil Laws	13	0*	20	0	10	4
Challenge	−8	2*	4	−4	−11	4
Security	10	5*	15	8	−15	11*
Must Work	11	5*	13	0	15	6
Like Work	−10	5*	−13	0	−15	6

Key: * Not significantly different from Southern Catholics

The EVS provides a twelve-item list of people a respondent would not like to have as neighbours:

People with a criminal record
People of a different race
Left-wing extremists
Heavy drinkers
Right-wing extremists
People with large families
Emotionally unstable people
Muslims
Immigrants/foreign workers
People who have AIDS
Drug addicts
Jews
Hindus

Southern Catholics are more TOLERANT than both Northern Catholics and Protestants. There is no difference between the two Northern groups on this tolerance measure. Irish Catholics (in the South) continued to be the most tolerant people in the English-speaking world, as Ward and I reported of the 1981 EVS study (Ward and Greeley, 1990), and Northern Irish among the most intolerant, whether Catholic or Protestant.

There were three 'morality' factors to be found in the EVS data set. On only one were there differences among the three Irish communities, a factor I call CIVIC VIRTUE:

> Please tell me for each of the following statements whether you think it can always be justified, never be justified, or something in between:
>
> Taking and driving away a car that belongs to someone else
> Taking the drug marijuana or hashish
> Someone accepting a bribe in the course of their duties
> Buying something you knew was stolen
> Sex under the legal age of consent

Northern Catholics are more likely to reject approval of these activities (as represented by the factor score) than are Southern Catholics, though there is no difference between Northern Protestants and Southern Catholics. It is possible that this is a phenomenon which represents an over-adjustment of the minority group to the perceived norms of the majority.

One item in the long morality battery may have special implications for an island in which civil unrest seems endemic, a question which asks whether political assassination is ever moral. Nineteen per cent of Southern Catholics think that it may on occasion be moral as opposed to 11 per cent of the Northerners of both denominations. In Britain 30 per cent think it may be moral as do 23 per cent of Americans. The average support for assassination in the EVS is 22 per cent. If this item be taken as a measure of support for political violence, the Southern Catholic percentage is not particularly high, but the Northern percentage, for both Catholics and Protestants, is exceptionally low—perhaps because both communities have had the chance to see the impact of political assassination. The gunmen patently do not speak for the people.

The final four items in Table 3 are based on responses to questions about work. The first two deal with what makes a job attractive, the second two with why one works. The questions which create the first two factors are:

Which one of the following do you personally think are important in a job:

Pay
Security
Interesting
Opportunity for promotion
Useful
Responsibility
Respect

The first two cluster on a factor that is called SECURITY and the remaining five on a factor called CHALLENGE.

Irish Protestants do not differ on these factors from Southern Catholics, but Northern Catholics are more likely to reject challenge and opt for security. As is perhaps not untypical of a minority, they want to take no chances.

Finally, a number of items seek to determine why people work:

The more I get paid the more I do.
Working for a living is a necessity.
I will always do the best I can regardless of pay
I enjoy my work.

The first two items form a cluster called MUST WORK; The second two constitute LIKE WORK.

As we would now come to expect with regard to the EVS data, Northern Catholics are higher than the other two communities on the MUST WORK factor and low on the LIKE WORK factor; and there are no differences between Southern Catholics and Northern Protestants.

The pattern in the Value Study data seems to be that the Northern Catholics are either more like the Northern Protestants than Southern Catholics or at least tend to be unlike Southern Catholics. Only on moral ABSOLUTISM are they not significantly different from Southern Catholics. Moreover, on most variables they are significantly different from

Southern Catholics even when Northern Protestants are not significantly different from Southern Catholics. This pattern strongly suggests a values system which has been heavily influenced by minority status, by the experience of a group which has been 'on the bottom' for a long time as opposed to a group which has been 'on the top' for a long time. One might argue that these variables are graphic proof of the impact of the Northern Ireland polity and culture on its Catholic citizens. Since virtually none of the variables are affected by either age or education, the data do not present a very hopeful picture for the future. Contrary to the dictum of the character in Roddy Doyle's *The Commitments*, the 'Negroes of Europe' are not those who live on the North Side of Dublin, but rather Catholics who live in the North.

ISSP 94: The Environment

Attitudes towards the environment may be an important effect of religions because they may represent a stance towards life and its purpose. A series of fifteen questions about the threat of chemical pollution, industry, water pollution and nuclear energy and the dangers of these to one's family generated four factors of which three differentiated among the three Irish communities: CHEMICALS, TEMPERATURE and NUCLEAR.

On all three factors (Table 4) Southern Catholics are substantially more concerned than Northern Protestants, and on CHEMICALS Southern Catholics are also more concerned than Northern Catholics. Northern Catholics are also more concerned than their Protestant neighbours about the dangers of nuclear energy. Table 2 establishes that concern about the nuclear threat among Irish Catholics (of North and South) is notably greater than not only of the Protestant community but also of the citizens of the United States and Great Britain. Indeed the concern of Irish Catholics about nuclear power is the highest in the world[19]—and this in a country where there are no such stations.

It may be that the liberal wing of the Irish Church has scored points with its people by insisting on the danger of nuclear energy, an insistence which is cost-free in a country that does not have any nuclear energy— just like attacks on the policies of the United States in Latin America are cost free. Moreover, the Catholic respect for nature as sacramental may account in part for the Irish horror of meddling with the power of the atom. Finally a well-publicised nuclear incident in Britain and fear of what would happen if there were an incident across the Irish Sea in Wales, may

---

[19] At least in the twenty-three nation world studied by the ISSP.

Table 4. Environmental Concerns (ISSP 93) (%).

	All		Higher Education		Young	
	North Catholic	North Protestant	North Catholic	North Protestant	North Catholic	North Protestant
Chemicals	−22	−29	−6	−8	−12	−13
Temperature	−1*	−10	−9	−19	−6	−10
Nuclear	0*	−22**	9	−31	9	−31

Key: * Not significantly different from Southern Catholics
        ** Significantly different from both Northern and Southern Catholics

be of considerable importance in explaining the intensity of Irish feelings on the subject.

One should also note that in the South both education and youthfulness predict greater differences than they do in the North. In the more relaxed and open society of the South (in recent years very open indeed and becoming more so) the usual demographic variables have a substantially greater impact than they do in the more constrained society of the North.

Summary and Conclusion

There can be little doubt that there are two different religions on the island of Ireland. Northern Protestantism and Southern Catholicism are not completely different. They are both Christian, European, Western and English speaking. Yet of the twenty-six variables we used in trying to trace out rough outlines of religion and religiously related culture, only on the 'happiness' measure is there no significant difference between the two communities. One supposes that this finding surprises no one, though it might be deemed worth while to have documented it. Moreover, there is no indication that the differences are diminishing among the university trained and those under the age of thirty-five.

The third religion of Ireland presents a more complex and intricate picture. It is Catholic (in the sense of being like Southern Catholicism) in its faith, devotion, morality and some of its attitudes (feminism, sympathy for criminals, tolerance for cheating, two attitudes towards the environment), but it is not like Southern Catholicism in its world views or much of anything else. It is significantly different from Southern Catholicism on twenty of the twenty-six variables. It is significantly different from Northern Protestantism on DEVOTION, CRIME attitudes, FEMINISM and CHEATING. On the various work values it is different from the Catholicism of the South in matters on which the Northern Protestants are not different from Southern Catholics. The religion of Northern Catholics fits nicely into the model of a (repressed) minority group torn between its traditional heritage and the cultural environment in which it finds itself. To test this thesis I compared Catholics in the North with Catholics in the counties which border the North, which includes the three counties of historic Ulster which are not part of the North. There is no decline in the differences between Catholics in the North and Catholics in the South when one limits the comparison to the border counties. Whatever the reason for the difference between the two Catholic religions in Ireland it is limited to the six counties and the experiences within their border.

Finally one might argue that Northern Anglicans constitute yet a fourth Irish religion, different from their Presbyterian neighbours and Southern Catholics in that they are less DEVOUT and in that they are less PELAGIAN than the Catholics and less CALVINIST than the Presbyterians.

In terms of the theory that religion is a story (or a collection of stories) which explain the meaning and purpose of life there are four important conclusions to this chapter:

1 There are three (or perhaps four) religions in Ireland, all of them Christian, which have rather different stories.

2 Two of these religions are Catholic. Thus it is clear that the raw religious materials of a religion, especially one as luxuriant in its metaphors as Catholicism, can be shaped into rather different stories, depending on the circumstances in which groups of Catholics might find themselves.

3 Apparently the experience of being a minority religion, and one that is, to state the matter mildly, under cross pressures, accounts for the different Catholic story in Northern Ireland.

4 There is no evidence that the differences among the religions of Ireland are being substantially affected by either age or educational attainment.

One can deny reality indefinitely of course, especially in Ireland. One can pretend that there is not a third religion on the island, a religion of a repressed minority and be none the worse for such a pretence. But then one ought not to be surprised that peace efforts are less than successful.

References

Akenson, D. H. (1993) *The Irish Diaspora*, Toronto: P.D. Meany Company.

Ester, P., Halman, L. and de Moor, R. (1993) *The Individualizing Society: Value Change in Europe and North America*, Tilburg: Tilburg University Press.

Greeley, A. (1995) *Religion as Poetry*, New Brunswick N.J.: Transaction Publishers.

Greeley, A. (1996) 'In Defense of Surveys.' *Society*, 33(4): May June.

Jagodzinski, W. and Greeley, A. (1997) 'Hard Core Atheism, Socialism and Supply Side Religion', Köln: ZA.

O'Connor, F. (1993) *In Search of a State: Catholics in Northern Ireland*, Belfast: The Blackstaff Press.

Ward, C. and Greeley, A. (1990) 'Development and Tolerance: The Case of Ireland', *Eire-Ireland*, 25(4) (Winter).

Whelan, C. T. (ed.) (1994) *Values and Social Change in Ireland*, Dublin: Gill and Macmillan.

Crime in Ireland 1945–95*

JOHN D. BREWER, BILL LOCKHART
& PAULA RODGERS

The State of Criminological Research in Ireland

ON ANCIENT MAPS, CARTOGRAPHERS USED TO DESCRIBE those territories whose boundaries they did not understand or whose people they knew little or nothing of, and did not much care to find out, as places where 'here be dragons'. It is a phrase synonymous with any unexplored and unknown issue, something easily and readily dismissed, and not seen as worth addressing. Ordinary crime in Ireland is a modern example, mapped by criminologists only by reference to terrorism, everything else about which to do with crime is ignored and unexplored. While there was some research in the manner of the Continental 'moral statisticians' during the mid-nineteenth century, when agrarian crime in Ireland was at its zenith, and some initial research by people in the criminal justice system in the Irish Republic in the 1960s when crime in modern times first began to rise, there is no tradition of academic criminology in Ireland; Rolston and Tomlinson (1982: 25) consider criminology Ireland's 'absentee discipline', and criminologists in Britain have completely ignored Ireland, including Northern Ireland.

Thus, there are remarkably few studies of crime in Ireland, with comparative studies between North and South non-existent (McCullagh's 1996 volume on crime in the Irish Republic, the first book of its kind, makes no mention of the North). One exception is Rottman (1989) who provided a brief but instructive overview of crime both before and after partition, making some comparisons between North and South, urban and rural,

* This paper is based on research which forms part of a larger project funded by the Northern Ireland Office, entitled *Crime in Ireland 1945–95: 'Here be Dragons'*, and published by The Clarendon Press, Oxford, 1997.

Proceedings of the British Academy, **98**, 161–186. © The British Academy 1999.

and Belfast and Dublin, using both recorded indictable crime statistics and victimisation survey results. Rottman's earlier study (1980) provides a comprehensive summary of statistical trends in crime in the Irish Republic from 1951 to 1972. O'Mahony (1993) followed this up and reported results for the Republic of Ireland for the period 1973 to 1991. McCullagh (1996) covers the period 1961 to 1991. Thus, in the case of the Republic, we have a fairly complete commentary on crime trends during the period 1951 to 1991. This contains mainly descriptions of crime trends in major crime categories but also attempts to link these to broader socio-economic change. This material is supplemented by other publications, such as Dooley's (1995) analysis of homicide in the Republic of Ireland during the period 1971 to 1991 and another recently published victimisation survey by O'Connell and Whelan (1994). This survey allows some comparisons with an earlier survey by Breen and Rottman (1985).

The reporting and analysis of crime trends in Northern Ireland is even more bleak than for the Republic, because there has been no criminological research (one exception is the edited collection by Tomlinson, Varley and McCullagh, 1988, which includes some references to the North; the North also features in van Dijk, Mayhew and Killias, 1990). Most information on crime trends comes from officially published government sources. Northern Ireland has not had an equivalent to the British Crime Survey, which is carried out on a regular basis by the Home Office in England and Wales (although a survey of a similar nature was carried out in early 1995 and is currently undergoing analysis). The nearest equivalents have been the basic questions on crime contained in the Continuous Household Survey and the Northern Ireland Social Attitudes Survey, which are undertaken on a regular basis.

The dragons, as it were, have been removed recently by the authors' research (Brewer *et al.,* 1996) on comparative crime trends in Ireland between 1945 and 1995. The comparative focus was made possible because both parts of Ireland come from a common legal system which was in place before partition, resulting in broad concordance on crime classification, particularly up to 1987. The major index of crime used was indictable crime, which, since 1987, has been called notifiable crime in Northern Ireland, to bring recording measures in line with England and Wales.[1] In addition to

---

[1] Indictable crimes are crimes, usually of a more serious nature, which have to be recorded by the police, whether a suspect is charged or not, and while they have limitations as a measure of the 'real' level of crime, no other measure exists to permit comparisons over long periods of time. Summary crimes, for example, are usually those of a less serious nature (including assaults, minor offences of dishonesty, and road traffic offences) which are dealt with in a Magistrates Court or the District Court in the Republic of Ireland. They are often only recorded officially when a person is charged. They are even less reliable as an indication of levels of crime and ignored here. Since 1987 the Northern Ireland figures refer to notifiable

examining crime profiles at the national level we also compared similar trends for Belfast and Dublin, and for specific categories of crime over time, such as homicide, rape, burglary, drug offences and juvenile crime. Crime figures were located in a sociological profile, which included demographic changes, industrialisation, urbanisation, unemployment, the development of consumership, changes in transportation and other larger social changes, enabling us to examine the social indicators of crime in Ireland.

The problems of using official police statistics on crime are well known (for an overview see Bottomley and Pease, 1986; Breen and Rottman, 1984; Maguire, 1994; O'Mahony, 1993) and the practice of using officially recorded police statistics as an index of the real level of crime is highly suspect. Thus, it was necessary to supplement the official statistics with data from other sources where they existed, such as victim surveys and self-report delinquency studies. Although these measures are not without problems, their incorporation allowed a more critical assessment of the official figures and a better understanding of crime trends. Even so, statistics do not capture people's experiences of crime or how they manage crime locally in the absence of reporting it to the police. Thus, an important dimension of our study was ethnographic research in two closely matched areas of Belfast, enabling us to contrast largely Protestant east Belfast with largely Catholic west Belfast.[2] This research design enabled us to address crime in Ireland at national, city and local levels.

crimes—these are similar but slightly different from indictable crimes. The variation is marginal. Indictable crimes in the Republic are essentially those for which proceedings can or must be heard before a Crown Court. These include indictable motoring offences, such as reckless driving, which are excluded from notifiable crimes in Northern Ireland. Similarly, all criminal damage is included as indictable crime whereas only those where damage exceeds £200 are included as notifiable. The effect of this is that the number of notifiable crimes in Northern Ireland will be somewhat lower than in earlier periods when indictable crime was used to measure crime levels. Notifiable crimes are, nonetheless, the only measure available and are a useful proxy for the indictable classification used in earlier years. Furthermore, while indictable crime in the Republic of Ireland excludes some commonly committed crimes, it is the only measure on which there is a time series permitting comparison between the North and South of Ireland. Trends in crimes which are excluded from the indictable category in the Republic are dealt with fully elsewhere (see Brewer, Lockhart and Rodgers, 1996). References throughout the text to indictable crime are taken to include the change in nomenclature in Northern Ireland to notifiable crime.

[2] Ethnographic studies of criminal activity are common place, but research on related issues, such as how communities deal with their criminals in the absence of reporting them to the police, are less so. The ethnographic part of the study focused on issues such as people's perceptions of the crime problem in their locality, levels of fear of crime, people's reporting behaviour, local crime management in the absence of reliance on the police, the frames of reference through which people approach crime, such as perceived levels of crime in other societies or historical comparisons with the past, and people's fears about future crime in their areas after the ceasefire.

The recent emphasis in social science on the process of globalisation is affecting criminology, so that crime is increasingly being understood as part of a global process. Modernity, however, is at once both a globalising and localising process because it throws into sharper relief the differences that remain locally under broad social transformations, and criminology also stresses the importance of locality and place on crime ('environmental criminology' gives fullest expression to the importance of place on crime; for summary statements see Bottoms 1994; Bottoms and Wiles 1996). This paper considers some of the environmental dimensions to crime trends in Ireland. After a brief reference to crime at the beginning of the century, it concentrates on a statistical comparison of crime rates for indictable crime in the North and South of Ireland, and Belfast and Dublin, between 1945 and 1995 in order to illustrate some broad convergences in the experience of crime in the island. However, a comparison of crime rates North and South points to a paradox which highlights some of the peculiarities of Ireland. Brief reference is made to the ethnographic material, where we consider the influence of locality on experiences of crime and its management in Belfast. This suggests that criminological attention in Ireland should, in future, be focused as much on localities as on national trends.

Crime in Ireland at the Beginning of the Twentieth Century

Irish crime trends at the beginning of the twentieth century show the pattern that reflects crime at the end: it is overwhelmingly urban and dominated by property crime. In this, Ireland is typical of industrial societies generally. Rottman (1989) points out that in the nineteenth century, crime in Ireland was largely agrarian in origin and location, with many disputes over land tenure and boundaries. Interestingly, Irish urbanisation at the beginning of the twentieth century coincided with an initial decline in overall crime rates, although the pattern of crime reflected the influence of urbanisation, with a switch from violent crimes, such as murder and assault, towards property crime and a concentration of crime in urban areas. The large ports of Dublin and Belfast, indeed, had amongst the worst crime rates in the United Kingdom. In 1910, only Liverpool exceeded the indictable crime rates in Dublin and Belfast; Dublin's rate was three times higher than that for London, related to the fact that it was a garrison city and port. But because there were so few urban areas in Ireland, the overall level of crime for the country as a whole was low. Judicial statistics for the year 1915, for example, show a total of only 7,873 indictable offences for the whole of Ireland. Of these 31 per cent occurred in the Dublin Metropolitan Police District and 21 per cent in the Belfast city area. This meant that just over half of all the crime recorded in Ireland occurred in two urban areas. Extrapolating to the land areas which now form the Republic of Ireland and Northern Ireland, 5,231 (66 per cent) indictable crimes occurred in the South and 2,642 (34 per cent) in the North. Dublin accounted for 47 per cent of the crimes in the South and Belfast 66 per cent of the crimes in the North.

National Trends in Crime 1945 to 1995

Total levels of indictable crime in both jurisdictions for the period 1945 to 1995 reveal that at the beginning of the period, the figures for Northern Ireland were only about one third of those for the Republic (with 5,709 and 16,786 crimes respectively), which is similar to the case in 1915 and to be expected since Northern Ireland is much smaller in population. However, as the period progresses the differential becomes much less. Overall there was no substantial change in either jurisdiction between the late 1940s and the early 1960s, from whence crime increases markedly, although faster for the North. This rise continued almost unabated until 1983 in the Republic, when a peak of 102,387 indictable crimes was recorded. This was by any standards a huge increase from 1945 of more than sixfold. In Northern Ireland a peak came a little later in 1986, when a total of 68,255 indictable crimes was recorded. Since that time there have been modest drop backs, although by 1995 the total had again risen to a new peak of 68,808 crimes in Northern Ireland and 102,484 in the Republic of Ireland.

For comparative purposes, however, it is conventional to compare crime between countries or over periods of time in terms of the crime rate per 100,000 population. This gives a clearer picture than simply using incidence figures. Population estimates can be derived at any given time from census figures.[3] Figure 1 shows a graph of the number of indictable crimes per 100,000 population for both Northern Ireland and the Republic over the period 1945 to 1995. For most of the period up to 1960 the rates are fairly similar, after which Northern Ireland has had a consistently

---

[3] There have been regular censuses carried out in both parts of Ireland since the Second World War. In the Republic censuses have taken place every five years since 1946, with the exception of 1976 when the census was delayed until 1979; it resumed its five yearly cycle in 1981. In the North it was carried out every ten years during the period concerned, with an additional one in 1966. It is possible to retrospectively estimate population sizes on a mid-year annual basis by adjusting for births, deaths and migration figures. Clearly such adjustments can introduce a source of error. However, of greater concern is the considerable under-enumeration for the 1981 census in Northern Ireland when, because of civil unrest, large sections of the community refused to make census returns. Nonetheless, the estimates subsequently released are believed to be sufficiently accurate for estimating crime rates per 100,000 population.

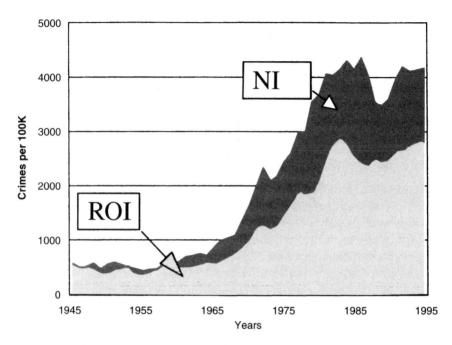

Figure 1.   Indictable/notifiable crimes per 100K population: ROI and NI 1945–1995. *Note*: NI = Northern Ireland, ROI = Republic of Ireland. *Sources*: RUC Chief Constable's Report and Gardai Report on Crime.

higher crime rate, although there have been substantial increases in both jurisdictions. Interestingly, in spite of the common belief that crime in Northern Ireland really only began to increase after the advent of 'the Troubles' in 1969, the rate in 1965 was already 53 per cent greater than that in the Republic. This differential grew to 60 per cent by 1985 and has remained at between half and two-thirds greater than that in the Republic throughout the period since 1965. The crime rate thus suggests there are some divergences in Northern Ireland's experiences of crime compared to the Republic.

Overall the indictable crime rate in the Republic grew by a factor of almost fivefold between 1945 and 1995, while that for Northern Ireland increased by almost ten times during the same period. By any standards these represent very considerable increases in both countries, and even more so for the North, although they would not be out of keeping with rises in the crime rate in other industrial societies over that time span. Comparable figures in England and Wales, for example, are 1,094 crimes per 100,000 in 1950 and 9,465 in 1995, an increase of almost ninefold. The comparative profiles of indictable crimes per 100,000 population for England and Wales, Northern Ireland and the Republic of Ireland are shown in Figure 2.

The comparison with England and Wales is worth emphasising. Crime rates rose in Ireland's nearest neighbour at nearly double the rate of the South, and on a par with the North, despite the quarter-century of civil unrest experienced in Northern Ireland. And the rise starts from a larger base in terms of gross number of crimes. If we look at the profile for recorded crime in England and Wales from 1946 to 1995, there are differences from that for Ireland. Crime has not risen in the two Irelands to the levels in England and Wales, and the rate began to rise steeply almost a decade later in Ireland. This reflects Ireland's late social and economic development; socio-economic changes into which rises in crime have to be located in industrial society occurred later in Ireland. This is characteristic of other islands on the fringe of Europe (for example Cyprus, Malta and Iceland) which have low crime rates in comparison to mainland countries. As another comparative case, crime in Sweden, in some respects a society similar to the Republic and also on the edge of Europe, saw an increase in recorded crime from the early 1950s, fifteen years or so before the Republic, although the rate of increase has been similar (Adler 1983, discusses Ireland as a low crime country).[4]

Variations in Crime at the City Level

It is worth examining trends at city level to demonstrate a further convergence in crime trends in both parts of Ireland and one which shows continuity down the century and further differences with crime trends in England and Wales. Patterns of urbanisation in both parts of Ireland are very similar, with a disproportionate amount of the urban population living in the capital city and surrounds, and crime trends in Belfast and Dublin dominate their respective national profile. The Gardai Commissioner's annual report normally cites the figures for recorded indictable crime in the Dublin area. From this it is possible to build a time series which allows the levels of indictable crime in Dublin to be compared with the levels recorded in the Republic as a whole. This has been done in Figure 3. The two profiles are very similar, demonstrating how strongly the incidence of crime in Dublin influences the profile for the whole country.

---

[4] The rate of increase in Sweden between 1950 and 1988 was fivefold, similar to that of the Republic but less steep than for Northern Ireland and England and Wales.

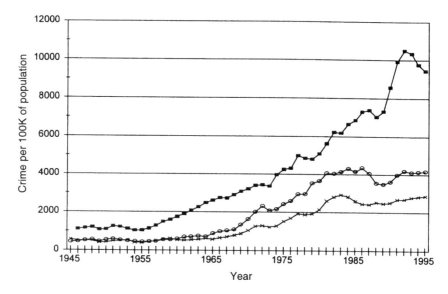

Figure 2. Indictable/notifiable crime per 100K of population: 1945–1995. (■) England and Wales, (○) Northern Ireland, (×) Republic of Ireland. *Sources*: Home Office Crime and Criminal Justice Unit: Research and Statistics Directorate.

Typically the incidence of crime in Dublin has been running at around 50–60 per cent of that of the whole country whereas, based on the 1991 census of population, the Dublin metropolitan area accounts for only 29.8 per cent of the total population.

It is instructive to convert the crime figures into prevalence rates per 1,000 population. Clearly the areas covered have changed boundaries over time, thus working out the population living there can be awkward. In more recent years the Gardai Commissioner's report has given indictable crime rates per 1,000 population by each police division. This is presented in modified form in Figures 4 and 5 for the period 1980–95 covering six geographic areas.[5] As expected the Dublin area has by far the greatest indictable crime rate per 1,000 population, followed by Cork East, which

---

[5] These areas were chosen to give a spread of different types of division. Limerick and Cork East represent the next largest cities to Dublin; Louth/Meath offers a reasonable sized east-coast division located North of Dublin and going right up to the border with Northern Ireland. It contains the sizable towns of Drogheda and Dundalk, the latter significantly affected by civil unrest in the North. By contrast Mayo is included to represent a large rural division in the West, without any large urban population centres.

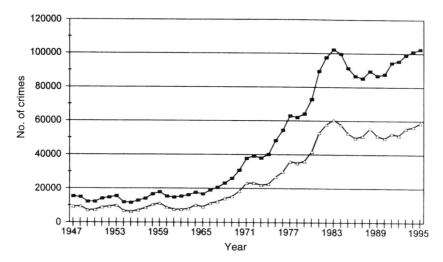

Figure 3. Indictable crime Republic of Ireland and Dublin: 1947–1995. (△) Dublin, (■) Republic of Ireland. *Sources*: Gardai Report on Crime and RUC Chief Constable's Report.

appears to have been experiencing substantial recent increases after a dip in the mid-1980s, which superficial evidence suggests might be due to police action against drug users and pushers. Limerick, by contrast, after peaking in 1982/83, has been showing significant decreases since then. Louth/Meath has had a fairly steady rate, averaging around 20 crimes per 1,000 during the period but still tends to be somewhat higher than the average for the rest of Ireland (excluding Dublin), perhaps reflecting both its relatively high urban population and the fact that the main road between Dublin and Belfast passes through a number of its urban centres. The police division with by far the lowest crime rate is Mayo. The crime rate has been uniformly low during the period and has not risen above 7.95 crimes per 1,000 population (in 1995) and was as low as 4.5 crimes in 1989. Although not shown in the figure, the only police division to rival the low crime rate of Mayo was Clare which had a crime rate of 11.8 in 1995. It is very apparent that crime tends to concentrate in large urban areas in the Republic. This is true for the North as well.

From the inception of the Northern Irish state in 1921 until 1970, the RUC was organised on a county basis, with the addition of two administrative areas for Belfast Borough Council and the Derry city area. There appear to be no published statistics based on these eight administrative areas, making it impossible to dissaggregate crime on a county

John D. Brewer, et al.

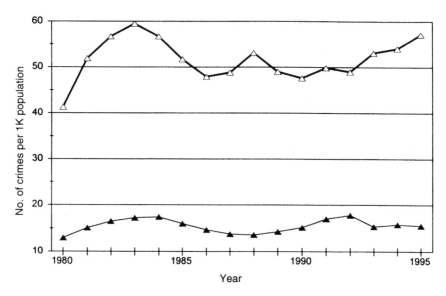

Figure 4. Indictable crime rates per 1K Republic of Ireland: Selected garda divisions. (△) Dublin MA, (▲) Outside Dublin MA. *Source*: Gardai Report on Crime.

basis.[6] Consequently, it is only since the restructuring of the RUC in 1970 that it is possible to get a break down of crime by police divisions. These divisions have been subject to significant changes in boundary since 1970, especially in 1990, which means that it is very difficult to construct a meaningful time series by region. This has been done for 1991 (after new divisional boundary changes) and 1995, as shown in Table 1.

The rank order by division for each year is largely similar. 'A' division recorded the highest number of notifiable offences in both 1991 and 1995, and covers the commercial centre of Belfast and also has a large number of public houses, clubs and places of entertainment. In both years the divisions covering the rural West of the province ('K' and 'L') had the lowest incidences of notifiable crime. If one combines the scores for the four Belfast divisions, Belfast accounts for 61.5 per cent of the total notifiable crime recorded in 1991 and 55 per cent in 1995 while having 42 per cent of the total population of Northern Ireland.

---

[6] It is known that at the opening of each county assizes the County Inspector of the RUC would give a report on crime to the presiding judge; however, extensive enquiries with the Public Records Office and the RUC Museum have unfortunately failed to uncover any of these reports.

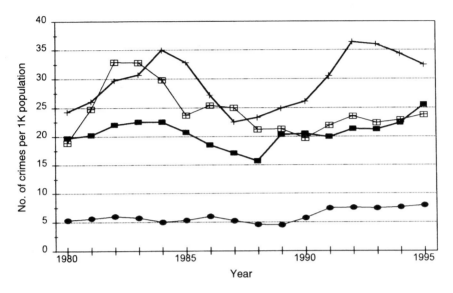

Figure 5. Indictable crime rates per 1K Republic of Ireland: selected garda divisions.
⊞ Limerick, (+) Cork East, (■) Louth/Meath, (●) Mayo. *Source*: Gardai Report on Crime.

Table 1. Breakdown of notifiable crime by RUC police divisions 1991 and 1995.

	Police division	Crimes known 1991	Crimes known 1995
A	(Musgrave St, Belfast)	13,838	12,252
B	(Grosvenor Rd, Belfast)	6,469	7,257
D	(Queen St, Belfast)	12,407	10,917
E	(Strandtown, Belfast)	6,315	7,133
G	(Newtownards)	3,429	5,073
H	(Armagh)	3,138	3,657
J	(Portadown)	3,546	3,603
K	(Cookstown)	1,630	2,310
L	(Enniskillen)	2,204	3,301
N	(Strand Road, Derry)	3,700	5,259
O	(Coleraine)	2,729	3,394
P	(Ballymena)	4,087	4,352

Source: Chief Constable's Reports.

This is characteristic of industrial societies generally because modern crime is overwhelmingly urban. However, the crime rate in Ireland's urban areas is still lower than in Britain's cities. If we compare the crime rates per 100,000 population in Belfast and Dublin in recent years, with those in Liverpool and Manchester, for example, we find that Irish cities have considerably lower rates. Figure 6 shows a

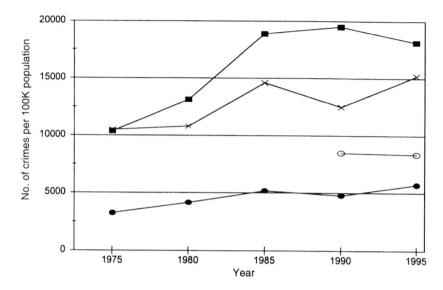

Figure 6. Indictable/notifiable crimes per 100K: Liverpool, Manchester, Belfast and Dublin. (×) Liverpool, (●) Dublin, (○) Belfast, (■) Manchester. *Sources*: RUC Statistics, Garda Report on Crime, Greater Manchester Police and Liverpool Constabulary.

plot over five-year intervals since 1975 for the four cities concerned, although the Belfast figures only start in 1990 because radical boundary changes from that year make it impossible to construct a time series before this. It can be safely concluded that the lower Irish crime rates are not simply a reflection of lower urbanisation in the island as a whole.

Victimisation Surveys

The crime rate for Dublin may be affected to an unknown degree by the exclusion of some popularly committed crimes, like drug offences, from the classification of indictable crime (although this does not distort statistics for Belfast), and by the under-reporting of crime that occurs in all official statistics. Victimisation surveys, however, support the contention that crime is lower in Ireland than elsewhere in the British Isles and under-reporting appears to occur less in Ireland than in Britain. There is no established tradition of victimisation studies in either part of Ireland, and nothing to compare to the regular national British crime surveys. Summarising the results from successive sweeps of the British crime survey, Maguire (1994) showed that there has been considerable under-reporting of crime in Britain, although much of the unreported crime is very petty in nature, with roughly one in every four crimes being reported to the police. Crime surveys in Britain also indicate that the increase in crime has been less steep than official statistics suggest, indicating that rapid rises have tended to occur more in those crimes that people feel are serious enough to report or have to report for insurance purposes (such as burglary and auto crime). Crime surveys and official statistics are both dominated by auto crime and both show low levels of violent crime; the main difference is that vandalism is much more prominent in crime surveys than in police statistics, reflecting its annoyance value to members of the public.

There are no time series victimisation surveys in Ireland, but Breen and Rottman (1985) did a pioneering snap-shot study in 1982/83, which allows some conclusions to be drawn. Comparing the victimisation results with Gardai figures for six specific crimes, they estimated that 88 per cent of burglaries are reported, 91 per cent of car theft but only 46 per cent of theft from around dwellings, for example, and 64 per cent of theft from persons. Comparing the incidence of crime in victimisation surveys in Ireland and Britain for four specific crimes, they concluded that the rate of incidence was higher in the Republic in all, save for theft from vehicles. Police statistics suggested the opposite, although differences in comparability of the surveys led them to qualify their remarks and their findings only related to four crimes. More recent surveys confirm the phenomenon of under-reporting but suggest, if anything, that crime rates in the Irish Republic flatter Britain rather than Ireland. Describing research undertaken in 1994, O'Connell and Whelan (1994) estimated that in Dublin the crime rate was 170 per 1,000 rather than the 49 suggested by Gardai figures. However, they argued that the level of disparity between victimisation survey data and official statistics on crime was less in Ireland than in Britain, estimating that one in three crimes are reported in the Republic compared to one in four in British surveys. Indeed, McCullagh claims that reporting in the Irish Republic is even higher than this but the Gardai fail to record many of the reported incidents (1996: 17). Thus, a comparison of crime rates in Ireland and Britain minimises rather than exaggerates the 'real' levels of crime in the two countries.

There is comparable data on Northern Ireland. Data from the Continuous Household Survey, which has fragmentary evidence on crime, shows that crime is under-reported, but suggests that more crime is reported than British surveys reveal. The Northern Ireland Office's 1986 commentary on Northern Irish crime statistics, for example, compared the data from Northern Ireland and Britain on four crimes in the early 1980s. Official statistics in Northern Ireland may under-estimate theft of vehicles by a factor of two and a factor of three for theft from vehicles. Similar under-reporting occurred in burglary for example, but the comparison shows that three-quarters of crime is reported in Northern Ireland, compared to 68 per cent in Britain, while 55 per cent of the reported incidents were recorded by the RUC compared to 48 per cent by local constabularies in Britain. Victimisation data showed that Northern Ireland experienced much less theft of, and from, vehicles than in Britain and slightly less burglary. This supports the conventional picture of lower crime rates in Northern Ireland compared to Britain. However, caution must be exercised in interpreting these results because the Continuous Household Survey is not designed as a victimisation survey. There are also important differences in methodology and procedure in all surveys, which makes comparison suspect.

Convergences and Paradoxes in Irish Crime Trends

Leaving aside comparisons with Britain, there are noteworthy similarities in crime between Northern Ireland and the Irish Republic. Rates of crime in the two parts of Ireland have a similar profile in incidence and rate of change. Crime rose in both Irelands at nearly the same time, from the late 1950s in the North and the mid-1960s in the Republic. Although increases occurred well before they are believed to have done by lay people, the rise was slightly later than other industrialised societies because of the slower rate of social change in Ireland. Levels of violent crime are higher in Northern Ireland than the South, linked to 'the Troubles' in the North; offences against the person, for example, comprise roughly one per cent of Dublin's total recorded crime, but are about 7 per cent of all recorded crimes in Northern Ireland. Rates for homicide, robbery and rape are all lower in the South. However, overall crime profiles in the two jurisdictions are similar because property crime so dominates crime trends in both societies. This ensures that most recorded crime in both societies is urban based and is not against the person. The main urban conurbation in each society has a disproportionate amount of the nation's crime because they provide an opportunity for property crime, but this skewed effect is about the same for Belfast as for Dublin. Violent crime is not disproportionately skewed toward the conurbations because its opportunity is unaffected by urban concentration. While crime is rising in both parts of Ireland, set in comparison to their European and Western neighbours, crime rates in Northern Ireland and the Republic are still lower, despite the fact that under-reporting of crime occurs in Ireland on a large scale. However, despite these convergences, there are critical differences in the crime rates of Northern Ireland and the Republic which point to some peculiarities within Ireland.

Between 1945 and 1960, the crime rate per 100,000 population in both parts of Ireland was very similar; it was never more than one third higher in one than the other and mostly only marginally different. They oscillated, sometimes annually, between who had the highest rate. However, from 1960 crime in Northern Ireland grew faster than in the Republic, so that the rate of crime per 100,000 of the population in the North rapidly outstripped that in the Republic, and it has been consistently greater ever since. The outbreak of civil unrest in 1968/69 reinforced what was already an identifiable trend, only widening the gap between their crime rates that had existed for a decade before. For a very long time, Northern Ireland was more industrialised and modernised than the Republic. Today it still remains more urbanised. The Republic's economic and cultural modernisation really only began in the late 1950s, at precisely the time when its crime rate was outstripped by Northern Ireland. Crime rates in the South rose as a result of these social and economic changes (see McCullagh, 1996: 30– 59), but they rose faster in the North. There are two puzzles within this one conundrum: why the Republic for a long time had a similar crime rate while ostensibly being a more traditional society than the North, and why they diverged just at the point when the Republic began to throw off its vestiges of tradition. This is paradoxical, for crime rates in Ireland appear to contradict conventional wisdom in the criminological literature that higher crime rates occur with industrialisation and modernisation.

However, the 'traditional' versus 'modern' dichotomy has long been abandoned in the development literature and its application to understanding social change in Ireland is particularly suspect. More complex transitions were occurring which help to explain the paradox of Irish crime rates. This divergence in crime rates must be set against a whole array of socio-economic, demographic and political changes which differentiated the two parts of Ireland. Northern Ireland's industrial development was characterised by its narrow economic base, dependent on the staple industries of shipbuilding, engineering and textiles. While these prospered, so did the Northern Ireland economy relative to the Republic's. Industrial output in Northern Ireland between 1950 and 1959 was almost double that of the Irish Republic and Northern Ireland had up to 75 per cent higher average income per head (O'Dowd, 1995: 140), although comparisons with Britain were to the disadvantage of the Northern Irish, with Northern Ireland always being the United Kingdom's poorest region (see Wichert, 1991: 66). Impressive though it was compared to the South however, Northern Ireland's industrialisation took on traditional forms, being structured by two solidaristic communities segregated by religion. Modernisation expressed itself in traditional form because it was structured by Northern Ireland's sectarian divide (a view particularly associated with the work of O'Dowd, 1986; 1995). Religious differences ensured the survival of separate communities, and through such processes as endogamy, residential segregation, distinct cultural and political associations and a segregated school system, the social organisation of the two communities ensured their effortless self-perpetuation in traditional forms. Industrialisation helped reproduce these traditional forms by reproducing sectarian division through largely segregated work-forces and communal patterns of recruitment, often reinforced by industrial development being located in one or other of the segregated communities. Industrial development in Northern Ireland thus took place in a way that helped to reproduce two close-knit, homogeneous, traditional communities divided by religion. Relative economic advancement compared to the South, from the 1920s onward, does thus not affect the judgment that Northern Ireland had deep elements of traditionalism, despite its impressive economic growth and development relative to the Irish Republic.

Moreover, the image of the Irish Republic up to the 1960s as a traditional society, often based on outdated anthropological studies of rural Ireland, is overdrawn (for a critical review of this anthropological literature see Fahey, 1995; Hannan, 1979; Tovey, 1992). Peasant proprietorship in rural Ireland was a very recent invention and undermined by massive depopulation. By 1960, researchers found demoralisation in the west of Ireland rather than a strong sense of tradition (see Gibbon, 1973). The typical peasant society of the west of Ireland had been in decline from the 1930s (Hannan, 1979: 18), class differences in rural areas had sharpened and depopulation ensured little continuity or stability in family and occupational structures (something evident in ethnographic fieldwork in the west of Ireland in 1975, see Curtin, 1988). There was massive internal migration to Dublin from rural areas in search of work, and a big turnover in the Dublin population due to emigration. Dublin holds a dominant position in Irish urbanism; half of the entire urban population resides in Dublin and surrounds, and its population is many times higher than the next largest city (see McKeown, 1986: 365). The transitory nature of Dublin's population due to emigration and seasonal labour migration can be unfavourably contrasted with the more stable Belfast population. Similarly, Irish Catholicism was a more 'modern' phenomenon than its continental counterparts in terms of moral and social attitudes and practices. Southern industry was not comprised of the substantial staple traditional sector, with stable patterns of communal recruitment, but more volatile smaller firms, often with short lifespans. The contrast in the crime rates of Northern Ireland and the Irish Republic up to the 1950s can thus be located in the different dynamics of their respective modernisation.

During the 1960s, however, Northern Ireland's industrial sector changed significantly with the decline in Northern Ireland's old staple industries and the growth of the service sector. With the decline of the traditional industries there simultaneously began an erosion of the traditional communities they helped to reproduce. The traditional forms in which industrialisation had up to that point occurred began to be replaced in the 1960s by a service and public sector that did not so readily reproduce close-knit, segregated traditional communities. Recruitment patterns were not so communally based and tended toward the employment of women and part-time labour. The religious social boundaries which defined these traditional communities also started to change as sectarian patterns were challenged in the 1960s by the rise of the Catholic middle class, improvements in Catholic access to higher education and the emergence of campaigns for civil rights. Therefore, Northern Ireland's move from traditionalism was as profound at this time as was that of the Irish Republic. This challenge to tradition in the 1960s coincided with social changes of other kinds. The North was more receptive than the Republic to the influence of British mass popular culture because of television, media and other cultural links with Britain, and thus also to the social changes in which Britain's own crime rise in the 1950s are located. The Republic of Ireland's susceptibility to British popular culture was inhibited, for example, by the fact that television was not introduced until 1962, and then there were only 127,000 television licences purchased in the entire country (McCullagh, 1996: 36), roughly 4.5 per cent of the total population, although the number of licences is likely to have an uncertain relationship to the number of sets.

There was also intensified emigration from the Republic in the 1950s, particularly of young adults, who are also the most likely to offend. The rate of emigration from the Irish Republic in this decade was the highest since the 1880s, and the 1956 population figure was the lowest recorded for any previous census. The South's total population decreased by 5 per cent between the census of 1951 and 1961 compared to an increase of 3.9 per cent in the North; the number of males decreased by 6.2 per cent in the South and increased by 4 per cent in Northern Ireland. Table 2 provides a comparison of the 1951 and 1961 census data for age distribution and shows that the proportion of young males was always smaller in the Republic than Northern Ireland and fell more dramatically in the ten-year period in the South; the number of males in the 25–9 cohort rose by two-thirds between 1951 and 1961 in Northern Ireland and fell by a fifth in the Republic.

John D. Brewer, et al.

Table 2. Percentage distribution of males in age groups 1951–61.

	15–19 years		20–24 years		25–29 years	
	1951	1961	1951	1961	1951	1961
Irish Republic	8.3	8.5	7.0	5.7	5.1	6.6
Northern Ireland	8.3	8.7	7.3	6.8	7.2	11.9

Source: Census 1951, 1961, Northern Ireland and Irish Republic.

Other demographic variations within the island are important. Differences in age structure of the populations can be a significant factor in explaining variations in crime rates. If one country has a higher proportion of children (defined officially as between 0–14 years) in the population it could have a lower rate of crime because such children are less likely to engage in indictable crime (as distinct from anti-social behaviour). The proportion of children (0–14 years) in both parts of Ireland at each common census between 1951 and 1991 reveals that the Republic has had a consistently higher number of children per 100,000 population than Northern Ireland, although the size of the difference is too small to be the major factor in explaining the large divergence in crime rates which emerged from the 1960s onwards.[7]

Political change also differentiated the two Irelands at this time. Once civil unrest broke in Northern Ireland at the end of the decade, the escalation in ordinary crime provoked by the violence widened the gulf in the crime rates between Northern Ireland and the Republic, although, paradoxically, the continuance of sectarian strife ensured that the remnant of these traditional close-knit communities survived, reducing the criminogenic effect of civil unrest. The Irish Republic surged ahead in terms of industrial development in the 1970s and 1980s: the industrial centre of gravity of the island shifted to the South by the mid-1970s, while Northern Ireland experienced continued deindustrialisation. Yet the crime rate in the Republic did not catch up that of the North because of civil unrest in Northern Ireland which increased the levels of ordinary crime. Therefore, crime in the South was on a par with the North before 1960 because its traditionalism was more apparent than real and because of the North's deep elements of traditionalism despite its apparent modernisation and urbanisation, and crime grew slower after 1960 because of the socio-

---

[7] Furthermore, the relatively large difference in number of children in the 1981 census should be treated with caution because of the under-enumeration which occurred in this census for Northern Ireland.

economic, demographic and political circumstances which differentiated it from Northern Ireland.

Locality and Place in Belfast

This section reports on some aspects of the ethnographic data.[8] It will not discuss criminal activity in Belfast but the related issue of crime management, which is much neglected in the criminological literature. This focus helps to inform interpretation of crime trends in Ireland because it illustrates how crime in Belfast is differentially experienced among people and places and how crime statistics are socially constructed by the public's willingness to report crime to the police. This is of particular importance in Northern Ireland because crime management is contested. 'Official' crime management by the RUC is challenged by 'popular' or local forms, and a consideration of 'popular' crime management in Belfast confirms the marked differences that exist in the local experiences of crime within one city, let alone in Ireland as a whole compared to other industrialised societies. It illustrates that some areas within the same city have had different fortunes under modernity, making them better able to respond to or cope with criminogenic processes. The local experience of crime in Belfast is that the criminogenic tendencies of social change are being mediated in some localities by social processes which reflect the persistence of social control, slowing the rate of social breakdown, with obvious effects on crime and its management.

In effect, very traditional communities have persisted in the North, based on the traditional forms within which its modernisation occurred in earlier decades. This helps to explain why Belfast, for example, has a lower crime rate per 100,000 of population than Liverpool or Manchester, despite a quarter-century and more of civil unrest, although the rate is higher than that of Dublin. It is not just the case, therefore, that the persistence of traditional communities in Belfast displaces crime elsewhere (which it does), it also helps relatively to suppress it and thus counter-act

---

[8] Data were collected exclusively by the use of in-depth interviews, which were conducted solely by one of the authors. Interviews were conducted with 115 individuals and with ten groups. Interviews were recorded on tape, except where people objected. There are ninety-two hours of tape recordings. Two closely matched study areas were selected, based on police subdivisional areas, one each in largely Protestant east Belfast and largely Catholic west Belfast, although we also gave attention to enclave areas within each. We worked through local community groups, enabling us to select a cross-section of client groups and avoid political unrepresentativeness. Both study areas included a variety of housing areas, extending from inner city to suburban areas. Interviews took place over twelve months between 1994/95, with six months spent in each area. The paramilitary ceasefire pertained for most of this period, facilitating candour amongst respondents.

the criminogenic tendencies that exist in the city. These traditional social forms have a profound effect on crime management. By the local management of crime, we mean those structures in the local neighbourhood and community which have a role in preventing and suppressing crime and offer alternative ways of dealing with it once committed. Not all localities in our two study areas contained these structures, so that popular crime management is a localised phenomenon, structured by processes embedded primarily in the communal structures and class dynamics of certain neighbourhoods within our two study areas. Most elderly respondents sensed a loss of community, but other respondents in certain neighbourhoods recognised that community structures in the locality had survived, such as extended family kinship patterns, a strong sense of neighbourliness and a vivid sense of locality and community identity. It is within these social processes that 'popular' crime management is sociologically embedded, illustrating that it extends beyond the policing role of paramilitary organisations.

Senses of community and neighbourhood identity are very localised, contingent upon the frames of reference people use, the locality in which they live and personal experiences of the quality of relationships that exist in their neighbourhood. Local experiences of community were mediated by class, being stronger in the inner city and working-class neighbourhoods in our study areas, and by the senses of community that survived in these localities. Social change, population relocation and housing redevelopment have affected localities in varying degrees, but not everywhere have they destroyed a sense of community and local identity.

People from most west Belfast neighbourhoods portray the areas as having a strong sense of community. Community is not experienced in the same way as it was in the past, but most people in west Belfast, save the elderly, recognise that it has not been lost. This sense of community is on the whole weaker in parts of east Belfast, where there is a sense of greater social change, housing relocation and social dislocation. Neighbourhoods there have not lived under the same sense of siege. Far greater numbers of residents from the east Belfast study area reflected on a decline in the sense of community in their neighbourhood. A resident said, 'I think the community spirit is not as strong now. People tend to keep themselves to themselves. Years ago everybody minded everybody else's business, if you saw a child misbehaving you disciplined it'. However, there are localities in east Belfast where people commented that community structures had survived. Some people live in working-class neighbourhoods where the old streets have not been redeveloped. One resident described his area: 'a lot of good living people, close-knit families, not a lot of movement, so people have been here for several generations, there is a stable social fabric.'

Local crime management is rooted in the social processes related to community and local identity, neighbourliness and an extended family kinship pattern. These processes provide, first, for the survival of a local moral economy. The values of this moral economy were expressed most frequently in the form that 'you don't steal from your own'. This runs entirely counter to local crime surveys in Britain, which show that most crime is committed by locals from the neighbourhood. In summarising results from crime surveys, Maguire (1994: 265–6) argued that most crime in Britain is predatory, it involves a continuing relationship between offender and victim, and the most vulnerable are people in council-owned dwellings primarily from people like themselves. Members of a mother and toddler group on a large housing estate in west Belfast explained, however, that 'you would get people in the private estates to talk more about crime, they're more burgled than we are. Off the record, we are sort of cocooned from criminals, they don't steal from their own'. An east Belfast worker with young offenders repeated the view: 'individuals who commit the crime have a lot of respect for the area that they live in, they don't break in in their own area.' This moral economy therefore rules out crime in certain close-knit areas, at least by its own local criminals, displacing it elsewhere. But it also rules out crime against certain categories of people who are protected by the local moral economy. Thus, several people identified that crimes against children, the elderly and Church property were defined as beyond acceptable bounds locally. An east Belfast community worker said of his neighbourhood: 'this is a parochial community around here and if the crime is against a pensioner, nobody will be spared. I have known a case where a parent actually contacted the police when they found out that their son had broken into a pensioner's house.'

This moral economy only works for criminals who are from the area and who share the code. Local crime is often perpetrated by outsiders who are escaping the constraints of the moral economy in their area or by people who do not subscribe to the code. The anti-social behaviour by local youths inflicted on elderly people, for example, seems to suggest that the values are not shared by all. Changes are occurring in the moral economy as structural adaptations to the changed circumstances young unemployed people find themselves in, and some people comment on the decline in the ethical code of local lags. But even if local criminals defy the code, the existence of a moral economy results in greater outrage, with its knock-on effects of increased effort to apprehend them by the community itself or by the paramilitaries, or successfully overcoming resistance to involve the police in official crime management.

Another factor involved in local crime management that arises from the survival of community structures is the existence of a 'local grapevine', a

network of informal contacts which passes on knowledge about perpetrators, the whereabouts of stolen property, and of the sorts of people who can
best apprehend or provide immediate satisfactory justice in the absence of
reporting it to the police. The grapevine is also the mechanism by which the
local moral economy is socially disseminated. As a resident from west
Belfast said, 'if a crime happened against an old person or a child, maybe
if it happened in [name of area], everybody would be talking about it'. A
young adult from west Belfast indicated how the grapevine worked even on
a large estate. 'Although this is a large estate, there is always somebody who
knows something, always somebody. There is not too many people that
keep things to themselves. There is always "did you hear about that", and
then it works its way around the grapevine.' The grapevine ensures that
knowledge is passed on to victims or even the relatives of perpetrators,
which is where neighbourliness and an extended family kinship network
come in particularly useful in local crime management. A very young girl,
associated with a youth club in west Belfast, described how this network of
contacts constrained her. Referring to possible victims of crime she said,
'they would always know who you are or know your ma or something. This
is a close knit community and people often do tell your ma or friends of
your ma sees you'.

This permits do-it-yourself policing. Many respondents told of how
they responded as victims when they knew the perpetrator as a result of
the local grapevine. Some went straight to the paramilitaries, some to the
police. Others, however, used the neighbourhood's network of informal
contacts to confront the parents. A member of a women's group in west
Belfast, explained how she would respond: 'you wouldn't like to see a child
get punished in a beating, you wouldn't like to see your own harmed, so we
went around and let the parents know.' A women from east Belfast said the
same, 'you would just go to the family'. Do-it-yourself policing thus
depends for its efficacy precisely on the survival of neighbourhood
networks.

Because a sense of community survives, the neighbourhood is able to be
readily mobilised to manage crime locally. One of the resources that can be
mobilised is the remnant of legitimate authority which community representatives still possess, such as teachers, priests and pastors, and community and youth workers. This authority has diminished compared to the
past, since many people experience social change as a decline in respect for
authority among the young, but the data reveal that many of these figures
are still drawn into the management of crime. A youth worker in east
Belfast, for example, explained how local people have come to her to
deal with specific incidents concerning youngsters rather than go to the
police. Clerics repeated the point. A priest in west Belfast said he was like a

policeman sometimes, being called out before the RUC: 'the people wouldn't ring the police, they'd ring you directly, you got out and you went and dealt with it.' Other community resources that can be mobilised in local crime management are the skills, finances and manpower of community organisations in the development and servicing of local initiatives against crime.

Social changes wrought by twenty-five years of civil unrest therefore have clearly not eroded some forms of social control in certain parts of Belfast, furnishing effective mechanisms for popular crime management in some localities. Social change has facilitated local crime management in another way, because different mechanisms have developed as adaptations to new structural conditions. Most notable of these new mechanisms are the paramilitary organisations. Their role in local crime management is heavily conditional upon the social processes associated with community structures. These networks disseminate the information that makes paramilitary policing possible and efficacious, and provides the push for the paramilitary organisations to engage in it in the first place.

Some respondents extolled the contribution made by the paramilitaries to the relatively low crime rate in their area: 'I think it is to the credit of the IRA that crime has been kept so low, because it has nothing to do with the RUC, absolutely not.' In east Belfast the paramilitaries were described by several people as the unofficial police force. 'The paras get things done', said one youth worker, 'things are done'. Some of the policing methods by which paramilitaries 'get things done' depend in part upon social processes associated with community structures in local neighbourhoods. One method is that of 'shaming', particularly associated with Republican paramilitaries, which requires for its effectiveness that communal disgrace will be experienced as a constraint by offenders. In west Belfast people have been forced to stand in public places (especially outside churches and supermarkets) with placards; some are tied to lamp posts to ensure they stay put. There is also a primitive 'house protection scheme', whereby paramilitary organisations place a sticker in the window of a house warning that criminals enter at their peril. Mostly, however, people perceive force as the main policing method of the paramilitaries. Some people perceive that this force comes in proportional degrees depending on the circumstances of the crime and the criminal background of the perpetrator, although others claim it to be quite arbitrary (on the gradation in paramilitary punishment beatings see Thompson and Mulholland, 1995). These informal disciplines almost appear as a form of customary law in a situation where state law is deemed to be without legitimacy or effect, making them similar to disciplines used by indigenous groups in North America and Australasia.

Local crime management is thus a phenomenon embedded in communal structures that are localised to specific places in Belfast, depending upon experiences of class, communal development, population relocation and other social transformations locally. Civil unrest, however, has also played its part in differentiating local experiences of crime management. In certain neighbourhoods 'the Troubles' have had the effect of inhibiting the processes of social dislocation and community breakdown. In some areas where it is most intense, civil unrest has produced a voluntary ghettoisation by restricting geographic mobility and population relocation, producing socially homogeneous districts in religious, ethnic and class terms. In-group solidarity has been reinforced by conflict with an out-group. This cohesion is reflected in structures such as the survival of extended kinship networks, close-knit neighbourhood structures and a sense of living in solidaristic communities, with their own local moral economy. Other ethnographies of crime in working-class neighbourhoods, for example, show them to be less vibrant and communal as equivalent localities in our study areas (see, for example, Robins, 1992, and Williams, 1989). Some of this is due also to benevolent housing policy (Northern Ireland has not seen the infamous tower block to any great extent) or employment restrictions on geographic mobility. Northern Ireland is also small, so families tend not to be disrupted even where geographic mobility occurs. For all these reasons, some localities in Belfast have not experienced social dislocation and breakdown.

Conclusion

Crime rates in Ireland have some interesting features when set against those of neighbouring countries, and a comparison between the two parts of Ireland illustrates how crime needs to be located in the socio-economic, demographic and political circumstances which differentiate North and South. Crime trends in Ireland, however, also need to be contextualised by understanding the social behaviours and communal structures which differentiate localities in modern Ireland. The local experience of crime in some areas of Belfast, for example, is that the criminogenic tendencies of social change are being mediated by social processes which reflect the persistence of social control, slowing the rate of social breakdown, with obvious effects on crime and its management. The future of criminological research in Ireland lies in identifying these micro-environmental variations in order to better understand the social behaviours that go to make up trends in Irish crime rates.

References

Adler, F. (1983) *Nations not Obsessed with Crime*, Littleton, Col.: Rothman.

Bottomley, K. and Pease, K. (1986) *Crime and Punishment: Interpreting the Data*, Milton Keynes: Open University Press.

Bottoms, A. (1994) 'Environmental Criminology' in M. Maguire, R. Morgan and R. Reiner (eds), *The Oxford Handbook of Criminology*, Oxford: Oxford University Press.

Bottoms, A. and Wiles, P. (1996) 'Explanations of Crime and Place', in J. Muncie, E. McLaughlin and M. Langan (eds), *Criminological Perspectives*, London: Sage.

Breen, R. and Rottman, D. B. (1984) 'Counting Crime: Potentials and Pitfalls', *Social Studies*, 7: 271–81.

Breen, R. and Rottman, D. B. (1985) *Crime Victimisation in the Republic of Ireland*, General Research Series, Paper No. 121, Dublin: ESRI.

Brewer, J. D., Lockhart, B. and Rodgers, P. (1996) *Crime in Ireland since the Second World War*, Belfast: Northern Ireland Office.

Curtin, C. (1988) 'Social Order, Interpersonal Relations and Disputes in a West of Ireland Community', in M. Tomlinson, T. Varley and C. McCullagh (eds), *Whose Law and Order?*, Belfast: Sociological Association of Ireland.

Dooley, E. (1995) *Homicide in Ireland 1972–1991*, Dublin: Stationery Office.

Fahey, T. (1995) 'Family and Household in Ireland', in P. Clancy, S. Drudy, K. Lynch and L. O'Dowd (eds), *Irish Society: Sociological Perspectives*, Dublin: Institute of Public Administration.

Gibbon, P. (1973) 'Arensberg and Kimball Revisited', *Economy and Society*, 2: 479–98.

Hannan, D. (1979) *Displacement and Development: Class, Kinship and Social Change in Irish Rural Communities*, Paper no. 96, Dublin: ESRC.

Maguire, M. (1994) 'Crime Statistics, Patterns and Trends: Changing Perceptions and their Implications', in M. Maguire, R. Morgan and R. Reiner (eds), *The Oxford Handbook of Criminology*, Oxford: Oxford University Press.

Maguire, M., Morgan, R., and Reiner, R. (eds) (1994) *The Oxford Handbook of Criminology*, Oxford: Oxford University Press.

McCullagh, C. (1996) *Crime in Ireland: A Sociological Profile*, Cork: University of Cork Press.

McKeown, K. (1986) 'Urbanisation in the Republic of Ireland: a Conflict Approach', in P. Clancy, S. Drudy, K. Lynch and L. O'Dowd (eds), *Ireland: A Sociological Profile*, Dublin: Institute of Public Administration.

O'Connell, M. and Whelan, A. (1994) 'Crime Victimisation in Ireland', *Irish Criminal Law Journal*, 4: 85–112.

O'Dowd, L. (1986) 'Beyond Industrial Society', in P. Clancy, S. Drudy, K. Lynch and L. O'Dowd (eds), *Ireland: A Sociological Profile*, Dublin: Institute of Public Administration.

O'Dowd, L. (1995) 'Development or Dependency? State, Economy and Society in Northern Ireland', in P. Clancy, S. Drudy, K. Lynch and L. O'Dowd (eds), *Irish Society: Sociological Perspectives*, Dublin: Institute of Public Administration.

O'Mahony, P. (1993) *Crime and Punishment in Ireland*, Dublin: Round Hall Press.

Robins, D. (1992) *Tarnished Vision: Crime and Conflict in the Inner City*, Oxford: Oxford University Press.

Rolston, B. and Tomlinson, M. (1982) 'Spectators at the "Carnival of Reaction"? Analysing Political Crime in Ireland', in M. Kelly, L. O'Dowd and J. Wickham (eds), *Power, Conflict and Inequality*, Dublin: Tureo Press.

Rottman, D. B. (1980) *Crime in the Republic of Ireland: Statistical Trends and their Interpretations*, General Research Series, Paper No. 102, Dublin: ESRI.

Rottman, D. B. (1989) 'Crime in Geographical Perspective', in W. Carter and A. Parker (eds), *Ireland: Contemporary Perspectives on the Land and its People*, London: Routledge.

Thompson, W. and Mulholland, B. (1995) 'Paramilitary Punishments and Young People in West Belfast', in L. Kennedy (ed.), *Crime and Punishment in West Belfast*, Belfast: The Summer School, West Belfast.

Tomlinson, M., Varley, T. and McCullagh, C. (1988) *Whose Law and Order?*, Belfast: Sociological Association of Ireland.

Tovey, H. (1992) 'Rural Sociology in Ireland: a Review', *Irish Journal of Sociology*, 2: 96–121.

Van Dijk, J. J. M., Mayhew, P. and Killias, M. (1990) *Experiences of Crime Across the World*, Deventer: Kluwer Law.

Wichert, S. (1991) *Northern Ireland Since 1945*, London: Longman.

Williams, T. M. (1989) *The Cocaine Kids: The Inside Story of a Teenage Drug Ring*, Reading, Mass.: Addison-Wesley.

Educational Inequality in Ireland, North and South

RICHARD BREEN, ANTHONY F. HEATH
& CHRISTOPHER T. WHELAN

Introduction

OVER THE COURSE OF THE POST-WAR PERIOD all economically advanced societies have expanded their provision of public education. This has led to increased rates of educational participation among their populations. Such expansion, however, does not necessarily imply a reduction in class differentials and the issue of persisting class barriers to educational participation and attainment has, in recent years, generated a good deal of debate, at the centre of which have been differing expectations concerning the consequences of the social and economic changes experienced by industrial societies (Shavit and Blossfeld, 1993).

On the one hand, the 'liberal theory' of industrialisation views the expansion of the educational system as a response to the functional requirements of industrial society. From this perspective, ascription gives way to achievement as educational qualifications become more important for occupational placement and educational selection becomes more meritocratic. On the other hand, it is argued that this approach takes too simplistic a view of the extent to which the forces of competition will lead to change in the process of social reproduction. Educational attainment is only one among several strategies that can be used in seeking to attain a more desirable occupation and privileged groups within society possess the capacity to adjust such strategies in the light of changing circumstances. As a result the liberal theory underestimates the extent to which education will come to be not only a means by which people can be allocated to jobs but also a factor mediating and, to a degree, maintaining class privilege (Erikson and Goldthorpe, 1993: 303–7).

Proceedings of the British Academy, **98**, 187–213. © The British Academy 1999.

As Erikson and Jonsson (1996: 47) note, the Republic of Ireland provides a particularly appropriate test of the ascription to achievement hypothesis since, as a consequence of late and rapid industrialisation, recent surveys include cohorts whose members have experienced the transformation of agrarian society alongside those whose formative experiences preceded such change. Even by 1960, 36 per cent of males at work in the Republic were either themselves self-employed in agriculture or were occupied in assisting self-employed relatives. By 1990 this figure had been halved. Associated with this transformation of the occupational structure was a growth in the importance of educational qualifications as a means of acquiring a position.

Northern Ireland provides a point of comparison with the Republic of Ireland in assessing the move from ascription to achievement as well as being an interesting test case in its own right. Here, free post-primary education was introduced some 20 years earlier than in the South. However, although Northern Ireland has the same examination system—namely GCSE and A-level—as England and Wales, its educational system continues to be organised selectively, with pupils allocated to more or less academically orientated post-primary schools on the basis of tests taken at the age of 11. Thus a comparison between the systems of Northern Ireland and of England and Wales could yield a potentially interesting study of the effects of institutional selectivity within a common examination system (though we do not pursue this issue here).

In this paper our primary goal is to examine how class and gender differentials in educational attainment may have changed over the course of the second half of this century in Ireland, North and South. Do the rather different institutional arrangements for post-primary education in the two parts of the island give rise to differences between them, or does the logic of industrialism impose on them a commonality irrespective of such differences? Our secondary goal is to examine whether (and, if so, how), within Northern Ireland, educational inequality between the two major ethnic groups—Protestants and Catholics—has shown any signs of change over the same period.

We begin with a brief description of the educational systems in the two parts of Ireland. We then go on to discuss our data and the methods of analysis we employ. The results of our two analyses—the North/South comparison and the comparison of Catholics with Protestants in Northern Ireland—follow. The paper concludes with a summary of our findings.

The Development of the Educational Systems of Ireland

Northern Ireland

Our analysis of educational attainment in Northern Ireland is based on respondents who received their post-primary education within the system established after the Northern Ireland Education Act of 1947 (which was very similar to the 1944 Act applying to England and Wales). Following this Act post-primary education was reorganised into a tripartite structure, comprising grammar, secondary intermediate and technical intermediate schools (Dunn, 1993). Selection into grammar schools was by means of the so-called '11-plus' exam. Between 1948 and 1965 this consisted of tests in arithmetic and English supplemented by an intelligence test. From 1966 onward the selection procedure used a combination of scores on two verbal reasoning tests and scaled rankings from the primary school of pupils' suitability for a grammar school course (Sutherland, 1993: 108). The procedure was further amended in 1990 but this is not relevant to our analysis since the youngest members of our sample would have transferred to post-primary education no later than 1981.[1]

The other major change of relevance to our study is the raising of the minimum school leaving age from 15 to 16 in the school year 1972/73. This would have affected the youngest cohort in our data, the oldest of whom would have reached the age of 15 in 1973. We therefore might expect to see some change in the pattern of educational attainment among this cohort.

Within the post-primary educational system of Northern Ireland, Protestants and Catholics are, by and large, educated separately.[2] This arose as a result of historical opposition to the state's attempts to establish a non-denominational system of schools. Three types of school evolved: controlled, maintained and voluntary, each differing in its management and financial structures. Controlled schools are almost all Protestant; maintained schools are almost all Catholic, while voluntary schools are all grammar schools and can be either Catholic or Protestant. Figures for 1993/94 indicate that 98.6 per cent of pupils attended schools in the controlled, maintained or voluntary sector. Only 1.4 per cent of pupils attended integrated schools (Breen and Devine, 1999).

It is widely accepted that under the Stormont regime (1922–71) Catholics were subject to discrimination in housing, the labour market and in the electoral system (Whyte, 1983; 1990). It was also the case that, until very recently, Catholic maintained schools received less generous state support

---

[1] See Sutherland, 1993: 109 for details.

[2] This segregation is less marked at the primary level and does not extend to the higher or further education sectors.

than so-called controlled (but in effect, Protestant) schools. It is therefore of interest to compare Catholic and Protestant educational attainment. Furthermore, in recent years there has been a noted growth in the size of the Catholic middle class (Cormack and Osborne, 1994; O'Connor, 1993), which is believed to have come about primarily through increasing levels of educational attainment among Catholics. This has obvious implications for the Protestant/Catholic comparison but it may also have implications for the trend in the relationship between class origins and education.

In addition to focusing on class, we also look at the impact of gender. One of the most striking shifts in patterns of educational attainment over recent years has been the very rapid erosion of gender differentials that formerly favoured men over women. In Northern Ireland, examination results show that gender and religion enjoy a complex relationship. This is then reflected in the finding that the Catholic middle class, when compared with its Protestant counterpart, contains a much higher proportion of women (Duffy and Evans, 1997). This also points to the possibility of a complex pattern of change in the relationship between class origins and educational attainment that varies by both religion and gender.

The Republic of Ireland

A separate vocational/technical school system had also been present in the Republic of Ireland from the mid-nineteenth century onwards, but was greatly strengthened and expanded after the 1930 Vocational Education Act. These schools had separate vocationally oriented curricula and a specific final examination—the Group Certificate. Although both curriculum and examination were nationally standardised, they were directed towards the needs of local labour markets (Coolahan, 1981; Hannan and Boyle, 1987). Vocational schools were predominantly working class in composition, even to the extent of the social origins and separate vocational/technical training of the bulk of their teachers. These schools were free—at least up to the age of 14. By contrast, secondary schools provided access to university education and to a range of white-collar occupations and were mainly middle class in social composition. Such schools charged fees until the late 1960s, although these were often quite modest.

In 1967 all post-primary education was made free of charge through the replacement of secondary-school fees with an annual state capitation grant (though a small number of secondary schools remained outside the 'Free Scheme' and continued to charge fees). At the same time free transport to school was also made available to all pupils. These reforms were quickly followed by curricular and examination reforms which incorporated the vocational system into the mainstream second-level system and allowed them, for the first time, to teach the full range of secondary subjects leading to a common examination system. Community and comprehensive schools were established which integrated the curricula of both pre-existing school types.

There has been a rapid growth in educational participation levels since 1960. Currently almost all students remain at school to sit for the Junior Certificate examination, usually taken around age 15, and almost 80 per cent of boys and 90 per cent of girls take the Leaving Certificate (the terminal post-primary examination) at age 17 or 18. Following the reforms of the 1960s there was disproportionately rapid growth among community and comprehensive schools. Nevertheless, the voluntary secondary sector still has around two-thirds of all pupils. Furthermore, most of the growth in senior cycle provision in the comprehensive sector has been in academic, rather than technical subjects as these schools have come into competition for pupils with secondary schools.

The reforms of the 1960s were, in part, a response to research which showed the high degree of class differentiation that was characteristic of local secondary and vocational schools at that time. Despite the growth in educational participation since that time, these sorts of distinction are still evident. Active selection of local schools by parents is the norm, particularly among the middle class, in the absence of any state regulation of local inter-school competition. As a result vocational schools report severe local competition for pupils—a competition in which they suffer most from 'cream-off' (Hannan *et al.*, 1996). The result is the persistence of class differences in the composition of secondary and vocational schools. On average, half of the intake of secondary schools comes from the middle class compared with 25 per cent in vocational schools. Fifty-five per cent of the pupil intake to the latter are drawn from the working class as against just over 30 per cent for secondary schools (Ibid.: 82). Besides this class selectivity, selection on the basis of academic criteria is almost as marked. One-third of the intake to vocational schools have general ability scores one standard deviation below the average, while this holds for just over 10 per cent of those in secondary schools (Ibid.: 86).

Data, Variables and Method

Data for the Republic of Ireland come from the Living in Ireland Survey which was conducted in 1994 by The Economic and Social Research Institute, Dublin. The survey provides a random sample of non-institutional households and of adult members within such households.

The data have been reweighted in line with independent population estimates.[3] Restricting our analysis to those aged between 25 and 49 years yields 4,994 valid cases. We confine our analysis to this range because at ages less than 25 a large proportion of respondents would still be in full-time education, while for older respondents information concerning father's class background is not available in the Northern Ireland data.

Data for Northern Ireland come from the annual Northern Ireland Continuous Household Survey (CHS) which is closely modelled on the General Household Survey (GHS) in Britain. Interviews are carried out with all adults in a simple random sample of households in Northern Ireland and the data include a record for each resident in the sampled households. We use five rounds of the survey: 1986, 1987, 1988, 1989–90 and 1990–91.[4] In total there are 17,528 respondents. When we omit those for whom we lack relevant information this is reduced to 13,649.

In our comparative analysis we use four variables. These are the cohort in which the respondent was born, the respondent's gender, highest educational qualification achieved, and social class origins.

The three birth cohorts are 1937–43; 1944–56; and 1957–70. In the North the final cohort would have been the only one potentially to benefit from the raising of the school-leaving age and, similarly, in the South, this is the only cohort that could have taken advantage of the introduction of free post-primary education in 1967. We should therefore expect that, if any changes over time are to be found, they will be evident in the comparison between the two older and the youngest cohort.

Our measure of highest educational qualification distinguishes four levels:

> *No Qualification.* In both Northern Ireland and the Republic of Ireland this includes anyone terminating their post-primary education without a qualification.
> *Junior Cycle Qualification.* In the North this comprises apprenticeships, CSE, GCSE, O-level or equivalent. In the South it covers those with the Intermediate, Group or Junior Certificate.
> *Senior Cycle Qualification.* For Northern Ireland this is defined as A-level or equivalent (such as HNC) and all qualifications above A-level but less than a degree (for example, nursing qualifications). In the South it includes the Leaving Certificate, Post-Leaving Certificate courses and non-degree third level qualifications.
> *University Degree.* In both cases this includes a university first or higher degree.

---

[3] Further details of the sample are provided in Callan *et al.*, 1996.

[4] Data are also available for the 1991–92 survey but neither father's socio-economic group nor the information needed to code it are available.

The class origins variable is based on the categorisation of father's socio-economic group (SEG) in the North[5] and, in the South, on detailed occupational information about the main breadwinner in the family when the respondent was growing up. Both have been recoded to the CASMIN class schema (Erikson and Goldthorpe, 1992). We employ a five-category version of the schema in our analysis with the constituent classes of the CASMIN schema indicated below by Roman numerals.

Professional and Managerial or Service Class (I + II)
Routine Non-Manual Class (IIIa)
Petty Bourgeoisie, including farmers (IV)
Skilled Manual (V/VI)
Non-Skilled Manual (IIIb + VIIa+b)

For analyses within Northern Ireland we draw the further distinction between Catholics and Protestants. For our purposes, origin religion (that is, the religion in which the respondent was raised) is the relevant variable, although the data refer to *current* religion. Given the very low rates of inter-religious mobility in Northern Ireland (Breen and Hayes, 1996), its use as a proxy for origin religion is not problematic. The exception is those who report themselves as having no religion. We know (Ibid.) that around 99 per cent of Northern Ireland adults were born into a Christian religion; accordingly we exclude those of no religion from our analysis. We also exclude those of non-Christian religions, many of whom were probably not brought up in Northern Ireland and who, in any case, comprise a very small group.

Our analysis is based on the so-called 'Mare model' (Mare 1980; 1981) which focuses on the odds of attaining a given educational level, conditional on having attained the previous level. In this model our four educational levels define three transitions: from no qualifications to a junior cycle qualification; from junior to senior cycle qualifications; and from senior cycle to a degree. This model follows from a random utility specification in which the decisions to continue to a further level of education are made sequentially (Pudney, 1989: Chapter 3). That is to say, pupils and their families decide whether to continue to the next level of education,

---

[5] In the CHS if the respondent's father is not resident in the same household information for coding father's SEG is requested from the respondent. If the respondent's father is in the same household, this information is included in the father's own record. It thus becomes necessary to take this information from his record and attach it to the respondent's. We are grateful to Naomi McCay for doing this. In addition, the recorded SEG in the CHS data does not distinguish subgroups within groups 1 and 2 (employers and managers) and 5 (intermediate non-manual) according to number of workers employed or supervised. We are grateful to Iain Bryson and Naomi McCay for adding these distinctions to the data set.

given that they have completed the current level. This is a more plausible behavioural assumption than that which underlies the use of a multinomial or ordered logit model, since these models would imply that the decision of which educational level to attain is made at the outset of an individual's educational career.

Trends in Educational Attainment

In our analysis of trends over time we make use of age groups from a set of cross-sectional surveys to make inferences about the experience of birth cohorts. This is sometimes referred to as the use of 'synthetic cohorts' and it is well known that the method has a number of potential difficulties although these are often ignored in practice (Breen and Jonsson, 1997). If this exercise is to be valid then it is necessary that these synthetic cohorts are indeed representative of the age cohorts of which they are a part. Put more precisely, we require that attrition of the original birth cohorts should be independent of the variables of interest in the study. In countries with histories of large-scale emigration—such as both parts of the island of Ireland—this is likely to be problematic. If emigrants are disproportionately drawn from among the less well-educated, analyses such as ours will tend to overstate the level of educational attainment in the true cohorts. But when, as here, the focus is on change over time in the effects of class, gender and religion, then we need to look at differentials in migration according to educational attainment between different classes, religions and genders. For example, if it were the case that the distribution of emigrants according to educational attainment or class origins (which is a proxy for educational attainment) differed as between the various religions, then conclusions concerning religious differences in educational attainment would be suspect. Consider the case in which Catholic emigrants were disproportionately drawn from the working class or from those of low educational attainment when compared with Protestant emigrants. This would make the educational attainment of those Catholics who remained, and who constitute our synthetic cohorts, higher, relative to Protestants, so leading us to erroneous conclusions about religious differences in educational attainment. If this disproportion changed over time, then we would be led to invalid conclusions about changes in the pattern of religious differences in attainment. These *caveats* should be born in mind in what follows. We will return to this issue in a later section of this chapter.

In Table 1 we set out the trend in educational qualifications across cohorts for both North and South. The most striking feature of the table is the significantly higher level of educational achievement in the South across all three cohorts. In the oldest cohort, 61 per cent of the Northern respondents are classified as having no qualification, compared to 54 per cent of the Southern respondents. In both countries there is a sharp decline over time in the number without qualifications although the difference between them—of around ten percentage points—remains roughly constant. As a result in the youngest cohort just less than 20 per cent in the South and 30 per cent in the North are without qualifications. Differences in intermediate levels of qualification are fairly slight, although at the higher levels the advantage once again rests with the South. Here there has been a dramatic increase in the percentage completing senior cycle, while the corresponding figures in the North remain fairly static.

It is possible that the A-level qualification represents, on average, a higher level of qualification than the Leaving Certificate (which is analogous to the Scottish 'Highers') and, as we shall see later, the transition rate from A-level to university degree is higher than from Leaving Certificate to degree. Nevertheless, whether one looks at senior or secondary education as a whole, it is clear that expansion of educational opportunity has been substantially more rapid in the Republic of Ireland than in Northern Ireland. However, in evaluating the figures for degree level, it is necessary to take into account the fact that, although our Southern and Northern data relate to the same cohorts, the Northern surveys were conducted at earlier dates. Consequently, the youngest cohort in the North will have had less opportunity to achieve a degree than will its Southern counterpart. Thus the figure of 6.6 per cent for the most recent birth cohort in the North should not be considered reliable, particularly in view of the fact that it is lower than in the 1944–56 cohort. Clearly, however, in the earlier cohorts at least, the percentage with a degree is higher in the South.

These results may cause some surprise, particularly those relating to the earlier cohort. However, the finding of higher participation rates in the South is not new. Tussing (1978) showed that in 1970 school participation rates at age fifteen and above were significantly higher in the Republic of Ireland than Northern Ireland and indeed a good deal higher than those for the UK as a whole (Tussing, 1978: 91–2.)[6] Furthermore he noted that by the late 1960s senior cycle participation rates in Ireland compared favourably with other OECD countries. Tussing (Ibid.: 54–9) suggests several factors to explain how a rural society such as the Republic of Ireland could have afforded such a highly developed system. Schools were operated in a spartan and frugal manner; resources for education were marshalled by the Catholic Church and the religious orders themselves

---

[6] See also *Investment in Education* (1965: 20).

contributed both in terms of school building and the provision of teachers; and, lastly, the educational system economised by emphasising subjects which required little in the way of costly equipment.

While the reforms in the 1960s were originally intended to produce expansion in enrolment at the post-primary stages, mainly in more vocational subjects, both the influence of educational interest groups and the substantial increase in service employment ensured that expansion occurred largely within the traditional secondary framework. Change took the form of across the board increases in participation rather than involving selective increase in provision aimed at serving the needs of the economy. Paradoxically, this general upgrading of human capital is now seen as one of the most important factors underlying the recent success of the southern economy (Duffy *et al.*, 1997).

While Irish education was provided at a relatively low cost, prior to free education it was still necessary for parents to pay fees, even though these were usually modest. The comparatively high rates of participation suggest that a high value was placed on participation and one reason for this may have been the lack of alternative paths to advancement available in more advanced industrial societies such as the United Kingdom. The Northern Ireland rates of educational participation appear to form part of the broader UK pattern which is characterised historically by a high degree of selectivity at second level and the absence of strong linkages between the educational system and industry. Low participation rates are likely to be a consequence both of the structure of the educational system and a somewhat different evaluation of the balance of costs and benefits than in the Southern case.

Table 1. Educational qualifications by cohort for the Republic of Ireland and Northern Ireland.

Level of Qual.	1937–43		1944–56		1957–70	
	Republic of Ireland	Northern Ireland	Republic of Ireland	Northern Ireland	Republic of Ireland	Northern Ireland
None	53.6	61.2	37.7	46.4	19.1	30.2
Junior Cycle	17.9	21.7	24.7	32.3	28.0	48.0
Senior Cycle	21.1	13.4	27.4	13.7	41.9	15.2
Degree Level	7.4	3.6	10.2	7.5	11.0	6.6
N	755	1,794	1,983	5,983	2,388	5,870

Class Inequalities in Educational Attainment, North and South

In Table 2 we present a preliminary analysis of class inequalities in educational attainment, ignoring for the moment differences between cohorts. It is apparent from this table that the higher levels of educational attainment in the South are accompanied by striking class differences. The five classes we have identified form a clear hierarchy in terms of educational outcomes. In the Republic of Ireland less than 4 per cent of respondents from the service class are without qualifications but this rises steadily to 47 per cent of respondents from the non-skilled manual class. The former thus have a relative advantage of 13:1. The corresponding figures for having a university degree are just less than 40 per cent and less than 3 per cent and the relative advantage enjoyed by the service class is thus 13.7:1. The product of these two ratios gives us a figure of 179:1. This is the odds ratio which summarises the outcome of the comparison between the classes with the least and the most resources to achieve the most favoured, and avoid the least favoured educational outcomes.[7]

The same comparison for Northern Ireland shows that 16.5 per cent of those from service-class origins report no qualifications compared to 59.1 per cent of the non-skilled manual class. This gives a ratio of 3.6:1 compared to 13:1 in the South. For a degree qualification the respective figures are 18.0 and 2.3, giving a ratio of 7.8:1 compared to the Southern figure of 13.7:1. The resulting Northern odds ratio of 28:1 would need to be multiplied by 6.4 to reach the Southern figure. While the extent of the differences between the two parts of the island will vary depending on the pairs of classes and educational destinations which enter into the comparison, the finding of stronger class effects in the Republic of Ireland is a general one and the pattern of class effects is such that the disparities in educational achievement between the two parts of the island are relatively greater for the higher than for the lower social classes.

Almost immediately, then, we see a striking contrast between Northern Ireland and the Republic. While levels of educational attainment are generally higher in the latter, so are class inequalities. As a result, despite the fact that respondents originating in the non-skilled manual class in the North, for example, enjoy a greater degree of equality of opportunity than their counterparts in the South, they are nevertheless 1.25 times more likely to be without qualifications and 2.7 times less likely to have achieved at least a senior cycle qualification.

---

[7] This observed figure will, of course, be subject to a large sampling error.

Table 2. Educational qualifications by social class for the Republic of Ireland and Northern Ireland.

Level of Qual.	Professional and Managerial		Routine Non-Manual		Petty-Bourgeoisie		Skilled Manual		Unskilled Manual	
	RoI	NI	RoI	NI	RoI	NI	RoI	NI	RoI	NI
None	3.6	16.5	10.0	28.4	28.5	37.0	31.1	40.9	47.2	59.1
Junior Cycle	9.6	37.8	15.1	45.3	24.5	36.6	30.5	36.6	28.1	31.7
Senior Cycle	47.2	27.7	54.0	18.2	39.2	18.1	33.0	15.1	21.8	6.9
Degree	39.6	18.0	20.9	8.0	10.4	8.3	5.3	8.3	2.9	2.3
N	464	1,736	271	735	1,523	3,203	1,006	4,072	1,669	3,901

Notes: RoI: Republic of Ireland, NI: Northern Ireland

The Effect of Migration to Britain

In the introduction to this paper we raised the question of the degree to which emigration might vitiate our results, based, as they are, on data concerning those who remained in Northern Ireland and the Republic of Ireland and excluding those who, though educated in Ireland, no longer live there. We can gain some limited insight into the likely magnitude of this problem by drawing on data on Irish immigrants to Britain contained in the General Household Survey (GHS). In 1982 and in 1985 through to 1992 the GHS collected data which allows us to assign respondents' fathers to a class position, so proxying respondents' class origins. We then take the same age cohorts as we have used thus far and we create tables of highest educational attainment by class origins and highest educational attainment by cohort for respondents born in Northern Ireland and for those born in the Republic of Ireland. These are shown in Table 3, panels A and B. Comparing these with Tables 1 and 2 allows us to assess the extent to which the trends over time and the overall class differences in educational attainment that we have found among non-migrants are also evident among migrants to Britain. This will allow us to form a judgement as to whether the comparisons we have made between the North and South might, in fact, be biased by selective emigration. Of course it would also be desirable to carry out a similar analysis to assess whether the pattern of change in ethnic (that is to say, Protestant/Catholic) differences in Northern Ireland over time or in gender differences in both parts of the island were also sensitive to the impact of selective migration. However, as is evident from Table 3, the numbers of GHS respondents on which we could base such an analysis are too small to sustain any firm conclusions.

Table 3, panel A, shows that the trends over time are consistent with those already noted among non-migrants, with increasing percentages acquiring higher educational qualifications in the later cohorts. There is no evidence that this trend differs between Northern and Southern migrants: the model that posits the same trend among both groups provides an adequate fit to these data.[8] But what is noticeable in this table is that the migrants from Northern Ireland have somewhat higher levels of qualification than those from the Republic—the opposite of what we found among non-migrants. Similarly, when we examine Table 3 panel B we find that the association between class origins and educational qualifications differs as between Northern and Southern migrants[9]—but this is because class differences in qualifications are rather less among Southern migrants than among Northern. This is, again, the opposite of what we found among the non-migrants.

Taken together these results suggest that the two major differences between North and South that emerged from our analysis based on data for non-migrants—namely that the North had a more open educational system but that levels of qualification in the South were rather higher—would, in fact, be somewhat less marked were we also to take account of the educational experiences of migrants.

Educational Transitions

In Table 4 we show the rates for the three educational transitions on which we focus, namely, from no qualification to a junior cycle qualification; from junior cycle to senior cycle; and from senior cycle to a university degree. We distinguish between Northern Ireland and the Republic of Ireland and between our three cohorts. Inspection of the table shows, as we would have anticipated, that the transition rate to a junior cycle qualification is somewhat higher in the South for each of the cohorts. The rate increases rapidly across cohorts for both parts of the island but the South continues to enjoy an advantage with the difference rising from 7 percentage points in the oldest birth cohort to 11 points in the most recent one. For the transition to senior cycle the Southern rates, which are relatively constant at around 0.60, are once again substantially higher than for the North where they decline from 0.44 to 0.31 across cohorts. On the other hand,

---

[8] Deviance of 6.8 with 6 df.

[9] The model of common educational fluidity fails to fit the data returning deviance of 27.6 with 12 df, p = .006.

Richard Breen, et al.

Table 3. Educational qualifications of Irish migrants (%).

Panel A: Qualifications by age cohort by country of origin.

Educational Quals	1937–43		1944–56		1957–70	
	RoI	NI	RoI	NI	RoI	NI
None	75	64	66	41	57	25
Junior	8	10	11	17	14	19
Senior	14	16	17	24	21	21
Degree	3	9	7	19	8	35
N	285	106	441	218	160	94

Panel B: Qualifications by class origins by country of origin.

Educational Quals	Professional and Managerial		Routine Non-Manual		Petty Bourgeoisie		Skilled Manual		Semi/ Unskilled Manual	
	RoI	NI	RoI	NI	RoI	NI	RoI	NI	RoI	NI
None	44	12	55	39	65	33	69	58	83	69
Junior	14	8	9	17	10	18	10	18	9	16
Senior	24	32	33	22	22	31	13	17	8	8
Degree	19	48	3	22	3	18	7	7	1	7
N	119	102	33	18	270	78	222	125	211	74

Notes: RoI: Republic of Ireland, NI: Northern Ireland

Table 4. Educational transition rates by cohort for the Republic of Ireland and Northern Ireland.

Cohort	Junior Cycle		Senior Cycle		Degree	
Education Level	RoI	NI	RoI	NI	RoI	NI
1937–43	0.46	0.39	0.61	0.44	0.26	0.21
1944–56	0.62	0.54	0.60	0.40	0.27	0.35
1957–70	0.81	0.70	0.65	0.31	0.21	0.30

Notes: RoI: Republic of Ireland, NI: Northern Ireland

with the exception of the earliest cohort, the transition rates to degree level are higher in the North.[10] These results point to the very selective nature of the A-level system in Northern Ireland which, in contrast to the senior cycle in the Republic of Ireland, caters to a smaller proportion of each cohort, but whose output is then more likely to go on to acquire a degree.

We turn now to the use of the Mare model to analyse the multivariate relationship between educational transition rates, gender and social class origins in the two parts of Ireland. The crucial advance represented in the Mare model is that it yields parameter estimates whose values are not affected by educational expansion per se, but instead reflect the degree of inequality of opportunity in educational transitions associated with factors such as gender and class origins. Under this model the educational attainment process is viewed as a sequence of transitions from one level of education to the next highest level.

Tables 5A and 5B show the rates at which the individuals in our Northern and Southern samples make these transitions, differentiated according to class and gender. We seek to capture variation in these rates using a log-linear model where the object is to find a model which provides an accurate but also parsimonious account of the data. The details of the models we fitted are reported in the Appendix to this chapter. Here we concentrate on the main findings that emerge from our analysis.

In both Northern Ireland and the Republic of Ireland, the greatest class difference in transition rates is found at the transition to a degree. For men in both North and South the major increase in transition rates between cohorts occurred in respect of the first transition, that is, to a junior cycle qualification. In neither part of the island is there any evidence that class differences in rates have declined over time, despite the various educational reforms that took place during the period covered by our data. In the North, however, women's position relative to men improves markedly in the youngest cohort and, among women in the Republic of Ireland, transition rates increased at all transitions as we move from the oldest to the youngest cohorts. However, once again we find that class inequalities in transition rates are much higher in the Republic of Ireland than in Northern Ireland. For example, in the South the odds of making the transition to junior cycle are 25 times greater for children from the professional and managerial class than from those of the non-skilled manual class. However, this ratio of 25:1 compares with a figure of just less than 6:1 for men in the North. Similarly the advantage enjoyed by the routine non-manual class over the non-skilled manual class in the South exceeds 12:1 while the

---

[10] This is true despite the fact that as explained earlier we are almost certainly underestimating the rate for the final cohort in the North.

Table 5A.   Educational transition rates by class by cohort by sex for the Republic of Ireland: percentage successful.

	Men			Women		
Class	Junior Cycle	Senior Cycle	Degree	Junior Cycle	Senior Cycle	Degree
1937–43						
Prof. & Managerial	95.1	84.7	53.5	98.1	87.6	19.0
Routine White-Collar	82.7	78.2	—	90.3	66.6	17.2
Petty Bourgeoisie	40.0	65.9	50.5	54.7	58.9	15.7
Skilled Manual	41.1	36.9	31.2	43.9	71.8	0.0
Unskilled Manual	27.9	41.7	21.2	30.2	36.7	0.0
1944–56						
Prof. & Managerial	95.4	94.0	64.7	94.4	86.7	41.8
Routine White-Collar	88.5	83.9	39.4	81.4	75.1	20.1
Petty Bourgeoisie	63.0	62.8	25.4	79.2	67.0	14.0
Skilled Manual	66.2	52.0	22.4	54.6	44.1	20.0
Unskilled Manual	45.5	44.5	30.8	42.9	60.7	11.4
1957–70						
Prof. & Managerial	99.5	91.7	43.7	95.7	90.6	42.1
Routine White-Collar	95.3	83.8	40.7	94.8	92.6	22.3
Petty Bourgeoisie	89.6	55.2	20.7	90.2	85.3	19.3
Skilled Manual	83.6	53.3	15.9	78.8	64.6	7.9
Unskilled Manual	69.5	42.2	10.0	65.4	56.8	5.2

respective figures for men and women in the North are 6:1 and less than 4:1. Differences for the comparison involving the skilled manual group are more modest but conform to the same pattern—that is to say, one of substantially greater class inequality in the South than the North.

Educational Transition Rates Among Catholics and Protestants in Northern Ireland

Within Northern Ireland, as noted earlier, the two ethnic groups—Catholics and Protestants—are educated separately. Has this led to different levels of educational attainment and to different patterns of change over time and, more generally, is the relationship between class, gender, cohort and educational attainment different among Northern Irish Catholics and Protestants?

To address this issue we once again fit a set of log-linear models to tables showing transition rates between our four educational levels according to class origins, gender and cohort for Catholics and for Protestants.

Table 5B. Educational transition rates by class by cohort by sex for Northern Ireland.

	Men			Women		
Class	Junior Cycle	Senior Cycle	Degree	Junior Cycle	Senior Cycle	Degree
1937–43						
Prof. & Managerial	69.7	60.4	31.3	73.0	66.4	19.1
Routine White-Collar	59.0	53.8	28.6	56.3	50.0	15.0
Petty Bourgeoisie	34.8	48.7	40.5	51.1	43.0	9.6
Skilled Manual	50.2	38.2	26.2	32.7	33.7	10.0
Unskilled Manual	25.4	32.3	22.7	16.7	32.7	11.8
1944–56						
Prof. & Managerial	79.7	61.1	59.1	84.7	56.5	33.5
Routine White-Collar	72.6	37.6	40.6	63.9	42.5	24.4
Petty Bourgeoisie	68.5	39.7	49.7	63.9	50.8	24.9
Skilled Manual	67.5	29.6	40.6	53.0	31.7	22.6
Unskilled Manual	53.0	26.3	35.6	30.4	26.1	20.8
1957–70						
Prof. & Managerial	84.2	51.5	34.4	88.6	49.5	27.5
Routine White-Collar	76.8	31.0	52.8	79.8	31.9	20.8
Petty Bourgeoisie	68.5	31.6	32.3	83.0	41.9	29.9
Skilled Manual	67.5	21.6	31.4	68.8	25.4	18.7
Unskilled Manual	53.0	17.9	26.6	56.4	18.5	22.9

Table 6. Educational transition rates for Catholics and Protestants in Northern Ireland.

	Transition: Cohort	1	2	3
CATHOLICS	1937–43	0.34	0.54	0.23
	1944–56	0.46	0.41	0.27
	1957–70	0.65	0.31	0.32
PROTESTANTS	1937–43	0.41	0.40	0.20
	1944–56	0.59	0.39	0.40
	1957–70	0.73	0.31	0.29

Doing this we find that the best-fitting model for these data is one which allows changes in transition rates to vary by class, gender, cohort and religion, and in which the patterns of differences in transition rates according to social class differ for men and women, and in which the change in transition rates over cohorts is different for Protestants and Catholics. This model returns a deviance of 108.22 with 98 df, so yielding a satisfactory fit to the observed data.

Since the variation in transition rates by gender and class has already been noted in our earlier analysis we can here simply concentrate on the changes over time in religious differences. Further, since the effects of class and gender on transition rates are conditionally independent of religion, we can discuss the latter without referring to the former, since, although the odds of making the various educational transitions are influenced by class and gender, religious *differences* in such odds are not. Accordingly, Table 6 shows the transition rates in the Northern data broken down by religion. For the first transition (no qualifications to O-level or equivalent) the standard errors around these rates are less than 0.02, while for the second and third transitions they are less than 0.03 and 0.04 respectively. There we see that in the oldest cohort, Protestants had a much higher chance of reaching O-level or equivalent, but thereafter, among those who reached O-level, Catholics were more likely than Protestants to continue, and the rate of transition from A-level to a degree showed no significant difference between the two. In the second cohort the overall transition rate to O-levels increases markedly, but particularly so among Protestants. In addition, in this cohort the Catholic advantage at the second transition disappears and Protestants also become more likely to make the transition from A-level to a degree. However, by the time we reach our youngest cohort, religious differences in transition rates have almost disappeared. At the first transition Protestants did better than Catholics but their advantage has been eroded by the very large increase in the Catholic rate in the youngest cohort compared with the second. The transition rates from O- to A-level and from A-level to a degree now show no religious differences.

In all, the pattern of religious differences in Northern Ireland shows Protestants to have had a relatively slight advantage over Catholics in the oldest cohort, a widening of this difference in the second cohort, followed by their diminution and virtual disappearance in the youngest. It is perhaps not entirely surprising that religious differences were relatively small in the oldest cohort: Catholics had their own educational system (albeit one which received less generous funding than the state system) so there could be no religious discrimination within the system and, as McGarry and O'Leary (1995: 209) point out, the complaint of the civil rights campaigners in the late 1960s 'was not that they had received a bad education, or had been denied access to state schools and universities, but that they were not receiving the jobs for which their qualifications entitled them'. And while the widening of religious differences in the 1944–56 cohort is puzzling, the fact that, in the youngest cohort, Catholics made up most of this ground can be taken as evidence for the widely held view that it was the Catholic community in particular which benefited from free education.

Conclusions

Both Northern Ireland and the Republic of Ireland have seen large increases in levels of educational attainment. This growth seems to have been more rapid in the South but this cannot simply be attributed to some 'catching-up' process whereby the South industrialised later and thus invested in education at a later date. Rather, we find, even in our oldest cohort, a smaller proportion with no qualifications, and a higher proportion with a degree in the Republic than in Northern Ireland. Thus, these differences predate the period of rapid industrialisation in the South. This is particularly surprising given that one would expect a more rural and less industrial society to have lower levels of educational provision. And, although our analysis of migration suggested that less-educated people from the South were likely to migrate to Britain while more-educated people from the North did so, it seems unlikely that this could account for all the differences between the two.

An explanation must, rather, be sought in more long-standing differences between the two parts of Ireland. During the later nineteenth century and the first part of the twentieth, the Catholic Church was chiefly responsible for the provision of education in Ireland. As Inglis (1987: 218) among others, has argued, this occurred with the support of the British government which saw the Catholic Church as a more effective means of social control in Ireland than the repression in which it had engaged in the seventeenth and eighteenth centuries. But it is also clear that, once it established itself during the latter part of the nineteenth century, the Church and its educational system became a focus for anti-imperialism and for the propagation of a distinct Irish identity (as witnessed by, for example, the role of the clergy in the 'gaelic revival' of the late nineteenth century). However, while this might provide an explanation for the unusually high level of educational provision in Ireland—albeit of a rather frugal and often spartan kind—it cannot explain differences between the two parts of Ireland in their rates of participation. In particular, given that the Catholic Church's activity in education has not been confined to what is now the Republic, one might reasonably wonder why there should be a such stark difference in Catholic participation rates between North and South.

To answer this question we must focus on the framework within which individual educational decisions are made. The Catholic Church and, particularly in Northern Ireland, the state, provided the necessary institutional setting for high rates of educational participation, but differences in the extent to which these opportunities were taken up can only be explained in terms of the alternatives to which individuals and their families had access. And here the economic differences between North and South would seem to be of central importance. The industrialised labour market of Northern Ireland, like that of Britain, offered employment to those with few or low levels of qualification within industrial establishments and also provided avenues for upward mobility outside the school system—most notably, of course, via apprenticeships. But this was less true in the Republic where, in the absence of large industrial employers, the prospects for those who lacked educational qualifications were bleak. This distinction also explains why rates of emigration among the unqualified were higher in the South than the North. For the unqualified, prospects within the Republic were poor: education offered almost the only avenue through which those who would not inherit a family farm or business could find a reasonably comfortable position in society.

Notwithstanding this striking difference between the two parts of the island, in recent decades they have also shared in some trends in educational participation that are common to very many other Western societies. On the one hand, gender inequalities in transition rates have narrowed over time, although they have not been completely eliminated in the transition to university education. On the other hand, there is no evidence, either North or South, of any trend towards declining class inequalities in educational opportunity.

However, while class differences are equally resilient in the two societies they are much stronger in the South than in the North. This is consistent with what has been found in research on social mobility (see Breen and Whelan, this volume), although once again the observed differences between North and South may have been exaggerated by the effect of migration. Nevertheless, our analysis shows that, while class inequalities are not unduly low in the North, they are particularly high in the Republic. This is the case despite the fact that a reduction of such inequalities was one of the most important objectives of the educational reforms initiated in the 1960s. Breen *et al.* (1990: 136) argued that the lack of state control over the educational system is an important part of the explanation of why the effects of such changes were quite unlike what seems to have been envisaged. *Investment in Education* (1966) showed clearly the degree of class differentiation that was characteristic of local secondary and vocational schools at that time. In the absence of appropriate structural reform these inter-school class distinctions continue to be extremely strong. Whelan and Hannan (forthcoming) argue that the structure and nature of the educational system in the Republic of Ireland and its connection to local stratification systems, which, in their turn, are linked to local and national economic structures, are such as to promote particularly high levels of educational inequality.[11]

More generally, one might suggest that in a society, like the Republic of Ireland, in which education counts for so much in terms of life chances, and in which other avenues of social advance are absent, not only will levels of educational attainment be high, but so will levels of class inequality. This is because families are prepared to devote substantial resources to ensuring their children's success in the system. In the absence of state intervention the consequence of this is that the probability of educational success comes to be closely associated with class position.

Overall, the two parts of Ireland differ in quite marked ways, which might be summarised by saying that the Northern educational system is characterised by low class inequalities and low average levels of educational attainment, while the Southern system demonstrates higher inequalities and higher average levels of attainment. These distinctions between the two are not of recent origin and any explanation of them must be sought in the long-standing economic and other differences between the two parts of the island of Ireland.

APPENDIX: Fitting models to the transition data

While our aim is to fit a joint model for both parts of the island, it is convenient to begin with separate discussions of the results for North and South. In each case the baseline model is the one that allows for only main effects and thus posits that transition rates are affected by cohort, gender, class origin and type of transition but that there is no interaction between these variables. Thus, for example, this model would specify that the effect of gender, transition and class is the same across cohorts and so on. From Table A1 we can see that for Northern Ireland this model (1A) produces a deviance of 913.73 with 80 df and clearly does not provide a satisfactory fit to the data. A model which allows for all two-way associations except that between class and cohort (1B), and which therefore assumes no change in

---

[11] Comparative analysis of the educational system in the Republic of Ireland has tended to represent it as a highly standardised (in the sense of having a national curriculum and a set of standardised examinations) but weakly stratified system with an absence of specific vocational linkages (Müller and Shavit, 1998). However, the connection between education and class position has then been found to be a good deal stronger than might be expected on the basis of this particular profile (Breen and Whelan, 1998). It may then be hypothesised that strong standardisation overrides weak differentiation. However, a more convincing case can be made for the argument that both standardisation and stratification are potent factors in the system. The form of stratification although though not adequately captured by a distinction between academic and vocational education has deep historical roots and pervades the system (Whelan and Hannan, forthcoming).

class inequalities across time, has a deviance of 118.44 with 60 df. In order to produce a statistically satisfactory fit it is necessary to use a further four degrees of freedom to capture specific three-way interactions between class (excluding the petty bourgeoisie), gender and the transition to senior cycle and between the petty bourgeois class, gender and the transition to third level. With the inclusion of these additional terms this model (1C) gives a deviance of 77.05 with 56 degrees of freedom and constitutes our final model. It represents a reduction of 91.2 per cent in the deviance statistic compared with the baseline model (1A).

The two-way effects for the North capture the following substantive effects.

- There is a significant increase in success rates over time for the first transition but a slight decline for senior cycle completion among those who achieved a junior cycle qualification. There is no clear trend over time in the transition rate to third level among those in possession of a senior cycle qualification.
- In the youngest cohort there is a significant improvement in the relative position of women. The relative position of women is poorest at the final transition.
- The effect of social class, for men and women, is weakest at the transition to third level.
- The impact of social class is stronger for women except among the petty bourgeoisie. In other words the routine non-manual and manual classes experience greater disadvantage relative to men in the likelihood of making a given educational transition than do women in the professional and managerial classes. However, among the petty bourgeoisie the position is reversed and women are, in general, more likely to be successful than men .
- Class differences in the pattern of transition rates have remained constant over time.

Finally, the three-way interaction terms capture the following features:

- Within the petty bourgeois class women are more likely than men to make the first two transitions but less likely to make the transition to third-level education.
- For women the impact of social class is weaker at the second as well as the third transition. The pattern for women is therefore close to that observed in a number of other countries where the effect of class declines as one advances through the educational hierarchy (Shavit and Blossfeld, 1993).

For the Republic of Ireland the baseline model (2A) gives a deviance of

482.55 with 80 df. The model of all two-way associations except that between class and cohort (2B) has a deviance of 143.83 with 60 degrees of freedom and clearly does not provide as good a fit as in the North. In order to provide such a fit it is necessary to:

1 use two degrees of freedom to allow for variation between cohorts in the impact of being in the petty bourgeoisie;

2 use seven degrees of freedom to include certain three-way interactions which capture the fact that:

    a transition and cohort interact in a rather different fashion for women than for men;

    b transition by cohort effects have a distinct pattern for the petty bourgeoisie;

    c the consequences of being a women in the petty bourgeois class are different for the final transition compared with the earlier ones.

These modifications use a total of nine degrees of freedom. However, in the final model we only allow for gender differences in the transition odds among the petty bourgeoisie, rather than within all classes. This saves three degrees of freedom and as a consequence there is a difference of six degrees of freedom between models (2B) and (2C). The latter yields a deviance of 68.91 with 54 df.

The model for the South captures the following substantive effects:

- For men, just as in the North, the success rate increases across cohorts for the first transition but not for the others. For women, however, the pattern of gain is spread more evenly across the transitions. The gender difference is particularly striking at third level where women in the South started out in the oldest cohort at a particularly heavy disadvantage.

- Unlike the North, social class has an equal impact across gender except for the fact that, as in Northern Ireland, the propensity for men to inherit farms and businesses is reflected in the significant educational advantage that women in the petty bourgeoisie have in comparison with their male counterparts.

- The effect of class is significantly lower at entry to third level.

- The impact of being in the petty bourgeois class interacts with cohort and transition in a manner that results in a significant improvement in the transition rates of that class across cohorts for the first transition, a deterioration at the third transition and no clear trend at the second.

- Otherwise the effect of class across cohort does not vary.

- As in Northern Ireland, the advantage enjoyed by women in the

Table A1. Goodness of Fit Statistics.

Northern Ireland	Deviance	df	% Reduction in Deviance
1A: all main effects	913.73	80	
1B: 1A + all two-way effects except CL*C	114.44	60	87.0
1C: 1B + CL(2)*T(2)*S(2) + CL(4)*T(2)*S(2) + CL(5)*t(2)*S(2) + CL(3)*T(3)*S(2)	77.05	56	91.2
Republic of Ireland			
2A: all main effects	482.55	80	
2B: 2A + all two way effects except CL*C	143.83	60	70.4
2C: (CL*T + S*C + S*T + T*C + CL(3)*S + CL(3)*C) + (T(2)*C(3)*S(2) + T(3)*C(2)*S(2) + T3*C(3)*S(2) + T(2)*C(3)*CL(3) + T(3)*CL(2)*CL(3)+T(3)*C(3)*CL(3) + T(3)*S(2)*CL(3)	68.91	54	85.7
Joint Models			
3A: main effects constant by country	2,015.80	169	
3B: main effects varying by country	1,396.3	160	30.7
3C: 1B + 2B	262.3	120	87.0
3D: 1C + 2C	146.96	110	95.2
3E: 3D (Holding Constant (T*C + S*C + S*T + T*(CL2 + CL4 + CL5)) + S(2)*C(3)*CO(1) + T(3)*C(3)*CO(1) + S(2)*T(3)*CO(1)	161.09	122	94.0

Note: CL = class; S = sex; C = cohort; T = transition; CO = country.

petty bourgeois class at the earlier transitions is not evident at the third transition.

Finally, we pool the two data sets and Table A1 reports results for models applied to Northern Ireland and the Republic of Ireland jointly. The baseline model (3A) gives a deviance of 2,015.8 with 169 df. Model 3B which allows the main effects to be different for the North and South results in a deviance of 1,396 with 160 df and reduces the baseline deviance by 31 per cent, indicating the extent to which differences North and South can be accounted for by allowing the effects of class, gender and transition to vary but constraining each factor to operate uniformly across categories of the other factors. Fitting all two-way effects except class by cohort (3C) but allowing the parameters to vary across country produces a deviance of 262.3 with 120 df and reduces the baseline deviance by 87 per cent. A model which combines the best fitting models for both countries gives a deviance of 146.96 with 110 degrees of freedom and reduces the baseline deviance by 95.2 per cent. Constraining gender and the two-way interactions between transition and cohort, gender and cohort, gender and transition, and transition and class (except for the petty bourgeoisie) to be equal across country would give a model with 125 degrees of freedom. However, in order to achieve a satisfactory fit it is necessary to fit three terms that capture specific sex by cohort, transition by cohort and sex by transition variations across country. With the addition of these terms Model 3D gives a deviance of 161.09 with 122 degrees of freedom (p = .0102) and accounts for 94.0 per cent of the baseline figure.

The joint model captures the following similarities and differences between North and South:

- Transition rates are significantly higher in the South at the first and, more particularly, the second transition.
- In both countries success rates increase across cohorts for the first transition but not for the remaining transitions. The exception to this is women in the South who start out with extremely high levels of comparative disadvantage and for whom the pattern of gain is more even.
- With the exception of the petty bourgeoisie in the South no trend in class effects across cohort is observed.
- Class interacts with gender differently in the two countries. In the North women in the routine non-manual and manual classes are more strongly disadvantaged than those in the professional and managerial class. No such effect is observed in the South. However, in both the North and the South among the petty bourgeoisie it is women who have higher transition rates, although this advantage largely disappears at the final transition.
- Finally, class effects are significantly stronger in the South.

References

Breen, R. and Devine P. (1999) 'Segmentation and the Social Structure' in P. Mitchell and R. Wilford (eds), *Politics in Northern Ireland*, Boulder, Col.: Westview Press.

Breen, R. and Hayes, B. C. (1996), 'Religious Mobility in the United Kingdom', *Journal of the Royal Statistical Society, Series A*, 159, Part 3: 493–504.

Breen, R. and Jonsson, J. O. (1996) 'How Reliable are Studies of Social Mobility? An Investigation into the Consequences of Unreliability in Measures of Social

Class', in M. Wallace (ed.), *Research in Social Stratification and Mobility*, volume 15, Greenwich, Conn.: JAI Press.

Breen, R. and Whelan C. T. (1993): 'From Ascription to Achievement? Origins, Education and Entry to the Labour Force in Ireland', *Acta Sociologica*, 36 (1): 3–18.

Breen, R. and Whelan, C. T. (1998): 'Investment in Education: Educational Qualifications and Class of Entry in the Republic of Ireland', in W. Müller and Y. Shavit (eds), *From School to Work*, Oxford: Oxford University Press.

Breen, R., Hannan, D. F., Rottman, D. and Whelan, C. T. (1990) *Understanding Contemporary Ireland: State, Class and Development in the Republic of Ireland*, London: Macmillan.

Callan, T., Nolan, B., Whelan, C. T. and Williams, J. (1996) *Poverty in the 1990s: Evidence from the 1994 Living in Ireland Survey*, Dublin: Oak Tree Press.

Coolahan, J. (1981) *Irish Education: History and Structure*, Dublin: Institute of Public Administration.

Cormack, R. J. and Osborne, R. D. (1994) 'The Evolution of the Catholic Middle Class', in A. Guelke (ed.), *New Perspectives on the Northern Ireland Conflict*, Aldershot: Avebury.

De Graaf, P. M. and Ganzeboom, H. B. (1993) 'Family Background and Educational Attainment in the Netherlands for the 1891–1960 Birth Cohorts' in Y. Shavit and H.-P. Blossfeld (eds), *Persistent Inequality: Changing Educational Attainment in Thirteen Countries*, Boulder, Col.: Westview Press.

Duffy, D., Fitz Gerald, J., Honohan, P. and Kearney, I. (1997) 'Interpreting the Recent Irish Growth Experience', in D. Duffy, J. Fitz Gerald and I. Kearney, *Medium Term Review*, Dublin: Economic and Social Research Institute.

Duffy, M. and Evans, G. (1997) 'Class, Community Polarization and Politics', in L. Dowds, P. Devine and R. Breen (eds), *Social Attitudes in Northern Ireland, The Sixth Volume*, Belfast: Appletree Press.

Dunn, S. (1993) 'A Historical Context to Education and Church-State Relations in Northern Ireland' in R. Osborne, R. Cormack and A. Gallagher (eds), *After the Reforms: Education and Policy in Northern Ireland*, Aldershot: Avebury.

Erikson, R. and Goldthorpe, J. H. (1993) *The Constant Flux: A Study of Class Mobility in Industrial Societies*, Oxford: Clarendon Press.

Erikson, R. and Jonsson, J. O. (1996) *Can Education be Equalized? The Swedish Case in Comparative Perspective*, Boulder, Col.: Westview Press.

Fienberg, S. E. (1977) *The Analysis of Cross-classified Categorical data*, Cambridge, Mass.: MIT Press.

Goodman, L. (1971) 'The Analysis of Multidimensional Contingency Tables: Stepwise Procedures and Direct Estimation Methods for Building Models for Multiple Classifications', *Technometrics*, 13: 339–44.

Hannan, D. F. with Boyle, M. (1987) *Schooling Decisions: The Origins and Consequences of Selection and Streaming in Irish Schools*, Dublin: Economic and Social Research Institute.

Hannan, D. F., Smyth, E., McCullagh, J., O'Leary, R. and McMahon, D. (1996) *Coeducation and Gender Equality: Exam Performance, Stress and Personal Development*, Dublin: Oak Tree Press.

Heath, A., Mills, C. and Roberts, J. (1992) 'Towards Meritocracy? Recent Evidence on an Old Problem', in C. Crouch and A. F. Heath (eds), *Social Research and Social Reform*, Oxford: Clarendon Press.

Hout, M. (1989) *Following in Father's Footsteps: Social Mobility in Ireland*, Cambridge, Mass.: Harvard University Press.

Inglis, T. (1987) *Moral Monopoly: The Catholic Church in Modern Irish Society*, Dublin: Gill and Macmillan.

Investment in Education (1965), Dublin: Stationery Office.

Jonsson, J. O., Mills, C. and Müller W. (1996) 'A Half Century of Increasing Educational Openness? Social Class, Gender and Educational Attainment in Sweden, Germany and Britain' in R. Erikson and J. O. Jonsson (eds), *Can Education be Equalised? The Swedish Case in Comparative Perspective*, Boulder, Col.: Westview Press.

Mare, R. D. (1980) 'Social Background and School Continuation Decisions', *Journal of the American Statistical Association*, 75 (370): 295–305.

Mare, R. D. (1981) 'Change and Stablity in Educational Stratification', *American Sociological Review*, 46 (1): 72–87.

McGarry, J. and O'Leary, B. (1995) *Explaining Northern Ireland: Broken Images*, Oxford: Blackwell.

O'Connor, F. (1993) *In Search of a State: Catholics in Northern Ireland*, Belfast: Blackstaff Press.

Pudney, S. (1989) *Modelling Individual Choice: The Econometrics of Corners, Kinks and Holes*, Oxford: Basil Blackwell.

Müller, W. and Shavit, Y. (1998) 'The Institutional Imbeddedness of the Stratification Process: A Comparative Study of Qualifications and Occupations in Thirteen Countries' in Y. Shavit and W. Müller, *From School to Work*, Oxford: Oxford University Press.

Shavit, Y. and Blossfeld H.-P. (1993) *Persistent Inequality: Changing Educational Attainment in Thirteen Countries*, Boulder, Col.: Westview Press.

Smith, D. J. and Chambers, G. (1991) *Inequality in Northern Ireland*, Oxford: Clarendon.

Sutherland, A. (1993) 'The Transfer Procedure Reformed?' in R. Osborne, R. Cormack and A. Gallgher (eds), *After the Reforms: Education and Policy in Northern Ireland*, Aldershot: Avebury.

Tussing, A. D. (1978) *Irish Educational Expenditures—Past Present and Future*, Dublin: Economic and Social Research Institute.

Whelan C. T. and Hannan, D. F. (forthcoming) 'Trends in Educational Inequality in the Republic of Ireland', *Economic and Social Review*.

Whyte, J. (1983) 'How much Discrimination was there under the Unionist Regime, 1921–68?' in T. Gallagher and J. O'Connell (eds), *Contemporary Irish Studies*, Manchester: Manchester University Press.

Whyte, J. (1990) *Interpreting Northern Ireland*, Oxford: Oxford University Press.

Sick Man or Tigress?
The Labour Market in the
Republic of Ireland

PHILIP J. O'CONNELL

Introduction

LABOUR MARKET PROBLEMS HAVE A LONG HISTORY in the Republic of Ireland. At the outset of political Independence in 1922 the Southern economy was highly specialised in agricultural production for the British market and its small industrial sector remained underdeveloped. Mass exodus from agriculture was the principal dynamic of change in employment from the 1920s until the 1960s. Between 1926 and 1961 employment in agriculture declined from 53 per cent to 36 per cent of total employment. While this decline in agriculture was counter-balanced to some extent by an expansion of positions in the industrial and service sectors, total employment never-theless fell—from 1.2 million in 1926 to just over 1 million in 1961 (Kennedy, Giblin and McHugh, 1988). Unemployment remained compara-tively high throughout this period, although the main effect of the failure to provide work for all resulted in substantial emigration; net emigration amounted to about 500,000 in the first three decades of Independence.

Labour market problems reached critical proportions in the 1950s, with stagnation in both agriculture and industry giving rise to increased un-employment and a renewed surge of emigration. During the decade of the 1950s alone, net emigration rose to over 400,000, reducing the population by almost 14 per cent of its 1951 level. The adoption of policies to encourage export-oriented foreign-owned manufacturing after 1958 gave rise to a substantial increase in employment and services over the next two decades, which more than offset an accelerated decline in agricultural employment, with the result that total employment increased by about 14 per cent between 1961 and 1980. Unemployment generally remained below 5 per cent until the recession of the mid-1970s and net emigration

Proceedings of the British Academy, **98**, 215–249. © The British Academy 1999.

slowed substantially in the 1960s, and, for the first time in over a century, there was substantial net immigration during the 1970s as some of those who had left during the 1950s returned to take up jobs in the booming economy. The boom times were relatively short-lived, however, and, with the onset of world recession in 1980 following the second oil price shock, employment fell rapidly throughout the first half of the 1980s, unemployment soared to over 17 per cent of the labour force, and emigration resumed.

At the end of the 1980s, there was widespread despondency among academic commentators at the scale of the crisis confronting Irish society, the most manifest indications of which were: mass unemployment, resurgent emigration, a massive public debt, and sluggish economic growth. Breen, Hannan, Rottman and Whelan (1990: 209) argued that

> Despite the enormously bloated role of the state as an economic intermediary, it has been monumentally unsuccessful either in ensuring sustained economic growth or in moderating inegalitarian tendencies in the class system.

They concluded (1990: 143):

> Since the foundation of the State, Ireland has been unable to create jobs on a scale sufficient to meet the requirements of its potential growth in population. The consequences of such failure have been high levels of unemployment among the employee labour force and high rates of emigration.

In more pessimistic vein, Lee (1989: 521) commented:

> It is difficult to avoid the conclusion that Irish economic performance has been the least impressive in western Europe, perhaps in all Europe, in the twentieth century.

Lee's account of the malaise is a culturalist interpretation which seeks an explanation for Irish failures in factors inherent to the society: national institutions which reward mediocrity, an inability to harness intellectual resources, and failings of national character and identity. There is no apparent escape from the dilemma. Lee's pessimism is shared by O'Hearn's (1990) account, which however, lays emphasis on external factors; the determining effects of Ireland's peripheral position in the international economy. Breen *et al.* (1990) set the state at centre stage, although they situate the state in class structure and mobilisation, and within the objective constraints given by late industrialisation and the position occupied by the Southern economy in the international division of labour. The crisis of the 1980s is thus seen as the failure of a highly interventionist state lacking the capacity to impose rational and progressive policies, not least because of the extent of State entanglements with sectional interests. While Breen *et al.*, share the despondency of their contemporary commentators, there is nothing in their interpretation to suggest that the crisis of the 1980s was inevitable, nor, therefore that the situation was entirely irreparable.

In fact, in 1987, in response to the crisis, the State took the lead in negotiating a corporatist-style solidaristic agreement between government and social partners, the Programme for National Recovery (PNR) from 1987–90, covering incomes as well as fiscal policy, which augured in a period of fiscal discipline, and which was combined with a macro-economic policy stance incorporating low inflation, stable exchange rates, and tax reform. This policy framework has been largely maintained during the 1990s and is widely perceived to have provided the institutional and policy framework for rapid growth in both output and employment.

Output has grown by more than 5 per cent per annum since 1990, and, assuming appropriate domestic policies and a continuation of moderate growth in the international economy, these trends are forecast to continue over the short to medium term. This exceptionally strong performance has resulted in unprecedented employment growth. Total employment increased by 136,000, or 12 per cent, between 1993 and 1996, and the ESRI forecast is for a further 3.4 per cent per annum increase in employment between 1996 and the end of the century (Duffy, Fitz Gerald, Kearney and Shorthall, 1997).

Popular accounts have, accordingly, begun to talk of the Republic of Ireland as a 'European tiger'—evoking comparisons with the rapid economic growth and development achieved by the Asian newly industrialising countries—and officials of the European Commission like to refer to Ireland as the success story of the cohesion strategy. In labour market terms, given that about 60 per cent of the recent increase in employment is accounted for by women, this characterisation of the sudden transformation—from 'sick man of Europe' to European tiger—appears to have misconstrued the gender of the animal.

This paper examines these recent changes in the labour market and situates them in longer-term developments in both State policy and the labour market. Taking the longer view, I argue that the labour market in Ireland has been characterised by a process of polarisation, with upgrading of positions for those at work combined with the exclusion of those lacking market capacities to compete for access to work.

Principal Developments in the Labour Market

The decade of the 1980s was particularly severe for the Southern economy. Table 1 shows how the numbers at work declined over the first half of the 1980s while the size of the labour force increased, due both to natural population growth and increasing labour force participation by women. Contraction in employment combined with labour force growth resulted in an increase in the unemployment rate from just under 10 per cent of the labour force in 1981 to over 17 per cent in 1986. Since then, economic performance has fluctuated: 1988/89 was a period of expansion in GNP and employment, but this was followed by a period of sluggish growth in both. More recent years have seen very rapid growth in both output (of about 5 per cent per annum) and in employment (which grew by 136,000 or 12 per cent between 1993 and 1996). Under these conditions unemployment fluctuated between 13 per cent and 18 per cent of the labour force during the 1980s, and stood at 15.5 per cent in 1991, increased to almost 17 per cent in 1993 and fell to less than 13 per cent in 1996.

Emigration has fluctuated in accordance with demand in both domestic and external labour markets. It rose dramatically in the late 1980s and peaked in 1989, when net emigration (in-migration minus out-migration) rose to 44,000 individuals, representing almost 3.5 per cent of the labour force in that year. Net emigration subsequently fell, and in 1996 inward migration exceeded out-migration by about 6,000. The demographic structure is skewed towards the younger age groups, with the result that, in the absence of emigration, the labour force has the capacity to expand by up to 25,000 each year (i.e., by 1.5 per cent to 2 per cent).

State Policy and Employment

The active role of the State in the Republic in the restructuring of the economy through its promotion of the export-oriented development strategy, and attraction of foreign direct investment since the late 1950s has already been well documented (Breen *et al.*, 1990). In our analysis of the development of the welfare state (O'Connell and Rottman, 1992) we

Table 1. Numbers (in thousands) at work, unemployed and net migration, 1971–96.

Year	At work	Unemployed	Labour force	Unemployment rate (%)	Net migration
1971	1,049.4	60.7	1,110.1	5.5	−5
1976	1,063.8	105.0	1,168.8	9.0	16
1981	1,145.9	125.7	1,271.6	9.9	2
1986	1,080.9	227.5	1,308.4	17.4	−28
1991	1,134.0	208.0	1,342.0	15.5	−2
1993	1,148.0	230.0	1,378.0	16.7	−2
1996	1,284.0	190.0	1,474.0	12.9	6

Sources: Censuses of Population and Labour Force Surveys.

demonstrated how state policies were instrumental in setting the transformation of the economy and labour market in motion, while policies in other areas, particularly in relation to public employment and social welfare policy were equally influential in reshaping the class structure. We argued that the increasing salience of the state mediation of life chances was evident in:

1 State policies that fostered public employment;

2 Welfare state policies that created jobs not only for public employees, but also for self-employed professionals;

3 Economic, social and taxation policies which underwrote property-based market capacities that would not otherwise be viable, and which became manifest in the growth of self-employment;

4 Regional policies which redistributed industrial jobs from urban to rural areas.

Table 2 shows the transformation of the structure of employment between 1971 and 1995. The number at work in agriculture continued its secular decline and the share of agricultural employment fell from 26 per cent in 1971 to just over 11 per cent in 1995. By 1996, the numbers at work in agriculture had fallen to 136,000, representing a decline of 50 per cent over the twenty-five years from 1971. Kearney (1992) shows that this fall in the agricultural work-force was not caused primarily by farmers becoming unemployed or leaving the land to find alternative employment, but was due mainly to retirement and a reduced rate of entry. Kearney also argues that even after the persistent decline in recent decades, there is still a surplus of labour in agriculture, with the result that agricultural employment is expected to continue to contract into the next century.

Employment in manufacturing currently accounts for about 21 per cent

Table 2. Persons at work by sector 1971–95 (%).

	1971	1981	1986	1991	1995
Agriculture	25.9	17.1	15.5	13.7	11.3
Manufacturing	23.1	22.9	21.6	21.7	21.2
Building	8.0	8.8	6.7	6.9	6.6
Transport	5.7	6.1	6.0	5.8	6.2
Distribution	13.6	14.6	15.1	15.1	15.0
Other Market Services	11.4	13.5	15.5	17.9	39.7
Non-Market Services	12.3	17.0	19.5	18.8	
Total	100.0	100.0	100.0	100.0	100.0
Number (1,000)	1,049.4	1,145.9	1,080.9	1,134.0	1,233.6

Note: Percentages do not always sum to 100.0 owing to rounding.
Sources: Censuses of Population and Labour Force Surveys.

of total employment. In numerical terms, manufacturing expanded somewhat during the 1970s (from 242,000 in 1971 to 262,000 in 1981) and declined during the recessionary period between 1981 and 1986 (to about 234,000). Recent years have, however, seen some expansion in manufacturing, with the result that the number employed in 1995 was about the same as in 1981. Accordingly, the Republic is one of the few EU countries in which manufacturing employment is expanding, mainly due to the continued influx of inward investment, prompted by the range of tax and grant incentives, as well as the moderate cost structure.

Aggregate data on manufacturing employment conceal significant changes over time in its composition. Irish manufacturing comprises an indigenously owned sub-sector, trading mainly in traditional products (such as clothing, textiles and food processing) and largely oriented toward the domestic market, and a foreign-owned, more high-tech sector (concentrated in engineering, instrumentation, computers and chemicals), oriented mainly to export markets. The foreign-owned sub-sector has been the more dynamic, expanding continuously over the last three decades, and in the early 1990s accounted for about 46 per cent of total manufacturing employment. The indigenous sector was subject to severe decline, particularly during the 1980s, when uncompetitive Irish firms proved unable to withstand competition from larger and better established producers in the European core. This was the downside of the outward-oriented strategy, and it resulted in large numbers of industrial workers being displaced by the process of economic restructuring. Workers displaced from traditional uncompetitive indigenous firms did not necessarily possess the requisite skills to compete for jobs in the expanding foreign-owned sectors, giving rise to the emergence of a substantial problem of long-term unemployment, which is discussed later in this paper. In the more recent employment expansion since 1993, growth has occurred in both the indigenous and foreign-owned sub-sectors, suggesting that the lengthy period of weeding out of the uncompetitive firms from the indigenous sector may be near completion.

Employment has expanded markedly in the services sector over the past two-and-a-half decades, with total employment increasing from 587,000 in 1971 to over 750,00 in 1995, an increase of 28 per cent. Most of the employment in services has taken place in non-market services—mainly public sector activities, and particularly in education and health. Employment in this sector increased from 12 per cent of the total in 1971 to almost 20 per cent in 1986. Until the mid-1980s the rate of expansion in the public sector outstripped the rate of growth in the total labour force (O'Connell and Rottman, 1992), and by the early 1980s, if employment in state-sponsored bodies is included, the public sector employed one-third of the non-agricultural workforce (Humphries, 1983). Public sector employment contracted somewhat following austerity measures introduced to cope with the public debt crisis in 1987, although expansion of public sector employment has resumed in recent years. Employment in 'other market services' (which includes a broad range of business, professional and personal services) also increased steadily over the period, accounting for 12 per cent of the total in 1971 and almost 18 per cent in 1991.

These sectoral changes in the structure of employment, dominated by the expansion of employment in the public sector, combined with changes in the occupational structure *within* sectors to produce a far-reaching transformation of the class and occupational structures. Table 3 provides a summary of the transformation of class positions of both men and women at work between 1961 and 1991.

Between 1961 and 1991 the total number at work, as measured by the Census, increased by almost 100,000. This resulted from offsetting trends: the number of men at work declined by about 4 per cent over the period, while the number of women at work increased by 46 per cent, with the result that women's share of total employment increased from 26 per cent in 1961 to 35 per cent in 1991.

Perhaps the most marked change that can be observed over the thirty-year period is the decline in the number of employers and self-employed individuals deriving their income from property ownership—from almost 40 per cent of the total in 1961 to 22 per cent in 1991—and the consequent increase in the numbers of wage and salary dependent workers. This is, of course, one of the common effects of industrialisation, and what is most noticeable in the Irish context is the rapid pace of that transformation. The most important source of the decline in the importance of property ownership is the decline in agriculture discussed above—from 30 per cent of class positions in 1961 to 12 per cent in 1991. Among men, the decline in agricultural employment and self-employment was from 36 per cent to 16 per cent of all positions (and if we include agricultural labourers the decline in agricultural positions was from 45 per cent of the total in 1961 to less than 20 per cent in 1991). By 1991 women had almost disappeared from agriculture.

Outside of agriculture there was some increase in the proportion of employers, from 1.5 per cent to 4 per cent, while the proportion self-employed was about the same in both 1961 and 1991 (although there was a decline in the latter years until the early 1980s, and a subsequent recovery over the following decade). Among men, there was a marked increase in the proportion of employers—from 1.6 per cent of the total in 1961 to over 5 per cent in 1991, and self-employment also increased from 6 per cent to 8 per cent. Among women, however, there was a much smaller growth in the proportion of employers from 1 per cent to 2 per cent, and both the number and proportion of self-employed women fell.

Among the expanding categories of employees, the most dramatic change was the growth in middle-class positions. Between 1961 and 1991, the proportion of upper-middle class employees—including professionals, managers and salaried employees—more than doubled: from just under 10 per cent of total employment to over 22 per cent. Within the upper-middle class there were important gender differences. The proportion of men occupying higher professional positions doubled from 2.2 per cent to 4.3 per cent, while the corresponding proportion of women in the higher professional category declined (although the number remained constant). Among women, however, there was a very substantial increase in the lower professional category—from less than 9 per cent of total women's employment in 1961 to over 19 per cent in 1991. Most of the increase in this category can be attributed to the marked expansion over this period of lower professional employment in health and education in the public sector.

The lower-middle class also expanded, although less dramatically, from 23 per cent in 1961 to 31 per cent in 1991. Women predominate in this class category, which includes a rather diverse range of white-collar occupations, including clerical workers, shop assistants and personal service workers. By 1991, lower-middle class positions accounted for almost half of all women's employment but just over one-fifth of men's employment.

Skilled manual work increased slightly, from 10 per cent of total employment in 1961 to 12 per cent in 1991, but these aggregate figures also conceal offsetting trends between men and women. The proportion of skilled manual male employees increased from 12 per cent to almost 17 per cent while the proportion of women in skilled manual occupations declined from 6 per cent to 3 per cent over the thirty-year period. There was a steady decline in semi- and unskilled manual work—from 19 per cent in 1961 to 12 per cent in 1991. That decline was particularly severe among men, with the share of unskilled manual work declining from 21 per cent to less than 13 per cent.

Finally, Table 3 also shows that unemployment increased dramatically—from 5 per cent of the labour force in 1961 to almost 15 per cent in 1991. Unemployment among men increased from almost 6 per cent in 1961 to 16.5 per cent in 1991, while the increase among women was from 3 per cent to almost 12 per cent. The increase in unemployment was due partly to rapid growth in the labour force, a factor which was relieved by high rates of emigration, particularly in the latter half of the 1980s: net outward migration averaged 14,000 between 1981 and 1986 and 27,000 per annum between 1986 and 1991, the latter representing a net annual outflow

Table 3. Men and women at work by class position, 1961–91 (%).

	Men		Women		All	
	1961	1991	1961	1991	1961	1991
EMPLOYERS AND SELF-EMPLOYED						
Agriculture						
(i) Employers	1.8	1.4	1.1	0.2	1.6	1.0
(ii) Self-employed and						
relatives assisting	34.3	15.0	13.9	3.2	28.9	10.9
Non-Agriculture						
(i) Employers	1.6	5.2	1.1	1.9	1.5	4.1
(ii) Self-employed and						
relatives asisting	6.2	7.9	6.5	4.1	6.3	6.5
EMPLOYEES						
(i) Upper middle class	7.6	19.2	14.8	28.3	9.5	22.4
Higher Professional	*2.2*	*4.3*	*5.0*	*3.5*	*3.0*	*4.0*
Lower Professional	*1.7*	*5.2*	*8.9*	*19.4*	*3.6*	*10.2*
Employers/Managers	*2.0*	*6.9*	*0.8*	*4.3*	*1.7*	*6.0*
Salaried Employees	*1.6*	*2.7*	*0.0*	*1.1*	*1.2*	*2.1*
(ii) Lower middle class	15.6	21.9	42.7	48.8	22.8	31.4
Inter Non-manual	*8.6*	*11.7*	*24.7*	*36.7*	*12.8*	*20.5*
Other Non-manual	*7.1*	*10.1*	*17.9*	*12.1*	*10.0*	*10.8*
(iii) Skilled manual	12.0	16.8	5.8	2.8	10.3	11.9
(iv) Semi/Unskilled manual	20.9	12.7	14.1	10.6	19.1	11.9
(a) agriculture	*8.4*	*2.8*	*0.2*	*0.4*	*6.2*	*2.0*
(b) non-agriculture	*12.5*	*9.9*	*13.9*	*10.2*	*12.9*	*10.0*
Total	100.0	100.0	100.0	100.0	100.0	100.0
Total at work	774,540	743,948	277,999	405,132	1,052,539	1,149,080
Percent Unemployed	5.7	16.5	3.0	11.6	5.0	14.8

Note: Percentages do not always sum to 100.0 owing to rounding.
Sources: Census of Population of Ireland, 1961 and 1991.

equivalent to about 2 per cent of the labour force in those years (Sexton and O'Connell, 1996).

The transformation of the structure of the labour market was more far-reaching than just a shift from agriculture to industrial and service sector employment, or from manual to non-manual activities, although both of these changes did take place. The new types of occupation required either qualifications or personal skills which had not been required by traditional employment, or which were unnecessary to inherit the family business in a class structure dominated by property ownership. Many of the changes in the structure of labour market positions coincided with the removal of at least some of the impediments to women's participation in the labour market, with the result that many of the newly created opportunities were taken by women, contributing to the substantial increase in women's employment over the three decades. Among the losers in the transformation were those who lost jobs in traditional industries, and, particularly older workers who, lacking the qualifications and skills to compete for the newly created positions, became unemployed and, eventually long-term unemployed, a group to which we return later in this paper.

Reviewing the transformation of the Southern labour market over the thirty-year period 1991–61 revealed in Tables 2 and 3, five overarching trends can be observed:

1   A secular contraction in agriculture, and more generally, a substantial decline in the importance of positions deriving income from property ownership, and consequently, an increase in the importance of wage and salary dependent employment;

2   A marked expansion in public sector employment;

3   A general upgrading of the quality of positions in the labour market, with well over half of all those at work occupying middle-class positions by 1991;

4   A substantial increase in the number of women at work; and

5   A marked increase in unemployment—itself entailing a further augmentation of the numbers dependent on the state for their income.

The growth in women's employment is worth investigating somewhat more fully, not least because at the outset of industrialisation women's labour force participation in the Republic was well below the European average, and because the increase in women's labour force participation which might have been expected to result from industrialisation or modernisation did not in fact materialise in the first two decades of the process (Pyle, 1990; O'Connor and Shortall, this volume). It has, however, increased rapidly since the mid-1980s. Table 4 shows the numbers of men and women at work, unemployed and in the labour force, and labour force participation rates for the period 1971–96. The total labour force increased steadily over the twenty-five year period, and the overall labour force participation rate fluctuated between 52 per cent and 54 per cent. This stability in the labour force participation rate, however, resulted from very different trends for men and women. The number of men at work traces the dominant trends in the economy and labour market over the period: it increased over the 1970s, fell dramatically in the early 1980s, rose slightly in 1991, fell again in 1993 and increased in 1996, but at 796,000 was still lower than its level in 1981. In contrast, the number of women at work increased steadily throughout the period, in spite of the economic downturns, from 276,000 in 1971 to 488,000 in 1996. There was an overall net increase in unemployment between 1981 and 1996 for both men and women, and although the number of men at work fell in the period, the number of men in the labour force showed a net increase.

The number of women participating in the labour force increased by almost 90 per cent, from 287,000 in 1971 to 541,000 in 1996. This trend for increased female participation in the labour force is confirmed by the labour force participation rate for women, which rose from just under 28 per cent in 1971 to 30 per cent in 1981, and to 38.6 per cent in 1996.[1] Over the same period the labour force participation rate for men fell from 81 per cent in 1971 to 69 per cent in 1996.

Part of the reason for the sluggish growth in women's labour force participation may be attributable to the State, which throughout the 1960s and early 1970s continued to implement discriminatory employment policies. The subsequent increase may be due to the abandonment of explicitly discriminatory employment policies with the removal of the marriage bar in the Public Service in 1973, the Anti-Discrimination (Employment) Act of 1974, the Anti-Discrimination (Pay) Act of 1975, the Employment Equality Act of 1977, and the introduction of statutory right to maternity leave in 1981. This is an effect which can take some time to work itself out, since earlier policies had the effect of removing women from the labour force in a near-permanent fashion. Thus, for example, Walsh (1993) shows that the participation rate for women in the 25–34 year age group was 28 per cent in 1971, and that the rate remained unchanged for this group in 1991 (then aged 45–54 years). Empirical studies of the increase in women's labour force participation have related the increase in the 1980s to increased wages, itself a consequence of employment equality legislation, (Callan and Farrell, 1991) and to increased social welfare benefit and declining birth rates (Walsh, 1993).

Part of the reason for the more recent increase is also likely to be due to increased educational attainment among women—a result of the general increase in educational participation at senior cycle secondary and third level which followed the introduction of free second-level education in the late 1960s and the subsequent expansion of enrollment at both second and third level since the 1970s.

It has also been argued that the continued low rate of participation of women in the Southern labour market is due to the continuation of state policies which promote gender discrimination within the household, even after the abandonment of discriminatory policies in the labour market (Pyle, 1990). The most obvious example of such policy is the continued

---

[1] Women's labour force participation rates actually declined from 32.5 per cent in 1936 to 28.6 per cent in 1961, and between 1961–71, the first decade of rapid industrialisation the decline continued, albeit slightly, to 28 per cent in 1971.

Table 4. Numbers at work, unemployed (in thousands) and labour force participation rates by gender (%), selected years 1971–96.

	At work	Unemployed	Labour force	Labour force participation rate
Men				
1971	774	50	824	80.7
1981	809	104	913	76.4
1986	741	174	915	73.6
1991	747	156	903	71.0
1996	796	138	934	69.0
Women				
1971	276	11	287	27.9
1981	337	22	359	29.8
1986	339	54	393	30.9
1991	387	52	439	33.4
1996	488	52	541	38.6
Persons				
1971	1,049	61	1,110	54.2
1981	1,146	126	1,272	53.0
1986	1,081	227	1,308	52.0
1991	1,134	208	1,342	51.9
1996	1,284	190	1,474	53.5

Sources: Censuses of Population and Labour Force Surveys.

absence of state supported child care, or even of tax allowances to compensate parents for child-care expenses.

In this context, it is significant that a substantial part of the growth in women's employment over the past decade has been in part-time work, with the result that the proportion of women working part-time increased from 11 per cent of the total in 1983 to almost 20 per cent in 1995.

The incidence of part-time working has increased significantly since the mid-1980s. Table 5 shows that the share of part-time workers in total employment rose from 5 per cent in 1983 to over 10 per cent in 1995, or in absolute terms from 56,000 to 124,000. For men the proportion of part-timers rose from 2 per cent to 4.5 per cent, while for women the increase was from 11 per cent to nearly 20 per cent. The large majority of part-time workers are women and in 1995 they accounted for 72 per cent of all part-time work. Women's labour force participation has thus partly increased in response to an increase in the demand for part-time workers—an arrangement which allows women greater scope to combine working with child rearing and other domestic work.

Part-time work accounted for all of the modest increase in total employment that occurred between 1983 and 1993; in fact the numbers in full-time employment declined during this time. Part-time employment rose by some 43,000 but this was partially offset by a fall of 21,000 in the numbers in full-time jobs, leaving a net overall rise of 22,000. However the balance between growth in full- versus part-time work has altered again with the recent surge in employment: total employment increased by 87,000 between 1993 and 1995. Men's employment increased by 43,000, of which only 7,000 were part-time jobs. Women's employment increased by 45,000 over the same two years, but 18,000 were part-time jobs.

The increase in part-time work in recent years, as well as the strong growth in women's labour force participation, suggests that there is substantial demand for access to work, a demand which confounds conventional boundaries between unemployment, labour force participation and economic inactivity. This is confirmed by a recent survey of 700 individuals classified as 'inactive'—i.e., in retirement or home duties (Fynes *et al.*, 1996). Almost 98 per cent of respondents were women. The survey found that about 11 per cent had actively tried to find work within the previous three months. When asked, however, whether they would be realistically interested in taking up a part-time job on a job-sharing basis outside the home if such were available, a total of 60 per cent responded that they would. The study concluded that there is a substantial pool of women, not presently classified as unemployed, who express a strong interest in the

Table 5. Total employment 1983–95 (in thousands), distinguishing part-time workers.

Year	Total	Full-time	Part-time	Part-time share (%)
Men				
1983	777.6	761.3	16.3	2.1
1986	741.4	725.8	15.6	2.1
1991	747.0	726.5	20.5	2.7
1993	736.0	708.2	27.8	3.8
1995	778.8	743.8	35.0	4.5
Women				
1983	346.4	306.6	39.8	11.5
1986	339.5	301.8	37.7	11.1
1991	387.0	331.6	55.4	14.3
1993	410.2	339.2	71.0	17.3
1995	454.8	365.6	89.2	19.6
Persons				
1983	1,124.0	1067.9	56.1	5.0
1986	1,080.9	1027.6	53.3	4.9
1991	1,134.0	1058.1	75.9	6.7
1993	1,146.2	1047.4	98.8	8.6
1995	1,233.6	1,109.4	124.2	10.1

Sources: Annual Series of Labour Force Surveys.

kind of jobs which increased work sharing could make available. Extrapolating from these data to a national basis would suggest that about 420,000 women, equivalent to about 85 per cent of the women currently in paid work, could potentially be attracted back into the labour force by an increase in job availability. These findings thus indicate enormous pent-up demand for work, particularly part-time work, among women currently regarded as outside of the labour force.

Part-time work tends to be concentrated in particular types of activity, with 50 per cent of the total in service-related activities (Sexton and O'Connell, 1996). There has been little research to date into part-time work in the Republic, so little is known about pay and conditions, about how much of part-time work is voluntary or otherwise, nor about the stability of such work.

Unemployment Trends

The Republic of Ireland has suffered from mass unemployment over a prolonged period. We have seen in Table 1 above that unemployment has climbed steadily since the 1970s and accelerated over the 1980s. Empirical studies of the sharp increase in unemployment in the early 1980s suggest a complex of factors, including external economic conditions, domestic fiscal policies and, to a lesser extent, demographic growth (Barry and Bradley, 1991).

The Republic also suffers from an exceptionally high level of long-term unemployment: the proportion of the unemployed who have been out of work for a year or more is one of the highest in the European Union. Figure 1 shows total and long-term unemployment, expressed as a proportion of the labour force for selected EU countries in 1994. Spain had the highest unemployment rate (24 per cent) of any EU country, and it was also the country with the highest rate of long-term unemployment—13 per cent of the labour force. The unemployment rate in Ireland was 15 per cent of the labour force, with 9 per cent unemployed for one year or more. This compared with an EU average of 12 per cent unemployment and almost 7 per cent long-term unemployment.[2] Estimates from the 1994 Labour Force Survey indicate that the share of long-term in total unemployment in Ireland was nearly 63 per cent, compared with an EU average of 48 per cent.

Figure 2 shows total unemployment and long-term unemployment in Ireland for the period 1983–96. Total unemployment increased from

---

[2] EU average unemployment rates relate to the 15 EU member countries, not just to those displayed in Figure 1.

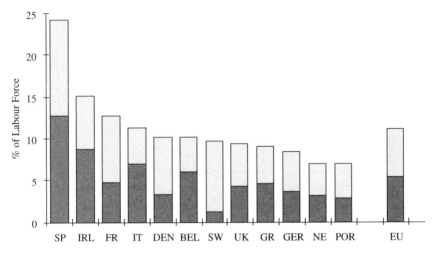

Figure 1. Unemployment rates in selected EU countries, 1994. ▢ <1 year, ▨ >1 year.
Source: European Commission, *Employment in Europe*, 1996.

194,000 in 1983 to 239,00 in 1987. Over the same period, long-term unemployment increased rapidly from 67,000 to 152,000, with the result that the proportion of the unemployed who were long-term unemployed increased from 35 per cent of the total in 1983 to almost 64 per cent in 1987. Thereafter, however, the numbers of long-term unemployed declined, particularly after 1988 when economic conditions improved. By 1990 the number of long-term unemployed had fallen to just under 110,000, even though this still constituted 64 per cent of total unemployment due to a concomitant decline in the overall numbers out of work. However, with the economic downturn of the early 1990s, there was a corresponding increase in both total and long-term unemployment, and the latter increased to 127,000 in 1994. The rapid expansion of the economy since 1993, however, gave rise to a substantial decrease in long-term unemployment in 1995, the numbers falling to 102,000, or just over 58 per cent of total unemployment, although there was virtually no change in the subsequent year.[3]

The trend data indicate that long-term unemployment is much more

---

[3] These estimates are based on ILO definitions, and are not available prior to 1983. It should be noted that the trend in long-term unemployment can be affected by the numbers on state employment schemes, as many participants in such schemes are recruited from among the long-term unemployed. Total participation in such schemes rose from 17,000 in 1993 to 41,000 in 1995, of which about two-thirds had been recruited from among the long-term unemployed. This suggests that long-term unemployment would have been even higher in 1994 were it not for these schemes, and that some of the decline in long-term unemployment observed between 1994 and 1995 is attributable to this source.

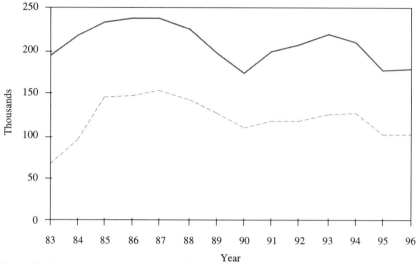

Figure 2. Total and long-term unemployment, 1983–95. ———— Total, - - - - Long-term.
Sources: (a) Special tabulations from the Annual Series of *Labour Force Surveys* (b)
EUROSTAT (1993).

significantly affected by cyclical changes in the economy than had here-
tofore been thought. Previous analyses of trends in long-term unemployment, which were based on the Live Register of unemployment, suggested
that the total number of long-term unemployed tends to increase following
recessionary periods, but that the number does not fall to any significant
degree when economic conditions improve (O'Connell and Sexton, 1994;
Breen and Honohan, 1991).[4] The data based on the *Labour Force Survey*
data presented in Figure 1 would suggest that such a hysteresis effect may
have been operative during the early part of the 1980s, when the number of
long-term unemployed increased from 67,000 in 1983 to 145,000 in 1985,
and the incidence of long-term unemployed increased from 35 per cent to
62 per cent of total unemployment. Since then, however, the trend in long-
term unemployment has been much closer to the trend in total unemployment, and more responsive to fluctuations in prevailing macro-economic
conditions.

---

[4] Most labour market analysts have now ceased to use the Live Register as a basis for
measuring either total unemployment or unemployment duration, both because of the growing discrepancy between Live Register and *Labour Force Survey* based estimates, which
suggests that the former is a better measure of the numbers claiming unemployment-related
social welfare payments than of the true incidence of unemployment, and because of a recent
study conducted by the Central Statistics Office (1996) which revealed that substantial
numbers of people who are not classified as unemployed in the *Labour Force Survey* are
nevertheless included in the Live Register total.

Table 6 shows the unemployed classified by age category and duration of unemployment for 1994. In 1994, 127,000 (nearly 64 per cent) out of 210,000 total unemployed had been unemployed for one year or more, and 87,000 (nearly 43 per cent) had been unemployed for more than two years. The long-term unemployed are predominantly male—men account for two-thirds of total long-term unemployment—and the incidence of long-term unemployment is higher among men (67 per cent of unemployed men are long-term unemployed) than among women (56 per cent).

Duration of unemployment is associated with age and is much more prevalent among the older age categories. Table 6 shows that while the share of long-term unemployment in total unemployment was just over 50 per cent in 1994 for those aged less than 25 years, it rose to nearly 63 per cent of persons aged between 25 and 39 years, and to well in excess of 70 per cent for persons aged over 40 years. The ratios were particularly high for those aged over 55, although it should be borne in mind that the absolute numbers involved are relatively small.[5]

If we focus on the age composition of long-term unemployment, we find that in 1994 about 25 per cent of the long-term unemployed were less than 25 years of age and a further 40 per cent were aged between 25 and 39. Thus about 65 per cent of the long-term unemployed are in age categories in which their expected labour force participation extends over two to four decades, rendering it particularly imperative to promote their reintegration into the world of work. The remaining 35 per cent of the long-term unemployed are aged over 40, and by virtue of their age alone, are likely to face severe difficulty in finding work.

One of the main impediments to effective labour market participation by the long-term unemployed is their generally poor educational qualifications. Table 7 shows educational qualifications by employment situation in 1991. Just under one-half of those at work had, at best, a junior second-level qualification, 30 per cent had taken the Leaving Certificate examination, and thus completed second level, and one-quarter had attended third-level education. The distribution of qualifications among the unemployed was less favourable, with 40 per cent having no qualifications, and about one-quarter having completed second-level education, including almost 7 per cent who had attended third level. The aggregate data for the unemployed, however, conceal important differences between the short-term and long-term unemployed. The long-term unemployed had a particularly poor educational profile—about 47 per cent had no

---

[5] The small numbers in the older age categories also give rise to rounding errors, with the result that the long-term unemployed share of total unemployment (78.3 per cent) appears to be less than the corresponding ratio for either men or women.

Table 6. The unemployed (in thousands) classified by age group and duration of unemployment, 1994.

Age	<1yr	1–2yrs	2yrs+	Not stated	Total	LTU	LTU share (%)
Men							
15–24	16.4	8.1	11.8	2.3	38.6	19.9	54.8
25–39	16.0	8.6	23.0	0.9	48.5	31.6	66.4
40–54	8.2	5.2	21.2	0.3	34.9	26.4	76.3
55+	1.7	1.2	5.6	0.2	8.7	6.8	80.0
Total	42.3	23.1	61.6	3.43	130.7	84.7	66.6
Women							
15–24	13.5	6.1	5.2	1.8	26.6	11.3	45.6
25–39	13.3	7.8	10.1	0.4	31.6	17.9	57.4
40–54	5.8	3.2	8.0	0.1	17.1	11.2	65.9
55+	0.4	0.5	1.5	0.3	2.7	2.0	83.3
Total	33.0	17.6	24.8	2.6	78.0	42.4	55.9
Persons							
15–24	30.1	14.3	17.1	4.1	65.6	31.4	51.1
25–39	29.2	16.4	33.1	1.4	80.1	49.5	62.9
40–54	14.2	8.3	29.2	0.4	52.1	37.5	72.5
55+	2.5	1.8	7.2	0.4	11.9	9.0	78.3
Total	76.0	40.8	86.6	6.3	209.7	127.4	62.7

Note: These estimates are based on ILO definitions. LTU: Long-term unemployed. Totals do not always sum to 100.0 owing to rounding
Sources: Special tabulations from the *Labour Force Survey*, 1994.

Table 7. Educational qualifications of those at work, unemployed and long-term unemployed, 1991.

	At work	Unemployed			
		All	Short term	Long term	Long term ≥35 yrs
No quals	21.7	40.1	24.3	47.2	65.1
Junior 2nd	26.2	34.5	37.7	33.2	22.4
Senior 2nd	30.7	18.6	26.9	14.9	8.3
3rd level	21.3	6.7	11.1	4.8	4.1
Total	99.9	99.9	100.0	100.1	99.9

Note: Totals do not always sum to 100.0 owing to rounding.
Source: *Labour Force Survey*, 1991 (Special tabulation).

qualifications whatsoever, and a further 33 per cent had only a junior-level qualification. The most educationally disadvantaged were the long-term unemployed aged over 35 years, 65 per cent of whom had no qualifications and another 22 per cent of whom had only a junior level qualification. While more than half of those at work in 1991 had completed upper secondary (and 20 per cent had attended third level), less than 20 per cent of the long-term unemployed had completed secondary education, and only 12 per cent of the older long-term unemployed had achieved this level of education.

The analysis of educational qualifications of the unemployed helps to explain why long-term unemployment has increased to such alarming levels in Ireland. In a situation of constant excess supply, caused partly by an influx of young new labour force entrants, the existing unemployed (particularly those who are older or disadvantaged), get pushed further down the queue of jobless and into long-term unemployment. The position has been exacerbated by the process of industrial restructuring which has caused the displacement of sizeable numbers of older workers, many with outdated skills. This 'queuing' phenomenon tends to further reinforce the problem, since a person who is marked with the stigma of long-term unemployment becomes less employable in the eyes of employers and it becomes increasingly difficult to escape from that state (Whelan *et al.*, 1990).

Our review of the age composition and educational qualifications of the long-term unemployed suggests that long-term unemployment represents a formidable problem with a significant structural dimension. While the fluctuation of trends over time in long-term unemployment may indicate that it is more susceptible to economic forces than previously envisaged, the total number of long-term unemployed has remained above 100,000 since the mid-1980s, and while it fell between 1994–95, it remained virtually unchanged between 1995–96. Furthermore, since it is the best equipped among the long-term unemployed who tend to find work first, it may be increasingly difficult of achieve further significant reductions in long-term unemployment, as the remaining body of long-term unemployed will tend to have an increasingly disadvantageous education and skills profile. There is, therefore, a need for continuing strenuous and well-targeted intervention on the part of the state if they are to be reintegrated into the labour market.

Youth Unemployment

As total unemployment soared over the course of the 1980s and again in the 1990s, so also did unemployment among young people. In 1981 almost 15 per cent of labour force participants in the 15–24 year age group were unemployed, compared to about 9 per cent of those aged over 25. The unemployment rate among young people reached its peak in 1993, when at over 27 per cent of the young labour force, it was almost double the unemployment rate among older labour force participants (14 per cent) (O'Connell and Sexton, 1994). This sharp increase in youth unemployment occurred despite a fall in the numbers of young people participating in the labour force.

Table 8 shows labour force and population data for young people in 1983 and 1995. The total population aged 15–24 increased only slightly over the period, due largely to high rates of emigration which peaked in the late 1980s.[6] Over the same period, however, the number of young people participating in the labour force declined by one quarter, from 359,000 in 1983 to 269,000 in 1995. This decline in the labour force participation rate—from 59 per cent to 44 per cent of the population age group, was due to a dramatic increase in educational participation—from 36 per cent of the population age group in 1983 to 53 per cent in 1995.

Over the entire period from 1983–95, the number of young people at work fell by one quarter, from 287,000 to 212,000, representing 47 per cent of the population age group in 1983, but only 35 per cent in 1995. While the absolute number of young people who were unemployed fell between 1983 and 1995, the decline in labour force participation meant that the un-employment *rate* among young people increased slightly between 1983 and 1995, although in 1995 the rate was substantially lower at 21 per cent than it had been in 1993 (27 per cent).

The decline in the number of young people at work, and the continua-tion of relatively high rates of unemployment among the 15–24 year age group, despite falling labour force participation, suggests that over time young people have found it increasingly difficult to find a foothold in the world of work. In 1983, workers aged 15–24 accounted for over 25 per cent of total employment, but by 1995 their share of total employment had fallen to 17 per cent. This fall in youth employment is mainly due to a closing off of the traditional ports of entry for young people, particularly in the case of clerical and junior professional openings, and skilled and semi-skilled work. O'Connell and Sexton (1994) show that young people bene-fited little from the employment surge of the late 1980s: between 1989 and 1991 youth employment actually fell while employment among those aged over 25 increased by 57,000. Young people have benefited more from the more recent expansion since 1993, although not to the same extent as older workers: employment of those aged 15–24 increased by 5 per cent between 1993 and 1995, while employment among those aged over 25 increased by 8

---

[6] Net outward migration amounted to over 200,000 between 1983 and 1995. Net migration is emigration less inward migration. The former tends to be concentrated among the younger age groups, while inward migration is more evenly spread across age groups, so net migration data is likely to underestimate the extent of out-migration among young people.

Table 8. Labour force and population trends among those aged 15–24, 1983 and 1995.

	1983		1995	
Principal Economic Status	(000)	%	(000)	%
At Work	286.6	47.0	212.3	34.6
Unemployed	71.9	11.8	56.4	9.2
Labour Force	358.5	58.8	268.7	43.9
Education	219.9	36.0	322.6	52.7
Other Non-Active	31.8	5.2	21.5	3.5
Population 15–24	610.2	100.0	612.7	100.0
Unemployment Rate		20.1		21.0
Youth Employment as a Percentage of Total Employment		25.5		17.2

Note: Totals do not always sum to 100.0 owing to rounding.
Source: *Labour Force Surveys*, 1983 and 1995.

per cent. In this respect Ireland differs from other countries, such as the United Kingdom and the United States, where young people have been recruited in disproportionately greater numbers than adults during economic upturns (Freeman and Wise, 1982; Makeham, 1980).

The marked growth in participation in education among the younger age groups has meant that the supply of well qualified candidates for jobs has increased. In a crowded labour market, young people with low or intermediate levels of qualification compete for jobs with somewhat older candidates who have higher levels of qualification, or work experience, or both. The problems confronting young labour force participants are very evident from Figure 3 which compares the proportion unemployed in each educational group for the younger age group (15–24) and those aged 25–64.

Figure 3 shows that at each level of educational attainment, young people were at very substantially higher risk of unemployment than their older counterparts. Those most at risk were young people with no quali-fications, 58 per cent of whom were unemployed, compared to 27 per cent of the older age group. Young people with the Junior Certificate faced a higher risk of unemployment than older people with no qualifications whatsoever. The unemployment rate of young people who had completed senior cycle secondary education (20 per cent) was well over twice that of the older group with a similar level of qualification (8 per cent), and the unemployment rate of young people who had attended third level was over three times the corresponding rate for the older age group.

Over the course of the 1990s, labour market prospects for young labour market entrants have generally improved in response to buoyant demand for labour. Nevertheless, while the employment prospects of those who left

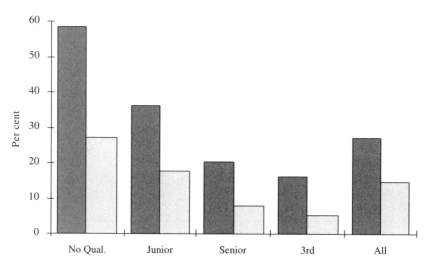

Figure 3. The risk of unemployment by age group and educational attainment in 1993. ▓ 15–24, ▢ 25–64. *Source: Labour Force Survey, 1993.*

after completing second-level education improved, the prospects of those with no qualifications or with only a junior level qualification continued to deteriorate; between 1991 and 1994 the proportion of those who left school with, at best, a junior level qualification, who were employed one year later decreased, while the proportion who were unemployed increased (O'Connell and McGinnity, 1997a).

Clearly the most disadvantaged young people in the labour market are those who leave school with no qualifications, although these are followed closely by those leaving on completion of the junior cycle of secondary education. The educational system produces an unacceptable number of poorly qualified early school leavers, ill equipped to compete in the labour market, although it should be acknowledged that the numbers of such poorly qualified school leavers have fallen substantially over the past decade. Both educational attainment and early school leaving are closely related to social class and children from lower socio-economic groups face a much greater risk of leaving school with inadequate qualifications than the children of higher socio-economic groups (Breen *et al.*, 1990; ESF Programme Evaluation Unit, 1996). Thus, despite the dramatic expansion of educational participation achieved in recent decades, class inequalities continue to be reproduced in the educational system, thus generating inequalities which then determine the distribution of opportunities in the labour market.

Breen and Whelan (1996) show that unemployment is very strongly related to social class. They found that the incidence of unemployment among the professional and managerial class is close to zero and is relatively modest among non-manual workers. Among skilled manual workers, however, the risk of unemployment at a given point in time increases to 20 per cent, and this increases to over 40 per cent among the unskilled manual group. Focusing on the duration of unemployment, they found that the average number of weeks of unemployment over the previous year was less than one week in the case of the professional and managerial group, but that this increased to 9 weeks in the case of the skilled manual group and to over 19 weeks in the case of the unskilled manual group. Both the risk of unemployment and the incidence of long-term unemployment is thus heavily concentrated toward the lower end of the social class hierarchy.

Given changes over time in the demand for labour, resulting in a general up-grading of available positions, as well as extended educational participation among the younger age groups, educational attainment has become the most significant labour market currency. Under these conditions, and in an overcrowded labour market, young people entering the labour market with inadequate qualifications are marginalised, as are older displaced workers with skills rendered obsolete by structural change.

State Labour Market Policies for the Unemployed

It has become conventional to distinguish between passive measures, which provide protection for unemployed workers, and active measures which are designed to improve the skills and competencies of the unemployed and support the search process in the labour market. Over the past two decades, in the Republic of Ireland, as in most other European countries, labour market policies have undergone a shift in emphasis to active measures to promote the reintegration of the unemployed into employment. This has meant that passive measures have been reformed in order to reduce the effects of unemployment traps and other barriers which derive from the structure of the taxation and welfare system and which can create disincentives for the unemployed to return to work, while active measures to provide training and subsidise employment have been expanded.

Most of the debate in recent years in relation to passive measures has focused on incentives and the relationship between incomes when in and out of work. Studies comparing Irish replacement rates—the ratio of out-of-work income (mainly from social welfare) to previous or potential net earnings, with those in other European countries have found that Irish replacement rates are not as high as in other European countries, although they are higher than in the United Kingdom. Such comparisons are, however, extremely sensitive to the income base for the comparison and the number of dependents involved (OECD, 1994). Similarly, comparative studies of the tax wedge—the gap between what it costs an employer to hire an employee and what the employee receives in take-home pay—suggests that Ireland is not significantly out of line with other European countries (NESC, 1993; OECD, 1994) Nevertheless, the tax wedge did increase rapidly in the early to mid-1980s, and may have created pressure to increase nominal wages and thus contributed to the decline in employment discussed earlier in this paper. Econometric evidence confirms that wage setting is influenced by the tax wedge (Bradley, Whelan and Wright, 1993). Recent initiatives in taxation and social welfare policy have sought to remove work disincentives by reducing both the numbers facing high replacement rates and the relative extent of the tax wedge, particularly for those on low incomes.

The state in the Republic has been particularly active in developing active labour market policies, and over the last decade such measures have become central to the policy response to unemployment. During the 1960s labour market policy in Ireland was mainly confined to the organisation of apprenticeship training and facilitating the efficient matching of supply and demand for labour. In the late 1960s two agencies were established; the National Manpower Agency, to facilitate placement, and AnCO, to provide and regulate training, but both were primarily oriented toward meeting the needs of employers and workers in employment. Active labour market policies as such, that is, designed specifically to meet the needs of the unemployed, were not developed until the onset of recession and the initial growth of unemployment in the 1970s. At that point employment subsidies and training schemes targeted on the unemployed were introduced (NESC, 1986). These were followed in the 1980s by temporary employment schemes, by which time active labour market policies had taken centre stage in the state response to mass unemployment. These policies were based on the premise that structural difficulties on the labour market are primarily on the supply side of the market, leading to a renewed emphasis on earlier policies to mobilise the supply of labour. This gradual shift in emphasis in Irish policy was consistent with the recommendations of the OECD (1990) and the European Commission (1994) to shift labour market expenditures from passive measures which provide protection for unemployed workers, to active measures which mobilise labour supply, improve the skills and competencies of the labour force, and strengthen the search process in the labour market.

By the end of the 1980s the Republic of Ireland was one of the leading countries in the share of national income devoted to active labour market policies and operated a wide range of differing programmes catering to a diversity of target groups among the unemployed and other socially excluded groups.

Table 9 presents a summary of active labour market programmes in Ireland, showing the numbers of participants (measured by throughput, the number completing programmes) and expenditure in 1994. A total of almost 93,000 individuals participated in such programmes in 1994, equivalent to 6.6 per cent of the labour force, or to almost 43 per cent of the total number unemployed, in that year.[7] Our estimates of expenditures for 1994 show that Irish expenditure on active measures amounted to 1.7 per cent of GNP, compared to an OECD average of 1 per cent (O'Connell and McGinnity, 1997a).

Table 9 distinguishes between four types of active labour market programme, two types of programme influencing labour supply—general and skills training—and two demand oriented measures—subsidies to employment in the private sector and direct employment or job creation schemes.

General Training includes a range of measures to provide basic or foundation level training in general skills. Most of the programmes are designed for those with poor educational qualifications experiencing labour market difficulties. This category includes second-chance education opportunities, programmes designed for women returning to work after a prolonged absence (usually in home duties), and older long-term unemployed males; measures targeted at young school leavers; community training, oriented towards the development of community resources; and training for people with disabilities. In 1994 there were almost 18,500 participants in general training programmes, representing 20 per cent of all active labour market participants in that year

Specific Skills Training courses provide training in specific, employable skills. The courses are market oriented and usually in skills areas linked to local labour market needs. The category includes skills training by FAS, the national education and training authority and CERT, the state tourism training agency. All these courses are characterised by high rates of placement in employment post-programme placement rates. They are open to all unemployed, although, in practice, many courses require minimum educational standards. In 1994 nearly 18,000 individuals participated, representing a further 20 per cent of all active labour market programme participants.

---

[7] These proportions are simply indicative of the scale of provision: a substantial proportion of participants in active labour market programmes are drawn from among those not actively participating in the labour force—including young labour market entrants, particularly early school leavers, and women returning to the labour force after a voluntary interruption in labour force participation.

Table 9. Distribution of activity on active labour market measures, 1994 (%).

Type of Measure	Participant Throughput %	Expenditure %
General Training	20	29
Skills Training	19	12
Employment Subsidies	23	8
Direct Employment Schemes	38	51
Total	100	100
Total Number/Expenditure	93,000	IR£420m

Source: O'Connell and McGinnity, 1997a: 28, Table 2.2.

Employment Subsidies provide subsidies to the recruitment or self-employment of unemployed workers in the private sector. They include:

1 Subsidies to employers in the form of either direct payments or social insurance contribution exemptions in respect of new additional hires;
2 Subsidies to employees, in the form of continued social welfare payments at reduced and declining rates for the first three years of employment; and
3 Subsidies to self-employment, in the form of income allowances or continued social welfare support for the initial years of business start-up.

Total participation in Employment Subsidies measures accounted for over 21,000 individuals in 1994, 23 per cent of all participants in active labour market programmes. Most, but not all, employment subsidies are targeted at the long-term unemployed, and are administered by differing agencies— mainly FAS and the Department of Social Welfare.

Direct Employment Schemes provide temporary part-time employment in community based work, together with personal and skills development opportunities. Community Employment is targeted mainly at long-term unemployed adults and, with over 32,000 participants, was the biggest single employment intervention in Ireland in 1994. The category also includes Teamwork which is targeted at unemployed young people, bringing the total who participated in direct employment schemes in 1994 to approximately 34,500, almost 40 per cent of all programme participants.

Preliminary indicators for 1995 suggest that Direct Employment Schemes continued to grow, and accounted for up to half of participants in programmes for unemployed people in that year, the number participating in Employment Subsidies measures declined to about half the 1994 provision, and the number receiving training increased somewhat. Thus, while the number of places in active labour market programmes for unemployed people continues to expand, the bulk of that growth is accounted for by Direct Employment Schemes, principally Community Employment.[8]

The international literature on active labour market policy suggests that the impact of such policies in creating additional employment is limited, with the exception of direct job creation measures (OECD, 1993). The research on the impact of such policies on the employment prospects of their participants shows a great deal of confusion, with empirical results often appearing to contradict each other (O'Connell and McGinnity, 1997a; Fay, 1996). Training policies may generate additional employment under conditions of skills shortages, and there is some evidence to suggest that training may have such positive effects in the Irish context, mainly because of the relatively low level of in-company training in Irish firms (Sexton and O'Connell, 1996). Effective and well-targeted measures may, however, serve to redistribute employment opportunities to less advantaged labour market participants.

A number of recent studies have attempted to assess the impact of labour market schemes in the Republic by tracking post-programme for performance of participants. The most recent such comprehensive analysis is that by O'Connell and McGinnity (1997a; 1997b) which covered about 3,500 former participants across a wide variety of publicly funded schemes. This research, which covered performance over a period of up to 18 months after leaving the schemes in question, revealed placement rates of 60 to 65 per cent for skilled training activities and employment subsidy programmes, rates of just over 30 per cent for general training schemes but as low as 25 per cent for direct employment schemes. When account is taken of individual characteristics (such as age, education and previous labour market experience) and participants are compared with a control group of non-participants, they find that in the short term, participation in any type of programme increased the probability of employment. However over the longer term involvement in market oriented programmes such as specific skills training or employment subsidies continued to result in a higher probability of employment, while participation in programmes with weak market linkages, such as general training or direct employment schemes, had no lasting effect on job prospects. They also found that programmes with strong linkages to the labour market led to greater subsequent employment stability and higher earnings than did programmes with weak market linkages.

We argue, however, that these findings should not be interpreted to suggest that the latter programmes are of no value and should be discontinued. For

---

[8] For a more detailed description of current provision in active labour market programmes see Sexton and O'Connell, 1996: Chapter 8.

many of the unemployed their educational qualifications or skills may be so inadequate that participation in general or foundation level training, or in temporary work experience offers the only hope of eventual reintegration into the labour market. The findings do suggest, however, that general training or temporary employment supports are of themselves unlikely to significantly improve the job prospects of participants unless they are followed by progression to more advanced schemes which have better linkages with the open labour market. This suggests the need for reintegration paths designed to allow the long-term unemployed and socially excluded to progress through a series of programmes tailored to their particular needs with the ultimate objective of securing sustainable employment.

There has been a dramatic increase in the numbers participating in active labour market programmes in Ireland in recent years. Total participants in all active labour market support measures increased from about 55,000 in 1992 to almost 93,000 in 1994, or from 4 per cent of the labour force in 1992 to 6.6 per cent in 1994. Despite this increase in activity, however, there is a marked absence of a coherent strategic approach to combating unemployment, and moreover, some evidence of a lack of coordination between different state agencies.

First, those most disadvantaged in the labour market—including the long-term unemployed, young early school-leavers, and women seeking to return to work—are more likely to participate in basic level training or in direct job creation measures than in skills training or in measures which subsidise employment/self-employment in the private sector (McGinnity, 1996). Relatively low placement rates from such programmes are partly due to the low qualifications and poor previous labour market experiences of participants, but they also reflect the quality of the programmes, and where it is provided, the level of training.

Second, direct employment schemes have expanded dramatically in recent years, but such schemes have been found to achieve low rates of placement in employment (O'Connell and Sexton, 1995; O'Connell and McGinnity, 1997a; 1997b). The Community Employment Scheme is the largest such programme targeted on the long-term unemployed and socially excluded, and currently provides temporary half-time employment for over 50,000 individuals. The scheme includes a training module, but in 1994 less than half of participants were receiving training, and in any event, the training component typically amounts to 20 days. It is difficult to imagine how 20 days of training could be expected to counteract the educational disadvantages of most Community Employment participants.

Moreover, the provision of large-scale programmes to absorb large numbers of the long-term unemployed in temporary job creation measures represents a policy choice for an expansion in the quantity of provision rather than an improvement in the quality of programmes. Such a policy appears to be predicated on an assumption that long-term unemployment does not respond to cyclical movements in the economy and improvements in labour market demand. Our review of trends over time in long-term unemployment above suggests that this assumption is unwarranted. If long-term unemployment declines during upturns in the labour market, as occurred in the late 1980s and again between 1994–95, then it is likely that a creaming-off process occurs, whereby the best-equipped among the long-term unemployed find work first. Such a creaming-off process leaves a residual group of long-term unemployed with particularly poor labour market prospects. If this group is to be reintegrated then it would require particularly well targeted interventions of a substantially more intensive nature than is currently available to most of the long-term unemployed.

Third, programmes targeted on marginalised groups suffer from a general weakness in not facilitating progression to further education and training—despite the fact that most participants in such programmes are in greater need of such progression opportunities than any other group of labour market participants. Recent reforms in certification systems have led to some improvement in progression options at foundation level training, although there remain strong elements of segregation between the training and educational system—rendering it difficult, for example, for an early school leaver who has completed a training course to access further education, rather than further training. Ultimately, removing barriers to progression problems is a matter of ensuring both resources and adequate training standards and certification arrangements to facilitate participants to gain access to further education and training opportunities.

Finally, in recent years there has been a proliferation of employment subsidy programmes targeted at differing groups with shifting responsibilities between differing agencies, leading to difficulties in coordinating services and confusion among both the unemployed and potential employers regarding availability, eligibility and administration of the various subsidies. Moreover, it is well established that employment subsidies suffer from high levels of dead-weight, whereby a substantial proportion of recruits would have found jobs in the absence of subsidies (Breen and Halpin, 1989). Targeting of employment subsidies to groups particularly hard to place (without subsidies) may serve to reduce that dead-weight (OECD, 1993). Policy formation has been slow to take account of such evidence, however, with the result that some of the new employment subsidies have been targeted broadly (at the unemployed in general) rather than specifically targeted on the long-term unemployed and other hard-to-place groups, running the risks of creaming off the more advantaged among the unemployed, and thus excluding the most marginalised, and incurring high dead-weight costs.

Recent changes in active labour market policies have entailed a substantial increase in activity on active programmes to combat unemployment. However, most of the additional resources appear to have been used to achieve an expansion in the quantity of provision rather than an improvement in the quality of programmes. The evidence on the effectiveness of programmes suggests that there is a need to improve the quality of programmes, particularly those targeted at the most disadvantaged, as well as to ensure progression to effective programmes in the final phase of reintegration paths which have the ultimate objective of securing sustainable employment. Such an approach would require the allocation of substantially greater resources targeted specifically at those most disadvantaged in the labour market, an issue which raises major political decisions about how the fruits of the recent economic growth are to be distributed in society.

Conclusion

This paper has reviewed the principal developments in employment and unemployment and in state policy in the Republic over the past three decades. Over that period we can observe an overarching trend towards increasing polarisation between those who possess capacities to compete in the labour market and those who do not; between those who work and those who do not. The polarisation process entailed a general upgrading of positions for those at work and the social exclusion of those unable to compete for jobs in the changing economy. Increased inequality during a period of industrialisation is generally expected under modernisation theories of the development process, although this is usually understood to derive from market processes. In the Republic, however, the increase in inequality has taken place as part of a developmental process initiated and fostered by a highly interventionist state.

In the world of work we can see four interrelated trends over the past thirty years:

1 A substantial decline in the importance of positions deriving income from property ownership, driven mainly by the contraction of employment in agriculture, and a consequent increase in the importance of wage and salary dependent employment;

2 A marked expansion of employment in the public sector;

3 A general upgrading of positions in the labour market, with well over half of all those at work occupying middle-class positions by the early

1990s, and a decline in the demand for semi- and unskilled manual work; and

4 A substantial increase in the number of women at work.

Coinciding with these changes in the world of work we also see a steady increase in the ranks of the unemployed, beginning in the 1970s and accelerating throughout the 1980s. Mass unemployment represents the failure of a state interventionist strategy which promoted economic restructuring, facilitated the upgrading of occupational positions and assisted the winners in the transformation process to compete for the newly created positions through free and subsidised education.

Within the ranks of the unemployed, the paper identifies two particularly marginalised groups: firstly, the long-term unemployed, accounting for about 60 per cent of total unemployment, many of whom were displaced in the process of economic restructuring, and lack the requisite skills to compete for jobs in today's labour market; and secondly, young early school leavers, similarly ill-equipped to compete in the labour market, facing extremely high rates of unemployment, and ultimately joining the ranks of the long-term unemployed with little hope of finding a place in the world of work. Both of these socially excluded groups are drawn disproportionately from manual working-class groups, with the result that class inequalities have remained largely undisturbed by economic restructuring, and, moreover, continue to be reproduced in the educational system.

Active labour market policies have come to represent the principal state response to mass unemployment. The Republic of Ireland is one of the leading countries in the share of national income spent on active labour market programmes, and it has developed a wide range of programmes catering to a diverse target population accounting for a very substantial proportion of the unemployed and other marginalised groups. Nevertheless, state policy on unemployment is characterised by the absence of a coherent strategic approach to combating unemployment and social exclusion, resulting in sub-optimal usage of resources and, in general, a failure to reintegrate the most marginalised. Thus, despite a great deal of activity, state intervention achieves little to counteract social exclusion.

How then, should we interpret the recent growth in employment in the context of this broader picture of the labour market in the Republic? It must be acknowledged that the surge in economic growth and employment represents a significant achievement, particularly in comparison with the sluggish performance of other European countries. Continued growth of similar magnitude is essential if unemployment is to be reduced.

More generally, these recent trends represent a continuation of well established trends. With regard to those at work, the upgrading of positions in the labour market continues, with most of the expansion in employment forecast to occur in the professional, managerial and proprietorial occupations, but with significant growth also at the lower end of the occupational spectrum in sales, security and service occupations (Canny, Hughes and Sexton, 1995). The strong growth since 1993 also continues the increase in the number of women at work — with about 60 per cent of the net increase being accounted for by women. If trends observed during the earlier half of the 1990s are continued, about 30 per cent of the net increase is accounted for by part-time jobs. These part-time jobs have been predominantly taken by women, and while there has been little research on the conditions of part-time work in the Republic, it is likely that this sector is characterised by wide diversity, and that a substantial proportion of the jobs are in low-paid and unstable employment.

With regard to unemployment, it should be noted that the net increase in employment of 136,000 between 1993–96 resulted in a decline in unemployment of about 40,000, and that the increase in total employment of 55,000 achieved between 1995–96 served to reduce unemployment by only 1,000. The persistence of high unemployment despite rapid growth in employment is due to the strong growth in the labour force, and serves as a reminder that there is a huge pent-up demand for work, not only among young entrants to the labour force, but also among women currently classified as economically inactive. Finally, with regard to long-term unemployment, I have argued that recent changes in state labour market policies are unlikely to be sufficient to achieve a significant improvement in the labour market prospects of the most marginalised among the unemployed.

Acknowledgements. I would like to thank John Bradley, Anthony Heath, Frances McGinnity and Chris Whelan for valuable comments on an earlier draft. Many thanks to Frances McGinnity for research assistance on both drafts.

References

Barry, F. and Bradley, J. (1991) 'On the Causes of Ireland's Unemployment', *Economic and Social Review,* 22: 253–86.

Bradley, J., Whelan, K. and Wright, J. (1993) *Stabilization and Growth in the EC Periphery,* Aldershot: Avebury.

Breen, R. (1991) *Education, Employment and Training in the Youth Labour Market,* Economic and Social Research Institute, General Research Series Paper No. 152, Dublin: ESRI.

Breen, R. and Halpin, R. (1989) *Subsidising Jobs: An Evaluation of the Employment Incentive Scheme,* Economic and Social Research Institute, General Research Series Paper No. 144, Dublin: ESRI.

Breen, R., Hannan, D., Rottman, D. and Whelan, C. (1990) *Understanding Contemporary Ireland: State, Class and Development in the Republic of Ireland*, London: Macmillan.

Breen, R. and Honohan, P. (1991) 'Trends in the Share of Long-term Unemployment in Ireland', *The Economic and Social Review*, 23: 73–92.

Breen, R. and Whelan, C. (1996) *Social Mobility and Social Class in Ireland*, Dublin: Gill and Macmillan.

Callan, T. and Farrell, B. (1991) *Women's Participation in the Irish Labour Market*, Dublin: National Economic and Social Council, Report No. 91.

Callan, T., Nolan, B. and O'Donoghue, C. (1996) *What has Happened to Replacement Rates?*, Paper to Irish Economic Association Annual Conference, April 1996.

Canny, A., Hughes, G. and Sexton, J. J. (1995) *Occupational Employment Forecasts 1998*, FAS/ ESRI Manpower Forecasting Studies, Report No. 3. Dublin: ESRI.

Central Planning Bureau (1995) *Replacement Rates: A Transatlantic View*, Working Paper No. 80, The Hague: Central Planning Bureau.

Central Statistics Office (1996) 'Study of the Differences between the Labour Force Survey Estimates of Unemployment and the Live Register', Cork: Central Statistics Office.

Department of Enterprise and Employment (1996) *Growing and Sharing Our Employment*, Dublin: Stationery Office.

Department of Labour (1991) *Economic Status of School-Leavers 1990*, Dublin: Department of Labour.

Dublin Inner City Partnership and Scheme Workers Alliance (1995) *Community Employment: Options and Opportunity*, Dublin: Inner City Partnership and Scheme Workers Alliance.

Duffy, D., Fitz Gerald. J., Kearney, I. and Shortall, F. (1997) *Medium Term Review: 1997–2003*, Dublin: ESRI.

European Commission (1994) *Growth, Competitiveness, Employment: The Challenges and Ways Forward into the 21st Century*, White Paper, Luxembourg: European Commission.

European Social Fund (ESF) Programme Evaluation Unit (1996) *Evaluation Report: Early School Leavers Provision*, Dublin: ESF Programme Evaluation Unit.

Eurostat (1995) *Population and Social Conditions: Labour Costs in Industry, 1992*, Luxembourg: European Commission.

Expert Working Group on the Integration of the Tax and Social Welfare Systems (1993) *Interim Report*, Dublin: Stationery Office.

Fay, R. (1996) *Enhancing the Effectiveness of Active Labour Market Policies: Evidence from Programme Evaluations in OECD Countries*, Paris: OECD.

Freeman, R. B. and Wise, D. A. (1982) *The Youth Labour Market Problem: Its Nature, Causes and Consequences*, Chicago: Chicago University Press.

Fynes, B., Morrissey, T., Roche, W., Whelan, B. and Williams, J. (1996) *Flexible Working Lives: The Changing Nature of Working Time Arrangements in Ireland*, Dublin: Oak Tree Press.

Humphries, P. (1983) *Public Service Employment: An Examination of Strategies in Ireland and Other European Countries*, Dublin: Institute of Public Administration.

Kearney, B. (1992) 'Trends in the Farm Labour Force', *FAS Labour Market Review*, 3(1): 1–11.

Kennedy, K. A., Giblin, T. and McHugh, D. (1988) *The Economic Development of Ireland in the Twentieth Century*, London: Routledge.

Lee, J. J. (1989) *Ireland 1912–1985: Politics and Society*, Cambridge: Cambridge University Press.

Makeham, P. (1980) *Youth Unemployment*, Research Paper No. 10, Department of Employment, London: Department of Employment.

McCoy, S. and Whelan, B. J. (1996) *The Economic Status of School Leavers 1993–1995*, Dublin: ESRI.

McGinnity, F. (1996) 'Long-term Unemployment and Access to Active Labour Market Programmes in Ireland', Poster paper presented to the European Science Foundation Conference on Social Exclusion and Social Integration in Europe, Blarney, March 1996.

National Economic and Social Council (NESC) (1986) *Manpower Policy in Ireland*, NESC Report No. 82, Dublin: NESC.

National Economic and Social Council (NESC) (1993) *A Strategy for Competitiveness, Growth and Development*, NESC Report No. 96, Dublin: NESC.

O'Connell, P. (1996) 'The Effects of Active Labour Market Programmes on Employment in Ireland', ESRI Working Paper Series No. 72, Dublin: ESRI.

O'Connell, P. and McGinnity, F. (1997a) *Working Schemes? Active Labour Market Policy in Ireland*, Aldershot: Avebury.

O'Connell, P. and McGinnity, F. (1997b) 'What Works, Who Works? The Impact of Active Labour Market Programmes on the Employment Prospects of Young People in Ireland', *Work, Employment and Society*, 11(4) 631–61.

O'Connell, P. and Rottman, D. (1992) 'The Irish Welfare State in Comparative Perspective', in J. H. Goldthorpe and C. T. Whelan (eds), *The Development of Industrial Society in Ireland*, Oxford: The British Academy and Oxford University Press.

O'Connell, P. and Sexton, J. J. (1994) 'Labour Market Developments in Ireland, 1971–1993', in J. Cantillon, J. Curtis and J. Fitz Gerald (eds), *Economic Perspectives for the Medium Term*, Dublin: ESRI.

O'Connell, P. and Sexton, J. J. (1995) 'An Evaluation of Measures to Assist Young People and the Long-Term Unemployed under Objectives 3 and 4 of the Community Support Framework', Report to the European Commission, DGV, Dublin: ESRI.

OECD (1990) *Labour Market Policies for the Nineties*, Paris: OECD.

OECD (1993) *Employment Outlook*, Paris: OECD.

OECD (1994) *The OECD Jobs Study: Part II: The Adjustment Potential of the Labour Market*, Paris: OECD.

OECD (1995) *Employment Outlook*, Paris: OECD.

Office of the Tanaiste, (1995) *Report of the Task Force on Long-term Unemployment*, Dublin: Stationery Office.

O'Hearn, D. (1990) 'The Road from Import Substituting to Export Led Industrialisation in Ireland', *Politics and Society*, 18: 1–38.

O'Malley, E. (1989) *Industry and Economic Development: the Challenge for the Latecomer*, Dublin: Gill & Macmillan.

Pyle, J. L. (1990) *The State and Women in the Economy: Lessons from Sex Discrimination in the Republic of Ireland*, Albany: State University of New York Press.

Sexton, J. and O'Connell, P. (eds) (1996) *Labour Market Studies: Ireland*, Luxembourg: Commission of the European Union.

Walsh, B. (1993) 'Labour Force Participation and the Growth of Women's Employment in Ireland 1971–1991', *The Economic and Social Review*, 24: 369–400.

Whelan, B. J., Breen, R., Callan, T. and Nolan, B. (1990) *A Study of the Employment Possibilities of the Long Term Unemployed*, Study carried out for the Department of Labour, Dublin: The Economic and Social Research Institute.

The Northern Ireland Labour Market

GRAHAM GUDGIN

Introduction

DESPITE BEING ONE OF THE FASTEST GROWING REGIONS of the UK, Northern Ireland has always been better known for its economic and social problems than for its successes. More than anything it is high unemployment which has differentiated the Northern Ireland economy from the rest of the UK and indeed from much of the rest of Europe. In recent years, however, and particularly since August 1996, this unenviable situation has changed. Unemployment has fallen to its lowest level since the 1970s, and the unemployment gap between Northern Ireland and Great Britain is at a historic low. Many of the EU states now have unemployment rates well above that of Northern Ireland, although this is as much to do with rising unemployment in the EU as with falling unemployment in Northern Ireland. One well-known contrast, however, remains within Northern Ireland: Catholics continue to have unemployment rates twice as high as those of Protestants.

This chapter focuses on two problems. The first is why unemployment in Northern Ireland has traditionally been so high, and particularly the issue of why the unemployment rate should be higher than that in Great Britain when Northern Ireland has had one of the most favourable records of job creation of any UK region. The second is why Catholic unemployment should remain persistently higher than Protestant unemployment despite the fact that Catholic employment has grown more rapidly than that of Protestants. The second section begins with a review of the salient characteristics of the Northern Ireland labour market. This is followed in the third section by an analysis of the dynamics of labour-market change to investigate how migration and wage levels act as adjustment mechanisms to

Proceedings of the British Academy, **98**, 251–284. © The British Academy 1999.

bring the supply and demand for labour into balance, albeit a balance at a high level of unemployment. The fourth section examines the question of why unemployment is so much higher among Roman Catholics than among Protestants. The chapter concludes that high levels of local unemployment are determined to a significant extent by high rates of natural increase in population and by migration propensities which are insufficiently large to bring labour supply into balance with demand at low unemployment rates.

The Salient Characteristics of the Northern Ireland Labour Market

For most of this century Northern Ireland has suffered the misfortune of having the highest unemployment rate of any UK region. During the decades of close to full employment in the UK, in the 1950s and 1960s, Northern Ireland was virtually the only region with a significant unemployment problem, with unemployment rates usually close to 6 per cent of the labour force. Unemployment had even been moderately high during the Second World War, to the embarrassment of the Stormont and Westminster governments given the acute labour shortages of those years.

Since 1973 unemployment has been both high and fluctuating throughout the UK, as in much of the rest of Europe. Whatever the level in Britain, it has always been the case that the unemployment rate in Northern Ireland has been higher (Figure 1). Indeed for the first 15 years of the post-1973 era

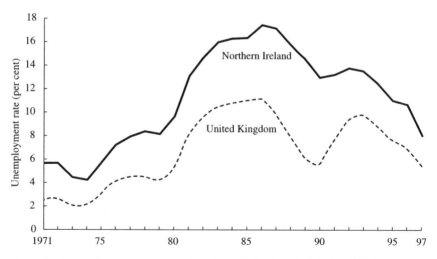

Figure 1. Unemployment rates for Northern Ireland and Britain 1971–97. *Source*: Department of Employment. Labour Market Trends.

of high unemployment, the gap in unemployment rates between Northern Ireland and Great Britain widened remorselessly and by 1989 the unemployment rate in Northern Ireland was a record nine percentage points above that in Great Britain. Since 1989 an equally remarkable reconvergence has occurred. Unemployment in Northern Ireland in 1996, although remaining well above the British level at 11.2 per cent (compared with 7.6 per cent in Great Britain), was closer to the British rate than at any time since the early 1970s when rapid out-migration connected with the Northern Ireland 'Troubles' temporarily depressed unemployment levels.

The unemployment gap between Northern Ireland and Great Britain appeared to stabilise from 1993 onwards, at three percentage points above the British average, and this gap could be interpreted as a dynamic equilibrium at which inflows and outflows into unemployment were balanced. Since August 1996 a further remarkable change has occurred. Claimant unemployment fell by over a third in the following twelve months, reducing the number of unemployed from 87,000 in August 1996 to 60,000 in August 1997 (Table 1).

This dramatic and unexpected decline in unemployment paralleled a similar change in Great Britain, although the rate of decline was twice as rapid in Northern Ireland. In neither Northern Ireland nor Great Britain was the fall in unemployment mainly due to any acceleration in job creation. The reduction of 27,000 in the number of unemployed over twelve months was matched by the creation of only 9,000 extra jobs. Instead, most of the reduction is likely to reflect a change in the administrative

Table 1. Salient characteristics of the Northern Ireland labour market (in thousands).

	Employed and self-employed	Unemployed	Absent from work due to sickness and invalidity	Numbers on training and temporary employment schemes	Working age population
1971	574	35	42	n.a.	879
1981	577	86	49	19	903
1991	634	95	66	24	970
1997	658[1]	60[2]	99[3]	27[4]	1,020[5]

Notes: 1 May 1997 for employees in employment, excludes HM Forces; June 1996 for self-employed.
    2 August 1997.
    3 December 1996.
    4 April 1997.
    5 Estimate based on 1995 NISRA mid-year estimates, cohort survival and projected migration.

Sources: Department of Economic Development, Northern Ireland Registrar General.

arrangements for unemployment benefits. The introduction of the new Job Seekers' Allowance in August 1997 has tied benefits more closely to the active search for work. The coincidence of the introduction of more stringent rules for job search, and the subsequent large reduction in unemployment, suggests that many of those previously registered as unemployed may not have been actively seeking work. The introduction of the fraud telephone 'hotline' in February 1996 may also have contributed to a reduction in fraudulent claimants.

The reduction in unemployment has been shared equally between short-term and long-term unemployment, and Northern Ireland's extraordinarily high rate of long-term unemployed claimants has moved closer to the average in Great Britain. As a result, the overall unemployment rate is currently only 2.5 percentage points above the British rate, and this may represent a new long-term equilibrium, perhaps more accurately reflecting realities in the labour market. The reduction has also been greatest in areas of highest unemployment, which in Northern Ireland are also mainly areas of majority Catholic population, chiefly located in the west of the Province.

The majority of the 60,000 people registered as unemployed in mid-1997 were males, and the rate of registered unemployment for males was more than double that of females (Figure 2). For much of the 1980s close to one in five males in Northern Ireland was registered as unemployed. Males also form the majority of people on Incapacity Benefit which, we argue below, probably includes a substantial number of what might be termed the disguised unemployed.

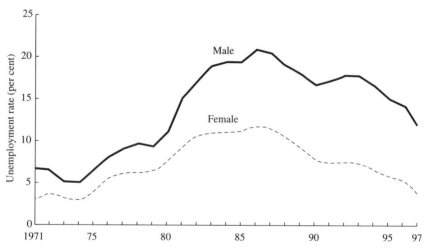

Figure 2. Male and female unemployment rates in Northern Ireland 1971–97. *Source*: Department of Employment. Labour Market Trends.

The large differences between male and female registered unemployment is not unique to Northern Ireland and is a long-standing characteristic of the UK labour market. In Northern Ireland it appears to be a real
difference, not greatly distorted by methods of recording unemployment.
In the UK system, in operation until mid-1998, females seeking work did
not necessarily register as unemployed, for three main reasons. Firstly,
many jobless women are not eligible to claim unemployment-related
benefits. For example, some jobless women may have an unemployed
partner who is claiming unemployment-related benefits on her behalf.
Other women may have a partner in full-time, well-paid employment,
and so will not be eligible to claim means-tested benefits.

Secondly, jobless women who have children may find it difficult to meet
some of the availability-for-work criteria, which are central both to survey-
based definitions of unemployment and to the 'claimant count' of those
receiving benefits associated with unemployment. For example, an unemployed mother must be able to have child-care arrangements in place within
24 hours in order to be eligible to claim unemployment-related benefits.

Thirdly, the term 'unemployed' can be ambiguous for many jobless
women. For example, survey evidence has shown that many jobless women,
particularly those with children, are reluctant to describe themselves as
unemployed because they associate the term with 'doing nothing'
(McLaughlin, 1993: 136).

The claimant count on which Table 1 is based is often viewed as an
inappropriate measure of female unemployment. A better measure is used
in the Labour Force Survey (LFS), based on the International Labour
Office (ILO) definition of unemployment. 'ILO unemployment' is an internationally recognised definition of unemployment, according to which an
individual is classified as unemployed if she or he (a) is not in employment,
(b) has looked for work in the previous four weeks and (c) is available to
start work within the next two weeks. The latest figures from the Labour
Force Survey (LFS) show that around two-thirds (66 per cent) of married
women in Northern Ireland who are ILO unemployed do not claim unemployment-related benefits. This compares to around one-quarter (24 per
cent) of single women and a similar figure for men. In the UK as a whole,
most unemployed females are not claiming benefits (Table 2). The LFS
figure thus shows a much higher level of female unemployment than the
claimant count, and can be regarded as a more accurate measure of female
unemployment.

The position for females, however, differs considerably between Northern
Ireland and Great Britain. In Northern Ireland a higher percentage of the
ILO unemployed are claimants, and at the same time there are more
claimants who are not actively searching for work. This may mean that there

Table 2. Comparison of ILO unemployed and claimants. Winter 1995/96 (% of economically active).

	Northern Ireland		Great Britain	
	Male	Female	Male	Female
ILO Unemployed and Claimants	9.5	3.0	6.9	2.3
ILO Unemployed, Non-Claimants	3.1	2.7	2.8	4.0
Claimants, Non-ILO Unemployed	5.1	2.9	4.4	1.8
All Claimants	14.6	5.9	10.2	4.0
All ILO	12.6	5.7	9.7	6.3

Source: Labour Force Survey, March 1996, Table 20; Northern Ireland Labour Force Survey, Winter 1995.

are more discouraged females in Northern Ireland. It may also indicate a greater success among ILO unemployed females in claiming benefits. Whatever the causes, it remains true that for females the ILO and claimant count definitions are considerably closer together in Northern Ireland than in Great Britain. One consequence is that in 1995/96 Northern Ireland had the highest rate of female unemployment for any UK region on the claimant count, but the second lowest rate on the ILO definition (Table 2).

The Labour Force Survey also provides a better measure of the number of males actively seeking work despite being based on a sample. It is generally true that there are greater numbers of unemployed males in the claimant count statistics than in the LFS (Table 2). This indicates that a number of the male unemployed claim unemployment-related benefits but are not actively seeking work. These males might be described as discouraged workers, but this total may also include people fraudulently claiming benefits.

The majority of unemployed males in Table 2 were both claimants and ILO unemployed (i.e., actively seeking work). In Northern Ireland in 1996, 9.5 per cent of the economically active were in this category. A further 3.1 per cent were seeking work but were not claiming benefits. Finally, 5.1 per cent were claimants who were not actively seeking work. It is this 5.1 per cent which includes both discouraged workers and fraudulent claimants. As Table 2 shows this category was larger in Northern Ireland than in Great Britain.

Incapacity Benefit Claimants

The existence of discouraged workers who are jobless but neither registered as unemployed nor actively seeking work means that both the claimant and

LFS figures are likely to be underestimates of unemployment. An important source of underestimation has been the growth in the number of people not at work due to illness or invalidity. Numbers in this category have grown from 42,000 in 1971, when Invalidity Benefit was introduced, to 96,000 in 1996 (Figure 3).

The increase in self-reported sickness, outlined above, is puzzling in light of the fact that, according to medically based measures, health status in Northern Ireland has improved significantly over the same time period. For example, the infant mortality rate, which is generally regarded as a fairly robust indicator of general health status among the adult population (Allsop, 1995), fell by around 7 percentage points between 1981 and 1994 from 13 per cent to 6 per cent. Similarly, average life expectancy for males increased from 69 years to 73 years. Similar arguments have been made for the UK as a whole and for other industrialised countries (Blondal and Pearson, 1995).

The main incentive to transfer from Unemployment Benefit to Incapacity Benefit lies in a higher and non-means tested benefit level. Also, there is no requirement to search for work. In the past the certifying authority has usually been the local GP, and the likelihood that certificates were issued on a less than totally rigorous basis led to a change in the rules from April 1996. The benefit, formerly named Invalidity Benefit, now relies on a panel of full-time doctors to assess applicants. The likelihood is that the rise in Incapacity Benefit claimants will cease, and total numbers may diminish. It has yet to be seen whether this will swell the numbers of the claimant unemployed.

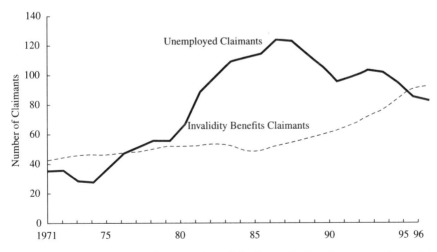

Figure 3. Numbers claiming Sickness and Invalidity/Incapacity Benefits compared with the number unemployed for Northern Ireland 1971–96. *Source*: NI Department of Economic Development, and Social Security Agency.

The rise in numbers claiming sickness and invalidity has accelerated markedly over the last ten years. The numbers claiming the benefit were broadly stable from its introduction in September 1971 until 1985. Since then, the numbers have doubled to 96,000. The 1996 figure is 50,000 above the average for 1971–85 and this may be taken as one measure of disguised unemployment in Northern Ireland. The particularly steep rise since 1992 coincides with a period of steadily falling unemployment. What is striking is that the 22,000 rise in sickness and Invalidity Benefit claimants between 1992 and 1996 is very close to the 20,000 reduction in the numbers unemployed over the same period.

The number of jobs also rose sharply during the 1992–96 period, by 38,000 (6.2 per cent), and a substantial reduction in unemployment was thus expected. At the same time however the labour supply has been boosted by a net migration inflow. This turn-around in migration in the 1990s compared with the 1980s has boosted labour supply by 30,000 over the course of the 1990s up to 1996. Hence, the rise in employment seems to have had its main impact, not on unemployment (however measured), but upon migration, with a small net annual outflow in the 1990s contrasting with the substantial net outflow each year prior to 1990.

Long-Term Unemployment

One of the key characteristics of the Northern Ireland labour market is the exceptionally high proportion of long-term unemployed, i.e., those out of work for more than one year. In 1995 47,400 registered unemployed had been out of work for more than one year. This comprised 57 per cent of all claimant unemployed. Of these, 18,000 people had been out of work for more than five years. Even these very high figures may under-represent the problem. In the 1991 Census of Population 50,000 people described themselves as economically active but with no job in the previous ten years. Some of these were young people who may have been unemployed for less than ten years, but the great majority were over 25 years old.

The problem of long-term unemployment in Northern Ireland is much more an issue for males than for females. Almost two out of every three unemployed males (61 per cent) has been jobless for more than one year whether measured on the claimant count or the LFS. For females the proportion is lower at 41 per cent in the claimant count, and much lower at 27 per cent in the LFS. Although there may be reasons why females would be less likely to classify themselves as long-term unemployed, contrasts in employment trends for men and women suggest that differences may be real. The proportion of the unemployed who have been out of work for more than 12 months has always been much higher in Northern Ireland than in Great Britain, and is well above the proportion in every other UK region. In Northern Ireland the number of long-term unemployed has been close to or above 50,000 (7 per cent of the labour force) since the early 1980s. Remarkably the number changed little between 1982 and 1996 despite the creation of an extra 100,000 jobs in the period. It seems clear that job creation alone has been insufficient to reduce numbers of long-term unemployed.

The gap in unemployment rates between Northern Ireland and Great Britain is chiefly one of long-term unemployment. Short-term unemployment rates have converged over the 1990s (Table 3) and Northern Ireland's short-term unemployment rate differed little from the UK national average over most of the 1990s. In 1997, short-term unemployment has unprecedently fallen below the UK average on claimant count figures. LFS data for autumn 1997 do not confirm this remarkable change but they do show that there is little difference in short-term unemployment rates between Northern Ireland and Great Britain.

Northern Ireland's rate of long-term unemployment on the other hand has for a long time been over twice as large as that in Great Britain (Table 3). Although the gap between Northern Ireland and Great Britain has narrowed, the long-term unemployment rate in Northern Ireland is still close to double the national average. Insufficient research has been undertaken on the long-term unemployed in Northern Ireland, but it seems clear that they form a block of people who are relatively detached from the labour force. As Scott (1993) showed, the flows into and out of

Table 3. Long-term unemployment in Northern Ireland and UK.[1]

	Percentage of unemployed out of work for more than 12 months		Long-term unemployment rate[2]		Short-term unemployment rate[2]	
	NI	UK	NI	UK	NI	UK
1979	27.9	24.6	3.0	1.3	5.0	2.8
1982	39.4	33.6	7.2	4.1	7.4	5.5
1987	51.1	42.6	8.9	4.4	8.4	5.7
1990	51.3	31.6	7.1	1.8	6.1	4.1
1992	48.9	32.6	7.3	3.3	6.7	6.4
1996	55.3	36.1	6.4	2.8	5.1	4.9
1997 (April)	54.5	36.2	4.6	2.5	3.5	4.3

Notes: 1 Claimant count.

   2 Per cent of total economically active.

Sources: Department of Employment, Labour Market Trends; Northern Ireland Abstract of Statistics.

long-term unemployment have traditionally been low. For the category of those out of work for three or more years, the inflow and outflow from the category in 1992 were both 21 per cent. For those unemployed for between one and three years the inflow was greater at 58 per cent and the outflow was 59 per cent. The longer the period of unemployment the lower the probability of leaving unemployment in any one year. This pattern is similar to that in Great Britain except that a lower proportion of the long-term unemployed leave the register each year in Northern Ireland (NIEC, 1994; 1996). Even in 1997, after a rapid fall in the numbers of long-term unemployed, almost two-thirds of the long-term unemployed had been out of work for more than three years.

The reasons for the high proportion of long-term unemployed in Northern Ireland are unclear. One possibility is that long periods of high unemployment lead to greater proportions of long-term unemployment (White, 1991; 1994). This association was seen in both Northern Ireland and Great Britain in the 1980s. With its higher level of total unemployment, it is likely that more people will have drifted into long-term unemployment, but this is unlikely to be the whole explanation. Other possibilities are differences in the rigour with which the Restart Scheme was operated after its introduction in 1986. The Restart interviews were a way of guiding the unemployed into training or back into work. In Great Britain they coincided with the employment boom which led to a return to near full employment in much of southern England. In Northern Ireland unemployment, and particularly male unemployment, remained very high. In these circumstances it seems possible that Employment Service officials in Northern Ireland may not have promoted the Restart interviews as resolutely as their colleagues in Great Britain. If so, the result is likely to have been a lower rate of turnover within the unemployed.

A further possibility is a high level of social security fraud in Northern Ireland. As the only UK region with a land border, cross-border working and claiming is a possibility. Secondly, difficulties in applying the law in some areas, and a greater antipathy to state authorities than in Britain, may also increase the likelihood of deception. The fact that the new Jobseekers' Allowance introduced in 1996, and the introduction of a social security telephone fraud 'hotline' in February 1996, appear to have contributed to the large reduction in long-term unemployment after more than a decade of near stability, suggests that some fraudulent claiming may have been present in Northern Ireland. However, the Jobseekers' Allowance is designed to increase job search activity, and this itself may also have accelerated the pace at which the long-term unemployed get jobs.

Measures of Labour Market Pressure

Unemployment rates are one key indicator of labour market pressure, with high unemployment indicating that the supply of labour substantially outstrips the demand for labour. Using unemployment as a definition, Northern Ireland has until recently had easily the slackest labour market of any part of the UK (Table 4), and this has been the case throughout the last half-century. The next highest unemployment rate has usually been that of the Northern region, with unemployment close to two percentage points below that of Northern Ireland. The gradation across the UK is relatively clear, with the lowest unemployment rates in southern England and the highest in the regions of northern England (North West, Yorkshire, Humberside and North). Although the hierarchy of unemployment rates in 1996 remained close to the traditional pattern, the gap between regions has been narrower in the 1990s than previously. What seems to have happened is that the great employment boom of the 1980s sucked labour into the regions of southern England, while the subsequent recession of 1990–92 did not lead to an equivalent reduction in labour supply. Unemployment thus rose further in southern England than in peripheral regions, such as Scotland and Northern Ireland, which were least affected by the cycle of boom and bust. However, the situation is complicated by the rise in concealed unemployment, not recorded in either the claimant count or the LFS (Beatty *et al.*, 1997).

Unemployment rates are not the only measure of labour market

Table 4. Unemployment, participation and employment rates 1996.

	Unemployment Rate[1]	Economic Activity[2]	Employment Rate[3]
Northern Ireland	**11.2**	**73.0**	**65.6**
Southern England	6.7	80.4	74.7
Midland England	7.1	75.5	69.8
Northern England	8.3	72.7	66.3
Scotland	7.9	74.2	68.2
Wales	8.0	71.6	65.8
UK	7.4	76.5	70.6

Notes: 1 Claimant unemployment October 1996 - seasonally adjusted.

2 Economically active as percentage of population of working age (16–60/65).

3 Employment rate is employed plus self-employed as a percentage of population of working age. The employment rate equals the participation rate multiplied by one minus the unemployment rate.

4 South East, East Anglia and South West regions.

5 Northern Region, North West and Yorkshire and Humberside.

Sources: Department of Employment Labour Market Trends; OPCS Population Trends; Northern Ireland Department of Economic Development, Registrar General.

pressure, and other measures modify the simple picture of Northern Ireland as the region with the greatest imbalance between supply and demand for labour. Two alternative measures are the *employment rate* and the *participation rate*. In both of these measures the entire population of working age is used as a denominator, in place of the economically active population which is used in calculating unemployment rates. The *employment rate* is simply employment (including self-employment) as a percentage of the population of working age. In many ways this is a better measure of labour market pressure than the unemployment rate because it avoids the definitional and measurement problems inherent in measuring unemployment.

Northern Ireland's employment rate at 65.6 per cent in 1996 lay five percentage points below the UK average, but was very similar to the rates in Wales and the average for the regions of northern England (Table 4). It was also two percentage points above the employment rate in the northern region of England alone. On this measure we might argue that the main distinction is between the tight labour markets of southern England and the rest of the UK including Northern Ireland. This conclusion is not altered by the large fall in unemployment since mid-1996.

Hence we reach the conclusion that unemployment is high in Northern Ireland compared with Wales or the regions of northern England not because there are fewer jobs in relation to the population, but because a higher proportion of the population is economically active in Northern Ireland than in these regions (Table 4). This could reflect the gender composition of employment. A high proportion of females in employment will tend to boost economic activity rates by bringing more females into the labour force. Although Northern Ireland has a slightly higher proportion of females in employment than the UK average, the difference is small, and is unlikely to be the main reason accounting for an economic activity rate higher than in Wales or the northern regions of England. Other potential reasons for the higher rate in Northern Ireland could be a greater resistance to discouragement from economic activity, or indeed a larger black economy (resulting in the double-counting of individuals as both employed and unemployed, hence exaggerating the size of the labour force).

Northern Ireland's economic activity rate was well below that of all UK regions in the 1950s and 1960s, but was boosted by the dramatic increase in size of the public sector following the imposition of Direct Rule in 1972. Between 1971 and 1977 employment in the public sector rose by 40,000 jobs (43 per cent), with many of these jobs, especially in education and health, being taken by females. This increased the female economic activity rate.[1]

---

[1] It also incidentally increased incomes for many families, leading to a house-price boom during the worst years of the Troubles.

After converging towards the UK average over the 1970s, the economic activity rate in Northern Ireland slowly diverged once again in the 1980s as Northern Ireland missed out on much of the UK service sector boom. In the 1990s it converged once more, until the recent large fall in unemployment, which has taken Northern Ireland's economic activity rate back down to 72 per cent, or 4 percentage points below the UK average. What is clear is that Northern Ireland's labour market, like those of Wales or the regions of northern England, is much less tight than the labour markets of southern England. The employment rate in Northern Ireland is almost 10 percentage points below that in southern England (Table 4). This reflects both a much lower economic activity rate in Northern Ireland, and a higher proportion of unemployed among the economically active.

The employment rate (or its inverse the non-employment rate) is probably the single best measure of labour-market pressure. As a rule of thumb we might regard an employment rate of 80 per cent as indicating full employment. This figure of 80 per cent was for instance the rate reached in south-east England at the height of the 1980s boom. With this definition of full employment, in 1997 Northern Ireland had a rate of joblessness equal to 14.4 per cent of the population of working age, whereas measured unemployment in 1997 was equivalent to under half of this level at 6.3 per cent. The difference between the two figures is a measure of the concealed unemployed. This includes many 'discouraged workers' not included in either the claimant count or the LFS figures. Many of these people are on Incapacity Benefit.

The above review of the various measures of labour-market pressure leads to the conclusion that Northern Ireland faces a chronic over-supply of labour relative to demand, but that Northern Ireland's degree of labour-market slackness is not unique within the UK. On some measures the northern region of England may have an even less tight labour market than Northern Ireland, and Wales and the north-west region of England are only a little tighter than Northern Ireland.

Wages and Salaries

The law of supply and demand leads us to expect low wage levels in slack labour markets. This expectation is borne out in Northern Ireland, where average wage levels are typically 10–15 per cent below the UK average, and 20 per cent below the level of south-east England.

Average weekly earnings in 1996 were 13 per cent below the UK average for males and for manual females (Table 5). The gap was smaller for non-manual females since almost 70 per cent of these work in health,

Table 5. Gross weekly average earnings of full-time employees on adult rates in Northern Ireland 1996 (GB = 100).

		All Sectors	Manufacturing	Services
Male	Manual	86.8	83.8	89.8
	Non-Manual	87.9	78.5	90.1
Female	Manual	87.6	86.2	86.2
	Non-Manual	92.2	79.5	93.2

Source: New Earnings Survey, 1996.

education and other public sector activities in which wage levels are generally the same across all regions of the UK. The wage gap between Northern Ireland and Great Britain is smaller in the service sectors than in manufacturing for the same reason.

The wage gap between Northern Ireland and Great Britain is a long-standing feature of the Northern Ireland labour market. In the 1970s there was some convergence in regional wage levels across the UK, reflecting the influence of wage controls and a growing tendency towards centralised pay bargaining within companies. Since 1980 the opposite has been true. Wage controls have been abolished and pay policies abandoned. Companies have increasingly tended to decentralise their wage bargaining (Walsh and Brown, 1991). As a result of these factors, and of relatively tighter labour markets in Britain compared with Northern Ireland in the 1980s, Northern Ireland's wage gap with Britain widened over the 1980s. Despite the convergence of unemployment rates in the 1990s the wage gap has remained wide (Table 6).

Table 6. Average gross weekly earnings of adult full-time male employees (UK = 100).

	1971	1979	1989	1997
South East	109	107	116	117
East Anglia	92	94	94	92
South West	94	91	94	94
East Midlands	93	96	90	90
West Midlands	102	97	92	92
Yorkshire and Humberside	92	98	91	89
North West	98	98	93	95
North	93	98	90	89
Wales	96	96	89	89
Scotland	95	100	93	92
Northern Ireland	**88**	**90**	**86**	**87**

Source: New Earnings Surveys.

Around half of the UK's wide regional dispersion of male wages in 1996 is due to differences in the balance of manual and non-manual occupations. Male wage levels in the south-east of England are boosted by around 9 per cent by an occupational structure more heavily weighted towards non-manual occupations than is the case in other regions. This has relatively little impact on Northern Ireland however, since a large public sector gives a representation of non-manual employees which is unusually high for a region in the northern half of the UK.

Not all of the wage gap between Northern Ireland and Great Britain can be accounted for by a slack labour market. As already noted this factor has little influence in the public sector, which still accounts for 30 per cent of employees in Northern Ireland. In manufacturing, a major influence on wage levels in any company is labour productivity, including the need for specialised skills in high productivity industries. An industry-by-industry comparison, at a high (4 digit) level of disaggregation, suggests that half of the wage gap in manufacturing between Northern Ireland and Great Britain is due to the concentration of low-productivity industries in Northern Ireland. Half of the manufacturing employment in Northern Ireland is, for instance, in the relatively low-productivity food, drink, textile and clothing industries, compared to 21 per cent in Great Britain.

Another factor responsible for the low wage levels of Northern Ireland manufacturing is the predominance of small firms, since small firms normally pay lower wages than large employers. One-quarter of employees in Northern Ireland manufacturing work for firms with less than 50 employees. This is the highest proportion of any UK region except south-east England and is double the proportion in the northern region. The proportion of Northern Ireland employees in small firms has also doubled since 1971 and partly accounts for the widening wage gap between Northern Ireland and Great Britain in manufacturing.

A further factor is the need for exporting companies to compensate for higher transport costs than their competitors in Great Britain. The transport cost penalty relative to Great Britain varies by product but the average is 2 per cent of the value of sales (PIEDA, 1984). A reduction in wages to a level 10 per cent below the British average compensates most exporting companies for this cost disadvantage. Partly offsetting this is an advantage of similar magnitude for the 40 per cent of sales made by Northern Ireland companies into markets within Ireland.

Econometric analyses demonstrate a link between high unemployment and low wages. An econometric study of Northern Ireland manufacturing between 1967 and 1983 found that a 10 per cent increase in unemployment led to a 7 per cent decline in wages (Borooah and Lee, 1991). However, econometric work undertaken for this chapter suggests a weaker relationship in the different labour market conditions of the 1990s (details are available from the author on request). This may reflect the fact that registered unemployment is no longer a reasonable measure of labour availability.

The Geographical Variation in Unemployment Within Northern Ireland

One of the notable characteristics of unemployment in Northern Ireland is its uneven incidence across both areas and communities. In May 1997 the unemployment rate in the Ballymena Travel to Work Area (TTWA) in north-east Ulster was 5.7 per cent. This was below the UK average and below the level of most UK regions. At the other extreme, the rate in Strabane on the western border of Northern Ireland was 12.9 per cent (down from 18.6 per cent in 1996). This was more than double the UK average and above the rate in all British TTWAs. The 10 percentage point range between TTWAs in Northern Ireland was almost as great as between the much greater number and diversity of TTWAs in Great Britain. Even this level of diversity in Northern Ireland is much less than before the recent large fall in unemployment.

The general pattern of unemployment is one of high rates in the west of Northern Ireland including many rural areas (Table 7). Belfast, the largest city, has an unemployment rate below the average for Northern Ireland and close to the average for large cities in the three regions of northern England, Wales or Scotland.

It is commonly believed both within and outside Northern Ireland that the very high unemployment rates in the west of Northern Ireland reflect

Table 7. Unemployment rates in Northern Ireland travel to work areas May 1997 (% of work-force).

East of Northern Ireland		West of Northern Ireland and Borders	
Ballymena	5.6	Magherafelt	7.8
Craigavon	6.4	Dungannon	9.3
Belfast	7.0	Omagh	9.4
Coleraine	9.6	Enniskillen	9.5
		Cookstown	9.9
		Newry	11.0
		Londonderry	11.6
		Strabane	12.9

Note: Northern Ireland average in May 1997 was 8.0 per cent. The UK average was 6.4 per cent.

Source: Department of Employment, Labour Market Trends, September 1996.

low levels of job creation, but there is no foundation for this belief. The west of Northern Ireland has had a faster rate of growth in employment over the last 25 years than the east (Gudgin, 1994a). Growth in employment in the west of Northern Ireland has also been above the average for the UK.

There is in fact almost no relationship between job creation and unemployment across Northern Ireland. Figure 4 shows unemployment rates for Northern Ireland TTWAs in 1991 plotted against growth in employment over the previous 20 years. Unemployment rates in areas of rapid job creation are similar to those in areas where employment has stagnated. The inference is that increases in the demand for labour lead to concomitant rises in the supply of labour. This may occur through migration, commuting, or increases in participation rates. Beatty and Fothergill (1996) show a similar lack of association for coalfield areas in Britain where the collapse in employment has had little impact on registered unemployment.

Unemployment rates in Northern Ireland TTWAs are clearly related much more to religious denomination than to job creation. All of the TTWAs with high unemployment have majority Roman Catholic populations. The areas of low unemployment have majority Protestant populations. Where Presbyterians form the majority, rather than Church of Ireland members, unemployment rates are lowest of all. It is argued below that persistently high unemployment in Northern Ireland

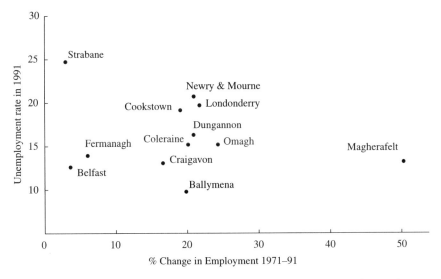

Figure 4. Unemployment and employment growth in Northern Ireland travel-to-work areas. *Source*: Northern Ireland Censuses of Population 1971, 1991.

represents an equilibrium between rapid natural increase in population and slower (although nonetheless quite rapid) rates of job creation. The likelihood is that this equilibrium also occurs at the local scale, resulting in high unemployment in areas with high levels of natural increase in population.

The weak association between job creation and unemployment can be shown perhaps more dramatically in a UK context. Figure 5 shows unemployment rates in 1991 for each UK county plotted against growth in employment over the previous 20 years from 1971–91. The counties of Northern Ireland are amalgamated into the eastern counties, Antrim, Down, Armagh and the western counties, Fermanagh, Tyrone, Londonderry. In the context of a much greater diversity of employment growth it is obvious that, for the UK as a whole, a relationship does exist between employment change over 20 years and unemployment at the end of the period. However, the impact of job creation remains low. A 110 percentage point difference in employment growth (between 80 per cent growth and 30 per cent decline) would reduce the unemployment rate by only 8 percentage points.

Figure 5 shows that the eastern counties of Northern Ireland fit within the broad relationship characteristic of counties in Great Britain, albeit at the high end of the unemployment spectrum along with Merseyside and Teeside. The western counties of Northern Ireland are completely outside the broad relationship. These counties have a growth rate for employment which is above the average for counties in Great Britain. However their unemployment rate, at 17.5 per cent, is double that of counties in Great

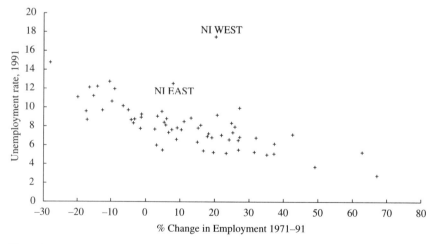

Figure 5.   Unemployment rate and change in employment, UK counties. *Source*: NOMIS and NI Department of Economic Development.

Britain with similar rates of job creation. This seems most likely to reflect the high rate of natural increase in population in these areas, combined with a rate of out-migration insufficient to bring unemployment rates into equality with other areas in Northern Ireland and Great Britain.

Religious Differences in Employment and Unemployment

Perhaps the most controversial aspect of the labour market in Northern Ireland is the large and persistent gap in unemployment rates between Protestants and Roman Catholics. It is this difference which underlies many of the geographical contrasts noted in the previous section. Unemployment rates for Catholic males have been between 20 and 30 per cent during most of the years up to 1994, and have always been between 2 and 2.6 times higher than unemployment rates for Protestant males (Table 8). Whereas Protestant males have an unemployment rate which is usually below the UK average, Roman Catholic males have an unemployment rate close to double the UK average.

Unemployment rates are also higher for Roman Catholic females than for Protestant females, but the gap is much smaller. The LFS figures for 1994 show an unemployment rate for Roman Catholic females at 8 per cent compared with 5 per cent for Protestants. The ratio in this case is 1.6:1.

Although it is the unemployment difference between Roman Catholics and Protestants in Northern Ireland which attracts most attention, it is also true that there is a significant difference between Presbyterians and Church of Ireland members within Northern Ireland. Church of Ireland

Table 8. Catholic and Protestant Unemployment Rates for Males in Northern Ireland.

Year	Source	Catholics	Protestants	Ratio
1971	Census	17.3	6.6	2.6
1981	Census	30.2	12.4	2.4
1983–4	CHS	35.8	14.9	2.4
1985–7	CHS	35.5	14.2	2.5
1988–90/1	CHS	27.2	12.2	2.2
1990	LFS	21.7	11.0	2.0
1991	Census	28.4	12.7	2.2
1991	LFS	22.8	9.3	2.5
1992	LFS	24.2	10.1	2.4
1993	LFS	23.0	11.0	2.1
1994	LFS	22.0	11.0	2.0

Sources: Northern Ireland Census of Population; the Northern Ireland Labour Force Survey (LFS) and the Northern Ireland Continuous Household Survey (CHS). The census values are uncorrected for those who do not state a religion.

members had an unemployment rate 45 per cent higher than for Presbyterians in 1991.

It was noted in the previous section that travel to work areas with highest unemployment in Northern Ireland had Catholic majorities, but did not exhibit slow growth in employment. This geographic pattern hides a more striking tendency for employment growth to have occurred among the Catholic population but not among Protestants. In the intercensual period 1971–91, Catholic employment rose by 14 per cent while Protestant employment fell by 0.5 per cent. This difference in employment growth has accelerated in the 1990s. Data collected annually by the Fair Employment Commission shows Catholic employment rising by 13 per cent between 1990 and 1995. Protestant employment in contrast rose by only 0.5 per cent. In both periods there was a rise in female employment for both Catholics and Protestants, although the rise was twice as rapid in the Catholic case. Male employment tended to fall. The decline occured in both periods for Protestant males. For Catholic males there was a small decline of 2 per cent in the 1971–91 period but a substantial increase of 11 per cent after 1990.

These large disparities in employment growth largely reflect differences between Catholic and Protestants in the growth of the economically active population. The combination of high Catholic unemployment with a relatively high employment growth demonstrates that Catholic employment has failed to fully keep pace with the increase in the Catholic economically active population. It is the balance between changes in employment and changes in economically active population which holds the key to understanding the Northern Ireland labour market, and it is to these dynamic factors that we now turn.

A Dynamic Analysis of the Northern Ireland Labour Market

Descriptions of unemployment and its associations with related variables, taken at one point in time or in a single period, provide a range of insights into the causes of unemployment. However, they cannot demonstrate the key equilibrating mechanisms which balance the supply and demand for labour over time. This is an important shortcoming in attempting to understand economies like that of Northern Ireland where potential labour supply and actual demand are constantly diverging.

Natural Increase in Population of Working Age

An important starting point in a dynamic analysis of unemployment in Northern Ireland is the rapid natural increase in population. This section focuses on the dynamics of the male labour market since this is where the greatest problem of unemployment lies. Natural increase in the male population of working age (16–65) consists of additions to the labour force (for example by school leavers) less withdrawals due to retirement or death. In Northern Ireland the natural increase in the working-age population since 1971 has averaged 1.5 per cent per annum. In Great Britain the rate of natural increase over the same period has been 0.3 per cent per annum. This means that the male population of working age in Northern Ireland rises on average by 7,000 each year due to natural increase, and by 5,500 in excess of the rate of natural increase in Great Britain. Over the 25 years from 1971 to 1996 natural increase added a potential 157,000 men to the working-age population of 439,000, an increase of 36 per cent. The equivalent increase in Britain over the same 25 years was 9 per cent.

The slow increase in the working-age population in Great Britain means that an equally slow growth in employment can be consistent with only a small rise in unemployment, little net out-migration and a stable economic activity rate. In Northern Ireland the much more rapid natural increase in population of working age inevitably leads to a large potential surplus of labour, unless employment grows much faster than in Great Britain. Rapid population growth can itself produce some acceleration in employment growth, for example via increased demand for public services if the local budget constraint is met by an external subvention (as it is in Northern Ireland). However, total employment will generally not keep pace with population increase unless economic competitiveness is sufficiently high to increase Northern Ireland's share of UK domestic markets and/or export market.[2]

There is some evidence that rising competitiveness has allowed employment in Northern Ireland to grow faster than the virtually static rate in Britain. Even so, employment growth in Northern Ireland has been much slower than the rate of natural increase in population. As a result, a number of mechanisms have reduced the huge potential labour surplus and brought it towards an equilibrium with the demand for labour. The history of unemployment in Northern Ireland suggests that equilibrium is reached when the Northern Ireland unemployment rate is 3–4 percentage points above that in Britain (although the introduction of the Jobseekers Allowance may have reduced this equilibrium to 2–3 percentage points). The various balancing mechanisms are discussed below, but first we turn

---

[2] This statement assumes that public expenditure will only rise to the point where levels of per capita service provision in Northern Ireland become equal to those in Britain. Similarly it assumes that public subsidies to private industry will be insufficient to accelerate employment growth by enough to match the rapid growth in labour.

briefly to the dynamics of employment change in Northern Ireland over the
last quarter-century.

Employment Change

For most of the 1970s and 1980s employment in Northern Ireland grew at a
rate broadly similar to that in Great Britain. Since 1990 Northern Ireland's
performance has been much more favourable than that in Great Britain
(Figure 6). At the level of individual regions, Northern Ireland has usually
been the third fastest growing of the UK's eleven standard regions over the
last three decades, out-performed only by the less urban regions flanking
the south-east, i.e., East Anglia and the south-west. Surprisingly, Northern
Ireland's job creation record over this period has been better than southern
England as a whole (i.e., south-east, East Anglia and the south-west), and
much better than any other UK region.

Employment in Northern Ireland grew faster than in Great Britain over
most of the 1970s as a rapid expansion in public sector jobs followed the
imposition of Direct Rule in 1972. Public sector employment was also
rising in Britain, but faster expansion in Northern Ireland added around
30,000 jobs to the Northern Ireland total. This was offset over the 1970s by
low growth in the private sector, held back by high levels of political
violence. An estimated 15,000 jobs were lost due to the Troubles and the
net gain to Northern Ireland over the 1970s was 15,000 jobs or 3 per cent.

The expansion of public sector employment slowed down after 1979

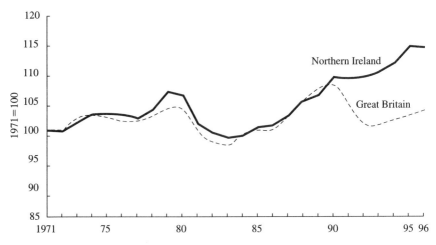

Figure 6.   Total employment in Northern Ireland and Britain 1971–96. *Source*: NOMIS, NI
Department of Economic Development.

and soon ceased. Employment growth in Northern Ireland fell steadily behind that in Great Britain where growth was rapid due to the debt-induced boom of the 1980s. The latter had only indirect benefits for Northern Ireland, and by 1989 employment in Northern Ireland had fallen behind what it would have been at national rates of growth to the extent of 30,000 jobs or 5 per cent of total employment.

Since 1989 a remarkable resurgence has occurred. Northern Ireland largely avoided the deep UK recession of 1990–92, which was itself a consequence of the preceding boom concentrated in southern England. Northern Ireland has also grown faster during the national recovery since 1992. The result has been an extra 72,000 jobs in 1996 over and above what would have been created at the British rate of employment growth. By 1996, employment was 10 per cent above what it would have been at natural average rates of growth.

As in Great Britain, all of the net addition to jobs since 1972 have been taken by females. Male employment fluctuated over the period but remained slightly lower in 1996 than in 1971. Female employment has in contrast risen by 45 per cent since 1971. In the case of females the growth of employment has kept pace with the natural increase in population of working age, albeit often in the form of part-time jobs. For males the lack of any net increase in the number of jobs has meant a huge potential job shortfall over the last 25 years.

Equilibrating Mechanisms in the Northern Ireland Labour Market

The remainder of this chapter measures the size of the shortfall in jobs over the last 25 years, and examines the ways in which the supply of labour has adjusted to this shortfall. A change in the shortfall in jobs over a period of time can be calculated as:

> **the natural increase in the population of working age**
> *less*
> **the increase in employment and self-employment**
> *all multiplied by*
> **the base-year participation rate**

An increase in employment shortfall will then lead to three consequent changes. These are changes in:

> **the level of migration;**
> **the participation rate;**
> **the number of unemployed.**

The first two of these three changes usually act to bring the supply of labour towards equilibrium with the demand. The change in the number of unemployed forms a residual in which equilibrium can be said to be reached when employment rates are equalised across the UK. The formal derivation of the relations between these variables is contained in Appendix A to this chapter.

In the case of males in Northern Ireland, the increase in the job short-fall over the 24 years from 1971 to 1995 was 166,000 (46 per cent of 1971 employment). This is made up of:

	thousands
Natural increase in working age population 1971–95	+157
Change in employment	−9
Change in job shortfall	+166

The consequences of this rising shortfall were then:

	thousands	*% of shortfall*
Net out-migration	95	57
Decrease in participation	29	18
Increase in unemployment	42	25
Change in total shortfall	166	100

Over half of the potential shortfall was reduced through out-migration. Around 18 per cent was reduced by a decline in the participation rate. Male participation declined from 89 per cent in 1971 to 83 per cent in 1995. This includes higher rates of staying on in education and early retirement. It also includes an increase in numbers on Incapacity Benefit and government employment schemes. The rise in unemployment over the 24 year period was only 25 per cent of the total potential shortfall.

Full equilibrium in the labour market is sometimes considered to be a state in which unemployment is at some frictional minimum. This state is achieved in theory through a fall in wages. In practice wage levels are insufficiently flexible and a net surplus of labour leads to high unemployment. Within an economic union like the UK we might define a regional equilibrium as one in which unemployment rates are equalised across regions. Migration is the main mechanism for achieving this result, but changes in relative wages across regions also play a small part. In addition there is a government policy response in which attempts are made to accelerate the rate of job creation through grants and subsidies to the private sector, and through a direct expansion of the public sector. These measures act on top of the more automatic regional stabilisers in which local spending is boosted through additions to public spending (e.g., unemployment benefits) and reduction in taxation. These mechanisms usually ensure that unemployment rates tend towards regional uniformity, but they are too weak to result in full equality of unemployment rates.

In the Northern Ireland context, net migration is a function of the difference between rates of unemployment in Northern Ireland and Great Britain, and of the difference in wage levels (Gudgin and O'Shea, 1993). As unemployment in Northern Ireland rises above the UK level, out-migration increases. At the same time the rising unemployment gap tends to reduce wages in Northern Ireland (although not by much), and this in turn accelerates the flow of out-migration. Out-migration in turn reduces labour supply in Northern Ireland, and hence reduces unemployment, leading towards labour market balance. Falling wages (relative to Britain) will also in principle increase the level of employment but again this link is relatively weak.

The evidence from Northern Ireland is that these mechanisms have tended to balance when the unemployment rate is around three to four percentage points above the UK average. At this point wage levels are some 15 percentage points below the UK average, and net migration flows are sufficient to offset the annual national increase in the population of working age. For this reason, unemployment in Northern Ireland is likely to remain around three to four percentage points above the UK average (although as stated above the introduction of the Jobseekers Allowance may have reduced the level of this equilibrium a little). An equilibrium rate of unemployment at 4 percentage points above the UK also characterises the Republic of Ireland (Honohan, 1992), although Fitzgerald (1996) thinks that this equilibrium may be lower in future.

High unemployment in Northern Ireland is driven fundamentally by a combination of a high rate of natural increase in population and an incomplete clearing of the labour market via either migration or wages. The fact that migration flows do not lead to a full equalisation of Northern Ireland and British unemployment rates reflects a range of factors. Some authors blame the UK housing market with its low stock of privately rented houses in all UK regions (McCormick, 1991). However, part of the reason may be a personal attachment to the home region which leads to a delay in migration and in some cases a lack of migration in the face of high local unemployment (Sheehan and Tomlinson, 1996: 73). Finally the lack of flexibility in wage levels reflects both institutional arrangements, including unionisation and social security benefits, and a division of the labour market into insiders and outsiders with little competition between them. Insiders gain specialist experience in their work and hence are partially protected from competition from the unemployed and from new entrants to the labour market.

Catholic and Protestant Unemployment in Northern Ireland

A number of studies have been undertaken to attempt to explain the large gap in unemployment rates between Catholics and Protestants in Northern Ireland. Most of these studies have been cross-sectional, focusing on how much of the unemployment gap can be ascribed to 'structural' character-istics of the two populations. Such characteristics include age, qualifica-tions, socio-economic status, location, marital status and housing tenure. Chambers (1987), Smith and Chambers (1991) and Murphy and Armstrong (1994) employed logit analysis, while Compton (1991) and Gudgin (1994b) used shift-share techniques. Four of these five studies concluded that structural influences accounted for close to half of the unemployment gap. The exception was Compton (1991) who argued that structural factors accounted for most of the gap. However Gudgin (1994b) argues that his methodology is likely to bias upwards the impact of structural factors. The shift-share studies indicate that location and occupation/socio-economic status each account for around a quarter of the unemployment gap. Age structure is a relatively unimportant factor.

One notable aspect of Roman Catholic and Protestant unemployment in Northern Ireland is the relative stability of the ratio of unemployment rates over a long period of time. Gudgin and Breen (1996) show that the ratio might have been expected to fluctuate much more widely as aggregate unemployment has varied over the 25 years to 1996. It transpires that when aggregate unemployment is at 10 per cent, a Catholic:Protestant un-employment ratio of 2:1 is equivalent to a 3 percentage point 'gap' between the Roman Catholic share of jobs and the Roman Catholic proportion among the economically active.[3] If aggregate unemployment rises to 20 per cent, this gap would need to widen to 6 percentage points in order to maintain a stable unemployment ratio. The question is why the gap should move in this way to maintain a stable ratio.

Cross-sectional methods are unable to account for the stability in the unemployment ratio. Neither are they able to incorporate dynamic influ-ences including differences in population growth due to natural increase and migration. These dynamic factors were investigated by Gudgin and Breen (1996) using a stylised simulation model. The model incorporated differences in Catholic and Protestant rates of natural increase and migration, for males in both cases (Table 9). Catholic natural increase was over three times as great as for other denominations. Although

---

[3] For instance in 1971 the Catholic share of the economically active was 34 per cent while the Catholic share of the employed and self-employed was 31 per cent. The 'gap' was 3 percentage points.

Table 9.   Population changes and migration 1971–91 (in thousands).

	Roman Catholic	Other Denominations	Total
Estimated Natural Increase in Population of Working-Age	61.3	21.9	35.5
Actual Change in Population of Working-Age	27.9	4.4	12.6
Difference (Net Out-Migration)	33.4	17.5	23.0
Annual Average Rate of Net Out-Migration 1971–91	1.15%	0.62%	0.84%

Source: Northern Ireland Census of Population 1971, 1991.

Catholic migration was also proportionately higher, it was not high enough to equalise unemployment rates.

The Gudgin and Breen model incorporated two equilibrating processes, which together maintained the unemployment ratio at a stable level. The first of these was migration. As the unemployment gap between Catholics and Protestants rises, due to differences in population natural increase, Catholic migration rises more rapidly that Protestant migration and in doing so checks the widening gap in unemployment. The second was a sharing of jobs in proportion to the number of job seekers. Since the Roman Catholic population had both a larger proportion of school leavers and higher unemployment, it received a proportionately large share of jobs, including both new jobs and jobs becoming vacant due to labour turnover. This again tended to damp down the tendency for the unemployment gap to widen. Both processes together tend towards an equilibrium in the unemployment gap, and this equilibrium is reached quite quickly irrespective of starting conditions.

The Gudgin and Breen study shows that, taken in isolation, Catholic disadvantage in obtaining and retaining jobs can account for only half of the higher Catholic unemployment rate. In order to account for the other half we must allow for differential population growth and differential migration propensities, and the manner in which such factors interact with Catholic disadvantage. In Gudgin and Breen (1996) this disadvantage is such that a Catholic job seeker would on average have a probability of success in obtaining a job which was 30 per cent lower than for a Protestant. Since this disadvantage on its own produces an unemployment gap similar in magnitude to the impact of structural factors measured in the cross-sectional studies, Gudgin and Breen (1996) deduce that the two are the same. Their conclusion is that Roman Catholic unemployment could be double that of Protestants as a result of differences in structural character-istics plus differences in natural increase and migration. Some of these factors have relatively small impacts on unemployment when acting in isolation. For example, the impact of higher Catholic natural increase in population is relatively slight when considered alone, raising the long-term unemployment ratio by only around 10 per cent. However, in combination with other factors its impact is increased, and its impact would be substantially greater if the rate of labour turnover fell much below 10 per cent. Gudgin and Breen emphasise that 'We are of course not suggesting that discrimination is absent from Northern Ireland or that chill factors are irrelevant. These things are clearly present in Northern Ireland. Our conclusion is different. It is that it appears perfectly possible to generate a stable unemployment ratio close to that observed in Northern Ireland, assuming only that degree of Catholic disadvantage which is normally described as structural' (1996: 40).

These conclusions remain controversial not least because this approach places no reliance on discrimination to maintain a large gap in unemployment between Catholics and Protestants. The principal critiques of this approach have come from Murphy (1996) and Rowthorn (1996). Murphy makes two main points. Firstly, he argues that a 30 per cent Catholic disadvantage in hiring cannot be equated with the structural disadvantages identified in the cross-sectional studies. Secondly, he argues that the migration function in the Gudgin/Breen model is not sufficiently well specified.

This conclusion on the first point is based on Murphy and Armstrong (1994) which included a cross-sectional analysis of transitions into employment. Based on LFS data for 1985–91, Murphy and Armstrong confirmed that Catholic job seekers were only 'about 70% as likely to get a job as Protestant job seekers'. However, their probit analysis suggested that only one-third of this disadvantage was due to structural factors. There is thus some difference between Gudgin and Breen, and Murphy and Armstrong, in their measurements of the importance of structural factors in the lower Catholic than Protestant chances of success in getting a job.[4]

Rowthorn has few criticisms of the general character of the Gudgin and Breen model and does not view Murphy's criticism of the migration function as significant. But Rowthorn accepts that the Murphy and Armstrong results on flows into employment 'if accurate, provide a better source of evidence than the studies of unemployment differentials which Gudgin and Breen cite in their support'. Rowthorn argues that, using this evidence, there would still be a gap between the predictions of the simulation model and

---

[4] Subsequent unpublished work by Gudgin however, closes much of this gap by annualising the Gudgin/Breen simulation model, by distinguishing RUC jobs from general employment, and by reweighting the different chances of success of unemployed job seekers and other job seekers irrespective of religion. Details are available from the author on request.

the actual ratio of Catholic to non-Catholic unemployment. Discrimination and the chill factor would be a natural explanation for this gap. His conclusion is that 'this discussion suggests that there is a great deal of uncertainty about the influence of discrimination or chill factors on unemployment'.

Rowthorn also finds it 'difficult to believe that Gudgin and Breen are right in implying that [discrimination and chill factors] have had virtually no effect on the evolution of the Catholic to non-Catholic unemployment ratio since 1971'. He expects that discrimination in the early 1970s in engineering industries should show up in the model. While it was certainly difficult for Catholics to gain jobs in large engineering firms in this period, the fact that these had declining employment over this period, and accounted for only 7 per cent of Protestant male jobs even in 1971, may however, make the point of limited significance. Rowthorn's final conclusion is that there is room for more empirical investigation on this issue.

Dynamic modelling of Catholic and Protestant unemployment provides the first comprehensive quantified theory of religious differences in unemployment in Northern Ireland. Complex modelling exercises of this type are always likely to remain controversial and open to debate about their technical properties. As a result it is easy for a widespread belief in discrimination, as an explanation of high Catholic unemployment, to persist despite a lack of quantitative evidence. In this context it is instructive to note that it is quite possible for large unemployment gaps to persist between religious groups in conditions where discrimination is not an issue. This is the case in the Republic of Ireland where Catholic unemployment rates remain 60–70 per cent higher than those of Protestants (Gudgin 1994b). In the border counties of the Republic with significant Protestant minorities, Catholic unemployment rates remain double those of Protestants in the 1991 Census, and this gap is greater than in the adjacent county on the Northern side of the border.

Summary and Conclusions

Unemployment remains one of the most serious social and economic problems in Northern Ireland. The official claimant count figures for August 1997 suggested that 60,000 people (8 per cent of the labour force) were out of work. However, another 50,000 people claiming Incapacity Benefit may also constitute a form of disguised unemployment, and a further 27,000 people were on government unemployment and training schemes.[5] Other

---

[5] About half of the 27,000 people on government schemes were in youth training. Some, but not all, of these would be likely to be unemployed if the scheme did not exist.

people seeking work are, for various reasons, excluded from the claimant count. The true figure for joblessness may thus be well in excess of 100,000, and could be close to double the official estimate.

Although Northern Ireland is not unique within the UK in having an unemployment problem of this magnitude, it does have a unique combination of high unemployment together with what, by UK standards, is a relatively favourable record of job creation. The reason for this apparently contradictory combination of circumstances lies in Northern Ireland's high rate of natural increase in its working-age population. With the highest birth rate of any European region, Northern Ireland will always have a large potential surplus of labour unless employment expands at a rate much above the UK and European averages.

Over the 25 years to 1996 the natural increase in the male labour force has for instance outpaced the change in employment by close to 180,000 jobs. Only a high rate of out-migration and falling economic activity rates prevented a huge rise in unemployment over this period. Even with these important adjustments of labour supply, male unemployment rose by a significant amount.

The working of the Northern Ireland labour market can be seen as a process of adjustment in which migration has risen to a level which offsets most of the annual natural increase in the labour force. The unemployment gap between Northern Ireland and Great Britain acts as an important influence on the magnitude of migration flows, and unemployment in Northern Ireland thus tends to rise above the level in Great Britain to an extent which is sufficient to induce enough migration to stem any further rise in unemployment. For these reasons unemployment rates in Northern Ireland are likely to remain above those in Great Britain until the level of natural increase converges to the British level. This is already happening in the Republic of Ireland, but the evidence for Northern Ireland is that full convergence may take a long time. Compton (1995) estimates that Catholic birth rates in Northern Ireland will converge on Protestant rates within ten years. At that point Northern Ireland's natural increase in population will be close to the UK and European average. It will however take a further 15–20 years for this convergence to feed through into the labour market.

The argument of this paper is thus that high unemployment in Northern Ireland represents a dynamic equilibrium between a high rate of natural increase in the working-age population and a slower rate of job creation, even if the latter is quite favourable in comparison with Great Britain. Similarly, it is argued that the persistently higher level of Catholic unemployment relative to Protestants within Northern Ireland also represents a dynamic equilibrium, again between high Catholic natural increase and lower (although nevertheless quite high) levels of job creation.

In some senses high unemployment in Northern Ireland can be said to represent the consequence of local preferences. Compton (1995) argues that high Catholic birth rates in Northern Ireland are due to preference: 'Catholics simply prefer larger families' (73), and 'socio-economic structure plays a relatively small role' (73). Preferred family size has been shown to be a direct function of religiosity, with preferred family sizes of strongly religious Catholics at over 4 children in 1983 (Compton and Coward, 1989). However, as David Coleman points out in his chapter in this volume with reference to international trends, '"Catholic fertility" simply does not work as a general proposition'. Coleman concludes that 'The particularly high fertility of Catholics in Northern Ireland . . . has, it seems, correctly been held up as a specific example of the "minority status effect" on birth rates', that is Catholic teaching has an impact on birth rates when the Church is held in high esteem, for instance when it is an important symbol of identity as in Quebec. Similarly, a lack of full market clearing through migration may itself represent a degree of preference for local residence as Sheehan and Tomlinson (1996) suggest in the case of West Belfast. The reluctance of Catholics to move to, or seek jobs in, majority Protestant areas in Northern Ireland (and vice versa), may be due to their beliefs or experiences of sectarian intimidation. However, the absence of mobility within Northern Ireland would seem to be of little account in explaining higher Catholic unemployment rates, given the geographical pattern and thus sectarian distribution of job creation in recent years. In this respect differential propensity to emigrate in relation to ethnically specific employment rates is of greater importance.

The situation is however changing. Northern Ireland's birth rate is converging on the British average, and Catholic birth rates are converging on Protestant rates. Short-term unemployment rates in Northern Ireland are now below the British average. The key remaining problem is how to get the long-term unemployed back into work, or alternatively into satisfactory retirement.

APPENDIX A: The Algebra of Employment Shortfalls

Change of Job Shortfall between year 0 and year n equals:

$p_0.NI - \Delta E$.

Where NI is the natural increase in working-age population, E is employment, P_0 is the participation rate in year 0, and Δ indicates a change between year 0 and year n.

And $p_0.NI - \Delta E = p_0. WMIG + \Delta p. W_n + \Delta U$

Where WMIG is the net number of out-migrants of working age. W_n is the population of working age in the final year and U is the number of unemployed. The labour force L is the sum of the employed and the unemployed.

Derivation

As

$$p_0. (NI - WMIG) = p_0. \Delta W$$

And

$$p_0. \Delta W + \Delta p \ W_n = p_n. W_n - p_0. W_0 = \Delta L$$
$$= \Delta U + \Delta E.$$

It follows that:

$$p_0.NI = p_0 WMIG - \Delta p.W_n + \Delta U + \Delta E$$

and

$$p_0.NI - \Delta E = p_0.WMIG - \Delta p.W_n \ \Delta U.$$

References

Allsop, J. (1995) *Health Policy and the NHS Towards 2000*, London: Longman.

Beatty, C. and Fothergill, S. (1996) 'Labour Market Adjustment in Areas of Chronic Industrial Decline. The Case of the UK Coalfields', *Regional Studies*, 30(7): 627–40.

Beatty, C., Fothergill, S., Gore, T. and Herrington, A. (1997) 'The Real Level of Unemployment', Centre for Regional Economic and Social Research: Sheffield Hallam University.

Blondal, S. and Pearson, M. (1995) 'Unemployment and other Non-Employment Benefits', *Oxford Review of Economic Policy*, 11: 136–69.

Borooah, V. and Lee, K. (1991) 'The Regional Dimension of Competitiveness in Manufacturing Productivity, Employment and Wages in Northern Ireland and the UK', *Regional Studies*, 25(3).

Bower, A. and Mayhew, K. (1991) *Reducing Regional Inequalities*, London: NEDO.

Chambers, S. G. (1987) 'Equality and Inequality in Northern Ireland: The Work-place', London: Policy Studies Institute.

Compton, P. (1991) 'Employment Differentials in Northern Ireland and Job Discrimination', in P. J. Roche and B. Barton (eds), *The Northern Ireland Question, Myth and Reality*, Aldershot: Avebury.

Compton, P. A. (1995) *Demographic Review of Northern Ireland 1995*, Belfast: Northern Ireland Economic Council.

Compton, P. A. and Coward, J. (1989) *Fertility and Family Planning in Northern Ireland*, Aldershot: Avebury.

Fair Employment Commission (1990) 'A Profile of the Northern Ireland Workforce', *Monitoring Report No. 7*.

Fair Employment Commission (1996) 'A Profile of the Workforce in Northern Ireland', *A Summary of the 1990 Monitoring Returns. Research Report No. 1*.

Fitzgerald, J. (1996) 'The Republic of Ireland after 2000. The Icarus Complex', Dublin: ESRI.

Gudgin, G. (1994a) 'The Distribution of Jobs between Communities in Northern Ireland since 1971', *Standing Advisory Commission on Human Rights. Annual Report 1994*.

Gudgin, G. (1994b) 'Catholic and Protestant Unemployment in Ireland North and South', Working Paper No. 10, Belfast: NIERC.

Gudgin, G. and Breen, R. (1996) 'Evaluation of the Ratio of Unemployment Rates as an Indicator of Fair Employment', *Studies in Employment Equality Research, Report No. 4*, Belfast: Central Community Relations Unit.

Gudgin, G. and O'Shea, G. (1993) 'Unemployment Forever? The Northern Ireland Economy in Recession and Beyond', Belfast: NIERC.

Honohan, P. (1992) 'Fiscal Adjustment in Ireland in 1980s', *Economic and Social Review*, 23(3): 285–315.

McCormick, B. (1991) 'Migration and Regional Policy', in A. Bower and K. Mayhew (eds), *Reducing Regional Inequalities*, London: NEDO.

McLaughlin, E. (1993) 'Unemployment', in J. Kramer and P. Montgomery (eds), *Women's Working Lives*, Belfast: HMSO.

Murphy, A. (1996) 'Comments', in G. Gudgin and R. Breen 'Evaluation of the Ratio of Unemployment Rates as an Indicator of Fair Employment', Belfast: Central Community Relations Unit.

Murphy, A. and Armstrong, D. (1994) 'A Picture of the Catholic and Protestant Male Unemployed', *Employment Equality Review*, Research Report No. 2, Belfast: Central Community Relations Unit.

Northern Ireland Economic Council (NIEC) (1994) *Autumn Economic Review Report 113*, Belfast.

Northern Ireland Economic Council (NIEC) (1996) *The 1995 UK Budget and its Implications For Northern Ireland*, Belfast.

PIEDA (1984) 'Transport Costs in Peripheral Regions', *PPRU Occasional Paper No. 7*, Belfast.

PPRU (various dates) 'Labour Force Survey Religion Report', *PPRU Monitor 2/93*. Belfast: Parliament Buildings.

Rowthorn, R. (1996) 'Comments', in G. Gudgin and R. Breen (eds), *Studies in Employment Equality Research*, Report No. 4, Belfast: Central Community Relations Unit.

Scott, R. (1993) 'Long-term Unemployment and the Policy Response', in G. Gudgin and G. O'Shea (eds), *Unemployment Forever?* Belfast: NIERC 1993.

Sheehan, M. and Tomlinson, M. (1996) 'Long-term Unemployment in West Belfast', in E. McLaughlin and P. Quirk (eds), *Employment in Northern Ireland*, Belfast: SACHR.

Smith, D. J. and Chambers, G. (1991) 'Inequality in Northern Ireland', Oxford: Clarendon Press.

Walsh, J. and Brown, W. (1991) 'Regional Earning and Pay Flexibility', in A. Bower and K. Mayhew (eds), *Reducing Regional Inequalities*, London: NEDO Policy Issues Series.

White, M. (1991) 'Against Unemployment', London: Policy Studies Institute.

White, M. (1994) 'Unemployment and Public Policy in a Changing Labour Market', London: Policy Studies Institute.

Does the Border Make the Difference? Variations in Women's Paid Employment, North and South

PAT O'CONNOR & SALLY SHORTALL

Introduction

THE GENDERED NATURE OF IRISH SOCIETY, North and South, is very much a taken for granted reality. Connell (1987) has argued that although we think of gender as a property of individuals, it is necessary to go beyond this and to see the social landscape as being more or less 'gendered' in the sense that its practices and structures are more or less mapped by gender. He suggests that gender divisions are a fundamental feature of the capitalist system ('arguably as fundamental as class divisions') and that 'capitalism is run by, and mainly to the advantage of, men' (Connell, 1987: 104). The concept of patriarchy is useful to describe this phenomenon 'in the limited sense of a short hand for describing male dominance' (Pollert, 1996: 655). It has been defined by Walby (1990: 120) as 'a system of social structures and practices in which men dominate oppress and exploit women'. It also has an ideological reality in the sense that women's position is seen as natural, inevitable or what women want rather than being due to the 'active social subordination of women going on here and now' (Connell, 1987: 215). Not surprisingly, the use of the concept as an overarching framework for understanding variation in women's position North and South is likely to provoke resistance. Equally, it is recognised that the identification of North and South as states may be seen as problematic and we recognise the difficulties implicit in doing this (see O'Dowd, 1991 and Rottman, this volume).

It is argued that the patriarchal nature of both states is reflected firstly in the fact that, to varying degrees, they are both male breadwinner states, in the sense that they are organised on the presumed existence of a male breadwinner and a financially dependent wife. Secondly, most women in both states are in a limited range of occupational positions, and at the

Proceedings of the British Academy, **98**, 285–318. © The British Academy 1999.

lower levels. It is suggested that by locating the similarities and differences in women's paid employment, North and South, in this context we can get an insight into the 'implicit gender contract underpinning social and economic organisation' which, to varying degrees, exists across Europe (*Bulletin on Women and Employment in the E.U.*, 1996, 9:1).

It will be shown that married women, particularly older married women in the North, have a higher level of participation in paid employment than their counterparts in the South, and we will suggest that this can be explained in terms of historical factors related to the demand for women's labour in occupations which were not affected by the marriage bar. It will be shown that more women are working part-time in the North and that more women are involved in low-paid work there. It is suggested that these patterns reflect the low levels of male wages; the deregulatory processes operating in the labour market and the creation of part-time opportunities by the state. It is suggested that these patterns can also usefully be located in the context of taxation arrangements; benefit systems and facilities as regards the care of children and generally reconciling work and family life. In this context the North emerges as a modified male breadwinner state insofar as it combines contradictory elements, such as individual taxation with means-tested benefits and little or no childcare provision (*The Bulletin on Women and Employment in the E.U.*, 1996, 9). On the other hand the South emerges as a strong male breadwinner state with married women's lower levels of participation in paid employment co-existing in a context where there is, effectively, household-based taxation and benefits, as well as little state-funded child-care. In both cases there is the presumption of a male breadwinner and a dependent wife (Lewis, 1992; 1993). In this respect it is argued that they differ from those E.U. countries where the assumption is that all adults of working age will be in paid work; where taxation and benefits are more individualised; where child-care is provided by the state, and where there is a less firm line between public and private responsibility. Scandinavian governments have consciously decided to move towards such a dual breadwinner model, with the state being committed to a heavy social service burden, partly to service family needs, but also partly to allow women, like men, to choose paid work (Crompton, 1995).

On the other hand it will be shown that women in the South, reflecting their higher levels of education, make up a higher proportion of those in the professional services (Breen, Heath and Whelan, this volume). However, women in the South, despite their occupancy of such positions of 'prestige', are less likely than those in the North to occupy positions of 'authority' (Savage, 1992) i.e., positions at the upper echelons of administrative and

managerial occupations. This may well reflect the impact of equality monitoring despite the prioritising of religion rather than gender as the ultimate
criterion of acceptability in the North and the limited efficacy of such
monitoring.

It will be shown that both North and South, as indeed across the EU,
women are disproportionately represented in low paid, part-time work;
they are overwhelmingly concentrated into a narrow range of 'semi-
domesticated areas' (Mann, 1986: 45) and they are overwhelmingly
excluded from positions of administrative or managerial power. It is
suggested that these trends reflect what Mann (1986) has referred to as
the neo-patriarchal nature of the society—what Walby (1990) has called
public patriarchy. Some of these gendered practices and processes will be
described here, although a detailed exploration of them lies beyond the
scope of this paper. What evidence we have suggests that they exist in
other European countries—their impact being reduced by political
philosophies and collective bargaining arrangements which stress indivi-
dualisation and the protection of the low paid (Norris, 1987; Whitehouse,
1992; Rubery and Fagan, 1993).

Structures, however, are not monolithic. Thus particular parts of the
state apparatus pursue conflicting policies (Mann, 1993; O'Connell and
Rottman, 1992). This is most obvious as regards the tension between the
state's endorsement of the rhetoric of equality and degendered citizenship
and the continuing support for the male breadwinner framework both
North and South. There is a further tension between the creation of
employment for women consequent on the expansion of the state apparatus, North and South, and the state's support for the male breadwinner
model. Equally there is a tension between this model and the demands of
the labour market for cheap flexible female labour.

The interpretation of these patterns is necessarily speculative. Sexton
and O'Connell (1997) noted that in the South there was no clear
consensus regarding the factors underlying even the growth in women's
participation in paid employment, or their differential importance.
Hence this chapter is organised so as to allow the reader to reach his/
her own conclusions. Thus, women's participation in paid employment
North and South is first described and specific features highlighted.
Then the weight of evidence in favour of various explanations is
assessed, focusing first on those related to the labour market supply;
then to labour market demand, and then to more broadly contextual
explanations related to equality policy, collective bargaining and organisational factors—the latter group being seen as particularly important
in explaining women's position, as opposed to their participation, in the
labour market.

Pat O'Connor & Sally Shortall

Women's Participation in the Labour Force, North and South: An Overview

Participation Rates: All Women

The pattern of women's participation in the labour force was quite stable from partition until 1981 in the South. In 1926, 30 per cent of all women in the South were economically active, as compared with just under 30 per cent in 1981 (see Table 1). However from the mid-1980s the proportion of women who were economically active (using principal economic status) increased steadily in the South, reaching 33.4 per cent in 1991, and 38.5 per cent in 1996. Furthermore this measure, as opposed to the ILO one, served to underestimate the proportion of women who were economically active. By 1995, the proportion of women who were economically active in the South using the ILO definition was just under 40 per cent, reaching 41 per cent in 1996 (*Irish Labour Force Survey*, 1996 [1997]).

In the North, the pattern has been somewhat different. Thus the proportion of women who were economically active was slightly higher (36 per cent) in 1926. The increase in the proportion of women who were economically active began earlier than in the South, and hence the increase

Table 1. Economically active women in Ireland, 1926–95.

	North	South	North	South
	Married women active as % of all married women	Married women active as a % of all married women	All women active as a % of all women	All women active as a % of all women
1926	14.6	5.7	35.7	30.3
1936	—	5.6	—	32.5
1951	14.6	4.7	34.5	30.6
1961	19.5	5.2	35.3	28.6
1971	29.3	7.5	36.0	27.2
1981	40.6	16.7	41.6	29.7
1991	48.9	27.4	45.2	33.4
1995	64.8	34.2	61.0	36.5
1996	64.2	36.6	62.0	38.5

Notes: 1926: 12 yrs and over
1951: 14 yrs and over
1961/71: 15 yrs and over
1981/91: 16 yrs and over
1995/96 NI women of working age (16–59)

Sources: Calculated from the Census of Population, Northern Ireland and Republic of Ireland. ROI figures taken from Fahey, 1990; NI and Republic of Ireland Labour Force Surveys, 1995 and 1996 (PES).

in the 1980s was less dramatic—42 per cent of all women being economically active in the North by 1981, and 45 per cent by 1991. Thus the
proportion in the North was similar to the EU average, which was 45
per cent in 1995 (Eurostat, 1997) while the proportion in the South, despite
the dramatic increases in the 1980s, was below the average, even in 1996.

Labour Force Participation Rates: Married Women

The differences between North and South were more pronounced as
regards the proportion of married women who were economically active.
In the South, almost 6 per cent of married women were economically
active in 1926, compared with 15 per cent in the North. Again this
pattern remained fairly stable in the South until the early 1970s. In the
North by comparison, it had reached 29 per cent by 1971, while it
remained much the same, at 7.5 per cent, in the South (Durkan *et al.*,
1995). By 1981 participation had increased to just under 17 per cent in
the South and it continued to increase dramatically. In 1996, just under
37 per cent of married women in the South were economically active as
assessed on the basis of principal economic status (just under 41 per cent
of married women being economically active using the ILO definition:
Irish Labour Force Survey, 1996 [1997]: 29, 55). In the North married
women's participation increased dramatically in the 1970s, and by 1981 it
had reached 41 per cent; and by 1991, 49 per cent. The EOC figures
(1995: 13) show that just under 56 per cent of married or cohabiting
women were economically active in the North.

These overall trends conceal substantial age variation, both North
and South. Using the ILO definition of labour force participation, 63
per cent of married women aged 25–34 years in the South were in the
labour force in 1996 as compared with 25 per cent of those aged 55–59
years (*Irish Labour Force Survey*, 1996 [1997]: 55). A virtually identical
proportion of young women (20–34 years) were economically active in the
North. On the other hand a much higher proportion (42 per cent) of
married women in the 55–59 year age group were economically active in
the North.

Thus variation in the economic activity rates of married women North
and South (EOC, 1995: 13) reflects differences in the activity rates of the
older cohorts and the longer tradition of paid employment for married
women in the North. In this context then the key issue becomes one of
explaining both the similarity in economic activity amongst the younger
cohorts and the differences in the economic activity rates amongst the
older cohorts.

Both North and South, equal pay legislation was introduced following membership of the European Community. It has been argued that at
the EU level the Directive was driven by France who already had such
legislation and did not wish to be economically disadvantaged on this
account (McGauran, 1996). In any case the most significant single
change in the wage differential in the North and South followed the
implementation of the Equal Pay Act in 1970 in the North, and 1975 in
the South. In the North, women's earnings were 63 per cent of men's
earnings in 1973, and by 1980 they had increased to 75 per cent. This
change was across all occupations, and at all levels. In the South
women's hourly earnings relative to men's, amongst manual workers in
the manufacturing area, increased from just under 60 per cent in 1973 to
69 per cent in 1980 (Callan and Wren, 1994). The differential has
remained relatively stable since then (Durkan *et al.*, 1995). The focus
on hourly earnings underestimates the male/female differential since it is
widely recognised that men are more likely to receive overtime and other
additional payments.

Callan and Wren (1994) found that women's hourly earnings across all
kinds of paid employment in the South was 80 per cent of men's—half of
that difference being explained by what they called 'productivity related
characteristics'—mainly labour market experience. Women's hourly earnings relative to men's (at 85 per cent) were slightly higher in the North. In
Britain, women who worked full time earned 80 per cent of men's hourly
wage (EOC, 1996). The narrower pay gap in the North is due to the lower
male wages.

Both the South and the North lack minimum wage agreements. Focusing on full-time women workers with earnings below two-thirds of the
median earnings, it is clear that the situation in Northern Ireland (and
indeed in the UK as a whole) is considerably worse than in the South or in
the rest of Europe. In Northern Ireland, 40 per cent of women who work
full time are low paid by this definition (as defined by the Low Pay Unit
[LPU]) compared with just under 30 per cent in the South (EOC, 1995: 25).
Furthermore, the LPU deals only with full-time employees, thus under-
stating the extent of female low pay, since many are in low paid, part-time
employment.

In 1991, women were equally or over-represented among the full-time
low-paid workers in every member State in the EU (Rubery *et al.*, 1993).
Thus, quite clearly although there is some divergence between North and
South as regards the proportion of women who are low paid, it is very clear
that there is convergence (across Europe indeed) as regards the over-
representation of women amongst the low paid.

Part-Time Work

Maruani (1992) has noted that part-time paid employment is, generally speaking, characteristic of women in Northern Europe. Part-time workers are particularly common in the UK and indeed also in the Netherlands. The UK as a whole has the second highest proportion of female employees working part-time in the EU and is well above the EU average, while the South is below the EU average (EOC 1995: 18). In Northern Ireland the proportion of part-time female employment is lower than in the rest of the UK (37 per cent versus 45 per cent, in 1993) but very much higher there than in the South, where only just over 19 per cent of women were in part-time work.

There has been a rapid increase in part-time employment in the South since the mid-1980s. An increase in part-time employment was characteristic of most of the EU countries in the 1984–94 period. For many of them this was related to the relaxation of restrictive employment legislation regarding part-time work. This legislation did not however, apply in Ireland or Britain. Nevertheless the second largest increase, both in overall terms, and (separately) for women and men occurred in the South over that period. The share of part-time employment also almost doubled in the South over the same period (from 6 per cent in 1985 to just under 11 per cent in 1994: NESF, 1996). The growth in part-time employment in the South accounted for almost three-fifths of the total employment increase over that period—being most important in the pre-1993 period (O'Connell, this volume). In the South it is likely that the increase reflected an increasing state commitment to the service sector which is typically linked to the growth in part-time employment.

Broadly similar trends emerged in the North, although the expansion in part-time employment began earlier there and accounted for a greater proportion of employment growth. Thus, the growth in female part-time employment in the North from 1971–92 accounted for 95 per cent of the net gain in female employment over the period (Dignan, 1996) and has been closely related to the expansion in the public service, and in particular, in education, health and welfare. Apart from these areas, part-time work in the North in general involves people with few qualifications doing low-skilled jobs. The earnings of part-time workers reflect their industrial and occupational distribution (Trewsdale, 1992).

In both the South and the North (as indeed in most of the EU) women are more likely than men to be working part-time. The majority of the women in part-time employment are married (NESF, 1996: 13). In the South, four out of five part-time workers are employed in services, and they are (rather surprisingly) concentrated in the business and professional areas (NESF, 1996: 13). Indeed, in 1996, nearly three out of five of those women who were working part-time worked either in the professional services or in commerce, insurance, finance or business services (*Irish Labour Force Survey*, 1996 [1997]: 58).

There has been some research on women's part-time work in the North (NIEC, 1992), but little research on the South (O'Connell, 1996). In any case the examination of part-time work as a uniform category of people who work thirty hours or less is fraught with difficulties. Nevertheless, it is clear that part-time work is very much more common in the North than in the South.

Occupational Segregation

Maruani (1992: 1) has stressed that the increase in women's participation in the labour force 'does not mean that women have won occupational equality. . . discrimination and segregation continue to reign'. The embedding of gender in occupations is reflected in persistent patterns of gender segregation, as well as in the reproduction of the gendered identity of jobs and occupations (Acker, 1990). This gendering may be extremely subtle and reflected in the conception of the nature or value of the skills involved in a task. Thus for example, the skills involved in cleaning or air hostess work, social work, etc., may be 'invisible' and seen as simply characteristic of the women who typically occupy these positions. The perception of these skills as 'natural' is used simultaneously to define these jobs as low skill, as suitable for women and as low paid; women's negotiating positions in such areas being often further weakened by weak unionisation.

After partition, the North was much more industrialised than the South. While agriculture was important on both sides of the border, it was more important in the South. The industrialised North featured many industries that traditionally employed a higher proportion of women than men viz., textiles (mainly linen) and clothing. These two industries accounted for over 80 per cent of women's employment until the 1940s. With the decline of these industries from the 1950s to the present day, there was an occupational shift from clothing and textiles to the service sector as sources of female employment.

The different labour market structure North and South not only affected the type of work women were engaged in, but also the accuracy of estimates of the extent to which married women were employed. Figures for married women's participation in paid employment do not include the farm work that many married women undertake on family farms (Fahey, 1990; 1993). Agriculture was much more important as a sectoral source of

employment in the South than in the North up to the 1950s. Indeed, until
the 1970s, farm work was the most important form of economic activity for
married women in the South. Thus the pre-1970 figures on the South may
have underestimated the extent of married women's economic activity. The
apparent increase in married women's participation in paid employment in
the South since the 1970s may reflect a changing balance between agriculture and non-agricultural sectors, and, in particular, married women's
movement from unpaid and invisible agricultural work, to paid work which
is being recorded in the labour force statistics. We have no way of assessing
the extent to which this is so.

Horizontal and vertical segregation are well recognised features of
women's participation in the labour force, with women being huddled
into a narrow range of predominantly female occupations and being
congregated at the bottom of career hierarchies. North and South, the
service sector currently accounts for approximately 80 per cent of female
employment. Currently in the North, clerical, secretarial and sales occupations account for almost half of the jobs held by women. In the South in
1996, 70 per cent of the women who were in paid employment were in three
occupational groups: clerical workers, professional and technical workers,
and service workers (*Irish Labour Force Survey*, 1996 [1997]). Both North
and South, women generally tend to work with other women. In the South,
77 per cent of clerical workers are women, with service and sales also being
highly feminised. Just over half (53 per cent) of the professional and
technical workers in the South are women, and in these areas too women
tend to be concentrated into a small range of occupations such as nursing
and teaching. Durkan *et al.* (1995) noted that the extent to which men and
women worked in different types of jobs had changed little since the early
1980s. He noted that just under 58 per cent of women in 1981, as compared
with 51 per cent in 1992 would have had to shift to male-dominated
occupations to eliminate occupational segregation. The validity of indices
of horizontal occupational segregation has been challenged (Blackburn *et
al.*, 1993). However, the clustering of women into areas of predominantly
female employment is very much a reality. It is not of course peculiar to
North and South, but is a very well recognised feature of women's participation in the labour force across Europe.

Vertical segregation also exists North and South. In the North, men
retain a disproportionate share of managerial and senior administrative
posts. Women in the North make up 26 per cent of managers and administrators, which is low by comparison with the UK (where they make up 33
per cent: EOC 1995: 18). It has been recognised that there are considerable
difficulties comparing the proportion of women in such positions internationally, because of variation in the definition of what constitutes a

management post (Rubery and Fagan, 1993). However, there is some evidence to suggest that the proportion of women in such positions is lower in the South. Thus a United Nations (1995) Report indicated that just under 23 per cent of administrators and managers in the UK were women, as compared with just over 15 per cent in the South.

The proportion of women in administrative/managerial positions varies considerably across Europe. Only in Hungary did women make up more than half of those holding these positions; with women constituting 39 per cent of those in these positions in Sweden. The United Nations Report showed that typically in Europe women constituted a much larger proportion of professional and technical workers. Thus, for example, they made up 63 per cent of such workers in Sweden; 40 per cent in the U.K. and 45 per cent in Ireland. The trends are even more extreme when one focuses simply on employees in the professional services. Here, women made up 65 per cent of those in these occupations in the South (*Irish Labour Force Survey*, 1996 [1997]: 25) as compared with 45 per cent of employees in these positions in the North (EOC, 1995: 18). Thus it seems possible to tentatively suggest that women make up a higher proportion of 'positions of expertise' in the South but a lower proportion of those in 'positions of authority' (Savage, 1992).

'Labour Market Supply' Explanations

Labour market supply theories have been the most common kinds of explanations put forward as regards married women's participation in paid employment. They include those involving the presence or age of children; taxation and benefit systems; individual choice; and educational level. Each will be briefly discussed in the following.

Children

The presence of children is widely seen as central to an explanation of the extent and nature of women's participation in the labour force. Frequently, the issue is implicitly or explicitly presented as if the presence of children had inevitable consequences as regards women's employment. In the North, using 1985–91 Labour Force Survey data, Dignan (1996) estimated that if a woman's youngest child was under two years, this reduced her participation rate by 27 per cent compared to a woman whose youngest child was 9 years or over. Similarly, Callan and Farrell (1991) showed that in the South women's participation in paid employment halved with each additional child.

However, the *Bulletin on Women and Employment in the EU* (1995: 6) clearly showed that focusing on mothers aged 20–39 years old, with a dependent child aged 14 years or less there was a very wide range of variation in mother's employment participation across the EU—ranging from 76 per cent in Denmark to 32 per cent in Ireland (see Table 2). It will be shown that such participation is also affected by education—with 95–98 per cent of young mothers with graduate education being in paid employment in Denmark and in Portugal, as compared with 68 per cent in Ireland.

Thus, quite clearly, the impact of bearing and rearing children is mediated by the state, and/or through the structure of the labour market, in the context of social norms and practices concerning women's role in the family. In Denmark, widespread state-funded child-care ensured that the overwhelming majority of women, with or without children, were in paid employment (motherhood effect = +2). In the South, the effect of motherhood on women's participation was negative and it was the highest in the EU (at −51) with the UK being in an intermediate position (at −34) (see Table 2).

Being a mother thus has very different implications in various EU countries—which tells us more about the way in which motherhood is constructed by the state, and the social norms and expectations about motherhood, than it does about the presence/absence of children. Furthermore, these patterns did not reflect a country's degree of economic development since the employment rate for mothers in Portugal (at 71 per cent) was very similar to Denmark (at 76 per cent)—despite their very different stages of economic development (United Nations, 1995). Equally, the presence of dependent children was not universally associated with high levels of part-time employment amongst women. It was clear that in some countries, full-time and part-time employment for mothers co-existed (e.g., Denmark); while in others, part-time employment was by far the dominant pattern, (e.g., Netherlands); while elsewhere (e.g., Spain), full-time employment was the dominant pattern.

Variation in Child-Care Provision and in Family Friendly Policies

In so far as child-care is not provided by women, it potentially can be provided by the state, the market and/or by other family members (for example, the husband). North and South differ little in terms of men's low involvement in housework and child-care (Montgomery, 1993; McWilliams, 1991; Rogers, 1993; Kiely, 1995; European Commission,

Table 2. Activity rates for women aged 20–39 by educational attainment and maternal status, 1991.

	Women without dependent children				Mothers[3]				
	Compulsory	Post-compulsory	Graduate	All	Compulsory	Post-compulsory	Graduate	All	Motherhood effect[2]
B	72.1	88.8	94.6	83.9	58.2	76.9	86.1	70.3	−16
DK	75.9	85.3	94.2	85.6	82.4	89.4	95.2	87.6	+2
D	77.4	86.7	92.9	85.4	44.8	53.9	61.8	51.9	−39
GR	50.6	70.9	89.5	61.1	37.4	47.7	81.2	47.4	−22
E	62.2	81.0	92.2	73.7	39.1	61.2	83.9	46.8	−37
F[1]	na	na	na	84.3	na	na	na	69.9	−17
IRL	71.9	84.3	91.1	82.7	29.5	46.8	68.1	40.7	−51
I	64.9	83.5	94.6	73.9	42.4	67.4	88.6	51.6	−30
L	78.5	95.1	93.4	83.2	41.0	48.9	68.6	43.5	−48
NL	76.1	84.0	93.1	84.0	36.3	53.9	69.5	48.1	−43
P	78.7	80.0	98.1	81.7	73.7	86.8	96.2	76.9	−6
UK	89.2	89.8	94.4	90.3	56.0	64.3	74.0	59.2	−34
EUR12	77.1	85.9	93.6	83.7	48.3	60.0	76.2	57.8	−31

Notes: 1. Comparable education data are not available for France. Data relate to women who are the household head, either individually or as part of a couple.

2. Motherhood effect = (activity rate of mothers − activity rate of women without dependent children)/activity rate of women without dependent children × 100.

3. Mothers are defined as women with a dependent child aged 14 years or less.

B = Belgium, DK = Denmark, D = Germany, GR = Greece, E = Spain, F = France, IRL = Ireland, I = Italy, L = Luxembourg, NL = Netherlands, P = Portugal, UK = United Kingdom.

Source: Bulletin on Women and Employment in the E.U. (1995): April: 8.

1997). Neither is there a significant difference in the level of state provision of child-care North and South, nor in the economic activity rates of young married women. Thus it is not clear to what extent such provision is important in affecting women's participation in paid employment, although the fact that Portugal, with a very low level of state provision, has a high level of female economic activity is certainly provocative.

The absence of such provision does however, signal a certain disinterest by the state in publicly facilitating the reconciliation of work and family life. The UK, with the South and the Netherlands, is one of the three countries in the EU with the lowest levels of publicly funded child-care services for children of all ages. Until recently, Northern Ireland had the poorest provision within the UK (EOC, 1995). In the South, public funding for children under six years, other than through early entry to the primary school system is very low (European Commission Network on Child Care, 1996). It is often argued that the availability of child-care facilities influences women's decision to opt for part-time work. This does not hold up however when we consider that the three EU countries with the lowest levels of publicly funded child-care have very different proportions of women in part-time employment.

Callan and Farrell (1991) noted the importance of the costs of substitute care in affecting women's participation where women's wage rates were low. Yet these trends sit uneasily with the fact that despite the absence of state funding for child-care, in 1991 the South, which had the lowest participation rate for mothers with children under ten years old, had the third largest increase in their participation over the 1985–91 period. Furthermore, in the South, unlike most other EU countries this increase largely reflected an increase in full-time as opposed to part-time employment. These trends clearly suggest that even in a situation where the state does not facilitate women's paid employment, young mothers' participation in paid employment can increase dramatically.

The limited evidence available suggests that both in North and South there is a good deal of interest amongst employees in arrangements to facilitate the reconciliation of work and family life—both as regards the provision of pre-school care, school holiday care, job sharing and flexible hours (Turner et al., 1994; Trewsdale and Kremer, 1996; EEA, 1996; Fynes et al., 1996). For the most part this demand has not been recognised by the state or by employers. Thus, although the real availability of child-care facilities to all mothers in a society is useful as an indicator of that society's concern with maximising choices, there is little difference between the North and South in this area.

Benefits

In both North and South the social security systems are, by and large, organised around the principle of a male breadwinner. In this situation women derive their rights to benefits from their partners, and their access to such benefits is typically means tested. Additionally, women are less likely than men to get benefits since they are more likely to have a spouse whose income places them outside the scope of means-tested benefits. Furthermore, means-tested systems often effectively discourage spouses' participation in paid employment by taxing their income.

A number of studies in the North have found that having an unemployed partner increases the likelihood of a married woman being unemployed (Dignan, 1996; Davies *et al.*, 1995; McLaughlin, 1993). There are many reasons why so few married women with unemployed partners are in employment, such as the likelihood of shared labour market characteristics (Gallie *et al.*, 1994). However, the importance of the way in which the benefit system operates cannot be eliminated. It penalises part-time work by the partner of an unemployed man, by proportionately reducing the man's out-of-work benefits. In addition, no allowance is made for travel or child-care costs. Dignan (1996) estimated that the effect on women's participation where a spouse is employed as opposed to unemployed is almost 20 per cent. Similar patterns emerge in the South (and indeed right across the EU) with women being much more likely to be pulled into unemployment by the unemployment of their spouse than vice versa (*Bulletin on Women and Employment in the E.U.*, 1996, 9: 4).

Benefit policies in the South have steadily underpinned the position of the male breadwinner. Prior to the EU Directive on equal treatment for men and women in the social security system, married women were paid lower rates of benefit than men for shorter periods of time; they were not paid unemployment assistance and married men could claim for their wives as dependants, regardless of what these women were earning. As part of its attempt (1978–95) to implement the Directive, equal payments for various kinds of benefits were introduced in the South over the 1984–86 period. In introducing such payments, the State directed that, unless these wives were earning less than IR£50 per week, married men could no longer claim for them as dependants (Fourth Report of the Fourth Joint Oireachtas Committee, 1996). In an attempt to buffer the effect of this reduction in married men's income, compensatory payments were introduced in November 1986, and these were not discontinued until 1992. These payments (up to IR£20 per week), which were only paid to married men, were seen as part of an attempt to implement the equal treatment directive. They were judged to be discriminatory in the European Court in 1995. Their introduction vividly illustrates the extent to which indirect discrimination has become so embedded in state practices and procedures that it is literally not even perceived.

Taxation

Differences in the taxation systems North and South make it more or less worthwhile in economic terms for married women to be in paid employment. In the North, as in the UK, separate taxation for husbands and wives is now automatic and universal. Furthermore, the additional tax allowance which is granted to married couples can be allocated to either or it can be split between them (European Observatory, EC, 1996). On the other hand in the South (and arguably reflecting its stronger endorsement of the male breadwinner model) double tax allowances and double tax bands are allocated to a married couple, regardless of whether or not the wife is in paid employment. This implicitly challenges the economic wisdom of a married woman participating in paid employment, particularly part-time and/or low-paid employment (Mahon, 1994). Furthermore, unless couples specify otherwise, double tax allowances and tax bands are given to the husband automatically, if they married before 1993–94, and to the highest earner (who is likely to be the husband) if they married after that (Monitoring Committee, 1996). Thus, apparently innocuous automatic arrangements as regards tax assessment in the South create a context which implicitly discourages married women's participation in paid employment, and implicitly reinforces the male breadwinner's position.

Individual Choice

Hakim (1991; 1995; 1996) argued that women are responsible adults who choose to be either home-centred (uncommitted workers), or committed workers. However as Breugel (1996) points out, this argument pays little attention to the context in which the choice is made. The context involves a variety of factors including the cost of child-care (insofar as it is not provided by the state or the family), the wages available to women, taxation arrangements, the structure of the labour market and the legal situation. The situation may be further exacerbated by the common practice for child-care costs to be met out of the wife's income. These factors may well create a situation where the perceived economic benefit of married women participating in paid employment is very low indeed. In this situation not surprisingly, married women in the South and in the North often referred to family/personal reasons for opting out of the labour market (Fine-Davis, 1988; Trewsdale, 1987).

Normative expectations as well as economic considerations can be expected to shape the choices made. In the South, the Roman Catholic Church endorsed an ideological position stressing the importance of women's role within the home—a position which Cousins (1996: 13) has suggested was 'not unrelated to the fact that there was always a comparatively high level of unemployment and underemployment amongst Irish men'. Women in Ireland are more likely than any other European women to favour a situation where the wife is not in paid employment (Rubery and Fagan, 1993). However, the proportion doing this was roughly the same size as the proportion favouring a husband and wife having equally demanding jobs—the co-existence of these two opposing views being unusual in European terms, and possibly reflecting differences in age and education.

It is increasingly accepted that women have the right to 'choose' to seek paid work, but the popular perception is that men 'ought' to seek paid work (Callan and Wren, 1994). Insofar as alternatives are not available, it is women who are more constrained in their attempts to decide 'how they shall live', since it is they who are seen as ultimately responsible for child-care, and so it is they who must consider how to combine child-rearing and domestic work with paid work (Crompton, 1995). There are real costs to women in terms of labour market returns because of child-related interruptions, effectively reducing women's wages relative to men's. They affect in purely economic terms the process of internal bargaining between couples, even those with identical preferences and similar capabilities (Callan and Wren, 1994). This kind of analysis illustrates the importance of examining the context within which women make choices. Hence a model such as Hakim's (1991; 1995; 1996) which implicitly ignores structural constraints seems less than satisfactory. Women in various societies do make choices about their paid working lives, but they do so under varying conditions, and largely not of their own making. Rational choice theory also fails to account for the fact that full-time work for women with children under five is restricted to those with higher educational qualifications (Ginn *et al.*, 1996). A plausible explanation for this is the considerable cost of private child-care—a cost which only those with high incomes can meet.

Education

In every EU country, participation in the labour force is associated with women's educational level. It is not clear to what extent these patterns reflect the greater economic return that such women can expect, their different attitudes as regards the importance of mothers being at home full-time, or their smaller family size (*Bulletin on Women and Employment in the EU*, 1995, 6: 8). Level of education had an effect in every country, although the strength of this effect varied even amongst young women with dependent children. Thus, for example the impact of education was modest in Denmark. It was stronger in Portugal, and greater still in (Southern) Ireland. Thus there was a difference of 38 per cent in the economic activity rates of mothers with compulsory and graduate education in the South (see Table 2). Dignan (1996) estimated that in the North having a degree increased women's participation rate by some 26 per cent compared to those without qualifications. Thus quite clearly right across the EU higher educational levels are associated with women's—even young mothers—participation in education, with the impact of education being somewhat greater in the South than in the North.

The educational attainment of women, North and South (like those in the rest of Europe) has increased dramatically since the 1960s. Thus for example 67 per cent of women aged 25-9 years in the South completed second-level education, as compared with 33 per cent of those aged 50-9 years (Eurostat, 1995, 12: 4). These differences are probably not unrelated to the very substantial differences in the economic activity rates of older and younger women in the South. Younger and older women in the North do not display the same differences in employment participation rates. Educational level as such then, cannot explain the differences in women's participation in paid employment, North and South.

Labour Market Demand Explanations

A good deal less attention has been paid to explanations related to the structure of the labour market, although it is of course obvious that the extent and nature of women's economic activity will be affected by the demand created by such structures, both in their own right and as they are shaped by state policies and practices.

The Marriage Bar and the Reintegration of Women in Paid Employment

The labour market is not always allowed to operate without manipulation. The classic example of such manipulation was the imposition of the 'marriage bar' by the state. Similar to many Western European countries, women in the North and South were subject to a marriage bar, whereby women in public sector employment had to leave paid employment on marriage. The imposition of this bar reflected and reinforced the male breadwinner model. In the South, the marriage bar was lifted in 1957 for primary school teachers, and not until 1973 for other public sector employees (e.g., civil servants and secondary school teachers). Although the marriage bar was not legally enforced in many other areas of paid employment, such as the banks, up to 1973 there was a clear expectation that women would retire on marriage and this was institutionalised through the marriage gratuity (i.e., a lump sum paid to women on their marriage and subsequent retirement). Thus directly or indirectly the marriage bar affected the participation of women who entered the labour force prior to that time i.e., those women who are currently in their forties or older.

In Britain, the marriage bar was removed in 1946 (Bagilhole, 1994), but not in Northern Ireland until the early 1970s. Fahey (1990) noted that the marriage bar was not a straightforward state policy on gender employment, but was rather the outcome of a complex and shifting interplay of labour market forces, cultural attitudes and state regulation. This would help explain the later removal of the bar in Northern Ireland where there was a greater labour surplus than in the rest of the UK. The interaction with the labour market also explains why, despite a similar marriage bar, there was a higher percentage of married women in paid employment in the North. Textiles and clothing were the main source of employment for women there, and these industries were not subject to the marriage bar. The much higher proportion of older married women in paid employment in the North reflects these factors.

The reintegration of middle aged married women into the labour force is particularly important in the South since their low level of economic activity was fostered by the social and economic policies of the state, by employers and trade unions. Such women face considerable difficulties as regards reintegration. Even if they define themselves as unemployed and attempt to register as unemployed, they find that, having been out of work for a period of time, they are not entitled to receive unemployment benefit, and frequently do not have enough insurance contributions to register for credits. If their husband is in paid employment, the level of the household income (regardless of how it is distributed) will determine whether or not they will be entitled to the means-tested unemployment assistance. If their husband is unemployed himself and is unwilling to 'swap eligibility', this option is closed to them. Because of the way it is done, 'splitting the claim', which is technically possible, is likely to reduce the total household income, and so it is likely to be an unattractive option. Hence married women are unlikely to be officially registered as unemployed (i.e., on the Live Register). It has been estimated that only 48 per cent of unemployed women are on the Live Register as compared with 85 per cent of unemployed men (Conroy Jackson, 1991).

Employment and training schemes in the South are overwhelmingly targeted at those who are on the Live Register. They are thus very effective in excluding women. Insofar as such schemes are basically concerned with the reintegration of people into paid employment 'there is no justification for any Live Register requirement' and it has been suggested that it may constitute indirect discrimination contrary to the Employment Equality Act (Cousins, 1996: 4). Thus through a myriad of apparently innocuous gender neutral rules and regulations, most courses and employment training are effectively targeted at men rather than women. This is particularly ironic since such training is substantially funded by the EU to facilitate reintegration, on the specific understanding that it will be gender audited.

It is suggested, therefore, that the continued low level of participation by older married women in the South reflects not only the marriage bar, but the ongoing implicit endorsement by the state of the male breadwinner model, as reflected in these policies and practices.

Industrial Policy

It is now widely recognised that in the South, state directed industrial policy contributed to the relatively low level of women's economic activity from the 1920s until the mid-1980s. The 1936 Conditions of Employment Act allowed the minister to restrict the employment of women in an industry so as to arrest any tendency to increase female over male labour (Daly, 1992: 122–3). In the 1960s and 1970s, the state directly and indirectly influenced the gender composition of the work forces of foreign firms entering the South (Pyle, 1990). Export-led industries preferred female labour, but the state actively tried to encourage foreign firms to provide employment for men. The semi-state body with particular responsibility for attracting foreign investment stated explicitly in the late 1960s that they were 'seeking employment that will employ predominantly men'. Their 1970/71 annual report stated that 75 per cent of new jobs should be for males (Pyle, 1990: 75). Even into the mid-1980s, there continued to be a preference for multinational companies who would provide 'male' manufacturing jobs. Pursuing male employment fitted with both the Constitution and Church ideology. It also reflected the state's perception of unemployment as a male social problem.

The higher participation rate of women in paid employment in the North after partition should not be construed as indicating that there was greater benevolence towards women's employment there. It is more accurate to see it as something that was accepted, rather than desired (McLaughlin, 1989a). As in the South it was male unemployment that was seen as a social problem (McLaughlin, 1989b). The image of Derry as a city of female breadwinners was used by nationalists after partition as proof of an oppressive Unionist sectarian state that would not provide employment for (Catholic) men (McLaughlin, 1989a). A report in 1971 stated that Derry was a place where too many women were in paid work, even though at that time female employment represented 20 per cent of all employment in the city (McLaughlin, 1986). Even in 1985/86, 70 per cent of the jobs created in Derry's Enterprise Zone were for men (McLaughlin, 1989a). Male unemployment, and reliance on female breadwinners west of the river Bann (the traditional Catholic marker), was perceived as evidence of the partisan nature of the Northern state. Beyond this however, the primacy of the male breadwinner model was not challenged.

On the other hand, however, both in the North and South the expansion of public sector employment generated a demand for female labour, mostly in the health and related welfare areas (Smyth, 1997; O'Connell, 1996). This occurred right across Europe, although it was strongest in Sweden where, because of its well developed welfare state, over 40 per cent of total employment, and over 60 per cent of women's employment was in the public sector in 1994. In the South, over 25 per cent of all employment and 40 per cent of women's employment was in these areas in 1994 (*Bulletin on Women and Employment in the E.U.*, 1996, 9: 2). In the North (but not the South) the growth in the public sector also accounted for most of the part-time employment growth during the 1970s and 1980s. In the South, the state implicitly and explicitly endorsed full-time paid employment as the norm. This was illustrated by the fact that although job sharing was technically available in almost four-fifths of public sector organisations in the South, and was predominantly used by women, the state as their employer effectively penalised those who opted for it by reducing their increments. The European Court of Justice ruled in 1997 that this was indirect discrimination (Honan, 1997).

The Structure of the Economy

In the South the decline in agricultural employment, and in semi-skilled and unskilled employment over the past 30 years, together with the expansion of middle-class positions (O'Connell, 1996) potentially favoured women, since they were less likely than men to own land and more likely than men to do well at school (Hannan *et al.*, 1996; Lynch and Morgan, 1995). O'Connell (this volume) notes that over the 1961–91 period the overall proportion of employees in upper-middle class occupations increased from under 10 per cent in 1961 to over 22 per cent in 1991. The increase occurred amongst both men and women—the proportion of women in such occupations rising from 15 per cent in 1961 to 28 per cent in 1991. Similar, although less dramatic trends occurred amongst lower-middle class employees so that by 1991 more than three-quarters of the women at work were middle-class employees as compared with roughly two-fifths of the men (Ibid.). Similar patterns have been observed across Europe, leading Maruani (1992: 1) to note that 'The feminisation of the working population, especially in white collar jobs, is one of the most important social developments of the late twentieth century'. However, there were clear limits to such opportunities in the South since, for example, within the upper-middle class the proportion of men in the higher professional category almost doubled, while the proportion of women declined by about one-third (O'Connell, this volume).

Walsh (1993) noted that increases in the importance of the service sector were associated with employment opportunities for women. In 1995, right across the EU, the main area of employment (and of employment growth) was in services: 65 per cent of all EU employment being in this sector, compared with 60 per cent in the South (Eurostat, 1996: 4). Just under 80 per cent of women across the EU (and in the South) were in the services sector. However, in the South, right up to the late 1980s, the state effectively disregarded the service sector, encouraged the industrial sector and tried to bulwark the agricultural sector—both areas of predominantly male employment. Jobs—'proper jobs'—were seen as being in the manufacturing and agricultural areas, a kind of focus which was very compatible with a focus on male employment.

In their analysis of women's participation in the labour market in the North, Heaton *et al.* (1993: 179) argued that non-service industries were organised along the lines of a 'male' model of employment, with full-time work being very much the norm for men and women. On the other hand, the service sector was characterised by having many 'small' jobs. It is certainly true that in the North and South there are very different opportunities for full-time and part-time work depending on the occupation and the sector. The increase in part-time work, North and South, has been linked to increased employment in the service sector. It is difficult, however, to know to what extent the reliance on part-time workers in this sector reflects weak unionisation rather than the intrinsic nature of the job.

Wider Contextual Factors

Women's participation in paid employment is affected by wider contextual factors as well as by labour market policy. Attention is focused on three of these here: namely equality policy, collective bargaining and organisational factors. It is suggested that these are particularly relevant to understanding variation in women's position within the labour market.

Equality Policy

Equality legislation represents the most direct attempt to ensure labour market equality and economic independence for women. Over the past 20 years, the legal and constitutional framework provided as regards women's position in society both North and South has come under a great deal of scrutiny. Initially, this arose in the context of entry to the European Community in 1973. As signatories of the Treaty of Rome, Ireland and the UK became bound by a series of Directives regarding equal pay and equal treatment in the area of access to employment, vocational training and social security. Such directives have been widely seen as an attempt by the EU to give concrete expression to a gender-neutral concept of citizenship.

In the North the passing of the Equal Pay Act (1970), the Fair Employment Act (1976), the Sex Discrimination (Northern Ireland) Order (1976) and the establishment of the Fair Employment Agency (1976) and the Equal Opportunities Commission (1976) were all part of this development. A plethora of equal opportunity directives have emerged since the 1970s, prompted by religious inequalities, but increasingly including gender as a category (for example Policy Appraisal on Fair Treatment). Largely due to economic and international political pressure, and the threat to internal stability, attempts have been made to tackle religious discrimination (Osborne and Cormack, 1989). They include monitoring the composition of the work-force, affirmative action, contract compliance and grant denial for employers who fail to meet their statutory obligations—the very measures long advocated by the sex, race and disability lobbies in both Britain and Northern Ireland (Maxwell, 1989; 1993). These raised the issue of 'read across' i.e., the question of why a strengthened policy could be promoted in Northern Ireland but not in the rest of the UK. By confining the new policy to religion (and not gender or disability) it could be depicted as of relevance only to Northern Ireland—'a place apart' (Osborne and Cormack, 1989: 293). Such an approach reflects the state's limited commitment to gender equality.

Jewson and Mason (1986) argue that the dominant approach to such equal opportunities initiatives was a liberal one. Theoretically, an attempt was made to deal with the value of women's work through Equal Value Legislation. It was introduced in the UK in 1984, following an EU ruling, but seems to have had little impact in Northern Ireland. Maxwell (1989; 1991) noted that the legislation was tortuous, complex and ambiguous. She argued that with hindsight it was difficult to resist the view that it was specifically designed to minimise any progress. Thus she noted that a limiting feature of the Sex Discrimination Order (1976) was its reliance on individual proceedings to eliminate wage discrimination. In reality, wage discrimination is rarely an individual rights issue, and more usually a structural or collective issue.

In the South, similar sorts of legislative and institutional changes occurred in the 1970s with the passing of the Anti-Discrimination (1974) and Employment Equality Act (1977), and the establishment of the Employment Equality Agency (1977). Because of ambiguous wording in the Employment Equality Act (1977) it has been almost impossible up to now to establish the existence of indirect discrimination since 'the Irish courts and tribunals have generally applied the law of indirect discrimination in a way that exposes subtle and institutionalised forms of sex discrimination' (Fourth Report of the Fourth Joint Oireachtas Committee, 1996: 13). This approach was fostered by the wording of Section 2 (c) of the 1977 Equality Employment Act. The Nathan v Bailey Gibson case, which drew on the Equal Treatment Directive and case law from the European Court of Justice, established for the first time that it was sufficient to show that a practice bore more heavily on one sex than another to constitute indirect discrimination and so nullified 'the impossible requirements of section 2 (c)', (Honan, 1997: 12).

More recently the Employment Equality and Equal Status Acts (1997) were passed by the Oireachtas but referred by the President to the Supreme Court for an assessment of their constitutionality. It is questionable to what extent either of them are concerned with actively promoting gender equality (as opposed to outlawing certain kinds of discrimination). Thus for example, certain kinds of positive action are allowed, but not required in the Employment Equality Act. In any event, particular parts/sections of the Equality Act (15, 16, 35 and 63 [3]) were found to be unconstitutional, and it will have to be redrafted. None of these sections were specifically concerned with gender.

Women's low pay is recognised as being related to their concentration in particular occupational groups which then tend to be defined as low skilled and poorly paid and which are not amenable to equal pay legislation (Trewsdale, 1987; Rubery and Fagan, 1993: 2; EOC, 1996). At EU level in an attempt to tackle the problem, a Code of Practice was adopted in

1996 on Equal Pay for Work of Equal Value. It aims to do away with discrimination in job classification and job evaluation schemes (European Commission, 1997: 10). However, it is not a legally binding instrument. There is also a proposal to include a reference to 'equal work of equal value' in the new European Treaty. It remains to be seen what effect, if any, such initiatives will have.

It is not clear that either state, North or South, is seriously committed to improving or even monitoring the effectiveness of the legal machinery in the employment equality area. While equal opportunities legislation exists in both places, there is no powerful interest group pressuring the state to implement or extend it in the area of gender. By contrast, equal opportunities legislation in Northern Ireland relating to religion is very much more rigorously monitored.

Collective Bargaining

Bercusson and Dickens (1996) and McCrudden (1993) have highlighted the inadequacies of legislation as a way of promoting equality. Collective bargaining is seen as potentially an alternative or supplementary route, although it is recognised that collective agreements may perpetuate discriminatory practices—particularly in situations where women have little power within the union, and where there is little importance attached to equality bargaining. Neither in the North nor in the South was equal pay legislation campaigned for by the unions. In fact, in both cases the unions negotiated on the basis of a male-female wage differential. In Scandinavian countries there is a much lower wage differential between men and women's earnings than in either the North or the South. This has been attributed to centralised wage negotiations and a commitment to limiting wage dispersion and it has proved more effective than legislation in minimising wage differentials (Callan and Wren, 1994; Lester, 1987). Thus while the South and the UK theoretically have better legislative protection than places like Denmark, the wage gap is lower in the latter (Lester, 1987; Bercusson and Dickens, 1996). The existence of a national minimum wage (which is currently attracting support in the UK and the South) is also advantageous to women since they are particularly likely to be amongst the low paid. However, it is interesting that the proposal by the Conference of Religious Ireland (CORI) (Clark and Healy, 1997) giving a basic income to every adult, and so representing the complete ending of the male breadwinner system, was greeted with derision by senior civil servants.

Whitehouse (1992) found that across OECD countries the size of the (hourly) wage differential between men and women was affected by the existence of collective bargaining, while there was no clear evidence as regards the effect of legislative measures. She recognised that in some cases the capacity of the unions to regulate the labour market hindered the influx of women into paid employment. Indeed this kind of pattern can be seen in the South where, at least up to the late 1980s, the unions were mainly concerned with the creation of full-time 'male' jobs in manufacturing industries. In the North, on the other hand, casualisation and deregulation were accepted at an earlier stage and hence facilitated women's participation in paid employment. In both cases however, the effectiveness of the Unions in protecting the wages and working conditions of part-time workers was limited. Whitehouse argues, however, that this need not necessarily be so. Thus for example in Sweden, union control over the conditions associated with part-time work (which is predominantly done by women) was such that employers had to look for other ways of achieving flexibility, apart from creating low security, poorly paid, part-time jobs.

Even in Sweden however, it has been noted that at particular points in time and in particular sectors (such as banking in the 1980s) managers acquired greater discretion to set individual weekly wages over and above those agreed collectively. Thus for example they decided at what point on the scale employees entered, when they should be promoted, and how merit payments should be distributed. Acker (1991) noted that overwhelmingly in these situations the net effect was to increase the wage differential. Thus like Rubery and Fagan (1993) and Whitehouse (1992) she concluded that wage differentials were likely to be minimised by wages being collectively negotiated. It is impossible to say why it should be so, although Pollert's (1996: 654) observation that 'Male dominance feeds on itself in terms of vested interests defending the status quo' is provocative.

Organisational Factors

These factors are seen as particularly important in explaining the position of women within the labour force, and in particular, in explaining the persistence of vertical segregation. It has been widely argued that women's absence from senior administrative and management positions reflected the impact of the marriage bar and/or the presence of children. Both of these explanations are increasingly seen as questionable in view of international evidence. Thus for example the proportion of women in senior positions in the Civil Service in the UK is much the same as in Ireland although the marriage bar was removed there in the 1940s. The proportion of women in such positions varies considerably across Europe but is very similar in Denmark and Ireland despite their very different levels of state support for child-care: (14.4 per cent and 15.1 per cent respectively: United Nations, 1995: 84). Variation also appears to be unrelated to stage of economic development.

Similarly, it appears that although women's educational levels can play a part in increasing their possibilities as regards access to such positions, educational level may facilitate access to positions of expertise but not authority (Savage, 1992). Norris (1987) suggested that socialist/left-wing governments were most likely to reduce vertical segregation—with the presence of right-wing parties being most likely to increase it. However, although this seems plausible in terms of the proportion of women in such positions in Sweden or Hungary, it is obviously not a sufficient explanation since the proportion of women who were administrators or managers was roughly the same in the United States as in Sweden. Furthermore, in the United States and indeed also in Australia, in contrast to the typical European pattern, women's educational expertise appeared to be more than proportionately reflected in their access to positions of authority (United Nations, 1995).

Women in the South show the typical European pattern i.e., constituting a very high proportion of those in the professional services area, and a very low proportion of those in the administrative and managerial areas. These trends reflect various aspects of organisational structure and culture in both the public and private sectors which the state has failed to challenge. For example, the virtual absence of women from senior positions in the local authorities in the South can be seen as reflecting the narrowness of the 'channel' from which such positions are recruited (Mahon, 1996). The absence of women in senior positions in the Health Boards can be seen as related to similar factors, compounded by the absence of a career path from areas of predominantly female employment, such as nursing, into mainstream management positions; and reflecting the tendency for areas of predominantly female employment to be remote from decision-making structures. The absence of women from senior positions also reflects both the very low ratios of promotional posts in female dominated areas of employment and men's greater access to them (the possibility of promotion being 28 to 1 in the case of women moving from staff nurse to assistant matron/matron, as compared with 14 to 1 for men in a similar position; and a 1 in 2 chance for male clerical officers to move into supervisory positions in the administrative structure in the health boards: O'Connor, 1998). Organisational procedures which militate against women's promotion in the public and private sectors, such as all-male interview boards, frequently chaired by retired men whose ideas reflect a stereotypical view of women, are also likely to be important (Mahon, 1996; O'Connor, 1996) as is the tendency to allocate high profile tasks to men (Mahon, 1991; O'Connor,

1998). The persistence of an organisational culture characterised by male prejudice which 'chills' women out has also been highlighted (Mahon, 1991; Barker and Monks, 1994; O'Connor, 1996; 1998). Such phenomena are not, of course, peculiar to Ireland. For the most part however they have been virtually ignored by the state in the South—the persistence of patterns of vertical segregation being perceived as 'natural'. Such a view seems highly questionable in view of the fact that such patterns changed dramatically over an eight-year period in the case of applications for and appointments to principalships in primary schools in the South (Lynch, 1994).

In the North, there is some evidence to suggest that although women are less likely than their counterparts in the South to be in the professional services, they are more likely to be in administrative or management positions. There are methodological difficulties in making such comparisons. However, it is interesting to note that similar trends emerged in the case of senior academic appointments—with women constituting 4 per cent of those at professorial position in the South, where such positions are typically linked to administrative responsibilities, as compared with just over 9 per cent in the North where they are not (Smyth, 1996; Ince, 1996). These differences may also reflect the more rigorous monitoring of appointments in the North. They cannot however, obscure the fact that in both states the overwhelming majority of such positions are held by men.

Summary and Conclusions

In this chapter, we have explored the extent and nature of women's participation in paid employment, North and South. However, mindful of the caveat that there are methodological difficulties in making such comparisons, the most striking differences are the higher proportion of older married women who are in paid employment in the North; the higher proportion of women who are working part-time and the higher proportion who are low paid. These trends are compatible with the depiction of the North as a modified male breadwinner state, where, traditionally and currently, women's participation in paid employment is facilitated, in the context of an expectation of economic dependence on a husband. Low provision of child-care, individual taxation, means-tested benefits, and a deregulated employment policy are currently associated with this pattern in the North.

The South appears to be a strong male breadwinner state insofar as more systematic attempts have been made to exclude women from the labour force and to inhibit their reintegration. A non-individualised taxation system, together with a low level of child-care, means-tested benefits, and an employment policy focused on the creation of full-time jobs in areas of predominantly male employment further reflects this strong male bread-winner ethos.

Young women in both North and South have similar levels of parti-cipation in paid employment. Today, most women North and South work in the service sector, in broadly similar kinds of occupations. Paradoxi-cally however, the commitment of the state in the South to education and to the expansion of middle-class service occupations within the state apparatus, combined with women's high educational performance, has created a situation where roughly two-thirds of those in professional services are women. In the North the proportion of women in profes-sional services is lower, reflecting women's lower educational levels (Breen, Heath and Whelan, this volume). In the North however, women constitute a higher proportion of those in administrative or managerial positions than they do in the South, possibly because of more assiduous monitoring of appointments.

Equal opportunities legislation has been introduced in both North and South since the 1970s. The extent of either state's commitment to the implementation of such legislation in the area of gender is ques-tionable, particularly where it conflicts with policies premised on the idea of a male breadwinner. In a situation where collective bargaining is weak and/or unconcerned with gender issues it is difficult to challenge the kind of organisational practices and processes which perpetuate discrimination.

For both North and South, explanations which focus on individual choice are attractive since they ignore the very real structural parameters within which such choices are made. In particular they make it possible to ignore the prevalence of women amongst the low paid, and men amongst the publicly powerful. They make it possible to ignore the fact that both the North and South are patriarchal societies.

Individual choice explanations also ignore the question of who benefits from the existence of a male breadwinner and from neo-patriarchal patterns within the paid employment areas. Depicting such patterns as freely chosen plays an important part in their legitimation and obscures part of the reality of women's experiences North and South.

Acknowledgements. The authors would like to thank the editors, the participants in the Oxford Conference, the anonymous reviewers, as well as Tony Fahey, Emer Smyth, Bernie Hayes, Ron Keegan, Eithne Mclaughlin, Maura Sheehan and Janet Trewsdale for helpful comments.

References

Acker, J. (1990) 'Hierarchies, Jobs, Bodies: A Theory of Gendered Organisations', *Gender and Society*, 4(2): 139–58.

Acker, J. (1991) 'Thinking about Wages: The Gendered Wage gap in Swedish Banks' *Gender and Society*, 5(3): 390–407.

Bagilhole, B. (1994) *Women, Work and Equal Opportunity*, Aldershot: Avebury.

Barker, P. and Monks, K. (1994) *Career Progression of Chartered Accountants*, Dublin: Dublin City University Business School.

Bercusson, B. and Dickens, L. (1996*) Equal Opportunities and Collective Bargaining in Europe*, Dublin: European Foundation for Living and Working Conditions.

Blackburn, R., Jarman, J. and Siltanen, J. (1993) 'The Analysis of Occupational Gender Segregation Over Time and Place: Considerations of Measurement and Some New Evidence', *Work, Employment and Society*, 7(3): 335–62.

Breen, R., Hannan, D., Rottman, D. and Whelan, C. (1990) *Understanding Contemporary Ireland*, Dublin: Gill and Macmillan.

Breugel, I. (1996) 'Whose Myths are They Anyway? A Comment', *The British Journal of Sociology*, 47(1): 175–7.

Bulletin on Women and Employment in the E.U. (1994) April. No. 4 Brussels: European Commission.

Bulletin on Women and Employment in the E.U. (1994) October, No. 5 Brussels: European Commission.

Bulletin on Women and Employment in the E.U. (1995) April, No. 6 Brussels: European Commission.

Bulletin on Women and Employment in the E.U. (1995) October No. 7 Brussels: European Commission.

Bulletin on Women and Employment in the E.U. (1996) April, No. 8 Brussels: European Commission.

Bulletin on Women and Employment in the E.U. (1996) October, No. 9 Brussels: European Commission.

Callan, T. (1991) 'Male-Female Wage Differentials in Ireland', *The Economic and Social Review*, 23(1): 55–72.

Callan, T. and Farrell, B. (1991) *Women's Participation in the Irish Labour Market*, Dublin: NESC.

Callan, T. and Wren, A. (1994) *Male-Female Wage Differentials: Analysis & Policy Issues*, Dublin: ESRI.

Clark, C. and Healy, S. (1997) *Pathways to a Basic Income*, Dublin: CORI.

Cousins, M. (1996) *Pathways to Employment for Women Returning to Paid Work*, Dublin: EEA.

Connell, R. W. (1987) *Gender and Power*, Cambridge: Polity Press.

Connell, R. W. (1994) 'The State, Gender and Sexual Politics: Theory and Appraisal', in H. I. Radtke and H. J. Stam (eds), *Power/Gender: Social Relations in Theory and Practice*, London: Sage.

Conroy Jackson, P. (1991) 'The Investment of Women in the Labour Market', Discussion paper for Combat Poverty: Referred to in the *Report of the Second Commission on the Status of Women, 1993*, Dublin: Government Publications.

Crompton, R. (1995) *Paying the Price of Care: Comparative Studies of Women's Employment and the Value of Caring*, Working Paper 4, Demos: London.

Daly, M. (1992) *Industrial Development and Irish National Identity 1922–1939*, Dublin: Gill and Macmillan Ltd.

Davies, C. and McLaughlin, E. (eds) (1991) *Women, Employment and Social Policy in Northern Ireland: A Problem Postponed?*, Belfast: Policy Research Institute.

Davies, C., Heaton, N., Robinson, G. and McWilliams, M. (1995) *A Matter of Small Importance? Catholic and Protestant Women in the Northern Ireland Labour Market*, Belfast: The Equal Opportunities Commission.

Davies, C., Sheehan, M., Osmani, L. and Taylor, M. (1996) *Women and Economic Policy—A Gender Perspective*, Belfast: EOCNI.

Department of Equality and Law Reform (1994) *Report on a Survey of Equal Opportunities*, Dublin: Government Publications.

Dignan, T. (1996) *Demographic Change and Labour Availability*, Belfast: EOC.

Durkan, J., O'Donohue, A., Donnelly, M. and Durkan, J. (1995) *Women in the Labour Force*, Dublin: Government Publications.

EEA (Employment Equality Agency) (1995) *Women in Figures*, Dublin: EEA.

EEA (Employment Equality Agency) (1996) *Introducing Family Friendly Initiatives in the Workplace*, Dublin: EEA.

Employment in Europe (1994) Com(94) 381. Brussels: EC.

EOC (Equal Opportunities Commission) (1993) *Where do Women Figure?* Belfast: EOC.

EOC (Equal Opportunities Commission) (1995) *Women and Men in Northern Ireland*, Belfast: EOC.

EOC (Equal Opportunities Commission) (1996) *Briefings on Women and Men in Britain: Pay*, Manchester: EOC.

Equal Opportunities Unit (1996) *Section 31 Review: Queen's University Belfast.* Belfast: QUB.

European Commission (1997) *Social Europe: Progress Report on the Implementation of the Medium Term Social Action Programme 1995–97. Luxembourg: Official Publications*, DG for Employment, Industrial Relations and Social Affairs.

European Commission Network on Childcare (1996) *A Review of Services for Young Children in the European Union* 1990–1995, Brussels: DGV.

European Equality Agency (1994) *Maternity Protection*, Dublin: EEA.

European Observatory on National Family Policies (1996) *Families and Policies: Evaluation and Trends*, Brussels.

Eurostat (1995) *Women and Men in the European Union: A Statistical Portrait*, Luxembourg: Office for Official Publications.

Eurostat (1996) *Statistics in Focus: 3 Population and Social Conditions Labour Force Survey*, Luxembourg.

Eurostat (1997) *Statistics in Focus: 1 The Economic Activity of Women in the European Union*, Luxembourg.

Fahey, T. (1990) 'Measuring The Female Labour Supply: Conceptual and Procedural Problems in Irish Official Statistics', *The Economic and Social Review*, 21(2): 163–91.

Fahey, T. (1993) 'Review Article: Review of NESC Report No 91: Women's Participation in the Irish Labour Market, and J. Pyle: The State and Women in the
Economy', *The Economic and Social Review*, 24(2): 199–210.

Fine-Davis, M. (1988) 'Changing Gender Role Attitudes in Ireland 1975–1986',
Report of the Second Joint Oireachtas Committee on Women's Rights, Dublin:
Government Publications.

Fourth Report of the Fourth Joint Oireachtas Committee on Women's Rights
(1996) *The Impact of European Equality Legislation on Women's Affairs in
Ireland*, Dublin: Government Publications.

Fynes, B., Morrissey, T., Roche, W. K., Whelan, B. J. and Williams, J. (1996)
Flexible Working Lives, Dublin: Oak Tree Press.

Gallie, D., Marsh, C. and Vogler, C. (1994) *Social Change and the Experience of the
Unemployed*, Oxford: Oxford University Press.

Ginn, J., Arber, S., Brannen, J., Dale, A., Dex, S., Elias, P., Moss, P., Pahl,
J., Cerridwen, R. and Rubery, J. (1996) 'Feminist Fallacies: A Reply to Hakim
on Women's Employment', *The British Journal of Sociology*, 47(1): 167–74.

Hakim, C. (1991) 'Grateful Slaves and Self Made Women: Fact and Fantasy in
Women's Work Orientations', *European Sociological Review*, 7(2): 97–120.

Hakim, C. (1995) 'Five Feminist Myths about Women's Employment', *The British
Journal of Sociology*, 46(3): 429–57.

Hakim, C. (1996) 'The Sexual Division of Labour and Women's Heterogeneity',
The British Journal of Sociology, 47(1): 178–88.

Hannan, D., Smyth, E., McCullagh, J., O'Leary, R. and McMahon, D. (1996) *Co-
Education and Gender Equality*, Dublin: Oak Tree Press.

Heaton, N., Robinson, G. and Davies, C. (1993) 'Women in the Northern Ireland
Labour Market', in P. Teague (ed.), *The Economy of Northern Ireland: Perspectives for Structural Change*, London: Lawrence and Wishart.

Honan, M. (1996) 'Nathan and Indirect Discrimination: a New Beginning?', *Equality
News*, 6: 10–12.

Honan, M. (1997) 'Recent Developments on Indirect Discrimination', *Equality
News*, 9: 16.

Ince, M. (1996) 'Chipping Away at the Glass Ceiling', *The Times Higher*, 26 July:
16–17.

Irish Labour Force Survey, 1996 (1997) Dublin: Government Publications.

Jewson, N. and Mason, D. (1986) 'The Theory and Practice of Equal Opportunities
Policies: Liberal and Radical Approaches', *The Sociological Review*, 34(2):
307–34.

Kiely, G. (1995) 'Fathers in Families', in I. Colgan McCathy (ed.), *Irish Family
Studies: Selected Papers*, Dublin: Family Studies Centre.

Lester, A. (1987) 'The Sex Discrimination Legislation and Employment Practices',
in Equal Opportunities Commission, *Equality in employment conference report*
Belfast: EOC.

Lewis, J. (1992) 'Gender and the Development of Welfare Regimes', *Journal of
European Social Policy*, 2(3): 159–73.

Lewis, J. (1993) 'Introduction, Women, Work, Family and Social Policies in Europe', in J. Lewis (ed.), *Women and Social Policies in Europe: Work, Family and
the State*, Hants: Edward Elgar Publishing House.

Lynch, K. (1994) 'Women Teach and Men Manage: Why Men Dominate Senior Posts in Irish Education', in *Women for Leadership in Education*, Dublin: Education Commission of the Conference of Religious in Ireland.

Lynch, K. and Morgan, V. (1995) 'Gender and Education: North and South', in P. Clancy *et al.* (ed.), *Irish Society: Sociological Perspectives*, Dublin: IPA.

Mahon, E. (1991) 'Motherhood, Work and Equal Opportunity', *First Report to the Third Joint Oireachtas Committee on Women's Rights*. Dublin: Government Publications.

Mahon, E. (1994) 'Ireland: a Private Patriarchy?', *Environment and Planning* A, 26: 1277–96.

Mahon, E. (1996) 'Women in Management in Local Administration', in *Second Report of the Fourth Joint Oireachtas Committee on Women's Rights*, Dublin: Government Publications.

Mann, M. (1986) 'A Crisis in Stratification Theory?', in R. Crompton and M. Mann, (eds), *Gender and Stratification*, Oxford: Polity Press.

Mann, M. (1993) *The Sources of Social Power Volume II*, Cambridge University Press, Cambridge.

Maruani, M. (1992) *The Position of Women in the Labour Market: Trends and Developments in the Twelve Member States 1983–1990*, Women of Europe Supplements no. 36, Brussels: Commission of the European Communities.

Maxwell, P. (1989) 'The Impact of Equal Value Legislation in Northern Ireland', *Policy and Politics*, 17(4): 295–300.

Maxwell, P. (1991) 'Equal Pay Legislation—Problems and Prospects', in C. Davies and E. McLaughlin (eds), *Women, Employment and Social Policy in Northern Ireland: A Problem Postponed?*, Belfast: Policy Research Institute.

McCrudden, C. (1993) 'The Effectiveness of European Equality Law: National Mechanisms for Enforcing Gender Equality in the Light of European Requirements', *Oxford Journal of Legal Studies*, 13: 320–67.

McGauran, A. M. (1996) 'The Effects of EU Policy on Women's Employment', *Irish Journal of Feminist Studies*, 1(2): 83–102.

McLaughlin, E. (1986) 'Maiden City Blues', Unpublished Ph.D. Thesis, Queen's University Belfast.

McLaughlin, E. (1989a) 'In search of the Female Breadwinner: Gender and Un-employment in Derry City', in D. Hastings and G. McFarlane (eds), *Social Anthropology in Northern Ireland*, Aldershot: Avebury.

McLaughlin, E. (1989b) 'Women and Work in Derry City: A Survey', *SAOTHAR 14 Journal of The Irish Labour History Society.*

McLaughlin, E. (1993) 'Ireland: Catholic Corporatism', in A. Cochrane, and J. Clarke (eds), *Comparing Welfare States*, London: Sage.

McWilliams, M. (1991) 'Women's Paid Work and the Sexual Division of Labour', in C. Davies and E. McLaughlin (eds), *Women, Employment and Social Policy in Northern Ireland: A Problem Postponed?*, Belfast: Policy Research Institute.

Montgomery, P. (1993) 'Paid and Unpaid Work', in J. Kremer and P. Montgomery (eds), *Women's Working Lives*, Belfast: EOC.

Monitoring Committee (1996) *Second Progress Report of the Monitoring Committee on the Implementation of the Recommendations of the Second Commission on the Status of Women*, Dublin: Goverment Publications.

NESF (National Economic and Social Forum) (1996) *Jobs Potential of Work Sharing*, Dublin: Government Publications.

Norris, P. (1987) *Politics and Sexual Equality*, Sussex: Wheatsheaf.

*Northern Ireland Labour Force Survey (*NIEC*) 1984–1995/6.*

O'Connell, P. and Rottman, D. (1992) 'The Irish Welfare State in Comparative Perspective', in J. Goldthorpe and C. Whelan (eds), *The Development of Industrial Society in Ireland*, Oxford: Oxford University Press.

O'Connor, P. (1996) 'Organisational Culture as a Barrier to Women's Promotion', *The Economic and Social Review*, 27(3): 205–34.

O'Connor, P. (1998) *Emerging Voices*, Dublin: Institute of Public Administration.

O'Dowd, L. (1991) 'The States of Ireland: Some Reflections on Research', *Irish Journal of Sociology*, 1: 96–106.

O'Dowd, L. (1987) 'Church, State and Women: The Aftermath of Partition', in C. Curtin, P. Jackson and B. O'Connor (eds), *Gender in Irish Society*, Galway: Galway University Press.

Osborne, R. and Cormack, R. (1989) 'Fair Employment: Towards Reform in Northern Ireland', *Policy and Politics*, 17(4): 287–94.

Pollert, A. (1996) 'Gender and Class Revisited: or, the Poverty of "Patriarchy"', *Sociology*, 30(4): 639–59.

Pyle, J. L. (1990) *The State and Women in the Economy — Lessons from sex discrimination in the Republic of Ireland*, New York: State University of New York Press.

Rogers, S. (1993) 'Equal Opportunities', in J. Kremer and P. Montgomery (eds), *Women's Working Lives*, Belfast: EOC.

Ruane, F. and Dobson, E. (1990) 'Academic Salary Differentials: Some Evidence from an Irish Study', *Economic and Social Review*, 21: 209–26.

Rubery, T. and Fagan, C. (1993) *Occupational Segregation of Men and Women in the European Community*, Social Europe Series, EC and Manchester.

Savage, M. (1992) 'Women's Expertise, Men's Authority', in M. Savage and A. Witz (eds), *Gender and Bureaucracy*, Oxford: Blackwell/Sociological Review.

Second Commission on the Status of Women (1993) *Report to the Government*, Dublin: Government Publications.

Sexton, J. J. and O'Connell, P. (1997) *Labour Market Studies in Ireland Series No. 1 Employment and the Labour Market*, Luxembourg: Office for Official Publications of the EU.

Smyth, A. (1996) 'Reviewing Breaking the Circle: A Pilot Project', in O. Egan (ed.), *Women Staff in Irish Colleges*, Proceedings of the HEEU Conference in U.C.G. Cork: UCC.

Smyth, E. (1997) 'Labour Market Structures and Women's Employment in Ireland', in A. Byrne and M. Leonard (eds), *Women and Irish Society: A Sociological Reader*, Belfast: Beyond the Pale Publications.

Trewsdale, J. (1987) *Womanpower No. 4: A statistical survey of women and work in Northern Ireland*, Belfast: Equal Opportunities Commission.

Trewsdale, J. (1992) *Part-time Employment in Northern Ireland*, Belfast: Northern Ireland Economic Council, Report 98.

Trewsdale, J. and Kremer, J. (1996) 'Women and Work', in R. Breen, P. Devine and L. Dowds (eds), *Social Attitudes in Northern Ireland*, Belfast: Appletree Press.

Trewsdale, J. and Trainor, M. (1979) *Womanpower No. 1: A Statistical Survey of Women and Work in Northern Ireland*, Belfast: Equal Opportunities Commission.

Turner, I. (1993) 'Childcare', in J. Kremer and P. Montgomery (eds), *Women's Working Lives*, Belfast: EOC.

United Nations (1995) *Human Development Report*, Oxford: Oxford University Press.

Walsh, B. (1993) 'Labour Force Participation and the Growth of Women's Employment in Ireland 1971–1991', *The Economic and Social Review*, 24(4).

Whitehouse, G. (1992) 'Legislation and labour market gender inequality: an analysis of OECD countries', *Work, Employment and Society*, 6(1): 65–86.

Walby, S. (1990) *Theorising Patriarchy*, Oxford: Blackwell.

Social Mobility in Ireland:
A Comparative Analysis

RICHARD BREEN & CHRISTOPHER T. WHELAN

Introduction

IN THIS PAPER WE COMPARE PATTERNS OF SOCIAL MOBILITY between the Republic of Ireland and Northern Ireland in order to address four questions. First, how do the class structures of North and South differ from each other? Secondly, are there differences in relative mobility, such that class inequalities are greater in one part of the island than another? Thirdly, are differences in mobility according to gender more or less marked in one or other part of Ireland? And, finally, in the case of Northern Ireland, are mobility patterns also distinctive with respect to ethnicity?

In the next section of the paper we discuss the historical background relevant to these questions, and set out what we believe the answers to these questions are likely to be. The third section describes the data we use and the fourth reports our results. In the fifth section we examine the extent to which migration from both parts of Ireland might influence the conclusions we draw concerning patterns of social fluidity. The final section provides answers to our four questions and we discuss some implications of our findings.

The Historical Background

The partitioning of the island of Ireland under the Government of Ireland Act of 1920 (and subsequently agreed in the 1921 Anglo-Irish Treaty) resulted not only in the formation of an overwhelmingly Catholic Free State (later the Republic of Ireland) and a mainly Protestant Northern Ireland, it also led to the former losing almost all of its industrial base. At the time virtually all of Ireland's industrial exports originated in the Belfast

Proceedings of the British Academy, **98**, 319–339. © The British Academy 1999.

region (Cullen, 1972: 156–70). The effect of partition on the Southern economy, was, as one commentator later put it, 'as if Scotland had obtained self-government with Glasgow and the Clyde left out' (O'Brien, 1962: 11).

Thus, at the time of partition, despite having shared a common history as part of the United Kingdom, the two parts of Ireland were economically quite distinct, and this was reflected in substantial differences in their class structures. The Republic of Ireland had a predominantly rural, agricultural economy[1] and thus a class structure containing a very large proportion of farmers and agricultural workers. By contrast, Northern Ireland's class structure approximated much more closely to that of an industrial society. But this difference was overlaid by another. Whereas the Republic of Ireland was religiously and ethnically homogenous (with over 90 per cent of the population Catholic) this was not the case in Northern Ireland. Although the border had been drawn so as to ensure a Protestant/Unionist majority, nevertheless Northern Ireland contained a substantial minority of Catholics, most of whom, it seems fair to assume, were Nationalists (roughly one-third of the population of 1.5 million was Catholic). Thus Northern Ireland was, and continues to be, an ethnically heterogeneous society, in which the two main ethnic groups[2] possess different (and, in this context, antagonistic) senses of national identity. The primary marker distinguishing members of these two groups is religious affiliation, though they also display a range of other cultural differences. But this ethnic distinction is not simply one of heterogeneity: it is also one of inequality, with the Catholic community suffering disadvantage relative to Protestants. There is widespread agreement that, under the Stormont regime (1922–72), Catholics were subject to discrimination in the allocation of public housing, in the electoral system and in the labour market (Smith and Chambers, 1991: 14–22).

The history of the class structures of the two parts of Ireland since partition has been one of very gradual convergence. The post-1958 industrialisation of the Republic, the decline in the importance of farming, and the growth of the service sector have acted to bring its class structure closer to that of Northern Ireland where recent industrial decline and the impact of 'the Troubles' have led to surprisingly little change. Table 1 compares the class structures of Northern Ireland and the Republic in 1961 and 1991.

---

[1] In the 1920s agriculture accounted for three-quarters of the Republic of Ireland's exports.

[2] We refer to the two communities in Northern Ireland as ethnic groups since each comprises 'a named human population, with a myth of common ancestry, shared memories, and cultural elements; a link with a historic territory or homeland; and a measure of solidarity' (Smith, 1993).

Table 1. Percentage distribution of men and women at work by class categories, Republic of Ireland and Northern Ireland.

	Men				Women			
	RoI		NI		RoI		NI	
Employees and Self-Employed	1961	1991	1961	1991	1961	1991	1961	1991
Self-Employed								
Agriculture	36.0	16.4	13.4	5.5	15.0	3.4	2.2	0.3
Non-Agriculture	7.9	13.1	4.8	13.3	7.6	6.0	3.2	3.2
Employees								
(i) Upper-Middle Class	7.6	19.2	11.5	21.0	14.8	28.3	14.7	26.7
(ii) Lower-Middle Class	15.6	21.9	10.6	10.5	42.7	48.8	29.1	34.9
(iii) Skilled Manual	12.0	16.8	27.1	27.9	5.8	2.8	13.0	3.2
(iv) Semi/Unskilled Manual	20.9	12.7	32.8	21.8	14.1	10.6	37.9	31.5
(a) Agricultural	8.4	2.8	6.2	1.2	0.2	0.4	0.3	0.4
(b) Non-Agricultural	12.5	9.9	26.4	20.6	13.9	10.2	37.6	31.4

Note: NI: Northern Ireland, RoI: Republic of Ireland.

Source: NI: Censuses of Northern Ireland, 1961 and 1991, recoding of socio-economic groups, omitting all those without a job for the last 10 years, members of the armed forces, those who did not state a job or whose job could not be classified and those on government training schemes. In the NI figures for 1961 some non-agricultural employers are included in the upper-middle class. RoI: O'Connell, this volume Table 3.

The differences between the two are readily apparent. For men the Republic has a much larger share of those at work in agriculture and a much smaller share in the skilled and semi/unskilled (non-agricultural) manual classes. These differences are much more pronounced in 1961. Between 1961 and 1991 the class structures have been subject to very similar change: a decline in the importance of agriculture and unskilled manual employment, and a growth in the middle classes. Nevertheless, both class structures continue to carry a strong historical imprint. Among men, Northern Ireland has a somewhat larger upper-middle class and substantially larger manual classes while in the South the agricultural classes and the lower-middle class are larger. Among women, the proportion in agriculture was much greater in the South than the North in 1961, but this difference had largely disappeared by 1991. The absence of opportunities for women in the South in traditional manufacturing industries is reflected in the much smaller percentage of women in the non-skilled manual classes than are found in the North, and although this difference has diminished over time it continues to be substantial, with the figure of over 30 per cent for the North being almost three times greater than that for the Republic of Ireland. In the former the lower-middle class dominates with almost half of all women being found in this class. As Table 2 shows, in 1961 labour force participation for women was higher in Northern Ireland, particularly for married women. Married women's participation rates rose dramatically between 1961 and 1991 so that in both parts of Ireland the rates for all women and for married women are virtually identical, although with higher overall rates of women's labour force participation in the North.

We should expect quite substantial differences between North and South in absolute mobility flows, largely due to the very substantial contrasts in their class structures in earlier years and the persistence of these differences, albeit in a weaker form. In terms of patterns of relative mobility—or social fluidity—we should expect to see rather more openness in the North than the South. The distinction between absolute and relative mobilty (or social fluidity) is commonly drawn. Absolute mobility refers to the size of the flows (possibily standardised as percentages) between various origin and destination classes. Social fluidity concerns the extent to which the chances of being found in one rather than another class destination differ between people according to the class from which they originated. If we look at the factors commonly supposed to influence social fluidity—such as class differences in educational attainment and the extent of equality in the distributions of income and wealth—then, at least as regards the former, a North-South comparison would lead us to suppose that the North would fare better. Northern Ireland has enjoyed free post-primary education since 1947—20 years in advance of the Republic—and, even though this was within the context of a selective educational system compared with a (nominally) non-selective system in the Republic of Ireland, research reported elsewhere in this volume (Breen, Heath and Whelan, this volume) shows that class inequalities in educational attainment are substantially less in Northern Ireland than in the Republic. In the latter such class differences are particularly marked and notably persistent over time (Breen and Whelan, 1993). In addition, it is well known that inequalities of income and wealth are particularly great in the Republic of

Table 2. Female labour force percentage participation rates, Republic of Ireland and Northern Ireland.

	NI		RoI	
	1961	1991	1961	1991
All Women	35.3	55.8	28.6	33.4
Married Women	19.5	55.0	5.2	31.3

Source: As for Table 1.

Ireland and are larger than in the UK, though it is less clear here whether a Republic of Ireland versus Northern Ireland comparison would show any substantial differences. The North has high levels of poverty while the middle classes, particularly those employed in the public sector or large companies and who are paid according to UK-wide salary scales, can enjoy a much higher standard of living than their counterparts in Britain.

On the other hand, it might be more judicious to expect that variation in such factors will have at best a minor impact on social fluidity. The results of the CASMIN project (Erikson and Goldthorpe, 1992) and other cross-national studies of mobility show that, although there are usually statistically significant differences in social fluidity between countries of the industrialised world, these tend to be relatively minor (Breen and Rottman, 1995: 114). As Erikson and Goldthorpe (1987: 162) conclude:

> A basic similarity will be found in patterns of social fluidity . . . across all nations with market economies and nuclear family systems where no sustained attempts have been made to use the power of the modern state apparatus in order to modify the processes or outcomes of the processes through which class inequalities are inter-generationally reproduced.

One thing that both parts of Ireland share in common is the absence of such sustained attempts.

Turning to ethnic differences in social mobility within Northern Ireland, it is generally accepted that, while discrimination against Catholics in Northern Ireland in the electoral system and in housing has been eradicated, the degree of discrimination in employment continues to be a much debated issue among the public, politicians, policy makers and academics (see Cormack and Osborne, 1991, for a review of this debate; also Whyte, 1990: Chapter 3; Smith and Chambers 1991; Murphy and Armstrong, 1994; Gudgin and Breen, 1996). What is not in doubt is that Catholics suffer much higher levels of unemployment than Protestants and that there are also some differences in their class distributions. According to the 1991 Census, 49 per cent of Protestants are in one of the non-manual classes (using the Registrar General's classification), compared with 40 per cent of Catholics. This has shown some change from Aunger's (1975) study, which, using data from the 1971 Census of Population, revealed that 31 per cent of Catholics were in a non-manual occupation, as opposed to 41 per cent of Protestants. We might therefore reasonably expect to see some differences in absolute mobility patterns and in class structure between Catholics and Protestants in Northern Ireland, though whether this will also extend to patterns of social fluidity is not certain. This will depend on the extent of intra-ethnic-group class inequality, and very little is known about this. Recently much has been made of the growth of the new Catholic middle class (Cormack and Osborne, 1994), suggesting increased upward mobility among this group, and thus, possibly, greater social fluidity.

In summary, although they occupy the same island, Northern Ireland and the Republic of Ireland are in many ways quite different societies. One might expect two societies that were originally part of the same state to have diverged from a common starting point: yet the Irish experience has, if anything, been the opposite of this. In terms of their class structure the two parts of Ireland have become more alike while still retaining some substantial differences. To the extent that their mobility regimes will show any particular similarity over and above that which appears to characterise all industrial societies there is some reason to suppose that Northern Ireland may display a somewhat more open pattern of social fluidity than the Republic.

Data

In order to examine patterns of social mobility in the two parts of the island of Ireland we form six separate mobility tables, cross-classifying an individual's class of origin (defined as the social class position of his or her father during the respondent's mid-teen years) by his or her current or most recent class position. In this we use the CASMIN class schema[3] and we here identify, in both origins and current class, five categories as follows:

  1 Professionals, administrators and managers (the 'service class' comprising classes I+II of the CASMIN schema);
  2 Routine non-manual employees (class III);
  3 The petty bourgeoisie, of small proprietors and farmers (class IV);
  4 Skilled manual workers and supervisors of manual workers (classes V+VI);
  5 Unskilled manual workers (class VII).

The six mobility tables that we form using this classification are for men and women in the Republic of Ireland; Catholic men and women in Northern Ireland; and non-Catholic (henceforth 'Protestant') men and women in Northern Ireland.[4]

The data we use come from two sources. For the Republic of Ireland they come from the Living in Ireland Survey conducted in 1994 by the

---

[3] The Comparative Analysis of Social Mobility in Industrial Nations project made comparable and analysed social mobility collected, for the most part, in the 1970s from a number of European countries (Erikson and Goldthorpe, 1992).

[4] We assign individuals to a religion in Northern Ireland on the basis of the religion in which they were brought up, rather than their current religion.

Economic and Social Research Institute (ESRI), Dublin. This yields a random sample of households and of individual adults resident within them. For the purposes of these analyses the total sample size is 3,000 men and 1,425 women aged between 21 and 65. For Northern Ireland the data come from a mobility survey carried out in 1996 and funded by the Economic and Social Research Council.[5] This survey yields a random sample of adults aged 21–65 years from the population of Northern Ireland. In the data used in this paper the sample sizes are 538 Catholic men, 816 Protestant men, 587 Catholic women and 801 Protestant women.[6]

Analyses

We begin our analysis by examining the class structures of Ireland, North and South. These are shown in Table 3 which reports the percentage distribution of respondents to our surveys according to their origin class and their current class position, distinguishing the six groups for which we have formed mobility tables. One simple means of judging the degree to which these distributions differ is to calculate the percentage of one distribution who would have to be allocated to a class other than the one in which they are found in order to make that distribution identical with another. This measure is termed the 'index of dissimilarity' or delta. Turning first to the origin distributions, perhaps the most interesting difference is between Protestants and Catholics in Northern Ireland. For men delta has a value of 15 and for women 10. In their class origins Protestants are over-represented relative to Catholics in the professional and managerial classes and in the skilled manual class, while Catholics are more numerous in the petty bourgeoisie and the non-skilled manual class. The larger share of Catholics in the non-skilled manual class and the greater proportion of Protestants in the service class and the skilled manual and supervisory class, indicate the disadvantaged position that Catholics held in Northern Ireland during the period when our respondents were teenagers. However, for women, this contrasts sharply with the distribution of current class position where hardly any differences between Protestants and Catholics can be discerned and the value of delta falls to one. Catholic men, on the other hand, continue to be under-represented in the service class relative to

[5] The data were collected under ESRC grant R000235397, *Social Mobility, Political Preferences, Attitudes and Behaviour in Northern Ireland*.
[6] Because of the traditionally low rates of female labour force participation in the Republic of Ireland we have restricted our analysis to women who are currently in the labour force. However, the data for Northern Ireland refer to all women. As we note below, defining the Northern sample in the same way as the Southern leads to results that do not differ at all from those presented in this paper.

Table 3. Percentage distributions in class origins and current class.

| | RoI | | NI | | | |
| | | | Catholics | | Protestants | |
Class	Men	Women	Men	Women	Men	Women
Class origins						
I+II	9	14	15	12	20	18
III	9	14	3	3	5	4
IV	32	31	28	24	21	22
V+VI	21	19	21	25	29	28
VII	28	23	33	36	25	28
Current Class						
I+II	20	27	28	25	32	25
III	15	49	7	32	7	32
IV	19	4	18	4	16	4
V+VI	25	8	25	8	24	10
VII	20	12	26	30	20	29

Note: Key to classes: I+II Professionals, administrators and managers (the 'service class'), III Routine non-manual employees, IV The petty bourgeoisie, V+VI Skilled manual workers and supervisors of manual workers, VII Unskilled manual workers.

Source: NI: 1996 Northern Ireland Mobility Survey. ROI: 1994 Living in Ireland Survey.

Protestants, though the differences are less than in the origin distributions and the value of delta declines to 8.

There are substantial differences between the class origin distributions in the South and the North. The former has a larger petty bourgeoisie class and smaller manual classes. In addition in the North the professional and managerial class is larger and the routine non-manual class smaller than in the South.[7] A good deal of convergence is evident in the current class distributions, notably in respect of the size of the petty bourgeoisie and the manual classes, while the number of women in routine non-manual work also displays a dramatic increase in both countries. However, the rather different distributions of respondents between the non-manual classes persists. In the case of women we also observe some divergence with a significantly greater decline in the numbers in non-skilled manual work in the South with the consequence that women in the North are almost two-and-a-half times more likely to be found in this class.

As we might have anticipated, however, it is in the comparison between

---

[7] The size of the routine non-manual class for women in the Republic of Ireland is consistent with the historical absence of opportunity in manufacturing industries. The relatively high figure for men may be related to the low rates of participation of married women in the labour force which prevailed until recent years.

men's and women's current class distributions that the greatest differences are evident. In the Republic of Ireland the index of dissimilarity between men and women is 40; in Northern Ireland it is 30 among Catholics and 34 among Protestants.[8] In both parts of the island women are over-represented in class III and under-represented in classes IV and V+VI. Gender differences are exacerbated in the Republic of Ireland by the under-representation of women in class VII—a phenomenon not evident in Northern Ireland for reasons already referred to.

Absolute Social Mobility

From Table 4 we can see that overall levels of absolute mobility do not differ across the countries. In both cases, consistent with evidence from other studies, we find that the level for women is higher than that for men (Breen and Whelan, 1995; Erikson and Goldthorpe, 1992). Focusing on mobility into the professional and managerial class, we find that, while there is relatively little difference between women North and South, for men such mobility is significantly higher in the North with 21 per cent of Protestants and 18 per cent of Catholics moving up the hierarchy compared to 15 per cent of men in the South. If we restrict our attention to mobility from the working class into the professional and managerial class the contrast between North and South is even more striking. Only 6 per cent of men and women in the South achieve such mobility but in the North the figure rises to 11 per cent for men and 9 per cent for women. Finally, long-range downward mobility shows little variation by country for men, and is higher for women (although this pattern is clearer in the North.) The improvement in the situation of Catholic women suggested by the earlier analysis employing the dissimilarity index is supported by the findings relating to upward and downward mobility. Among Catholic women 6 per cent more had been mobile into the profes-sional and managerial class than had been downwardly mobile into the non-skilled working class; for Protestant women the figure is one per cent. Among men, however, the advantage lies with Protestants for whom the figure is 10 per cent compared with 5 per cent for Catholics.

Relative Mobility

Now we turn from an examination of absolute mobility to an analysis of the pattern of association between class origins and current class position,

---

[8] It should be kept in mind that while the figures in Table 1 for the Republic of Ireland exclude the unemployed they are included here on the basis of their last occupation. Thus the survey figures show a larger manual class than is evident in the census data.

Table 4.   Absolute class mobility levels in Northern Ireland and the Republic of Ireland.

	Republic of Ireland		Northern Ireland			
			Protestants		Catholics	
	Men	Women	Men	Women	Men	Women
Mobile	62.0	76.4	62.0	75.2	65.5	75.1
Mobile into the Professional and Managerial Class (I+II)	14.9	20.6	21.3	17.4	18.4	21.0
Mobile into the Professional and Managerial Class from the Working Class (V, VI, VII)	6.5	6.2	11.3	8.7	10.6	10.9
Mobile into the Non-Skilled Working Class (VII)	11.2	12.7	11.4	16.4	13.0	15.2

Note: Key to classes as Table 3.

Source: NI 1996 Northern Ireland Mobility Survey. ROI: 1994 Living in Ireland Survey.

or 'social fluidity' as it is usually termed. By social fluidity we mean the degree to which there is a statistical association between the class a person was born into and the class they currently occupy. Were there no such association then the percentage distribution of people across the current class categories would be the same, irrespective of the class from which they originated. This state of affairs is called 'perfect mobility' and it would represent complete openness in social fluidity. Needless to say, this is never observed, and there is always some relationship such that there are patterns of association between being born into particular classes and being found in particular classes. Perhaps the strongest association in many mobility tables is found in the propensity of people to remain in their class of origin. This is particularly marked where the class in question is one where the requirements for entry can be directly inherited and is most apparent in the petty bourgeoisie where the means of production can be passed from a parent to a child. However, mobility tables generally tend to display a clustering of cases in the cells on the main diagonal recording the number of people who are in the same class as the one in which they were brought up.

   Patterns of association between origins and current class are modelled using odds-ratios. An odds, in this context, is measured by the proportion of people from a given class origin who are found in one, rather than another, class destination, and an odds-ratio, as its name suggests, is the ratio of odds as between people of two different class origins. If an odds-ratio is equal to one, the relative chances of being found in one rather than another destination class are the same regardless of which of the two origin classes in question an individual came from. Odds-ratios less than or greater than one arise when these relative chances differ. Thus odds-ratios capture the pattern of association between origins and destinations, net of the marginal distributions of these variables. Equally, we can say that they measure the degree of inequality in access to more, rather than less, desirable class destinations as between people of different class origins; or, again, that they capture the pattern of social fluidity. In analyses of social mobility we are usually more interested in social fluidity than in studying the distributions of class origins and current class position. This is because the extent of social fluidity is taken as an indicator of the degree of equality of opportunity or 'openness' in a particular society. Clearly, not all inequality in the chances of access to desirable class positions arise as the result of inequalities of opportunity, but research suggests that a substantial part of it does (e.g., Marshall and Swift, 1993; 1996; Breen and Goldthorpe, 1999).

In comparing Northern Ireland with the Republic of Ireland, men with women and Catholics with Protestants, our starting point is the assumption that social fluidity is common. That is to say, we allow the marginal distributions of origins and destinations to differ as between our six mobility tables but we assume that they all show the same pattern of social fluidity. As with all the models we fit, we assess the plausibility of the assumptions that underlie it by assessing how closely the expected frequencies generated by the model match the actual frequencies in our mobility tables.

It is perhaps not surprising that the common social fluidity model does not provide a statistically adequate fit to the data, returning a deviance of 183.72 with 80 degrees of freedom, but what is surprising is how small this deviance is given the strength of the assumption of common social fluidity.[9] If we then allow social fluidity to differ by nation, this yields a deviance of 98.27 with 64 degrees of freedom (p = 0.0038)—a reduction in deviance of 85.45 with 16 df (p <0.0001).[10] In other words, patterns of social fluidity are clearly different in the Republic of Ireland than they are in Northern Ireland. Furthermore, if we then allow social fluidity to differ by religion within Northern Ireland the effect is not significant (the change in deviance is 23.69 with 16 df, p = 0.097). Patterns of social fluidity of Protestants are no different from those of Catholics. If, however, we allow social fluidity to

---

[9] The deviance, when considered in relation to the degrees of freedom, provides a measure that tells us whether or not a given model provides an adequate account of, or fit to, the observed data.

[10] That is to say, under this model social fluidity is the same among men and women in the Republic of Ireland, and it is also the same in the four Northern Ireland tables—for Catholic men and women and for Protestant men and women.

differ by gender we find a significant effect (the change in deviance is 29.29 with 16 degrees of freedom, p = 0.0225). However, these gender difference arise for three specific reasons. First, women in the Republic of Ireland are less likely than men to enter class IV from an origin in class III; Protestant women in Northern Ireland are less likely than Protestant men to enter class V+VI from an origin in class III, or to remain in class V+VI having been born into it; and, thirdly, Catholic women in Northern Ireland are less likely than Catholic men to be upwardly mobile from origins in class V+VI into class I+II. If we replace the gender difference in social fluidity by four dummy variables (which we can label 'affinity terms' to adopt the terminology of Erikson and Goldthorpe, 1992) that capture these effects we find that the model yields an acceptable fit to the data (deviance of 74.86 with 60 degrees of freedom, p = 0.0938).[11]

Thus a rather clear picture emerges of differences in social fluidity in our data. There is no significant difference in social fluidity between Catholics and Protestants in Northern Ireland. This result echoes findings based on the only other social mobility data set for Northern Ireland which was collected in 1973 (Miller, 1983; Hout, 1987: Chapter 7). There are some specific and relatively minor differences in social fluidity between men and women both North and South, but substantively, social fluidity is virtually the same among men as among women. However, between Northern Ireland and the Republic of Ireland there is a substantive difference in patterns of social fluidity. Now we turn to the question of the nature of this difference.

One parsimonious way of modelling differences in social fluidity between two or more mobility tables is the so-called 'unidiff' model (Erikson and Goldthorpe, 1992; Xie, 1992). This model posits that the pattern of association between origins and destinations is the same among the different tables, but it allows the strength of this association to differ by a uniform amount, so allowing for more or less marked inequality in social fluidity. To apply this model we first fit the model of common (across all six tables) social fluidity to our data, but also including the affinity terms that capture gender differences. This yields a deviance of 160.22 with 76 degrees of freedom. We call this model A. As we have already seen, allowing the pattern of social fluidity to vary between North and South yields a model with deviance of 74.86 and 60 degrees of freedom. The difference in deviance between this latter model and model A—namely 85.36 with

---

[11] If we omit women in Northern Ireland who were not currently in the labour force, so defining the samples of women North and South in exactly the same way, this particular model returns a deviance of 75.18 with 60 df. In general, changing the criteria for our Northern sample in this way has no effect on our results.

16 degrees of freedom—is a measure of how much of the variation in social fluidity between the six tables this latter model explains. If we now apply the unidiff model to the same data we find that it yields a deviance of 115.84 with 71 degrees of freedom (p = 0.001). Clearly this model does not fit the data. However, if we take the difference between its deviance and that of model A, the result (44.38 with 5 degrees of freedom) is equal to 52 per cent of the total variation in social fluidity that we have been able to explain.[12] The failure of the unidiff model to fit the data statistically shows that the difference between the Republic of Ireland and Northern Ireland in their social fluidity is not simply due to their having the same pattern but a different level of inequality. Nevertheless, the unidiff model explains about half of the difference in social fluidity between North and South.

Since the unidiff model allows only for uniform differences, variation in social fluidity is captured by a single parameter for each table. In our case, if we express these parameter values relative to the value for men in the Republic of Ireland we find that the values for the other five tables are as set out in Table 5. Since negative values indicate more openness than is found among men in the Republic of Ireland these results are very clear cut. There is no difference between men and women in the Republic of Ireland, nor are there any differences between any of the four groups in Northern Ireland. However, these four display patterns of social fluidity that are significantly more open than those found in the Republic of Ireland. On average, odds-ratios in the Northern Ireland tables are around two-thirds of the magnitude of those found in the Republic. Of course, this is not the whole story, because the unidiff model leaves unexplained about half of the difference in social fluidity between the two parts of Ireland, and a more detailed investigation into the pattern of differences and similarities in social fluidity is an issue we hope to address in later work. However, one possible explanation for the differences which are not captured by the unidiff model concerns the larger role played by property ownership in the origin distribution of the Republic of Ireland than in the North: in other words, the petty bourgeoisie (class IV) is much larger in the former's origin distribution than in the latter's. Given that it is in this class that family advantage takes a very concrete form in the ability of parents to pass on the means of production to their children, we might expect that some part of the lower level of social fluidity in the South would be due to the greater influence of the petty bourgeoisie. And, accordingly, if we rerun our analyses omitting all those who were born into that class, we do indeed find

---

[12] The unidiff model reduces the deviance compared with model A by 44.38 while the model that allows social fluidity to vary between North and South in an unrestricted fashion reduces it by 85.36, 44.38 is then 52 per cent of 85.36.

Table 5.   Uniform difference parameters relative to men in the Republic of Ireland.

	Unidiff Coefficient	Standard Error
Men in Republic of Ireland	0.000	
Women in the Republic of Ireland	−0.043	0.11
Catholic Men in Northern Ireland	−0.511	0.11
Catholic Women in Northern Ireland	−0.484	0.13
Protestant Men in Northern Ireland	−0.373	0.09
Protestant Women in Northern Ireland	−0.430	0.11

Source: NI: 1996 Northern Ireland Mobility Survey. ROI: 1994 Living in Ireland Survey.

that while there are still differences in social fluidity between North and South (the model of common social fluidity still fails to fit returning deviance of 88.52 with 56 df, p = 0.0036) the unidiff model now very nearly fits the data (deviance of 69.22 with 51 df, p = 0.0456). There still remains a statistically significant difference between the unidiff model and the observed data, but it is clear that this is now relatively minor. There seem, therefore, to be two main ways in which social fluidity differs between North and South. The Republic of Ireland is a less open society, and competition for more desirable class positions is more heavily biased by class origins than it is in the North. This gives rise to the differences in parameter values in the unidiff model. But the unidiff model fails to fit the data because of another source of difference in social fluidity between the two parts of the island which arises as a compositional effect. The class in which class position can most readily be inherited—namely the petty bourgeoisie—makes up a larger share of the class origin distribution in the South than in Northern Ireland.

As is usual in comparative studies of social mobility, variation in absolute mobility patterns owes more to differences between marginal distributions than to differences in social fluidity. We can see this more clearly if (following Breen, 1985) we decompose the total mobility variation in our data into that which arises from marginal differences and that which is due to differences in social fluidity. We define the total mobility variation as equal to the difference in deviance between our best fitting model for the data (74.86 with 60 df as above), and a model which sets social fluidity and all marginal distributions to be identical across our six mobility tables (though allowing for differences in sample sizes). Such a model yields a deviance of 1893.4 with 120 df. Table 6 then shows how this total mobility variation is partitioned into that due to differences in the class origin distribution, the current class distribution and social fluidity. As Table 6 shows, much more of the difference in mobility patterns is due to marginal effects than to social fluidity, and, indeed, as we have seen,

Table 6. Partitioning of total mobility variation.

	Deviance	df	Percentage of total mobility variation[1]
1. Common margins and social fluidity	1893.4	120	
2. + differences in origins	1553.4	100	18.7
3. + differences in current class	183.72	80	75.3
4. + differences in social fluidity	74.86	60	6.0

Note: 1 Total mobility variation is defined as the difference in deviance between model 1 and model 4.

Source: NI: 1996 Northern Ireland Mobility Survey. ROI: 1994 Living in Ireland Survey.

almost all of the within-country variation in mobility patterns derives from the former source. Within the former it is differences in the current class distribution that are of overwhelming importance.

The Effects of Migration

Since the mid-nineteenth century the island of Ireland, and particularly the Republic of Ireland, have been notable for high levels of emigration. This raises the question of how, if at all, this might have affected patterns of social fluidity. In general, migration per se will have no such effect unless it is differentiated in some way with respect not simply to class origins, but also to those factors that more directly influence an individual's mobility chances. Consider, for example, a situation in which people from one class origin were substantially more likely to migrate than people from other classes. Of itself this would not have any impact on observed patterns of social fluidity, providing that the migrants from this class were a random sample of everyone who originated in that class. In this case we can conclude that the social fluidity experiences of those who remained in Ireland was what those who emigrated would also have experienced had they not done so.[13] But suppose, instead, that those who migrated from this class were those who were most likely to be downwardly mobile in Ireland because they lacked some particular resource associated with mobility: they might, for example, have particularly low levels of educational attainment. In this case the migrants would not be a random sample of everyone originating from that class, and so the observed experiences of the non-migrants could not be assumed to be indicative of what would have happened to them had they chosen to remain in Ireland. Rather, had

[13] In fact, we do not require the migrants to be a random sample in an absolute sense. Rather they should be a random sample with respect to the factors that influence mobility chances.

they remained we would have observed less upward mobility from this class than we in fact saw. Suppose now that the class in question were the service class: then observed social fluidity will be rather less than it would have been had there been no emigration. This is because, in the absence of migration, the service class would have contained a larger proportion of people who were likely to be downwardly mobile and so the advantaged position of this class, vis-à-vis the others, would be somewhat eroded. Conversely, if the class in question were the skilled manual class, say, then the migration of those with the fewest mobility resources will cause observed social fluidity to be somewhat greater than it would be were the migrants to have remained within an Irish mobility regime. However, suppose that these patterns of selective migration were true of all classes. Then social fluidity would be unaffected because, in this example, those with the poorest mobility chances would be removed from consideration in all classes.

So, for emigration to affect our conclusions about social fluidity we require that two conditions be met. First, migration should be selective within classes with respect to the factors that influence mobility chances; and secondly, this selective migration must operate differently among people from different class origins. In this chapter, however, our concern is with a comparison of social mobility and social fluidity between the two parts of Ireland and we therefore need to ask not only whether emigration affects conclusions about fluidity but also whether this operates in different ways in the Republic of Ireland and in Northern Ireland. If it does, then the results of a comparison based, as ours is, on only non-migrants will have to be treated with some care. Thus a third condition is needed. If migration is to cast doubt on the results of our North/South comparative analysis, then differences in the operation of selective mobility as between classes must themselves be different in the two parts of the island.

To test whether any of these conditions are met we therefore require data on the class origins and the mobility resources possessed by individuals in Northern Ireland and the Republic of Ireland and by migrants from these two jurisdictions. We have, in fact, already analysed such data in the chapter in this volume dealing with education (Breen, Heath and Whelan, this volume). Given that educational qualifications are possibly the most important resource for social mobility, we here return to the data set used in that chapter to answer the question of whether any of these conditions are met. Here we compare data from the Northern Ireland Continuous Household Survey (CHS) with that from the British General Household Survey (GHS) (for details of these data sources see Breen, Heath and Whelan, this volume) and the ESRI's Living in Ireland Survey. We draw on the GHS data to form tables of class origin by highest educational qualification (using the same four levels of educational qualification as in the earlier chapter) for migrants to Britain from both Northern Ireland and the Republic of Ireland; and we use the CHS and Living in Ireland data to form tables of class origins by highest educational qualification for respondents living in Northern Ireland and the Republic of Ireland, respectively. Overall, this yields a five class by four educational levels by two migrant status cross-tabulation for both Northern Ireland and the Republic of Ireland.

When we analyse these two cross-tabulations we find a quite striking result: namely, that educational fluidity is constant among migrants and non-migrants in Northern Ireland (deviance = 13.65 with 12 df, p = 0.324), whereas it is not for those who originated in the Republic of Ireland (deviance = 53.36 with 12 df, p <0.0001). This means that, so far as people born in Northern Ireland are concerned, the relationship between class origins and education is the same among migrants and non-migrants. In this case, it appears that migration is not likely to have had any biasing effect on conclusions about social fluidity based on data for non-migrants only. But in the Republic of Ireland this is not so. The failure of the common educational fluidity model to fit the data points to a different relationship between class origins and educational attainment among those who remained in Ireland, compared with those who migrated to Britain. And, further analyses show that there is rather more educational fluidity among the migrants than the non-migrants: that is to say, educational qualifications are less closely tied to class origins among migrants than among those who did not migrate. The evidence for this is twofold. First, the pattern of residuals from the model of common educational fluidity shows a clear tendency for cells that associate more advantaged class origins and lower levels of qualification, or less advantaged origins and higher levels of qualification, to be under-fitted by the model among migrants. Secondly, if we fit the unidiff model to the Southern data we find that it fails to fit the data (deviance = 25.96 with 11 df, p = 0.007) but the unidiff parameter shows that the association between class origins and education among migrants (as measured by odds-ratios) is significantly less than among non-migrants.

Of course, as the analyses reported in the education chapter of this volume show, the distribution of educational qualifications is quite different among migrants and non-migrants from both parts of the island. But here our focus is on whether the pattern of association between qualification levels and class origins shows comparable differences. Our conclusion is that there is such a difference in the case of the Republic of Ireland, but not for Northern Ireland. This gives us strong evidence to suspect that conclusions about social fluidity in the Republic, but not the North, drawing on data only for respondents who did not migrate, might have been rather different had there been no migration.

Such differential effects of migration then need to be taken into account in our comparison of social fluidity in the two parts of Ireland. Greater educational fluidity among migrants from the Republic implies a weaker relationship between class origins and the major proximate factor influencing social mobility (namely, educational qualifications). Had migrants been included in the Southern mobility data we may well have seen rather more social fluidity than we in fact observed and the difference in social fluidity between the two parts of Ireland would then have been rather less—though, given the data at our disposal, it is not possible to quantify this.

Several caveats must be entered when drawing conclusions from these findings. The data relate only to migrants to Britain and, although this has been the main destination for Irish emigrants during the post-war period there have nevertheless been significant migratory flows to other destinations. Furthermore, our data only relate to one mobility resource, namely educational qualifications, and this is a fairly obvious limitation since we know that patterns of social fluidity far from simply reflect the differential distribution of educational qualifications. Nevertheless, our results do lead us to suspect that the lower level of social fluidity found in the Republic of Ireland may owe something to the effects of selective migration.

Conclusions

We set out to address four questions concerned with differences and similarities in patterns of class structure and social fluidity in Ireland, North and South. For the most part our results have been surprisingly clear-cut. Our analyses of class structure showed a general trend towards convergence in the two parts of the island, albeit with the persistence of the kind of gender differences which are familiar from previous research in many other countries. But perhaps the most striking finding here was the convergence in the class distributions between Protestant and Catholic women in Northern Ireland, and the advantage enjoyed by the latter in relation to long-range upward and downward mobility. Among men, while there has also been some convergence, Catholics are still disadvantaged, being less likely to be found in the professional and managerial class and more likely to be located in the non-skilled manual class, and the advantage in relation to long-range mobility continues to lie with Protestants. However, the magnitude of these ethnic difference pales when set against the extent of gender difference in the current class distribution which is far larger in both the North and South and among Catholics and Protestants.

The bulk of our analysis focused on patterns of social fluidity. Differences between men and women in both the Republic of Ireland and Northern Ireland certainly exist, but they are small relative to the degree of commonality between them. In Northern Ireland (and in common with studies using data from the early 1970s) we could find no difference in social fluidity between Protestants and Catholics of the same gender. The one clear source of variation in social fluidity in our data is cross-national: the Republic of Ireland is substantially less open than is Northern Ireland. That is to say, mobility chances are more closely tied to class origins in the former and, we can infer, equality of opportunity is less.

This finding should come as no surprise in the light of earlier research which has shown the Republic of Ireland to have class inequalities considerably greater than most other European countries including England and Wales.[14] As we have seen, there are two sources of difference between the two parts of Ireland in their pattern of social fluidity. On the one hand there is a compositional effect: class origins in the petty bourgeoisie are much more numerous in the South, almost inevitably leading to less openness in social fluidity. But, on the other hand, even taking this into account, social fluidity among people of other class origins is uniformly less in the South than in the North. However, further analyses suggest a third factor that might be acting to accentuate differences in social fluidity between North and South. In the Republic of Ireland, though not in Northern Ireland, selective migration had the effect of removing a disproportionate share of better qualified people from less advantaged class origins. The effect of this would be to increase the association between class origins and educational qualifications among those who remained, probably leading to lower rates of social fluidity. Such conclusions, however, are necessarily tentative.[15]

Patterns of social fluidity are primarily shaped by three considerations: the relative desirability of different class destinations; the barriers to mobility into particular classes; and the resources available to individuals to allow them to overcome these barriers and enter the more desirable class destinations (Goldthorpe, 1980/87: 99). Since we can reasonably assume that the relative desirability of different classes is common to both parts of

---

[14] For a summary see Breen and Whelan (1996).

[15] Of course, one might equally well argue that, far from selective migration being the cause of lower social fluidity it was the consequence, in as much as well-qualified people from less-advantaged classes migrated precisely because they believed that low social fluidity would prevent them securing the returns on their qualifications that they might obtain elsewhere.

Ireland, the reasons for lower social fluidity in the South must be sought in an examination of differential barriers and the differential distribution of resources. Both issues may be important. On the one hand, since odds-ratios are uniformly higher in the Republic, rates of class inheritance must also be higher: thus, insiders appear better able to retain their class position here than in the North. On the other, evidence presented by Breen, Heath and Whelan (this volume) shows that class inequalities in education are more substantial in the South than in the North. In so far as educational attainment is a resource for social mobility, it follows that some of the difference in social fluidity may arise from this source.

References

Aunger, E. A. (1975) 'Religion and Occupational Class in Northern Ireland', *Economic and Social Review*, 7(1): 1–18.

Breen, R. (1985) 'A Framework for Comparative Analysis of Social Mobility', *Sociology*, 19: 93–107.

Breen, R. and Goldthorpe, J. H. (1999) 'Class Inequality and Meritocracy: A Critique of Saunders and an Alternative Analysis', *The British Journal of Sociology*, 50(1) March.

Breen, R. and Rottman, D. B. (1995) *Class Stratification A Contemporary Perspective*, London: Harvester, Wheatsheaf.

Breen, R. and Whelan, C. T. (1992) 'Explaining the Irish Pattern of Social Fluidity', in J. H. Goldthorpe and C. T. Whelan (eds), *The Development of Industrial Society in Ireland*, Oxford: University Press.

Breen, R. and Whelan, C. T. (1993) 'From Ascription to Achievement? Origins, Education and Entry to the Labour Force in Ireland', *Acta Sociologica*, 36(1): 3–18.

Breen, R. and Whelan, C. T. (1995) 'Gender and Class Mobility: Evidence from the Republic of Ireland', *Sociology*, 29(1): 1–22.

Breen, R. and Whelan, C. T. (1996) *Social Mobility and Social Class in Ireland*, Dublin: Gill and Macmillan.

Britten, N. and Heath, A. (1983) 'Women, Men and Social Class' in E. Gamarnikow, D. Morgan, J. Purvis and D. Taylorson (eds), *Gender, Class and Work*, London: Heinmann.

Callan, T., Nolan, B., Whelan, B. J., Whelan, C. T. and Williams, J. (1996) *Poverty in the 1990s: Evidence From The 1994 Living in Ireland Survey*, Dublin: Oak Tree Press.

Cormack, R. J. and Osborne, R. D. (1991) 'Disadvantage and Discrimination in Northern Ireland', in R. J. Cormack and R. D. Osborne (eds), *Discrimination and Public Policy in Northern Ireland*, Aldershot: Avebury.

Cormack, R. J. and Osborne, R. D. (1994) 'The Evolution of the Catholic Middle Class', in A. Guelke (ed.), *New Perspectives on The Northern Ireland Conflict*, Aldershot: Avebury.

Cullen, L. M. (1972) *An Economic History of Ireland Since 1660*, London: Batsford.

Erikson, R. and Goldthorpe, J. H. (1987) 'Commonality and Variation in Social Fluidity in Industrial Nations, Part II: The Model of Core Social Fluidity Applied', *European Sociological Review*, 3: 145–66.

Erikson, R. and Goldthorpe, J. H. (1992) *The Constant Flux: A Study of Class Mobility in Industrial Societies*, Oxford: Clarendon Press.

Goldthorpe, J. H. (1980/1987) *Social Mobility and Class Structure in Britain*, Oxford: Clarendon Press.

Gudgin, G. and Breen, R. (1996) *Evaluation of the Ratio Unemployment Rates*, Studies in Employment Equality, Research Report No. 4, Belfast: Central Community Relations Unit.

Hayes, B. C. and Miller, R. L. (1993) 'The Silenced Voice: Female Social Mobility Patterns with Particular Reference to the British Isles', *British Journal of Sociology*, 44: 653–72.

Heath, A. and Britten, R. (1984) 'Women's Jobs Do Make a Difference', *Sociology*, 18: 475–90.

Hout, M. (1989) *Following in Fathers' Footsteps*, London: Harvard University Press.

McGarry, J. and O'Leary, B. (1995) *Explaining Northern Ireland: Broken Images*, Oxford: Blackwell.

Marshall, G. and Swift, A. (1993) 'Social Class and Social Justice', *British Journal of Sociology*, 44: 187–211.

Marshall, G. and Swift, A. (1996) 'Merit and Mobility: A Reply to Peter Saunders', *Sociology*, 30(2): 375–86.

Miller, R. L. (1983) 'Religion and Occupational Mobility' in R. J. Cormack and R. D. Osborne (eds), *Religion, Education and Employment: Aspects of Equal Opportunity in Northern Ireland*, Belfast: Appletree Press.

Murphy, A. with Armstrong, D. (1994) *A Picture of the Catholic and Protestant Male Unemployed*, Employment Equality Review Research Report No. 2, Belfast: Central Community Relations Unit.

O'Brien, G. (1962) 'The Economic Progress of Ireland 1912–1962', *Studies*, 51: 9–26.

Smith, A. (1993) 'The Ethnic Sources of Nationalism' in M. E. Brown (ed.), *Ethnic Conflict and International Security*, Priceton: Princeton University Press.

Smith, D. J. and Chambers, G. (1991) *Inequality in Northern Ireland*, Oxford: Clarendon Press.

Whelan, C. T., Breen, R. and Whelan, B. J. (1992) 'Industrialisation, Class formation and Social Mobility in Ireland', in J. H. Goldthorpe and C. T. Whelan (eds), *The Development of Industrial Society in Ireland*, Oxford: Oxford University Press.

Whyte, J. (1990) *Interpreting Northern Ireland*, Oxford: Clarendon Press.

Xie, Y. (1992) 'The Log-Multiplicative Layer Effect Model for Comparing Mobility Tables', *American Sociological Review*, 57: 380–95.

Industrial Relations in the
Two Irish Economies

PAUL TEAGUE & JOHN McCARTNEY

Introduction

THIS PAPER EXAMINES THE DEVELOPMENT OF INDUSTRIAL RELATIONS in the two parts of Ireland with a view to identifying the key themes or dynamics in each system. With regard to the Republic of Ireland, the theme that stands out is the extent to which employment practices in the country are influenced by British ideas and procedures. It is argued that for the first 50 years of Independence, Irish industrial relations more or less replicated the British 'voluntarist' model. However, since the early 1970s, the two systems have gradually drifted apart. The arrival of multinationals, the country's enthusiasm for Europe and a new breed of leader in trade union and employer organisations have all contributed to the decline of the British influence. The demise of voluntarism in the Republic has not led, however, to the emergence of an alternative employment model. Contemporary Irish industrial relations are fragmented, with many different ideas influencing the organisation of the employment system.

In relation to Northern Ireland, two main themes have dominated industrial relations. One is the industrial relations dimension to the vexed questions of Catholic labour market disadvantage and the drive towards fair employment in the region. This paper argues that it is naïve to think that work practices or labour market institutions played no part in the religious bifurcation of the employment system. At the same time, it suggests that Catholics fared less well than Protestants in employment more as a result of the unintended consequences of particular labour market practices rather than deliberate acts of discrimination. While certain industrial relations procedures may have contributed to Catholic labour market disadvantage, successive governments have seen other

Proceedings of the British Academy, **98**, 341–368. © The British Academy 1999.

labour market practices as holding the key to fair employment. In particular, through a series of legal moves, governments have obliged enterprises to adopt certain human resource management policies in an effort to end religious disadvantage at work. We argue that these actions have considerably improved the position of Catholics in employment.

The other big issue with regard to Northern Ireland industrial relations is the extent to which it is integrated into a wider UK system. One view is that because the region is half in and half out of the British economic and political system, it should develop its own system of labour market governance to improve economic performance. The counter-argument is that to reinforce the Union, Northern Ireland should tie itself to UK-wide arrangements. This paper suggests this debate is a side-show. For a start, it argues that talk about integrating the local system into wider British arrangements is a misnomer as the UK no longer has an established pattern of industrial relations. Furthermore, the case for a regional industrial relations systems is blunted by the under performance of local labour market institutions. Overall, Northern Ireland industrial relations fails to promote fairness in the employment systems or to contribute greatly to economic performance. In this situation, important changes have to occur to existing arrangements which set out to reform the nature of the British connection and the activities of regional industrial relations bodies.

Living with the British Legacy

Political independence in 1921 did not end British influence in the Republic of Ireland. For the most part, the new Free State inherited a British method of governance. Like many other parts of the administrative structure, little attempt was made to recast the established industrial relations arrangements by the early governments of the Free State. As a result, an ethos of voluntarism continued to govern relationships between labour and management. Indeed industrial relations in Britain and Ireland remained virtually indistinguishable until the mid-1970s.

Voluntarist industrial relations in Ireland influenced the organisation and behaviour of employers and trade unions. As for organised labour, its most pronounced feature was its fragmented structure. Every occupational segment, no matter how small, seemed to have its own trade union organisation. Moreover, trade unions frequently competed for similar types of worker, a practice compounded by several large British trade unions continuing to recruit in the Republic after Independence. A second feature of trade union organisation was its decentralised orientation. On the one hand, the authority of the Irish congress of Trade Unions (ICTU), the federal body for organised labour, was carefully circumscribed so that its main role was one of coordination. On the other hand, local shop stewards enjoyed considerable autonomy, thereby ensuring that they were frequently the pace setters on industrial relations matters. Employer organisations displayed many of the characteristics of the trade unions. Although not particularly fragmented, national employer organisations were relatively weak bodies with little capacity to drive an industrial relations agenda from the centre. In one sense this was not a problem since the predilection of employers was for decentralised industrial relations.

Thus voluntarism ensured that the social partners in Ireland progressed along a different path to that emerging in other parts of continental Europe. In countries like Germany and Sweden, a contrasting organisational structure was unfolding for trade unions and employers. Here, both social partners developed more ordered and coherent internal structures. In addition, national federations played a prominent role in deciding the general strategic direction of capital and labour. Thus each side of industry approximated towards the Olsonian idea of *encompassing* institutions with the national leadership of trade unions and employers able to formulate collective strategies, negotiate collective obligations and implement collective policies. These institutional characteristics resulted in associative orders being established in many national labour markets in Europe. Key features of such an order were a strong reciprocity between trade unions and employers, even though they had competing interests, and a special public status being conferred on them by government (Schmitter and Streeck, 1985). A contrasting organisational logic emerged in the Anglo-Irish industrial relations system. The core reflex of this system was adversarialism which tended to encourage mistrust and suspicion between labour market actors. This is an important contrast, for it meant that both Ireland and Britain stood apart from the institutional dynamics that underscored the evolution of Social Europe.

Trade union and employer behaviour in Ireland was strongly influenced by voluntarist principles. In particular a sectionalist approach to collective bargaining was promoted in which both sides of industry sought to realise the narrow interests of their members. For many leading British industrial relations academics, such as Alan Flanders (1968), this was a perfectly acceptable and reasonable approach. But the consequence was a lack of integration between industrial relations and the wider national strategy of economic development. The gap between the two is exemplified by the roller-coaster history of attempts at national pay agreements between 1948 and 1980. Successive Irish governments established national wage determination arrangements to tie pay to other national economic objectives, but invariably many of these initiatives were short-lived. The chequered history of these programmes is well documented (see Hardiman, 1988; 1992; Roche 1994; and Durkin, 1992), but the basic problem was that governments were attempting to build a national wage strategy on unsuitable institutional foundations.

Voluntarism ensured that legal regulation played a relatively minor role in Irish industrial relations and also made policies to promote a greater consensus in the employment relationship more difficult. For the most part, both sides of industry eschewed the juridification approach to industrial relations whereby legal rules govern labour market behaviour. Such an approach was common in continental countries such as France, Belgium and Italy. But in Ireland, labour law interventions were regarded as a direct threat to collective bargaining and to the autonomy of both sides of industry in deciding their own destiny. For the trade unions, excessive labour law would sound the death knell of solidaristic action whereas employers found it menacing as it would place them inside the straightjacket of state regulation. Thus both sides of industry favoured taking their chances in a free collective bargaining tussle rather than allow government the opportunity to lay down the boundaries of permissible and nonpermissible industrial relations action.

In Ireland, there was not the strong antipathy towards the principle of worker participation which existed in Britain. Many British trade unions rejected out of hand proposals for worker democracy as a cunning capitalist ploy to first incorporate and then subjugate organised labour. Irish trade unions were more phlegmatic on the matter; they were neither overly in favour nor opposed to the principle of participation. But the institutional characteristics of Irish voluntarism meant that it was exceptionally difficult to implement worker participation schemes within organisations (McCarthy, 1975). A fascinating report under the chairmanship of Michael Fogarty (1969) highlighted how the fragmented trade union structure created enormous organisational barriers to the enactment of an employee involvement arrangement.

All these developments added up to Irish industrial relations being the twin sister of the system that prevailed in Britain. Despite formal political independence, the umbilical cord was still there. Another way the close association between the two countries manifested itself was by Irish trade unions engaging in pattern bargaining. The term 'pattern bargaining' was invented by American industrial relations scholars to describe the process of trade unions in one part of the United States formulating bargaining demands by examining collective agreements reached in other parts of the country. Underpinning pattern bargaining therefore, is the view that trade union demands are heavily influenced by (i) normative sentiments about a group of workers' position relative to other workers; and (ii) the availability of information since only when workers have information about wages and employment conditions for other workers can they make a judgement. Mostly, pattern bargaining is practised within countries. Previously in Britain, for example, most firms in the engineering sector waited for Ford and other large car manufacturers to set the pattern for collective bargaining demands before entering negotiations with their own workforce.

Many trade unions in Ireland, particularly in the 1960s and 1970s, regarded pay deals concluded in Britain as a legitimate comparison and thus sought to shadow particular UK collective bargaining agreements. Britain being an orbit of comparison for Irish wage setting was facilitated by three factors. First, the existence of a currency union between the two countries removed any possible centrifugal influences arising from the exchange rate illusion. The argument here is that separate currencies discourage trade unions from engaging in any normative comparisons. Second, by engaging in collective bargaining in Ireland, British-based trade unions represented a ready-made organisational channel for the transmission of information from one area to the other. Thirdly, the large flows of Irish workers in and out of the British labour market created the all-important social foundations to pattern bargaining.

Escaping the British Model

Thus for fifty years after 1921, Irish industrial relations more or less followed the pattern of British labour market governance. But since the 1970s the apparently seamless boundary between the two employment systems has been gradually coming apart. No one episode has been responsible for the rupture. Instead, it is the result of four factors operating in Ireland and one large factor working in Britain. With regard to Ireland, the first important factor to prompt a reorientation of industrial relations, and wider economic and political structures for that matter, was the arrival of multinationals. After the programme of self-sufficiency had all but brought the country to its knees, the political and administrative elite in Dublin engineered a complete policy reversal and a regime of unfettered economic openness was put in place. Generous tax incentives were created to attract foreign direct investment and many multinationals were enticed to take up the offer.

Much has been written about how multinationals have come to dominate the tradeable sector in Ireland, and the benefits and weakness of this situation. It is not appropriate to review this literature here, since the concern is with the impact of multinationals on the industrial relations environment. In the industrial relations literature an important distinction is made between multinationals acting as ethnocentric and policycentric organisations. Ethnocentric multinationals transfer the dominant employment practices of the home country when establishing a subsidiary in a host country. By contrast, polycentric multinationals adopt the employee relations practices of the host country. No systematic study has been carried out on which industrial relations strategy tends to be pursued by multinationals in Ireland, but the balance of evidence is that ethnocentric practices are more widespread. Roche and Geary (1994) argue that multinationals have played a significant role in the importation of new employee relations ideas such as the non-union firm and US models of human resource management that emphasise team-working and multi-skilling. McCartney and Teague (1997) in an in-depth survey of three economic sectors in Ireland, reached similar conclusions.

Many new workplace employment practices inside multinationals are a direct challenge to old-style voluntarist industrial relations. For example, under voluntarism trade unions gained influence over the social structure of the enterprise through joint management-trade union committees. But now work practices such as team-working and employment involvement arrangements are, in many areas, dissolving the traditional boundaries between management and labour and are thus making such committees obsolete. Moreover, it is unlikely that these workplace innovations will remain completely confined to the foreign-owned sector. Managers who have worked for multinationals leave and join indigenously owned companies, taking with them fresh ideas about managing the internal labour market. Owners of Irish companies sometimes compare themselves to foreign subsidiaries to assess whether they can copy human resource practices to improve their competitive performance. More generally, a process of societal spill-over invariably takes hold through which the employment practices of certain companies gradually modify the social conventions governing the labour market. This type of slow reorientation appears to have taken place in Ireland: voluntarism is no longer a widely accepted labour market convention.

Membership of the EU is a second factor encouraging a recasting of Irish industrial relations. European integration has generated both formal and informal influences. On the formal side, Irish entry into the EU coincided with a relatively large shrinkage of the indigenous industrial base. Through the process of trade creation, whereby inefficient productions are exposed to more competitive organisations from other member states, many Irish-owned companies went to the wall, unable to live in a world without protective barriers. It was not that these companies were a bastion of voluntarism—they were in the main just poorly managed, inept even at voluntarist industrial relations—rather their closure was significant in that it removed from the industrial structure a group of enterprises that would have been a drag on industrial relations change. In other words, the corporate shake-out that took place with EU membership resulted in an increase in the capacity of organisations to diffuse workplace innovations. A higher diffusion capacity spelt a bigger threat to the traditional relations system.

Another formal influence arising from European integration was EU social policy. Like other member-states, Ireland is obliged to comply with employment laws and policies adopted by the EU. At the start, this proved a difficult enough task. For example, the 1975 Equal Pay Directive threw the Irish Government into convulsions, with ministers declaring that they had no intention of placing such sex equality legislation onto the statute book. Twenty years later, although not problem-free, Dublin is more comfortable dealing with EU social legislation. A measure of the new confidence was the passage in 1993 of a law giving part-time workers a plinth of rights which was more or less modelled on a draft EU Directive: to show that it was a good European, the Irish government implemented the initiative even before it became EU law. Large-scale Europeanisation of policy making in Ireland accounts for the positive attitude in Dublin to EU initiatives. This process had several dimensions, but all with implications for the voluntarist system of industrial relations.

Probably the most important dimension was that the EU became an important external reference point for Irish governments when developing labour law initiatives. Previously, Dublin administrations had either relied on British legal thinking or the International Labour Organisation when formulating industrial relations legislation. Unsurprisingly, therefore, a strong voluntarist ethos underpinned much of the Irish labour law before 1970. With the EU legal influence becoming more prominent, Irish thinking on employment matters has shifted towards the juridification model, found in continental Europe. In addition to this legal dimension, EU membership allowed Irish civil servants to participate in Europe-wide policy networks. As a result, government officials became exposed to differing institutional models of the labour market. In particular, they learnt more about the associative industrial relations systems of many north European countries where the emphasis has been on management and labour developing mutual interdependence strategies. Irish trade unions and employers too, have been more exposed to such systems by participating in various committees for the social partners in Brussels. It would be wrong to argue that the EU has ended the British influence in Irish industrial relations, but European integration has certainly weakened it.

In addition to these formal factors, European integration also gave rise to a range of informal influences. Across Irish society, European integration is regarded as involving much more than meeting the obligations of EU membership or participating in EU institutions in Brussels. It is also seen as embodying a model of development that combines social equity and economic efficiency which ought to be diffused into Ireland. Thus, European integration represents an imagined economic and social order which should guide policy in Ireland. This informal European influence, for example, has played a big part in the commitment of the trade union movement to the recent national wage agreements. In other words, the dynamics of European integration has become embedded in the cognitive structures of the Irish labour market.

A third factor encouraging industrial relations change was the deep economic crisis that lasted from the late 1970s until the early 1990s. For most of that decade Ireland stood at the edge of the economic abyss. Huge budget deficits, rampant inflation, accelerating unemployment and large-scale migration threatened to rip apart the economic and social fabric of the country. The country faced nothing less than an economic emergency which required an all-embracing, inclusive institutional response by government and the social actors. Voluntarist industrial relations, with the capacity to promote a 'them and us' mentality, were ill-suited to this policy imperative. To have pursued sectionalist demands in such bleak economic times would have been exceptionally cavalier. Thus, both employers and trade unions stepped back from voluntarism and joined the country-wide solidaristic alliance to combat the economic crisis. Tying their own actions to wider national priorities was a decisive step away from voluntarism and towards cooperative industrial relations. The national pay deals that were first signed in the teeth of the gales of economic crisis, and which have lasted the arrival of calmer, more prosperous times, are an indication of the new commitment towards consensual labour market behaviour.

A fourth factor that accounts for the demise of voluntarism has been strategic change by the social partners themselves. There is widespread agreement in the academic industrial relations community that economic and social factors alone do not fully account for trade union or employer action. In most circumstances, both have a range of strategic options open to them. This factor has been at play in Ireland. In the early 1980s, a new brand of trade union and employer leader emerged in the country, unhappy that the Irish employment system was driven by free collective bargaining. The common view was that the British voluntarist model of employee relations was ill-suited to modern Ireland. As a result, both sides of industry became more amenable to industrial relations change.

The demise of voluntarism was accelerated by the rise of Thatcherism in Britain. A cornerstone of the Thatcher economic programme was industrial relations without trade unions. Labour exclusion policies have considerably weakened the British trade union movement. Trade union density rates have declined, as has trade union recognition. Moreover, multi-tier collective bargaining has been broken up, leading to decentralised and disorganised industrial relations. The lessons of the Thatcher years have not been lost on Irish trade unions. Neo-liberalism rewrote the industrial relations ground rules: the traditional choice between concertation or voluntarism was buried and trade unions, almost everywhere, faced the stark reality that if they were not cooperative they would be excluded. Thatcherism delivered the knock-out blow to voluntarism as a credible organising principle for employee relations. Little wonder, when in 1989 the then Irish Prime Minster, Charles Haughey gave the trade unions the option to participate in a national stabilisation programme, the offer was immediately accepted. Economic times may have been hard, but the trade unions were at least assured a future.

Contemporary Irish Industrial Relations: A Cohabitation of Different Models

The National Wage Agreements: Towards Social Corporatism?

The institutional edifice of the new consensual industrial relations is the national pay agreements that have been in place since 1987. In one sense these pay deals are unremarkable since an evergreen in Irish economic policy has been attempts at centralised wage formation. But for many they mark a new beginning as they are seen to embody the end of voluntarism in Ireland and a decisive move towards a more European model of labour market management. Whilst some of the claims made about the latest national wage agreement are too exaggerated, they nevertheless appear to stand apart from previous arrangements. Not only have they lasted for much longer, but they also seem to be underpinned by a qualitatively different relationship between the social partners: a greater spirit of partnership seems to prevail between employers and trade unions than hitherto.

A number of features of the national pay agreements stand out. One is that they have held down wages in Ireland's tradeable sector. Some commentators, such as Walsh (1993), have been critical of the various national wage deals for failing to control wages in the private sector. But little justification exists for this assessment: without the national agreements, wages in the private sector would have been much higher (Teague, 1995). A second and more important aspect of the agreements is how they have dovetailed with the country's macro-economic strategy. Since the mid-1980s Ireland has pursued monetary and fiscal policies to make it better placed to join a monetary union in Europe. Every agreement explicitly states that the pay deals must be consistent with the country's efforts to be part of an EU single currency club. Fituossi (1995) describes such a macro-economic strategy as *competitive disinflation*. Tying wage formation to a tight fiscal and monetary regime marks off the Irish national pay deals from the social corporatist arrangements found in most Nordic countries in the 1970s and 1980s (Rowthorn, 1992).

Third, while private sector pay has been constrained, the same is not true for the public sector. For the past decade, employees in the non-market sector have received annual wage increases above inflation. Moreover, because of the regular comparability assessments, pay, particularly for higher grade public sector workers, is regularly topped up. As a result, it is questionable whether public sector workers would have done so well under free collective bargaining. Sooner or later the imbalance between private and public sector wage formation will have to be addressed. Without any redress, private sector workers are likely to grow disillusioned with centralised pay fixing, causing the agreements to fall apart.

A fourth feature of the agreements is how they have more or less concentrated on redistribution—how to divide up the macro-economic pie. This is unlike other national collective bargaining systems which also have an active role in the productive side of the economy, mostly through the provision of collective labour market goods. Thus, in Germany national partnership between trade unions and employers is not simply embodied in the system of coordinated wage bargaining, but also in the renowned apprenticeship system. Labour market collective goods are important for productive activity as they can reduce negative economic externalities. For example, without proper, functioning training institutions it is difficult to establish an adequate pool of skilled workers. When skill shortages arise, firms invariably start to poach labour from each other, thereby triggering wage inflation. Collective labour market goods frequently prevent these distortions and thus contribute to economic efficiency. For the most part, the centralised wage agreements in Ireland have yet to create such arrangements for the productive side of the economy. By and large, this can be attributed to the weak links between the national pay deals and the employment practices of enterprises.

Overall, the Irish national wage agreements have operated in a highly distinctive way, containing both positive and negative features. Thus some of the uncritical accounts that are emerging about the pay deals are perhaps overblown. Nevertheless, it would be churlish not to accept that they have played an important part in the present economic recovery. For the social partners, but particularly the trade unions, the big prize is that they have emerged from the dark days of economic recession at the centre of economic decision making. The theme of partnership now appears at the centre of all government programmes. This is unlike Britain, where the trade unions are out in the cold. With the return of better economic times, the opportunity now exists for the trade unions and employers, through the national collective agreements, to help promote a new social agenda for the country. In terms of narrow industrial relations matters, the key issue will be whether or not the partnership principle can be diffused into enterprise-level employment systems. The extent to which this can happen depends on the character of employee relations on the ground.

Enterprise-Level Employment Systems in Ireland

Only a fragmentary picture exists with regard to ground-level industrial relations. As a result, it remains uncertain, for example, whether companies are introducing new human resource policies such as employee involvement and team-working or whether they are sticking with tried and tested employment practices. In an effort to gain more information about employee relations inside organisations the authors conducted a survey covering three sectors of the Irish economy—electronics, financial services and food, drink and tobacco—to assess the extent to which workplace innovations are being diffused in the country. In total, in-depth interviews were carried out with 102 organisations.

A number of important findings emerge from the survey. First, team-working is the least likely workplace innovation to occur. Only about one in four enterprises have adopted this type of workplace reform. The results with regard to job rotation are interesting, for they show that whereas 56.9 per cent of companies have introduced this practice to some of their core workers, only 38.2 per cent have enacted the policy at the 50 per cent level. This suggests that job rotation has been introduced by firms as much to remove job demarcations as to promote multi-skilling or multi-tasking. Breaking down demarcations between job tasks has been a common strategy in British companies in an effort to obtain internal functional flexibility. Thus one interpretation of this result is that human resource managers inside companies in Ireland continue to be influenced by British thinking on the employment relationship. But the figure also suggests that many skilled workers have been able to resist moves towards functional flexibility.

Total quality management (TQM) has been the most common employ-ment innovation introduced by firms: about 70 per cent of the sample diffused this practice in some form, (workers in each establishment are involved in this effort). However, in a good many cases TQM initiatives mainly involve a company-wide ethos and have not involved any large-scale changes to work organisation. Thus some companies appear to have only introduced minimalist, symbolic workplace innovations with few far-reaching implications. But perhaps the main finding from the survey is that no overall pattern exists to workplace change in the country. This conclusion is broadly in line with other studies which suggest that ground-level employee relations in Ireland are fragmented (Roche, 1994). It is also consistent with the observation that whilst human resources managers in Ireland are moving away from voluntarist industrial relations, they have no preferred alternative model: they are being influenced by a number of different developments with regard to the employment relationship. In particular, some appear influenced by the British flexibility model; others are closer to the American human-resource management model; still others by the partnership principle through which workplace reform is introduced via working with established trade unions.

Thus although there appears to be a decisive shift away from the voluntarist model of industrial relations at the enterprise level, no coherent new system is emerging. Elements of different models of the employment relations are sitting side-by-side with each other. This conclusion has implications for how the central industrial relations arrangements connect with employment systems on the ground. Perhaps the key lesson from the above discussion is that it would be misguided to tie organisations to any one particular employment practice. Only loose connections between the centre and enterprises appear feasible, suggesting that Ireland cannot develop a distinctive industrial relations model. Actually to even use the language of an 'employment model' is to cut against the grain of social and economic change.

At the moment, economies are going through a huge wage of innovation and experimentation. The scale and direction of these changes have made well-understood categories of the labour market governance more or less redundant. For example, innovations such as lean production make it no longer possible to talk about a high road and a low road to economic success. In the new emerging complex economy, systems of governance lose their capacity to order and stabilise productive systems. They certainly lose the ability to tie enterprises to particular labour market practices. All that can be achieved is a form of open-ended coordination which establishes fluid and loose institutional supports for strongly decentralised forms of corporate decision making. As a result, it is inevitable that ground-level employee relations will be diffuse. At the same time, the industrial relations centre still has an important role, particularly by generalising good employment practices. In addition, industrial relations institutions should adopt 'learning by monitoring' procedures (Sable, 1994) whereby the centre interprets and codifies the type of social and economic changes taking place to guide and support unfolding labour market changes.

Almost by accident, Irish industrial relations have arrived at this open-ended coordination arrangement. On the one hand, ground-level employment systems are fairly fragmented. On the other hand, the industrial relations centre continues to have a key role, especially in relation to wage formation. Until recently, the national pay agreements have been mostly concerned with macro-economic management. With macro-economic stability more or less restored, the social partners can encourage a dialogue about the nature of enterprise-level employment systems. Indeed, as part of the latest agreement, the national social partners are likely to set down general principles to encourage employee voice at the workplace. This is exactly the type of policy suggested by the open co-ordination model; rather than tying individual enterprises to one particular arrangement, for example, works councils, the centre sets out broad policies. Thus the general outlook for Irish industrial relations is bright. After a generation of living with a model it did not want, the country has developed alternative arrangements that are in line with the new flexible economy.

Industrial Relations in Northern Ireland

Whereas the story of industrial relations in the South is essentially about the gradual atrophy of the British voluntarist model, no single overarching theme is evident for the employment system in the North. Instead, discussions about industrial relations in the region must address two relatively separate trends: (i) the relationship between industrial relations and the religious divide in the labour market; and (ii) the extent with which Northern Ireland is part of a wider British industrial relations system. Each of these themes are discussed below.

Industrial Relations and the Religious Divide in Northern Ireland

Industrial relations institutions are perhaps most accurately seen as mediating mechanisms that connect economic and social structures; they are an attempt to secure an accommodation between the human resource needs of enterprises with worker aspirations for decent wages and working conditions. Thus, industrial relations arrangements help create a form of economic citizenship by establishing rights and obligations through which people are incorporated into working life. We can say, for example, that Germany has a different model of economic citizenship than Britain largely as a result of contrasting industrial relations systems. In relation to Northern Ireland, this line of analysis raises the sensitive question of whether industrial relations practices have played a role in the unequal employment status of the two communities.

That differential employment status exists in Northern Ireland is now more or less beyond controversy. The literature on the religious divide in Northern Ireland labour markets has arrived at the following stylised facts:

1　Catholic males are more than twice as likely to be unemployed than Protestant males;

2　Protestants are over-represented in professional, managerial and skilled occupations;

3　Catholics are over-represented in semi-skilled and unskilled jobs;

4　Catholic males are hugely under-represented in security-related occupations;

5　While Catholic women are under-represented in administrative and managerial jobs and in clerical, secretarial and sales employment they are over-represented in professional jobs;

6　Economic inequality within each religious bloc has increased.

Agreement rapidly breaks down when it comes to explaining why Catholics have fared worse than Protestants in the employment system. Part of the debate on this matter concerns the role of industrial relations institutions in segmenting the regional labour market along religious lines. One view, which can be called the vulgar incorporation thesis, suggests that trade unions were docile, if not open accomplices, with the Unionist domination of the regional labour market, particularly during the Stormont years (Boyd, 1984; Tomlinson, 1980). As for the formal workings of the trade union movement, this argument is not convincing. Cradden (1993), in a copious and illuminating study of the Northern Ireland labour movement, shows that the Northern Ireland Committee of the Irish Congress of Trade Unions (NIC-ICTU) continually exhorted government to move against religious discrimination in employment. Individual trade unions frequently demanded similar action. Thus, from the very outset of the Northern Ireland state, the formal trade union position has been unequivocal in its opposition to sectarianism and religious bigotry.

A contrasting picture emerges when the focus shifts to the informal side of industrial relations. Here, the argument is that the actions of workers and employers outside established collective bargaining structures, and sometimes within them, ensured that Protestants did better than Catholics in employment. There are malign and benign versions to this story. According to the malign version the informal workings of the labour market were fairly straightforward. On the one hand, many employers when recruiting simply preferred Protestants to Catholics. On the other hand, Protestant workers inside enterprises, with considerable incumbency rights, acted to protect their insider status in a way that excluded Catholic outsiders. Thus the malign view is that the minority community encountered deliberate, widespread, if not systematic, labour market discrimination.

The benign story is somewhat different. It suggests that Catholic labour market disadvantage has in large measure been the unintended consequence of particular employment practices. Consider Harland and Wolff, the large ship-building company. Traditionally, this company operated a dense local employment system in mainly Protestant East Belfast, in a way that blurred the boundary between the company and the local community. In particular, a highly developed, extended internal labour market existed in the district whereby local people formed a queue for a job in the company. When a vacancy arose, it was filled from this waiting list through an informal recruitment channel. Both Harland and Wolff and the local community benefited from this informal employment system. This loose industrial relations system was not peculiar to Belfast: other communities elsewhere in Britain and Europe which housed large traditional industries, such as steel and coal, developed similar employment practices. But one negative side-effect from such systems can be local labour market closure as social barriers to entry are erected, making it difficult for outsiders to gain employment inside the community or district. Two unfortunate consequences arose in Northern Ireland as a result of local labour market closure. One was that Catholics were effectively excluded from many engineering jobs. The other was that a deep association emerged between Protestantism and manufacturing activity. In other words, it was a battery of industrial relations practices along with other social processes that ossified the occupational structure along religious lines, and not some innate propensity for Catholics or Protestants to favour one type of employment over another.

Economic change has all but washed away traditional extended internal labour markets in Northern Ireland. As a result, the high-profile local employment systems which appeared to typify the deep religious schisms in the regional labour market have declined. In recent years, there has been some discussion about the relatively large number of small private sector organisations with mainly Catholic or Protestant employees. Frequently, this religious segregation of corporate life is attributed to what is known locally as the chill factor: the reluctance of individuals from one religion to join organisations where the other religion is dominant because of a perceived threat of intimidation, personal injury, or in the extreme case death. Whilst clearly an important factor, it is questionable whether the chill factor is the sole influence at play. Even at the height of the violence, there were many trouble-free areas where the chill factor was relatively weak, yet there still existed a high number of mono-religious enterprises.

A more convincing explanation for this development is that segregation in employment is only reflecting the growing residential segregation of the two communities. Over the past twenty years gradual, almost unnoticed, shifts in population have been occurring, resulting in the concentration of Catholics and Protestants in particular parts of the region. For instance, there appears to have been a virtual exodus of Protestants from the border areas and in many residential areas a more pronounced clustering of the Catholic community has taken place. Since many (small) private sectors firms tend to recruit from the immediate surroundings, it may be that mono-religious enterprises are the by-product of the residential concentration of Catholics and Protestants. Industrial relations influences played a relatively minor part in this development. Yet paradoxically the emergence of religiously homogenous workplaces may impact benignly on employee relations as they might encourage the social bonds of loyalty established in communities spilling over into enterprises.

Overall, industrial relations arrangements have played a part in the religious bifurcation of the Northern Ireland labour market. It would be almost impossible to quantify the exact role of such factors since we are dealing with informal social processes. Determining the relative importance of the benign and malign influences of industrial relations institutions would be equally difficult. Employers did overtly discriminate against Catholics (and Protestants), and Protestant workers did operate in a way that intimidated Catholics from particular firms. Probably more important however, have been industrial relations practices with the unintended consequence of crowding Catholics into the lower end of the labour market. Thus, Catholic disadvantage was not some grand conspiracy on the part of Unionists or Protestants, but, in part, the result of 'normal' labour market processes becoming entangled in the local religious divide.

Industrial Relations and Fair Employment

Although industrial relations and human resource management practices are implicated in the religious divide in the labour market, policies in these areas are also seen as important to realising fair employment. Fair employment legislation has been on the statute book since 1976, but it was only after the law was revised in 1989 when an effective anti-discriminatory regime emerged in the labour market. The updated and revised Act of that year places strong obligations on enterprises to become fair employers. Table 1 outlines the various fair employment policies that enterprises have to pursue and others that could be used. At the very minimum, enterprises have to introduce a range of actions aimed at compliance with the law and the 'key duties' placed upon employers. As a next step an employer could make some improvements in general employment practices in line with the 'Fair Employment Code of Practice'. For the most part, this code sets out a 'soft' human resource management (HRM) approach to fair employment involving the formalisation of procedures relating to recruitment, promotion and redundancy and the introduction of new disciplinary arrangements to deal with religious harassment at work. More radically, the employer could take steps to bring about significant organisational change to promote fair employment. In general terms, such an approach can be termed 'hard' HRM policies for fair employment. Whilst not completely jettisoning the merit principle, measures under this banner represent a more far-reaching attempt to reduce religious imbalance inside the enterprise.

Table 2 shows that in the years since the Fair Employment legislation has been strengthened, the proportion of Catholic men and women in the workforce has increased in almost every occupational grouping. An interesting question is whether the 1989 Act encouraged the adoption of new employment practices by enterprises and the extent to which these contributed to the improved labour market performance of Catholics. In 1992 a survey of public and private sector organisations was carried out to

Table 1.   The range of fair-employment policies.

Compliance	Soft fair-employment policies	Hard fair-employment policies
Registration with the Fair Employment Commission	Written policy for equality of opportunity	Enacting a strong fair employment culture
Annual monitoring of the workforce	Consultation with trade unions or employee representatives	Targeted training
Review of personnel policies on three yearly basis	Formalised recruitment and selection procedures	Fast-track promotion
Programme of affirmative action, if necessary	Redundancy procedures based on efficiency critera	Performance indicators to include equality targets
	Improving managerial competence in relation to fair employment	Organisation relocation to achieve a better balance of workforce's community background
	Outreach activities	
	Anti-harassment policy	
	Policy on flags and emblems	

Table 2.   Change in the Catholic proportion of the Northern Ireland workforce, 1990–94.

	Men			Women		
	1990 %	1994 %	Change %	1990 %	1994 %	Change %
Managers and Administrators	28.5	32.2	+3.7	36.0	39.1	+3.1
Professional Occupations	29.6	34.4	+4.8	41.4	46.1	+4.7
Associate Professional and Technical Occupations	32.8	34.8	+2.0	45.3	46.8	+1.5
Clerical and Secretarial Occupations	34.9	39.3	+4.4	33.9	36.4	+2.5
Craft and Skilled Manual Occupations	32.2	32.6	+0.4	42.7	43.1	+0.4
Personal and Protective Service Occupations	20.0	22.0	+2.0	40.5	40.5	0.0
Sales Occupations	26.0	31.1	+5.1	34.7	37.0	+2.3
Plant and Machine Operatives	36.5	39.0	+2.5	42.3	46.7	+4.4
Other Occupations	40.5	40.9	+0.4	36.8	39.5	+2.7
Total	32.0	34.2	+2.2	38.5	40.6	+2.1

Source: Fair Employment Commission, Profile of the Workforce in Northern Ireland, Summary of the 1994 Monitoring Returns, FEC, 1995.

find out the experience of employers in complying with the 1989 Act. The results show that the new legislation had an impact on the employment practices of a sizeable proportion of companies, but by no means a majority. For example, personnel practices were reported to have been revamped in one way or another in 40 per cent of companies as a result of the legislation. Staff recruitment procedures was the area most commonly changed, particularly among larger companies. Just under a third of companies canvassed also introduced affirmative action measures and, of these, just under half had also incorporated goals and timetables.

The most recent evidence for change comes from the three-yearly reviews of companies undertaken by employers themselves. An analysis of these reviews by the Fair Employment Commission (FEC) shows that the overwhelmingly majority have adopted at least some of the soft fair-employment policies recommended in the Code of Practice (FEC, 1995). For example, 89 per cent of companies have a written equal opportunity policy, and a similar proportion have a policy governing the display of flags and emblems. Also, the vast majority (85 per cent) have made discrimination and harassment a disciplinary offence.

In relation to recruitment and selection, it appears that a greater degree of formality is being introduced. This is particularly the case with regard to management jobs. However, informal methods (factory notices, word of mouth) continue to be used for manual recruitment in about 20 per cent of companies. In addition, informal recruitment methods have been important for school leavers in gaining employment (Shuttleworth, 1994) which is a worry, since disadvantages experienced at the start of a career are likely to have an important influence on future work prospects.

Initiatives in the 'hard' range of policies remain the exception. A few large private sector companies, as well as certain public sector organisations, have adopted radical human resource management innovations to secure a more religiously balanced workforce. One enterprise, for example, has pursued a corporate decentralisation strategy with the explicit aim of increasing its presence in predominantly Catholic areas. Parts of the public sector have introduced far-reaching changes to internal structures and procedures to ensure that the organisation's employment system does not operate in a manner that disadvantages Catholics. Such high profile changes however, are in the minority. Overall the trend is for enterprises to do enough to comply with the legislation or to introduce 'soft' HRM policies to promote fair employment.

Political systems require a range of attributes to make them stable and governable. But an indispensable ingredient is an inclusive form of citizenship that not only makes people feel protected by the law but also enables them to actively engage in social and public life if they so wish. Should any formal or informal barriers exist to the full social participation of any particular group then the legitimacy of the entire political system invariably is called into question. Northern Ireland has never really enjoyed a stable system of governance precisely because of the absence of an all-embracing citizenship. The main factor behind this problem is the big religious divide in the region, which has been sustained over time by the complex interplay of a variety of social and cultural institutions. It has been argued here that industrial relations arrangements, mostly in the form of informal influences, did contribute, particularly during the Stormont years, to economic citizenship being truncated and deformed. More recently, however, active government initiatives, particularly the adoption of fair employment legilisation, have gone a long way to addressing this shortcoming in the *formal sense*. Industrial relations institutions formally promote an inclusive form of economic citizenship. Moreover, informal industrial relations processes can no longer be regarded as generating unequal status in the labour market. Yet for all these encouraging developments, a genuinely inclusive citizenship in Northern Ireland has yet to be established. The large political divisions that remain between the two communities continue to hold back other positive moves towards social integration. Northern

Ireland remains an unstable democracy, despite the overhaul of many social and economic institutions.

Regional or British Industrial Relations

A long-running controversy has been whether Northern Ireland should be fully integrated into a wider British system of industrial relations or whether it should develop its own regional labour market governance structures. In a number of papers, Black (1984; 1985; 1987) argues that in spite of a number of local peculiarities, Northern Ireland is essentially part of a wider British employment system. While this conclusion is broadly correct, it would be misleading to suggest that local arrangements are insignificant: Northern Ireland has a more developed institutional architecture for industrial relations than any other UK regions. Thus for instance there is the Labour Relations Agency which provides a more developed regional arbitration, conciliation and mediation service for the local economy than other parts of the UK. In addition, the only regional Equal Opportunities Commission in the UK exists in Northern Ireland. The same is also true for health and safety matters. Furthermore, the local Training and Employment Agency enjoys considerable autonomy in developing skill-formation policies. For instance, the strategy of the UK central government of creating local Training and Enterprise Councils (TECs) never crossed the Irish Sea.

Many of these distinctive, regional industrial relations institutions are a by-product of the Stormont years when Northern Ireland enjoyed devolved government: regional administrations have a propensity to create decentralised institutions to help manage economic and political affairs. Although Northern Ireland has been without a devolved institution for more than 20 years, an ethos of doing things differently still lingers. For instance, the strong anti-corporatist stance of successive Conservative governments has never been actively pursued in Northern Ireland. Local trade unions and employers still have an input into government decision making. At the same time, it is not at all apparent that these regional industrial relations institutions operate to maximum potential. First of all, there appears to be a lack of coordination between the various bodies. For example, many would be hard pressed to remember any policy collaboration between the Labour Relations Agency and the local Equal Opportunities Commissions. In addition, there is a relative dearth of innovatory regionally specific industrial relations policies. Local industrial relations institutions cannot be considered policy entrepreneurs eager to make full use of the autonomy they enjoy.

Despite having its own regional labour market institutions, Northern Ireland is tied in key ways to the wider UK system of industrial relations. Many of the legal rights and obligations governing the workplace in the region are set by Westminster. Over the years, collective bargaining in the region has been fully incorporated into the British system. Thus, for example, although important areas of the public sector in Northern Ireland, such as local government, have their own regional institutional structures for collective bargaining, these normally only act as *conduits* for the local introduction of agreements concluded in London: little attempt has been made to reach regional bargains on pay and terms and conditions. All sorts of other anomalies exist; for example many local civil servants are members of Northern Ireland-only trade unions, but this does not affect them being covered by national-level collective bargaining arrangements. Virtually every public sector worker in the region is governed by a UK-wide pay determination system.

In the 1980s, it was fashionable to argue that national collective bargaining in the public sector turned those on the government payroll in Northern Ireland into privileged insider employees. Public sector unions were incensed by the portrayal of their members as some new type of labour aristocracy. But this fury could not disguise the fact that public sector employment was on the whole more attractive than jobs in the private sector—there was a greater level of job security, pay was relatively good due to national pay bargaining, and prospects for training and career development were much better. But the 1990s have seen several significant changes to the employment system in the public sector. In the first place, contracting out and the introduction of quasi-markets in many parts of the government sector have put the squeeze on public sector employment. Moreover, job insecurity has increased, with many people uncertain about whether redundancy is just around the corner. In addition, because of cash limits and meagre pay awards, public sector productivity has grown rapidly. Few government workers are now capturing insider rents (obtaining wages in excess of productivity performance). A more accurate picture now is of public sector workers stretched to the limits. Thus even though a UK-wide system of employment rules still prevails, the relatively privileged position of public sector workers in Northern Ireland has been undermined.

For the most part, this new situation is the result of large-scale and on-going organisational change. In almost every sphere of public sector activity there has been a growth of autonomous organisational units with considerable capacity for independent action. So far, national collective bargaining has remained unaffected by these developments. But it is scarcely credible that this situation will last for much longer. The new breed of public sector managers that are now in control will soon be demanding scope to develop their own human resource management systems, un-hindered by national rules. In other words, UK public sector industrial relations are on the threshold of fragmentation, with far-reaching implications for Northern Ireland.

What is threatening to happen in the public sector has already occurred in the private sector. As a result of concerted action by Conservative governments, national pay bargaining in key parts of the private sector has collapsed. The effect has been far-reaching since it is no longer credible to talk about an organised system of industrial relations in the UK. Hardly any private sector workers in Northern Ireland are now covered by national collective bargaining deals. Decentralised, enterprise-level pay determination has become the norm. The impact of this new industrial relations environment has been considerable. From the early 1970s to the mid-1980s, private sector wages in Northern Ireland gradually converged with the UK average. But since the mid-1980s, this trend has been reversed and the pattern is now one of divergence. Private sector wages in Northern Ireland are not much lower than any other UK region (Dickens and Machin, 1995).

This development has been bad news for the private sector worker in Northern Ireland. Decentralised industrial relations have resulted in their real wages not keeping up with the UK trend, although they have increased in real terms. At the same time, the new low wage environment is likely to have contributed positively to the impressive employment growth in the region over the past six or seven years. By any standards, recent job generation figures have been impressive. In the main, service sector activity lies behind the recent increase in employment. Since the late 1980s, job growth in financial and business services has been growing at about 5–6 per cent a year. Jobs in other non-tradeable sectors, such as retailing, and hotel and catering, have also expanded rapidly. During the past decade, the number of jobs lost in manufacturing has outweighed the number of jobs created, but behind the aggregate total, the job market in this sector has behaved fairly erratically.

The factors behind this impressive performance are not fully under-stood. But it would be surprising if cheaper labour were not part of the equation. Certainly some aspects of the labour market appear to resemble an 'American'-style deregulated, flexible employment system. Evidence is emerging of much higher rates of turnover in many parts of the economy. Higher turnover rates cause unemployment inflows and outflows to be larger. Previously, if a person lost a job in Northern Ireland they would normally experience a lengthy spell of unemployment, if not a fall into long-term unemployment. But in recent years there has been an improve-ment in short-term joblessness rates. Thus a new pattern of labour market behaviour is emerging; although many workers are still prone to experiencing unemployment, they are more likely to leave it once they are there. People are getting jobs, leaving them more frequently, and returning to another job sooner. This is exactly the type of labour market behaviour that exists in the United States and it is closely associated with the widespread availability of low-wage, unskilled jobs.

This rise in flexible labour markets has raised concern about the regional economy falling into a low-skills, bad jobs trap. On the one hand, workers have little incentive to improve their human capital since relatively high skilled, well-paid jobs are not available, the private rates of return to education and training are low. On the other hand, firms do not provide good jobs either because they do not require a high skilled labour input or because there is a relative scarcity of well-trained people. When such market failures operate simultaneously on the demand and supply side, the labour market becomes locked into a low-skills equilibrium that makes it difficult for the economy to compete on the basis of high skilled, high value-added activity. The worry is that the poor quality of some of the new commercial activity may be turning the local economy into a site for low value-added and unskilled jobs.

Thus the decline of national collective bargaining systems has squeezed the equity dimension in the regional labour market. This should not be surprising as multi-tier collective bargaining tends to create an employment safety net by establishing a floor of workers' rights. With the breaking up of this floor, the regional labour market has become monopsonistic in character, it operates as a captive market for employers. Restoring an acceptable balance between labour market equity and efficiency in Northern Ireland will be difficult. One option is to include the region in a UK-wide collective bargaining system. But after nearly two decades of Conservative rule, it is hard to see how an organised national system of employee relations can be restored in the UK: the shift towards decentralised pay determination appears irreversible.

In the short term, perhaps the only way equity can be restored in the Northern Ireland private sector is if the Labour government introduces a minimum wage. Many uncertainties exist about the implementation of a minimum wage in the UK. One controversy concerns the rate at which the minimum wage should be introduced. At the time of writing, the Low Pay Unit is calling for a rate of £4.80 per hour, while the TUC figure is £4.40. Other calculations suggest a lower rate. For instance, if the average basic hourly earnings level of Wage Councils before abolition is updated, the minimum wage would be £3.20. Figure 1 sets out the number of Northern Ireland workers in certain sectors covered by the minimum wage at various rates. If a minimum wage was introduced at £4.50, approximately the TUC

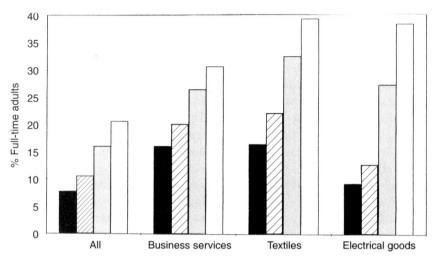

Figure 1. Percentage of full-time adults in Northern Ireland earning less than the specified hourly rates (1996 £). ■■■ £3.60, ⊿⊿⊿ £3.80, ▭ £4.20, ▭ £4.50.

figure, the impact on Northern Ireland would be enormous. Nearly 40 per cent of all workers in textiles and electrical goods would be covered by the policy. This is totally out of line with the labour force coverage of minimum wages in most European economies where only about 7–8 per cent of workers are affected by such arrangements. To approximate to the European norm would mean setting a rate of about £3.60 for Northern Ireland, but even then the impact on individual low pay sectors would be considerable. Overall, a minimum wage is likely to have a greater impact on Northern Ireland than any other part of the UK such is the low level of private sector wages. Clearly careful attention would have to be given to how this policy would impact on job creation.

Overall, two points arise from the above analysis. One is that existing regional industrial relations institutions under-perform. In the literature, a range of positive benefits are seen as arising from regional forms of labour market governance: employment policies are more in line with the needs of enterprises, and public institutions can contribute more to the formation of trust relations between employers and workers. But industrial relations institutions fail to create such an environment in Northern Ireland. The other is that the fragmentation of the UK system of collective bargaining has weakened the equity dimension in the regional labour market. As a result, Northern Ireland needs a new balance betwen equity and efficiency in its employment system. For this to happen, both the regional and British components to the industrial relations system need reform: thus these two components are not in collision but are actually complementary and potentially mutually reinforcing. Of course, behind this argument is the view that it is preferable to have an industrial relations system that at once improves the competitiveness of the local economy and increases the living standards of citizens in the region. But it is far from certain that this system will arise. An equally plausible scenario is that industrial relations in the region will remain lacklustre.

Conclusions

Clearly, there are similarities between the industrial relations systems, North and South. The frequency of strikes and industrial disputes have been declining in both economies; trade unions find it difficult to recruit atypical workers in the two parts of the island; companies each side of the border are concerned with the impact of labour market rules on corporate competitiveness. While important, these similarities should not be over-stated as they are trends common to virtually all European economies. These shared patterns can be regarded as exogenous influences that are pushing industrial relations systems in the same direction. Beyond these common features, large differences remain between the two industrial relations systems on the island.

At root, two factors account for the distinctiveness of labour market governance in the two Irish economies. One is that whereas the Republic is a national system of industrial relations, the North is only a regional system. This difference has considerable implications for the organising capabilities of both trade unions and employer organisations, the type of trade-offs that can be made between pay bargaining and wider economic policy objectives, and the range of incentives and constraints that can be created by industrial relations institutions. In other words, national sovereignty has a big impact on the institutional architecture and key dynamics of an industrial relations system. The other main source of difference between the two industrial relations systems is that one part of the island is a stable political democracy and the other is not. In the Republic, the enactment of the national pay deals has been made easier by the high level of legitimacy enjoyed by the political system. Not only has this legitimacy been absent from Northern Ireland, but industrial relations arrangements have become intertwined with both the lack of inclusive citizenship and the search for a more stable form of governance in the region. The result is that the character, texture and orientation of the industrial relations systems on the island are quite contrasting.

This assessment has implications for the topical debate about promoting closer institutional links between the two economies. For the over-riding message is that borders continue to matter, at least in relation to labour market management. Claims that economic globalisation, along with European integration, are washing away national boundaries, whether in Ireland or wherever, should be treated with scepticism. Borders have not atrophied largely because they signify that national territories still create the necessary institutional and social structures for economic and commercial activities. Frontiers represent the end of one economic and social order and the beginning of another. The German economic system is different from that of France which in turn contrasts with the organisation of economic activity in Britain.

Thus even with the undoubted rise of economic globalisation, national systems are not obsolete. Actually, basic economic theory tells us why this should not be surprising. The consensus now in economic theory is that markets are decentralised and characterised by limited information. In this situation buyers and sellers cannot explore all possible transactions and thus usually only explore a restricted number of commercial deals. As a result, close and repeated 'customer' connections emerge between buyers and sellers, which normally give rise to long-term relationships. Thus although decentralised markets are fragmented and incomplete they are frequently associated with established social relations that sustain long-term relationships and which compensate for limited information and high levels of uncertainty. In other words, decentralised markets are usually socially embedded. Moreover, because full information is absent, decentralised markets cannot be seen as self-clearing; on many occasions they fail. When market failures occur, institutional interventions, normally in the form of government policies, become necessary to avoid distortions. This is the classical reason why governments have to create public goods in areas such as education, health and transport. Thus decentralised markets are also institutionally embedded. Institutional and social support structures to organise and sustain decentralised markets are normally formed within distinct national territories. Economic structure and national institutional and social processes become contiguous.

One manifestation of this coincidence is the idea of distinct national models of economic and social developments. Sometimes the notion of national models is used in a fairly vacuous way, but developed properly it can yield penetrating insights. It can show how different bargains emerge, and are sustained between different economic and social interests—for example between industrial and financial capital. It can highlight how different forms of economic and social citizenship arise in different national contexts. The way people are incorporated into work—the skills they possess and the rights they enjoy—are quite diverse in Britain and Germany for example. Some countries have a more comprehensive welfare state than others, with their citizens prepared to pay the price in terms of higher taxes. Thus although we live in a global era, which generates common pressures across countries, there is still considerable diversity to national economic and social life.

This analysis has important implications for the current debate about the potential for North-South economic cooperation. For it suggests, at least for labour market governance, that far-reaching programmes to bring the two economies together may not succeed. Partly this is because the industrial relations institutions are so different. It is hard to envisage how genuine coordination could be secured between the two systems without root and branch institutional change either in the North or South, or perhaps even both. Another factor is that the two industrial relations systems are directly tied to contrasting models of economic and social citizenship. Therefore, obtaining close labour market coordination between the two parts of the island may involve undermining the economic and political sovereignty of one of the jurisdictions. Thus without major constitutional change, only relatively low level, ad hoc connections between the North and South appear feasible.

References

Black, B. (1984) 'Trade Union Democracy and Northern Ireland—a Note', *The Industrial Law Journal*, 3(4): 443–7.

Black, B. (1985) 'Collective Bargaining Structure in Northern Ireland: Dimensions, Determinants and Developments', *Journal of the Statistical and Social Inquiry Society of Ireland*, XXV(2): 69–85.

Black, B. (1987) 'Collaboration on Conflict—Strike Activity in Northern Ireland', *Industrial Relations Journal*, 18(1): 84–102.

Boyd, A. (1984) *Have the Trade Unions Failed the North?*, Dublin: Mercier.

Cradden, T. (1993) *Trade Unionism, Socialism and Participation: the Labour Movement in Northern Ireland*, Belfast: December Publications.

Dickens, R. and Machin, S. (1995) 'Minimum Wages in Britain: Issues Involved in Setting a Minimum Wage', in TUC, *Arguments for a National Minimum Wage*, London: TUC.

Durkin, J. (1992) 'Social Consensus and Income Policy', *Economic and Social Review*, 23(3): 347–63.

Easterly, W. (1996) 'When is Stabilisation Expansionary? Evidence from High Inflation', *Economic Policy*, 22: 65–108.

FEC (1995) *Annual Report*, Belfast: FEC.

Fitoussi, J. P. (1995) *Le débat interdit, Monnaie, Europe, Pauvreté*, Paris: Editions Orléan.

Flanders, A. (1968) *Trade Unions*, London: Hutchinson.

Fogarty, M. (1969) *Report of the Committee on Industrial Relations in the Electricity Supply Board*, Dublin: Stationary Office.

Hardiman, N. (1988) *Pay, Politics and Economic Performance in Ireland, 1970–1987*, Oxford: Clarendon Press.

Hardiman, N. (1992) 'The State and Economic Interests', in J. Goldthorpe and C. T. Whelan (eds), *The Development of Industrial Society in Ireland*, Oxford: Oxford University Press.

Kochan, T. and Osterman, P. (1994) *Towards the Mutual Gains Enterprise*, Cambridge, Mass.: Harvard University Press.

McCarthy, C. (1975) 'Workers' Participation in Ireland: Problems and Strategies', *Administration*, 23(2): 97–121.

McCartney, J. and Teague, P. (1997) 'Workplace Innovation in the Republic of Ireland, School of Public Policy, Economics and Law', University of Ulster, mimeograph.

Monks, K. (1996) 'Global or Local? HRM in the Multinational Company: The Irish Experience', *International Journal of Human Resource Management*, 7(3): 721–35.

Roche W. K. and Geary, J. (1994) 'Attenuation of "Host Country Effects"? Multi-nationals, Industrial Relations and Collective Bargaining in Ireland', Working Paper IR-HRM No. 94–5, Graduate School of Business, University College Dublin.

Roche, W. (1994) 'Industrialisation and the Development of Industrial Relations', in T. Murphy and W. Roche, *Irish Industrial Relations in Practice*, Dublin: Oak Tree Press.

Rowthorn, R. E. (1992) 'Centralisation, Employment and Wage Dispersion', *Economic Journal*, 102(3): 506–23.

Sabel, C. (1993) 'Decentralised Production Systems and Trust Relations', Cambridge Mass,: Department of Politics, MIT, mimeograph.

Sabel, C. (1994) 'Learning by Monitoring: the Institutions of Economic Development', in N. Smelser and R. Swedbeg (eds), *Handbook of Economic Sociology*, Princeton: Sage.

Schmitter, P. and Streck, W. (1985) 'Community, Market State—and Associations? The Prospective Contribution of Interest Governance to Social Order', in W. Streck and P. Schimitter (eds), *Private Interest Government*, London: Sage.

Shuttleworth, I. (1994) 'An Analysis of Community Differences in the Pilot Northern Ireland Secondary Education Leavers Survey', Research Report, No. 3, Belfast: CCRU.

Teague, P. (1995) 'Pay Determination in the Republic of Ireland: Towards Social Corporatism', *British Journal of Industrial Relations*, 33(2): 372–401.

Tomlinson, M. (1980) 'The Limits of Trade Unionism', in L. O'Dowd, B. Rolston and M. Tomlinson, *Northern Ireland: Between Civil Rights and Civil War*, London: Pluto Press.

Walsh, B. (1993) 'Credibility, Debt and the ERM: the Irish Experience', *Oxford Bulletin of Economics and Statistics*, 55(3): 512–31.

Whyte, J. (1991) *Interpreting Northern Ireland*, Oxford: Clarendon Press.

Nationalism and the Continuation of Political Conflict in Ireland

BRIAN GIRVIN

The Persistence of Nationalism

ONE OF THE CENTRAL QUESTIONS OF POLITICAL THEORY has been how societies can achieve a level of accommodation which would provide for the stability of the political system while at the same time allowing for political change. In liberal democratic societies achieving this aim may be difficult unless most voters accept some minimum set of rules about how the political system should function (Girvin, 1994b). In the absence of such agreement, it may be impossible for a political system to evolve peacefully. National-ism can provide one of the strongest sources for political legitimacy but it may be the main source of instability if national identity or sovereignty are in dispute. Mill (1861: 207–8) suggested that at least three conditions are required to achieve stable norms:

> The people for whom the form of government is intended must be willing to accept it; or at least not so unwilling as to oppose an insurmountable obstacle to its establishment. They must be willing and able to do what is necessary to keep it standing. And they must be willing and able to do what it requires of them to enable it to fulfil its purposes. The word 'do' is to be understood as including forbearances as well as acts. They must be capable of fulfilling the conditions of action, and the conditions of self-restraint, which are necessary either for keeping the established polity in existence, or for enabling it to achieve the ends, its conduciveness to which forms its recommendation.

In the contemporary world, the most likely source for undermining these conditions is nationalism, and to a lesser degree religion and race.

This view has been rejected for post-war western Europe by some writers (Deutsch, 1953; Dogan, 1994; Kearney, 1997), but nationalism and national identity continue to provide an essential building block for political stability. Some studies on nationalism confuse the absence of

Proceedings of the British Academy, **98**, 369–399. © The British Academy 1999.

conflict over nationalism with the disappearance of nationalism (for criticism see Kellas, 1991; Connor, 1994: 28–66). An alternative approach takes the view that nationalism is now a universal phenomenon and will remain so, even in Western Europe. The reason for this is that nationalism provides a sense of political identity and emotional satisfaction for the vast majority of people which no other political value does. Moreover, with its emphasis on community, territory and sovereignty, nationalism offers a source of moral superiority to its members, expressed through patriotism.

There are a number of features which characterise nationalism. The first of these is its universal nature. Though each nationalism is particularist in its historical origin, all nationalisms share common features. There are recurrent themes in each variety of nationalism, including distinctness, common origin, shared history and unique traits. Secondly, all nations claim special rights as a consequence of nationality. This is a very powerful emotional tool for nationalism when challenging a numerical majority in a state. Though a numerical minority in a state, a nation will claim special recognition for its status as a nation. On this basis, it will argue that the statistical basis for making decisions must be the majority of the nation *not* the state.[1] Once nationalism has acquired moral superiority in respect of other political forms, it will become the means by which all political communities express political demands. This process is ineluctable, otherwise a community will be designated a cultural minority within a state and will not gain the rights usually ascribed to nations. If the only method of acquiring rights is through the assertion of nationality, then the likelihood is that when a majority and minority culture clash within a state each will claim sovereignty and self determination on the basis of its nationality. This process has accelerated in the course of the twentieth century and is likely to continue.[2]

That nationalism has not been exhausted in Western Europe can be appreciated from the importance of nationalist political movements in Scotland and Catalonia, and from the deep regional divisions which affect Belgium and Italy. Moreover, it would be mistaken to ignore the latent influence of nationalism in either Germany or France. Yet nowhere is the influence of nationalism more potent than in Ireland. Whether in Northern Ireland or in the Irish Republic, nationalism seems to retain its emotional

---

[1] This tension between the majority in a state and a majority nationality within a region of a state can give rise to conflicting notions of legitimacy. This is of particular importance in Northern Ireland, but can be appreciated from other examples such as Quebec in Canada.

[2] This discussion is based on a review of the literature on nationalism. Important contributions are Gellner, 1983; Kellas, 1991; Connor, 1994; Smith, 1991; Hutchinson, 1994; Hutchinson and Smith, 1994; Anderson, 1991; Giddens, 1985; Llobera, 1994. This is not an exhaustive list, as the literature is now expanding exponentially.

strength even when, as in the latter case, it is a force for stability rather than division. Nor in this context should the relevance of national identity be ignored in the British case; not only is this true of Scotland but it also has a resonance in England and Wales. The Irish case is not unique, although the conflict in Northern Ireland may be seen to be because of the violence. This conflict can be understood as a by-product of the particular historical circumstances which led to the growth of political nationalism in modern Ireland. This historical sequence established the context within which nationalism can contribute to either stability or instability in very similar sets of circumstances.

History and Identity in Ireland

The appearance of nationalism and unionism in Ireland reflected one possible outcome in the process of modernisation and democratisation which characterised Europe from the middle of the eighteenth century. Prior to this time, identities were often localised and linked to discrete (and often overlapping) cultures (Kearney, 1989). In Ireland, three distinct sub-cultures can be identified: Catholic, Presbyterian and Anglican. Each of them had a distinct history, and in the case of Presbyterians were concentrated in the north-east of the island. Nationalists (Gallagher, 1957; Lemass, 1959; Adams, 1986) have argued that all those who live on the island are members of the Irish nation and that state formation should reflect this. Unionists have challenged this view (Foster, 1995; Porter, 1996), emphasising the distinct and separate evolution of Protestant Ireland. Nationalism and unionism are engaged in different exercises in this argument. Unionists focus on actual outcome and draw attention to the existing political divisions in Ireland. Nationalists engage in a thought experiment involving the belief that unity is (and was) possible if the right circumstances exist(ed). Whatever merit there may be in what might have been, the important question is why the current situation remains so polarised.

Outcomes are never inevitable, but decisions taken at particular historical moments can affect how the outcome will look. In the Irish case a number of features can be identified. Among the most important is the failure of the English crown to successfully integrate Ireland into its state. In this respect Ireland is different from Scotland and Wales, regions which were successfully integrated. The Reformation further compromised relations between the English and the Irish, giving divisions a decidedly religious flavour by the seventeenth century (Ellis, 1991; Lennon, 1994). The wars of the seventeenth century compounded these divisions, creating, as Bradshaw (1988/89; 1994) has argued, the core historical myths for both the Irish Catholic and the Ulster Protestant. The crucial moment, however, may have been the failure to realise Wolf Tone's objective of uniting the three religious sub-cultures in a common national movement in the 1790s (Elliott, 1989; Curtin, 1994). Not only was this period a fluid one politically, but it also coincided with the dawn of nationalism as a political movement. If, and it is a big if, a unified political movement had been successful, a single Irish nationality might have emerged (Girvin, 1994c: 53–81).

This did not prove to be the case and the Act of Union integrated Ireland institutionally into the British state. However, due to the Protestant nature of the British state Catholic grievances were not addressed and this alienated significant sections of Catholic opinion. Daniel O'Connell successfully mobilised Catholic opinion by emphasising religious issues while linking them to nationalist aims (Girvin, 1991). The nature of this movement excluded most Irish Protestants, though this was not O'Connell's intention. By the 1830s Irish nationalism had taken on the form it was to maintain thereafter. It was democratic, Catholic in composition (but not essentially priest ridden), anti-British and separatist in aims. It was also a political movement which was predominantly English speaking, anti-liberal and with a strong rural social base (Hindley, 1990; Girvin, 1997). Irish Catholicism may have been unusual in the nineteenth century, but Irish nationalism was the model for many other subsequent types of nationalism (Kellas, 1991). For the most part the appeal of Irish nationalism has been limited to Catholics and its imaginative reach (Anderson, 1991) has never extended to the Protestant population in the north-east.[3]

While the majority of Catholics became nationalists by the 1830s, the majority of Protestants became unionist in the sense that they believed that political and institutional arrangements should be maintained within the British state. However, this was not simply a relationship to the union as an institution, but reflected the growth of a British consciousness among Protestants, especially those in the north-east (Gibbon, 1975; Miller, 1978; Coulter, 1994). It was relatively easy for Presbyterians and Anglicans to become British as it was possible for them to identify with what Colley (1992: 5–8) characterises as the main features of Britishness: the monarchy, Protestantism, the Empire and patriotism. Ulster Protestants could share in notions of Britishness while remaining Irish in the same way that the Scots and Welsh could. For them, at least, there appeared to be no contradiction between being Irish and British (Robbins, 1990: 4–18). The richness of Ulster Protestant history has yet to be integrated into an understanding

---

[3] Individual Protestants have, of course, been nationalists, but were probably rarer than unionist Catholics.

of the Irish historical process, and this prevents a deeper appreciation of the complexities of the relationship between the two main identities in Ireland. A contrast should be drawn, however, between the Anglican ascendancy which dominated the Catholic majority in the southern regions and the Presbyterian majority in the north-east. The Presbyterians were a self-conscious, independent and distinct culture. Strong links with Scotland provided a cultural milieu which allowed for autonomous political development independent of London or Dublin. In religion, politics, culture and trade Presbyterian Ulster was more like Scotland than Ireland or England (Brooke, 1987; McBride, 1993; Walker, 1995).[4]

What nationalist writers have often failed to recognise (see Lee, 1989: 1–14) is that the attractions of nationality were just as strong among Ulster Protestants as Irish Catholics. They were expressed in different terms, but unless one wishes to deny the legitimacy of these attributes they need to be recognised. For some writers (Anderson, 1980; Adams, 1986) Ulster Protestants do not constitute a nationality, for others (Whyte, 1978; Ruane and Todd, 1996) any such claim has limited application. Yet this is to ignore the political reality that Ulster unionism has provided consistent evidence for its political difference from nationalist Ireland. Electoral politics as early as the 1830s reflected the tensions between nationalism and unionism in Ulster (Coakley, 1986) and this was to continue through-out the century. When Home Rule appeared in the 1880s, Ulster Protes-tants quickly developed a self-conscious notion of separateness from Irish nationalism, a clear identification with Britain and a distinct sense of themselves in Ulster (Heslinga, 1971; Hennessey, 1993). McBride (1996: 1–18) emphasises the importance of the association between Ulster and Britishness at this time: 'The invention of "Ulster" as a separate entity, endowed with particular characteristics and virtues, constitutes one of the central themes of the period.' While nobody denies the existence of an Irish nation with specific rights, there is an extreme reluctance to concede such status to the Ulster Protestants (Whyte, 1978: 262–3; Ruane and Todd, 1996: 82; however see Gallagher, 1990; 1995 for an alternative view). The available evidence suggests that there has never been a single nation on the island of Ireland, that when an Irish nationalism did emerge it was predominantly Catholic and that another distinct nationality emerged in the northern area which considered itself to be Irish (or Ulster), British and overwhelmingly Protestant. This leads to a further conclusion; that is that partition in Ireland predates the political arrangements of the

---

[4] I have stressed Presbyterianism in this section because of its crucial contribution to the creation of the identity of the Ulster Protestant. Such an emphasis is not intended to exclude Anglican or other Protestant denominations from consideration.

early 1920s. What the Government of Ireland Act 1920 and the 1922 Treaty settlement did was institutionalise an already existing social and political reality. That Irish nationalism has refused subsequently to accept partition is closely linked to the refusal to recognise a separate nationality in Northern Ireland.[5]

Irish Nationalism After 1922

Partition did not resolve the conflict in Ireland, but it did change its nature. It became more polarised and sectarian. Both sides failed to achieve what they had sought to do before 1914, but neither did they fully accept the outcome in 1920 or 1922. Britain changes most after 1920; the state distanced itself from the Irish question in the belief that most outstanding difficulties had in fact been resolved. Nationalists however, were outraged at the outcome. Despite any evidence to the contrary, nationalists continued to insist that the island of Ireland should be a single political unit. The island was considered to be a 'natural' unit unjustly divided by the British. From the Home Rule period to the War of Independence, Irish nationalism in all its expressions refused to acknowledge that a distinct community existed within Ireland which refused in turn to acknowledge the Irish nationalist version of history (Saorstat Eireann, 1923; Gallagher, 1957; Adams, 1986)

Though the two parts of Ireland developed in quite different ways after 1920, the nationalist insistence on sovereignty and the alienation of Northern Irish Catholics from the Unionist government combined to weaken the possibility of accommodation between North and South and within the North. Nor did the actions of the Unionist government after 1920 contribute to creating the conditions in Northern Ireland for consensus or conciliation. In retrospect, Direct Rule from Westminster would have been a more appropriate policy for such a divided region. Yet considerable possibilities for accommodation did exist, especially after the Irish civil war and the establishment of the first Cumann na nGaedheal government after the 1923 general election. Garvin (1996: 183–5) has shown that W. T. Cosgrave accepted the right of the North to remain outside the Free State. He accepted this reluctantly and with regret, but nevertheless his government's policy was to pursue a policy based on Northern Ireland remaining in the United Kingdom. The foreign policy of the new state implicitly upheld this position until Fianna Fáil's election in 1932 (Harkness, 1969). Cumann na nGaedheal were realists, believing

---

[5] I discuss the nature of unionist nationalism in more detail below, in particular the approach taken by Gallagher (1995).

that more could be achieved by negotiation and by defending the Treaty than by destabilising the politics of Northern Ireland. This effective recognition of the North and the possibilities it held out was undermined by the Irish government's mishandling of the Boundary commission, by a failure to insist on repartition and by the success of Fianna Fáil in providing a more nationalist alternative to the incumbent government by 1932 (Girvin, 1989; 1999).

Fianna Fáil rejected the underlying assumptions of the Free State, especially those in respect of Northern Ireland. De Valera had little understanding and no sympathy for Irish unionists (Coogan, 1993; Garvin, 1996). In contrast with the liberal constitutionalism of the outgoing government, de Valera redefined the character of the Free State by making it more Catholic, nationalist and Gaelic. In articles 2 and 3 of the 1937 Constitution, de Valera effectively withdrew the recognition of Northern Ireland and insisted on the unification of the entire island under Dublin's jurisdiction. This remained the official position of successive Irish governments until May 1998, though as discussed below, the emphasis had already changed prior to this. After de Valera's retirement in 1959, his successor Seán Lemass, while moderating his approach, continued to insist on the integrity of the island. However, the main difference between Lemass and de Valera is important. De Valera was inflexible on Northern Ireland, a simple assertion of right seemed adequate for him. In contrast, Lemass recognised the complex loyalties which existed and understood that traditional nationalism had failed to either undermine the unionist government or to attract the unionist population into a united Ireland. Moreover, Lemass became Taoiseach at a time when the Irish Republic was suffering unprecedented economic dislocation. The response to this had economic and political consequences for the future of the Republic, but it also opened the opportunity for a more innovative and conciliatory approach to Northern Ireland for the first time in thirty years (Girvin, 1997).

The changes which took place in the Republic during the 1960s are significant and include a greater openness to the Orange and Unionist traditions; for example 12th of July marches were reported as cultural events for a short period, unthinkable since the early 1970s. The exchange of visits between Taoiseach and Prime Minister reflected this openness further, although Lemass was in a stronger position politically to do so than Terence O'Neill (Herz, 1986; Cochrane, 1996). Perhaps the most important departure was the willingness to reconsider the nature of the Irish Constitution. The Committee on the Constitution (1967) recommended that significant changes should be considered, and that the claim to jurisdiction over Northern Ireland should be revised. The importance of

this discussion can be overrated. Public opinion remained solidly nationalist, even while reform was being considered. The fiftieth anniversary of
1916 served to remind nationalists and unionists of their differences,
rather than what they had in common (Keogh, 1994: 284). Furthermore,
changing attitudes in the Republic were restricted to a fairly narrow elite.
Outside of this elite, more traditional views were dominant, though they
were no longer asserted with the conviction of de Valera. The breakdown
of public order in Northern Ireland in 1969 dissolved any consensus in
the Republic for decisive change. The primordial nationalist consensus
quickly came into play (Smith, 1991) and public opinion identified with
the nationalist population under threat in the North. What is of interest
after 1969 in the North and the South is how quickly each community
identified with its historical culture and mobilised in terms of this
relationship. Between 1969 and 1973 views hardened within Northern
Ireland and between North and South. Ironically, the most significant
adaptation during these years took place in Britain, where there was
increasing support for the withdrawal of British troops from Northern
Ireland (Hayes and McAllister, 1996: 65–70).

Within the Republic the onset of conflict and violence destabilised the
political system. Fianna Fáil was most seriously affected by this as it was in
government and was also the most nationalist of the political parties (Joyce
and Murtagh, 1983; Lee, 1989; Keogh, 1994). Serious divisions emerged in
the party around the issue of how to respond to the escalating violence. It is
possible to identify a number of possible approaches to the question within
nationalism by the middle of the 1970s. The most extreme would involve
the active support for the IRA by the Dublin government. There is some
evidence to suggest that arms were shipped to the IRA and a number of
former Fianna Fáil cabinet ministers were charged, and then acquitted, of
complicity in such action (Keogh, 1994: 306–14). Another option, and one
not inconsistent with the first, would have involved sending the Irish army
into Northern Ireland in the event of a major crisis. In 1970 some 17 per
cent interviewed in the Republic believed that this might be necessary
under certain circumstances. However, on the one occasion when popular
opinion might have sustained such a move, after Bloody Sunday in 1972,
the government decided not to pursue such action. This confirms a long-
standing feature of liberal democracy, that democratic states do not go to
war with one another (Russett, 1993). Other approaches from within a
nationalist framework included United Nations deployment, repartition
and British withdrawal, all of which received some support during this
time. The more moderate nationalist approaches included revising the
Constitution, reforming aspects of Irish society and generally making the
Republic more attractive to Northern Protestants. While moderate nation-

alists sought to attract unionists into a united Ireland the more traditional view usually involved an element of coercion (Fitzgerald, 1973).

Opinion in the Republic during the 1970s may have been more volatile and hard-line in relation to the North than is sometimes suggested (see Davis and Sinnott, 1979), with some polls reporting that as many as one in five were prepared to support violence in Northern Ireland. However, the strategy of the Fianna Fáil government up to 1973 and the coalition government which succeeded it (1973–77) involved containing violence within Northern Ireland, supporting the nationalist minority there and negotiating a 'solution' with the British government. There is little evidence that at the level of the political elites any significant change had taken place in respect of traditional nationalist aims or objectives. A survey of the parliamentary elite in 1973/74 (Sinnott, 1986: 15–31) highlighted some differences between the main parties. Fianna Fáil members were more likely to emphasise British withdrawal and improving the Irish economy to make the Republic more attractive to unionists. No Fianna Fáil respondent was prepared to de-emphasise the goal of Irish unity, whereas 46 per cent of Fine Gael and 36 per cent of Labour respondents were. Another significant difference is evident in respect of the IRA; whereas 35 per cent of Fine Gael and 27 per cent of Labour respondents considered action against the IRA to be a central feature of Northern policy, 3 per cent of Fianna Fáil took this view (see also Cohan, 1977).

Although these are elite responses, they are important in that political elites are frequently in a position to implement their policy priorities. The tension between elite and popular opinion was highlighted when a Fine Gael-Labour coalition government was elected in 1973. Fianna Fáil was highly critical of government policy for much of this time, but was incensed by the position taken by Conor Cruise O'Brien on Northern Ireland. O'Brien became Minister for Posts and Telegraphs in the new government and proved to be the most persistent critic of Irish nationalism between 1973 and 1977 (Akenson, 1994: 374–425). O'Brien's book *States of Ireland* (1972) provided the cornerstone for his criticism, while his subsequent intervention in controversy changed the nature of the debate in the Republic. He challenged the self-image of Irish nationalism, claiming that Irish unity could not be achieved without violence and that in any event there would be a violent backlash from the unionist population to prevent this happening. In effect, O'Brien was claiming that one of the main objectives of Irish nationalism should be abandoned. He further outraged opinion by highlighting the denominational nature of Irish nationalism and the Catholic ethos of the Irish state. His intervention led to accusations that he was 'anti-national' and a unionist (Murphy, 1978: 156–60; Hume, 1980/81). In contrast to O'Brien, Garret FitzGerald

(1973) provided a more moderate, if still nationalist, approach but one which sought reconciliation. O'Brien and FitzGerald agreed on the need to defeat the IRA and protect the state, but they drew radically different conclusions from their respective surveys of history, especially in respect of policy towards Northern Ireland (FitzGerald, 1982)

At the very time when this debate was underway, a survey in Dublin (MacGréil, 1977) identified some changes in popular opinion. Some 27.5 per cent of respondents agreed that the British army are 'cruel and brutal', 36 per cent claimed not to like the British government, while 17 per cent would be happy if Britain 'were brought to her knees'. Over a third believed that violence was necessary 'for the achievement of non-Unionist Rights', while a majority agreed that unity was required to obtain a just solution to the conflict. Paradoxically, over 40 per cent considered that Northern Ireland and the Republic constituted two separate nations. University educated respondents and those in higher professional positions were more likely to endorse the use of violence and to reject the existence of separate nations. Yet these same groups were less willing to support a 32 county republic and were more open to federal options. There was also a gender difference; women were more likely to believe that two nations existed and less likely to endorse violence. What is surprising given the levels of violence at this time is that the 'nationalist' questions did not receive stronger support (MacGréil, 1977: 336–81).

Despite the polling evidence, there was little change in government policy during the 1970s. All parties in the Republic seemed mesmerised by the escalating violence in Northern Ireland and by the failure to achieve a settlement or an agreed government there. The failure of the power-sharing executive in 1974 hardened nationalist attitudes to the British government and the unionist population. FitzGerald (1991: 234–44) suggests that the British army could have broken the Ulster Workers Council (UWC) strike, but does not address O'Brien's view (1994: 165–7) that the insistence on the Council of Ireland provided the basis for weakening Protestant support for Brian Faulkner (Girvin, 1986a: 121–5). While power-sharing failed, it also provided some evidence for changing attitudes. Some sections of unionism had wished for accommodation, though this search was weakened by divisions within the political community. For the first time since the 1920s an Irish government had recognised the status of Northern Ireland, even if this was a rather qualified acceptance. In particular, the Irish government accepted that change in Northern Ireland had to be based on the stated wishes of the majority before the status could be changed. This posed a dilemma for Irish nationalism and government policy. It remained clear that the overwhelming majority of Protestants and some Catholics wished to retain the union (Rose, 1971;

Moxon-Browne, 1983), but if this were to be recognised how were Protestants to be persuaded to accept a united Ireland? In contrast to the IRA, constitutional nationalists were opposed to the direct coercion of unionism, but by the end of the 1970s there was a belief that the British should play a more active role in persuading unionists that their future should be in a united Ireland.

The Failure of Traditional Irish Nationalism

By the end of the 1970s the nationalism of de Valera and of the Independence generation had failed to either persuade the British to leave Northern Ireland, the unionists to accept a united Ireland, or to protect nationalist communities from Protestant extremists. The IRA argued that constitutional nationalists could not achieve nationalist goals and only a war of liberation could assure success (O'Malley, 1983: 258–88). In contrast to this, O'Brien called for the abandonment of the entire project. Neither of these positions received support from the Republic's population, though Mair (1987b: 90–1) reports on polls between 1978 and 1984 which found that a third or more of respondents admired the ideals and motives of the IRA, but disapproved of their methods. Consequently there was considerable ambiguity among nationalists about how to proceed. One response was to modify the traditional nationalist approach. A neo-traditional strategy was adopted by John Hume and Charles Haughey which involved persuading the British government that it should no longer guarantee the union between Northern Ireland and Britain. The reasoning behind this approach was that once the guarantee was removed the unionists would negotiate a settlement (Hume, 1980/81; Hume in O'Malley, 1983: 100–6). This was accompanied by a demand for British withdrawal leading to Irish unity by the SDLP and Fianna Fáil (Haughey in Mansergh, 1986: 327–38; 450–81; Girvin, 1994a: 18–22). These policies were vigorously prosecuted by Haughey when he became Taoiseach in 1979 and maintained throughout the early 1980s, a period of considerable tension due to the H-Blocks campaign and the Falklands War.

However, another approach to this question also appeared within Irish nationalism. A more moderate and gradualist position, often associated with Garret FitzGerald and Fine Gael, emphasised the need for reconciliation, for changes in the Republic to make the state more attractive to Protestants and for a less confrontational stance in respect of Britain. In 1981 FitzGerald launched his 'constitutional crusade' in an attempt to transform Irish political culture and reform the constitution. While there was some support for the initiative in general, most of the polls carried out

in 1981 indicated that on specific issues opinion remained quite conservative. Thus, while a plurality considered that FitzGerald had the best policy
on Northern Ireland (39 per cent), a majority believed that constitutional
change would not improve prospects for a united Ireland and 46 per cent
disapproved of any change in the claim over Northern Ireland in the
constitution (*Sunday Tribune*/IMS Poll, 1981). FitzGerald, in the event,
was unable to achieve his objectives even when he formed a stable government in 1982. Fianna Fáil remained resolutely opposed to change and in
the referendums on abortion in 1983 and on divorce in 1986 a majority of
those who voted did so to maintain or extend the denominational nature
of the Constitution (Girvin, 1993).

A further setback for FitzGerald's reformist nationalism occurred with
the publication of the New Ireland Forum Report (1984). The bipartisan
nature of the Forum and the need to sustain the SDLP against the electoral
challenge of Sinn Féin led to the primacy of neo-traditionalism over more
moderate approaches in the final report. Although the report produced
three options for the future of Ireland, Haughey insisted (*Irish Times*, 24
May 1984) that the unitary option was the 'only option which will bring
peace and stability'. In fact, FitzGerald also favoured this option, though
he recognised that this might not prove attractive to unionists (*Irish Times*,
7 May 1984). Despite this, subsequent developments highlighted the differences between neo-traditionalism and moderate nationalism by the mid-
1980s. Whereas Fianna Fáil and the SDLP continued to demand British
withdrawal and Irish unity, the Fine Gael/Labour government maintained
close contacts with the British government on issues such as extradition,
border security and general cooperation. This continuing process laid the
framework for the successful negotiation of the Anglo-Irish Agreement in
1985 (Girvin, 1986b; O'Leary, 1987; FitzGerald, 1991: 460–550).

The Anglo-Irish Agreement is the point of departure for the changing
relationship between neo-traditionalism and moderate nationalism in the
Republic, between North and South and between Britain and Ireland. The
detail of the Agreement has been examined extensively elsewhere (Girvin,
1986b; 1994a; Mair, 1987b), but its significance has been greatest for the
Republic. When the Agreement was signed the Tanaiste, Dick Spring,
claimed that it 'goes beyond a right to consult or be consulted'. The Irish
state for the first time gained considerable leverage within Northern
Ireland. The relationship between the Irish state and Britain also changed
out of recognition; in effect the Agreement provided the basis for a partnership between the two states in Northern Ireland. The Agreement also
weakened the position of unionism within the United Kingdom and
strengthened that of the SDLP explicitly. Moreover, the Agreement
weakened Fianna Fáil politically, prompting the expulsion of a leading

member of the party and the establishment of a new pro-Agreement party the Progressive Democrats. There was also a cooling of the relationship between the SDLP and Fianna Fáil, a consequence of the overwhelming support which the SDLP and the Catholic community in Northern Ireland gave to the Agreement. Nor did public opinion in the Republic support Haughey or Fianna Fáil in its principled opposition to the Agreement. Of those interviewed 59 per cent immediately after the Agreement approved of the Irish government signing it, while only 32 per cent supported Haughey in his opposition. One of the interesting features of the original poll was the realism of the respondents. While 66 per cent agreed that it would improve relations between Ireland and Britain and 50 per cent that it would bring about better relations with Northern Ireland, only 30 per cent thought it would bring a united Ireland closer and 31 per cent that it would improve life for the unionists (MRBI, 1985). A poll in February 1986 (MRBI, 1986) reported that support for Haughey's position had fallen further, even among Fianna Fáil supporters, but also that overall approval had reached 69 per cent. This poll also displayed greater optimism among the public on the possibility of reconciliation and ending violence.

The immediate impact of the Anglo-Irish Agreement on Irish politics was to generate considerable support for the government's moderate strategy. This successfully challenged the traditional *methods* of pursuing Irish unity, but not the objective itself. FitzGerald made clear on a number of occasions that while his ultimate aim was a united Ireland, in the short term he was more concerned with reconciliation than pursuing a narrow constitutional claim. In this he must have been disappointed as the evidence suggests (Cochrane, 1993: 1–20) that little was actually achieved within Northern Ireland in the five years after the Agreement. Increased violence and communal polarisation were the chief consequences of the Agreement *within* Northern Ireland (Cochrane, 1993: 19; O'Leary and McGarry, 1993: 271–4). Consequently, the impact of the Agreement has been greatest on the internal politics of the Irish Republic and on the diplomatic relationship between Britain and Ireland. A new moderate consensus on Northern Ireland was forged within Dáil Eireann, by 1987 a majority of TDs supported the government on this issue. Moreover, Fianna Fáil was placed on the defensive throughout the 1987 general election despite the unpopularity of the outgoing government. This election was the last opportunity for Fianna Fáil to challenge the moderate nationalism of the Agreement, but because of the strength of support for FitzGerald's position, Haughey had to concede that his party would maintain the Agreement if elected. Forty-one per cent believed that Fine Gael had the best policy on Northern Ireland, while only 29 per cent considered that Fianna Fáil's policy in this area was best. Furthermore,

21 per cent of Fianna Fáil supporters considered that Fine Gael had the best policy, with only 56 per cent supporting their own party position (*Irish Political Studies*, 1988: 139). Fianna Fáil went on to form a minority government, but the consensus on Northern Ireland was maintained, despite some criticism of the way in which the new government went about this process. Likewise, after the 1989 election, when Fianna Fáil formed an unprecedented coalition government with the Progressive Democrats, similar constraints on the neo-traditionalist position were maintained.

While the seam of neo-traditional nationalism was largely exhausted by 1989, this does not mean that nationalist aspirations have disappeared. The new consensus is a more moderate set of aspirations, operating in a context where gradualist assumptions take priority. In particular, there is a recognition that successful negotiations with the British government can bring about change even when there are obstacles to change within Northern Ireland. A 1988 poll (*Irish Political Studies*, 1989: 157) highlights the subtle shifts in opinion by this time. Three-quarters of those questioned believed that the Irish government should take steps to begin discussions with the unionists. When prompted on the possible objectives of such discussions, 49 per cent considered that improving North-South relationships should be the main aim while 27 per cent opted for political unity. This highlights an important contrast between those who believed a united Ireland should be the main objective of policy and other options which emphasise a reconciliation strategy.

Much of the support for the new departure was based on the premise that the process was changing the nature of power within Northern Ireland and between nationalists and unionists. The unionist response to the Agreement was easily defeated by the British and Irish governments, while by 1990 it was clear that any further changes would be in large part on terms acceptable to the Irish government and within the framework of the Anglo-Irish Agreement. Though a new departure, this process was not a radical change for Irish nationalism. This was confirmed in 1990 when the Irish Supreme Court rejected the claim by the McGimpsey brothers that the Anglo-Irish Agreement contravened Articles 2 and 3 of the Constitution (Incorporated Council of Law Reporting for Ireland, 1990). The Supreme Court concluded that the Agreement advanced the objectives of the Irish Constitution as contained in Articles 2 and 3 and did not therefore contravene it. The Supreme Court's finding confirmed both the fears of unionists and the claims made by moderate nationalists; that the Agreement promoted the aim of Irish unification. In a number of respects FitzGerald's moderate realism achieved more for Irish nationalism in under a decade than had been the case for physical force, traditional, or neo-traditional nationalism in over fifty years. By the early 1990s the

British were effectively neutral on outcome, while British opinion was broadly in favour of either an independent Northern Ireland or unification with the Republic. Less than a third continued to support the union (Hayes and McAllister, 1996: 68). The process further weakened the unionist position while enhancing that of the Irish government, if not always that of the nationalist population in Northern Ireland. This new set of relationships led to the Joint Declaration in December 1993, the IRA cease-fire in August 1994 and the Framework for the Future in February 1995 (for assessments see Girvin, 1994a; O'Leary, 1995). Between 1985 and 1995 the political and diplomatic initiative remained with the Irish government and, though weakened by the IRA's return to violence, this capacity remains strong. This capacity to influence the outcome also constrained the IRA's use of violence once it resumed its campaign. The IRA remained sensitive to the Irish government and to the reaction of public opinion in the South, a factor which contribtuted to the relatively low level of violence between February 1996 and July 1997. Nor did the resumption of violence lead to a breakdown in relations between the Irish and British governments. Despite some short-term difficulties, the two governments worked together to secure agreement within Northern Ireland.

The Nature of Opinion in the Republic of Ireland

Public opinion in the Republic also began to change in response to these developments. A debate in Dáil Eireann on a motion by the Workers Party to amend Articles 2 and 3 of the Constitution was only narrowly defeated by 74 to 66 votes in December 1990. Fianna Fáil was the only party to oppose the motion on principle, and the leader of Fine Gael John Bruton not only supported the motion but linked the constitutional aims with the terrorism of the IRA. This is a connection usually denied by constitutional nationalists. It is perhaps not surprising that the new leader of Fianna Fáil, Albert Reynolds, called Bruton 'John Unionist' during the 1992 general election. These features draw attention to the nuances of elite political debate, but show little enough about any changes in public opinion.

Large proportions of Irish public opinion consider themselves to be nationalists and believe that Irish unity is something to hope for, as can be seen from the responses to polls by MRBI, as shown in Table 1.

The responses to the questions posed are fairly uniform across age, party and class. When asked about the territorial extent of the nation a majority supported the 32 counties as the unit, whereas about one-third considered it to be the 26 counties. Of interest is the view that national identity in Northern Ireland is a complex one, as can be seen in Table 2.

Table 1. Attitudes to a united Ireland (%).

	1983	1987	1991
Something to hope for	76	67	82
Prefer not to happen	15	19	13
No opinion	9	14	5
N	1,000	1,000	1,000

Source: MRBI (1983, 1987, 1991).

Table 2. Percentage response to the question 'Do you consider the people of Northern Ireland to be:'

	1983	1987
Irish	41	33
British	13	15
Both	39	42
Neither	5	6
No opinion	2	5
N	1,000	1,000

Sources: MRBI (1983, 1987).

On this reading, opinion was subtle, with significant proportions of the public recognising the complex nature of identity in Northern Ireland. A survey carried out in 1988/89 (MacGréil, 1996: 235) reported that 44 per cent *disagreed* with the proposition that: 'Northern Irish Protestants have more in common with the rest of the Irish people than they have with the British.' The same survey (Ibid., 1996: 236) also reported that 49 per cent agreed that Northern Ireland and the Irish Republic were two separate nations, while 42 per cent disagreed. These views did not prevent 50 per cent of respondents from holding the belief that national unity was 'an essential condition for a just solution of the present Northern problem'; some 25 per cent disagreed.

Opinion in the Republic is fairly evenly balanced between a realistic assessment of what is possible and an idealistic hope for what might be achieved. This can be seen in Table 3.

The 1993 data (MRBI, 1993) highlights important differences between those who believe that unity will be achieved within 25 years and those who consider it will take 50 years or will never happen. The main difference appears to be concentrated on age, with those over 50 more likely to endorse the traditionalist view. In addition, women are more likely than men to take a realist view on unity. Fianna Fáil identifiers are more likely to

Table 3. Percentage response to the question 'When is a united Ireland likely to be achieved?'

	1983	1987	1991	1993
Never	39	49	30	34
100 years	9	11	9	6
50 years	16	13	15	12
25 years	17	9	21	16
10 years	9	7	20	23
No opinion	10	11	5	8
N	1,000	1,000	1,000	1,000

Source: MRBI (1983, 1987, 1991, 1993).

Tables 4. Percentage reponse to retaining Articles 2 and 3 of the Irish Constitution.

	1991	1992	1993	1995
Retain	58	41	28	20
Change	25	39	51	60
No opinion	17	20	21	20
N	1,000	1,000	1,000	1,000

Sources: MRBI (1991, 1992, 1993, 1995).

endorse the traditionalist view than other parties. There is, additionally, considerable resistance to paying higher taxation in the event of a closer relationship between the Republic and Northern Ireland; only 19 per cent of respondents were prepared to support such a suggestion. The refusal to pay for unification, in contrast to the situation in Germany since 1989, suggests that Irish support for unity may be quite weak, especially if the cost is considered to be high (MRBI, 1993).

In respect of Articles 2 and 3 one finds a mixture of realism and ideological sentiment, but with a willingness to change opinion in the light of evolving circumstances. Table 4 shows opinion on this question since 1991.

Three factors contributed to the change in opinion during the 1990s. The first was the recognition that unionist sensitivities had to be taken into account. The second was the hostility to IRA terrorism and a recognition that the Irish and British governments were making considerable progress in negotiations. The third factor was that the polling questions were changed from ones which offered a stark contrast between support for or opposition to the territorial claim to ones where the alternative provided was between retaining the claim and including an *aspiration* to unity. Furthermore, a poll in 1991 reported that 81 per cent of those questioned would be prepared to postpone efforts to achieve unity if this helped to

secure an internal settlement in Northern Ireland. In 1993 (MRBI, 1993)
81 per cent agreed with the view expressed by Dick Spring in his six
principles of government policy, that there could be no change in the status
of Northern Ireland without the support of a majority.

None of this means that Irish nationalism has changed its essential
nature. There appear to be no circumstances where Irish nationalism
considers that unity should be abandoned or that Northern Ireland should
remain in the United Kingdom in perpetuity. These are fixed 'Absolute
Presuppositions' (Collingwood, 1940) and as such seem immune to existing
political reality. This is not, however, to reject the view that Irish nationalism has changed some of its strategic priorities or that different political
coalitions are not now dominant. Traditional and neo-traditional nationalism has been appreciably weakened. Changes in the Fianna Fáil leadership in the 1990s moved the party towards a more realistic position within
constitutional nationalism, though it retains traditional instincts often
reflected in its unthinking anti-unionism. The changing nature of the Irish
political system has also contributed to this. Coalition government now
seems to be the norm and in these circumstances some, if not all, of the
parties which make up any coalition are on the realist wing of constitutional nationalism. Most importantly, perhaps, realist nationalism seems to
work. Although less demonstrable, and more volatile, is the impact of
opinion on nationalism. The polls discussed here highlight the continuing
importance of nationalism in Irish politics, but its impact may have
weakened somewhat in the 1990s. A significant proportion of the public
is more pragmatic in terms of options, more realistic in regard to Northern
Ireland and less tolerant of the use of violence by the IRA for the promotion of nationalist objectives. For example when, between January and
March 1994, Sinn Féin and the IRA effectively rejected the Joint Declaration, there was a considerable increase in the proportion of those who
agreed to exclude Sinn Féin from any talks process while violence continued. In addition, some three-quarters of those questioned supported a
security crackdown by the British and Irish governments if IRA violence
did not end (*Irish Political Studies*, 1995: 298, 319). This type of pressure,
along with that from the British, Irish and US governments, contributed to
the IRA's decision to call a second cease-fire in July 1997. The strength of
constitutional nationalism can be further demonstrated by the successful
negotiation of the Good Friday agreement in 1998, its endorsement at the
subsequent referendums in the North and the South while the elections for
the new Assembly held out the prospect of consensual government in
Northern Ireland. The referendum in the Irish Republic in May 1998
amended Articles 2 and 3 of the constitution, removing the most objectionable features contained in the original. The public response to the Omagh

car bombing confirmed the shift in opinion in the Republic, but also indicated that the commitment to constitutional politics had advanced significantly in Northern Ireland as well. With very limited exceptions, Irish nationalists in the North and the South are now committed to constitutional politics for the first time since the present conflict began in the 1960s.

Unionism as a Problem for Irish Nationalism

Despite the considerable changes within Irish nationalism over the past decade unionism as a political movement and as a source of identity remains a serious problem for those who believe there is one nation in Ireland and that a united Ireland is the only solution to the conflict. Unless unionist claims are ignored, as traditional and neo-traditional nationalists do, the existence of unionism and its assertion of self-determination is the weakness at the heart of the nationalist view of history and politics. In a context where Britain maintains that it has no 'selfish interest' in continuing partition and that it will support the wish of the majority in Northern Ireland to *change* its status, this traditional view is of diminishing relevance. What constitutional nationalism has yet to come to terms with is unionism as a distinct nationality with a status within Ireland and the United Kingdom, similar to that of Irish nationalism over the past two centuries and not as a cultural minority within the island or a cultural majority within Northern Ireland. The difficulty continues to be the refusal of Irish nationalism to give up its moral claim to control the North, while refusing to acknowledge the Ulster Protestants as a distinct nationality. There is a brutal logic to this: to accept that Ulster Protestants are a distinct nationality would undermine the moral legitimacy of the nationalist demand. To all intents and purposes this means that Irish nationalism continues to deny unionists the right to be unionists.

It is not the purpose of this section to provide a detailed discussion of unionism or a critique of its government in Northern Ireland (see Porter, 1996; and Bew this volume). It is however, to suggest that the polarisation and conflict in Northern Ireland and between Ulster Protestants and nationalist Ireland, is about conflicting views of nationality. It is also to insist that the criteria usually applied to nations can be successfully used in Ireland to demarcate distinct nationalities within the island and within the United Kingdom. The levels of polarisation are well known. Boyle and Hadden (1994: 6–66) have described in detail the extent of segregation between Catholics and Protestants, a gap which may have widened since 1968. The evidence presented to the Independent Review of Parades and

Marches (1997) highlights the lack of understanding between Catholics and Protestants on the issue of Orange marches, though this is simply a microcosm of more general divisions. What is painfully obvious is that Northern Ireland is a polarised and pillarised society, but one which does not have the institutional arrangements for consociational accommodation. Consociationalism has worked in deeply divided societies only when the sources of identity are shared, as in the Netherlands or Austria; where identity is contested it has proved to be virtually impossible to achieve the agreement necessary to achieve this (Lijphart, 1982; McGarry, 1990). In a crucial sense, if national identity is what is at stake the likelihood of agreement is limited.

Nor is this new; Rose's (1971: 334, 269) 1968 survey captured the continuing polarisation of Northern Ireland and the denominational basis for the distance between the two communities. Indeed, since the early nineteenth century questions of nationality and identity have polarised Catholics and Protestants in Northern Ireland, a confrontation which continues to be reflected in historical memory, anecdote and perception by each community. There are, in reality, two histories in Northern Ireland. This polarisation is expressed most directly in the political system. If Lipset and Rokkan (1967) are correct in suggesting that party alternatives freeze at certain stages of mobilisation, then alignments in Northern Ireland are a classic expression of this phenomenon. Rose (1971: 235–6) found that Protestants overwhelmingly voted for unionist parties, while a majority of Catholics voted for nationalists. When asked for a second preference, only 2 per cent of Protestants indicated that they would vote for a nationalist while 8 per cent of Catholics said they would vote for a unionist. A decade later this pattern had been maintained despite the fragmentation of the Unionist Party during the 1970s (Moxon-Browne, 1983: 65). The absence of a cross-over effect has been evident in every election and survey since 1968, reflecting the continuing distance between nationalists and unionists. As Breen (1996: 38) reports 'No Protestants call themselves Nationalists and no Catholics call themselves Unionists'. This is a society which is radically segmented on political issues. Not only do Catholics and Protestants not share the same political parties, but on a wide range of issues related to the status of Northern Ireland, the role of the Irish government and security matters the gap between Protestant and Catholic can be overwhelming (see *Irish Political Studies*, 1995: 316). This polarity in attitudes is reflected in Table 5.

There is a close relationship between religion, attitudes to a united Ireland and political identity evident in this table. This is reinforced from data in the Social Attitudes in Northern Ireland surveys (Breen *et al.*, 1996) In the 1994 survey 45 per cent of Catholics and 24 per cent of Protestants

Table 5. Attitudes towards a united Ireland (%).

	For a united Ireland	To remain in the UK	Don't know
Total	25	61	14
Ulster Unionist	0	100	0
Democratic Unionist	1	97	2
Sinn Féin	95	5	0
Social Democratic and Labour Party	52	33	16
Alliance Party	19	61	19
Conservatives (Northern Ireland)	9	87	4
Democratic Left	25	50	25
Protestant	3	90	7
Catholic	52	28	20
Other Religion	5	55	45
N	214	517	119

Source: Ulster Marketing Surveys for ITN, 17–18 December 1993 as reported in *Irish Political Studies* (1994: 225). Total sample 848.

claimed they were neither unionist or nationalist, but no Protestant claimed to be a nationalist and no Catholic claimed to be a unionist. Additionally, Catholic/neither and Protestant/neither voted for parties which expressed their traditional religious loyalties (Breen, 1996: 37–9). This emphasises how the two denominations inhabit quite separate and distinct political domains. The reason for this becomes clearer when the data in Tables 6 and 7 are assessed.

Protestants overwhelmingly identify themselves as British or Ulster, whereas Catholics identify themselves as Irish or Northern Irish; there is little overlap or shared identity. It would be significant if a Protestant identified as a nationalist or a Catholic as a unionist and if a Protestant who adopts the category 'neither' identified as Irish and supported a united Ireland or if a Catholic 'neither' choose to be British or opted to remain in the United Kingdom. The evidence for Protestants suggests that they do not identify as Irish, as nationalists, with nationalist political parties or support a united Ireland. Likewise, though not as strongly, Catholics do not perceive themselves as unionists, do not vote for unionist parties, tend to favour a united Ireland and do not identify themselves as British or Ulster.[6]

It is possible to accept the extent of polarisation described here, yet refuse, as most Irish nationalists continue to do, to accept that Ulster

[6] I am grateful to Richard Breen for access to data from the Social Attitudes in Northern Ireland surveys. This section contains very preliminary analysis of these data, which I hope to develop in more detail at a later stage.

Brian Girvin

Table 6. Protestant self-identity, 1968–94 (%).

	1968	1978	1989	1991	1993	1994
British	39	67	68	66	70	71
Irish	20	8	3	2	2	3
Ulster	32	20	10	15	16	11
Northern Irish	—	—	16	14	11	15
Other	9	5	3	3	3	—

Sources: For 1968, Rose (1971); for 1978, Moxon-Browne (1983); for 1989–94, Breen *et al.* (1996).

Table 7. Catholic self-identity, 1968–94 (%).

	1968	1978	1989	1991	1993	1994
British	15	15	10	10	12	10
Irish	76	69	60	62	61	62
Ulster	5	6	2	2	1	—
Northern Irish	—	—	25	25	25	28
Other	4	10	4	1	2	—

Sources: For 1968, Rose (1971); for 1978, Moxon-Browne (1983); for 1989–94, Breen *et al.* (1996)

Protestants have a distinct nationality. Indeed, despite a wealth of evidence highlighting the strength of this identity and its distinctiveness from Catholic and nationalist identity, there is a general reluctance to concede that the Ulster Protestants are indeed a nation. Various objections have been advanced for this. They include the religious basis of identity, the volatility of Protestant identity, that its Britishness might be a temporary phenomenon, that Britishness is not a nationality, that the British themselves do not acknowledge that the Ulster British are British as well as the conditional nature of Ulster Protestants' loyalty to the state (Whyte, 1978; 1990; Miller, 1978; FitzGerald, 1982; Lee, 1989; Gallagher, 1995; McGarry and O'Leary, 1995). Trew (1994; 1996; see also Benson and Trew, 1995) has explored this question in considerable detail. This research and that of Ruane and Todd (1996) draws attention to the distinct nature of identity in Northern Ireland, though they also suggest that new forms of identity (European or Northern Irish) may emerge to provide an alternative source of identity.

A number of these objections confuse state and nation. The conditional nature of loyalty to a state is quite congruent with the claim that a group is a nation. As noted earlier, the nation defines the majority not the state. Nations in a multi-national state will always have conditional loyalty, because their primary loyalty is to the nation not the state. The 'volatility' of Ulster Protestant identity cannot be sustained from the evidence. The change between 1968 and 1978 was a product of a challenge to the Protestant self-image as Irish and British. When Irish was appropriated by nationalism and the Britishness of the Ulster Protestant was challenged from that position, the vast majority of Ulster Protestants confirmed their identity explicitly as British. Opinion on identity among Protestants has been very stable since 1978. Nor is it likely that British identity is temporary, though if Northern Ireland were to be expelled from the United Kingdom a reformulation of identity might be expected. Even such a radical change would not affect the underlying sources of identity, however. The objection that British may not be a nationality has some strength, as this confuses state and nationality. There is some ambiguity between Britain as a state and Britain as a nationality, which is not easily resolved. Colley's view (1992) allows for a distinction to be made between state and nation while continuing to recognise the individual nations which compose Britain. On this view there is no necessary contradiction between English and British or Scottish and British and allows for British to be used in Northern Ireland for those who live in Ireland and identify with Britain to give expression to that. The refusal of the British to accept the Ulster British as British does not invalidate the latter's claim, though it does make it more difficult for them to gain support for their political aims. A stronger objection is that religion cannot be the basis for national identity (Oommen, 1997: 79–90). In a strict sense this is true, but it fails to recognise that nationalism and religion are not necessarily synonyms, but that the particular culture which forms the basis for the nation has a strong religious tradition which informs concepts of nationality. This aspect of nation formation is particularly strong when two religions confront one another in adjacent territories (Martin, 1978: 109). There is little evidence that new identities are forming in Northern Ireland; a more realistic reading of the evidence suggests that the two identities are as far apart as ever. This is to confuse the possibility of cooperation between the two nationalities to give effect to shared government with the dissolving of differences between them. While the first is possible, the latter reflects a lack of understanding of the nature of nationalism (Kellas, 1991).

These objections and suggestions misconceive the strength of nationalism in the modern world; even when multiple identities exist there is usually a dominant one especially if identity is challenged. National identity cannot easily be dissolved and is more 'hard wired' than some suggest (Kearney, 1997). Culture is the arena within which change takes place, not national identity (Girvin, 1997). A number of recent studies suggest that the existence of a distinct national identity among the Ulster

British should be considered seriously (Pringle, 1985; Hennessey, 1993; Coulter, 1994; Porter, 1996). Gallagher (1995) has made a careful analysis of the various theories in respect of the Ulster Protestants concluding that the most useful approach to the question of identity is a model which allows for 'three nations' or 'two nations and part of another'. This reluctance to accept the Ulster Protestants as a single nationality distinguishable from the English, Scots and Welsh on the one hand and the Irish on the other is based on the view that the divisions within the Ulster Protestant community are associated with national identity. This is an overstatement of the case. It is more accurate to link these differences to disagreement over political tactics and objectives, differences which exist in any political system. As Gallagher notes, Moxon-Browne (1983: 8) drew attention to the strong overlap between the Ulster and British identity among Ulster Protestants. While the evidence is open to a number of interpretations, the one most consistent with other evidence is that the differences between Ulster and British do not constitute differences based on nationality.

If Tables 6 and 7 are compared, opinion on identity within the Catholic community is just as diverse as within the Protestant. Yet this rarely raises questions about the identity of Catholics in Northern Ireland, who are normally presumed to be Irish. In contrast to Protestants who have increased their British identity since 1968, the percentage of Catholics who identify as Irish has actually declined; in 1994 more Protestants considered themselves to the British than Catholics considered themselves to be Irish. Nor is this diversity of opinion on questions of identity unusual in a comparative context. In Scotland, Catalonia, Andalucia and the Basque Country extremely complex notions of nationality and identity appear. It would be unacceptable to deny that Scotland, Catalonia or the Basques were nations despite the multiple responses to questions about identity (Moreno and Arriba, 1996; 78–97; Keating, 1995). A re-evaluation of these data is required, but it can be suggested that the position of Ulster Protestants is not unique in a comparative context; there are a number of examples where members of nationalities describe their identities in complex terms. This however, does not undermine their claim to be a nation, but draws attention to the sophisticated notions of identity and loyalty in the specific cases, particularly the relationship between state and nation. It might be concluded then that within Ireland and the United Kingdom and in a wider comparative context the position of the Ulster Protestants (or the Ulster British more accurately) is not an anomaly. Indeed, if the same criteria are applied to the Ulster British as are applied to Irish or other nationalisms, then it would be difficult to deny to it that status. If Irish nationalism were to acknowledge this status the political consequence for the future could be quite dramatic.

Conclusion

To accept that two nations exist in Ireland has various consequences. The most important is that each nation has to recognise the legitimacy of the other, and the rights and responsibilities concomitant with that status. If nationalism is the main source of identity in the contemporary world, the recognition of the equality of this status can change the context within which relations take place. Nationality has a different status to all other identities in existence and it is clear that once they have been formed, as they were in Ireland at the end of the eighteenth and early in the nineteenth century, it is almost impossible to break down the basis for it or to dissolve it into something else.

A thought experiment can conclude this chapter. Seamus Heaney (1983) once wrote angrily that:

> be advised
> my passports green.
> No glass of ours was ever raised
> to toast the Queen.

Heaney's rejection of British identity would probably be welcomed by most nationalists, but would they reject as easily the denial of the Ulster British that they are Irish? The same applies for the Ulster British in respect of Irish nationalism. Denial brings reassertion not assimilation and this leads to further conflict; the historical record is clear on this. It also allows more extreme forces to dictate the political environment. Porter (1996), writing as a unionist, has sought to provide an alternative approach by invoking a 'civic unionism' which could treat Irish nationalism as an equal in political terms. The move towards a civic understanding of nationalism in Ireland will only occur if due recognition is given to the status of each nationality. The changes which have occurred in 1998 go some way to providing this recognition. The actions of the political parties in the new Assembly and their ability to co-operate in governing Northern Ireland will provide the evidence of this over the coming years.

Acknowledgements. I would like to thank the participants at the symposium for their helpful comments on the version presented there. James Kellas has discussed aspects of Scottish identity with me on a number of occasions and supplied me with references. I am particularly grateful to Jack Jones of the Market Research Bureau of Ireland for his willingness to supply me with copies of the regular MRBI/*Irish Times* political polls.

References

Adams, G. (1986) *The Politics of Irish Freedom*, Dingle: Brandon.

Akenson, D. H. (1994) *Conor*, Montreal and Kingston: McGill-Queen's University Press.

Anderson, B. (1991) *Imagined Communities: Reflections on the Origin and Spread of Nationalism*, London: Verso.

Anderson, J. (1980) 'Regions and Religion in Ireland: a Short Critique of the "Two Nations" Theory', *Antipode*, 12(1): 44–53.

Ashford, S. and Timms, N. (1992) *What Europe Thinks*, Aldershot: Dartmouth.

Barton, B. and Roche, P. J. (eds) (1994) *The Northern Question: Perspectives and Policies*, Aldershot: Avebury.

Benson, D. E. and Trew, K. J. (1995) 'Facets of Self in Northern Ireland: Explorations and Further Questions', in A. Oosterwegel and R. A. Wicklund (eds), *The Self in European and North American Culture: Development and Processes*, Amsterdam: Kluwer.

Boyle, K. and Hadden, T. (1994) *Northern Ireland: The Choice*, London: Penguin.

Bradshaw, B. (1988/89) 'Nationalism and Historical Scholarship in Modern Ireland', *Irish Historical Studies*, 26: 329–51.

Bradshaw, B. (1994) 'The invention of the Irish', *Times Literary Supplement*, 14 October: 8–10.

Breen, R. (1996) 'Who wants a United Ireland? Constitutional Preferences among Catholics and Protestants', in R. Breen, P. Devine and L. Dowds (eds), *Social Attitudes in Northern Ireland*, Belfast: Appletree.

Breen, R., Devine, P. and Dowds, L. (eds) (1996) *Social Attitudes in Northern Ireland*, Belfast: Appletree.

Brooke, P. (1987) *Ulster Presbyterianism*, Dublin: Gill and Macmillan.

Coakley, J. (1986) 'The Evolution of Irish Party Politics', in B. Girvin and R. Stürm (eds), *Politics and Society in Contemporary Ireland*, Aldershot: Gower.

Cochrane, F. (1993) 'Progressive or Regressive? The Anglo-Irish Agreement as a Dynamic in the Northern Ireland Polity', *Irish Political Studies*, 8: 1–20.

Cochrane, F. (1996) '"Meddling at the Crossroads": The Decline and Fall of Terence O'Neill within the Unionist Community', in R. English and G. Walker (eds), *Unionism in Modern Ireland*, Dublin: Gill and Macmillan.

Cohan, A. S. (1977) 'The Question of a United Ireland: Perspectives of the Irish Political Elite', *International Affairs*, 53(2): 232–54.

Colley, L. (1992) *Britons: Forging the Nation 1707–1837*, New Haven: Yale University Press.

Collingwood, R. G. (1940) *An Essay on Metaphysics*, Oxford: Clarendon Press.

Committee on the Constitution (1967) *Report of the Committee on the Constitution*, Dublin: Stationary Office.

Connor, W. (1994) *Ethnonationalism: The Quest for Understanding*, Princeton, New Jersey: Princeton University Press.

Coogan, T. P. (1993) *De Valera*, London: Hutchinson.

Coulter, C. (1994) 'The Character of Unionism', *Irish Political Studies*, 9: 1–24.

Curtin, N. J. (1994) *The United Irishmen: Popular Politics in Ulster and Dublin 1791–1798*, Oxford: Oxford University Press.

Davis, E. E. and Sinnott, R. (1979) *Attitudes in the Republic of Ireland Relevant to the Northern Ireland Problem*, Dublin: The Economic and Social Research Institute.

Deutsch, K. W. (1953) *Nationalism and Social Communication*, New York: John Wiley.

Dogan, M. (1994) 'The Decline of Nationalisms within Western Europe', *Comparative Politics*, 26(3): 281–305.

Elliott, M. (1989) *Wolfe Tone*, New Haven: Yale University Press.

Ellis, S. G. (1991) 'The Inveterate Dominion: Ireland in the English state, a Survey to 1700', in H.-H. Nolte (ed.), *Internal Peripheries in European History*, Göttingen: Muster-Schmidt Verlag.

English, R. and Walker, G. (eds) (1996) *Unionism in Modern Ireland*, Dublin: Gill and Macmillan.

FitzGerald, G. (1973) *Towards a New Ireland*, Dublin: Torc Books.

FitzGerald, G. (1982) *Irish Identities*, London: BBC.

FitzGerald, G. (1991) *All in a Life*, Dublin: Gill and Macmillan.

Fitzpatrick, B. (1988) *Seventeenth-Century Ireland: The War of Religions*, Dublin: Gill and Macmillan.

Follis, B. (1995) *A State Under Siege: The Establishment of Northern Ireland 1920–25*, Oxford: Clarendon Press.

Forum for Peace and Reconciliation (1995) 'Report of Proceedings — Volume 1, 28 October 1994', Dublin: Stationary Office.

Foster, J. W. (1995) *The Idea of the Union*, Vancouver, British Columbia: Belcouver.

Gallagher, F. (1957) *The Indivisible Island*, London: Victor Gollanz.

Gallagher, M. (1990) 'Do Ulster Unionists have a right to Self-Determination?', *Irish Political Studies*, 5: 11–30.

Gallagher, M. (1995) 'How Many Nations are There in Ireland?', *Ethnic and Racial Studies*, 18(4): 715–39.

Garvin, T. (1996) *1922: The Birth of Irish Democracy*, Dublin: Gill and Macmillan.

Gellner, E. (1983) *Nations and Nationalism*, Oxford: Blackwell.

Gibbon, P. (1975) *The Origins of Ulster Unionism*, Manchester: Manchester Universtity Press.

Giddens, A. (1985) *The Nation State and Violence*, Cambridge: Polity Press.

Girvin, B. (1986a) 'National Identity and Conflict in Northern Ireland', in B. Girvin and R. Stürm (eds), *Politics and Society in Contemporary Ireland*, Aldershot: Gower.

Girvin, B. (1986b) 'The Anglo-Irish Agreement 1985', in B. Girvin and R. Stürm (eds), *Politics and Society in Contemporary Ireland*, Aldershot: Gower.

Girvin, B. (1987) 'The Campaign', in M. Laver, P. Mair and R. Sinnott (eds), *How Ireland Voted*, Dublin: Poolbeg.

Girvin, B. (1989) *Between Two Worlds: Politics and Economy in Independent Ireland*, Dublin: Gill and Macmillan.

Girvin, B. (1991) 'Making Nations: O'Connell, Religion and the Creation of Political Identity', in M. O'Connell (ed.), *Daniel O'Connell: Political Pioneer*, Dublin: Institute of Public Administration.

Girvin, B. (1993) 'Social Change and Political Culture in the Republic of Ireland', *Parliamentary Affairs*, 46(3): 380–98.

Girvin, B. (1994a) 'Constitutional Nationalism and Northern Ireland', in B. Barton and P. J. Roche (eds), *The Northern Question: Perspectives and Policies*, Aldershot: Avebury.

Girvin, B. (1994b) *The Right in the Twentieth Century: Conservatism and Democracy*, London: Pinter.

Girvin, B. (1994c) 'The Act of Union, Nationalism and Religion: 1780–1850' in J. Elvert (ed.), *Nordirland in Geschichte und Gegenwart*, Stuttgart: Franz Steiner.

Girvin, B. (1996) 'Church, State and the Irish Constitution: The Secularisation of Irish Politics?', *Parliamentary Affairs*, 49(4): 599–615.

Girvin, B. (1997) 'Ireland', in R. Eatwell (ed.), *European Political Cultures*, London: Routledge.

Girvin, B. (1999) 'The Republicanisation of Irish Society 1932–48', in *A New History of Ireland*, Vol. VII. Oxford: Oxford University Press.

Harkness, D. (1969) *The Restless Dominion*, London: Macmillan.

Hayes, B. and McAllister, I. (1996) 'British and Irish Public Opinion Towards the Northern Ireland Problem', *Irish Political Studies*, 11: 61–82.

Heaney, S. (1983) *An Open Letter*, Derry: Field Day Theatre Company.

Heaney, S. (1995) *The Redress of Poetry*, London: Faber and Faber.

Hennessey, T. (1993) 'Ulster Unionist Territorial and National Identities 1886–1893: Province, Kingdom and Empire', *Irish Political Studies*, 8: 21–36.

Herz, D. (1986) 'The Northern Ireland Policy of the Irish Republic', in B. Girvin and R. Stürm (eds), *Politics and Society in Contemporary Ireland*, Aldershot: Gower.

Heslinga, M. W. (1971) *The Irish Border as a Cultural Divide*, Assen: Van Gorcum.

Hindley, R. (1990) *The Death of the Irish Language: A Qualified Obituary*, London: Routledge.

Hume, J. (1980/81) 'Interview with John Hume', in *The Crane Bag*, 4(2): 39–43.

Hutchinson, J. (1994) *Modern Nationalism*, London: Fontana.

Hutchinson, J. and Smith, A. D. (eds) (1994) *Nationalism*, Oxford: Oxford University Press.

Incorporated Council of Law Reporting for Ireland (1990) *Irish Law Reports*, Dublin: Incorporated Council of Law Reporting for Ireland.

Independent Review of Parades and Marches, (1997) *Report*, Belfast: Stationary Office.

Irish Political Studies (1988) 'Data Section', *Irish Political Studies*, 3: 121–43.

Irish Political Studies (1989) 'Irish Political Data' *Irish Political Studies*, 4: 145–62.

Irish Political Studies (1995) 'Irish Political Data', *Irish Political Studies*, 10: 262–339.

Joyce, J. and Murtagh, P. (1983) *The Boss: Charles J. Haughey in Government*, Co. Dublin: Poolbeg.

Kearney, H. (1989) *The British Isles: A History of Four Nations*, Cambridge: Cambridge University Press.

Kearney, R. (1997) *Postnationalist Ireland*, London: Routledge.

Keating, M. (1995) *Nations Against the State: The New Politics of Nationalism in Quebec, Catalonia and Scotland*, London: Macmillan.

Kellas, J. G. (1991) *The Politics of Nationalism and Ethnicity*, London: Macmillan.

Kennedy, D. (1988) *The Widening Gulf*, Belfast: The Blackstaff Press.

Keogh, D. (1994) *Twentieth Century Ireland: Nation and State*, Dublin: Gill and Macmillan.

Laver, M., Mair, P. and Sinnott, R. (eds) (1987) *How Ireland Voted*, Dublin: Poolbeg.

Lee, J. J. (1989) *Ireland: 1912–1985*, Cambridge: Cambridge University Press.

Lemass, S. (1959) *One Nation*, Dublin: Fianna Fáil.

Lennon, C. (1994) *Sixteenth-Century Ireland: The Incomplete Conquest*, Dublin: Gill and Macmillan.

Lijphart, A. (1982) 'Consociationalism: the Model and its Application in Divided Societies', in D. Rea (ed.), *Political Cooperation in Divided Societies*, Dublin: Gill and Macmillan.

Lipset, S. M. and Rokkan, S. (1967) 'Cleavage Structures, Party Systems and Voter Alignment: an Introduction', in S. M. Lipset and S. Rokkan (eds), *Party Systems and Voter Alignments: Cross-National Prespectives*, New York: The Free Press.

Llobera, J. R. (1994) *The God of Modernity: The Development of Nationalism in Western Europe*, Oxford: Berg.

McBride, I. (1993) 'The School of Virtue: Francis Hutcheson, Irish Presbyterians and the Scottish Enlightenment', in G. Boyce, R. Eccleshall and V. Geoghegan (eds), *Political Thought in Ireland since the Seventeenth Century*, London: Routledge.

McBride, I. (1996) 'Ulster and the British Problem', in R. English and G. Walker (eds), *Unionism in Modern Ireland*, Dublin: Gill and Macmillan.

McGarry, J. (1990) 'A Consociational Settlement for Northern Ireland', *Plural Societies*, 20: 1–21.

McGarry, J. and O'Leary, B. (1995) *Explaining Northern Ireland*, Oxford: Blackwell.

MacGréil, M. (1977) *Prejudice and Tolerance in Ireland*, Dublin: College of Industrial Relations.

MacGréil, M. (1996) *Prejudice in Ireland Revisited*, Maynooth, Co. Kildare: Survey and Research Unit.

Mair, P. (1987a) *The Changing Irish Party System*, London: Francis Pinter.

Mair, P. (1987b) 'Breaking the Nationalist Mould: The Irish Republic and the Anglo-Irish Agreement', in P. Teague (ed.), *Beyond the Rhetoric*, London: Lawrence and Wishart.

Mansergh, M. (1986) *The Spirit of the Nation: The Speeches and Statements of Charles J. Haughey, 1957–1986*, Cork: Mercier.

Martin, D. (1978) *A General Theory of Secularization*, Oxford: Basil Blackwell.

Mill, J. S. (1861) 'Considerations on Representative Government', in J. Gray (ed.), *John Stuart Mill: On Liberty and Other Essays*, Oxford: Oxford University Press.

Miller, D. W. (1978) *Queen's Rebels: Ulster Loyalism in Historical Perspective*, Dublin: Gill and Macmillan.

Moreno, L. and Arriba, A. (1996) 'Dual identity in Autonomous Catalonia', *Scottish Affairs*, 17: 78–97.

Moxon-Browne, E. (1983) *Nation, Class and Creed in Northern Ireland*, Aldershot: Gower.

MRBI (1985) *The Irish Times/MRBI Poll*, Dun Laoghaire: Market Research Bureau of Ireland.

MRBI (1986) *The Irish Times/MRBI Poll*, Dun Laoghaire: Market Research Bureau of Ireland.

MRBI (1987) *Eire Inniu: An MRBI Perspective on Irish Society*, Dun Laoghaire: Market Research Bureau of Ireland.

MRBI (1991) *The Irish Times/MRBI Poll*, Dun Laoghaire: Market Research Bureau of Ireland.

MRBI (1992) *The Irish Times/MRBI Poll*, Dun Laoghaire: Market Research Bureau of Ireland.

MRBI (1993a) *21st Anniversary Poll*, Dun Laoghaire: Market Research Bureau of Ireland.

MRBI (1993b) *The Irish Times/MRBI Poll*, Dun Laoghaire: Market Research Bureau of Ireland.

MRBI (1995) *The Irish Times/MRBI Poll*, Dun Laoghaire: Market Research Bureau of Ireland.

Murphy, J. A. (1978) 'Further Reflections on Nationalism (reply to Conor Cruise O'Brien)', *The Crane Bag*, 2(1–2): 156–63.

New Ireland Forum (1984) *Report*, Dublin: Stationery Office.

O'Brien, C. C. (1972) *States of Ireland*, London: Hutchinson.

O'Brien, C. C. (1992) *The Great Melody: A Thematic Biography of Edmund Burke*, London: Sinclair-Stevenson.

O'Brien, C. C. (1994) *Ancestral Voices: Religion and Nationalism in Ireland*, Dublin: Poolbeg.

O'Leary, B. (1987) 'The Anglo-Irish Agreement: Meanings, Explanations, Results and a Defence', in P. Teague (ed.), *Beyond the Rhetoric*, London: Lawrence and Wishart.

O'Leary, B. (1995) 'Afterword: What is Framed in the Framework Documents?', *Ethnic and Racial Studies*, 18(4): 862–72.

O'Leary, B. and McGarry, J. (1993) *The Politics of Antagonism: Understanding Northern Ireland*, London: Athlone.

O'Malley, P. (1983) *The Uncivil Wars*, Belfast: Blackstaff Press.

Oommen, T. K. (1997) *Citizenship, Nationality and Ethnicity*, Cambridge: Polity.

Phoenix, E. (1994) *Northern Nationalism: Nationalist Politics, Partition and the Catholic Minority in Northern Ireland 1890–1940*, Belfast: Ulster Historical Foundation.

Porter, N. (1996) *Rethinking Unionism: An Alternative Vision for Northern Ireland*, Belfast: Blackstaff Press.

Pringle, D. G. (1985) *One Island, Two Nations?*, Letchworth: Research Studies Press.

Robbins, K. (1990) 'Varieties of Britishness', in M. Crozier (ed.), *Cultural Traditions in Northern Ireland*, Belfast: Institute of Irish Studies.

Rose, R. (1971) *Governing Without Consensus*, London: Faber and Faber.

Ruane, J. and Todd, J. (1996) *The Dynamics of Conflict in Northern Ireland*, Cambridge: Cambridge University Press.

Russett, B. (1993) *Grasping the Democratic Peace*, Princeton, New Jersey: Princeton University Press.

Saorstat Eireann (1923) *Handbook of the Ulster Question*, Dublin: Stationary Office.

Sinnott, R. (1986) 'The North: Party Images and Party Approaches in the Republic', *Irish Political Studies*, 1: 15–32.

Smith, A. D. (1991) *National Identity*, London: Penguin.

Teague, P. (ed.) (1987) *Beyond the Rhetoric*, London: Lawrence and Wishart.

Trew, K. (1994) 'What it Means to be Irish from a Northern Perspective', *The Irish Journal of Psychology*, 15(2–3): 288–99.

Trew, K. (1996) 'National Identity', in R. Breen, P. Devine and L. Dowds (eds), *Social Attitudes in Northern Ireland*, Belfast: Appletree.

Walker, G. (1995) *Intimate Strangers: Political and Cultural Interaction Between Scotland and Ulster in Modern Times*, Edinburgh: John Donald.

Whyte, J. (1978) 'Interpretations of the Northern Ireland Problem: an Appraisal', *Economic and Social Review*, 9(4): 257–82.

Whyte, J. (1990) *Interpreting Northern Ireland*, Oxford: Clarendon.

The Political History of Northern Ireland since Partition: The Prospects for North-South Co-operation

PAUL BEW

Introduction

THE POLITICAL HISTORY OF NORTHERN IRELAND since partition is perceived to be the weakest point in the efforts which have recently been made to present a 'modernising' or even 'liberal' case for Ulster unionism.[1] It is widely presumed that fifty years of unionist misrule in Northern Ireland (1921–72) constituted an appalling and discreditable story; revealingly even Roy Foster's (1988) revisionist *Modern Ireland 1660–1972*—the most influential general work of Irish history in this generation—accepts this consensus and it was, in turn, the only section of that book to be praised by *An Phoblacht/Republican News*, the organ of Provisional Sinn Féin. It is too early, in fact, to offer a definitive account of this period, but is worth pointing out one stultifying effect of the present consensus. It actually inhibits the possibility of an historic compromise in Ireland by failing to situate accurately what was at stake at moments of potential North-South understanding, such as the Craig/Collins pacts of 1922 or the O'Neill/ Lemass meetings of the mid-1960s. Unionists are presented with an exaggeratedly intransigent version of their own history while nationalists are encouraged not to reflect seriously on their own stance. These remarks have an historiographical context. Following the release of a massive amount of the material in 1977 (under the new, less restrictive public

---

[1] This paper does not attempt to deal with the 'core' historic experience of the unionist state after 1925—when it was formally recognised by Dublin in an international treaty, though this recognition was unilaterally withdrawn by the Irish constitution of 1937. There is no doubt that from 1925 to its abolition in 1972 the unionist state was responsive to populist sectarian Protestant pressures—though there were always elements in the elite who resisted the worst excesses—and this contributed mightily to Catholic alienation. This is the thesis of Bew *et al.*, 1979, and now published in a revised and extended edition, Bew *et al.*, 1996.

Proceedings of the British Academy, **98**, 401–418. © The British Academy 1999.

records regulation), the early landmark publications were by the academic historian Patrick Buckland, *The Factory of Grievances: Devolved Government in Northern Ireland 1921–39* (1979) and *James Craig* (1980); and self-confessed socialist republican Michael Farrell, *Arming the Protestants* (1983), which is considerably more interesting than his earlier, more polemical, but still useful *The Orange State* (1975), which was written before the release of documentation. Finally, there was the work of Paul Bew *et al.*, *The State in Northern Ireland: Political Forces and Social Classes* (1979), recently released in two heavily revised and extended editions, *Northern Ireland 1921–94* (1994) and *Northern Ireland 1921–1996* (1996). All these works took as their principal object the 'old Stormont regime'—though, of course, Stormont itself was not built until the 1930s. All were critical, with varying degrees of emphasis, of the sectarian rigidity of the regime. Post-1983, it has to be said that this historiographical debate, such as it then was, went to sleep rather for at least five years. Nor is there any evidence of this work's impact on public policy; it is, for example, quite likely that the framers of the Anglo-Irish Agreement of 1985 on either the British or the Irish sides, had not read any of it.

In recent years, however, the rate of publication within the field has begun to intensify again. In 1988 Dennis Kennedy published his *The Widening Gulf: Northern Attitudes to the Irish Free State 1921–48*. Kennedy clearly demonstrated—more decisively than any other writer—that unionist attitudes in the North were seriously affected not only by the nationalist violence directed against Southern Protestants in the period 1920–22, but also by their general treatment thereafter as Dublin moved ever more explicitly towards the adoption of the Catholic constitution of 1937. In 1993, the present writer (along with co-editors K. Darwin and Gordon Gillespie) published *Passion and Prejudice*, a collection of documents designed to illuminate both nationalist and unionist attitudes in the 1930s. In 1994 Eamon Phoenix published *Northern Nationalists: Nationalist Politics, Partition and the Catholic Minority in Northern Ireland 1890–1980*—which together with important new books on educational matters by Mary Harris (1993) and Sean Farren (1995)—helped to fill in the Catholic-nationalist world view. More recently, Colm Campbell's *Emergency Law in Ireland 1918–1925* (1995) and Bryan Follis' *A State Under Siege: The Establishment of Northern Ireland 1920–25* (1995) have offered new documentary material on the 1920s. Most recently of all Brian Barton's *Northern Ireland During the Second World War* (1995) with its revelation, based on the Dublin archives, that leading Northern nationalists placed their community under the protection of the Third Reich, is of great interest.

All of the books so far mentioned have a solid documentary basis. It is obviously more difficult to provide for the more recent period since the accession of Terence O'Neill to the position of Prime Minister for which, at best, only some cabinet papers, for example, are available. The historian has thus to rely rather more on interviews and the press. Nevertheless, some recent articles may be said to belong to a certain recognisable field of contemporary history—as opposed to political science or journalism. I have myself been involved in three books which cover the period from 1964 to the present day (Bew and Gillespie, 1993; Bew and Gillespie, 1996; Bew *et al.*, 1997) but pride of place must go to the recent Institute of Contemporary British History (ICBH) collection of papers, *The Northern Ireland Question in British Politics* (edited by Peter Catterall and Sean MacDougall) and a superb essay by Anthony MacIntyre 'Modern Irish Republicanism: The Product of British State Strategies' (1995).

This was the state of play before the release of a second most recent wave of documents. This new evidence is of two sorts—the normal release under the 30 year rule of material which now illuminates a part of the O'Neill/Lemass era, and secondly, in the autumn of 1996, some hundreds of documents relating to the earlier period of 1921–47 which had been withheld previously, largely for reasons of security sensitivity. These new security related papers (both of these in Kew and Belfast) reveal that there was rather more reason for unionist paranoia in the early 1920s than has traditionally been acknowledged by historians. Let us consider the nature of IRA violence throughout Ireland in the 1919–21 period. The new Public Records Office (PRO) files, released in November 1996, support the recent thesis of Peter Hart (and go rather against the comments in Campbell, 1995, on this point) that IRA violence was much more sectarian than has been acknowledged by scholars.[2]

Campbell advances some evidence which implies that a Southern Protestant willingness to act as British 'spies' might explain their casualty rate. Hart disagrees and is supported by the most important of the recently released files. Referring to the execution of so many so-called spies, the final 'end of term' lengthy report on the work of British intelligence services in Ireland makes it clear that the Southern Protestant community had long since been frightened into silence; in consequence it provided little information. This document offers a different explanation for the IRA's *modus operandi*:

> Numbers of ex-soldiers and others have been murdered during the rebellion, not so much because they were discovered in active espionage—indeed, few of these had ever given information—but they met their deaths partly

---

[2] See for a foretaste, Hart (1996).

because there was a possibility that they might become informers and partly in order to keep alive the reasons in which it was considered desirable to impose. The outside public knew not whether or not the man foully done to death was an agent or not. In the customary notice found pinned on his back, it was inferred that he was, and, when cases of this kind were numerous, the layman concluded that the rebel organisation had almost miraculous facilities for tracing a betrayer.[3]

However, perhaps the most important aspect of the new documentation is that it permits a more complete assessment of those conjunctures when it appeared that a new and more harmonious North/South relationship might be worked out. This is of particular relevance in the immediate aftermath of the Framework Documents of February 1995 which were designed to provide a model for such a transformed relationship. To a remarkable degree the language, and, more importantly the concepts underlying all three efforts—the Craig/Collins pacts of 1922; the O'Neill/Lemass meetings of the mid-1960s and the Framework Document of 1995—are similar; yet so far, no such effort has succeeded and in such a context there may be a lesson to be learnt from previous failures.

The Craig/Collins Pacts of 1922

The 1922 meetings between Sir James Craig, staunch Ulster Unionist Prime Minister, and Michael Collins, IRA leader and head of the new provisional government in Dublin, surprised many contemporaries. Yet, the immediate context is clear. Craig's intelligence services had told him that on the eve of the Anglo-Irish truce of July 1921 it had been 'the intention of the Sinn Féin authorities to send 500 men to Ulster to carry on guerrilla warfare'.[4] This latent danger obviously created a predisposition on Craig's part to deal with the new government in Dublin—perhaps its intentions since the signing of the Anglo-Irish Treaty in late 1921 were now peaceable? Craig later explained that he wanted to get on to the 'ground floor' before some damaging proposition was advanced on either side or indeed before the London and Dublin governments approached him with some unsatisfactory initiatives of their own. In the light of these considerations, the fact that Craig and Collins reached an agreement is perhaps less surprising than has sometimes been suggested. For as Collins' most sympathetic and well-informed biographer, Tim Pat Coogan, has argued, whilst Collins himself was a die-hard nationalist, he was well aware

---

[3] PRO 904/156/24. This document is clearly the work of Sir Ormonde Winter; see his *A Winter's Tale* (1955).

[4] PRONI SB 24/4710. Divisional Commissioner's report signed E. Gilligan and dated 2/12/1921.

of the fact 'that the bulk of the people in the twenty-six counties wanted a return to peace, not adventures across the border' (Coogan, 1991; see also Staunton, 1997). Collins also had particular and immediate concerns about the release of IRA prisoners. Both men wanted to sort any possible changes in the territory of Northern Ireland as quickly as possible; though they had very different views as to how extensive these might be. Craig wanted small adjustments whilst Collins was looking for something more radical. Collins wanted to see Catholic workers in Belfast receive better treatment; Craig wanted an end to the economic boycott of Northern businesses by the South—though largely for reasons of 'political atmosphere' as perhaps only 10 per cent of Northern businesses were affected in an economic sense. They were both willing to consider measures of practical cooperation on an 'all Ireland' basis. The terms of the agreement between the two men were published in the press:

> 1   The Boundary Commission as outlined in the Treaty to be altered. The governments of the Free State and of Northern Ireland to appoint one representative each to report to Mr Collins and Sir James Craig, who will mutually agree on behalf of their respective governments the future boundaries between the two.
>
> 2   Without prejudice to the future considerations of his government on the question of tariffs, Mr Collins undertakes that the Belfast boycott be discontinued immediately, and Sir James Craig undertakes to facilitate in every possible way the return of the Catholic working men—without tests— to the shipyards as and when the trade revival enables the firms to absorb the present unemployed. In the meantime a system of relief on a large scale is being arranged to carry out the period of distress.
>
> 3   Representatives of both governments to meet to facilitate a settlement of the railway dispute.
>
> 4   The two governments to endeavour to devise a more suitable system than the Council of Ireland for dealing with problems affecting all Ireland.
>
> 5   A subsequent meeting will take place at a subsequent date in Dublin between the signatories to discuss the question of prisoners. (*Irish Times*, 22 January 1992)

This result was 'a sensation', in the words of one journal, 'scarcely second in importance to the Treaty . . . Sir James Craig and Michael Collins can never again be to one another as they were' (*Co. Cork Eagle*, 11 February 1922). The joy of Southern unionism, in particular, was unconfined; Southern unionist opinion stressed that the provisional government was now likely to enjoy a better relationship with influential Protestants—particularly in the banking and financial sectors—within its own state. There was delight also that Craig and Collins had agreed some mechanism for mutual cooperation. The same journal noted that the agreement involved discarding the vague and ineffective Council of

Ireland—which was the only device the British parliament could invent for bringing North and South closer together. In its place there would be a more suitable system 'evolved through the combined efforts of the Irish governments'. The *Co. Cork Eagle* insisted: 'Whatever Mr Collins and Sir James Craig may design, it will have the supreme advantage over the discarded Council of Ireland, that it will be of Irish manufacture—racy of the soil and so better fitted for its work than the imported model' (28 January 1922). In his press conference afterwards, Sir James Craig declared that he had no idea in his mind of coming to a specific agreement on anything but as time went on he saw his opportunity and Mr Collins saw his. Craig added:

> For the credit of our land we were able to put our joint names to a document which, on the one hand, is an admission by the Free State that Ulster is an entity of its own, with a head with whom they can at any rate confer . . .
>
> At any rate, I think, our meeting has reassured the loyalists throughout the south and west, that we, by recognising the government formally, will greatly aid the unionists, loyalists and level-headed men throughout the country to rally to that government—which at all events is endeavouring to restore order and stave off separation and 'the Republic', which is the party cry of the other side. (*Co. Cork Eagle*, 4 February 1922)

To this end he was prepared to have a settlement which left the road open, at some future date for 'Ulster' to decide whether it joined the 'Free State' or not. This explained why he had not vetoed Collins' proposal for a constitutional conference for Ireland as a whole. Addressing 500 key members of his own party on 27 January, Craig was unrepentant: 'My duty was, in effect, to lead'. He added:

> What I was aiming at is Ulster's security, Ulster's close ties with Great Britain and the Empire, but as part of Ireland that it should be a free part of Ireland and not an Ireland at war. I have kept before my eyes all the time that in the long run it is better for the south and west and the Empire that we should be in the condition I have stated, because it seems to me we will be some little check on the hotheads in the south, if they know that by proclaiming the Republic, by trailing the Union Jack in the dust, by causing harm to the loyal people who belong to us—kith and kin of ours, that they only put the clock back for a century as far as any hope of getting Ulster in, whereas, as Lord Carson said in the House of Commons on a famous occasion: 'Ulster might be wooed by sympathetic understanding, she can never be coerced'.[5]

The more remarkable aspects of Craig's stand requires some analysis. In the first place, it is clearly predicated on the assumption—to use modern

---

[5] *Irish Times*, 28 January 1922. The reference is to the Carson speech of February 1914 discussed in Bew, 1994: 103.

Framework Document or Downing Street Declaration parlance—that Britain had no selfish strategic or economic interest in partition; in other words, it was for 'Ulster' and 'Ulster' alone—'Ulster' here meaning the six counties of Northern Ireland—to decide whether or not it chose to join up with the South. All that really matters for Craig is that the principle of consent be respected; this can be achieved most effectively through Dublin's recognition of the Northern parliament. There is also the willingness to take up the 'Council of Ireland' idea—purged of the unwieldy bureaucratic machinery proposed in the Government of Ireland Act of 1920—as a means of providing a forum for North/South contact in matters with an 'all-Ireland' dimension. Craig was challenged by angry grass-roots loyalists who argued that he had conceded too much, but he was able to carry the bulk of Ulster unionist opinion—especially business opinion—with him. As Craig himself said at the time—his duty was to lead, not to follow. It is, however, also worth noting that Craig laid great stress on the position of Southern protestants—in this he was, of course, strongly supported by Lord Edward Carson, whose roots were in that community. He signalled that this community should rally to the support of the Free State government as the least unpleasant available option—but he also argued that the North should signal a possible long-term willingness to come in with the South, in order to protect that community from republican onslaught in the South. In later years, as the Southern Protestant community went into rapid decline by the end of the 1920s—as a result of policies of violence, 'control' through language policy and breaking of professional links with the rest of the UK—this consideration ceased to have significant impact on Craig's approach.[6]

However, there was no corresponding satisfaction on the part of Michael Collins. Immediately after his meeting with Craig, he confessed his unease about the overall political situation in a letter of 27 January to one of his girlfriends, Kitty Kiernan (O'Broin, 1996). Even after this meeting with Craig, Collins at a cabinet meeting on 30 January still considered himself to be carrying out a policy of non-recognition of the Craig regime;

---

[6] Thus Craig, who had managed a rhetoric of 'minority rights' and 'North-South cooperation' in the difficult period of 1921–26, lapsed into a more stale vocabulary. By 1933 Craig was ignoring the complaints of Southern Protestants, in favour of the more simplistic notion of a confessedly Protestant state in the North and a confessedly Catholic state in the South. His patriarchalism with regard to the Protestant community, always an element of his political style—he furnished the Co. Down men under his command in the South African war with special rations, paid out of his own deep pockets – became his whole style. On the role of violence in reducing the size of the Protestant commnity, see Hart (1998), McDowell (1997), on matters such as language policy, intellectual life and the attacks on UK professional links see the material presented in Jones (1997a) and on professional links see Jones (1997b).

he was prepared to support school teachers and local bodies who refused to recognise the new state.[7] On 1 February, Collins and Griffith met a delegation of Northern nationalists and assured them they would insist on the transfer of large territories from the six counties—he reassuringly insisted that Northern nationalists were pushing at an 'open door' on this point. Even more ominously, Collins assured this deputation: 'There were only two policies—peace or war. He and his colleagues were going to try the peace policy first' (*Irish Times*, 2 February 1922).

Sir James Craig balefully noticed this delegation: he argued that the impact was a negative one. 'Yesterday', said Sir James Craig, 'Mr Collins adopted a very different attitude from that he showed at the first meeting . . . It appeared that he had been driven by the extremists to reverse his earlier policy of conciliation' (*Co. Cork Eagle*, 11 February 1922). Craig had assumed that had only meant adjustments of the border were at stake. Michael Collins, for his part, declared: 'Our attitude has been made perfectly clear and that we will not coerce any part of Ulster, which is desirous of remaining in the area controlled by the Northern parliament but neither will we allow coercion of any part of Ulster which votes itself into the Irish Free State'. As Collins privately told his cabinet, he then wished to wage a tariff war against a smaller Northern Ireland.[8] Hardly surprisingly, this time the Craig/Collins discussions broke down completely.

Worse still, the Free State government appeared to switch immediately into war-like mode. The *Irish Times* reported grimly:

> We deplore the unofficial but authoritative reports which suggest that the provisional government is dallying with the fatal notion of war upon Ulster. It says that an attempt may be made to smash the machinery of the Northern administration by reducing such services as the Post Office and the Land Commission to a state of chaos. (3 February 1922)

Yet, it is worth noting that the official public line of the new Free State government remained unchanged. In an ironic comment on de Valera's republican propaganda on partition, the *Free State* observed on 25 February: 'We have agreed with de Valera that we should not coerce Ulster, still agree not to coerce Ulster but have the power to make it worth while for Ulster to join with the rest of Ireland'. But such public language was increasingly compatible with rather more devious forms of private action. On the night of 7/8 February, Collins secretly approved a series of IRA raids across the border into Fermanagh and Tyrone which led to the kidnapping of 42 prominent loyalists, including the High Sheriff of Fermanagh: these were intended to be used as bargaining counters to

---

[7] SPO (Dublin), Provisional Government, cabinet conclusions, 30 January 1922.
[8] SPO (Dublin), Provisional Government, cabinet conclusions, 6 March 1922.

secure the release of IRA prisoners. Three days later 5 died (four B-Specials) in a clash between B-Specials and IRA in Clones: the rest of the Specials were arrested. This, in turn, provoked violent loyalist reprisals in Belfast, including a bomb attack which killed 6 children. Matters continued to deteriorate along these lines in March—in that month 35 Catholics and 18 Protestants were killed in Northern Ireland.

Blithely disregarding his own role in the deterioration, Collins sent an angry telegram to the British government on 6 March 1922:

> Belfast parliament apparently powerless or unwilling to prevent bloodshed or to bring criminals to justice. Invariably your troops are called against our people and feeling running very high against this course of action. Suggest you send an independent investigator and my statements can be shown to be correct. Cannot over-emphasise the seriousness of the situation. Absolutely imperative that some action be taken.[9]

At the end of the month, responding to such pressures, the British government sponsored an attempt to renew the Craig/Collins pacts. On the eve of this meeting, Sir James Craig claimed that his government did not blame the provisional government for IRA outrages in the North—though he noted language explicitly supporting Northern IRA violence had been used by senior figures closely associated with the regime such as Sean MacEoin, Eoín O'Duffy and P. McGrath. This rather tactful (if ambiguous) message clearly indicated that he was prepared to make a second serious effort to reach a settlement (*Irish Times*, 29 March 1922). After rather difficult discussions in which Collins apparently 'boasted'[10] of responsibility for outrages in the North, the terms of a new pact were dramatically announced:

1   Peace is hereby declared.

2   From today the two governments to cooperate in every way with a view to the restoration of peaceful conditions in the unsettled areas.

Its most important clause was the third one:

3   The police in Belfast to be organised in general accordance with the following conditions:

    a   The police in mixed districts to be composed of one half Catholics and of one half Protestants . . . All Specials not required for this force to be withdrawn to their homes and their arms handed in.

---

[9] PRONI, HA 31/1/28. Telegram from Collins to Churchill, 6 March 1922.

[10] Lady Spender's diary (6 April, 1922) records her husband Wilfrid Spender's view of these negotiations: 'Collins, who he says is like the hero of an American film drama, was very truculent . . . did not attempt to deny responsibility for outrages in Ulster . . . indeed he boasted of them'. Diary of Lady Spender in PRONI, D1633/2/24.

b An advisory committee composed of Catholics to be set up to assist in the selection of Catholic recruits for the Special Police. (*Irish Times*, 31 March 1922)

In addition the British government was to make available at least £500,000 for relief works—at least one-third of which was to go to Catholic workers. The essence of the new pact is clear: a reformed, non-sectarian Northern Ireland as far as security and employment policy was concerned, in exchange for an end to IRA violence (clause 6) and Dublin recognition. Many senior unionists felt that Craig had conceded too much ground—but the Prime Minister himself seems to have been determined to work the new arrangement.

Even so, this new pact was to fail as did its predecessor. In his explanation of that failure, Michael Farrell lays great emphasis on the failure of the Northern government to fulfil its part by investigating four particularly brutal reprisal murders of innocent Catholics in the Arnon Street/Stanhope Street area in retaliation for the earlier IRA murder of a policeman on the day after the pact was signed: 'Eye-witnesses in the area and a number of Catholic policemen claimed that they could identify the police involved and that they were led by the district inspector of the area, J. W. Nixon' (Farrell, 1983: 114, 330). In Michael Farrell's view, 'D.I. Nixon was a powerful and influential figure in loyalist, Orange and Ulster Special Constabulary circles'; but he adds, more controversially, 'it seems that Craig had to choose between confronting his own forces and undermining the pact. He chose the latter'. The difficulty with this interpretation is that it appears to overestimate the significance, undoubted though it was, of D.I. Nixon. It also underestimates the scale of mainstream unionist condemnation of the Arnon Street/Stanhope Street murders.[11] Farrell argues reasonably that the 'withholding of the file on Nixon even sixty years after the event inevitably sharpens suspicion about Nixon's role'. But one important file on Nixon has now been opened and it does not confirm his analysis.

The file actually opens with a complaint from Nixon that he, a district inspector, has been passed over for promotion to the rank of county inspector; worse still, in Nixon's view, he has been passed over in favour of Southern Catholic candidates. Nixon wrote:

> Some of the officers brought from southern Ireland have longer service than I have, and others have shorter service. I can not see why they should be brought from southern Ireland and appointed county inspectors over Ulster officers, Ulster sympathies, Ulster associations, and at least with as good police records . . .

[11] 'Mob Law at its Worst', *Weekly Northern Whig*, 8 April 1922.

It is a common saying here that loyalty to Britain does not pay but I hope the same will not be said about Ulster, but it is very hurtful to be rejected by those whom you considered your friends.

Personally, I attach little importance to the promotion itself, except that I feel that as if Sinn Feiners and their friends were laughing at me for getting left after all my exertions against them. In short, I can hardly conceive how the Home Secretary could bring District Inspector Regan and promote him over me.[12]

The Minister of Home Affairs, R. Dawson Bates, himself a rather shrewish Orangeman, was singularly unimpressed by this complaint. He wrote to a cabinet colleague, J. M. Andrews:

Much stress is placed on appointments not having been given to Ulstermen; but the analysis will show that more than half of the officers are in fact Ulstermen. Mr Nixon is not included in this category, but comes in under the heading of 'Irish' as, although the inference in his letter is that he is an Ulsterman, the fact remains that he comes from Co. Cavan.[13]

In fact, the RUC senior command had 58 officers; 12 of whom were Irish Catholics and the rest were English, Southern Protestant, or by far the largest category, Ulster Protestants (*Irish Times*, 17 October 1996). This is nevertheless a wry touch—consciously or unconsciously indicating— that Ulster had come to mean the 'six counties' as opposed to the 'historic' nine (including Cavan, Monaghan and Donegal) very early indeed in the life of the government of Northern Ireland. One sees here that birth of the 'little Ulsterist' mentality—so often to be rightly associated with a narrow bigotry, but here being comically turned against one of the great exponents of sectarian extremism. Anyway, as Bates told a Tyrone loyalist delegation who had wrongly assumed that a security 'leak' was due to the activities of a Catholic policeman: 'And do they think a police force could be carried on without Roman Catholics?'[14]

In 1924 Bates finally succeeded in easing Nixon out of the force—this despite a spectacular campaign of intimidation of even the high and mighty of the unionist hierarchy by Nixon's supporters—Bates commented: 'I never thought that the time would come when any group of persons who are loud in their protestation of loyalty would take their cue from Sinn Féin'. Bates argued that the public expression of private political opinions by the police—as Nixon had done on a number of occasions—would

---

[12] PRONI HA 31/1/254. Nixon's protest to R. Dawson Bates is dated 11 July 1922.
[13] Ibid.
[14] PRONI HA 31/1/467. Minutes of meeting of delegation led by Captain Hamilton Fyffe, solicitor, Co. Omagh. Though as Kevin Myers points out in *Irish Times* (17 October 1996) Collins used co-religionists to steal security files in the North and South; as Stephen Gwynn admitted in his *Observer* articles (see below) this was bound to affect unionist policy.

destroy the 'utility of our force'. The burden of this Nixon file is clear
enough; a government which felt strong enough to refuse Nixon promotion
at the expense of a Catholic policeman was hardly going to allow Nixon to
determine the fate of the Craig/Collins pact. There is no question that
Nixon—later a unionist MP at Stormont—was powerful enough to be a
thorn in the flesh of the government; no doubt also that he was suspected
of involvement in reprisals, reprisals which had been a common feature of
the police response to the IRA's campaign of murder of policemen all over
Ireland since 1919 and for which few policemen had been made account-
able because the 'authorities' regarded the practice as inevitable. But it is,
none the less, clear that the government felt no overwhelming need to
placate Nixon where his interests clashed with those of wider policy; Craig
undoubtedly did not want an enquiry into the working of his state
'security' forces but this was a context in which he and his officials clearly
believed that the peace proposals of the pact were not being worked
honourably by the Collins government: to accept an inquiry would imply
a possible major culpability for continuing disorder—a notion which
mainstream unionism bitterly rejected. David Lloyd George, the British
Premier, anxious to secure his accommodation with Michael Collins, was
sympathetic to Dublin calls for a full-scale judicial inquiry, but this eventually transmuted to a private inquiry by a senior official, S. G. Tallents,
which concluded at the end of June: 'I have no doubt that the failure to give
effect to clause 6 of the Agreement which provided for the cessation of IRA
activity in the six counties was the major cause of its failure'.[15]

The alternative view was expressed in the *Free State*, the organ of the
Irish government, which described government in the North as 'government by animals'. In this view, a reign of terror had been unleashed on the
Catholic minority which required Southern support—if only to maintain
its morale. These morale-boosting actions included the shooting of a
unionist MP, the destruction of the houses of others and even, at the end
of May, an 'invasion' of Fermanagh (at Belleek) by Free State forces. The
Northern government, in turn, believed that these were the real acts of
aggression. One captured document (13 May) from the north-east advisory
committee of nationalists—Collins' Northern representatives—in effect
spoke of a 'definite plan of campaign to be adopted by the nationalists
of the north-east whereby they can render impotent the so-called government of Northern Ireland'.[16] On 24 May 1922, Major General A. Solly-
Flood, the Northern Irish government's military advisor, prepared a
'Guide for City and County Authorities in Connection with the Defence

---

[15] PRO CO 906/30.
[16] PRONI, HA 32/1/206.

of Ulster'. Some of its proposals were draconian—in the event of 'war' disaffected areas were to be proclaimed; there was to be widespread use of censorship and black-lists of suspect officials were to be drawn up. The document concluded:

> The real difference between the precautionary period and the war period is that at this latter period the main duty of the Constabulary is to kill or capture the enemy, for it is by overcoming and evicting him from the six counties that peace can be restored. There must be no half measures when enemy forces are met.[17]

On 27 June 1922 S. Watt, a senior official of the Ministry of Home Affairs, summarised the position as he saw it:

> A very large number of outrages attributed to the IRA have been committed and documents and other evidence in the hands of the Intelligence Branch prove that the provisional government is fully cognisant of the activities of the IRA. These outrages include many cases of murder and wounding of members of the police forces, government officials and loyal subjects, ambushes, laying of mines, sniping across the frontiers, seizure of motor cars, arson etc., fifteen police and one civilian kidnapped prior to 30 March 1922 and seven police and seventeen civilians kidnapped since that date are still detained in southern Ireland. Some of these men were kidnapped in the Free State.
>
> On 20 May a wholesale series of raids and attacks on various police barracks and incidences in Counties Antrim and Down occurred which could only have been carried out in pursuit of an organised plan, while the forces which invaded Northern Ireland at Belleek and Pettigo would appear from the statement issued by GHQ at Beggars' Bush [see *Belfast Telegraph*, 6 June 1922] to have been troops who owed allegiance to the Free State.
>
> It is clear from documents found that the IRA are determined to make Ulster part of a free Irish Republic [see *Northern Whig*, 7 June] and to make the task of the northern government impossible.
>
> The boycott of Ulster has been reinforced more vigorously than ever [see Arthur Griffith's speech in *Newsletter* of 27 April where he admits this, though of course repudiating responsibility] and attacks have been made on Ulster firms in Dublin—the headquarters of the provisional government, looting of towns and seizure of northern goods still continue.
>
> No attempt has been made to restore to their homes the refugees driven from southern to Northern Ireland.[18]

Tallents regarded Watt as a 'partisan' figure but he seems to have accepted the validity of much of this analysis. It is clear, however, that Craig's earlier apparently genuine attempts to reach a compromise with Collins stood in good stead with London. In particular, Winston Churchill

---

[17] PRONI, HA 32/1/466.
[18] PRONI HA 5/139/6.

insisted that Craig's moderation implied that Britain had a duty to defend the North, thus, for example rebuff the Belleek/Pettigo invasion. But it does not follow that Craig had always intended only this outcome or that he was principally to blame for the failure of the two pacts.

The next major effort to achieve a measure of *rapprochement* on a North/South basis came with the O'Neill/Lemass meetings of the 1960s. Both Terence O'Neill, Northern Premier, and Seán Lemass, Irish Taoiseach, were self-proclaimed modernisers. Their meetings initially generated great optimism about the future of Ireland. However, the documents recently released in Dublin, Belfast and London serve to highlight the ambiguities of this process. Lemass was not perhaps as iconoclastic (with respect to nationalist pieties) as many have assumed. Professor Henry Patterson, the scholar who has worked most with this material, insists that there were contradictions in Lemass's policies on the North: in particular, he continued, whilst calling for greater North/South functional cooperation, to employ a relatively unreconstructed rhetoric on the national question. O'Neill—whose antennae were very sensitive to any signs of disapproval in London—picked up the notion that the London governments of Macmillan and Alec Douglas-Hume (that is to say, even before Harold Wilson) felt that the Northern government should respond to Lemass on themes of cooperation. O'Neill was responding to this external pressure: he was fully aware that Brookeborough's obstructive attitude towards a Lemass proposal for a North/South Free Trade Agreement— something which had support both from within the unionist cabinet (Lord Glentoran) and local businessmen—had annoyed London. London's view was that Lemass was such an improvement as compared with de Valera that the North should seize the new opportunity and not complain so much about the irridentist Articles 2 and 3 of the Irish constitution of 1937. The principal difficulty for O'Neill arose out of Lemass's tendency to present economic cooperation as leading to a relatively quick end to partition. Also, Lemass seems to have misunderstood the British position as being part of the broad sweep of 'wind of change' and 'decolonisation' policies. Because of these confusing signals from Dublin, O'Neill was never able to keep a dialogue on a pragmatic economic level and was always open to internal revolt, exacerbated by the rise of Paisleyism (Bew *et al.*, 1997: Chapter 1). Similar difficulties befell Brian Faulkner in 1974.

More recently, these difficulties have again been reprised in the controversy over the Anglo-Irish Joint Framework Document, published by both governments in February 1995. This text outlines the imaginary line of compromise between unionist and nationalist aspirations. On the British side, a significant influence on the Framework Document was an article by the late Dr John Whyte, Professor of Politics at The Queen's

University, Belfast. Dr Whyte drew attention to the large number of voluntary associations which had an all-Ireland identity and in which unionists participated freely. He noted that the secretary of his local Unionist Association was also the secretary of one of these all-Ireland bodies. The implication is clear: North-South bodies are already a significant part of Northern Irish life, and they might have a role to play in any compromise. Fresh bodies worked, in effect, on the basis of the principle of consent.

On the Irish side, a key concept was a rather unrefined concept of an 'island economy' perceived in a European context. The growing integration of the two economies, North and South, was intended to provide the basis of all-Ireland harmonisation. In fact, the greater integration between the two economies, a key intellectual prop of the Framework Document, now looks to be a rather more uncertain project. The decision by Ireland to join the single European currency while the UK stays out has seen to that. As the Lancaster House paper 'North-South Co-operation' reveals, it is difficult to talk, say, of harmonisation of financial services when the two countries will be inside different currency systems.

All of the current controversy and debate which surrounds the Framework Document and the current talks process cannot hide the fact that the underlying themes are those of Craig-Collins: the need to produce equality of treatment for Northern Catholics; the need to produce a system whereby the two governments, North and South, will work together on an all-Ireland basis—the same notion here reappearing in both the Craig-Collins agreement and the 'Heads of Agreement' promulgated at Stormont early in 1998—and the need for the Irish government to recognise the North. On this last point, the failure of the Dublin government to promise (in the event of an otherwise satisfactory negotiated settlement) that the words 'the territory of Ireland is the island of Ireland'—and thus the territorial claim—be removed from its constitution constituted a difficulty (Bew and Gillespie, 1996: 90). What is clear, however, is that we are not served by a history—unsupported by serious acquaintance with the latest available material archives—which exaggerates unionist intransigence on the matter of cross-border cooperation. It deprives those unionist leaders who wish to reach an understanding with Dublin of the necessary cultural and ideological resources. It is also a more hopeful sign that in a recent interview for *Parliamentary Brief* with the present author, the Taoiseach, Mr Ahern said: 'We have to make constitutional changes and we have to make them as clear and as acceptable as we can. I would be anxious that we do not create ambiguities and further difficulties'.

When the Craig-Collins pact was signed in April 1922, Stephen Gwynn, a former Protestant nationalist MP who had lost his seat to the new Sinn

Féin movement in 1918, offered an analysis in *The Observer* on 2 April 1922; he was confident that Craig was genuine in his policy of peace, even though he had earlier condemned Craig's failures to alleviate the condition of Belfast Catholics since the first pact—by contrast Gwynn felt that unionist restraint in rural border areas had been impressive—he now felt sure that Craig was sincere. He pointed out: 'If Ulster wanted war, Ulster only had to wait. With an IRA divided, raids across the border were certain and every raid was worth a British battalion to Ulster, if Ulster bided its time. Enough of such raids, borne without retaliation in the end, the war must have had full British support. It looks as if the strategists have decided that Ulster's interest was peace' (*Observer*, 19 February 1922). He noted that even while the negotiations leading to the new pact were ongoing, new policemen were killed by the IRA close to Monaghan on 29 March (*Observer*, 2 April 1922). Stephen Gwynn—and possibly here he was speculating over-much—saw as factors making for the pact the benign influence of Sir Henry Wilson, former Chief of the Imperial General staff and unionist MP, but also Joe Devlin, moderate Belfast nationalist MP, and prominent Southern Orangemen. This is perhaps less important than his analysis of the underlying principles involved: 'Generous recognition for differing interests without regard to their numerical strength is the saving formula for Ireland'. He might have added: the need to cooperate on an all-Ireland basis. As the *Weekly Northern Whig*, a staunch unionist supporter of the regime, put it in an important editorial on the pact:

> Friendly co-operation between north and south is not only perfectly practic-
> able but necessary in the interests of the populations on both sides of the
> border. Ulster's refusal to submit to the authority of a Dublin parliament
> does not involve refusal to recognise the palpable fact that the six counties
> and the twenty-six have much in common and that it is their duty to help each
> other to the extent of their capacity. (*Weekly Northern Whig*, 1 April 1922)

But the leader added 'Ulster' would never accept 'forceful incorpora-
tion in the Free State'—indeed, 'Every effort to bring it about is bound to result in further alienation of the people'. Seventy-five years later little has changed; though the large reduction in the size of the Southern Protestant population has made it more difficult for unionists to think in 32 county terms, on the other hand, the Ahern government is far more solid in its commitment to the principle of consent than the Collins one ever was.[19] This has to be a source of hope that this time a viable North-South arrangement will be achieved.

---

[19] For the most recent analysis of the 'devious northern policy' of Collins, see Fitzpatrick, 1998.

References

Barton, B. (1995) *Northern Ireland During the Second World War*, Belfast: Ulster Historical Foundation.

Bew, P. (1994) *Ideology and the Irish Question*, Oxford: Oxford University Press.

Bew, P. and Gillespie, G. (1993) *Northern Ireland: A Chronology of the Troubles 1968–93*, Dublin: Gill and Macmillan.

Bew, P. and Gillespie, G. (1996) *The Northern Ireland Peace Process 1993–96*, London: Serif.

Bew, P., Darwin, K. and Gillespie G. (eds) (1993) *Passion and Prejudice*, Belfast: Institute of Irish Studies.

Bew, P., Gibbon, P. and Patterson, H. (1979) *The State in Northern Ireland 1921–1972: Political Forces and Social Classes*, Manchester: Manchester University Press.

Bew, P., Gibbon, P. and Patterson, H. (1994) *Northern Ireland 1921–1994*, London: Serif.

Bew, P., Gibbon, P. and Patterson, H. (1996) *Northern Ireland 1921–1996*, London: Serif.

Bew, P., Patterson, P. and Teague, P. (1997) *Northern Ireland: Between War and Peace*, London: Lawrence and Wishart.

Buckland, P. (1979) *The Factory of Grievances: Devolved Government in Northern Ireland 1921–39*, Dublin: Gill and Macmillan.

Buckland, P. (1980) *James Craig*, Dublin: Gill and Macmillan.

Campbell, C. (1995) *Emergency Law in Ireland 1918–1925*, Oxford: Oxford University Press.

Catterall, P. and MacDougall, S. (eds) (1996) *The Northern Ireland Question in British Politics*, London: Macmillan.

Coogan, T. P. (1991) *Michael Collins*, London: Hutchinson.

Farrell, M. (1975) *The Orange State*, London: Pluto.

Farrell, M. (1983) *Arming the Protestants*, London: Pluto.

Farren, S. (1995) *The Politics of Irish Education 1920–65*, Belfast: Institute of Irish Studies.

Fitzpatrick, D. (1998) *The Two Irelands*, Oxford: Oxford University Press.

Follis, B. (1995) *A State Under Siege: The Establishment of Northern Ireland 1920–25*, Oxford: Oxford University Press.

Foster, R. (1988) *Modern Ireland 1660–1972*, London: Allen Lane.

Harris, M. (1993) *The Catholic Church and the Foundation of the Northern Ireland State*, Cork: Cork University Press.

Hart, P. (1996) 'The Protestant Experience of Revolution in Southern Ireland' in R. English and G. Walker (eds), *Unionism in Northern Ireland: New Perspectives on Politics and Culture*, London: Macmillan/Dublin: Gill and Macmillan.

Hart, P. (1998) *The Irish Republican Army and its Enemies: Violence and Community in Co Cork*, Oxford: Oxford University Press.

Jones, G. (1997a) 'Catholicism, Nationalism and Irish Intellectual Life', *Irish Review*, 20: 47–61.

Jones, G. (1997b) 'The Rockefeller Foundation and Medical Education in Ireland in the 1920s', *Irish Historical Studies*, xxx, No. 120, November, 1–17.

Kennedy, D. (1988) *The Widening Gulf: Northern Attitudes to the Irish Free State 1921–48*, Belfast: Blackstaff Press.

Macdowell, R. B. (1997) *Crisis and Decline: The Fate of the Southern Unionists*, Dublin: Lilliput.

McIntyre, A. (1995) 'Modern Irish Republicanism: The Product of British State Strategies, *Irish Political Studies*, 10: 97–123.

O'Broin, L. (ed.) (1996) *In Great Haste*, (revised extended edition) Dublin: Gill and Macmillan.

Phoenix, E. (1994) *Northern Nationalists: Nationalist Politics, Partition and the Catholic Minority in Northern Ireland 1890–1980*, Belfast: Ulster Historical Society.

Staunton, E. (1997) 'Reassessing Michael Collins' Northern Irish policy' *Irish Studies Review*, 20: 9–12

Whyte, J. (1983) 'The Permeability of the Irish Border', *Administration*, vol. 31.

Winter, O. (1955) *A Winter's Tale*, London: Richards Press.

Political Cleavages and Party Alignments in Ireland, North and South

GEOFFREY EVANS & RICHARD SINNOTT

Introduction

THE ORIGINS AND THE NATURE OF POLITICAL CLEAVAGES are central issues in any systematic comparison of the two parts of Ireland. One might even say that they are *the* central issues since, without these cleavages, we would not be comparing 'two parts of Ireland'; nor would there be a 'Northern Ireland problem'. This chapter addresses a limited aspect of this question, namely, the relationship between the cleavage system and the party system at the mass level. Parties are variously seen as articulators, or aggregators, or embodiments of conflicting interests. Whether parties articulate specific interests or aggregate a wide range of interests in a catch-all fashion and whether they embody or institutionalise basic cleavages or simply represent ad hoc coalitions of particular interests at individual elections, are questions of fundamental interest in terms of understanding party systems and electoral behaviour; in the context of the problems in Northern Ireland they are also of some practical interest in that they affect the role parties play in the generation, maintenance and resolution of political conflict.

The background to our analysis derives from Lipset and Rokkan's (1967) well-known 'freezing' hypothesis in which they argued that the cleavages underlying European party systems at the beginning of the twentieth century or earlier continue to form the basis of divisions in contemporary politics. In their account, certain historical junctures—Reformation and Counter-Reformation, centre-periphery relations during periods of nation and state-building, the timing of industrialisation—are held to have had a profound influence on the nature and on the extent of politicisation of divisions in any given country. These historical developments have tended to generate four major cleavages: centre-periphery,

Proceedings of the British Academy, **98**, 419–456. © The British Academy 1999.

church versus state, town versus country, employer versus worker; which of these, or which combination, comes to dominate depends on the historical path taken and upon the degree of social and cultural distinctiveness of the social groups involved (Bartolini and Mair 1990: 224). Thus the strength of a particular social cleavage will be conditioned by its institutionalisation in the party system at the onset of democratic competition. In the case of the two Irish political systems, the critical juncture can be dated to the process of mass electoral mobilisation and the institutionalisation of political competition in 1918 and the turbulent years that followed. A key aim of this chapter will therefore be to assess the influence of the political cleavages that existed at that time on the structure of present-day politics in the two systems. For this purpose we examine not only the political issues that might divide parties and their supporters, but also the social characteristics that have been thought to provide the basis of partisanship and mobilisation. In combination, these two sources of structure have been said to provide the key to understanding the stability of European party systems (Ibid.: 219). In particular, we consider what the current evidence suggests about the potential for change in the patterning of the two party systems: what is the current state of electoral mobilisation? What is the relationship between parties and voters? Are there emerging lines of cleavage that could form the basis of a political realignment? To what extent has Ireland, North or South, already embarked on a period of realignment and what would be the implications of such a development?

A systematic North-South comparison can be expected to be particularly useful in this context. Given the common origins of the two party systems, an important question is to what extent the differences between them can be understood, on the one hand, as regional variations in the island of Ireland that were institutionalised by partition or, on the other hand, as effects of the differences in their situations that have emerged since partition, particularly the presence or otherwise of unresolved conflict and the eruption of violence and terrorism. Part of this inquiry is to trace the ways in which the divergent paths of development following partition may have altered the salience of the constitutional issue, both in absolute terms and relative to the 'left-right' cleavage regarding inequality and the role of the state.

The first part of this chapter traces the common roots of the political parties on the island of Ireland from the mid-nineteenth century onward, noting the growing polarisation that occurred and focusing especially on the effects of partition on the emerging cleavage systems. It then attempts to tease out the implications of the particular form of the institutionalisation of cleavage, North and South, for involvement in the political process and for the contemporary bases of party choice. The empirical analysis then tests the implications of this account of the development of the party systems at the mass level by focusing on three aspects of political representation: voter turnout, levels of identification with parties and the structure of political divisions in the two societies.

The Origins of the Party Systems and the Effects of Secession

While the main foundations of the party systems in Ireland North and South are located in the period 1918–23, it is useful, particularly in the context of a North-South comparison, to trace the origins of the political parties in earlier periods of partial electoral mobilisation and party competition. In the early nineteenth century Irish political parties were simply extensions of the Tory and Whig parliamentary alliances that dominated British politics. This began to change in the period from 1832 to 1880, a period characterised by 'the metamorphosis of the Whigs into the Liberal party, which increasingly became the party of Catholic Ireland, and of the Tories into the Conservative party, which quickly became the party of Protestants' (Coakley, 1993: 6). The other development that occurred toward the end of this period was a strengthening of the link between the religious cleavage and an emerging territorial cleavage resulting, eventually, in the displacement of the liberals by the nationalists as the representatives of Catholic Ireland. The year 1885 saw a significant widening of the franchise and a step in the direction of mass electoral mobilisation. This intensified the religious/territorial cleavage and strengthened the position of nationalism. Its impact on the institutionalisation of cleavage was limited, however, both by the modest extension of the franchise involved and by the restraint on party competition imposed by the extensive territorial segregation of the competing groups (Garvin, 1981: 89–90).

The context of the 1918 election (1916 and all that) included the emergence of radical nationalism as an electoral force in the form of a remodelled Sinn Féin Party. Sinn Féin overwhelmed the moderate nationalist Irish Parliamentary Party in the South and mounted a very substantial challenge to the nationalist party in the North. Whereas in 1884 the electorate had increased from 8 to 31 per cent of the population aged 20 and over, in 1918 it went from 26 to 75 per cent. While there were still uncontested areas, a much fuller mobilisation occurred and this was followed, especially in the South, by a decade of intensive political activity and party building and the establishment of the real basis of the party system. The implications of these developments can be clarified by applying the Lipset-Rokkan framework to the analysis of the processes of electoral mobilisation and the development of the party systems and electoral alignments North and South, beginning, for reasons of ease of exposition, with the South.

Secession, Cleavages and Parties in the South

The insight which opened the way for the application to Ireland of the standard model of the development of European political cleavages and party systems is due to John Whyte. His focus at the time was on the development of cleavages and parties in the South. The positive implications of what he had to say for the comparability of the Irish case were perhaps obscured by his statement that 'It is, then, perhaps a comfort to comparative political analysts that Irish party politics should be *sui generis*: the context from which they spring is *sui generis* also' (Whyte, 1974: 648). Accompanying this apparently negative assessment of the comparability of the Irish party system, however, was a lucid comparative account both of the prevailing cleavages in the United Kingdom in 1918 (as seen from an Irish perspective) and of the effect of secession on the development of political cleavages in the South.

Reminding the reader of the four cleavage categories 'worked out by Lipset and Rokkan in their magisterial work on party systems and voter alignments' he argued that 'Ireland has handled all these conflicts to varying extents in exceptional ways' (Ibid.: 647). In particular, 'the centre/periphery crisis was . . . resolved in Ireland in an unusually absolute way: Ireland is a former part of the United Kingdom periphery that simply broke off'. The land-industry conflict 'again . . . was solved in an unusually absolute way. The agrarian sector broke off to found its own state' (Ibid.: 648). The same observation applies to the church-state conflict: the periphery and therefore the secessionist state was overwhelmingly and loyally Catholic. The owner-worker conflict was the only potential cleavage that was internal to the new state, but both its material and cultural bases were weak.

This view forms the basis of a fruitful application of the Lipset-Rokkan approach to the party system in the South. In the absence of major conflict along agrarian-industrial, church-state and owner-worker fault-lines, the dominant cleavage in what was to become the Republic of Ireland was based on a centre-periphery conflict in which Southern Ireland was the periphery and London the centre. Through the treaty split and the civil war, this centre-periphery cleavage became the bedrock of the Irish party system. The two parties (Anti-treaty Sinn Féin/Fianna Fáil and Cumann na nGaedheal/Fine Gael) became identified with opposing positions on the issue, though it must be emphasised that these positions were not nationalist versus anti-nationalist but radical nationalist versus moderate nationalist. Though these differences can be subtle and nuanced, residues of them are clearly discernible in the contemporary party politics of the Republic (Sinnott, 1986a; 1986b; Laver and Hunt, 1992). Two other consequences of the development and institutionalisation of cleavages in the South should be noted. The first is the persistent minority status of the Labour Party. The second is that the dominant role of the centre-periphery conflict in the building of the Irish party system left the two largest parties as free agents on other potential cleavage dimensions; as such, they have at various times pursued identical policies or even exchanged positions on a wide range of issues: on church-state relations, on public spending, on the role of the state in the economy, on the interests of industry and agriculture, and on free trade versus protectionism.

Given this background, the major feature of the Irish party system in recent years has been its vulnerability. This vulnerability arises, in the first place, because part of the original centre-periphery conflict (the Anglo-Irish relations part) was solved by the Anglo-Irish Treaty of 1938 and the declaration of a Republic in 1948 and the part that was not solved (the Northern Ireland problem) developed into so intractable and so bloody a conflict that it ceased to be a basis which could sustain overt inter-party competition. Secondly, from about 1960 onwards, Irish society underwent rapid economic, social and cultural change. Thirdly, partly as a result of these changes, potential alternative bases of cleavage emerged or at least threatened to emerge in the form of either embryonic left-right or secular-confessional conflict. Political scientists pored long and hard over the entrails of what seemed to be an emerging class conflict in the party system in the 1980s, while the possibility of a secular-confessional conflict in the same period also appeared to be substantial. The victory of Mary Robinson in the presidential election of 1990 was seen by some as indicative of the emergence of a combination of both and, certainly, as a 'cataclysmic event' (Finlay, 1991). It should also be noted that the vulnerability of the party system in the South is exacerbated by the electoral system variable (PR-STV), which facilitates party fragmentation and particularistic voting. We would expect therefore that, in the South, contemporary party choice will not be strongly determined by positions on the original cleavage issue (nationalism). Whether it is determined by positions on other issue dimensions—i.e., left-right or secular-confessional—will provide an indication of the extent of any realignment. The lack of *any* pronounced basis to partisanship would suggest dealignment.

Secession, Cleavages and Parties in the North

While creating a highly homogeneous society and institutionalising an external conflict between Britain and Ireland in the party system in the South, the secession of Southern Ireland strengthened the potential for conflict *within* Northern Ireland on three of the four Lipset-Rokkan cleavage dimensions. First and foremost, there was the centre-periphery (unionist-nationalist) conflict, which, with religion as an ethnic marker, split the new political entity into a two-thirds majority versus a one-third minority. This conflict would have existed whether or not state institutions had been established in Northern Ireland. The establishment of a government and parliament of Northern Ireland did, however, exacerbate the conflict by giving a local focus both to unionist possession and nationalist dispossession. But, over and above this potent mixture of religion, nationalism and considerable political autonomy, the establishment of the state added a further, sharper edge to church-state conflict: the state was a Protestant state and the Catholic Church went into opposition, nurturing and guarding institutions of cultural separation at every turn. Because religion is also the clearest ethnic marker in Northern Ireland, it is important to emphasise that church-state relations constituted a distinct dimension of conflict in addition to the nationalist/centre-periphery cleavage. Even if nationalism had been weak in Northern Ireland, there would have been a conflict between church and state; as it was, both conflicts were strong and, by and large, each reinforced the other.

The third line of cleavage that was intensified by the secession of Southern Ireland was that between owners and workers—the class cleavage most closely associated with industrialisation. In the South of Ireland, over 50 per cent of the work-force were engaged in agriculture and a mere 12 per cent in industry in the period immediately following secession. In the North, by contrast, only 26 per cent were engaged in agriculture and 39 per cent in industry (Harkness, 1983: 46). Clearly the potential for the political mobilisation of labour against capital was much greater in the North. In the event, a left-right cleavage played a very subordinate role in each jurisdiction. In the South, the minimal potential for left-right alignment that might have existed was definitively side-lined by the abstention of the Labour Party in the 1918 election. In the North, the conflict between capital and labour was not so much sidelined as subsumed into the overriding conflict between unionism and nationalism.

The outcome in Northern Ireland was not, therefore, the emergence of a fully developed multidimensional cleavage system (which might have led to some amelioration of conflict through cross-cutting cleavages). Instead, a centre-periphery cleavage, in which the marker of ethnicity was religion, emerged and dominated all other cleavages in the society. To this picture of reinforcing lines of cleavage must be added the fact that the very creation of the Northern Ireland state was the creation of a cockpit of conflict in which the lines of struggle were drawn with particular clarity and invested with a special intensity born of proximity, smallness of scale and historical longevity. This was exacerbated by the institutional combination of a local parliament operating on strict majoritarian and adversarial lines and, from 1929 until the abolition of Stormont in 1972, using a plurality or first-past-the-post voting system. This institutionalisation of a Protestant majority (which saw itself as a besieged minority) ensured that, for most of the period since partition, there was little prospect of Catholics having an effective political voice.

Against this background, one would expect a continuing intense partisan alignment in Northern Ireland. A number of considerations might, however, qualify this expectation. First, one-party dominance and the consequent reduction of party competition in a first-past-the-post electoral system may have injured the capacity of parties to represent the interests of voters. Secondly, the contemporary party system will inevitably have been affected by the intractability of the conflict, by the failure of repeated efforts at conflict resolution and by the partial displacement of parties by terrorist organisations as carriers of the putative interests of each side to the conflict. Given the manifest failure of the party system to manage the conflict, the level of attachment to political parties may well have declined over the last two decades. Thirdly, in the wake of the abolition of a representative assembly and the imposition of an alternative form of governance, it seems likely that a partial realignment did in fact occur, with the addition of a further layer to Northern Ireland's cleavage structure through the growth of parties (the Democratic Unionist Party and Sinn Féin) drawing their force from the interests of groups that were not adequately represented by the established unionist and nationalist parties (see Evans and Duffy, 1997: 52–5). Despite these qualifications, however, the most plausible prediction for the North is the maintenance of the original alignment, in which party choice is determined mainly by position on the ethnic/centre-periphery cleavage, possibly complemented by position on a left-right axis of more recent vintage.

Analysis

In testing the expectations set out above, three sets of data will be examined. The first is data on electoral turnout, for all types of elections in both jurisdictions. Secondly, we use Eurobarometer data to analyse the

evolution of party attachment over time. The advantages of the Eurobarometer in this context are obvious: it provides twice-yearly data for
Northern Ireland and the Republic since the late 1970s. The disadvantage
is that, in the case of Northern Ireland, the sample in each survey is only
300. In the analysis that follows, this is partly overcome by combining the
two samples in each year; even so, sample size is less than would be
desirable, particularly when we proceed to compare attitudes in the two
communities. The third data set, which we use to examine the bases of
party choice, consists of coordinated studies of national identity and of
attitudes to the Northern Ireland problem carried out in 1995 and 1996.
Sample sizes in this case are approximately 1,000 in each area.

Turnout North and South, 1920–96

High turnout is both a condition of the maintenance of an electoral
alignment and an indicator of its strength and stability. Figure 1 shows
turnout in general elections, local elections, presidential elections and
European Parliament elections in the South. Across the different kinds
of elections, average turnout has ranged from 45 per cent in non-
concurrent European elections to 70 per cent in general elections. Over
time, turnout in general elections has ranged from 60 per cent in 1923,
through 80 per cent in 1933, to 66.7 per cent in 1997. The first point to note
about this line in the graph, however, is that the sharp rise in general
election turnout between 1923 and 1932 needs to be substantially dis-
counted because of problems of redundancy in the electoral register in
the 1920s.[1] Turnout in 1997 was therefore, in all probability, the lowest
since the foundation of the state, surpassing the previous low of the snap
war-time election of 1944. The 1997 figure confirms a modest but indis-
putable downward trend in turnout in general elections since 1981 when
turnout was 76.2 per cent. That this is part of a general trend is suggested
by the decline in turnout in local elections since 1967, a slight decline in
turnout over the two European Parliament elections that have not been
linked to another more substantial electoral contest[2] and by the turnout of
42 per cent in the presidential election of 1997. The increase in turnout in
the presidential election of 1990 might have been regarded as confounding
any suggestion of a declining trend, but the 1997 presidential turnout put
paid to that notion. The relatively high turnout in 1990 may have been due

---

[1] This redundancy occurred mainly in western and north-western areas (see Sinnott, 1995:
84–87).
[2] European Parliament elections coincided with local elections in 1979 and with a general
election in 1989.

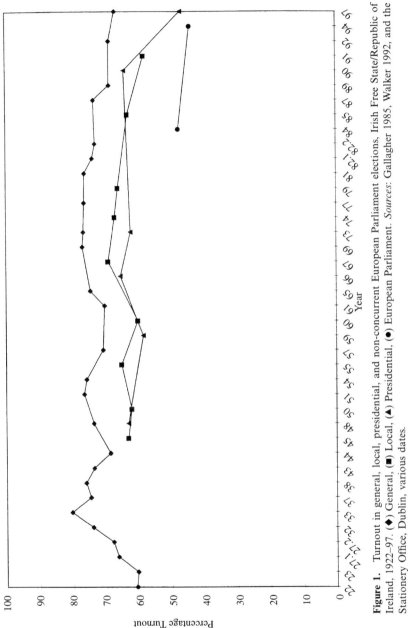

Figure 1. Turnout in general, local, presidential, and non-concurrent European Parliament elections, Irish Free State/Republic of Ireland, 1922–97. (◆) General, (■) Local, (▲) Presidential, (●) European Parliament. *Sources:* Gallagher 1985, Walker 1992, and the Stationery Office, Dublin, various dates.

to the novelty of the event (the previous one had been in 1973); if it was due, on the other hand, to a more fundamental process of mobilisation, this would give no comfort to the existing party system. Whether or not the 1990 presidential election was cataclysmic may be debatable; what is not debatable is that it was a contest that challenged rather than reinforced existing electoral alignments and the established party system.

At first sight, the turnout data for Northern Ireland present a strange picture: as measured in the normal way, i.e., voters as a proportion of the total electorate, turnout in Northern Ireland Parliament (Stormont) elections appears to have plummeted in the first decade or so of the existence of the state, to have recovered somewhat between 1938 and 1949, but then to have fallen sharply again in the early 1950s, and not to have recovered until 1969 or even 1973 (see Figure 2). The picture of turnout in Westminster elections is stranger still: starting from an extremely low level in 1922 and 1923, it seems to gyrate on a two-election cycle until 1955 when it settled down to a more normal level and a more normal pattern. The explanation of these enormous fluctuations in the rate of recorded participation in elections in the early decades of the existence of Northern Ireland is a simple but, in terms of our inquiry, quite significant one: relatively large swathes of the Northern Ireland electorate did not have a regular opportunity to vote in Northern Ireland Parliament elections from 1925 to 1969 and in Westminster elections from 1922 to 1951. This is illustrated in Figure 3, which presents bargraphs of the proportions of the electorate in contested constituencies and a line graph of voters as a percentage not of the total electorate but of the electorate in the contested constituencies. The absence of contests was a function of a combination of safe seats and the abstentionist policies pursued by nationalist parties. The temporary disenfranchisement of the voters was particularly widespread in 1922 and 1923 (both Westminster elections), in 1931 (Westminster) and 1933 (Stormont) and was at quite a high level (40 per cent or more) in all Stormont elections between 1929, when plurality voting was introduced, and 1965. This absence of competition clarifies the anomalies that are apparent in the turnout data for the early decades in Figure 2 and confirms that the turnout estimates from 1955 on for Westminster elections and from 1973 on for Northern Ireland Assembly elections can be relied on but that the earlier figures require radical adjustment to allow for non-contested constituencies. On the basis of the adjusted turnout figures for the early years we can make at least some tentative observations (see Figure 3). Turnout in Westminster and especially in Stormont elections went through two periods of decline: it fell between 1921–22 and 1945 and then, following a notable increase in turnout in 1949–50, declined again between then and the mid-1960s. It

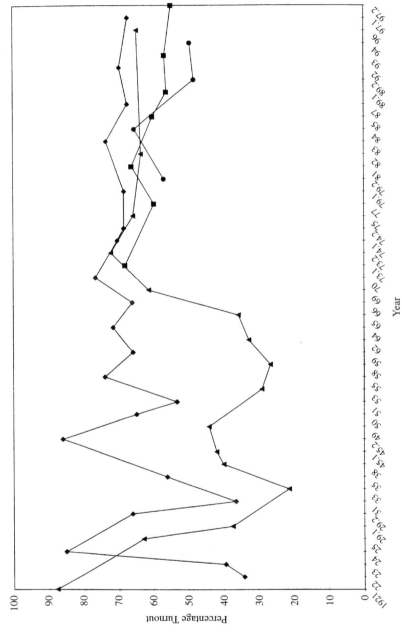

Figure 2. Turnout as proportion of total electorate in Northern Ireland Parliament/Assembly, Westminster, district council and European Parliament elections, 1921–97. (▲) NI Parliament/Assembly, (◆) Westminster, (■) District Council, (●) European Parliament.
Sources: Flackes and Elliot 1994, Walker 1992, *Irish Political Studies,* 1995, 1997, 1998.

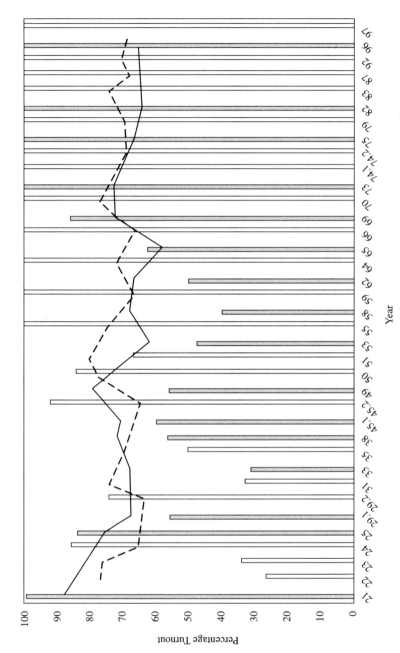

Figure 3. Proportion of total electorate and turnout in contested constituencies, Northern Ireland/Assembly and Westminster elections, 1921–97. ▨ Electorate in contested constituencies – NI Parliament/Assembly, ☐ Electorate in contested constituencies – Westminster, ——— Turnout – NI Parliament/Assembly, - - - - Turnout – Westminster. *Source*: As Figure 2.

recovered in Stormont elections in 1969 and in Westminster elections in 1970.

Given the oddities of the turnout data for Northern Ireland in the early years, the best approach to North-South comparisons is to concentrate on the period since 1970 when we have both reliable data and data from a variety of types of elections. As with the South, we have data from four types of elections for this period: Westminster, Northern Ireland Assembly, District Council and European Parliament. Taken as a whole, these data indicate a significant decline in turnout since the early 1970s: from 77 per cent in 1970 to 68 per cent in 1997 in the case of Westminster; from 72 per cent in 1973 to 64.7 per cent in 1996 in the case of the Assembly; from 68.1 per cent in 1973 to 54.7 per cent in 1997 in the case of the District Councils and from 56.9 per cent in 1979 to 49.4 per cent in 1994 in the case of the European Parliament. Taken together, all of this suggests a degree of demobilisation in Northern Ireland more or less on a par with the South; this demobilisation is in conflict with the general expectation that electoral alignments would have been more strongly maintained in Northern Ireland.

Party Attachment in Ireland, North and South, 1973–95

If parties are the carriers or sources of the maintenance of political cleavage as suggested by Lipset and Rokkan, one would expect that levels of attachment to parties would be high and stable over time. Although controversies may rage about how it should be measured, about its applicability across systems and about its consequences for voting choice, party attachment has been an enduring concept in the study of voters and parties. Indeed, the classic 'Michigan model' of voting behaviour (Campbell *et al.*, 1960) sees party identification as the primary mechanism by which the structure of political cleavages is reproduced over time.

The basic concept is a simple one: voters do not make a fresh choice of party at each election; rather, they possess what has been variously described as a degree of affective support for, a standing decision in favour of, a sense of loyalty or a feeling of closeness to, or an identification with a certain party. In any given election voters may vote otherwise than in accordance with this prior sense of commitment; nevertheless, so the argument goes, the commitment remains an important attribute of the voters, affecting not only their propensity to vote for a given party but also their perceptions of politics and even the positions they adopt on issues. While party identification is the most popular label for the concept, it is probably preferable to use party attachment as the generic term;

identification, closeness, loyalty etc., can then be treated as particular operationalisations of the overall concept. The notion of party attachment fits in well with a Lipset-Rokkan style account of cleavages and party systems: party attachment is the carrier at the level of the individual of the systemic-level electoral alignment that is central to the theory. Application of the concept to the Irish party systems leads to two pertinent questions: has the alignment which originated in Southern Ireland between 1918 and 1923 survived in the form of enduring attachments to parties in the very different Ireland of the period since the late 1960s? Has attachment to party in the North, which one would expect to have endured in tandem with the persistence of the basic cleavage, survived the political failures and the party fragmentation brought on by the Troubles?

The two main operationalisations of party attachment are party identification and party closeness. In the following analysis we use the latter measure as implemented in Eurobarometer surveys since 1978. This enables us to compare Ireland North and South on this dimension over almost two decades and to compare trends in both parts of Ireland to trends in Europe as a whole.[3] Figure 4 presents the data on party attachment in the Republic, in Northern Ireland and in the European Community for the period 1978–94. The evidence clearly supports the dealignment hypothesis in the South: since 1978, party attachment has declined by some 20 percentage points from about 60 per cent in the late 1970s to less than 40 per cent in the early 1990s. The decline occurred in three stages: between 1980 and 1981, between 1983 and 1986 and between 1988 and 1991. The level of party attachment in Northern Ireland appears to have been significantly lower than that in the Republic at the outset of the period under consideration. Given that party attachment in the North did not show any consistent trend between then and the mid-1980s and given the already noted decline in party attachment in the Republic, levels of party attachment in the two systems became remarkably similar. The similarity indeed extends into the second half of the period considered as party attachment in both jurisdictions declined at more or less similar rates between 1987–88 and 1991.

---

[3] Irish-European comparisons of party attachment must be approached with caution. There are significant differences in the wording of the party attachment question in the Eurobarometer surveys, mainly between a relative question ('do you feel closer to one party than to the others?') and an absolute question ('do you feel close to any particular party?'). It can be shown that the relative question produces higher proportions with party attachment than does the absolute question. The relative question has been asked in most continental European Community member states of the European Community/Union and the absolute question has been asked in Britain, Northern Ireland and Ireland. This means that only the measures for North and South are directly comparable; the European average is included in Figure 5 to provide a yardstick only for comparing general *trends* in levels of attachment.

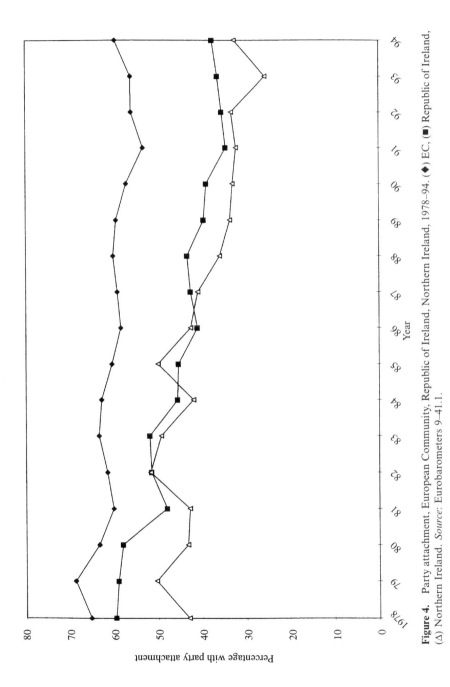

Figure 4. Party attachment, European Community, Republic of Ireland, Northern Ireland, 1978–94. (♦) EC, (■) Republic of Ireland, (△) Northern Ireland. *Source:* Eurobarometers 9–41.1.

If there are signs of similarity between North and South, there are substantial differences in party attachment within Northern Ireland, between
Protestants and Catholics. Figure 5 shows that except for two years (1978
and 1988), levels of attachment to party have been quite different in the two
communities, being substantially higher among Protestants than among
Catholics. Similar downward trends are, however, observable in both communities, the decline being precipitous among Catholics between 1978 and
1980 and more evenly spread over time among Protestants. In short, and
viewing the period 1978–94 as a whole, the level of party attachment has
been about the same in the Republic and in the Protestant community in
Northern Ireland and has been notably lower in the Catholic community;
the trends among all three groups have, however, been downward.

   It might be argued that these downward trends are simply part of a
general trend in Western Europe and that the evidence of party attachment
examined so far therefore sheds little or no light on specifically Irish
developments; there has after all been a lot of speculation in recent years
about just such a decline and about the more general phenomenon of
dealignment. Before writing off the significance of the Irish trends in this
way, however, we should note Schmitt and Holmberg's scepticism about a
general decline in party attachment: following a detailed analysis of all of
the available evidence, they concluded that '. . . specific developments, by
country and by party, are so varied that any "overall" view disguises more
than it discloses' (Schmitt and Holmberg, 1995: 121). This sceptical view
regarding any overall trends, up or down, is confirmed when we compare
the average trend in party attachment in the European Community as a
whole with the Irish trends: while there may be some slight evidence of a
decline across the Community as a whole, it is small compared to what
occurred in Ireland, North and, particularly, in the South (see Figure 4).
Indeed, one of the most striking features of Figure 4 is the absolute
discrepancy in party attachment in Ireland, North and South, and in the
European Union. We have already issued a severe health warning in regard
to drawing inferences from the absolute differences between Europe and
Ireland on the basis of the data in Figure 4. We have also noted, however,
that Eurobarometer data that make an adjustment for the differences in
question wording are available from the post-election Eurobarometer
survey of June-July 1994 (EB 41.1).[4] These data, which enable us to

---

[4] The adjustment was made by inserting a supplementary question, which asked all those
respondents who gave a negative answer to the initial question whether they 'feel a little closer
to one of the parties than to the others'. As hypothesised when this methodological test was
undertaken, the supplementary question produced larger additional proportions of attached
voters in countries in which the absolute question had been asked as compared with countries

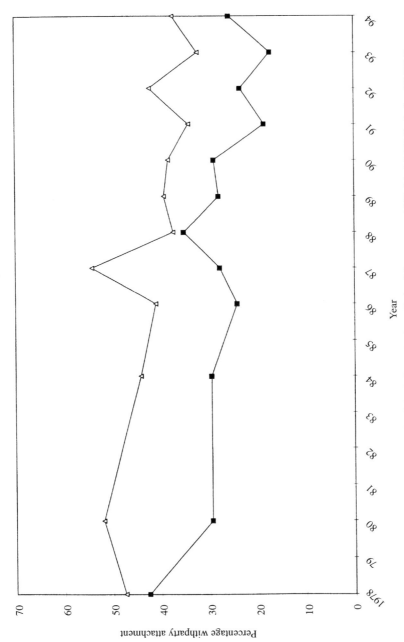

Figure 5. Party attachment, Northern Ireland Catholics, Northern Ireland Protestants, 1978–94. (■) NI Catholic, (△) NI Protesant.
Source: Eurobarometers 9–41.1.

make a direct comparison of levels of party attachment across all member states, are presented in Figure 6. This shows that the Republic of Ireland and, following close on its heels, Northern Ireland had the lowest levels of attachment to party across 14[5] European political systems in June-July 1994. However we may explain the decline in party attachment in the two systems, the process involved has left the two parts of Ireland looking very similar to each other and very different from the majority of member states of the Union with respect to this important party-system characteristic. It is perhaps significant that the only case that comes close to Irish levels of detachment from party is Belgium, a state that has also been characterised by a fundamental cleavage on the nationalist issue. Our original expectations were that party attachment would have declined in the South but would have been maintained in the North. The evidence confirms the first expectation but not the second. It is understandable that party attachment would be withering away in the Republic; it appears that, rather than maintaining or even intensifying attachment to party, the prolonged conflict in Northern Ireland is also associated with a reduced attachment to parties. The context of politics in each jurisdiction and the experiences and records of the parties North and South may have been very different; the results were, however, the same: similarly low levels and a continuing erosion of party attachment.

The Bases of Party Support, North and South

This brings us to the final and most complex part of this comparative exploration of electoral alignment in Ireland North and South: the basis of party choice. Our analysis of the structure of political cleavages in the two systems involves an assessment of, first, the extent to which voters' partisan preferences are structured by ideological cleavages or social characteristics and, secondly, the dimensionality or cross-cutting character of the relationships between partisanship and such underlying structures of cleavage as may exist.[6] Our consideration of events since partition led to opposing prognoses for North and South: in the North, party choice should be

---

in which the relative question had been asked (Sinnott, 1998). The data from the supplementary question can be used to construct a functionally equivalent measure of the overall levels of party attachment across all member states as of 1994.

[5] The comparison can be made across 14 cases by treating Northern Ireland (sample 300) and former East Germany (sample 1,000) as separate political systems.

[6] The relevance of cross-cutting issues and social cleavages to the situation in Northern Ireland has received detailed treatment by a variety of survey analysts (Budge and O'Leary, 1973; Aunger, 1981; Duffy and Evans, 1996). In the South, the question of the dimensionality of inter-party differences has been dealt with, for the most part, at elite level.

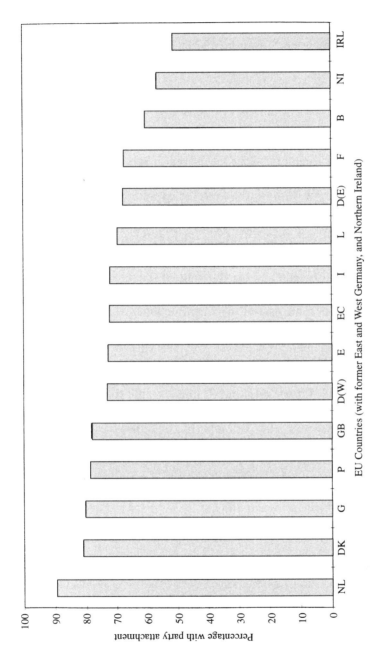

Figure 6. Total party attachment in the member states of the EU, June–July 1994 (with sub-samples for former East and West Germany and Northern Ireland). NL = Netherlands, DK = Denmark, G = Greece, P = Portugal, GB = Great Britain, D(W) = West Germany, E = Spain, EC = European Community, I = Italy, L = Luxembourg, D(E) = East Germany, F = France, B = Belgium, IRL = Ireland. *Source:* Eurobarometer 41.1.

significantly determined by position on the original cleavage, whereas in the South, the original cleavage should have withered to insignificance. At the same time, although these were our original expectations, the evidence examined so far on levels of turnout and on party attachment suggests that the long-term cleavage structures in both systems may have been undermined.

After 25 years of conflict involving numerous practical and theoretical efforts to devise constitutional solutions to the problem, the range of possible constitutional alternatives for the future governance of Northern Ireland is considerable and complex. The attempts of survey researchers to grapple with this complexity have meant that it is quite difficult to obtain comparable evidence on constitutional preferences across different surveys.[7] This paper draws on a coordinated survey effort conducted in the context of the comparative ISSP (International Social Survey Programme) study of national identity and the BSA (British Social Attitudes) and NISA (Northern Ireland Social Attitudes) surveys.[8] The constitutional preferences question was asked in an identical manner in Britain, Northern Ireland and the Republic of Ireland.[9] The question gave four basic options for the future governance of Northern Ireland: remain part of the UK, become part of the Irish Republic, be governed jointly by the UK and the Irish Republic or become an independent state. Each of the first three options was presented in two alternative forms, i.e., with or without a separate Parliament in Belfast.[10]

Table 1 presents the data derived from this question for Britain, for Northern Ireland Protestants and Catholics and for the Republic of Ireland. The contrast in attitudes between Protestants in Northern Ireland and the three other publics is striking: the constitutional preference of 84 per cent of Northern Irish Protestants is supported by 20 per cent of Northern Irish Catholics, 16 per cent of people in Britain and 9 per cent of people in the Republic of Ireland. Substantial majorities of both Northern Irish Catholics and of people in the Republic of Ireland express a preference for either a United Ireland or joint governance of Northern

---

[7] With sufficient effort, however, the evidence can be compared and is effectively marshalled in Hayes and McAllister (1996).

[8] The authors are grateful to the ISSRC and the Greeley Trust for support for the ISSP study in the Republic of Ireland.

[9] Unfortunately comparability is somewhat reduced by the non-coincidence of fieldwork dates; fieldwork was carried out in Britain and Northern Ireland in the spring of 1995 and in the Republic in the spring and summer of 1996.

[10] This question was designed by Geoffrey Evans and Brendan O'Leary to obtain a more informative measure of views on the constitution than can be gained from the standard two-option question used in the BSA and NISA surveys.

Table 1. Attitudes to future government of Northern Ireland among NI Protestants, NI Catholics, and in the Republic of Ireland and Britain (%).

	NI Protestants	NI Catholics	Republic of Ireland	Britain
Remain part of the UK without a separate parliament in Belfast	29	12	4	11
	84	20	9	16
Remain part of the UK but with a separate parliament in Belfast	55	8	5	5
Become part of the Irish Republic without a separate parliament in Belfast	0	18	23	14
	2	31	38	27
Become part of the Irish Repblic with a separate parliament in Belfast	2	13	16	13
Be governed jointly by the UK and the Irish Republic without its own parliament in Belfast	1	10	9	3
	5	28	22	16
Be governed jointly by the UK and the Irish Republic with its own parliament in Belfast	4	18	14	13
Become an independent state with its own parliament, separate from both the UK and the Irish Republic	4	7	17	11
Can't choose	6	14	13	20
N	674	431	997	1,058

Note: Question wording: Here are a number of different ways in which Northern Ireland might be governed in the future. Please tick one box to show which you would most prefer.

Ireland; it should, however, be noted that, in line with the conclusions drawn by Hayes and McAllister (1996) from their analysis of a wide range of surveys, the preference for a united Ireland in the Republic is substantially down on what it has been in the past. The question which most concerns us, however, is: how do the supporters of the various political parties in Ireland line up on this issue?

Table 2 shows that there is very little difference on this issue between party supporters in the South. In particular, the supporters of the two parties (Fianna Fáil and Fine Gael) that embodied the original nationalist cleavage differ only on the nuances and then only minutely. In fact, the

Table 2. Attitudes to future government of Northern Ireland by party support (Republic of Ireland) (%).

	Fianna Fáil	Fine Gael	Labour Party	Others	Don't know
Remain part of the UK without a separate parliament in Belfast	3	4	5	5	4
	8	11	11	10	8
Remain part of the UK but with a separate parliament in Belfast	5	7	6	5	4
Become part of the Irish Republic without a separate parliament in Belfast	27	21	33	16	14
	40	39	52	35	31
Become part of the Irish Republic with a separate parliament in Belfast	13	18	19	19	17
Be governed jointly by the UK and the Irish Republic without its own parliament in Belfast	9	9	6	8	13
	22	25	17	21	23
Be governed jointly by the UK and the Irish Republic with its own parliament in Belfast	13	16	11	13	10
Become an independent state with its own parliament, separate from both the UK and the Irish Republic	16	17	12	21	17
Can't choose	14	8	9	13	20
N	383	210	89	166	113

Note: Question wording: Here are a number of different ways in which Northern Ireland might be governed in the future. Please tick one box to show which you would most prefer.

party with the most distinctive supporters is the Labour Party, whose supporters are actually a shade greener in this respect than the supporters of the other parties. In stark contrast to the virtual inter-party unanimity on this issue in the South, this same question polarises the supporters of the parties in Northern Ireland: 91 per cent of UUP supporters and 89 per cent of DUP supporters opt for remaining part of the United Kingdom, while only 15 per cent of SDLP supporters do so. Conversely, a mere 2 to 3 per cent of the supporters of either of the Unionist parties support any one of the set of options that link Northern Ireland more or less closely with the Republic and that are chosen by 68 per cent of SDLP supporters.

Table 3. Attitudes to future government of Northern Ireland by party support (Northern Ireland) (%).

	Alliance	DUP	UUP	SF	SDLP	Others	None
Remain part of the UK without a separate parliament in Belfast	26	32	30	9	9	23	23
	65	89	91	12	15	50	51
Remain part of the UK but with a separate parliament in Belfast	39	57	61	3	6	27	28
Become part of the Irish Republic without a separate parliament in Belfast	1	1	0	27	20	8	4
	8	1	1	57	33	16	10
Be governed jointly by the UK and the Irish Republic with a separate parliament in Belfast	7	0	1	30	13	8	6
Be governed jointly by the UK and the Irish Republic without its own parliament in Belfast	4	1	0	0	12	5	4
	18	1	2	3	35	20	14
Be governed jointly by the UK and the Irish Republic with its own parliament in Belfast	14	0	2	3	23	15	10
Become an independent state with its own parliament, separate from both the UK and the Irish Republic	7	8	3	15	5	5	6
Can't choose	4	2	3	12	13	10	18
N	133	127	334	33	236	101	272

Note: Question wording: Here are a number of different ways in which Northern Ireland might be governed in the future. Please tick one box to show which you would most prefer.

The conclusion that there are virtually no differences between party supporters in the Republic on this issue and immense differences between the supporters of the parties in Northern Ireland is confirmed when we look at the other measure, i.e., attitudes to the role of the Irish government in the running of Northern Ireland. The maximum difference between the three main parties in the South is 8 percentage points and this and any other trace of difference that exists is confined to the limited question of whether the Irish government should have 'a great deal of say' or 'some say'

in how Northern Ireland is run. When these two categories are combined,
very similar and overwhelming majorities in all three parties come down on
the positive side of the scale (Fianna Fáil, 74 per cent; Fine Gael, 76 per
cent; Labour, 72 per cent). In Northern Ireland, on the other hand, the
scale again polarises the supporters of the parties: 83 per cent of DUP and
72 per cent of UUP supporters express outright rejection of any role for the
Irish government; on the other side of the political spectrum, 62 per cent of
SDLP supporters and 82 per cent of Sinn Féin supporters want at least
some say for the Irish government (see Table 3). Within the nationalist side,
however, the scale makes a further distinction between SDLP and Sinn
Féin supporters (respectively 22 per cent and 53 per cent 'a great deal of
say' for the Irish government in the way Northern Ireland is run).

    While the above crosstabulations go some way towards answering the
questions raised regarding the differing fate of the original centre-
periphery conflict in the two parts of Ireland, the answers provided are
quite incomplete without consideration of where these supporters also
stand on other key issues or of how positions on the full range of issues
might relate to one another. To display these we present a number of plots
of the mean positions of party supporters North and South on several
scales: a nationalist, left-right and pluralist-confessionalist scale in the
Republic (Figures 7 and 8) and a nationalist and left-right scale in Northern Ireland (Figure 9). At first sight, the nationalist scale seems to distinguish quite effectively between the supporters of the various parties in the
South. This is seen to be quite illusory, however, when it is realised that the
supporters of the three main parties are almost completely indistinguishable on this scale. This is as predicted; less predictable is the even greater
degree of similarity between the supporters of the parties on the left-right
scale which measures attitude to the role of government in reducing differ-

Table 4. Attitudes to Irish government involvement in running Northern Ireland by party
support (Republic of Ireland) (%).

	All	Fianna Fáil	Fine Gael	Labour Party	Others	Don't Know
A great deal of say	30	34	28	29	26	26
Some say	42	40	48	43	38	48
A little say	15	14	14	17	16	12
No say at all	9	8	9	8	15	5
Can't choose	5	5	1	3	5	9
N	989	383	210	89	166	113

Notes: Question wording: How much say do you think an Irish Government of any party
should have in the way Northern Ireland is run? Do you think it should have . . .

Table 5. Attitudes to Irish government involvement in running Northern Ireland by party support (Northern Ireland) (%).

	All	DUP	UUP	Alliance	SDLP	SF	Others	None
A great deal of say	9	0	1	0	22	53	12	8
Some say	20	4	6	24	40	29	27	23
A little say	20	6	6	24	40	29	27	23
No say at all	42	83	72	36	5	0	29	31
Can't choose	9	6	4	7	14	6	11	14
N	1,237	126	334	133	238	34	100	272

Notes: Question wording: How much say do you think an Irish Government of any party should have in the way Northern Ireland is run? Do you think it should have . . .

ences between rich and poor. The supporters of the three main parties are also virtually *ad idem* on a measure of pluralism versus confessionalism: the supporters of all parties are located on the pluralist side of the scale and the only substantial differences are between the supporters of the tiny Democratic Left and the supporters of the three main parties. Fine Gael and Progressive Democrat supporters are a shade more pluralist on this scale than the supporters of Fianna Fáil or Labour, who have almost identical scores.

In contrast to the pervasive political homogeneity in the South, in the North the role of the Irish government scale shows up a huge gulf between the DUP and UUP on the one side and Sinn Féin and the SDLP on the other. It also distinguishes clearly between Sinn Féin and SDLP supporters on the nationalist side and it shows that Alliance Party supporters are to the unionist side of the centre but remain quite a distance from UUP and DUP supporters. Attitudes towards the role of government in redistribution show some difference between party supporters on each side of the constitutional divide: DUP supporters are more left-wing than UUP or Alliance supporters; the same goes for Sinn Féin in comparison to SDLP supporters.[11]

In order to complete this account of the bases of partisan cleavage in Ireland North and South, it is also necessary to examine the possible impact of socio-economic and demographic factors: these may provide a foundation for party choice that may or may not be mediated through explicit policy preferences. Thus, in the South we should explore possible social class and religiosity correlates of voting in addition to ideological

---

[11] Similar findings obtain using a more comprehensive 'left-right scale' comprising five items concerned with inequality and redistribution, see Evans and Duffy (1997), who also provide a detailed discussion of divisions within nationalist and unionist camps.

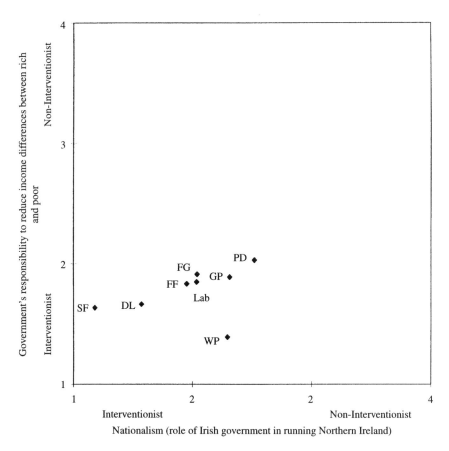

Figure 7. Mean scores of party supporters on a nationalist and a left-right scale, Republic of Ireland. SF = Sinn Féin, DL = Democratic Left, FF = Fianna Fáil, FG = Fine Gael, Lab = Labour, PD = Progressive Democrats, WP = Worker's Party, GP = Green Party.

and policy preferences; in the North we would obviously expect religious denomination to play an overwhelming role but class and urban-rural differences are also worth exploring. In all of this, we are particularly interested in teasing out the relative weight of different determinants of party preference. In order to do this we must take account of the simultaneous effect of all of these variables in a multivariate analysis.

Logistic regression is one of a group of multivariate techniques that calculate the odds of being in one response category rather than another (see Aldrich and Nelson, 1984). The response categories in this case are a series of dichotomies arrived at by comparing the choice between various pairs of parties or groups of parties. The first and most obvious pairing in

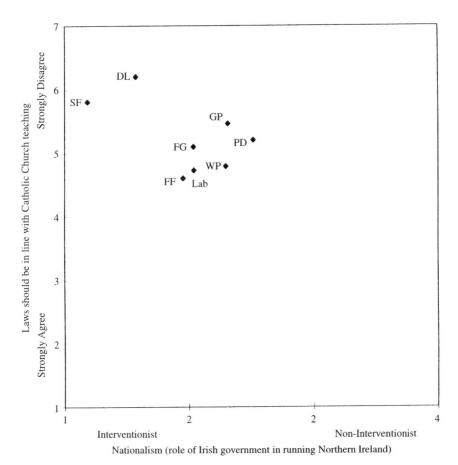

Figure 8. Mean scores of party supporters on a nationalist and a confessionalist scale. Republic of Ireland. SF = Sinn Féin, DL = Democratic Left, FF = Fianna Fáil, FG = Fine Gael, Lab = Labour, PD = Progressive Democrats, WP = Worker's Party, GP = Green Party.

the case of the Republic of Ireland is Fianna Fáil versus the rest.[12] This was for a long time assumed to be the basic fault line in the party system and is the dichotomy that should reveal any nationalist cleavage in the party system, if such exists. The main alternative cleavage is of course a division between left and right. This is explored in our second contrast: Fianna Fáil, Fine Gael and the Progressive Democrats, on the one hand, versus Labour, the Workers' Party and Democratic Left on the other. A third contrast that is in fact only a minor variation on this can also be explored:

[12] For the purpose of this analysis the small proportion of Sinn Féin supporters in the sample is omitted.

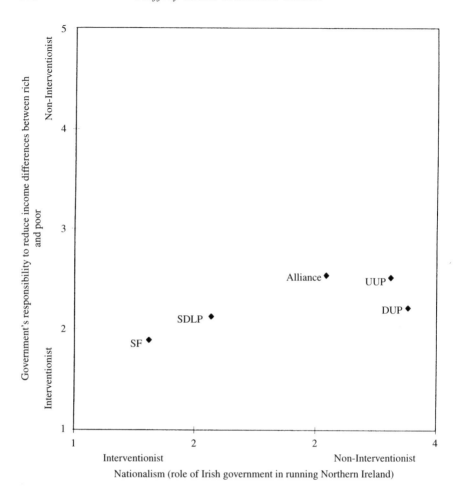

Figure 9. Mean scores of party supporters on a nationalist and a left-right scale, Northern Ireland. SF = Sinn Féin, SDLP = Social Democratic & Labour Party, Alliance = Alliance Party of Northern Ireland, UUP = Ulster Unionist Party, DUP = Democratic Unionist Party.

the so-called 'civil-war parties' (Fianna Fáil and Fine Gael) against the rest.[13]

The independent variables used in analysing these three contrasts are: preference regarding the amount of say an Irish government should have in running Northern Ireland; the importance of Irish identity; a measure of confessionalism-pluralism (whether laws should be independent of or in line with the teaching of the Catholic Church); frequency of religious

[13] These contrasts were chosen after a preliminary investigation of the structure of divisions among all of the main parties using discriminant analysis.

practice; attitude to income redistribution; age; self-identification as middle class and level of educational attainment. These variables provide a basis for testing for the existence of the three cleavages that we have focused on in our discussion of the Irish party system: nationalism, left-right ideological orientation and secularism-confessionalism.

The results of the test confirm the view that the original (nationalist) cleavage in the system has all but petered out; they also indicate that the gap has not been filled by either of the two alternative lines of conflict (left-right and secular-confessional) but that some limited divisions on both these lines have emerged. Thus, just three variables—frequent religious practice, a lower level of education,[14] and an emphasis on the importance of Irish identity—contribute to the prediction of the odds of being a Fianna Fáil supporter rather than a supporter of any of the other parties but the model does little to improve goodness of fit. The parameters which do attain significance are of modest size and, most importantly, attitude to the amount of say the Irish government should have in running Northern Ireland does not have any significant effect at all.[15]

Perhaps the original battle lines in the South over centre-periphery relations and nationalist issues have been replaced by conflict between left and right. The improvement in fit is a little better in the second model in Table 6, but the variables that predict support for the left have little to do with left versus right as traditionally conceived. The results indicate that the odds of supporting a left-wing party are affected by being young (specifically being between 25 and 34 years of age) while the odds are significantly reduced by a higher level of education and by frequency of religious practice. Most importantly, both subjective middle class identification and support for a government role in the redistribution of income are statistically insignificant.[16] There is some evidence here that the left-right divide between the parties may reflect a secular-confessional ideological divide. However, the reflection is, at best, subliminal since the direct measure of confessional ideological outlook (laws should be in line with the teaching of the Catholic Church) also has no significant effect.

---

[14] To ensure that socio-demographic effects were not being masked by attitudinal variables, all three socio-demographic variables were used in a first-stage, separate analysis. In the account that follows, attention will be drawn to any socio-demographic effects that appeared at this first stage but do not figure once attitudes are included in the model.

[15] If we rerun this analysis focusing on the contrast between Fianna Fáil and Fine Gael, which was after all the original embodiment of the conflict, none of the variables have a significant effect. This reinforces the point that, at the mass level, the original conflict in the party system has run its course.

[16] The class variable is significant in a model that consists only of socio-demographic variables. Thus there are class differences in support for parties of the left and right but the contrasts are more effectively captured by the variables in the final model reported in Table 6.

Table 6. Social characteristics, political attitudes and party preference in the Republic of Ireland, 1995.

	FF (1) vs the rest (0)	Left (1) vs the rest (0)	Civil War parties (1) vs the rest (0)
Irish goverment should have a say in the running of NI	0.08 (0.05)	0.01 (0.08)	0.13** (0.07)
Laws should be in line with teachings of Catholic Church	0.01 (0.04)	−0.03 (0.06)	0.03 (0.05)
Importance of being Irish	0.18* (0.10)	−0.16 (0.12)	0.33*** (0.10)
Attendance at religious services	0.08** (0.03)	−0.15*** (0.04)	0.19*** (0.04)
Govt should reduce income differences	−0.02 (0.06)	−0.16 (0.10)	0.15* (0.08)
Middle class (subjective)	0.07 (0.15)	−0.30 (0.22)	0.10 (0.19)
Education (no. of years)	−0.07** (0.03)	−0.10** (0.05)	0.01 (0.04)
Age under 25	0.01 (0.22)	0.47* (0.27)	−0.33 (0.25)
Age 25–34	−0.10 (0.15)	0.43** (0.20)	−0.42** (0.18)
Age 35–44	0.00 (0.14)	−0.24 (0.22)	−0.09 (0.18)
Age 45–54	−0.01 (0.15)	0.00 (0.22)	0.10 (0.20)
Age 55–64	0.00 (0.16)	−0.27 (0.26)	0.16 (0.22)
Age over 65 (reference category)	—	—	—
Constant	−1.72 (0.56)	0.92 (0.69)	−2.71 (0.64)
% classified accurately	60.7	86.6	76.0
Initial log likelihood	1,260.8	747.0	909.6
Improvement in fit	33.6, 12 df	48.0, 12 df	88.8, 12 df

Notes: The parameter estimates are logistic coefficients with standard errors in parentheses.
* significant at p <0.10 ** significant at p <0.05 *** significant at p <0.01.

Our final attempt to identify cleavage lines in the Irish party system pits the two 'civil war' parties against the rest. In the final model in Table 6, the improvement in fit (chi^2 88.75, for 12 df; represents a 9.8 per cent reduction in the log likelihood) is a little more impressive and several variables have significant parameters. Supporters of the 'civil war' parties are distinguished from the supporters of other parties in terms of age, religious practice, attitude to Irish identity and to policy on Northern Ireland, and, at the margin of statistical significance (0.07), by attitude to the role of government in redistributing income. Again it must be emphasised that the differences are modest: being older and more religious, placing more emphasis on Irish identity and being more supportive of a substantial role for the Republic in the running of Northern Ireland are characteristics that are linked to support for the 'civil war parties' but the relationships are far from being strong enough to warrant the conclusion that there are substantial cleavages underlying mass support for the political parties in the South.

The main conclusions of this analysis of the sources of party support in the South can be summarised briefly: the contemporary party system in the South is largely unstructured, whether we look for that structure in terms of ideological preferences or socio-demographic characteristics. To the extent that traces of such structure exist, they can be found mainly in degrees of religious practice; this makes some contribution to distinguishing between Fianna Fáil and the rest (including the left), between the left and the rest (including Fianna Fáil) and between the civil war and non civil war parties. The indicator of nationalism does not predict support for Fianna Fáil versus the rest (nor for Fianna Fáil versus Fine Gael) but it does play a modest role in distinguishing the civil war parties from the others. The measure of left-right ideological orientation does not pass the conventional minimum for statistical significance in any of the analyses we have conducted.

The structuring of party preference in the North is a very different story. As outlined above, we expect that party choice in Northern Ireland will be determined mainly by position on the ethnic/centre-periphery cleavage, possibly complemented by position on a left-right axis of more recent vintage. Given the nature of the conflict and the role of religion as an ethnic marker, it is very difficult to separate the effects of religion and nationalist preferences in the determination of party support. From a simple cross-tabulation of the survey data, we know, for example that more than 60 per cent of Protestants express support for one of the main Unionist parties (UUP and DUP) and that virtually no Protestants support either of the main nationalist parties (SDLP and Sinn Féin[17]); the remainder of the Protestant community either supports the Alliance (10 per cent) or gives a don't know/other minor party/no party response. Party support among Catholics is the mirror image of this. In this sense, religious affiliation is a good predictor of party support. But, how good? And, do nationalist preferences or other political attitudes also play a role?

---

[17] The number of respondents openly supporting Sinn Féin is clearly an underestimate—a common problem with surveys in Northern Ireland. Importantly for our purposes, however, comparison with analyses conducted on more extensive data indicates that this does not appear to have affected the relationships between Sinn Féin support and either social characteristics or the issue positions reported above (see Evans and Duffy, 1997).

What happens when we control for the effects of class[18] and other socio-demographic variables? Most importantly, what distinguishes party supporters within each camp (UUP versus DUP and SDLP versus Sinn Féin) and supporters of the more moderate party in each camp from Alliance supporters in the middle? This set of questions yields the five models presented in Table 7.[19]

The first model in Table 7 captures the pattern of division between unionist and nationalist camps. The blocs are formed by combining supporters of the UUP with those of the DUP to form the unionist bloc, and supporters of the SDLP and Sinn Féin to form the nationalist bloc. Unsurprisingly, the divisions are very firmly drawn: the initial log likelihood is reduced by no less than 87 per cent and 96.8 per cent of cases are accurately classified—and determined very much, but not completely, by respondents' denominational affiliations. The only additional significant predictor is the measure of attitudes towards the Irish government's involvement in the affairs of the North, which we use as a reasonably effective indicator of where respondents stand on the constitutional question.

It should be apparent, however, that even when analysing bases of partisanship that are distinct from the main nationalist versus unionist cleavage, all of the models in Table 7 display far greater levels of division than those observed in the case of the South (as indicated, for example, by considerably larger proportional reductions in the initial log likelihood). There are also major differences in the social and ideological content of the divisions. Thus although we expect the effects of denomination to be powerful, the most important patterns to observe in the subsidiary contrasts are that class and education effectively divide supporters of the more hard-line versus less hard-line parties: levels of support among middle class and more highly educated groups decrease as the distance from the political centre increases. The strong relationship between class position and

---

[18] Social class is measured using Goldthorpe's class schema (Erikson and Goldthorpe, 1992), in which class position is operationalised by a combination of distinctions in employment status (i.e., between employers, self-employed and employees) and on the basis of conditions of employment, degree of occupational security and career prospects among employees (see Evans, 1992). Allocation to a class position is derived from respondent's occupation and employment status, except when this is not available, when partner's occupational and employment status is used. Church attendance is measured using a scale from 'never' (1) to 'more than once a week' (6). Educational qualifications are measured with a 6-point scale ranging from 'none' to degree level.

[19] This structure has also been examined using discriminant analysis, which shows a very strong main function dividing the nationalist and unionist blocs, with a secondary division between social classes and educational groups in their preference for more or less hard-line constitutional parties, and with Alliance support remaining very much the preserve of the urban, educated middle-class voter on both sides of the communal divide.

Table 7. Social characteristics, political attitudes and party preference in Northern Ireland, 1995.

	Nationalist (0) vs Unionist (1)	UUP (0) vs DUP (1)	Alliance (0) vs UUP (1)	Alliance (0) vs SDLP (1)	SDLP (0) vs Sinn Féin (1)
Church of Ireland	7.49** (0.75)	—	—	−3.30** (0.45)	Na
Other Protestant	4.63** (0.88)	0.60* (0.27)	−0.07 (0.30)	—	Na
None	—	0.64 (0.44)	−2.24** (0.37)	—	−0.10 (1.21)
Catholic	—	Na	—	—	—
Urban residence	0.59 (0.53)	−0.18 (0.24)	−0.53* (0.27)	−0.94** (0.36)	0.64 (0.43)
Church attendance	−0.13 (0.20)	−0.07 (0.08)	−0.03 (0.08)	−0.09 (0.13)	−0.08 (0.21)
Middle class	−0.02 (0.73)	−0.73* (0.37)	−0.31 (0.31)	−0.88* (0.45)	−0.74 (1.09)
Educational Qualifications	0.48 (0.32)	−0.30* (0.15)	−0.36* (0.14)	−0.04 (0.20)	−1.31** (0.39)
Age 18–29 (ref. Cat.)	—	—	—	—	
Age 30–44	−0.06 (0.76)	−0.85* (0.33)	−0.57 (0.45)	0.08 (0.56)	−1.38* (0.62)
Age 45–59	0.68 (0.91)	−2.05** (0.41)	−0.46 (0.92)	−0.37 (0.59)	−2.58** (0.77)
Age 60+	−0.40 (0.94)	−1.67** (0.38)	−1.12* (0.48)	−0.27 (0.60)	−1.84* (0.70)
Support for redistribution	−0.11 (0.27)	0.28** (0.12)	0.00 (0.12)	0.33* (0.16)	0.11 (0.22)
Irish govt. role in North	−1.61** (0.32)	−0.50** (0.20)	−0.74** (0.16)	0.98** (0.22)	0.95** (0.31)
Constant	−9.67 (0.32)	−2.64 (1.08)	2.12 (1.04)	3.88 (1.16)	−2.65 (1.60)
% classified accurately	96.8	74.8	80.3	87.4	87.7
Initial log likelihood	954.3	535.6	550.0	476.5	203.9
Improvement in fit	830.5, 11 df	66.5, 11 df	123.7, 11 df	243.1, 10 df	47.4, 10 df

Notes: The parameter estimates are logistic coefficients with standard errors in parentheses. Catholic is the reference category for the effect of denomination in the nationalist vs unionist model. Church of Ireland is the reference category for the effect of denomination in the analyses of UUP vs DUP and Alliance vs UUP. Catholic is the reference category in the analyses of Alliance vs SDLP and SDLP vs Sinn Féin. * significant at p <0.05; ** significant at p <0.01.

educational qualifications leads to class effects (which are significant for all models when education is not controlled for) becoming non-significant except for the DUP versus UUP comparison when education is included in the models. This suggests that at least part of the preference for less hard-line nationalist and unionist parties among the middle classes may derive from their possessing more tolerant expressed attitudes as a result of greater experience of higher education,[20] which are probably complemented by differences in the rhetorical style of the competing unionist and nationalist parties.

Urban-rural divisions appear most marked among nationalists, with the SDLP picking up a noticeably higher proportion of its support from rural areas than either the Alliance Party or Sinn Féin. The marked effects of age on partisanship can probably be best understood in terms of political socialisation—both Sinn Féin and the DUP only started to compete electorally after many older voters had already developed attachments to the more established representatives of unionist and nationalist political visions. The recruitment of the young and unaligned was therefore an easier prospect (Evans and Duffy, 1997: 75–6). Church attendance, arguably a proxy for religiosity, has no effect, thus testifying to the political rather than theological nature of divisions in the North.

Finally, the coefficients for the two attitudinal variables show clear evidence of an asymmetry in the patterns of intra-community partisan differences among nationalists and unionists: among the former, the attitudinal bases of party choice concern only attitudes towards the constitutional issue; whereas among unionists the main partisan division derives its force not just from the position of parties on the constitutional issue but from interests relating to economic, left-right considerations (for more on this, see Evans and Duffy, 1997).

Conclusions

We have examined the development of political cleavages and party and electoral alignments in Ireland, with particular emphasis on how these have been affected in each jurisdiction by partition. Our findings confirm the main expectations formed in the course of this exercise but they also significantly modify other expectations or, perhaps more accurately, they strengthen some hunches at the expense of others. One of the striking

---

[20] This interpretation of the relationship between educational experience and intergroup tolerance has been advanced by many researchers (see, for example, Hyman and Wright, 1979; Lipset, 1981) although not without disputes about the conditions under which it occurs (see Weil, 1985).

features of the evidence we have presented is the similarity of certain aspects of party and electoral alignment in the two jurisdictions. Party alignments at the mass level are similar in two respects: relatively low and declining voter turnout and low and declining party attachment, the latter being markedly lower than that found in other West European societies. The contrasts arise when we turn to the cleavage structure underlying party choice. In the North, there are highly structured underlying cleavages: in addition to the main nationalist/unionist cleavage there are further intra-bloc cleavages in terms of both social bases and issue dimensions. In contrast, in the South there is very little evidence of a cleavage structure or structures underlying party choice. The nationalist cleavage has all but evaporated and, contrary to expectations in some quarters during the mid- to late 1980s, it has not been replaced by either a left-right or a secular-confessional conflict, though fragmentary evidence of both can be found.

Cleavages in the North remain entrenched despite the weakness of party attachment and voter mobilisation; differences of identity and of interest rather than of party provide the basis for the maintenance of conflict. Here we encounter another similarity between the two systems: parties are not in fact the embodiments of conflict in either jurisdiction; parties are marginal. The differences between these societies arise because there is an underlying homogeneity in the South and an underlying conflict in the North; both of these conditions are products of partition. In the North, partition institutionalised conflict. That conflict is, however, independent of and, in a sense, greater than the parties. This means that parties in the North can play only a limited role in brokering a solution, a conclusion reinforced by research which shows that, in Northern Ireland, parties that stray from the preferences of their constituencies are likely to lose them (Evans and O'Leary, 1997). Perhaps if parties had been more central to the conflict in Northern Ireland, rather than providing just another expression of entrenched divisions, it might have been easier to find a solution to the problem. In the South, secession institutionalised homogeneity; in the long term this has led to a weakening of the parties and resulted eventually in substantial dealignment. However, there is another aspect to the effect of partition in the South: it may have institutionalised homogeneity within the South but it also institutionalised a conflict between North and South and between Ireland and Britain. Looking at the South from this perspective, one can see that conflict was institutionalised not so much between political parties as between states. The politics of the parties in the South may at times appear to be post-nationalist; the politics of the state are certainly not. Paradoxically, while the weakness of parties that are prisoners of an entrenched conflict in the North may make the search for a solution more difficult, the weakness of post-alignment parties in the South may facilitate a solution by enabling political leaders, of whatever party or combination of parties, to redefine the objectives and orientations that were embedded in the structure of the state by partition.

References

Aldrich, J. and Nelson, F. (1984) *Linear, Probability, Logit and Probit Models*, Beverley Hills, California: Sage.

Aunger, E. A. (1981) *In Search of Political Stability: A Comparative Study of New Brunswick and Northern Ireland*, Montreal: McGill-Queen's University Press.

Bartolini, S. and Mair, P. (1990) *Identity, Competition and Electoral Availability: The Stabilisation of European Electorates, 1885–1985*, Cambridge: Cambridge University Press.

British Social Attitudes Survey (1995) The Data Archive, University of Essex.

Budge, I. and O'Leary, C. (1973) *Belfast: Approach to Crisis*, London: Macmillan, 1973.

Campbell, A., Converse, P., Miller, W. and Stokes, D. (1960), *The American Voter*, Chicago and London: The University of Chicago Press

Coakley, J. (1993) 'The Foundations of Statehood', in J. Coakley and M. Gallagher (eds), *Politics in the Republic of Ireland*, 2nd edition.

Davis, E. E. and Sinnott, R. (1979) *Attitudes in the Republic of Ireland Relevant to the Northern Ireland Problem: Vol. 1 — Descriptive analysis and some comparisons with attitudes in Northern Ireland and Great Britain*, Dublin: ESRI.

Duffy, M. and Evans, G. (1996) 'Building Bridges: the Political Implications of Electoral Integration for Northern Ireland', *British Journal of Political Science* 26: 123–40.

Erikson, R. and Goldthorpe, J. H. (1992) *The Constant Flux: A Study of Class Mobility in Industrial Societies*, Oxford: Clarendon Press.

Eurobarometer Survey, Zentralarchiv für Empirische Forschung, Köln.

Evans, G. (1992) 'Testing the Validity of the Goldthorpe Class Schema', *European Sociological Review*, 8; 211–32.

Evans, G. (1996) 'Northern Ireland during the Cease-fire', in R. Jowell, J. Curtice, A. Park, L. Brook, & K. Thomson (eds), *British Social Attitudes: the 13th Report*, Aldershot: Dartmouth.

Evans, G. and Duffy, M. (1997) 'Beyond the Sectarian Divide: the Social Bases and Political Consequences of Unionist and Nationalist Party Competition in Northern Ireland', *British Journal of Political Science*, 27: 47–81.

Evans, G. and O'Leary, B. (1997) 'Frameworked Futures: Intransigence and Flexibility in the Northern Irish Elections of May 30 1996', *Irish Political Studies*, 12: 23–47.

Finlay, F. (1991) *Mary Robinson: A President with a Purpose*, Dublin: O'Brien Press.

Flackes, W. D. and Elliot, S. (1994) *Northern Ireland: A Political Directory, 1968–93*, (Fourth Edition) Belfast: Blackstaff Press.

Franklin, M. N., Mackie, T. T. and Valen, H. (eds) (1992) *Electoral Change: Responses to Evolving Social and Attitudinal Structures in Western Countries*, Cambridge: Cambridge University Press.

Gallagher, M. (1985) *Political Parties in the Republic of Ireland*, Manchester: Manchester University Press.

Garvin, T. (1981) *The Evolution of Irish Nationalist Politics*, Dublin: Gill and Macmillan.

Harkness, D. (1983) *Northern Ireland since 1920*, Dublin: Criterion Press Limited.

Hayes, B. and McAllister, I. (1996) 'British and Irish public opinion towards the Northern Ireland problem', *Irish Political Studies*, 11: 61–82.

Hyman, H. H. and Wright, C. R. (1979) *Education's Lasting Influence on Values*, Chicago: Chicago University Press.

International Social Survey Programme (ISSP), various years, Zentralarchiv für Empirische Forschung, Köln.

Irish Political Studies (1995) 'Irish Political Data 1994', *Irish Political Studies*, 10: 262–339, PSAI Press.

Irish Political Studies (1997) 'Irish Political Data 1996', *Irish Political Studies*, 12: 148–210, PSAI Press.

Irish Political Studies (1998) 'Irish Political Data 1997', *Irish Political Studies*, 13: 211–79, PSAI Press.

Laver, M. and Hunt, B. (1992) *Policy and Party Competition*, London: Routledge.

Lipset, S. M. (1981) *Political Man: The Social Bases of Politics*, London: Heinemann.

Lipset, S. M. and Rokkan, S. (1967) 'Cleavage Structures, Party Systems and Voter Alignments: An Introduction', in S. M. Lipset and S. Rokkan (eds), *Party Systems and Voter Alignments*, New York: Free Press.

Mair, P. (1992) 'Explaining the Absence of Class Politics in Ireland', in J. H. Goldthorpe and C. Whelan (eds), *The Development of Industrial Society in Ireland*, Oxford: Clarendon Press.

Moxon-Browne, E. (1983) *Nation, Class and Creed in Northern Ireland*, Aldershot: Gower.

Northern Ireland Social Attitudes Survey (NISA), 1995, Data Archive, University of Essex, England.

Schmitt, H. and Holmberg, S. (1995) 'Political Parties in Decline', in H.-D. Klingemann and D. Fuchs (eds), *Citizens and the State*, Oxford: Oxford University Press.

Sinnott, R. (1986a) 'The North: Some Evidence on Party Images and Party Approaches in the Republic of Ireland', *Irish Political Studies*, 1: 15–32.

Sinnott, R. (1986b) 'Party Differences and Spatial Representation: the Irish Case', *British Journal of Political Science*, 16: 289–307.

Sinnott, R. (1995) *Irish Voters Decide: Voting Behaviour in Elections and Referendums since 1918*, Manchester: Manchester University Press.

Sinnott, R. (1998) 'The Measurement of Party Attachment in Eurobarometer Data: an Interpretation, a Test and some Implications', *British Journal of Political Science*, 28: 527–50.

Stationery Office, *Election Results and Transfer of Votes*, Dublin: The Stationery Office.

Walker, B. M. (ed.) (1992) *Parliamentary Election Results in Ireland, 1918–92: Irish Elections to Parliaments and Parliamentary Assemblies at Westminster, Belfast,*

Dublin, Strasbourg, A New History of Ireland Ancillary Publications V, Dublin: Royal Irish Academy.

Weil, F. D. (1985) 'The Variable Effects of Education on Liberal Attitudes: A Comparative-Historical Analysis of Anti-Semitism Using Public Opinion Data', *American Sociological Review*, 50: 458–74.

Whyte, J. (1974) 'Ireland: Politics Without Social Bases', in R. Rose (ed.), *Electoral Behavior: A Comparative Handbook*, New York: The Free Press.

Generations, Prejudice and Politics
in Northern Ireland

BERNADETTE C. HAYES & IAN McALLISTER

Individuals who belong to the same generation, who share the same
year of birth, are endowed, to that extent, with a common location in
the historical dimensions of the social process.

Karl Mannheim (1952: 290).

THE POLITICAL VIOLENCE THAT NORTHERN IRELAND HAS EXPERIENCED since 1968
is not new. Throughout the nineteenth century Belfast was the scene of
periodic communal rioting (Budge and O'Leary, 1973), and the widespread
disturbances that accompanied the 1886 Home Rule Bill resulted in 86
deaths across the province (O'Leary and McGarry, 1993: 21). The political
crises that have punctuated the past quarter century are also not new; for
example, the arming of the Ulster Volunteer Force in 1913 and the Curragh
mutiny a year later both produced major political upheavals (Stewart,
1967). Nor is paramilitary activity new. The republican and loyalist organisations which employ political violence are the descendants of groups
which used similar methods, for similar ends, at the turn of the century, and
more distantly, in the eighteenth century (Williams, 1973).

What *is* new is the scale of these events in Northern Ireland since 1968.
More people have died in communal violence in Northern Ireland—
currently over 3,000—in the past quarter century than in any similar
period in Ireland over the past two centuries, with the possible exception
of the 1922–23 Irish Civil War.[1] The depth and intensity of the political
crisis has also surpassed any other comparable period in Irish history. Since
1968, the British government has abolished the local parliament and made
three attempts—in 1973–74, 1975, and between 1982–86—to replace it

[1] The best examination of the violence and its parallels with previous periods of Irish history
is to be found in O'Leary and McGarry (1993: 8ff).

Proceedings of the British Academy, **98**, 457–491. © The British Academy 1999.

Table 1   Exposure to political violence in Northern Ireland, 1973–95 (%).

	1973	1978	1995
Witnessed:			
Vehicle hijacking	—	4	7
Riot	34	14	20
Explosion	12	20	21
Experienced:			
Personal injury	3	—	5
Family, close friend injured or killed	28	—	19
Intimidation	14	—	19
(N)	(2,401)	(1,277)	(982)

Note: The 1973 survey was conducted among men only. The 1978 and 1995 surveys were based on the adult population aged 18 years and over. The questions were as follows: (1973) 'Have you . . . been present when a riot or a confrontation took place? . . . been present when a bomb exploded/had your house or shop bombed? . . . experienced any kind of injury due to the Troubles . . . were any of your family/friends killed or injured due to violence? . . . experienced harassment in general?'; (1978) 'Have you ever witnessed an act of terrorism, for example a shooting, an explosion, a hijacking, or rioting?'; (1995) 'During the Troubles, were you ever . . . caught up in a hijacking? . . . caught up in a riot? . . . caught up in an explosion? Were you a victim of any violent incidents? . . . were you injured? Were any of your family or close relatives killed or injured due to the violence? Were you intimidated due to the Troubles?'

Sources: 1973 Ireland Mobility Survey; 1978 Northern Ireland Attitudes Survey; 1995 Northern Ireland Social Identities Survey.

with a more representative body; all have failed. And while no reliable statistics exist, it is likely that more people in Northern Ireland have participated in illegal paramilitary organisations than at any time since the United Irishmen rising of 1798.

The political violence has touched almost all sections of Northern Ireland society. In 1973, more than one in three adult men said that they had witnessed a riot, and one in eight an explosion (Table 1). By 1995, more than one in five of the adult population as a whole had witnessed an explosion. The statistics on intimidation also show their effects across the society: by 1995 nearly one-fifth said that they had been intimidated at some point due to the Troubles. A significant minority of the population have experienced personal injury, with a much larger group saying that someone in their close family or social circle had been killed or injured due to the violence.[2] This is, then, a conflict whose effects extend far beyond those who participate in the violence or live in areas where it is conducted; the effects extend to the society as a whole.

[2] For discussions of the patterns of violence, see Carroll (1981) and Poole (1983) and for an analysis of its consequences, Kelley and McAllister (1986).

The scale, intensity and duration of the conflict have undoubtedly influenced a large proportion of the population, but we would expect the impact to be greatest among the young, who have grown up and become politically aware in the midst of the violence. Some 15 per cent of the current adult population were born after the start of the Troubles in 1968, and a further 20 per cent will have had their earliest childhood memories punctuated by the violence. Theories of socialisation predict that it is this one-third of the adult population who will bear the imprint of the conflict for the rest of their lives. The extent to which this younger minority of the population emerge as more tolerant or more prejudiced as a result of their experiences may well hold the answer to whether or not the Northern Ireland problem can be resolved within the lifetimes of those presently alive.

Generational change has often been viewed as a solution to the Northern Ireland problem, with younger, more tolerant generations displacing their older, more prejudiced counterparts. In 1962 Denis Barritt and Charles Carter exemplified this view in their influential book *The Northern Ireland Problem* by arguing that the weight of outside events would come to shape the views of the young: 'a new generation will have a different sense of what is important' (1962: 154). This optimistic interpretation also underlines the arguments that are advanced for integrated education (see, for example, Fraser, 1973; Heskin, 1980). The contrary view is that it is the young rather than the old who are more extreme as a result of their experiences. It is the young who have been most exposed to the violence during their impressionable years, and it is the young who are most active in sustaining it through membership of paramilitary organisations. If that is the case, then the prospects for a political solution to the Northern Ireland problem are indeed grim.

In this chapter we examine the extent of tolerance or prejudice across the generations in Northern Ireland, and trace the consequences of those views for political outlooks. Such research is difficult without a panel survey, where the views of the same individuals are measured at different points in time. It is possible partly to compensate for the absence of panel data by using a cross-sectional survey to examine separate generations. Here, however, the problem is sample size and the small numbers that typically emerge within the generations that might be of analytic interest. We overcome this problem by combining the five Northern Ireland Social Attitudes (NISA) surveys conducted between 1989 and 1995. This produces a total sample of 5,643, which enables us to identify separate generations, and to analyse them separately by religion.

Generations and Political Change

The prediction that generational replacement will result in political change is based on the assumption that generations differ in their political attitudes. The explanations for why generations should differ in their political attitudes emphasise such factors as differing historical experiences, the impact of changing socio-economic conditions, and changes in the person's position in the lifecycle. Mannheim (1952) argues that there are most likely to be 'generational effects' during periods of rapid social and cultural change. But if there are no critical political events—if the political system is distinguished by stability when the person becomes politically aware—then all age groups are likely to be influenced in much the same way. This is what is often termed a 'period effect'.

The classic theories of generational effects emphasise the importance of critical historical events, which place an indelible imprint on the views of the young. Wars, revolutions, transitions to or from democracy, and major economic upheavals have all been viewed as critical events which have left their mark on the young and impressionable. In the twentieth century, the experiences of the Great Depression in the 1930s, the Second World War and, in the United States, the Vietnam War, have all been identified as events which moulded the political outlooks of an emerging generation and which have resonated through the years (Abramson, 1983; Davis, 1987; Glenn, 1989). Such defining events have less impact on older people because they are better equipped by their lifetime experiences to resist their influences.

A contrary view is that generational differences in political views are the result of a 'compositional effect', so that each new generation benefits from greater skills and opportunities, which in turn moulds their political views. Foremost among the compositional changes that have taken place in society are the greater opportunities for education. The rapid expansion of education in the post-war years has been used as the explanation for increased support for democratic values, notably tolerance and the defence of minority rights. This observation has been traced to the work of Samuel Stouffer (1955), who observed high levels of intolerance within the American population, and the link between education and support for civil liberties. Based on the post-war expansion of education in the United States, Stouffer predicted that tolerance would increase, a prediction that has largely been fulfilled (Davis, 1975; Nunn *et al.*, 1978).

The third explanation for generational differences focuses on 'lifecycle effects'. As persons move into adulthood they gain new responsibilities, such as maintaining a full-time job, raising a family and paying a mortgage. Later still, when the children have left the home, they are faced with new concerns over health care or social welfare. Lifecycle theories of attitude change predict that the impact of these shifting priorities help to shape political views. Moreover, the net effect of the lifecycle on the political system as a whole is marginal, since older generations are subject to the same influences as those who went before them, and those who will follow them. To the extent that there are variations attributable to the lifecycle, they are the result of minor changes in the size of particular generations.

To estimate the impact of these four potential factors—generation, period, composition and lifecycle—on political views in Northern Ireland, we hypothesise that generational effects will be mediated by the position of the particular generation within the lifecycle, by its social composition and by the period when the political views were recorded (Figure 1). Whatever variance is left unexplained by period, composition and lifecycle can then be attributed to generational effects—the influence of critical events on the views and beliefs of the particular generational groups. In defining political outlooks, we assume that certain underlying values about the nature of the Northern Ireland problem will structure political beliefs. In particular, we identify the level of tolerance shown towards either of the two religious communities as a prior set of values which will shape political identity.

The strength of these relationships has significant implications for resolving the Northern Ireland conflict. If political views are predominantly shaped by a generational-critical events explanation, then we would expect the post-1968 generations to be more extreme in their views than pre-1968 generations, an outlook which will accompany them for the rest of their lives. If the conflict is not resolved, then each succeeding generation will be socialised into extreme views, thus heightening the overall levels of polarisation in the society. If period effects emerge as significant, then we would expect a wider influence for these critical events, although their lasting impact would be on the emerging generations. By contrast, if social compositional effects are a major political influence, then we would expect the increasing proportion of educated persons in the Northern Ireland population to reduce extreme political views, so that the conflict would

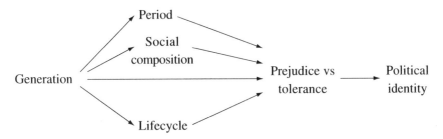

Figure 1.   Generational effects, prejudice and political identity.

largely be resolved in the course of time, as the society develops. Finally, if lifecycle explanations best explain political views, then we would expect stability, with little change in political opinions.

The Northern Ireland Conflict and the Young

Although sociologists have largely eschewed investigating the social consequences of the Northern Ireland conflict,[3] fortunately there is a major body of psychological research assessing its impact on the young. These studies have proved highly controversial with some researchers predicting serious long-term psychological damage to future generations (see, for example, Fields, 1973; 1977; Fraser, 1973), while others have argued that young people cope well with the stressful environment engendered by violence (see, for example, Harbison, 1983; 1989; Harbison and Harbison, 1980). This latter group has identified the stability of local communities and families as an essential mechanism which neutralises the potential effects of the civil conflict. Indeed, some researchers have even suggested that where psychological problems exist among children, they are caused not by the conflict but by economic and social deprivation.

There is extensive evidence to support the proposition that the Troubles have not caused long-term damage to the young. Psychological studies have consistently demonstrated that both Protestant and Catholic children who grew up in the turbulent late 1960s were neither more nor less likely to develop a higher degree of authoritarian or conservative attitudes than their Republic of Ireland or British counterparts (O'Kane and Cairns, 1988). Nor were these children more likely to have experienced a weakening in religious or moral values (Greer, 1984; 1990), or to have developed an unhealthy preoccupation with violent death (McWhirter *et al.*, 1983; McWhirter, 1982). Furthermore, terrorist-related offences still account for only a very small proportion of juvenile crime. This occurs, it is argued, because the majority of parents, many of whom are the original children of the Troubles, still continue to provide a secure and positive environment for their children, even in the most deprived areas (see Whyte, 1995).

This is not to say that children in Northern Ireland have grown up totally unaffected by the conflict. Research into the development of ethnic stereotyping suggests a continuing historical legacy of inter-group hostility and intolerance, particularly among Protestant children.[4] Not only does a negative evaluation of those of the opposite religion become apparent in

---

[3] There is, however, important anthropological work on Northern Ireland, most notably by Harris (1972) and Burton (1978).

[4] Cairns (1987) provides a comprehensive review of the earlier literature in this field.

children as young as six years of age, but the ability to distinguish ingroup or outgroup members is acquired by the age 10 or 11 (Houston *et al.*, 1990). Accompanying this process is a growth in the negative stereotyping of the outgroup and the positive reinforcement of ingroup attributes. While both religious groups have engaged in these practices, there is now increasing evidence to suggest that it is Protestant children and adolescents who are more likely than their Catholic equivalents to develop ethnocentric attitudes (Houston *et al.*, 1990; Stringer and Cook, 1985; Stringer and Cairns, 1983; Mercer and Cairns, 1981; Jahoda and Harrison, 1975).

Despite this wealth of empirical information, Cairns and Cairns (1995) note that one important, but largely neglected, area of investigation has been the long-term consequences of this phenomenon for the political behaviour and orientations of the young. The evidence suggests that whereas the vast majority of Protestant children and adolescents continue to define themselves in terms of both a British and Unionist national identity, Catholics see themselves as Irish and Nationalist (Trew, 1994; Wadell and Cairns, 1986; 1991; McClenahan *et al.*, 1991; Cairns and Mercer, 1984; Trew, 1983). Although a minority of both Protestant and Catholic youths are now more willing to accept a Northern Irish identity, Catholics still remain almost uniform in their rejection of either a British or Ulster identity, as are Protestants of an Irish identity (see Trew, 1994; Wadell and Cairns, 1991). Thus, as is also the case among the adult population (see Trew, 1996; Breen, 1996), national identity in Northern Ireland still follows a religiously based pattern.

When the development of other political attitudes is examined, the results are inconclusive.[5] Whereas Hosin and Cairns (1984) claimed that children and young people in Northern Ireland had little interest in politics, other studies have shown a high level of political knowledge, particularly on questions relating to politics outside Northern Ireland (see Whyte, 1983; 1995). With regard to the morality of political violence, an investigation of 3,000 schoolboys in 1971–72 found that a majority of both Protestants and Catholics were willing to endorse the use of political violence to achieve constitutional aims, such as the introduction of a united Ireland or the maintenance of the union with Britain (Russell, 1974). Later research, however, suggests an increasing 'war weariness' among the young. Two studies conducted in the 1980s found that a majority of young people actually condemned political violence (Hosin and Cairns, 1984; McWhirter, 1982) and that a desire for peace was, by far, the most preferred aspiration (McWhirter, 1983).

Despite the doomsday predictions of some researchers, the children of

[5] For a review of these findings, see Cairns and Cairns (1995).

the post-1968 Troubles do not represent a 'lost generation'. Whatever their childhood and adolescent experiences, they have not become amoral juvenile delinquents nor long-term adult psychiatric casualties. Some have even argued that because parental control and security was so great during the formative years of these post-1968 generations, the end result has been the creation of an over-conformist and politically stagnant section of the population (see Whyte, 1995; Harbison, 1983; Belloff, 1980; 1989). Nevertheless, while these post-1968 generations do not appear more likely to endorse violence or to support extreme political opinions than others, it remains unclear how far their views of the opposing community differ from those who grew up prior to 1968. It is also unclear how far the views of the other community shape their political beliefs. We examine these topics in the remainder of the paper.

Identifying Generations

Although scholars agree that generations are defined by critical historical experiences, there is no consensus on how to identify such periods of history: wars or cataclysmic events are the easiest to distinguish, but longer periods of minor change present classificatory problems. Nor is there consensus on the ages at which persons are most likely to bear the imprint of such events, however defined. Dalton (1977) argues that adults are most affected by economic conditions when they are 10 years old. Studies of voting and partisanship have usually seen the years following entry into the electorate—the late teens and early 20s—as the most formative (see Abramson, 1983), although political socialisation studies point to basic political views being acquired much earlier (Greenstein, 1969). Mannheim (1952) argues that impressionability is greatest in late adolescence and early adulthood, at about the age of 17, which he terms the age of 'personal experimentation with life'.

On the grounds that individuals will become aware of political violence at a much younger age than constitutional politics, we assume that each generation is most likely to be impressed by the prevailing political events at about the age of 12 years. Table 2 defines nine generations based on the predominant historical experiences when they were approximately this age.[6] In the case of the two world wars and the political events since 1968 the defining lines are clear. However, distinguishing between the generations that grew up between the end of the Second World War and

[6] Strictly speaking, a period in which there were no major crtitical events identifies a 'cohort' rather than a 'political generation', but for consistency we use the term generation to define all of these nine groups.

Table 2. Political generations in Northern Ireland.

Political generation	Percent	Age in 1995	Major political events
<1930	5	79+	First World War, partition
1930–39	13	69–78	Depression, creation of Irish Free State
1939–45	13	62–68	Second World War
1946–54	18	53–61	Post-war reconstruction, creation of Irish Republic
1955–61	12	46–52	IRA border campaign
1962–70	12	37–45	Civil rights, O'Neillism, start of Troubles
1971–76	9	31–36	Abolition of Stormont, internment, UWC strike
1977–83	12	24–30	Hunger strikes, Assembly
1984–present	7	18–23	Anglo-Irish Agreement, New Ireland Forum

Source: 1989–95 Northern Ireland Social Attitudes Surveys, combined file.

the start of the O'Neill period of government in 1963 is problematic.[7] For the purposes of this analysis, we have distinguished the post-war reconstruction period up to 1954 from the 1955 to 1961 period, when the IRA mounted a border campaign. Although the campaign was—by current standards—a minor one, we would hypothesise that it may have had some influence on the political outlooks of the emerging generation.

The numerically largest generation, which includes nearly one in every five adults in Northern Ireland, are those people who became politically aware during the period of post-war reconstruction, between 1946 and 1954. All of the remaining generations constitute between 12 and 13 per cent of the population, with three exceptions: the First World War generation—those coming of age prior to 1930—who make up 5 per cent of the adult population; the generation that experienced the abolition of the Stormont parliament and internment in the early 1970s who constitute 9 per cent; and the most recent generation, who make up 7 per cent. These generations form the basis for the analyses that follow.

Measuring Generational Change

Measuring generational change and testing the various explanations for it requires panel data; only by interviewing the same individuals at different points in time can we evaluate the extent to which attitudes change, and

---

[7] Terence O'Neill became the Ulster Unionist Prime Minister of Northern Ireland in 1963. Unlike his predecessors, not only did O'Neill support and eventually try to institute many of the civil-rights reforms demanded by Catholics, but he was also the very first Northern Ireland Prime Minister to officially invite and meet his Republic of Ireland counterpart—Seán Lemass, the Prime Minister of Ireland—at Stormont in 1965. In fact, it was because of these activities that he was eventually forced to resign in April 1969.

how far any such changes be attributed to particular experiences and events rather than to changes in social and economic circumstances. However, panel surveys are rare, largely because of the costs involved and the methodological difficulties associated with ensuring a sufficiently large response rate. In any event, no panel surveys have been conducted on the adult population in Northern Ireland. An alternative approach is to use cross-sectional surveys and to ask the respondents to recall past events or opinions. This approach is reliable where important factual data are concerned—for example, where respondents are asked to recall their father's occupation or their own first occupation (Broom *et al.*, 1980: 25ff)—but it is less effective when respondents are asked to recall their past opinions.

In the absence of data about the same individuals at successive time-points, the only alternative is to utilise cross-sectional studies, where different individuals are asked similar questions in different surveys. The difficulty with this approach is that it produces an identification problem: it is impossible to disentangle the generation and period effects from other effects which may be due to ageing. One way of mitigating the problem is to use theoretical specifications and knowledge that go beyond the available cohort data (Glenn, 1989: 754). Such situationally dependent information enable evaluations to be made of the types of influences that may be at work, and are used extensively in research on political behaviour (Abramson, 1983; Page and Shapiro, 1992: 302ff).

The identification problem becomes acute when a survey population is analysed as a whole, since generation, age and period cannot be entered simultaneously in the same analysis. However, if we disaggregate the population into generations and treat each generation as a discrete unit, this will control for the generation or cohort into which each individual was born. In practice, this is rarely feasible since most surveys include too few respondents to permit the creation of subgroups with sufficient sample sizes for reliable analysis. We overcome this problem by using a merged file created from the 1989, 1991, 1993, 1994 and 1995 NISA surveys. The merged file produces a sample size of 5,643, which not only enables us to identify the nine generations described in Table 2, but to conduct the analyses separately for Protestants and Catholics. This has the added advantage of permitting all possible interactions between the independent variables within a generational group from each of the two religious communities.[8]

---

[8] For example, we might expect the interactions between variables such as age and church attendance, or education and occupation, to vary not only by generation but also by religion. By analysing the data separately by generation and religion we permit such interactions to take place.

The problem of taking into account age or period effects in the model does, however, remain. We do not know, for example, to what extent any observed changes may be a consequence of exposure to the events of the time, or as a result of ageing. In practice, we can reduce the error involved in identifying the changes due to events in two ways. First, the models can control for the year in which the survey was conducted. The limited period of the surveys—just six years—reduces the utility of this method, but it does provide some statistical control. Second, we include a wide range of social composition and lifecycle variables within the models, many of which will control indirectly for ageing. In practice, then, we assume that most of the effects of ageing and the period when the survey was conducted have been taken into account.

A range of variables is used to measure social composition and lifecycle effects. Social composition is measured by education, reflected in the possession of a degree or a diploma, or by another post-school qualification. Occupation is measured by being employed in a non-manual occupation, and by whether or not the person supervised others. Supervision is used rather than other occupational measures, such as status or self-employment, because supervision involves the application of authority in the workplace (Kelley and McAllister, 1985) and might be expected to be linked to feelings of prejudice or tolerance. Table 3 shows that there are substantial educational and occupational variations across the generations, as we would expect. For example, within the civil rights generation almost one in four possess a degree or a diploma, compared to less than half that proportion in the two oldest generations.

The choice of the lifecycle measures presents more difficulties. Marital and labour force status are uncontentious; as Table 3 demonstrates, they reflect the stages through which individuals progress as they move through the lifecycle. The allocation of gender and church attendance to either composition or lifecycle is more problematic. Gender could be regarded as a compositional effect, since changes in the gender distribution reflect less lifecycle than social structure. It is included here under lifecycle on the grounds that it is also correlated with marital and labour force status, two of the key lifecycle measures. Church attendance is sometimes seen as a compositional effect, although religious behaviour (as opposed to religious belief) is highly dependent upon the lifecycle and more particularly on the presence or absence of children in the home (Argyle and Beit-Hallahmi, 1975). It is therefore included under lifecycle in Table 3.[9]

---

[9] One methodological problem concerns the specification of the model for each generation. Since all of the independent variables consist of one or more dummy variables, their effects are judged relative to the excluded category. In some cases—for example, in the case of marital status among the younger or older generations—there are few respondents in some of the categories. The exact model used for each generation is therefore modified to take account of these changes, normally by excluding a category that had fewer than 10 per cent of the cases.

Table 3. The social compositional and lifecycle characteristics of generations (%).

	First World War	Depression	Second World War	Recon-struction	IRA resurgence	Civil rights	Abolition of Stormont	Hunger strikes	Anglo-Irish Agreement
Social composition									
Education:									
No qualifications	79	70	63	57	45	36	30	21	12
Post-school qualification	14	21	25	28	37	40	49	60	77
Degree, diploma	8	9	12	15	18	25	21	19	11
Non-manual occupation	37	43	47	49	52	55	54	50	42
Supervisor	23	28	31	34	34	36	32	26	16
Lifecycle									
Male	30	42	43	47	48	44	43	42	45
Marital status:									
Married	20	38	53	69	75	76	70	48	11
Single	16	16	13	10	10	11	16	44	88
Divorced	1	3	8	10	12	13	13	8	1
Widow	63	44	26	11	3	1	2	0	0
Frequent church attender	49	56	54	53	48	44	36	32	40
Labour force status:									
Employed	1	6	27	56	71	68	68	68	62
Unemployed	0	0	4	11	11	10	9	13	19
Home duties	25	19	19	23	18	22	23	19	19
Retired	74	75	50	9	0	0	0	0	0
(N)	(398)	(655)	(497)	(641)	(647)	(951)	(702)	(688)	(277)

Note: Frequent church attendance refers to attendance once a week or more.

Source: 1989–95 Northern Ireland Social Attitudes Surveys, combined file.

Religion is measured by affiliation, with all of the Protestant churches being grouped into one general category. A recent trend has been for a growing proportion of the population to eschew a religious affiliation; this first emerged in the 1971 census, when the religion question was made voluntary and 9.4 per cent of the population left it unanswered. However, recent surveys have consistently found that about one in 10 of the adult population reject a religious affiliation (Hayes and McAllister, 1995), and in line with international trends these respondents tend to be younger (Glenn, 1987). The combined NISA surveys file contained 10.3 per cent who said that they were secular. These nominally secular respondents have been classified as either Protestant or Catholic based on their family religion on the grounds that our interest is less in the dynamics of religious affiliation than in generational change within the adult population as a whole.[10]

The generational distribution of Protestants and Catholics shows the consequences of differential fertility and emigration patterns between the two religious communities (Figure 2). The higher Catholic levels of fertility were traditionally offset by their higher levels of emigration, particularly among younger males—politically the most active group (Compton 1985; Grada, 1986). In the 1970s and 1980s, both Catholic emigration and Catholic fertility declined, resulting in a larger proportion of younger Catholics within the total adult population. The net result has been a convergence in the proportions of Protestants and Catholics within the generations growing up since 1968. For example, within the generation coming of age since the Anglo-Irish Agreement, Protestants have only a 2 per cent numerical advantage over Catholics, compared to an advantage of 42 per cent within the generation that grew up during the Second World War.

Measuring Religious Prejudice

The feelings of prejudice that exist within a society have important implications because they provide the context within which individual and group behaviour takes place. In particular, prejudice is usually viewed as an attitudinal prerequisite for the act of discrimination (Feagin, 1978). At first glance, the meaning of prejudice may seem obvious, particularly in a society such as Northern Ireland. In his classic study *The Nature of*

---

[10] Although 10.3 per cent of the total combined sample gave no religion in response to the affiliation question (compared to 0.6 per cent who did not answer the question), only 0.9 per cent said that they had been brought up in a home where their parents had no religion. These secular respondents are also proportionally distributed between Protestants and Catholics.

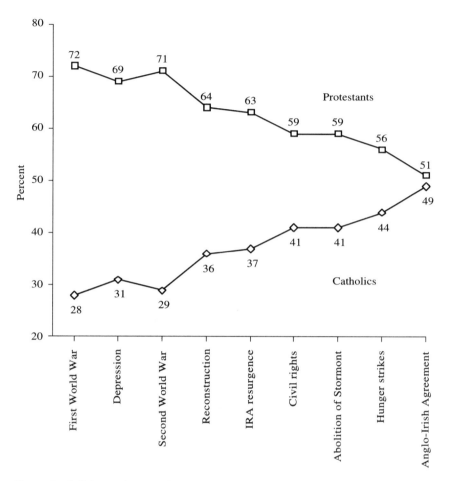

Figure 2. Religion and generation. *Source*: 1989–95 Northern Ireland Social Attitudes Surveys, combined file.

Prejudice, Gordon Allport defines prejudice as 'an antipathy based upon a faulty and inflexible generalisation. It may be felt or expressed. It may be directed toward a group as a whole, or toward an individual because he (or she) is a member of that group' (1987: 9). Prejudice, then, is a reaction to a person based on perceptions about group membership, rather than on an objective evaluation of that person—what Allport has called 'thinking ill of others without sufficient warrant' (1987: 7).

The apparent ease with which we can arrive at a suitable definition of prejudice belies the complex empirical ways in which researchers have attempted to measure it. The earliest social science research on prejudice was conducted by Emory Bogardus in the 1920s using a social distance scale to measure how close his subjects would allow a member of a particular 'target' group to approach them (Bogardus, 1928). The first post-war attempt to explain prejudice was the work of Theodore W. Adorno and his colleagues, who observed the relationship between authoritarian values and prejudice in Nazi ideology (Adorno *et al.*, 1950). The work of Henri Tajfel (1970) presents a third stage in understanding and measuring prejudice. In his famous 'minimal groups' experiment, Tajfel's found that even when the subjects had no information about the other people involved in the experiment, they still chose to be associated with those who they believed to be most like themselves.[11]

One means of measuring the extent of prejudice in Northern Ireland is to examine official government statistics, such as the reports of the Fair Employment Agency. The official statistics do, however, convey only one part of the overall picture. Many instances of discrimination or prejudice undoubtedly go unreported for a wide range of reasons; some may go undetected by those against whom they are aimed; others that are interpreted as discrimination may in fact be unwitting or innocent. Perhaps more importantly, individuals who are prejudiced may modify the more immediately visible aspects of their behaviour or conduct, but still harbour feelings of prejudice. This is what is termed 'symbolic racism': individuals may accept the principles of integration, but oppose the policies designed to bring such goals about (Carmines and Merriman, 1993: 238). Opposition to government policies is acceptable whereas support for prejudice is not; the former can be justified by commitments to individual liberty, curbing the power of the state, or by the preservation of freedom of choice.

By any standards, the respondents in the NISA surveys believe that there is considerable prejudice in their society, directed against both Protestants and Catholics (second panel, Table 4). Around one in every four Protestants believe that there is 'a lot of prejudice' against both religions, although marginally more against their own community than against Catholics. Just under half of all the Protestants interviewed believe that there is 'a little prejudice' against the two communities. Only a minority felt that there is 'hardly any prejudice'. Catholics are equally adamant that there is extensive prejudice in Northern Ireland, but with

---

[11] Tajfel's subjects were asked to count the number of dots which had been flashed briefly onto a screen; the subjects were then told that they had either under- or overestimated the number of dots, although in reality they had been assigned at random to one of the under- or overestimator groups. When they were asked to allocate rewards to two other people, Tajfel found that the subjects systematically favoured those who were in the same group as themselves. Tajfel's experiment with 'minimal groups' explained the essence of the problem of prejudice, and of the relationship between outgroups and ingroups.

Table 4. Personal and general religious prejudice in Northern Ireland (%).

	Protestants	Catholics
Personal		
A lot of prejudice	1	0.4
A little prejudice	16	8
Hardly any prejudice	83	91
(N)	(3,382)	(2,046)

	Against Prots	Against Caths	Against Prots	Against Caths
General				
A lot of prejudice	24	23	16	35
A little prejudice	48	44	55	51
Hardly any prejudice	28	33	30	14
(N)	(3,294)	(3,297)	(1,976)	(1,985)

Note: The questions were as follows. 'How would you describe yourself . . . as very prejudiced against people of other religions, a little prejudiced, or not prejudiced at all?' 'Now, thinking of Protestants/Catholics, do you think there is a lot of prejudice against them in Northern Ireland these days, a little or hardly any?'

Source: 1989–95 Northern Ireland Social Attitudes Surveys, combined file.

the difference that they believe—with more historical justification—that the discrimination is more likely to be directed against them. More than one in every three Catholics believe that there is a lot of prejudice against Catholics, more than twice the proportion who feel that there is the same level of prejudice against Protestants.

However, these beliefs about widespread prejudice are not consistent with the respondents' own levels of self-reported prejudice. The vast majority—83 per cent of Protestants and 91 per cent of Catholics—believe that they themselves are 'not prejudiced at all', while 16 per cent of Protestants and half that number of Catholics say that they are 'a little prejudiced'. One in a 100 or fewer see themselves as 'very prejudiced'. There is therefore little congruence between general perceptions of religious prejudice that are prevalent across the society and self-reports of the same phenomenon. People see considerable prejudice around them, but are unlikely to admit to harbouring such feelings themselves. These are, admittedly, highly subjective issues and require subjective judgements, so it is perhaps not surprising that the two sets of results do not match. But the extent of the difference, and the very small proportion who admit to possessing some significant level of prejudice, does clearly point to an unwillingness among many respondents to see themselves as prejudiced.

Those who admit to personal prejudice present no difficulty: they can be classified as religiously prejudiced. The measurement problem is to differentiate those in the large, apparently unprejudiced group who are tolerant from those who are prejudiced. One option is to use the responses to the question on prejudice across the society as a whole, on the grounds that those who are consciously or unconsciously concealing prejudice may be more willing to admit that there is prejudice around them. Using this method to classify the respondents, about one in five Protestants emerge as being very prejudiced, compared to half that proportion of Catholics (Figure 3). These are the respondents who self-report being 'very' or 'a little' prejudiced. A further 14 per cent of Protestants and 13 per cent of Catholics are somewhat prejudiced, having viewed themselves as not prejudiced, but observing 'a lot' of prejudice directed against either the Protestant or Catholic community within their society. The remaining two groups reflect those who responded by saying that they were not prejudiced and that there was little or hardly any prejudice against the two religious communities.

The results in Table 5 confirm the validity of this approach. Irrespective of whether Protestants or Catholics are considered, individuals who are classified as 'very' or 'somewhat' prejudiced are consistently more likely than those who are not to either exclusively restrict their contacts to

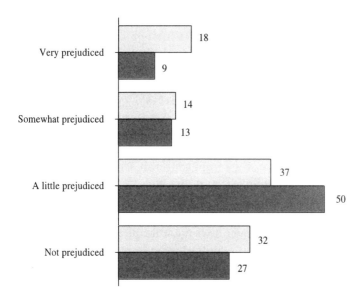

Figure 3.   Religious prejudice among Protestants and Catholics. *Note*: See text and Appendix to this chapter for details of estimation. ☐ Protestant ■ Catholic. *Source*: 1989–95 Northern Ireland Social Attitudes Surveys, combined file.

Table 5.   Religious prejudice and levels of religious segregation (%).

	Protestant		Catholic	
	Very/somewhat	Little/none	Very/somewhat	Little/none
Contacts of the same religion among:				
Neighbours	41	32	49	35
Friends	23	16	24	12
Relatives	52	48	44	40
Support for religious segregation in:				
Neighbourhood	40	22	30	14
Schools	47	36	52	39
Workplace	20	7	11	5

Note: The questions were as follows: 'About how many of your [neighbours, friends, relatives] would you say are the same religion as you—that is Protestant or Catholic?'; 'If you had a choice, would you prefer [a neighbourhood, school, workplace] with people of *only* your own religion, or in a *mixed-religion* [neighbourhood, school, workplace]?' Only individuals who reported that all their contacts were among individuals of the same religion and those who preferred to be with people of their own religion are included in the analysis.

Source: 1989–95 Northern Ireland Social Attitudes Surveys, combined file.

individuals of the same religion or to support religious segregation practices in the society at large. For example, whereas around one in every four Protestants who expressed feelings of prejudice had neighbours with exactly the same religious affiliation, the equivalent figure among the non-prejudiced is notably lower at 32 per cent. Among Catholics, the difference between the two groups is even larger: just under half of the prejudiced group as compared to only 35 per cent of those who are not. A similar, though more dramatic, pattern is found when attitudes towards religious segregation are considered. Irrespective of religious affiliation, not only do much larger proportions of individuals within the prejudiced category positively endorse religious segregation practices within their neighbourhoods, schools and workplace, but in all but one case—segregation in schools—this greater margin of support is at least double that of the non-prejudiced.

By any standards, religious prejudice is strongly related to generation (Figure 4). But contrary to the patterns of group prejudice that are found in most other countries, it is the young rather than the old who are more likely to be prejudiced. Furthermore, this relationship holds regardless of whether our combined measure or its individual component items are examined (see Table 6). The older generations, particularly those growing up in the period when partition took place, and those growing up during the Depression of the 1930s and the Second World War, show low levels of prejudice. By contrast, the highest levels are found among those who have grown up

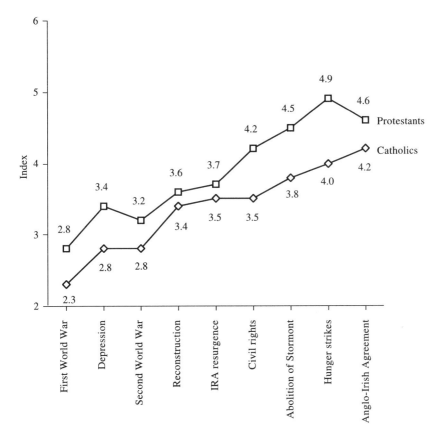

Figure 4. Religious prejudice by generation. *Note*: See text and Appendix to this chapter for details of estimation. *Source*: 1989–95 Northern Ireland Social Attitudes Surveys, combined file.

since the start of the Troubles in 1968; within these generations, prejudice is up to three quarters higher than among those who had grown up half a century before.

This contradicts most other research on racial and ethnic prejudice and on political tolerance which shows that it is older people who are more likely to be prejudiced than younger people, at least partly as a consequence of increased education among the young (Sullivan *et al.*, 1982). However, there is more recent research in the United States which suggests that the general trend towards more tolerant racial attitudes over the past twenty years has had little impact on the racial views of the young (Dowden and Robinson, 1993). But the strength of the trend in Northern Ireland suggests that the post-1968 Troubles may have had a significant impact in shaping religious prejudice, above and beyond the social changes

Table 6. Personal and general religious prejudice by generation (Means, scored 0 to 10)

	Protestant			Catholic		
	Personal	Against Prots	Against Caths	Personal	Against Prots	Against Caths
First World War	1.3	4.9	4.6	1.1	3.7	5.7
Depression	1.5	5.1	4.5	1.2	4.0	5.7
Second World War	1.5	4.9	4.4	1.1	4.3	5.6
Reconstruction	1.7	4.9	4.5	1.3	4.7	6.1
IRA resurgence	1.5	5.3	5.0	1.3	4.8	6.3
Civil rights	2.0	5.0	5.0	1.4	4.5	6.3
Abolition of Stormont	2.1	4.9	4.8	1.5	4.8	6.6
Hunger Strikes	2.2	5.3	5.4	1.5	5.0	6.4
Anglo-Irish Agreement	1.9	5.6	6.0	1.7	4.9	6.6

Source: 1989–95 Northern Ireland Social Attitudes Surveys, combined file.

that may have occurred in each generation. We test this hypothesis in the next section.

Testing the Generational Change Hypothesis

If generations do indeed bear the lifelong imprint of the events surrounding the period when they grew to maturity, we would expect each generation to display distinctive political views, even after compositional, lifecycle and period effects have been taken into account. In other words, once these potentially confounding effects have been controlled for statistically, the patterns that remain should reflect the net effect of the events experienced at the time that the group was young. As we have already noted, there are several important caveats to using such a methodology to infer generational change, the most notable being the problems associated with using cross-sectional data to distinguish generational from age effects. Nevertheless, we argue that controlling for a sufficiently wide range of potentially confounding effects should provide a reasonably reliable estimate of the extent to which particular generations have been influenced by the events of their youth.

The estimates are produced by calculating a regression equation to predict religious prejudice; this equation is calculated separately for each generation. Alternative regression analyses which included all nine generations simultaneously in the one equation suggested no substantive difference in findings.[12] In each equation, the full range of social composition and lifecycle variables defined in Table 3 are included in the equations,

[12] The results of this analysis also suggested that members of the older generations were consistently less likely to hold a more prejudiced position than their younger cohorts. More

together with dummy variables for the survey year, which controls for period effects. The equations are then evaluated at the mean to provide a net estimate of religious prejudice. Full details of the method are provided in the Appendix. The result of these calculations are shown in Figure 5.

The results suggest that there are strong generational effects for religious prejudice, even after a wide range of factors have been taken into account. Moreover, the broad pattern that emerges across the generations—with those in the post-1968 generations displaying the highest levels of prejudice—generally remains. Among Protestants, prejudice either remains stable or increases with each succeeding generation, with the exception of those who experienced the abolition of the Stormont parliament and the start of the Troubles. Within this generation, prejudice is greater than the levels found among those who grew up in the early years of the century and who experienced the violence that surrounded the birth of the Northern Ireland state. Among the generations with the highest levels of prejudice, two of the three are post-1968 generations, and the third is the civil rights generation, which experienced unprecedented Catholic demands for political reform.

There is a more complex pattern among Catholics. Contrary to the findings for Protestants, there is considerable prejudice among those who grew up in the immediate post-war years, while those with the lowest levels of prejudice grew up during the First World War and during the Depression of the 1930s. From then on, religious prejudice climbs steadily and then declines among those who grew up in the 1960s. Like Protestants, one of the most prejudiced generations within the Catholic community is a recent one, namely those for whom the defining political event was the experience of the Hunger Strikes. The other notable generations are Protestants whose defining events were the abolition of Stormont and the start of the Troubles, and Catholics who grew up in the post-war reconstruction and IRA resurgence periods. The overall conclusion is that the post-1968 Troubles have indeed made people more prejudiced, most notably for Protestants.

Generations and Political Identity

By any standards, the correlation between religion and politics in Northern Ireland is extraordinary (for a review, see Whyte, 1990: 72ff). The only advanced societies which approach Northern Ireland's levels of religious

---

specifically, when all but the youngest generation—the dropped out category of comparison—were entered as a series of dummy variables in a single regression equation, for each of five generations prior to the civil rights movement, the estimated partial regression coefficients were significant and consistently negative. Furthermore, this relationship held regardless of whether Protestants or Catholics were considered.

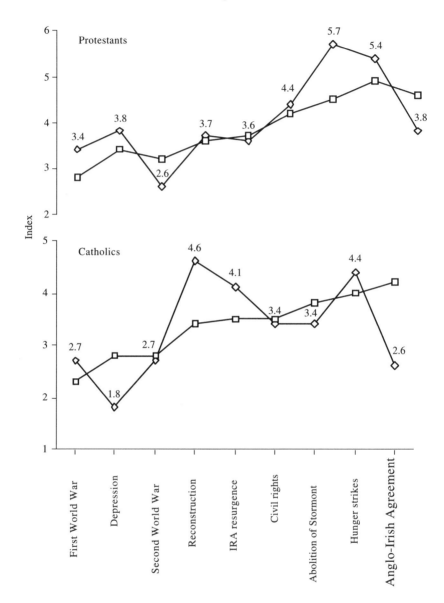

Figure 5. The impact of generational experiences on religious prejudice. *Note*: The actual estimates are the same as those in Figure 4, from where the exact estimates can be found. The regression estimates control for social composition, lifecycle and period effects. See text and Appendix to this chapter for details of estimation. (□) Actual estimate, (◇) Regression estimate. *Source*: 1989–95 Northern Ireland Social Attitudes Surveys, combined file.

voting are Switzerland and the Netherlands (Lijphart, 1975), but even here the correlations are about half those found in Northern Ireland and are, in any event, declining as a result of secularisation and the more general weakening of cleavage politics across the advanced democracies (Franklin, 1992). In the combined NISA surveys, among those who identify with unionism, 99.2 per cent are Protestant, and among those who identify with nationalism, 98.9 per cent are Catholic.[13]

These figures, however, ignore the growing proportion of respondents who apparently eschew either a unionist or nationalist political identity. In the surveys, 39 per cent of those interviewed said that they did not identify with either unionism or nationalism, a figure which is just short of the proportion who considered themselves unionist (43 per cent) and more than twice the nationalist proportion (18 per cent). This group divided almost equally between Protestants (49 per cent) and Catholics (51 per cent). These voters who reject the long-standing political identity of their religious community represent the centrist political tradition in Northern Ireland politics, which was carried on by the Northern Ireland Labour Party in the 1950s and 1960s (Walker, 1985), and since the start of the Troubles, by the Alliance Party (McAllister and Wilson, 1978). Although both parties have been committed to maintaining the union with Britain, they have sought to attract biconfessional support. In effect, they are the extreme moderates, since they represent the furthest each community can go without crossing the political divide (Rose, 1976: 58–9).

Although the surveys show that since 1989 four in every 10 Northern Ireland voters reject a unionist or nationalist political identification, the centrist Alliance Party has never managed to mobilise more than a minority of these apparently disaffected voters. The Alliance Party has rarely won more than one-tenth of the total vote; in the 1982 Assembly elections, for example, the party polled 9.3 per cent of the vote (O'Leary et al., 1988: 208); and in the 1992 general election they won 8.7 per cent of the vote, less than Sinn Féin, which contested two seats fewer than the Alliance (Butler and Kavanagh, 1992: 313). Part of the explanation for why the political centre does not mobilise more of these disaffected voters rests with the higher probability that disaffected voters will abstain.[14] Turnout has been declining in Northern Ireland: the 1982 Assembly

---

[13] This relationship yields a correlation of 0.75.

[14] The breakdown of party support among those who have neither a unionist nor a nationalist political identity is as follows: OUP (8 per cent); DUP (5 per cent); Alliance (21 per cent); SDLP (21 per cent); Sinn Féin (1 per cent); none (44 per cent).

election produced a turnout of 60.4 per cent, compared to 70.6 per cent in the 1973 Assembly election.[15]

Given the intensity of the post-1968 Troubles, what is remarkable about this large group of disaffected voters is, first, that they are much more likely to be found among those who have grown up since 1968 and second, that they have shown more rapid growth within the Protestant community. The NISA surveys asked both the direction and strength of political identity; Figure 6 shows the proportions of those rejecting a unionist or nationalist identity, together with the proportion who said that they held one or other of the identities very strongly. The results show that the proportion of disaffected Protestants has grown consistently over the years. Protestants who became politically aware during the First World War or afterwards are the strongest unionists: less than one in five do not consider themselves unionist and between one in four and one in five consider themselves very strong unionists. With the growing proportion of those rejecting the unionist identity—half or more in the two most recent generations—there has been a weakening in the strength of that identity.

There is a similar though much less dramatic trend among Catholics. Upwards of four in every 10 Catholics reject a nationalist identity, and that proportion increased gradually with each new generation until the civil rights generation. Since then, the proportion has remained reasonably constant, albeit with an increase among those whose first political experiences included the IRA hunger strikes of the early 1980s. The strength of nationalist identity has also declined, although not on a par with the level of decline among Protestants.

As we would expect, both the direction and strength of political identity has significant consequences for party support (Table 7). Among Protestants, strong unionist identifiers are more likely to support either of the two main Unionist parties—the Official Unionist Party led by David Trimble or the Democratic Unionist Party led by Ian Paisley—while those who reject unionism either predominate among those who claim no political affiliation or support the Alliance. There is a similar pattern among Catholics, with very strong nationalists being more likely to opt for Sinn Féin, somewhat weaker identifiers the Social Democratic and Labour Party, led by John Hume, and those who reject nationalism, the Alliance.

We are, therefore, left with two apparently contradictory patterns. The previous section showed that prejudice had increased among the younger generations, almost certainly as a consequence of the civil disturbances. On the other hand, this section has shown that there are more disaffected

---

[15] We are unable to test directly the proposition that these disaffected voters are more likely to abstain, since a voting recall question was not included consistently in the 1989–95 surveys.

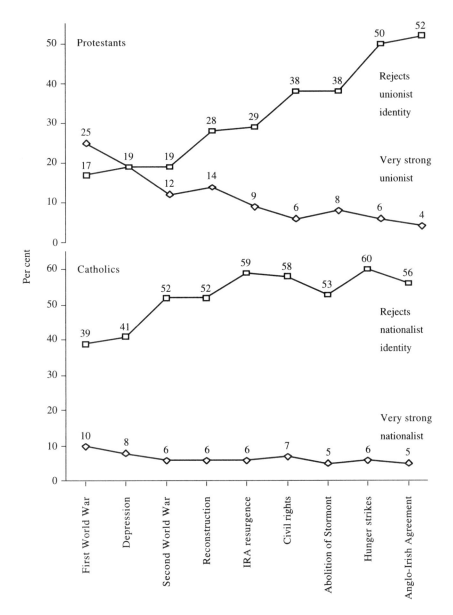

Figure 6. Unionist and nationalist political identities by generation. *Note*: See text and Appendix to this chapter for details of estimation. *Source*: 1989–95 Northern Ireland Social Attitudes Surveys, combined file.

Table 7. Party support by strength of political identity (%).

Party support	Very strong	Fairly strong	Not very strong	None
		Political identity		
Protestants:				
OUP	61	68	64	15
DUP	33	23	18	10
Alliance	4	6	8	27
Other/none	3	3	11	48
(N)	(366)	(940)	(849)	(900)
Catholics:				
SDLP	42	68	75	40
SF	51	19	6	2
Alliance	1	2	4	15
Other/none	6	11	15	43
(N)	(114)	(366)	(364)	(947)

Note: See text and Appendix to this chapter for details of estimation.

Source: 1989–95 Northern Ireland Social Attitudes Surveys, combined file.

voters in Northern Ireland within the younger generations, and among those who retain a traditional political identity, the strength of that identity is likely to be weaker. Given that prejudice is strongly correlated with political outlooks, how do we accommodate these two apparently contradictory findings?

The answer is that while popular support for the traditional political identities of each community has declined, among those who retain such identities and consider them important, prejudice has become a much more important determinant of political views. In other words, among the younger generations that have grown up since the start of the Troubles, religious prejudice is more likely to shape their political outlooks compared to those who grew up before the Troubles. For example, among Protestants who reject a unionist identity, the mean level of prejudice for the three post-1968 generations is 4.1; the same figure among those with a very strong unionist identity is 8.4, more than double. However, among the three oldest generations, those who reject a unionist identity have a mean of 3.1, compared to just 4.6 among those who see themselves as very strong unionists. There is a similar though less dramatic pattern among Catholics.

This greater political polarisation among the post-1968 generations can be shown more precisely by using a regression equation to predict political identity, and by including prejudice as an independent variable, along with social composition, lifecycle and period effects. If prejudice were causing a greater political polarisation among the younger generations, then we would expect the net impact of prejudice on political identity to increase the younger the generation. Figure 7 shows that this is precisely what happens, starting with the generation that experienced the IRA resurgence in the 1950s. Among Protestants, the impact of prejudice on political identity is at an historic low within this generation; it climbs consistently in each succeeding generation, with a slight decline within the Anglo-Irish Agreement generation.

The pattern among Catholics broadly follows that found among Protestants, with three exceptions. First, the impact of prejudice on political identity is actually lowest in an earlier generation—those whose formative experiences occurred at the time of the Second World War. Second, the most recent generation is by far the more polarised than any that went before it. And third, it is this oldest generation of Catholics, who experienced the First World War, the Home Rule movement and the partition of Ireland, who are the second most polarised of all in the way

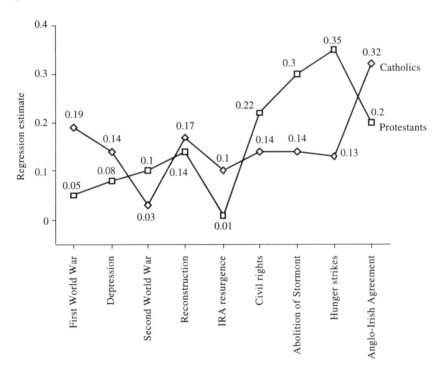

Figure 7. The consequences of prejudice for political identity. *Note*: Figures are regression estimates of the net impact of religious prejudice on political identity for each generation. See text and Appendix to this chapter for details of estimation. *Source*: 1989–95 Northern Ireland Social Attitudes Surveys, combined file.

in which they link prejudice and political identity. Among Catholics, then, it is the oldest and the youngest who are most likely to apply their prejudice to politics.

Consistent with our previous results, these estimates point to the impact that the civil disturbances have had on those who have grown up since 1968. The decline in the proportions displaying traditional political identities, as well as their weakening strength among those who retain them, belies the greater role that prejudice plays among those who retain a strong traditional political identity. Within this group, prejudice is more likely to figure as an element in their political world view and, we would hypothesise, as a greater motivation towards collective political action. The results are all the more significant when we consider that the models control for a wide rage of potentially confounding effects. It also empha-sises the impact that partition evidently had on the political outlooks of the younger Catholics of the time, in dramatic contrast to their Protestant counterparts.

Conclusion

The Northern Ireland problem has proved to be one of the most intract-able—if not *the* most intractable—political conflicts of the twentieth century. Scholars have disagreed widely both in their interpretation of the causes of the problem and in its possible solutions—a phenomenon that McGarry and O'Leary (1995: 355) call 'the conflict about the con-flict'. Some, such as Rose (1976: 139), argue that it is a problem which lacks a solution, since most territorial conflicts are based on the contested ownership of land and as a result are non-negotiable. The corollary to such a view is that only a solution which keeps the two sides apart, such as repartition, has any hope of success. Others, such as Whyte (1990) have been more cautiously optimistic, while not underestimating the difficulties in arriving at a political solution acceptable to the majority of both communities.

What is clear is that it is an internal conflict between the two religious communities, and that outside influences—such as those of the British or Irish governments—have relatively little impact on the trajectory of the conflict. The conflict is perpetuated by a range of social processes, such as family structure, the educational system and social interaction, which reinforce the values and outlooks which are particular to each religious community. Given the way in which these values and outlooks are inter-nalised by each community and transmitted from generation to generation, it is perhaps surprising that political scientists and sociologists have not examined in more detail the intergenerational dynamics of their transmission, since this, in many ways, holds the key to the future.

Our hypothesis was that the post-1968 Troubles have had a disproportionate impact on the generations growing up during the past quarter of a century, representing about one-third of the total population. Contrary to the findings of many psychologists, our results show that these generations have indeed been marked by the political violence. They are significantly more likely to display higher levels of religious prejudice, and such feelings of prejudice provide a more potent motive for political action than they do among the older generations. These findings endorse other research which has shown that indiscriminate violence generates rioting in response (Kelley and McAllister, 1986: 90); in the words of the old Chinese proverb, terrorists sow dragon's teeth and reap a harvest of violence in return.

These findings would appear to contradict the body of literature which suggests that the young have been relatively unaffected by the Troubles (O'Kane and Cairns, 1988; Greer, 1990). However, as Cairns and Cairns (1995) point out, little of this research has examined politics, and where studies have examined political values, the conclusion has been that ethnic stereotyping and political identities are at least as strongly entrenched among the young as the old.[16] Our finding that the young are more prejudiced and polarised than the old does not contradict this psychological research, since the young can have strong moral and religious values and low levels of delinquency, but still engage in political violence if they consider it legitimate. Indeed, the more a young person conforms to the norms of their community, the more likely it may be that they will engage in violence; in Northern Ireland it is the radicals who reject violence, and the conservatives who promote it.

The implications of the findings are threefold. First, if the violence continues at its present level or escalates, the numbers who will be affected by it will increase as a proportion of the total population. In turn, this will increase the levels of prejudice across the society and, via political identity, generate more support for extreme parties and groups. Second, if the conflict subsides, there will still exist within the population a large minority who have been marked by political violence and several decades will have to pass before the levels of prejudice decline through generational replacement. Third, the linkages between social processes and political outlooks undoubtedly reinforce the impact of the violence on each emerging

---

[16] As Harris (1972: 199) comments in her study of 'Ballybeg', 'Of course the senior generation was busily engaged in passing on its prejudices to the next; that is not a fact that can be overlooked.'

generation. It is perhaps here that researchers need to look to find possible solutions to the problem.

APPENDIX

Data. The Northern Ireland Social Attitudes surveys are conducted among a random sample of the adult population aged 18 years and over. Full details of the surveys and their methodology can be found in the appendices to the five reports that have been published, *Social Attitudes in Northern Ireland.* For the analyses presented herein, the five surveys were combined into a single file, producing a sample size of 5,643. The surveys differ in their individual sample sizes, with the 1989, 1991 and 1993 surveys being smaller (ns = 866, 906 and 842, respectively) than the 1994 and 1995 surveys (ns = 1,519 and 1,510). The combined file was not weighted to compensate for this bias since our interest was in the separate generations and, in any event, the regression analyses control for the survey year.

Variables. Generation is identified by age, according to the distribution in Table 2. This results in the following age distribution in each survey:

Table 8. Age distributions in the NISA Surveys.

Generation	1995	1994	1993	1991	1989
Anglo-Irish Agreement	18–23	18–22	18–21	18–19	—
Hunger strikes	24–30	23–29	22–28	20–26	18–24
Abolition of Stormont	31–36	30–35	29–34	27–32	25–30
Civil rights	37–45	36–44	35–43	33–41	31–39
IRA resurgence	46–52	45–51	44–50	42–48	40–46
Reconstruction	53–61	52–60	51–59	49–57	47–55
Second World War	62–68	61–67	60–66	58–64	56–62
Depression	69–78	68–77	67–76	65–74	63–72
First World War	79–98	78–98	77–98	75–98	73–98

Religion is measured by religious affiliation, with those who said that they had no religion being assigned to the religion that they were brought up in. The affiliation question was: 'Do you regard yourself as belonging to any particular religion?' The family religion question was: 'In what religion, if any, were you brought up in?' Prejudice is measured by the two sets of questions in Table 4, with those responding that they themselves harboured 'hardly any prejudice' being assigned to the three groups in the general prejudice question referring to both their own religion and that of the opposite community. In the analyses, prejudice is scored from a low of 1 to a high of 10. The range of independent variables are defined in Table 3; all are scored as dummy variables.

Method. The estimates reported in Figure 5 were made by calculating a regression equation for each generation, separately by religion, predicting prejudice from social composition, lifecycle and period effects, as defined in Table 3. The equations were then evaluated at the mean to estimate the net effect of generation once the independent variables had been taken into account. The estimates in Figure 7 are derived from a regression equation predicting political identity (scored from 1 to 4, using the categories described in Table 5), using the same social composition, lifecycle and period independent variables, but also including prejudice. The estimates in the figures are obtained by multiplying the mean for prejudice by its partial coefficient to show the net effect of prejudice on political identity.

Acknowledgement. The 1989–95 Northern Ireland Social Attitudes Surveys were co-ordinated by Social and Community Planning Research and funded by the Nuffield Foundation. We are grateful to Paula Devine for providing us with the combined dataset. The 1973 Irish Social Mobility Survey was collected by John Jackson and Robert Miller and funded by the Economic and Social Research Council. The 1978 Northern Ireland Attitudes Survey was collected by Edward Moxon-Browne and funded by the Nuffield Foundation. The 1995 Social Identities Survey was collected by Karen Trew and Denny Benson and funded by the Northern Ireland Central Community Relations Unit. We are grateful to Karen Trew for granting us access to the data. Our thanks to members of the Oxford meeting for their comments, and particularly to Anthony Heath and Christopher Whelan for detailed and constructive suggestions; the usual disclaimer applies.

References

Abramson, P. R. (1983) *Political Attitudes in America,* San Francisco: Freeman.

Adorno, T. W., Frenkel-Brunswik, E., Levinson, D. J. and Nevitt Sandford, R. (1950) *The Authoritarian Personality,* New York: Macmillan.

Allport, G. [1954] (1987) *The Nature of Prejudice,* Reading, MA: Addison-Wesley.

Argyle, M. and Beit-Hallahmi, B. (1975) *The Social Psychology of Religion,* London: Routledge and Kegan Paul.

Barritt, D. and Carter, C. (1962) *The Northern Ireland Problem,* Oxford: Oxford University Press.

Belloff, H. (1980) 'A Place Not So Far Apart: Conclusions of an Outsider', in J. Harbison and J. Harbison (eds), *A Society Under Stress: Children and Young People in Northern Ireland,* Shepton Mallet: Open Books.

Belloff, H. (1989) 'A Tradition of Threatened Identities', in J. Harbison (ed.), *Growing Up in Northern Ireland,* Belfast: Stranmillis College.

Bogardus, E. S. (1928) *Immigration and Race Attitudes,* Boston, MA: Heath.

Breen, R. (1996) 'Who Wants a United Ireland? Constitutional Preferences Among

Catholics and Protestants', in R. Breen, P. Devine and L. Dowds (eds), *Social Attitudes in Northern Ireland: The Fifth Report*, Belfast: Blackstaff.

Broom, L., Jones, F. L., McDonnell, P. and Williams, T. (1980) *The Inheritance of Inequality*, London: Routledge Kegan Paul.

Budge, I. and O'Leary, C. (1973) *Belfast: Approach to Crisis*, London: Macmillan.

Burton, F. (1978) *The Politics of Legitimacy*, London: Routledge Kegan Paul.

Butler, D. and Kavanagh, D. (1992) *The British General Election of 1992*, London: Macmillan.

Cairns, E. (1987) *Caught in the Crossfire: Children and the Northern Ireland Conflict*, Belfast: Appletree.

Cairns, E. and Cairns, T. (1995) 'Children and Conflict: A Psychological Perspective', in S. Dunn (ed.), *Facets of the Conflict in Northern Ireland*, London: St. Martin's Press.

Cairns, E. and Mercer, G. W. (1984) 'Social Identity in Northern Ireland', *Human Relations*, 37: 1095–102.

Carmines, E. G. and Merriman, W. R. (1993) 'The Changing American Dilemma: Liberal Values and Racial Policies', in P. M. Sniderman, P. E. Tetlock and E. G. Carmines (eds), *Prejudice, Politics and the American Dilemma*, Stanford: Stanford University Press.

Carroll, T. G. (1981) 'Disobedience and Violence in Northern Ireland', *Comparative Political Studies*, 14: 3–29.

Carter, C. F. and Barritt, D. P. [1962] (1972) *The Northern Ireland Problem*, Oxford: Oxford University Press.

Compton, P. A. (1985) 'An Evaluation of the Changing Religious Composition of the Population in Northern Ireland', *Economic and Social Review*, 16: 201–24.

Dalton, R. (1977) 'Was There a Revolution? A Note on Generational Versus Lifecycle Explanations of Value Differences', *Comparative Political Studies*, 9: 458–73.

Davis, J. A. (1975) 'Communism, Conformity, Cohorts and Categories: American Tolerance in 1954 and 1972–73', *American Journal of Sociology*, 81: 491–513.

Davis, J. A. (1987) *Social Differences in Contemporary America*, San Francisco: Harcourt Brace, Janovitch.

Dowden, S. and Robinson, J. P. (1993) 'Age and Cohort Differences in American Racial Atitudes: The Generational Replacement Hypothesis Revisited', in Paul M. Sniderman, P. E. Tetlock and E. G. Carmines (eds), *Prejudice, Politics and the American Dilemma*, Stanford: Stanford University Press.

Feagin, J. R. (1978) *Racial and Ethnic Relations*, Englewood Cliffs, NJ: Prentice-Hall.

Fields, R. (1973) *A Society On the Run: A Psychology of Northern Ireland*, England: Penguin.

Fields, R. (1977) *Society Under Siege: A Psychology of Northern Ireland*, Philadelphia: Temple University Press.

Franklin, M. (1992) 'The Decline of Cleavage Politics', in M. Franklin, T. Mackie and H. Valen (eds), *Electoral Change*, Cambridge: Cambridge University Press.

Fraser, M. (1973) *Children in Conflict*, New York: Basic Books.

Glenn, N. G. (1987) 'The Trend in 'No Religion' Respondents to U.S. National Surveys, Late 1950s to Early 1980s', *Public Opinion Quarterly*, 51: 293–314.

Glenn, N. G. (1989) 'A Caution about Mechanical Solutions to the Identification Problem in Cohort Analysis', *American Journal of Sociology*, 95: 754–61.

Grada, C. O. (1986) 'Determinants of Irish Emigration', *International Migration Review*, 20: 650–6.

Greenstein, F. I. (1969) *Children and Politics*, New Haven, Conn.: Yale University Press.

Greer, J. E. (1984) 'Moral Cultures in Northern Ireland', *Journal of Social Psychology*, 123: 63–70.

Greer, J. E. (1990) 'The Persistence of Religion: A Study of Sixth-Form Pupils in Northern Ireland, 1968–1988', *Journal of Social Psychology*, 130: 573–81.

Harbison, J. (ed.) (1983) *Children of the Troubles*, Belfast: Stranmillis College.

Harbison, J. (ed.) (1989) *Growing Up in Northern Ireland*, Belfast: Stranmillis College.

Harbison, J. and Harbison, J. (eds) (1980) *A Society Under Stress: Children and Young People in Northern Ireland*, Shepton Mallet: Open Books.

Harris, R. (1972) *Prejudice and Tolerance in Ulster*, Manchester: Manchester University Press.

Hayes, B. C. and McAllister, I. (1995) 'Religious Independents in Northern Ireland: Origins, Attitudes and Significance', *Review of Religious Research*, 37: 65–83.

Heskin, K. (1980) *Northern Ireland: A Psychological Analysis*, Dublin: Gill and Macmillan.

Hosin, A. and Cairns, E. (1984) 'The Impact of Conflict on Children's Ideas About Their Country', *Journal of Social Psychology*, 118: 161–8.

Houston, J., Crozier, E., Ray, W. and Walker, P. (1990) 'The Assessment of Ethnic Sensitivity Among Northern Ireland Schoolchildren', *British Journal of Developmental Psychology*, 8: 419–22.

Irish Social Mobility Survey (1973) The principal investigators of this survey were J. A. Jackson and R. L. Miller. Funded by the Economic and Social Research Council, the data is currently available from the data archive at the University of Essex, England.

Jahoda, G. and Harrison, S. (1975) 'Belfast Children: Some Effects of a Conflict Environment', *Irish Journal of Psychology*, 3: 1–19.

Kelley, J. and McAllister, I. (1985) 'Class and Party in Australia: Comparisons with Britain and the United States', *British Journal of Sociology*, 36: 383–420.

Kelley, J. and McAllister, I. (1986) 'Economic Theories of Political Violence in the Northern Ireland Conflict', in Y. Alexander and A. O'Day (eds), *Ireland's Terrorist Dilemma*, Dordrecht: Martinus Nijhoff.

Lijphart, A. (1975) 'The Northern Ireland Problem: Cases, Models and Theories', *British Journal of Political Science*, 5: 83–106.

Mannheim, K. (1952) 'The Problem of Generations', in P. Kecskemeti (ed.), *Essay on the Sociology of Knowledge*, New York: Oxford University Press.

McAllister, I. and Wilson, B. (1978) 'Bi-Confessionalism in a Confessional Party System: The Northern Ireland Alliance Party', *Economic and Social Review*, 9: 207–25.

McClenahan, C., Cairns, E., Dunn, S. and Morgan, V. (1991) 'Preference for Geographical Location as a Measure of Ethnic/National Identity in Children in Northern Ireland', *Irish Journal of Psychology*, 12: 346–54.

McGarry, J. and O'Leary, B. (1995) *Explaining Northern Ireland*, Oxford: Blackwells.

McWhirter, L. (1982) 'Northern Irish Children's Conceptions of Violent Crime', *Howard Journal,* 21: 167–77.

McWhirter, L. (1983) 'Contact and Conflict: The Question of Integrated Schooling', *Irish Journal of Psychology,* 6: 13–27.

McWhirter, L, Young, V. and Majury, J. (1983) 'Belfast Children's Awareness of Violent Crime', *British Journal of Social Psychology,* 22: 81–92.

Mercer, G. W. and Cairns, E. (1981) 'Conservatism and its Relationship to General and Specific Ethnocentrism in Northern Ireland', *British Journal of Social Psychology,* 20: 13–16.

Northern Ireland Social Attitudes Survey (1978) The principal investigator of this survey was E. Moxon-Brown. Funded by the Nuffield Foundation, the data is currently available form the data archive at the University of Essex, England.

Northern Ireland Social Attitudes Surveys (1989–1995) Funded by the Nuffield Foundation and the Northern Ireland Central Community Relations Unit, the data is currently available from the data archive at the University of Essex, England. Our thanks to P. Devine for merging these surveys and providing us with a combined dataset.

Northern Ireland Social Identities Survey (1995) The principal investigators of this survey were K. Trew and D. Benson. Funded by the Northern Ireland Central Communities Relations Unit, the data is currently available from K. Trew at the Department of Psychology, Queen's University, Belfast. Our thanks to K. Trew for granting us access to the data.

Nunn, C. A., Crockett, H. J. and Williams, J. A. (1978) *Tolerance for Non-Conformity,* San Francisco: Jossey-Bass.

O'Kane, D. and Cairns, E. (1988) 'The Development of Conservatism in Northern Ireland: A Cross-Cultural Comparison', *Journal of Social Psychology,* 128: 49–53.

O'Leary, B. and McGarry, J. (1993) *The Politics of Antagonism,* London: Athlone Press.

O'Leary, C., Elliott, S. and Wilford, R. A. (1988) *The Northern Ireland Assembly, 1982–86,* London: Charles Hurst.

Page, B. I. and Shapiro, R. Y. (1992) *The Rational Public*, Chicago: University of Chicago Press.

Poole, M. (1983) 'The Demography of Violence', in J. Darby (ed.), *Northern Ireland: Background to the Conflict,* Syracuse: Syracuse University Press.

Rose, R. (1976) *Northern Ireland: Time of Choice*, London: Macmillan.

Russell, J. (1974) 'Socialisation and Conflict', Glasgow: Ph.D. thesis, University of Strathclyde.

Stewart, A. T. Q. (1967) *The Ulster Crisis*, London: Faber.

Stouffer, S. A. (1955) *Communism, Conformity and Civil Liberties,* New York: Doubleday.

Stringer, M. and Cairns, E. (1983) 'Catholic and Protestant Young People's Ratings of Stereotyped Protestant and Catholic Faces', *British Journal of Social Psychology,* 22: 241–6.

Stringer, M. and Cook, N. M. (1985) 'The Effects of Limited and Conflicting

Stereotypic Information on Group Categorization in Northern Ireland', *Journal of Applied Social Psychology,* 15: 399–407.

Sullivan, J. L., Piereson, J. and Marcus, G. E. (1982) *Political Tolerance and American Democracy,* Chicago: University of Chicago Press.

Tajfel, H. (1970) 'Experiments in Intergroup Relations', *Scientific American,* 233: 96–102.

Trew, K. (1983) 'Sense of National Identity: Fact or Artefact?', *Irish Journal of Psychology,* 6: 28–36.

Trew, K. (1994) 'What It Means to be Irish Seen from a Northern Perspective', *Irish Journal of Psychology,* 15: 388–99.

Trew, K. (1996) 'National Identity', in R. Breen, P. Devine and L. Dowds (eds), *Social Attitudes in Northern Ireland: The Fifth Report,* Belfast: Blackstaff.

Wadell, N. and Cairns, E. (1986) 'Situational Perspectives on Social Identity in Northern Ireland', *British Journal of Social Psychology,* 25: 25–31.

Wadell, N. and Cairns, E. (1991) 'Identity Preferences in Northern Ireland', *Political Psychology,* 12: 205–13.

Walker, G. (1985) *The Politics of Frustration,* Manchester: Manchester University Press.

Whyte, J. (1983) 'Control and Supervision of Urban 12–Year-Olds Within and Outside Northern Ireland: A Pilot Study', *Irish Journal of Psychology,* 6: 37–45.

Whyte, J. (1995) *Changing Times: Challenges to Identity,* Aldershot: Avebury.

Whyte, J. (1990) *Interpreting Northern Ireland,* Oxford: Oxford University Press.

Williams, T. D. (ed.) (1973) *Secret Societies in Ireland,* Dublin: Gill and Macmillan.

Conclusions

ANTHONY F. HEATH, RICHARD BREEN
& CHRISTOPHER T. WHELAN

OUR AIM IN THIS VOLUME HAS BEEN TO EXPLORE the changes that have been taking place in Ireland North and South over recent decades. As David Rottman shows in his chapter, there has been very little work up until now comparing the two parts of Ireland; most previous work has treated the Republic as a 'critical case' for exploring general theories of social change, while the North has been of more interest as a test case for understanding 'settler societies' and the associated ethnic conflict.

Both the ideas of general theory of social change and those of conflict in settler societies are germane to our current interests in the evolution of the two parts of Ireland, but they are not the *raison d'être* of our inquiry. Rather, our concern is with the question of whether, and in what respects, the two parts of Ireland have been converging or diverging in their patterns of economic, social and political behaviour. On the one hand, the two parts of Ireland may be exposed to common social and economic processes as a result of economic development and modernisation, membership of the EU, diffusion of values and secularisation. Both North and South share common exposure to the global forces (and more European ones) of small open economies on the European periphery (Rottman, this volume: 11). These common processes may lead over time to some greater commonality between the two parts of Ireland.

On the other hand, the two parts of Ireland have had very different historical legacies, even before partition, and they have evolved many different institutions since then. The most evident difference between them was the existence of religious-ethnic divisions which had arisen in the north-east of Ireland for specific historical reasons and which were not found to anything like the same extent on the rest of the island. This difference was exaggerated after partition, as the South became ethnically

Proceedings of the British Academy, **98**, 493–516. © The British Academy 1999.

and religiously more homogenous while the North remained a mixed society with, in recent years, the numerical balance of the Catholic and Protestant populations becoming more even. In addition, the two jurisdictions inherited very different economies from the nineteenth century. These, plus more recent legacies, also shape the current patterns of social relationships.

Our interest in these processes derives ultimately not from a concern with sociological or economic theory *per se* but with the prospects for Ireland's future. Ireland's future, whether it eventually becomes a single unified Irish state, or some joint sovereignty is evolved, or the status quo persists, will undoubtedly depend on political contingencies and decisions that we as sociologists or political scientists cannot conceivably predict. However, these decisions will be made within certain temporal and sociological contexts that may to some extent limit the scope for manoeuvre or alternatively make new options available. What we can try to offer then, as social scientists, is not a blue-print for the future but some understanding of the context and constraints within which decisions will be made.

We begin in this concluding chapter with some discussion of the distinctive legacies that our chapter authors have noted and then turn to the common social processes that they have detected. We conclude with some more speculative comments about their implications for the future.

Historical Legacies

For much of the twentieth century, long before partition, the two parts of Ireland had very different economies, the North having a major industrial base centred on ship-building and textiles in Belfast, while the South remained largely agricultural and experienced a very late economic modernisation. The effect of partition on the Southern economy, was, as one commentator later put it, 'as if Scotland had obtained self-government with Glasgow and the Clyde left out' (O'Brien, 1962: 11 quoted by Breen and Whelan, this volume: 320). As Bradley writes 'The South embarked on a path of political independence with an economy that was without significant industrialisation, but was dependent on mainly agricultural exports to the British market. The North achieved a degree of regional autonomy within the UK at a stage when the perilous state of its strong industrial base was still hidden in the aftermath of the economic boom created by the First World War' (Bradley, this volume: 45–46). Bradley concludes that there were many changes both in the North and in the South between 1921 and the early 1960s, but few were of major significance compared with the legacy of the pre-1922 period. The South attempted to construct an industrial base behind a protective barrier of high tariffs, but with relatively little success. Meanwhile the North's staple industrial specialisations continued to decline. In this light it seems rather doubtful whether, in the absence of partitition, the main Northern industries could have provided the innovation and resources for industrialisation needed in the mainly agricultural South. As in other aspects of the socio-economic legacy, therefore, the South was clearly different from the North even before partition, but the North also inherited a legacy that set it apart from mainland Britain, with a much greater dependence on a few, declining industries.

Allied to its rural character and institutions and the lack of economic opportunities, the South also inherited a legacy of a highly distinctive demographic regime. After the great famine in the mid-nineteenth century, late age at marriage combined with high marital fertility, frequent celibacy and partible inheritance produced a remarkable demographic regime in which the South displayed an exceptional (by European standards) level of natural increase and an exceptional level of outward migration. 'Emigration is the most distinctive feature of Ireland's demography, even more than its high birth rate, in per capita terms the greatest of all the European nineteenth-century diasporas' (Coleman, this volume: 78). As Coleman argues in his chapter, migration enabled high rates of natural increase to continue without feeding back on to population size, and there was therefore no demographic incentive for a reduction in marital fertility.

The Republic's demographic exceptionalism continued until the mid-twentieth century and beyond, and while the North was clearly different from the South, it also showed a distinctively Irish fertility regime with higher fertility and migration than in the rest of the UK (with the exception of the Highlands and Islands). The two communities in the North were also sharply different, the Catholics showing both higher fertility and higher propensity to migrate than did the Northern Protestants. 'Throughout most of the twentieth-century Northern Ireland shows the sharpest demographic contrast between any two neighbouring communities outside Kossovo in Serbia' (Coleman, this volume: 90). As a result, the rate of natural increase (excess of births over deaths) remained about three times higher among the Catholic compared with the non-Catholic population, a difference which would translate directly into differences in rates of population growth in the absence of migration. The legacy of Catholicism (and in the North of Protestant institutions) in accounting for these differences in fertility and family policy is undoubtedly important, but it is also essential to interpret the role of Catholicism in context. Coleman argues that there is no general tendency for Catholic teaching to be associated with high fertility: Italy and Spain have some of the lowest fertility levels in the world. What we see in Ireland is probably, as Coleman suggests, a minority status effect: 'Roman Catholic influence, independent of socio-economic status, can only be shown to be important where Roman Catholicism acquired particular authority through being a focus for the national sentiments of a disadvantaged minority in a larger population' (this volume: 105–6).

Closely linked both with the agricultural character of the Republic and its remarkable demographic regime was a distinctive pattern of family policy. Fahey and McLaughlin argue in their chapter that, even before partition:

> The political and literary elite of the new nationalist movement and the clerical leadership of the Catholic Church joined forces to generate a far-reaching ideological glorification of the small family farm and to elevate the pastoral idyll into a framework for emerging national identity. This outlook defined the countryside as the repository of true moral values and contrasted the authentic rural way of life with the social and moral danger of the city (exemplified in Patrick Pearse's pledge that there would be "no Glasgows and Pittsburghs in a free Ireland"). Conservative, patriarchal and stable forms of family organisation were central both to this worldview and to the reality of the small-farm economy which underlay it. The groundwork was thus laid for the powerful rural focus of state ideology and state practice in the post-partition Free State, the consequences of which had a major effect on family policy as well as on the broad lines of national development in independent Ireland. (This volume: 122)

Fahey and McLaughlin go on to argue that this ideology demanded strong state support for Catholic moral regulation as an essential part of the cultural superstructure. The new independent state responded appropriately, with a particular focus on sex, reproduction, gender and childhood discipline. Censorship (1929), the banning of artificial contraceptives (1935) and the drive to control occasions of youth immorality (such as the Public Dance Hall Acts 1935) were the main measures in the sexual and reproductive arenas. The promotion of a domestic role for women was pursued in the 1930s through the 'marriage bar' against female employment in teaching and the public service, and, for working-class women, the introduction of 'protective' legislation against 'unsuitable' work practices such as nightwork and heavy manual labour. The family articles in the 1937 Constitution, which emphasised patriarchal rights, the domestic role of women and a Catholic view of the impermissibility of divorce, represented the culmination of this trend.

The North also had a legacy that was distinctly different both from the Southern one and from that of Britain. While the bulk of the post-war Beveridge welfare state was applied to Northern Ireland as well as to

Britain, nevertheless the post-war Northern welfare system remained distinctive, as Unionist politicians, civil servants and professionals sought to achieve the (populist) benefits of the British welfare state through means which '[were] more in keeping with Unionist principles than those adopted in the system across the water' (Connolly 1990). 'Modifications to the Beveridge welfare system took three forms: firstly, tighter restrictions on entitlement to cash benefits [intended to protect the boundaries of the northern state and inhibit population movement from the South], a greater role for unelected administrative bodies, and thirdly, more restrictive distributive public services and normative family law' (Fahey and McLaughlin, this volume: 128). These differences in family policy and demographic regime were also manifested in different profiles of women's participation in the labour market. As O'Connor and Shortall (this volume) show (Table 1) married women in the South have always had a lower participation rate in the wage labour market than married women in the North.

In one respect, however, the South has had a more favourable legacy than the North. As Breen *et al.*, demonstrate, the South has long been superior to the North in levels of educational attainment. While it is difficult to compare the two systems, since the nature of the qualifications offered to pupils are different, nevertheless it is clear that the proportion of Southern pupils leaving school with no formal qualifications has long been lower than in the North. The North has had, and continues to have, a highly selective educational system in which a minority of pupils were sponsored for educational success.

Moreover, within the Northern jurisdiction, Catholics do not appear to have been at the kind of major educational disadvantage relative to Protestants that they experienced in other fields. The role of the Catholic Church in organising education for Catholics in both North and South is certainly part of this story and can help to account for the apparent anomaly of an agricultural society like the South offering high levels of school attainment. Schools were operated in a spartan and frugal manner; resources for education were marshalled by the Catholic Church and the religious orders themselves contributed both in terms of school building and the provision of teachers; and, lastly, the educational system economised by emphasising subjects which required little in the way of costly equipment (Tussing, 1978).

At the same time, however, and probably due to the lack of alternative channels of mobility in the South, social class differences in education were (and continue to be) markedly higher in the South. Again these differences are long-standing (although as Breen *et al.*, emphasise in their chapter selective patterns of migration may well lead to some exaggeration in the surveys of the underlying differences). Similarly in the area of social mobility the South has a history of greater class inequalities and lower openness than other European countries, including Northern Ireland, Scotland, England and Wales (Breen and Whelan, 1996). This finding is consistent with Fahey's (1998: 415) recent argument that the primary purpose of social service provision for the Catholic Church was to disseminate and safeguard the faith, not to combat social inequality or reform society, with Catholic schools being structured in such a way as to reflect, and to some extent reinforce existing social hierarchies.

While the separate school systems for Protestants and Catholics in the North meant that there has been little overt educational discrimination, there has clearly been a history of discrimination in the allocation of public housing, in the electoral system and in the labour market. There is also a legacy of structural disadvantage suffered by Catholics in the North: the 1971 census showed 31 per cent of male Catholics in non-manual occupations compared with 41 per cent of Protestants, and a rate of unemployment among Catholic men more than two-and-a-half times that of Protestant men. As Teague and McCartney argue 'Employers did overtly disciminate against Catholics (and Protestants) and Protestant workers did operate in a way that intimidated Catholics from particular firms. Probably more important, however, have been industrial relations practices with the unintended consequences of crowding Catholics into the lower end of the labour market. Thus, Catholic disadvantage was not some grand conspiracy on the part of Unionists or Protestants but, in part, the result of "normal" labour market processes becoming entangled in the local religious divide' (this volume: 356).

Alongside the legacy of religion is of course the legacy of politics. As Hayes and McAllister emphasise 'The political violence that Northern Ireland has experienced since 1968 is not new. The republican and loyalist organisations which employ political violence are the descendants of groups which used similar methods, for similar ends, at the turn of the century, and more distantly, in the eighteenth century' (this volume: 457). They go on to argue that 'research into the development of ethnic stereotyping suggests a continuing historical legacy of inter-group hostility and intolerance, particularly among Protestant children' (462).

A number of our authors emphasise that we must avoid imprisoning ourselves within myths about Irish history. Bew argues that 'Unionists are presented within an exaggeratedly intransigent version of their own history while nationalists are encouraged not to reflect seriously on their own stance' (this volume: 401). But perhaps the key to understanding the political legacy is to recognise, as Girvin argues, that there are two nations in Ireland:

> The available evidence suggests that there has never been a single nation on the island of Ireland, that when an Irish nationalism did emerge it was

predominantly Catholic and that another distinct nationalism emerged in the Northern area which considered itself to be Irish (or Ulster), British and over-whelmingly Protestant. This leads to a further conclusion: that is that partition in Ireland pre-dates the political arrangements of the early 1920s. What the Government of Ireland Act 1920 and the 1922 Treaty settlement did was institutionalise an already existing social and political reality. That Irish nation-alism has refused subsequently to accept partition is closely linked to the refusal to recognise a separate nationality in Northern Ireland. (This volume: 373–74)

Girvin argues that there had perhaps once been a chance in the 1790s to realise Wolf Tone's objective of uniting the three religious subcultures (Catholic, Anglican and Presbyterian) and forge a single Irish nationality, but that chance has long since gone. Within Northern Ireland the survey evidence captures the continuing polarisation of the two communities in which the gap between Catholics and Protestants on a wide range of issues is overwhelming (Breen, 1996; Irish Political Studies, 1995). Girvin con-cludes that the two identities are as far apart as ever and one should not confuse the possibility of cooperation between the two nationalisms with the dissolving of differences. Conversely, it is clear that the hostility of the new Irish state towards Northern Ireland during the 1922/23 period, as documented by Bew, has given way to a complex evolution of attitudes, culminating, by the end of the 1980s, in what Girvin describes as the exhaustion of the seam of neo-traditional nationalism and the develop-ment of a new set of nationalist aspirations in which gradualist assump-tions take priority. Opinion polls in the South in the 1990s show the continuing importance of nationalism but the emergence of more prag-matic views in relation to options with, as Hayes and McAllister (1996: 80) show, Irish Unity becoming a minority preference and a large majority favouring changes to the constitution to accommodate political settlement.

However, one should not overemphasise the historical differences between the two parts of Ireland. In some respects political independence in 1921 did not end British influence in the Republic of Ireland. For example, a common legal framework was inherited from British rule before partition (Brewer, this volume: 162), and there were common industrial relations structures too. As Teague and McCartney argue, 'Like many other parts of the administrative structure, little attempt was made to recast the established industrial relations arrangements by the early governments of the Free State. Indeed industrial relations in Britain and Ireland remained virtually indistinguishable until the mid-1970s' (342). One aspect of this was the continued functioning of the Irish Congress of Trade Unions (ICTU) which covered both North and South. The South's economy also remained for a substantial period closely tied to Britain's, reflected also in the major flows of migration between the South and Britain.

Common Social Changes

As Bradley argues, both North and South entered the 1960s in a state where major policy changes were needed, and although the major policy changes that came were very different in the two parts of the Ireland, they produced not entirely dissimilar results. In the South the highly protectionist regime of the pre-war state was eventually abandoned with the First Programme for Economic Expansion in 1958 and the abolition of the Control of Manufactures Act,[1] which had prohibited foreign ownership, and its replacement by a policy which encouraged Foreign Direct Investment (FDI). Since then there has been a phenomenal growth of export-oriented FDI in the South which has led to a major modernisation of the Southern economy. Meanwhile the North struggled with the reverse problems of a declining industrial base and the consequent economic restructuring. FDI has not had the same impact as in the South, but, particularly after the imposition of Direct Rule in 1972, there have been major UK subsidies for inward investment and a substantial expansion of the public sector. Thus, starting from very different origins, the North and South have both been exposed to the forces of modernisation. While they have not yet converged, they both share some of the standard developments of modern Western economies—increasing proportions engaged in non-manual work, especially in the growing service sector. Up to the 1950s the South had been a rural society where 40 per cent worked on the land. Since then Southern Irish employment has shifted to urban, manufacturing and service jobs; by 1995 only 12 per cent worked in agriculture compared to 20 per cent in manufacturing, 8 per cent in utilities and 61 per cent in services. In Northern Ireland the comparable figures were 6 per cent, 19 per cent, 6 per cent and 69 per cent.[2]

Similarly Breen and Whelan argue that the 'history of the class structures of the two parts of Ireland since partition has been one of very gradual convergence. The post-1958 industrialisation of the Republic, the decline in the importance of farming, and the growth of the service sector have acted to bring its class structure closer to that of Northern Ireland where recent industrial decline and the impact of "the Troubles" have led to surprisingly little change' (this volume: 320).

Like other Western European countries, both North and South have seen dramatic increases in educational attainment. Breen *et al.*, (this volume) show that in the South, the proportion who have completed the

---

[1] The act was repealed completely in 1964. From 1958 it could be waived by ministerial order (via the Industrial Development [Encouragement of Investment]) Act.

[2] Source: NI: NIAAS, 1997 Republic of Ireland: ILFS, 1997.

junior cycle or above has risen from 46 per cent in their earliest birth cohort (educated in the 1950s) to 81 per cent in the most recent (educated in the 1970s and 1980s). The North shows almost as large an increase from 39 per cent to 70 per cent. This kind of expansion seems to be a fairly universal feature of contemporary Western societies (Shavit and Blossfeld, 1993), probably reflecting young people's growing recognition that jobs for the unqualified were becoming fewer and fewer in number. But what is particularly interesting is that, in both parts of Ireland, in common with most other industrialised countries increasing levels of educational attainment have not resulted in, or been accompanied by, a decline in class differences in attainment. These 'persisting class differentials' have been explained, in a rather general way, as the result of the greater ability of those with power and privilege to maintain their position in spite of changes that might be expected to threaten it. In a recent paper, Breen and Goldthorpe (1997) have tried to present a rather more detailed explanation of the phenomenon. They argue that more ambitious educational options carry higher risks for some social classes than others. Viewed from this perspective the large increase in overall educational attainment in both parts of Ireland can be seen as, in part, the result of inflation in the levels of educational attainment needed to secure a given class position, while the persistence of class differences is chiefly the consequence of the underlying, and unchanged, distribution of risks associated with the institutionally structured alternatives among which young people must choose.

As with other Western societies, both North and South have also seen a major reduction in gender inequalities in education. Married women's participation rates in the labour market also rose dramatically between 1961 and 1991 in both North and South, so that in both parts of Ireland the rates for all women and for married women have become virtually identical (this volume: Breen and Whelan, Table 2; O'Connell, Table 4). Conversely men's participation rate fell in both North and South, and hence much of the increase in total employment has been taken by women, especially in part-time work (reported both by O'Connell and Gudgin in their chapters). Declining male labour-force participation in the Republic of Ireland is principally due to a marked decline in participation in the younger age groups associated with increased educational participation, although there has been a trend towards earlier retirement among older males (aged over 45). While younger women's participation rates have also declined, this has been more than offset by a marked increase in participation among women aged over 25. From the mid-1980s to the early 1990s increased female participation coincided with a sharp increase in part-time working among women, although with the more recent employment

expansion most of the increase in women's employment has been in full-
time work. Again this is a feature shared with other European societies.

In both the North and South, too, there has been a reduction in the
male/female earnings gap following enactment of equal pay legislation
(O'Connor and Shortall, this volume: 290). In the North women in 1973
earned only 63 per cent as much as men, rising to 75 per cent in 1980; in the
South the comparable figures were 60 per cent in 1973, rising to 69 per cent
in 1980. Much of this equal opportunity legislation, O'Connor and
Shortall argue, 'arose in the context of entry to the European Community
in 1973. As signatories of the Treaty of Rome, Ireland and the UK became
bound by a series of Directives regarding equal pay and equal treatment in
the area of access to employment, vocational training and social security.
Such directives have been widely seen as an attempt by the EU to give
concrete expression to a gender-neutral concept of citizenship' (O'Connor
and Shortall, this volume: 306).

In the labour market, both North and South have also seen declining
frequency of strikes and industrial disputes, reflecting as Teague and
McCartney point out trends common to virtually all European economies.
Less fortunately, both South and North have a shared experience of
unemployment. 'In summary, the deterioration of the Northern labour
market from the late 1970s and throughout the 1980s was replicated in
the South, where over-shooting of employment growth after the fiscal
expansions of the late 1970s was unsustainable. In both regions a serious
problem of structural or long-term unemployment emerged.' (Bradley, this
volume: 53).

The combination of an expanding middle class and rising unemployment effectively means, as O'Connell argues, that the labour market in
Ireland has been characterised by a process of polarisation, with upgrading
of positions for those at work combined with the exclusion of those lacking
capacities to compete for access to work. It is likely that a similar process of
polarisation has been at work in the North too. Both parts of Ireland have
also witnessed, as Brewer and his colleagues describe, large increases in
crime rates and at nearly the same time—from the late 1950s in the North
and the mid-1960s in the South.

Partly as a result of these economic and educational changes, the South
(and also the North) has now gone through the same demographic transitions that other European countries have experienced, although the first
demographic transition came very late to the South, perhaps some sixty
years behind the times. As Coleman shows, dramatic changes took place in
the 1970s and 1980s. While Irish fertility, both North and South, is still
towards the higher end of the European range, it has in both parts of the
island fallen below replacement level. By 1994 the Total Fertility Rates had

fallen to 1.87 and 1.92. Coleman concludes that 'The distinctive Irish fertility regime is nearly over, [and will become] questions of recent history rather than of the contemporary world' (108).

Moreover, Ireland North and South have begun the second demographic transition with some gusto, before they have even quite finished the first. As elsewhere in north-west Europe, illegitimate births, once very rare, have increased sharply since the 1970s and the trend between North and South is scarcely to be distinguished. Although still well short of that in England, Wales or Scotland, rates in 1995 have comfortably exceeded levels in countries such as Italy and Spain, even though starting from a lower position, 'This indicates a startling change in attitudes; the end of a tradition of sexual restraint before long-delayed marriage' (Coleman, this volume: 88).

As Fahey and McLaughlin argue, 'The Catholic moral heritage in the fields of sex and marriage became more and more contentious. The initial major challenge came from an increasingly liberal Supreme Court in the 1960s and 1970s, most notably in the McGee judgement in 1973 which struck down the legal ban on contraceptives as unconstitutional. In the South throughout the 1980s and early 1990s public debate was convulsed by controversy over the "politics of the family".' On the surface the dominant outcome of the conflict has been to provide support for traditional approaches to the family. The constitutional referendums in the 1980s installed an anti-abortion clause in the constitution and rejected any change to the prohibition of divorce in Irish law. The 1995 constitutional amendment permitting divorce was passed by only the tiniest majority. However, these developments co-existed with decisive moves away from traditional approaches in order to accommodate new patterns of behaviour in family life (Whelan and Fahey, 1990). Similarly, a strong and apparently unshakeable anti-abortion consensus prevailed throughout the 1990s, yet in 1992 this consensus was thrown into turmoil by the 'X' case in which the Supreme Court ruled that a fourteen year old who was the victim of an alleged rape had a constitutional right to an abortion, on the grounds that her life was threatened by suicidal tendencies arising from her pregnancy. In the subsequent referendum the rights to travel abroad to have an abortion, and to disseminate information in Ireland on legal services available abroad were affirmed, while a proposed new and more restrictive amendment to the 1983 anti-abortion clause in the Constitution was rejected. Fahey and McLaughlin conclude that 'The general tenor of family policy has therefore tended to converge towards that in the North' (137).

The explanation of these processes of the first and second demographic transitions in Ireland are, as Coleman notes, highly complex but lying behind them are likely to be the common processes that seem to have operated elsewhere, namely 'the increased costs of higher quality children in a modern economy; the effects of near-universal literacy and higher education standards (especially among women), an open society offering rewards to those with skills and education, the parallel erosion of traditional and religious influences aided by greater geographical mobility and urbanisation, and the movement of married women into the workforce' (this volume: 100). This decline of traditionalism and community is also likely, as Brewer argues, to be associated with the rise in crime rates.

Religious change in Ireland has most frequently been considered in terms of models of secularisation defined as the process by which sectors of society and culture are removed from the dominance of religious institutions or symbols. In the South until recently, as Fahey observes, the Catholic Church's role as a social provider exceeded anything provided by any other non-state organisation in the nineteenth or twentieth century. The sheer scale of its resources enabled it to 'control the moral discourse and practice of the Irish people' and maintain a 'moral monopoly'. Today, the Church's role as a service provider is dwindling because falling vocations have left it without the personnel to sustain its role. Church attendance, which remained as high as 80 per cent weekly, has declined significantly in recent years, perhaps not entirely unrelated to a series of scandals which rocked the Church in the 1990s. Corish (1996) concludes that 'if Catholics could come to terms with accepting that the clergy numbered among them a small minority of deviants, they found it much more difficult to accept the mishandling of these cases by the hierarchy'. Hornsby-Smith and Whelan (1994) conclude on the basis of the European Values Survey that Catholics in the South increasingly reject the Church's right to speak with authority on matters of personal morality.

In the political sphere, too, Evans and Sinnott note that there have been some similar processes, again shared with several other Western European countries. Specifically, there has in both North and South been a substantial weakening of people's attachment to political parties. The South, with the North following close on its heels, had the lowest levels of attachment to party across fourteen European political systems in 1994. However we explain this decline in party attachment in the two systems, the process involved has left the two parts of Ireland looking very similar to each other and very different from the majority of member states of the Union. Evans and Sinnott note that 'It is perhaps significant that the only case that comes close to Irish levels of detachment from party is Belgium, a state that has also been characterised by a fundamental cleavage on the nationalist issue . . . it appears that, rather than maintaining or even intensifying attachment to party, the prolonged conflict in Northern Ireland is associated with reduced attachment to parties' (this volume: 436).

Thus in both countries we have seen, over the last thirty years or so, demographic transition, educational expansion, growth of the middle classes, increased participation of women in the labour market, a reduction of gender inequalities and in the political sphere a reduced attachment to the political parties. Less happily, both parts of Ireland have seen rising unemployment and rising crime rates. Many of these changes have been shared, in general character if not in extent, by other Western European countries. These changes have been a product of a variety of linked processes, especially economic modernisation, social liberalisation and possibly the weakening of religious values; but some have also in part been stimulated by membership of the EU and its common directives. Hence in many respects there has been convergence.

Persisting Differences

Despite these common processes of change, Ireland North and South have by no means wholly converged. For example, while much reduced and now below replacement level, fertility is still slightly higher in the South than the North, and in the North it is higher among Catholics than Protestants. Probably related to the historical differences in family size, we find that there are large remaining differences too in married women's labour force participation (this volume: Breen and Whelan, Table 2; O'Connor and Shortall, Table 1). The proportion of women working in the North was similar to the EU average, which was 45 per cent in 1995, while that in the South, despite the dramatic increases in the 1980s, remained below the EU average. As Callan and Farrell (1991) have shown, in the South women's participation in paid employment halved with each additional child, while O'Connor and Shortall show that the differences in participation are larger among the older cohorts, where the fertility differences were also larger. O'Connor and Shortall go on to argue that, although there are no significant differences in the level of state provision of child-care North and South, there are taxation differences, perhaps reflecting the South's continued stronger endorsement of the male breadwinner model. In particular, they argue that:

> Differences in the taxation systems North and South make it more or less worthwhile in economic terms for married women to be in paid employment. In the North, as in the UK, separate taxation for husbands and wives is automatic and universal. Furthermore, the additional tax allowance which is granted to married couples, can be allocated to either or it can be split between them. On the other hand in the South (and arguably reflecting its stronger endorsement of the male breadwinner model) double tax allowances and double tax bands are allocated to a married couple, regardless of whether

or not the wife is in paid employment. This implicitly challenges the economic wisdom of a married woman [in the South] participating in paid employment. (299)

Certainly, institutional differences between the two jurisdictions persist in this, and in other respects.

Crime rates, despite the rapid rises in both jurisdictions, are also slightly lower in the South, and indeed, as Brewer and his colleagues argue, there are greater differences now between North and South than there were before the recent period of the South's urbanisation and industrial development. Part of the explanation lies in the levels of violent crime in the North, linked to 'the Troubles': offences against the person, for example, comprise roughly one per cent of Dublin's total recorded crime, but are about 7 per cent of all recorded crimes in Northern Ireland (Brewer, this volume: 174). But even in Northern Ireland, crime rates are still lower than in the rest of the UK, and probably reflect the fact that community structures have to some extent persisted in both parts of Ireland despite modernisation.

Nor has convergence yet occurred with the class structures: 'for men the Republic has a much larger share of those at work in agriculture and a much smaller share in the skilled and semi/unskilled (non-agricultural) manual classes . . . both class structures continue to carry a strong historical imprint' (Breen and Whelan, this volume: 321). This historical imprint also remains on contemporary patterns of social fluidity and educational opportunity.

Andrew Greeley concludes that religion still provides very different world views, or 'stories' North and South. Indeed, he sees Ireland as having three religions. In the South Greeley sees a Pelagian worldview, which he names after the monk Pelagius 'who did battle with Saint Augustine on the issue of whether humans could do good without God's help'. Pelagius, who was Irish, held that they could. Southerners are significantly more likely to be Pelagians (this volume: 147). Greeley contrasts this with the Calvinist worldview of Northern Protestants who exhibit a sense of predetermination or predestination.

The third religion in Ireland is that of the Northern Catholics. 'It is Catholic (in the sense of being like Southern Catholicism) in its faith, devotion, morality and some of its attitudes ([on] feminism, sympathy for criminals, tolerance of cheating . . .), but it is not like Southern Catholicism in its worldviews or much of anything else' (Ibid.: 158). 'Northern Catholics are as pessimistic as their Protestant neighbours, perhaps because the culture of the six county majority has been absorbed by the minority community. The "story" of the meaning of life which Northern

Catholics tell is more like that of the Northern Protestants than that of the Southern Catholics' (148). Greeley concludes that the religion of Northern Catholics 'fits nicely into the model of a (repressed) minority group torn between its traditional heritage and the cultural environment in which it finds itself' (158).

On the conventional measures of secularisation, too, major differences persist between Catholics and Protestants, and between Ireland generally and most of Europe. Even by the 1990s almost four-fifths of Southern Catholics attended Mass weekly or more frequently and the vast majority continue to have their children baptised and confirmed, to be married and buried in church, and to draw comfort and strength from prayer. In the North the figure for Catholics was almost identical, while half of Presbyterians attended church at least once a month, and two-fifths of Anglicans did so. While the Protestant figures are much lower than the Catholic ones, they are still notable by European standards. In Germany or Britain for example, under two-fifths of Catholics attend church monthly and under one-fifth of Protestants do so (International Social Survey Programme, 1991).

Finally, there are two fundamental ways in which Ireland North and South continue to differ. First, Northern Ireland, unlike the Republic, remains an ethnically heterogenous and divided society, in which, on aggregate, the Catholic community continues to hold a disadvantaged position. This is perhaps most evident in the labour market, where Catholic men are twice as likely to be unemployed as Protestant men and are over-represented in unskilled manual jobs (although, in contrast, Catholic women are over-represented in professional jobs but under-represented in administrative and managerial occupations). High levels of residential segregation combined with higher rates of Catholic unemployment mean that areas of Northern Ireland with high unemployment rates have majority Catholic populations and areas of low unemployment have majority Protestant populations.

As Teague and McCartney note, agreement tends to break down when it comes to explaining why Catholics have fared worse than Protestants in the employment system and, in particular, on the role of discrimination. Econometric studies (Smith and Chambers, 1991 and Murphy and Armstrong, 1994) suggest that about half the unemployment differential between Catholics and Protestants can be accounted for by factors such as age, number of children, housing tenure, qualifications and area of residence. These are commonly labelled 'structural' factors. Opinion is then divided as to the degree to which the remaining half of the differential can be attributed to discrimination, whether this is direct, indirect, or the so-called 'chill factor'. The central thesis of the Gudgin-Breen (1996) study is that while some discrimination clearly does occur it is not currently of sufficient magnitude to contribute in any important way to the mainte-nance of the unemployment rate differential. This conclusion has been the subject of a sometimes rather technical debate (Bradley, 1997; 1998; Breen, 1998; Murphy, 1996; Rowthorn, 1996). Moreover, because the Gudgin-Breen study focused only on the 1971–91 period, it did not address the question of the extent to which the various disadvantages suffered by Catholics under the Stormont regime may have helped to shape some of the religious differences in the current distribution of structural factors—and, clearly, it would be difficult to deny either that this was the case, or that the resulting disadvantage was not then reproduced across generations.

The second major, and persisting, difference between the two parts of Ireland is simply that the Republic is a state while Northern Ireland is a region of a state. As a state, the Republic of Ireland possesses a degree of relative autonomy (Breen *et al.*, 1990) denied to a region of the UK. From this a number of important differences follow. One very clear example is found in the revival of neo-corporatism in the Republic in the late 1980s. As O'Donnell and Thomas (1998: 118) observe 'in a context of deep despair in Irish society, the social partners acting through the tripartite National Economic and Social Council—hammered out an agreed strategy to escape from the vicious circle of real stagnation, rising taxes and exploding debt'. The series of national agreements which followed played an important part in economic recovery through holding down wages in the tradeable sector, tying wage increases to a tight fiscal and monetary regime as part of the country's objective of achieving member-ship of EMU. Trade union commitment to such arrangements should be viewed in the context of European integration as an imagined economic and social order which shapes social policy in Ireland.

In Northern Ireland, on the other hand, Teague and McCartney con-clude that UK public sector industrial relations are on the threshold of fragmentation, and this process has already taken place in the private sector. Decentralised enterprise-level bargaining has become the norm, and private-sector wages in Northern Ireland are now much lower than in any other UK region. This new low-wage environment they conclude is likely to have been a significant factor in producing the impressive employ-ment growth in the service sector. Certain aspects of the labour market are coming to resemble an American-style deregulated, flexible employment system leading, as Teague and McCartney note, to a concern about a low-skills, bad jobs trap. Even within the manufacturing sector, as Gudgin (this volume: 265) documents, half of the manufacturing employment in North-ern Ireland is in the relatively low productivity food, drink, textile and clothing industries. As Teague and McCartney conclude, on the one hand Northern workers have little incentive to improve their human capital and on the other hand firms do not provide good jobs (either because they do not require high-skilled labour, or because there is a relative scarcity of high-skilled labour).

A similar distinction is evident in relation to macroeconomic policy. Within Northern Ireland economic policies are set mainly according to UK norms. While tax rates in Northern Ireland are identical to the UK rates, the pattern of public expenditure can be set with some limited discretion within the overall block grant made to the Northern Ireland Office. A case where this discretion has been used is in the design of generous subsidy-based industrial incentives. Nevertheless, the fact remains that policy norms in Northern Ireland are those designed with the wider UK in mind, and they can be unsuitable for a peripheral region. While the subvention assistance can be used to design and operate beneficial policies to address Northern Ireland's structural problems, some of these problems may originate in the first place from application of UK-wide policies to Northern Ireland.

The Future

As we argued at the beginning of this chapter, Ireland's future, whether it eventually becomes a single unified Irish state, or some joint sovereignty is evolved, or the status quo persists, will depend on political contingencies and decisions that we as social scientists cannot conceivably predict. However, these decisions will be made within specific historical and social contexts that may to some extent limit the scope for a political settlement or alternatively make new options available. What we have tried to offer then, as social scientists, is not a blue-print for the future but some understanding of the context and constraints within which political decisions will be made.

Many of the processes of convergence that we have noted in this chapter might be expected to make a lasting settlement of the Northern Irish question a more attainable option. The two jurisdictions are in many respects more similar today than they were at the time before partition, when they were under a single jurisdiction. And in several respects we can expect the North and South to develop in ways that continue to make them more alike. Extrapolation from past trends into the future is always hazardous, but Coleman expects the Irish demographic pattern to settle to that of north-west rather than of southern Europe. While the end of Ireland's demographic exceptionalism will not in itself solve any political problems, it may reduce some of the pressures on the two economies and, following Gudgin's line of reasoning one stage further, it may mean that unemployment rates generally, and the Catholic/Protestant ratio in particular, will be lower than would otherwise have been the case.

Demography will, however, leave the major political problem unchanged. The Catholic population in the North in 1991 was 42.1 per cent of the total according to the best estimate (from Breen, 1997). It seems likely that the Catholic population will stabilise, at or just less than, half of the population of Northern Ireland. Thus Northern Ireland will remain an ethnically divided society whose competing groups are of approximately equal size. This would seem to rule out any majority in favour of a change in the constitutional position of the region while ensuring that the nationalist minority remains sizeable.

Nevertheless, we may expect continuing changes both North and South, and among Catholics and Protestants alike, as both societies continue to become more highly educated, more liberal on social questions, and perhaps more secular, and less inclined to more extreme political views. Evans and Sinnott suggest that (net of the effect of age, on which more below), higher education does indeed lead to reduced support for hard-line political parties. These processes, it might be hoped, would lead eventually to shared attitudes and perhaps identities. Higher education elsewhere is associated with greater cosmopolitanism and reduced support for locally based nationalisms (Heath and Kellas, 1998). In the very long run we might anticipate that the higher-educated might tend towards more European-wide identities, although the impact these developments will have on Ireland, both North and South, will depend crucially on the economic opportunities available at home. The highly educated may be better placed to emigrate, and there is some evidence that it has been the better-educated who have in the past emigrated from the North. Moreover, education may be a two-edged sword: the highly educated are likely to have a greater sense of political efficacy and to be inclined towards political participation and activism, and as the history of new social movements shows, they are not always active in conventional ways. Uneven social and economic development may therefore solve few problems or even lead to unintended consequences. If the supply of graduates outstrips the labour-market's demand for graduates, increased political activism and protest rather than a liberal consensus on a middle way may follow.

On the economic front, continued convergence of the two economies and, in the North, of Catholic and Protestant economic fortunes, is not an unreasonable hope. As Teague and McCartney argue 'active government initiatives, particularly the adoption of fair employment legislation, have gone a long way to addressing . . . [the need for] an inclusive form of economic citizenship. Moreover, informal industrial relations processes can no longer be regarded as generating unequal status in the labour market' (this volume: 359). While there are still widespread perceptions of prejudice and discrimination in the North, we would argue that in the long run such perceptions will depend at least in part on the extent of actual discrimination. While it is quite possible for false beliefs to be self-sustaining, we see no need to be defeatist on this score.

On the political front, too, there is perhaps some cause for optimism. As Evans and Sinnott report, attitudes in the South have become substantially more favourable towards some kind of power-sharing. Hayes and McAllister (1996) have noted that the preference for a united Ireland is now substantially lower than in the past among Southerners. To be sure, Girvin rightly points out that 'None of this means that Irish nationalism has changed its essential nature. There appear to be no circumstances where Irish nationalism considers that unity should be abandoned or that Northern Ireland should remain in the United Kingdom in perpetuity . . . [but a] significant proportion of the public is more pragmatic in terms of options, more realistic in regard to Northern Ireland and less tolerant of the use of violence by the IRA for the promotion of nationalist objectives' (this volume: 386). Similarly in Britain there is substantial willingness for some kind of change to the present constitutional arrangements, either in the form of joint arrangements with the Republic or in the form of a united Ireland (Evans and Sinnott, this volume: Table 1). These developments give politicians on both the Southern and British sides greater freedom for manoeuvre.

There are, however, many grounds for pessimism, both economic and political. A continuation of the troubles would inhibit convergence of the two parts of Ireland in many respects. Not least it will make the North a less attractive site for the location of foreign direct investment, which may, in turn, lead to a growing gulf between the structure and nature of industry in the two parts of the island. As Bew points out, another issue which may act to exacerbate the differences between the two parts of the island is the different attitudes towards the EU in the UK and Republic of Ireland, respectively, and specifically, their different stances towards monetary union. As he points out, 'the greater integration between the two economies, a key intellectual prop of the [1995] Framework Document, now looks to be a rather more uncertain project. The decision by Ireland to join the single European currency while the UK stays out has seen to that' (this volume: 415). However, the consequences of the South's entry into monetary union for differences and similarities between it and the North are far from clear, not least because there is considerable uncertainty surrounding the likely effects of EMU on the Southern economy, and about the date at which the UK might also join.

Since Northern Ireland has no scope for independent monetary policy, the impact of monetary policy mismatch on cross-border interactions must also be viewed in the light of the decision of the Republic of Ireland to participate in EMU and the decision of the UK to stay out, at least initially. The biggest danger from monetary policy mismatch for North-South interactions could arise if sterling stayed out of EMU, was the target of large-scale speculation in international currency markets and became very unstable. In the light of the structural weaknesses of the Northern Ireland economy, a situation where sterling devalued or even moved erratically would undoubtedly disrupt cross-border trade and other forms of North-South interaction. The fact that the important small-firm sector in Northern Ireland is heavily dependent on the Republic of Ireland as an export destination exacerbates the problem.

The Republic of Ireland's experience during the early stages of its adherence to the narrow band of the EMS (1979–86) showed how long it can take for expectations to adjust to fundamental changes in monetary policy regimes. Hence, any uncertainty that endures about differences between UK and Republic of Ireland attitudes to EMU are likely to delay the deepening of North-South economic interactions, were this to be on the agendas of the authorities in both regions. In such a situation of uncertainty, Northern Ireland would tend to retain its focus on British policy as the most likely option for minimising economic disruption. One might therefore envisage a situation in which the Republic comes to look increasingly towards Europe and progressively reject Anglo-Saxon or liberal models in favour of continental models while the reverse happens in Northern Ireland.

It is also necessary to recognise that recent economic trends have led to growing economic polarisation within both societies, and again there is little reason to suppose that this trend will reverse itself. As O'Connell and Gudgin both point out, unemployment rates have been particularly high in both parts of the island of Ireland, and the incidence falls particularly harshly on young men. Even if the demographic convergence helps to contain this problem, polarisation has been a feature of other Western countries too, and we doubt if the two parts of Ireland will escape its consequences. Continuing high rates of unemployment can only be bad news for social integration, either within the two societies or for the integration of Ireland as a whole. High unemployment among unqualified young men, and the associated social exclusion, is a major concern for Europe generally and is surely likely to be especially worrying in the Northern Irish context.

Of similar cause for concern are the findings reported by Evans and Sinnott and by Hayes and McAllister suggesting that the younger generations in Northern Ireland may actually be more intransigent than the older generations. While we might have expected to find that rising levels of education would have made the young more liberal and tolerant in their attitudes, there appear to be specific generational features that counteract this liberalising tendency. Evans and Sinnott, for example, find that the young tend to show considerably greater support for the more hard-line parties within each community in Northern Ireland. Thus (net of class and education), younger Catholics are more inclined to Sinn Féin rather than the SDLP, while among Protestants there is a similar tendency for the young to support the DUP rather than the UUP. They argue that 'The marked effects of age on partisanship can probably be best understood in terms of political socialisation—both Sinn Féin and the DUP only started to compete electorally after many older voters had already developed attachments to the more established representatives of unionist and nationalist political visions. The recruitment of the young and unaligned was therefore an easier prospect' (Evans and Sinnott, this volume: 452). Similarly Hayes and McAllister believe that the answer to whether or not the Northern Ireland problem can be resolved within the lifetimes of those presently alive will depend upon whether this younger minority of the population emerge as more tolerant, or more prejudiced as a result of their experiences. Their own view is distinctly pessimistic. They take the view that, as it is the young who have been most exposed to the violence during their impressionable years, and it is the young who are most active in sustaining paramilitary organisations, then the prospects for a lasting political solution to the Northern Ireland problem may well be grim.

Just how pessimistic these findings should lead us to be depends ultimately on how much force Evans and Sinnott's, and Hayes and McAllister's generational explanations have. As Hayes and McAllister point out, the data themselves do not ultimately tell us whether generational or lifecycle interpretations of the differences are to be preferred. While theory does strongly suggest that a generational interpretation is plausible, it must be said that the findings on political disaffection are more likely to have a lifecycle interpretation (see Heath and Park, 1997): young people do seem to display lower levels of conventional political participation but many are likely to conform to more conventional modes as they grow older (and perhaps as they acquire greater family commitments and a greater stake in established society). Moreover, other evidence from Britain and the United States suggests that generational differences are by no means immutable and that the major component of attitude change over time tends to be due to 'period' experiences that affect all people alike. In other words, attitudes can shift (either in an intransigent or in a conciliatory direction) in response to contemporary changes. We agree with Hayes and McAllister that the Troubles have left their mark, but we suspect that the future may be more open than they allow—if only because both new and old generations may now have some experience of peace, however temporary.

Moreover, there is some evidence that senses of national identity can perhaps be shaped by emerging political institutions. For example the Catalan experience suggests that devolution and the meeting of some Catalan aspirations have been able to satisfy many Catalans and preserve their dual identity as both Spanish and Catalan (Kellas, 1991). The entrenchment of successful all-Ireland political institutions, which fall short of unification, could conceivably lead to the emergence of new, dual, senses of identity.

Above all, however, as social scientists we would emphasise the importance of taking a longer-term view in shaping not only political institutions but people's everyday experience. Here we would see an inclusive citizenship as paramount. As the Framework Document argues 'any new political arrangements must be based on full respect for, and protection and expression of, the rights and identities of both traditions in Ireland and even-handedly afford both communities in Northern Ireland parity of esteem and treatment, including equality of opportunity and advantage' (Para. 10: iv). This needs to be translated into matters of practical experiences and not merely of political rhetoric. One area in which this is essential is the labour market. If, for example, as the Gudgin Breen study would lead one to suspect, current discrimination is often overestimated as a cause of Catholic disadvantage, the need for policies that address the wider issues concerning the ways in which disadvantage is maintained becomes all the more urgent. To the extent that religious discrimination is no longer a major proximate factor in explaining Catholic disadvantage, then policies that concern themselves solely with religion are likely to be ineffective. Policies that seek to tackle the factors that directly influence individuals' chances of getting a job are likely not only to be more efficient, but have the very considerable advantage of being to the benefit of the disadvantaged in all communities.

References

Bradley, J. (1997) 'Evaluation of the Ratio of Unemployment Rates as an Indicator of Fair Employment: a Critique', *Economic and Social Review*, 28: 85–104.

Bradley, J. (1998) 'The Ratio of Unemployment Rates and Fair Employment: a Response to Richard Breen', *Economic and Social Review*, 29: 95–97.

Breen, R. (1996) 'Who Wants a United Ireland? Constitutional Preferences Among Catholics and Protestants', in R. Breen, P. Devine, and L. Dowds (eds), *Social Attitudes in Northern Ireland: The Fifth Report*, Belfast: Appletree.

Breen, R. (1997) 'Estimating the Size of the Catholic and Protestant Populations of Northern Ireland using Multiple Imputation with Non-Ignorable Non-Response', unpublished paper.

Breen, R. (1998) 'The ratio of Unemployment Rates and Fair Employment: a Reply to John Bradley', *Economic and Social Review,* 29: 87–93.

Breen R. and Goldthorpe J. H. (1997) 'Explaining Educational Differentials: Towards a Formal Rational Action Theory', *Rationality and Society,* 9: 275–305.

Breen, R., Hannan, D. Rottman, D. and Whelan, C. T. (1990) *Understanding Contemporary Ireland: State, Class and Development in the Republic of Ireland,* Dublin: Gill and Macmillan.

Breen, R. and Whelan, C. T. (1996) *Social Mobility and Social Class in Ireland,* Dublin: Gill and Macmillan.

Callan, T. and Farrell, B. (1991) *Women's Participation in the Irish Labour Market,* Dublin: NESC.

Connolly, M. (1990) *Politics and Policy-Making in Northern Ireland,* Hemel Hempstead: Philip Allan.

Corish, M. (1996) 'Aspects of Secularisation of Irish Society', in E. Casidy (ed.), *Faith and Culture in the Irish Context,* Dublin: Veritas.

Fahey, T. (1998) 'Progress or Decline? Demographic Change in Political Context', in W. Crotty and D. Schmitt (eds), *Ireland and the Politics of Change,* London: Addison Wesley.

Foreign and Commonwealth Office (1995) *White Paper Relating to Northern Ireland: Frameworks for the Future,* Cm. 2964, London: HMSO.

Gudgin, G. and Breen. R. (1996) 'Evaluation of the Ratio of Unemployment Rates', *Studies in Employment Equality, Research Report No. 4,* Belfast: Central Community Relations Unit.

Hayes, B. and McAllister, I. (1996) 'British and Irish Public Opinion Towards the Northern Ireland Problem', *Irish Political Studies,* 11: 61–82.

Heath, A. and Kellas, J. (1998) 'Nationalisms and Constitutional Questions', *Understanding Constitutional Change: special issue of Scottish Affairs,* Edinburgh: Unit for the Study of Government in Scotland.

Heath, A. and Park, A. (1997) 'Thatcher's Children?' in R. Jowell, J. Curtice, A. Park, L. Brook, K. Thomson and C. Bryson (eds), *British Social Attitudes: the 14th Report,* Aldershot: Ashgate.

Hornsby-Smith, M. and Whelan, C. T. (1994) 'Religious and Moral Values', in C. T. Whelan (ed.), *Values and Social Change,* Dublin: Gill and Macmillan.

International Social Survey Programme (1991) *1991 Module: Religion,* Cologne: Zentralarchiv für Empirische Sozialforschung, Universität zu Köln.

Irish Labour Force Survey (1966/1977) Dublin: Government Publications.

Irish Political Studies (1995) 'Irish Political Data', *Irish Political Studies,* 10: 262–339.

Kellas, J. (1991) *The Politics of Nationalism and Ethnicity,* London: Macmillan.

Murphy, A. (1996) 'Comments' in G. Gudgin and R. Breen, *Studies in Employment Equality, Research Report No. 4,* Belfast: Central Community Relations Unit.

Murphy, A. and Armstrong, D. (1994) 'A Picture of the Catholic and Protestant Male Unemployed', in *Employment Equality Review Research,* Belfast: Central Community Relations Unit.

Northern Ireland Annual Abstract of Statistics (1997) Belfast: Northern Ireland Statistics and Research Agency.

O'Brien, G. (1962) 'The Economic Progress of Ireland', *Studies*, 51: 9–12.

O'Donnell, R. and Thomas, D. (1998) 'Partnership and Policy Making', in S. Healy and B. Reynolds (eds), *Social Policy in Ireland*, Dublin: Oak Tree Press.

Rowthorn R. E. (1996) 'Comments', in G. Gudgin and R. Breen, *Studies in Employment Equality, Research Report No. 4*, Belfast: Central Community Relations Unit.

Shavit, Y. and Blossfeld, H-P. (1993) *Persistent Inequality: Changing Educational Attainment in Thirteen Countries*, Boulder, Col.: Westview Press.

Smith, D. J. and Chambers, G. (1991) *Inequality in Northern Ireland*, Oxford: Clarendon Press.

Tussing, A. D. (1978) *Irish Educational Expenditures—Past, Present and Future*, Dublin: ESRI.

Whelan, C. T. and Fahey, A. (1994) 'Marriage and the family', in C. T. Whelan (ed.), *Values and Social Change*, Dublin: Gill and Macmillan.

Index

Prepared by Margaret Cronan

Note. This index is arranged in word-by-word alphabetical order. Entries in **bold** type indicate contributions to this volume. The following abbreviations are used in subheadings: NI . . . Northern Ireland; RoI . . . Republic of Ireland.